S0-DNN-430

STENDHAL

BOOKS BY

MATTHEW JOSEPHSON

Stendhal

Galimathias (poems)

Zola and His Time

Portrait of the Artist as American

Jean-Jacques Rousseau

The Robber Barons

The Politicos

The President Makers

Victor Hugo

Empire of the Air

STENDHAL

After a painting by Dreux Dorcy
Museum Grenoble
Courtesy The Bettman Archive

STENDHAL

or The Pursuit of Happiness

by

MATTHEW JOSEPHSON

GARDEN CITY—MCMXLVI—NEW YORK

Doubleday & Company, Inc.

PRINTED IN THE UNITED STATES
AT
THE COUNTRY LIFE PRESS, GARDEN CITY, N. Y.

FIRST EDITION

Contents

CONTENTS

Introduction

STENDHAL (whose real name was Henri Beyle) has been my favorite author for more than twenty years. I have read and reread not only the principal works by which he is known, but his letters, journals, and merest fragments, with unfailing pleasure. M. Léon Blum, who is a most discerning literary critic as well as a man of politics, was quite right in saying that the habit of reading Stendhal "takes hold of one like a drug." A drug, one might add, stimulative and sedative at once. In America, as in Europe, I have met Stendhalians who read at least a page of his works every day; such adepts form a curious international freemasonry bound together by no other secrets than those of the wisdom and humor of Stendhal. One of these said to me recently: "I read him not as a dead author, but as an endlessly amusing and wise older friend who is always at my side."

But to read his books, as many familiar with them will agree, arouses the keenest curiosity about his personality. One thinks of him as being *alive*, as contemporary; and recalls with surprise that he was born during the reign of Louis XVI and died in the early years of Queen Victoria's regime. How, we ask ourselves, could he have arrived at opinions, ideas, and anxieties that we consider peculiarly the attributes of the twentieth-century mind? How could he have known, for instance, about suppressed desires or the inferiority complex—though he lived more than a hundred years ago? Or spoken in such "modern" terms about power politics, sex, religion, history, art, all the subjects that most absorb us today?

If Stendhal is now regarded as one of the most philosophical (and prophetic) of novelists, he was at all events no pedant nurtured in libraries, but an enemy to solemn dullness. As philosopher he must surely be classed as one of that breed we tend to call "intoxicated"—because they seem always drunk with the wine of life.

From the time of his youth the study of human nature, "the observation of the human heart and its passions," was his constant preoccupation. But where could he study the passions better than in himself? Though he lived exuberantly, submitting himself to experience with an abandon that few men of letters have really relished, he went on incessantly writing down everything that happened to him just as it happened. He had become so imbued with the late eighteenth century's spirit of scientific detachment that he was even led to perform some remarkable experiments upon himself—always in pursuit of light upon human morals, or "the passions"—then recorded that which he had experienced or witnessed with a sober objectivity designed to correct all tendency to romantic exaggeration. The more horrid his confessions—the more he blushed inwardly at human vices demonstrated in himself—the more unsparingly he recorded them; for he possessed, as Nietzsche said in after years, "the psychologist's eye," and was perhaps truly, as Nietzsche also added, "the last of the great French moralists."

No author ever told us more about himself than Stendhal, and yet no man was ever more difficult to know. For he lived under many different masks. He laid claim to having been a soldier, a man of fortune, a great lover, a society wit, a diplomat, a traveler, and even, sometimes, a revolutionary conspirator. (There was some truth in all these claims.) In his day he even acquired a passing reputation as an "immoral philosopher," and rather enjoyed that. He posed, and he travestied his own poses. He also loved to conceal his own identity—as if he felt himself forever hunted by the secret police, or persecuted by the Bureau of Censorship—under scores of different pseudonyms. Christened, in plain French, Marie-Henri Beyle, he called himself "Baron de Stendhal," or "Henri Brulard," or "Dominique," or "César Bombet," but most often "Stendhal," the name which he has made immortal.

He believed there was such a thing as an "art of life," and tended always to review mentally almost every act of his, whether at a polite gathering in a salon or in a stormy affair of love, in order to learn what lessons analysis and reflection might afford. One tenet of his system required that he must be constantly in love or falling out of love, so that pursuit of a series of women was his principal business in life—"and *after them* came my books." Yet he was no Casanova with a single-track mind; for, not pure act, but the sufferings or modulations of his sensibility were virtually the end-object of his adventures, so often comic or unhappy, so often misadventures.

Another article of his system stressed the enjoyment of a cosmopolitan culture; he played the "good European" long before that role was widely appreciated. A typical Frenchman by birth, he assailed and lampooned the ways of his own countrymen, preferred to live in Italy, and assumed a Teutonic nom de plume, though he felt little enough for Germany.

The history of Stendhal's reputation is in itself a singular thing in the annals of literature. Little read or relished by the public of his age—like Blake, Melville, and Samuel Butler—he was to be rediscovered and "revived" a full two generations after his time, to be proclaimed as a lost genius, a mute, inglorious Voltaire—nay, to moderns, wittier and more brilliant than Voltaire himself! Fifty years after his death he becomes one of the demigods of the world's letters, taking his place in the ranks of the great social writers who appeared toward the end of the last century, such as Ibsen and Tolstoy, Dostoevski, Zola and Bernard Shaw—as if he belonged naturally among them rather than in the company of romantic Byron, with whom he used to walk in Milan in 1818, or Hugo and Balzac, whom he knew in Paris.

This posthumous success he himself had foreseen, for he had written repeatedly in his letters or journals: "I shall be read only in 1880 or 1900." Or perhaps as late as 1930? Often he used to address himself to his future audience in invocations: "Oh, reader of 1880 or 1900 . . ."

By appealing over the heads of the public of his own time he pursued, with design, a "policy of immortality," as Paul Valéry has remarked. But there was good reason for it. He felt himself most distinctly a man of transition—one of a "lost generation," as we now say—trapped between two great swings, forward and backward, of the historical pendulum. In 1815, when, middle-aged, he first began to write his books in a weary, ravaged, postwar world, he was haunted by the sense of history.

Earlier, his boyhood and youth had been deeply molded by the coming of the great French Revolution; he had believed in the goddess of Reason, as in equality and liberty; willingly he had gone to fight in the armies of the Republic and of the young Napoleon who had appeared as the military instrument of the Revolution against old Europe's feudalism. Then, on the morrow of Waterloo, he had seen the restoration of the old regime, of legitimate throne and altar to absolute power. Fervent Jacobin that he was, liberal and materialist, it seemed to him that this return of Bourbon rule, by means of foreign armies, was a return to the Dark Ages. The long era of Metternich's political domination of Europe was, as Stendhal conceived, a time of "black reaction," directed by police and Jesuit priests who now looked to the education of the peoples. For him the lights had gone out.

Most other writers of his day chose conformity; they imitated Chateaubriand, the romantic Catholic, and other apologists of ultraroyalism. Stendhal continued to believe in the teachings of the preceding century's rational and democratic philosophers who were now discarded as "old-fashioned." In Restoration days he too was often treated as a belated reveler who had lost his way since the time of the eighteenth-century Enlightenment; yet he clung to his conviction that the recurrence of absolutism (paralleling that of fascism in our own century) would be limited in time; that further social upheavals impended; that the drives of common men toward self-improvement, shaped by reason, scientific method, and humane ideas, would, in the long run, govern the future and not the ideas of authoritarians and obscurantists. In fifty or a hundred years all the lying nonsense that his contemporaries wrote—to appease the censor or win favor before the king's ministers—would be forgotten in the rubbish heap of history. With admirable tenacity Stendhal steered his own course, away from fashionable or authorized ("right-thinking") modes of thought. Almost single-handed he carried on a resistance movement of his own, in a sort of intellectual Underground of his own, read by but few men, yet saying to himself: "I write what *I, myself*, think and not what *they* think."

Steadfastly he protested at his times, holding that they, and not himself, were out of key with realities. And it was in accord with his role as an eternal dissenter that he proceeded to break all the rules of style and literary form then enjoying credit, and to write novels that were severely condemned by the men of the Romantic School, whose camp he had quickly left. His pioneering in the social novel was ill regarded; his overwhelming interest in psychological analysis of the ego and of human passions, as in *The Red and the Black*, was held unpleasant, subversive, and immoral—though later generations saw him as one of the great precursors of modern psychology. For the twentieth century was to take a wholly different view of his case.

It is one of Stendhal's chief claims to the admiration of later men that, while he waited for the end of the political and cultural night that seemed to have fallen over Europe, he retained his sanity, his love of life, his readiness to laugh at himself and at the world, to an unusual degree. His protests were generally expressed with an irony that was good-humored as well as subtle. Thus he defended his own individuality, his own "sensibility," his vision, by use of a whole "system" of satirical stratagems and concealments that are a marked feature of the

Stendhalian wit. While his indirection was harmless in itself, and scarcely impugned his real honesty, Stendhal's strategy of resistance, as we may call it, enabled him to survive. It was to bring deep comfort to men who read him in later times as war-weary and confused as his own. For he spoke with the ripe wisdom and the stoicism of a man who was no dupe, who had seen the mutations of history and violent changes of fortune, yet refused to despair, refused to believe that men would surrender their heritage of knowledge to become the unthinking victims of regimes of retrogression.

The recurrent revivals of Stendhal are certainly traceable to the parallels between his situation and that of modern man. The line of descent from Stendhal to our great modern authors such as Marcel Proust, André Gide, and the earlier Joyce is clear enough. His powers as political seer have been less well estimated. For example, at the time of the Pact of Munich, in 1938, when it seemed that the very weaknesses of Western leadership prepared the way, inevitably, for new Dark Ages, how much consolation one could find in turning to read again the letters and journals of this man of singular humor and intelligence who had once served at the court of Napoleon and marched in the terrible retreat of the Grande Armée from Moscow. Nor was it surprising to learn some years later, after another big military despot had run his career, that during the occupation of France by German armies, from 1940 to 1944, there had been an impressive growth of interest in Stendhal among the French youths who carried on an unremitting secret resistance against the enemy.

"Our young writers have made a cult of Stendhal and of his Julien Sorel," I was told by a French author who came here on some war mission. Julien Sorel, hero of *The Red and the Black*, was, of course, the embodiment of Stendhalian dissent. Like him, many a young man of promise forfeited his life by entering the desperate Resistance movement. Thus my gifted friend, Robert Desnos, in 1945 was fated to die in a German concentration camp. Jean Prévost, who was also a devoted Stendhalian, fell the year before, fighting as an officer of the Maquis.

For those who hold that Stendhal was but a "master of disillusionment," we must call to mind the closing chapter of *The Red and the Black* with its account of the trial and sacrificial death of young Julien Sorel. Offered the alternatives of winning freedom by feigning a repentance he does not feel, or facing death at the guillotine, Julien rejects the course he holds shameful, saying: "And what would become of me if I despised myself? . . . One has his duties in accordance with the range of his spirit."

I have tried, by way of introduction, to mention but a few of the many grounds on which Stendhal appeals to us today, so that the American reader may be led to understand how he happened to become a legendary figure in European culture, and why his manner of life itself has fascinated whole regiments of literary scholars in France, Italy, and Germany in the last forty years. In his case, as in no other, knowledge of his personality is requisite to reading his books.

It is a great pity that Stendhal did not live to complete his memoirs, for the writing of which he showed both passion and genius, as evidenced by the fragment we have of *Henri Brulard*, reaching only to his seventeenth year. His novels were concealed autobiographies: all his life he prepared to write his memoirs, judging from the quantity of notes and reminders to himself found in his journals, on scraps of paper, or on the margins of books he happened to read. No Proust ever examined his memories or interrogated his ego more constantly than he.

But what Stendhal wrote, often with such terrible honesty, was for his private instruction or relief; it was scribbled in an almost illegible hand, in cryptograms, with names of persons, places, and dates altered. This excess of self-confession—assuming the form of a dispersed and confusing quantity of notations and reflections—has made him the joy and the despair of biographers. It has also spurred on a whole army of literary ferrets, orthographic experts, and manuscript collectors to search for long years through his voluminous private papers in the hope of solving the many contradictions and mystifications he seems to have included in them with design. The thing, obviously, has its grotesque side.

In France, the literature concerning Stendhal has grown until it has assumed almost unmanageable proportions, like Lincolniana in the United States. Its best productions as yet are chiefly monographs or special studies covering selected phases of his career and works. For example, almost half the seventy-four volumes of M. Henri Martineau's edition of the *Œuvres complètes* is made up of letters, unrevised journals, unfinished fragments, or mere notes, and of course the footnote commentaries of the editor. A mass of Stendhal material has accumulated since the 1880s, and yet, even in France, I believe, has not been fully sifted, or synthesized for the purposes of a comprehensive biography. (The more complete biographies, chronologically, like Chuquet's large work, date back to the early 1900s, and are partially obsolete; while a more recent study, by Professor F. C. Green of Cambridge University, one of two existing works by English writers, is done partly in French.)

INTRODUCTION

This book is an attempt to present Stendhal's life and character before the English-reading public as fully and completely as is now possible, in the light of new material compiled up to 1940, which in great measure has not been available previously in English. In performance of this task, admittedly full of perplexities, I have drawn upon the compilations of numerous French, Italian, and German scholars, and acknowledge my debt to them. Still more am I indebted to the editors of the elaborately annotated Champion edition of Stendhal's writings (still incomplete in 1940) and of the even more extensive Divan edition (by Martineau), whose versions of the works and letters I have mainly followed. For the paramount thing was to gather in the confidences of Stendhal himself, walking with him through life, as it were, sharing all the variety of his experiences, then, with him, reflecting upon them.

M. J.

April 20, 1946

STENDHAL

CHAPTER I

Father and Son

GRENOBLE, the birthplace of Stendhal, has always been esteemed as one of the most splendidly situated towns in all France. Though it lies in a level plain, on the banks of the Isère River, the ancient fortified capital of Dauphiné is all but encircled by the snowy mountain walls of the Western Alps. Quite suddenly, as one approaches Grenoble through those barren passes, the whole panorama of its valley comes into view; the sight of that rich, green floor, so intensely cultivated, so abounding in flowers, with the Isère serpentining through it, is a never failing surprise. It is still "the fairest garden of France," as one of the early dauphins, (later) King Louis XII, said over four hundred years ago.

Like Jean-Jacques Rousseau, who had lived long years in solitude on the other side of the Grande Chartreuse, above Grenoble, Stendhal loved mountainous Dauphiné. Not in sublime Lombardy, he declared, nor in the environs of Naples, nor even in the paintings of Titian, was anything to be seen that was more remarkable than that immense and incredibly verdant plain over which he roamed in his boyhood, with his eye always fixed on "those distant granite peaks that traced their dark red forms against the eternal snows."

But for the town of Grenoble itself, the city of his fathers, he felt only disgust. Now, in the latter part of the eighteenth century, Grenoble was reputed to be a center of elegant and pleasure-loving society. So Choderlos de Laclos, the author of *Les Liaisons dangereuses*, described the town at this period, after having served as an officer in its garrison. But Stendhal thought of it only as a place to flee from. "Everything that is provincial and bourgeois . . . everything that is low and mean in the middle-class style reminds me of Grenoble," he wrote in a singularly wrathful passage of his memoirs directed at the very family and class from which he sprang.

You feel something of the provincialism accursed by Stendhal in the old quarter of the town, in the tangle of narrow streets off the Grande Rue and near the river where he lived as a boy. Here the old gray buildings dating from the sixteenth and seventeenth centuries, some of them six stories tall, huddle together crazily to shut out the sunlight. In their shadow one can no longer see the mass of the Grande Chartreuse or the white cone of Mont Blanc still farther off. But it was here, closely confined within the ancient fortifications, and not in the mountain passes or in the open Grésivaudan Plain, that men dwelt under the old regime. The respectable burghers, merchants, advocates, and king's officers who were Henri Beyle's forbears lived out their lives in these houses, already old in the time of Louis XVI, that face the gloomy street with their front windows always shuttered, as if to hide the dramas of desire or avarice that were played behind their decent façades. It was in such a street, in the heart of the old quarter, at number 60 Rue des Vieux Jésuites (now Rue Jean-Jacques Rousseau), that four generations of the Beyle family dwelt and Henri Beyle, the last of their line, was born.

The Beyles were typical Dauphinois, and the Dauphinois are a people apart even among the highly diversified French. Though men of the *midi* they are quite unlike their Latin neighbors of Provence or the Lyonnais, for they are descendants of the ancient Allobroges, a Celtic mountain tribe of Roman times. Their southeastern border province came late into the family of France as a hereditary apanage of the crown prince who was named in its honor the *dauphin*. Grenoble, their capital, boasted its own Parlement and special municipal privileges; the Dauphinois cherished their semi-independence and were imbued with a strong regional feeling. By tradition the man of Dauphiné is tenacious, deliberate, and adroit of speech; "he thinks before he acts"; "he hates to be fooled." He has an intelligence and subtlety which one would seek in vain among the civilizations of Provence or of neighboring Burgundy. Where the Provençal pours out atrocious insults, for example, the Dauphinois ponders and takes counsel of his heart.[1] Crafty in trade, stubborn in argument, these "Normans of the South" are likened to the canny Scot or the sharp Yankee.

For two centuries before 1650 the Beyles, living in the vicinity of Sassenage, in the hills outside of Grenoble, had thrived as tillers of the soil. By the middle of the seventeenth century they appear as priests,

[1] *Vie d'Henri Brulard*, I, p. 29, Divan edition.

government officials, soldiers, and merchants. One of them, Jean Beyle, is listed as a village draper. But his grandson, Joseph Beyle, acquires education, becomes a lawyer, and practices in Grenoble in the 1690s. By a fortunate marriage he becomes proprietor of a sizable landed estate at Claix, a few miles south of Grenoble, and is able to purchase the house in the Rue des Vieux Jésuites that is to be the home of the Beyles for a century. At his death in 1739, his son Joseph Beyle, in accordance with old usage, inherits his legal practice and rises in his profession to be solicitor before the Parlement and advocate to the consistory. The great-grandfather of Henri Beyle was thus a man of note at the Palais de Justice and the bishopric of Grenoble, for the Beyles had close ties with the Church. In turn, his son Pierre and his grandson, Joseph-Chérubin Beyle, born in 1747, inherited these offices, almost in the manner of the hereditary magistrates.

The Beyles were an old and rich bourgeois family, close to the nobility, and moved for generations in a circumscribed little world that centered at the old Palais de Justice, with its buzzing courts of law. They lived within a jealous hierarchy of dignities and privileges, hemmed in between the nobility of the robe just above them, into whose choice circle they longed to climb, and the less fortunate members of the third estate, who envied them and whom they disdained.

At only twenty Chérubin Beyle became the responsible head of his family, owing to his father's early death. He inherited a fortune that approached perhaps 200,000 francs, which was wealth for those days; but as the only son, blessed with nine dependent sisters, he was burdened by his cares and made sober and cold in manner. The Beyles were shrewd, patient accumulators, and Chérubin seemed to show the family disposition for trade and its aptitude for the law.

"Money was the all-absorbing thought of my father," his son would write of him reproachfully. In this matter, Chérubin was, like all the Beyles before him, ready to spend whole days in haggling with a peasant over the purchase or sale of a half acre of land. As an attorney he was esteemed by the townspeople as both scrupulous and resourceful in his dealings. He loved to talk of legal chicane, and his family in time grew all too familiar with his dry jokes about "petitory" and "possessory" actions. On the other hand he had social pretensions, and considered himself a landed squire; he gave great attention to the management and improvement of the family property at Claix, and eventually assumed the non-hereditary title of *noble* Joseph-Chérubin Beyle, and a coat of arms.

It was only as he neared thirty-five that the reserved and prudent man determined to marry. His choice was Henriette Gagnon, daughter of Grenoble's leading doctor, himself a man of comfortable wealth and a social leader of the town. Though Chérubin was plain-looking and with an air a little too grave and pious, Henriette Gagnon, after some resistance, ended by accepting his hand, for he was a good match.

She was much younger than he and by all accounts very vivacious and pretty, though short and plump of figure. Her father, Dr. Gagnon, one of the most learned men of Grenoble, had brought her up with a kindly hand, in accordance with the teachings of Rousseau, the philosopher-hermit of nearby Savoy. She loved people, had many friends and all sorts of talents, including that of drawing. "Alas, what did she not do well?" her family said of her. She even read Dante in the original Italian. Indeed there was something "romantic" and "Italian" about her, her son relates.

The Gagnons were not native Dauphinois, Stendhal tells us; they had come from Avignon, in Provence, some seventy years before his birth. But what was more, as his aged great-aunt Elisabeth Gagnon used to tell him, they were really descendants of immigrants who, in the fifteenth century, had migrated from a still sunnier, warmer clime, "where orange trees grew in the ground" and not merely in tubs, as in the Public Gardens of Grenoble. In the Gagnon family the legend was nourished of an ancestor named something like Gagnone or Gagnoni who had fled from Florence after a fatal duel. Thus two contrasting family stocks, two different bloods, the spontaneous Italian and the cooler Celtic of the Dauphinois, were crossed in Henri Beyle, and, to his mind, his southern blood made for his deep attachment in later life to the people and sky of Italy. Nor was he wrong in his idea of his ancestry, for recent genealogical research has marked the Gagnons of Avignon as the Gallicized descendants of a soldier named Gaignoni who hailed from a village near Florence.

"Go away, you ugly fellow!" Henriette had said, according to the servants' tales, to Chérubin Beyle when he first came courting her. But he was persistent, and on February 20, 1781, led her to the altar of St. André's Church, then brought her to live in the gray house of the Rue des Vieux Jésuites. After the more spacious, sunlit home of the Gagnons that gave on the Place de Grenette, the central square of the town, the old Beyle house seemed immitigably dark and damp; its hallways, illuminated only by small iron-barred windows, were musty, its rooms were low-ceilinged; only the living rooms and the bedchambers on the street side, ornate with carved panels in Louis XV style, were cheerful, though they too were shuttered by old jalousies.

On January 23, 1783, Henriette Beyle bore a son who was named Marie-Henri, after his maternal grandfather. Three years later she gave birth to a daughter, and two years after that to a second daughter.

2

Henriette Beyle was twenty-five when her son was born. He was no beauty as an infant, but was fat, red-faced, and had a very large bald head. "*Père* Beyle, himself!" everyone exclaimed with laughter, for he bore a marked resemblance to a great-uncle who was a monk. Alas, he was not to be handsome like the Gagnons. But Henriette adored, pampered her first child; perhaps because there had been a stillborn son the year before, she surrounded him with a solicitude that was even a little excessive.

When he was able to walk, he showed himself an enterprising fellow, always rushing at everything impetuously on his short, sturdy legs, climbing to the top of fragile chairs, falling from them, breaking his front teeth, howling, and frightening everyone. One day, while walking with his nurse in the fields outside the town gate, he pricked a mule with a pointed stick, and was promptly kicked in the chest. Screaming, he was carried to his grandfather, who pronounced him sound, though saying: "A little more and he would have been killed."

The story of his childhood and boyhood is set forth in the most vivid detail in the fragment of his memoirs entitled, *The Life of Henri Brulard,* probably the most truthful and uninhibited confessions ever written. His own first sharply focused recollections date from the age of three and are characterized by anxiety and violence:

> My earliest memory is that of biting the cheek or the forehead of Madame Pisan-Dugalland, my cousin. . . . I see her still, a woman of twenty-five, plump and very much rouged. It was apparently the rouge at which I took offence.
>
> "Kiss me, Henri," she said to me. I did not want to. She was greatly vexed and I bit her hand. I can see the whole scene, no doubt, because I was at once reproached for it, as if I had committed a crime and because my family never stopped talking about it.[2]

[2]Cf. Chapter XIX, p. 373, for the discussion of *Henri Brulard,* written when Stendhal was fifty-three. In narrating his first sixteen years, Stendhal was one of the few who wrote neither to defend nor to apologize for himself, but to dissect his own direct memories, always carefully distinguishing between fact or after-impression or hearsay, in a finely scientific spirit. No memoirs ever written were less *retouched* than these, which hold all the elements of the fanciful, the unexpected, or the unconscious, and even the unexplained lapses in his memory, as fixed in his mind. It is a case

At three, he was already a "little monster." Not long after this the infant Beyle committed another dark deed. He was playing at the balcony of a window on the first floor, working with a small kitchen knife over a box of plants which he was trimming down and setting out as his own little garden. Suddenly the knife slipped from his hand and fell to the street, a few steps from a lady passing by, a certain Mme. Chenavaz, "the most ill-natured woman in all the town." His aunt Séraphie Gagnon, whom Henri disliked for her carping disposition, at once accused him of trying to "kill" Mme. Chenavaz. He was scolded by everyone, though he knew he had meant no wrong. At the very outset his life seemed to be filled with impressions of danger and injustice, and the drive of aggression.

From earliest years the obsession with death clung to him. It was associated at first with the memory of an imposing funeral, performed with military as well as religious ceremony, that he attended with his parents when he was only five. The records attesting the accuracy of his memoirs indicate that it was the burial service for Marshal Vaux that took place in Grenoble in 1788. In his house, by the window, he listened to the sound of the bells tolling endlessly at St. André's Church. Then at the church

> . . . the majestic sound of the bells moved me deeply. . . . The sight of that black catafalque illuminated in broad daylight by a great quantity of tapers, with the windows darkened, was a striking one. It was the idea of death appearing for the first time.

And at the cemetery, as the soldiers drew up to give the salute:

> So they were going to fire! And such a lot of soldiers! I was dying of fright; but kept an eye on the black carriage that was advancing slowly. . . . I waited trembling for the order to fire.

When at last the order was given and the roar of muskets followed at once, "a great weight was lifted from me."

Like the mysteriously organized sequence of a dream there remained fixed in his memory the episodes of public disorder that burst forth in Grenoble that same year. It was the historic "Day of the Tiles" (June 7, 1788), when the attempt of King Louis XVI to curb the traditional (judiciary) powers of the Parlement of Grenoble roused the people of the city to fight in the streets and even to hurl tiles from their roofs upon the heads of the King's troops. From a window of his grandfather's house on the central square Henri was the unwitting spectator of the

---

of a master of psychology operating upon himself; and one proceeds with the story of his early years as if in an embarrassment of riches.

first insurrectionary disorders in France, the starting signal for the drama of civil revolution that was to change his entire world. He could not understand, yet could never forget, the sight he had of a little old woman being pursued along the street by soldiers and screaming at them as she ran: *"Je me révorte, je me révorte!"* Did she mean *"révolte"*?

Then, soon afterward, a workingman, assisted with difficulty by two comrades, came tottering by on the Grande Rue, bright blood flowing from his back, for he had been stabbed with a bayonet. At the house across the street, the workingman was assisted up the winding, glass-enclosed staircase to the sixth-floor attic where he lived, almost expiring at every step from loss of blood. Stendhal relates:

> My parents scolded me and drove me away from the window of my grandfather's bedroom, so that I should not see this terrible sight, but I kept returning to it.

As at the funeral of Marshal Vaux, he was terribly afraid, yet could not avert his eyes.

But from all these immense perils, illusory or real, the imaginative and high-strung child had but one sure refuge: he could fly to the maternal breast, to weep there, to be protected and consoled, and to smile again.

"My mother . . . was a charming woman and I was in love with her," her son writes very simply in recollection fifty years later. But it was less simple than that.

Henriette Beyle was the soul of gaiety for her family. Aside from her the others seemed to have always taut nerves, and the darkening days of the Great Revolution that was upon them did not make them happier. It was his mother who brought a cheerful bustle into the Beyle household. She was forever inviting guests to dinner, and in her time, at dinner parties, the salon and dining room glittered with dozens of wax candles.

But it was no ordinary bond that united the mother and child. Examining his memories of his childhood in the 1780s, Stendhal says: "I find many things that surprise me in 1835." Then he bravely sets them down.

The love of his "noble and fresh young mother" he declares was the "principal affair of his childhood," and he avows, not without embarrassment:

> In loving her at the age of about six [1789] I had exactly the same character as when, in 1828, I loved Alberthe de Rubempré [his mistress] with mad passion. . . . Since then my way of seeking happiness has changed little, with but

the single exception that in what constitutes the physical side of love I was then what Caesar would be, if he came back to earth, with regard to the use of cannon and small arms. I should soon have learned, and it would have changed nothing in my tactics.

I wanted to cover my mother with kisses, and for her to have no clothes on. She loved me passionately and kissed me often. I returned her kisses with such ardor that she was sometimes obliged to run away. I abhorred my father when he came to interrupt our kisses. I always wanted to kiss her bosom. You must remember that I lost my mother in childhood when I was barely seven.

Turning over his "buried memories" late in life, Stendhal records in almost clinical terms, and yet without any trace of affectation, how he "loved his mother's charms with a mad passion . . . as criminal as possible," and how jealousy of his father dimly formed itself in his child mind. Then, as if troubled by these strange recollections, he adds briefly:

My mother cannot be insulted at the liberties I take with her in revealing that I loved her. If I ever met her again, I would tell her so again. Besides she took no [conscious] part in this sort of love. . . .[3]

On the afternoon of November 22, 1790, Henri, who was nearly eight years old, and his sister Pauline were sent out for a long walk with the maid, Marion, a Dauphinois peasant girl who was like a servant out of Molière, devoted to her masters, but ever speaking her mind freely to them. That evening they were brought to the house of their grandfather, at the Place de Grenette, given supper and put to bed there, instead of returning home. They were not supposed, of course, to know that their mother lay racked in child labor.

In the deep of night—it was two in the morning—the boy was awakened suddenly by the loud wailing and sobbing of his grandfather and his two maiden aunts, just returned from the Rue des Vieux Jésuites after seeing his mother die. Henri remembered every moment of the day that followed.

At first he felt more surprise than despair, he tells us. He did not understand what death was (like most children) and calmly interro-

[3]The passage cited from Chapter III of *Henri Brulard* is certainly one of the most remarkable psychological documents in all literature and astonished Freud himself when it was brought to his attention seventy-five years after it was written. These memoirs had lain hidden among Stendhal's posthumous papers for half a century after his death. What is remarkable is not the appearance of the mother fixation or Oedipus complex in his confessions, frequent enough in literature since ancient times, so much as Stendhal's clear recognition of its decisive importance and his "necessary statement" upon it, though he feared he might have to destroy his memoirs in the end because of such singular reflections.

gated Marion, the nursemaid who sat wailing beside his bed. How could it be that he would "never see her again"? She would be placed, he was told, in the cemetery. "But where is the cemetery?" he asked eagerly. "In the Rue des Mûriers, the one belonging to the parish of Notre-Dame." Henri finally fell asleep peacefully.

But the next morning, when he woke up, he was told to go and kiss his father—not his mother as he was accustomed to. Led into the dim bedchamber where the green curtains were drawn, he felt "an aversion for his father, and found it repugnant to kiss him." He notes: "My father appeared very ugly to me; his eyes were all swollen, and sobs overcame him at every moment." Henri had not been close to his father before this.

Gradually, from the way in which people around him talked or behaved it was borne in upon the boy's mind that he would really never see his mother again. A friend of the family, the Abbé Rey, arrived and, embracing Chérubin Beyle, said in a nasal voice: "Alas my friend, it is God's will!" To the boy these were terrible words the priest uttered. Not long after this, with the direct logic of a child, he began to "speak evil of God," according to Marion, who reproached him for it.

The next day, dressed in mourning, he sat by his father's knee in the parlor, while the friends and relatives of the family came to offer their condolences and attend the funeral. Dry-eyed, watchful, silent, he heard them turn easily from the subject of death to that of trade or to gossip of the law court. He noticed how his uncle Romain Gagnon had gotten himself up for his sister's funeral, in his finest coat, all scented and powdered, like the Lovelace he was!

Henri did not weep or wail. Even the day before, his aunt Séraphie, younger sister of his mother, observing this, had characterized him as a "heartless child." He was vexed, as nearly always at Aunt Séraphie, and resented being misunderstood. But now the one person who had always dissolved such misunderstandings and soothed such hurts was not there. Now for the first time he had no one to confide in; he could no longer run to weep and discharge his grief upon that breast which he had been wont to cover with his furious kisses. When, from the next room, he heard the loud bang of the coffin being sealed and presently carried out, he was ready to believe that his mother was dead. At the parish church of St. Hugues, where the services were held, he at last gave way to his choked-up emotions and made such signs of woe that his father was obliged to send him outside. Even as a grown man, returning to Grenoble, the sound of the church bells would produce in him "a dull and arid grief . . . akin to rage." At the cemetery, he became quite hysterical. When they threw earth upon his mother's coffin, he protested fiercely, tried to stop them, and cried out that "they would hurt her."

3

"Here begins my moral life," he wrote in after years as he looked back with such steady eyes at every moment of his childhood. It is plain that he means: "Here begins the inward conflict of my life," fixed by the death of his mother, at which point in time, he relates, all the joys of his childhood came to an end. In effect childhood itself comes to an end.

In the months that followed the sudden passing of his mother, Henri tasted the full measure of his loss. Instead of growing up as a normal child, surrounded with affection and sympathy, made happy, as he naturally tended to be, he felt himself alone, misunderstood, even "persecuted."

The vivacious Henriette Beyle's role had been to spread happiness in her family circle. With her demise the whole family was plunged in gloom, observed strictest mourning, and dropped all social life for many years. Even Dr. Gagnon, usually a merry soul, was in despair at the death of his favorite child.

Henri's father, that "rival" whom he feared and disliked, was so deeply affected by his wife's death that he ordered her bedchamber shut up, and kept it so, for ten years. The large salon also was left darkened and closed. Nor did Chérubin marry again, though he was in his early forties. "His piety was absurd," his son wrote, "and led him to deny himself and his children all pleasure." To carry on with the household and care for the upbringing of his children he invited Henriette's younger sister, Séraphie Gagnon, to come and live with them in the old house in the Rue des Vieux Jésuites. Aunt Séraphie was a thin woman of about twenty-seven, somewhat pretty, but devout to the point of bigotry, and afflicted with bad nerves and poor health. The spinster aunt was most faithful in caring for Henri, now eight, and his sisters Pauline and Zénaïde, five and three, respectively. But what a long face she made about it.

For the Beyles the times were now badly out of joint. The whole structure of the privileged society in which they lived "close to the nobility" was suddenly collapsing about them. The Bastille had fallen the year before; soon the Constitution was to be voted, and the country engulfed in war, civil and foreign. Catastrophic events followed each other step by step in the five years following Henriette Beyle's death. Chérubin Beyle, besides being secluded by mourning, was now more depressed than ever and showed even less desire than before to go out or seek amusement or receive people. In these dark days when money itself seemed worthless, and the King was being tried for his life, the Beyles and the Gagnons stayed closely within their family circle, suspicious of everyone, often moaning over their lot. Aunt Séraphie would inveigh against the godlessness of the times and even cursed those who, like their eloquent young neighbor, Barnave, had joined hands with the revolutionary leaders in Paris. The three Beyle children were as prisoners of their elders who were in mourning.

Mostly Henri and his sisters were kept indoors, or always accompanied by an older person when they went out. Their only relief was the daily visit at noon for *déjeuner* at the brighter quarters of their grandfather, with its sunny terrace overlooking the river Isère and the busy Place de Grenette, then the central square of the town. In the afternoon they would return to the dim, cheerless rooms of the Beyle house, do their lessons, eat their light supper, and go to sleep.

The great length of time, nearly half a century, that elapsed between those days and the written recollection of them did not soften the extraordinary father-hatred which Stendhal pictures as growing constantly in himself and making the central drama of his boyhood. In enumerating the members of his family as they were in 1790, he describes his grandfather as his "true father" and intimate, for he had transferred his affections to the learned and sympathetic doctor; his great-aunt Elisabeth Gagnon, whom he would also see daily at the Place de Grenette, is described as a truly noble and generous soul who held great sway over Henri; with similar indulgence he wrote of his uncle Romain, who became his model in gallantry.

But his aunt Séraphie was a "she-devil." And as for his father, he is mentioned last of all, described as wrinkled, ugly, and cold: "Never did chance associate two beings so fundamentally antipathetic as my father and myself. He could not say a word that did not displease me." It seemed impossible for him to love his son. "He did not love me personally as his son, but instead regarded me as the continuator of the family." Henri was expected to be like his father, assume his offices someday, direct the family affairs, tell people lawyers' jokes. Thus the pages of *Henri Brulard* are poisoned with father-hatred, expressed with an intensity seldom witnessed in all literature, and supported by many vividly told anecdotes, certainly most venomously colored, or exaggerated, but plainly not invented or fictitious. The remarkable thing is that, far from being uncommonly wicked or unjust, Chérubin Beyle was an average father as fathers went in the eighteenth century save for his avarice, and bore with a great deal from his singular son.

There have been notable conflicts throughout history between fathers and sons: one had occurred only recently between the great Mirabeau and his brilliant father, "the friend of man," who alternately tried to ruin his son or had him imprisoned for years by *lettre de cachet*. Chérubin, far from emulating the Marquis de Mirabeau, tried to help Henri according to his lights; kept him by his side, paid him many little attentions, and watched over him. That Chérubin was not incapable of deep affection is shown by his worshipping the memory of his wife, and locking up her room for ten years, during which he mourned and prayed for her—which did him honor even in Henri's unfriendly eyes. He gave money, though reluctantly, and the advantages of education to his son. But *he did not permit him to be happy.*

Despite the teachings of Rousseau, the life of French children of aristocratic or upper middle-class family was not a happy one in the eighteenth century. Henri and his sisters must be reared with a grave discipline; they must not play with "common children"; they must be tutored at home by religious mentors who had "severe faces." He might be taken riding in a carriage; but he would be seated by his carping aunt, forced to listen to her bromides, while enviously, out of the corner of his eye, he watched the lower-class children of the town running about the streets or the Public Gardens at liberty. Occasionally he would be permitted to meet a few children of noble birth whose parents were the clients of his father: the counts and barons de Monval, de Sinard or de Bérenger; but they were as stiffly dressed, as "suffocated" as himself. "Alas," he cries, "I was forbidden even to play marbles or spin a top."

At five he could read and write a passable French; at six he was set to studying Latin with a tutor. Because it was plain that he was precociously intelligent he was kept closely confined "as if under a glass jar." It was always with the soft words of tender solicitude that his "tyrants"—father and aunt—addressed him, or with homilies about paternal love and the duties of children. They were in mourning, they were fearful of the strange upheavals that convulsed all France. "In their dark humor, I was their unique occupation," he relates. "They adorned this process of torture with the name of education and probably meant it in good faith." Even the patience of his father, who administered physical chastisement to him only two or three times in his life, exasperated Henri. Impulsiveness—Henri sometimes gave extreme provocation—might have been better.

And Aunt Séraphie!—that "sour-minded believer" who, when he read books that gave him pleasure, snatched them from his hand—he speaks of her with a rage that is all but comic. His grandfather handed him, when he was ten, a book by Voltaire. "How can they give *such books* to a child?" Séraphie screamed. And she would run to his father with her complaints, while Dr. Gagnon prudently beat a retreat, disliking scenes, but also, as Henri observed, showing himself a timid soul.

On fine days, his father and aunt always took him for the same walk of five miles to the family "domain" at Claix up the cascading river Drac, Henri keeping exactly forty paces ahead of the couple. He loved the farm at Claix, with its old orchard, its vineyards, and its great views of mountain-cupped Grenoble. "But even the wonderful mountains of Dauphiné were spoiled for me," he complained—because his two cicerones were forever canting about the "beautiful scenery." Lying under an apple tree at Claix, one day, he lost himself in a copy of *Don Quixote* that Dr. Gagnon had given him and went off into peals of laughter as he read. His father, hearing him, dragged him off to inspect the work that was going on about the farm, the new stone sheep barns, or the drains that were being laid.

"They even objected to my laughter!" the boy would recall. As for his father's "obsessions" with his farming projects, the self-willed son refused to be interested in them.

When he was about six the Abbé Raillane, a Jesuit priest who lived for a time in a small house in the courtyard back of the Beyles', came into his life as his private tutor and afflicted it with his "dark tyranny." He is pictured as a thin, neatly clad man, with a very wrinkled and greenish, or jaundiced, complexion, hideously thick eyebrows, mean eyes, and a villainously hooked nose. The Abbé, who enjoyed an excellent reputation (though not for personal charm), taught the children of the leading families of Grenoble. That he was strong in his faith was shown by the fact that, after being forced into hiding during the Terror of '93, he would reappear secretly and conduct mass in private homes at the risk of his life. Under him Henri received a thoroughgoing religious instruction, and regularly sang in the choir at St. André's Church with admitted enjoyment—up to the age of twelve. He also studied rhetoric, arithmetic, and Latin (by rote). Taught to write Latin verses by the Abbé's authoritarian methods, and to read Virgil, he conceived a dislike for poetry and even for Virgil. Such were the unintended results of the "tyrant's" methods, he assures us.

The Abbé would report any small misdeed as a matter of duty to his pupil's father, and punishment of some sort would promptly follow. He expounded discipline and religious orthodoxy. When Henri, who became much interested in the natural sciences under his grandfather's encouragement, would speak his own inquiring, irritatingly logical and independent little mind, the Abbé Raillane would sternly order him to forget such notions. "But sir, it is true, that is what I feel."—"Never mind, my little friend, you must not say that, it isn't proper." Always he ended by saying that something wasn't done, wasn't proper. He taught the boy the Ptolemaic system, though Grandfather Gagnon came in one day and asked him why he continued to teach it when everyone knew it was false. "But it explains everything, and besides, it is approved by the Church." Dr. Gagnon, who was a Voltairian, would shake his head, laugh lightly, and make off. But in his good-humored way, he would mock at the ignorance of such servants of the Lord as Raillane, even imitating his manner: "*. . . besides, it is approved by the Church!*"

Henri never forgot the dreary walks around Grenoble that he was obliged to take in the company of the Abbé and two other proper little pupils every afternoon, at five in summer, at three in winter. In the river Isère, along whose bank they walked invariably, there was a charming islet of rock where the town boys went swimming in fine weather. Passing it, Henri and his comrades would look with longing, like "poor prisoners," at the boys in the river. Whereupon the Abbé Raillane would assure them that respectable children never bathed in the river; the boys who did so always ended by drowning. This gave Henri a childhood fear of water that nearly cost him his life in later days. The Abbé would go chattering by the hour on the "dangers of liberty"—until Henri could repeat the sermon by rote.

The boy tried to deceive his mentor by using a pony for his Virgil. Or, in prankish spirit, he tormented the Abbé's pet canaries, or injured his tubbed orange trees. But in this duel he usually came off second best, and gained only the punishment of being sentenced to eat supper alone in his room. When angered, the Abbé would berate him with a cold rage; on two or three occasions his father whipped him.

That the heart of Henri Beyle could easily be won by anybody who amused and interested him, or was simply kind to him, was well known in later years to his school friends, for his was in great measure, despite his shyness and self-consciousness, an affectionate, happy, and lusty nature. But such approaches were never used by his father or his tutor. Thanks to them, he relates, he became "somber, discontented, and *underhanded*." He adds: "The Abbé Raillane, for all his good intentions, might well have turned me into a thief."

The pinpricks, the petty scoldings, the continual homilies appeared to him as a massive system of persecution ranged against himself, and —in the absence of a mother—made him, in very self-defense, deceptive, calculating, and also melancholy. Often he would weep alone in his room. In the calmer mood of later years he writes: "I was perhaps very wicked and unjust toward my father and the Abbé Raillane . . . but they *poisoned* my childhood." He adds revealingly: "I hated the Abbé, I hated my father, the source of the Abbé's power, I hated still more the religion in whose name he tyrannized over me."

Thirty or forty years later, he would feel an instinctive aversion to people who had the same kind of nose as the Abbé Raillane. He would regale his friends in Paris, such as Prosper Mérimée, with stories of the morose priest who "persecuted" him for a harmless prank, or for tearing his clothes in play. He would mimic the old Abbé crying: "You are a disgrace to your family and your religion!"

When he was twelve, he declares, he hated his religion, he hated all priests. In his memoirs he describes them, with the exception of Raillane, as invariably dirty, greasy, gluttonous fellows who made clacking noises with their tongues when dining with the Beyles, or rolled their eyes madly at the sight of a suckling pig at the table. He hated his father, but also the religion and the priests who, supporting his father's authority, "oppressed the young and the weak." He hated even Grenoble, the city of his father, and drew up elaborate, secret plans to run away.

4

There were compensations: "My excellent grandfather . . . was really my true father and intimate friend. . . ."

How much happier were the sunlit rooms of his grandfather's large house, only three minutes distant, at the open Place de Grenette, where Henri came for lunch every day. The paternal tenderness that he lacked, he received from the sixty-year-old surgeon, who secretly disliked his son-in-law as much as he loved his grandson.

Henri Gagnon had studied medicine at the University of Montpellier, had become Grenoble's favorite doctor and passing rich. Like a true son of the eighteenth century he was a student of all the sciences, he was liberal and tolerant in his beliefs, and passed for one of the best talkers and most cultivated men of Grenoble. He loved literature also and "for forty years had been the head and front of all that was literary and liberal in Grenoble." His library, one of the most valuable in the town, still shows this, for it was bequeathed to the Bibliothèque Publique of which he was one of the founders and in which his portrait still hangs. It shows him a handsome man with delicate features, wearing a powdered wig with three rows of curls just as his grandson has described him.

The Gagnon house had a wing and a terrace back of it, which the doctor filled with beds of rare plants and flowers. Here he played the naturalist every morning, tending the flowers like a good disciple of Rousseau. At night he would walk his terrace scanning the stars and expound his astronomical lore first to his children, then to his grandson Henri.

The boy had the run of the doctor's library. Dr. Gagnon looked the other way even when he took "forbidden" books. At the age of ten Henri read not only Molière, but Voltaire, a favorite of his grandfather, who kept a little wooden bust of the philosopher on his desk. In his youth Dr. Gagnon had made a pilgrimage to Voltaire's home, Ferney, just over the Swiss border, and had been received there with every distinction.

Seeing that Henri was quick to read, he encouraged him by giving him such books as the Abbé Prévost's *Manon Lescaut* and Ariosto's *Orlando Furioso* in French. While others played in the sun, the lonely boy sat by the window overlooking the gardens and river, reading endlessly. Increasingly he lived in books, where in a dream world rid of his father, aunt, and tutor, he consorted with the brave knights and noble ladies of Ariosto, and even with beautiful courtesans like Manon Lescaut, who died for love. All sorts of romantic enthusiasms now gripped his imagination, and this disposition was fostered, not only by his reading, but by the influence of his great-aunt Elisabeth Gagnon.

This charming old lady, like her brother the doctor, showed much tenderness to the boy; calm and dignified of bearing, dwelling alone in her little apartment at her brother's house, she impressed him as a woman who lived in her dreams, and entirely "Spanish" or "Castilian" in her ideals. The stories she would tell him about "the good old days" strengthened this impression. For example, she had a proud way of avoiding all mention of money matters so constantly on the lips of the Grenoble bourgeois. Elisabeth, it was said, had remained unmarried as a consequence of some unhappy passion, but to Henri she was still beautiful in old age, and he said that it was she who formed his heart.

But while he acquired a taste for reverie that brought relief from the vexations his family circle inflicted, there was another side of him that developed strongly: a cool, curious, reasoning fellow who would pull against the romantic fellow in his transports. Medicine and science, as his grandfather expounded them, also fascinated him. "At twelve, a prodigy of science, I incessantly questioned my good grandfather, who took pleasure in instructing me." The doctor and naturalist, who had won some note for his papers on meteorology, read before learned societies, urged him to be exact and precise in his thought. He spoke of his experimental methods, and the boy learned from him what he could grasp of anatomy, or even of dissection. His grandfather opened the beautiful volumes of Diderot's Encyclopedia, and he found the new world of science mirrored in their magnificent engravings. Not only was his thirst for knowledge sharpened, but it was given an analytical and rational bent that conflicted strangely with the "enthusiast" in him.

"My grandfather also," as he tells us, "communicated nearly all his literary tastes to me." A man of measure, with Horace ever beside him, Dr. Gagnon always urged that clarity and restraint were the hallmarks of intellectual greatness, and in literature were exemplified by the great seventeenth-century writers, and those who preceded Rousseau in their own century. Rousseau was a favorite of Dr. Gagnon's, but what pretentiousness, overemphasis, and exaggerated eloquence he had inspired in his imitators! The grandfather himself seemed like a figure out of the preceding century, deliberate and precise in speech, full of good form, elegantly shunning quarrels and scenes, making jests with a light and dry wit—sometimes almost too light, even effete.

Uncle Romain Gagnon, who lived with his father, was also a man of charm in a somewhat different measure. He was as merry as he was handsome, and the recognized Lovelace of the town. On occasion the nephew was permitted to see his uncle do his entire toilet, an elaborate ritual which made the boy's eyes almost start out of his head. Romain wore embroidered coats with gold buttons that cost perhaps 1,000 *écus* (of three francs each!), and he poured perfume all over himself. His father certainly did not pay for these fine garments, and would lift his hands in dismay at seeing him thus. After the dandy's toilet was done Henri would proudly hold a great silver candlestick to light his way before him as he made his grand descent to dinner.

Romain, also a lawyer, but one who did not bother to have clients, would wink and roll his eyes as he dropped hints to his little nephew of the many noble ladies who pined for him. One woman of Grenoble's good but rather gallant society was actually heard to say: "Well, at any rate I did not yield to Romain Gagnon like all the others." Some of the others, according to an old southern custom, sometimes sent him gifts of jewels or even money. "It matters little," Romain would explain to Henri, when he was only twelve or so, "so long as one doesn't hoard such things." The gifts received from some plain dowager would, in good time, pass on to a poor but pretty little actress at the Grenoble Opera House.

Children reach adolescence early in life in southern France; and Henri, as a mere boy, had his uncle Romain as his sly mentor in gallantry. From him he learned how fine a thing it was to be lucky with women. Also, when he was scarcely twelve, he discovered in Romain's room a whole heap of libertine books, such as Voltaire's *La Pucelle d'Orléans*, or others by obscure authors with titles such as *The Weakness and Repentance of a Woman.*

It was Uncle Romain, moreover, who took him for the first time to the Opera House to see a performance of Corneille's *Le Cid*. The lights, the music, the sky-blue satin costumes of the actors, offered a vision of thrilling beauty and happiness. Henri had the impression that his uncle was one of those exalted characters who strutted the stage; that "every moment of his life must be as delicious as those I enjoyed at the play."

The time came when Uncle Romain made a good marriage and removed to his wife's estate at the border village of Les Echelles, in Savoy, several hours' carriage ride from Grenoble. Henri and his sisters at regular intervals, once or twice a year, came to visit their uncle and new aunt high up in the mountains, amid the fragrance of deep pine forests at a place of great natural beauty, by the waterfall of the river Guiers. His uncle's wife was not only gracious to him, but was so beautiful that Henri remembered being abashed at the sight of her, scarcely answering her questions, while devouring her with his eyes.

Like Marie Antoinette, they went on picnics in those days. The company was made up of young friends and relatives of the Gagnons, including some attractive young ladies, and always a young officer or two accompanying them. It was like a scene out of Rousseau, whose ghost certainly hovered here. Into the occasionally amorous dalliance of the older folk, Henri—perhaps boasting a little, in later years—remembered entering with precocious zeal. On one day, when one of the young ladies who had petted and kissed the small boy also showed favor to a young officer, suffering his embraces and kisses, the infant lover grew fiercely jealous and threw pebbles at them. The officer then picked up the boy and perched him in the branches of a low mulberry tree from which he could not climb down. But he jumped off, hurting his ankle, then ran away like a rabbit while everyone pursued him, shouting and laughing.

Henri was so lively at such parties that everyone was amused by him; these occasions were all the happier because his aunt Séraphie was usually absent. His grandfather, a man of the world, would say to him: "You are a homely little fellow but no one will mind that in you."

For him the holidays at Les Echelles, with their welcome change of scenery, brought "happiness, sudden, complete, perfect . . . like going to heaven; everything was enchanting." "Here," he says significantly, "everybody was a friend, everybody smiled at me. . . ."

Then the return to the old quarter of Grenoble, to his father and aunt, to the shuttered old house of the Beyles, to the Latin lessons he was supposed to have completed during the week's excursion.

His recollections color and exaggerate the gloom of his family life, which the sight of his uncle Romain's rural paradise by contrast made all the darker. Henri knew more happy hours than he owned: there were more picnics and excursions in those days than today. Parents also left their children much in the company of servants, who were their unaffected friends. Thus Henri was the confidant of the maid Marion; he was also the devoted admirer of Lambert, an attractive young man-servant of his grandfather's. But to his great sorrow, when Henri was about eleven, Lambert died suddenly in an accidental fall from a ladder, and Henri wept for him almost every night for many weeks. After having been reproached by Séraphie for his "unfeeling heart" at the time of his mother's death, he was now scolded for lying awake and sobbing at night. Later, examining his memories carefully, he tells us almost casually that for years after his mother's death he wept alone every night before he fell asleep.

5

The Abbé Raillane told him that while being the aptest of his pupils, he was "truly imprudent in speech." When his sense of indignation was aroused by unjust scolding, or by the cool reproofs of his father, he would reply with passion.

> One day, bored by my father's speeches, I said to him: "If you love me so much, give me five sous a day and let me live as I like. However, you can be sure of one thing: as soon as I am old enough, I shall enlist."

My father turned on me as if he would crush me with a blow. "You are nothing but an undutiful and impudent wretch," he exclaimed.

Henri learned that it was profitable to hold his tongue and hide his emotions. He grew morose or sullen. Sometimes he could be cruel to his sister Pauline and strike her with his fist—though later he became passionately fond of her—and he always detested his youngest sister Zénaïde-Caroline, his father's favorite and a talebearer. He felt himself "a slave," as he explains in his memoirs, and soon assumed all the worst qualities of that condition. To be truthful to his aunt and father, as the observant child noted, or to his tutor, was often costly. Did not the Abbé make statements that seemed, not so much true, as "proper"?

"I began to tell lies," he recollects. "The little happiness I was able to extract was preserved by lying." Outwardly, Henri was respectful enough toward his elders; but he was ready to employ almost any ruse to strike back at them or hurt them.

When he was eleven, he kept a tame thrush in the house. He regarded this pet as one of his few real friends. The thrush, though lame in one foot and walking with a funny hop, defended itself well enough against cats and dogs, and always came to hide under Henri's chair in the dining room at mealtimes. One day the thrush disappeared, nobody would say how. (Later, he ascertained that it was accidentally crushed under a door.) By his whole air, by his suspicious and resentful glances, Henri made it all too plain that he believed his father had killed the thrush, merely to spite him. His father sensed this and seemed hurt at Henri's suspicions, since he was blameless. At table one day, Chérubin Beyle, in his somewhat subtle, roundabout lawyer's speech, explained to the world at large that there were little accidents, sometimes leading to false accusations, yet only the result of chance. But Henri refused to show any faith in these explanations.

"I was sublime; I blushed to the roots of my hair, but did not open my lips." His father seemed hurt. "He pressed me for an answer, but was met only with silence. My eyes, which were doubtless very expressive at that age, must have spoken for me. Thus was I avenged, O tyrant!"

It was but a trivial incident, yet like so many other of his recollections, too truthful, too revealing to be disbelieved. In telling it he shows overtones of the morbid and neurotic: the son deliberately seeks to be unjust to the father, and seems ready to draw up the most terrible accusations against him.

Not only did he suffer from insecurity and hostility within his family circle since his mother's death, but the times in France were themselves calculated to inspire in persons of property the most painful feelings of insecurity, as the great Revolution now unfolded itself, each new stage more spectacular and violent than the last.

Hitherto the conflict between father and son had been instinctual. But now, as Stendhal's autobiography of his boyhood pictures it, the struggle assumed a higher, more objective form. "Soon politics came between us," he relates.

His family was, in sentiment, one of the most aristocratic in town—"which meant that I immediately felt myself a fanatical republican." He was thrilled like most young people at the news of the immense victory of French republican soldiers at Valmy over the trained foreign armies attempting to invade France. He saw the picturesque regiments of dragoons ride through Grenoble on the road to Italy. Some of them were quartered with the Beyles. Henri naturally longed to be one of them, wearing a plumed helmet. ". . . My eyes devoured them . . . my parents loathed them."

Perceiving the gloom of his father, as news came in the autumn of 1792 of the establishment of the Republic and the arrest of the King, Henri with instinctive malice made himself a little tricolor flag. Bearing it aloft, he paraded about the rooms of his house all alone on days of victory for Revolutionary arms. Aunt Séraphie and Chérubin caught him and snatched the flag from his hands, calling him an "abominable, impious child." In afterthought he wrote—one doubts that he had the same ideology at ten—"I felt myself a martyr for the fatherland; I loved liberty madly. . . ." On the walls of his room he scrawled in chalk the slogan: *Live free or die.*

The priests now went into hiding, some of them taking refuge in the Beyle or Gagnon house. To Henri's great delight the "tyrant" Raillane took to the hills for a time, and a lay instructor, named Durand, more amiable, if less acute, replaced him.

Each phase of the trial of King Louis XVI was followed by Henri's "relentlessly aristocratic and religious" family with the most intense anxiety.

"But *they* will never dare to carry out this infamous judgment," he remembered his father saying. Looking back, he thought that the attitude of his father and their friends who were royalists or priests was what made him "wish silently for the death of the king."

It must have been five or six days after the 21st of January 1793—the Abbé Raillane was still on hand—when the sound of the mail coach arriving from Lyons and Paris shook the house. His father went out to see the newspapers or hear the news. At length he came back and told them with a heavy sigh: "It is all over. They have murdered him."

"I was seized by one of the sharpest feelings of joy I have ever experienced in all my life," Stendhal relates in his autobiography. "The reader will perhaps think that I am cruel, but what I was at ten, I still am at fifty-two." At this moment Henri had been hoodwinking his family as usual by pretending to study his lessons, while reading a light novel by the Abbé Prévost, *Memoirs of a Man of Quality.*

"I could not go on reading my novel, so enraptured was I at this great act of national justice," he says. "I hid the book and placed in front of it the serious work, probably Rollin's *Roman History,* which my father was making me read, and I shut my eyes so as to be able to enjoy this great event unmolested."

Unconsciously he transferred the guilt of the King (whom the republican press accused of treason against the nation) to his father, who represented authority over him as the King over the people. The access of voluptuous pleasure he felt was doubtless inspired by seeing in imagination his own father-tyrant slain!

This is assuredly one of the more terrible confessions of his memoirs of boyhood, and Stendhal insists that the thought of the pleasure he felt in 1793 at the guillotining of Louis XVI stayed with him for forty-two years, proof enough of the degree in which he felt himself "persecuted" and goaded, in the depths of his unconscious mind, to secret revolt.[4]

In addition to the thought that he was "persecuted" there appears at this point in the uncontrolled, almost automatic statements of his memoir the idea: "At the bottom of my heart I was still jealous of my father." It was as if he charged his father—though this secret thought is never uttered, it is everywhere implied—with guilt for his mother's early death.

But the uncanny thing about his reminiscences is that, generations before the modern schools of psychoanalysis appeared, Stendhal asso-

[4]In retrospect, in *Henri Brulard,* Chapter X, he expresses the fear that his readers will think him "immoral" as well as cruel, but promises that "this is not the worst you will see of me." We cannot accept the suggestion once made by Sainte-Beuve concerning similar reminiscences or confessions that they are composed principally of "the untruths that an old man tells us about what he pretends his youth must have been." The passage in question is full of the most significant fancies, or thought-associations, that dwell upon the fixation of father-hatred in himself, written it must be remembered some seventy years before the Freudian contributions to psychiatry appeared. Also, we must note that he had never intended to publish those memoirs of early life in the unrevised, uncensored form in which they were found long after his death.

ciated his own individual secret rebellion against his family with the larger, collective, and political rebellion that was sweeping over France. Repeatedly he likened his own personal lot to that of the downtrodden people who rose against their ruler:

> In a sense, I was exactly in the position of the people of Europe at the present day: my tyrants always used the gentle language of the most tender solicitude, and religion was their firmest ally.

He universalizes rebellious youth in himself, in his own revolt against the family authority; and, perhaps for the first time, by implication associates such unconscious impulses with the more general uprisings of the peoples. We have here unmistakable clues that trace for us the psychical formation of the Rebel Type—the "infant Brutus"—who exclaims: "The death of a King is always useful, *in terrorem* . . . ."

He was only ten in that year of the great Terror in France, but bitterness at the parental constraints he suffered gained over him, and moved him to conspire and to lie, to attempt a still more active resistance, which to his dismayed family appeared as the most infamous betrayal, yet to him was but a blow for liberty.

CHAPTER II

The Struggle for Freedom

> These youths who had never known what it was to be young . . . these children of the new generation bore upon their brows the marks of the terrible times in which they came into the world. . . . A truly new generation! which would always be distinct and set apart, by its strange traits, from the times past and the times to come. . . . And their elders made moan at finding themselves more like strangers before their children, multiplying upon the face of the earth.
>
> —Sainte-Beuve: *Chateaubriand et son groupe littéraire.*

SURROUNDED by older people, who were in mourning, and feared for their very lives, the sensitive boy tended to withdraw into himself, living alone, with "an alienated heart." Not being permitted to play with children of his own age made him seem, later on when tardily he was sent to school, both awkward and oversensitive, older than his mates and yet less experienced than they. He would be made self-conscious in his relations with most people all his life, as his cousin Romain Colomb observed.

For early sorrow had made him prematurely introspective. As his grandfather noticed, he really lived in books from the age of six or seven. Longer than other children he knew nothing of life save what he read in books. And what books! Those he swiped from his rakish uncle Romain's room were simply licentious and stimulated his erotic curiosity. Others were irreligious or subversive in that they inspired their readers with grand illusions and vague longings to "escape." The works of Rousseau especially, which Henri read at ten, now so generally neglected, had the effect of arousing the youth of the eighteenth century, the young Robespierres and Bonapartes, to full revolt.

The dangerous thing was that his family did not know what was going on in that child mind which was both precocious and obsessed. They prated and scolded. He ended by believing that *everything* they or the Abbé Raillane told him was a lie. Did not his father calmly lie to him one day, saying that he had promised a reward of one franc if he did his lessons well, instead of one *écu* (three francs), as Henri clearly heard him say? Everyone lied. He need only pretend to believe or agree with them, he need only deceive them to diminish the superior power they held over him. Meanwhile the spirit of negation waxed in him; schemes for insurrection teemed in his head, as is indicated by a digressive passage of *Henri Brulard* in which certain antithetical thought combinations that used to haunt him as a boy are noted down by Stendhal in old age with a psychological acumen unique in his time. These were:

"father" versus "patriotism-Brutus"
"priest" versus "love," etc.

He himself was surprised to find such notions in his memory, clearly associated with the time when he was ten. It would be the task of future psychologists, he implies, to discover why a child of this age compiled a list of the *greatest regicides* of history, which his amiable grandfather was deeply shocked to find in one of his lesson books.[1]

But in the tragic springtime of 1793, the Reign of Terror reached even remote Grenoble; Henri's father feared for his neck as well as his property and status. In those days they could almost hear the thunder of artillery as dissident Lyons, on the other side of the mountains, was besieged by the Republicans. To the elder Beyle and Aunt Séraphie it seemed that this dark hour was made all the more trying by the boy's sly resistance to discipline and his increasing *esprit raisonneur,* his eternal argumentativeness.

At the end of April 1793, at the order of the Convention in Paris, two of the people's representatives or commissars arrived in Grenoble to impose stern measures aimed at crushing internal enemies and reinforcing the loyalty of the Dauphinois to the Republic. Soon they issued a decree for the arrest of all persons in the town who were regarded as *notoirement suspects,* a full list of whom were drawn up.

Among the first to be placed on the list of the "notorious suspects,"

[1]Plainly enough the father image represented tyranny, the servant of the church repression of sexual impulses, to his unconscious mind. He remarks: "I had a list of thought associations such as . . . *father* versus *patriotism,* or *Brutus*—who seemed to me the symbol of all that was sublime in literature. This was entirely my own invention. I had forgotten all about it for perhaps twenty-six years; I must come back to this subject." *Vie d'Henri Brulard,* I, 193, Divan edition.

and subject to imprisonment by the local Committee of Public Safety, was the Abbé Raillane. His precipitate flight into the mountains had been for young Beyle one of the great, tangible blessings born of the bloody Revolution. But what was worse, his father, Chérubin Beyle, one of the stanchest adherents of the Bourbons, was also on this list of the condemned. The attorney, however, simply moved across the street to his father-in-law's house and avoided showing himself in public.

The Terror was comparatively mild in Grenoble. Though the Dauphinois were enthusiastic Republicans, the first to rebel, they were reasonable men. The local revolutionary authorities knew where Citizen Beyle was, but after inquiring at his own home and learning that he was absent, paid no more attention to him. (Later in 1794, however, he was compelled to show himself and submit to a brief imprisonment of two or three weeks.) But while he waited, uncertain as to his fate, he uttered many a complaint at the "new order of things," as he contemptuously called it, and ventured the opinion that he was being persecuted chiefly because one of the heads of the Committee of Public Safety was a rival lawyer, named Amar, a Jacobin, who was eager to take over his clientele.

"But Amar has placed you on the list of those suspected of not loving the Republic, and it is *certain* that you do not love it," remarked his son brightly.

At this the father and all the family present were beside themselves with anger at the unfeeling boy; after a fierce slating he was banished from the supper table. But habitually he only thought of the logic or truth of what he had said, and of the injustice of his father: "What *right* had they to be angry with me?"

He wept and he longed for liberty. Outside, the gaily caparisoned cavalry of the Republic rode by every day. From his window he also watched longingly the "Roman" festivals, and those fraternal public dances about the Liberty Tree that were being held in all the towns of France in 1794, and in which other boys joined.

The boy's logic was cruel; but that he was capable of affection and generous passion was shown by his attachment for the manservant, Lambert, and his prolonged mourning for the man's death. Also by an incident related not by himself in those memoirs where he so often acts as his own worst witness, but long afterward by his young cousin Romain Colomb.

The Colomb family, related to Henri on his mother's side, had been even more actively royalist than the Beyles; Romain's father was hunted down and imprisoned in June 1794, and on the day of the arrest little Romain was brought to stay at the house of Dr. Gagnon, then regarded as a liberal. This was evidently one of the rare occasions when Henri could play with his cousin. After dinner the two boys went into the salon, and Romain fell asleep on the couch. But in the adjacent dining room Henri could hear his relatives discussing the case. They sat behind shuttered windows full of fear, and anxiously considered whether they had not increased their own danger by sheltering the child of an arrested suspect. It seemed to Henri that Aunt Séraphie particularly urged that little Romain be sent away somewhere. At this, he rushed into the other room and began to protest most vehemently at the very idea of forsaking his friend and cousin. They were shamed into keeping the little boy with them. As Colomb, who awoke and overheard their talk, relates: "Their design, so cowardly and heartless toward me, plunged Henri Beyle into despair, and he delivered himself in such vigorous terms as to strengthen forever the bonds of our friendship."[2]

Not long after the condemnation of his father as a suspect the spreading anti-clerical movement reached Grenoble. As in other cities a so-called Battalion of Hope was organized here by a certain unfrocked priest named Gardon; it was to be recruited from the boys and girls of the town who, instead of receiving religious instruction, were to meet at a sequestrated church and drill, parade, or hold public meetings designed to prepare them for patriotic service and to combat the alleged anti-republican agitation of the clergy and their flocks. Soon Henri could watch them parading gaily in the streets, as he stood with his nose pressed to the window. His proposal that he join with them was sternly rejected by his elders; but in love with all the excitement that the Revolution had wrought, he burned to play soldier and patriot with the other children and defend the Republic.

One morning, at the Gagnon door, a crude note was found, ordering Citizen Beyle to send his son to a meeting at St. André's Church, to be enrolled in the Battalions of Hope. The note ended with "Fraternal Salutations" and was signed simply "Gardon."

The Beyles and Gagnons were thrown into a panic at receiving this message from such a sinister figure. In imagination they saw themselves denounced and led to the block, and did not scan the note too carefully. However, a certain friend of the family, an ugly, hunchbacked fellow whom Henri detested, happened to be visiting with

[2]Romain Colomb, *Notice biographique*, p. ix, Paris, 1845.

them, and he, noticing that the message was written in a most childish hand, suggested that it might well be a forgery or a mere prank. Henri at once was sent out of the room while all of them compared the note with his writing in his lesson books. The evidence was damning, and they took it hard. Their child of eleven, outwardly so well bred, had all but betrayed them. Certainly the affair might have led to their being gravely compromised. Calling him into their presence again, they most solemnly and humorlessly indicted him.

The infant Machiavelli had been waiting in the salon, playing casually with a clay ball but really filled with fear and trembling. He had made resolutions to face them like a brave Roman, and declare firmly his determination to go to Citizen Gardon and serve his country in spite of all of them. But this statement when he made it frightened his family more terribly than anything else, even though it was delivered in a weak and timid voice. Even his grandfather, "pale with fear," now joined in the chorus of reproaches and cries of shame. Henri's sang-froid deserted him; he grew tearful, softened, and soon was begging to be forgiven. This time he was in for it, being sentenced to three days' banishment from the table. But rallying his spirits he exclaimed proudly as he marched out: "I would far rather dine alone than with tyrants who never stop scolding me!"

The Gardon affair left wounds. His father, who understood so little of the boy's nature, at once passionate and calculating, must have been startled at what he glimpsed that day. A wall was raised between them, and Henri grew less fond even of his good grandfather, though he admitted this with sorrow. Dr. Gagnon was after all but a timid compromiser. This prudent Voltairian had shrunk from serving the Revolution when nominated by some of his townspeople as their deputy to the Convention at Paris; he was still more afraid of his daughter Séraphie and her carping tongue.

In his struggle for liberation, the boy had used ruse and chicane. He had failed, but he would try again.

2

In the recollections of his early years he wrote shrewdly:

> If my parents had known how to bring me up they might well have succeeded in turning me into one of those dolts, of whom there were so many in the provinces. . . . The indignation I felt in childhood created, in spite of them, the character I have.

The ordeal of alienation and conflict in childhood made him refreshingly different from less passionate and more docile beings. It made him Stendhal.

He had naturally strong reasoning powers; he could detect little frauds or hypocrisies in his father, or his aunt, with a pitiless eye. But at the same time he had a quite extraordinary power of self-delusion; his imagination easily transported, intoxicated him.

Deprived of freedom and play, the "child misanthrope" (so he has been called) read books all the more voraciously, especially such as solaced his mind by affording escape to a world of romance and chivalry. The tender Corneille and Ariosto's *Orlando Furioso* fed his imagination and gave shape to his dreams. Reading the epic of the late-Renaissance poet, he relates, "I fell in love with Bradamante, whom I imagined as a buxom girl with a bosom of the most dazzling whiteness." Unlike his bourgeois parents he felt he must strive to be noble and courtly like Roland, even aristocratic or "Castilian," never mentioning any money matters such as forever occupied his father. For this reason Molière's *L'Avare* repelled him, when he first read it, because of the "vulgar details" used by the comic poet, which reminded him too much of his home life.

It was in reading the plays of someone like Destouches, the sentimental imitator of Rousseau, that Henri was most deeply stirred. These feeble love comedies set him dreaming and weeping. It was at this time that he resolved to go to Paris and write plays, as soon as he was old enough.

There were all sorts of forbidden books in the Gagnon house, and Henri knew their hiding place well. He would wait until the doctor was called away by a patient, then would snatch them up. In Pliny the Elder, he tried in vain to satisfy his curiosity about the "natural history of woman" when he was but twelve. At this time he also came upon one of those Louis XV studies in scatology that his rakish uncle collected, a book called *Félicie* (by André de Nerciat), and (in the company of his little cousin, Colomb) read it from beginning to end. He declares that this book made him absolutely mad with excitement, and that "the possession of a living mistress, then the object of all my desires, would not have plunged me into such a torrent of amorousness." Who could forget a heroine who cries: "Ah, to live for the moment, and die!" or: "God has made me as I am!" Finally in the same treasure trove of forbidden literature, he came upon Choderlos de Laclos' *Les Liaisons dangereuses*, a recent novel (1782) which was of a much higher order than the stories of fallen women in Uncle Romain's library.

Laclos' famous romance is much too rambling and diffuse by modern standards, but gives a most perceptive picture of the manners of the 1780s in France. Its hero, Valmont, by a quite methodical amorous strategy, carries out a series of conquests of more or less virtuous females. The setting is easily recognized as the garrison town of Grenoble itself.

Les Liaisons dangereuses became the "breviary" of the town's provincial gallants: they could almost recognize its female characters. Reading it at this most impressionable age, the calculating little Beyle was fascinated by its ingenious yet clear dissection of the passions, and its methodical, self-conscious approach to love. Love indeed was pictured as an everlasting war, in which knowledge of the adversary and mastery of all details yielded victory. The paramount role of planning and tactics—for the author, Laclos, was a soldierly fellow himself—in this rather cold romance undoubtedly helped to give a special bent to the disposition of the young Beyle in early adolescence.

But on the other hand he, like tens of thousands of other youths of his time, could not long escape the all-pervasive influence of Jean-Jacques Rousseau. Locking himself in his room, and curling up in bed, he read *La Nouvelle Héloïse* in all its length, as in a trance. The melancholy and enormously sensitive Rousseau expounded another way of love: that of self-sacrifice and virtue. His heroine was not one of the facile women of Laclos, but the "ideal mistress" who inspired and returned only the noblest passion. Feeling was *all.* Great feeling made one superior to others. Like Goethe, Chateaubriand, and Byron, Henri Beyle in youth fell completely under the spell of the eloquent philosopher of the expansive ego. He was all too ready to enjoy Rousseau's sentimental introspectiveness; like Rousseau he was a "lost child," like him a "superior soul," misunderstood and persecuted, pitying himself and mistrusting the world around him. Even Rousseau's attitude of timidity toward women was adopted by him. "*La Nouvelle Héloïse* taught me," he says, "to be good, despite my family." But the romantic philosopher also encouraged in his young readers an introspectiveness that fed on their own sorrow with a morbid self-pity; he stimulated a precocious affectation of world-weariness and disillusionment.

These two contrasting books, *Les Liaisons dangereuses* and *La Nouvelle Héloïse*, together with the *Confessions* of Rousseau, he read over and over again during his boyhood and youth. They represent the two poles of his nature, and its two conflicting directions: the one toward a knowing libertinism, to be pursued by what might be called coldly rational tactics and finesse; the other a longing for "ideal love" and surrender to the tenderest and most virtuous sentiments.

3

As the pretensions of the Beyles required that he be educated by a private tutor, so it was decided when he was eleven that he should take drawing lessons at the home of an artist named Leroy, who had recently come to Grenoble from Paris. Leroy's home was about ten minutes' walk from the Beyles', but by doubling his pace Henri gained whole quarter hours of freedom without the company of an elder person. He could loiter curiously about the crowded, noisome Central Market. Pushing farther on to the Public Gardens, he could even watch the town children who played there at liberty though he scarcely knew how to address them. To explain his delays he told various lies. But he was seen straying out of bounds by neighbors who were allies of Aunt Séraphie and reported him.

"Were you not at the Public Gardens?" she asked. He denied it. She cited her witnesses, and he would be scolded and punished. His first glimmer of physical freedom was suppressed by a new arrangement which required the drawing master to come to the Beyle house.

The repressive habits of his guardians sometimes made him fly into violent outbursts of temper; but more often, he was outwardly well behaved, while telling his little lies. Lying became a habit with him in youth.

But during 1794, when so many troubles beset his father, he found more and more opportunity to escape from parental surveillance. And each time he pushed farther afield. At dusk of one cold evening in 1794 he slipped off, saying that he was on his way to join his aunt Elisabeth in the neighborhood; then did what he had tremulously longed to do: he went to the sequestrated St. André's Church to attend a meeting of the Jacobin Club of Grenoble.

He felt himself a rebel and a Jacobin; his mind was full of the heroes of Roman history, such as Cincinnatus or Camillus—though he was also terrified at the thought of what evil might befall him if some spy of Aunt Séraphie's should see him here! But alas, his family had infected him with their aristocratic tastes, and the experiment was not a happy one. "I have too fine a skin, a woman's skin . . . hence perhaps my unbounded horror of all that seems dirty, dingy and dank."

The chairman addressed the meeting, then soon everybody, including all sorts of seemingly ill-favored, ill-clad persons, joined in and spoke at once, with considerable disorder and using absurd turns of speech. Henri remembered how his grandfather used to mock at these people and their ways of talking:

> It seemed to me at once that my grandfather was right. My impression was rather unfavorable. This narrow high church was very ill-lighted and damp, and I saw there many women of the lowest class. In a word, I was then what I am today; I love the people and hate their oppressors, but every moment would be a torture to me if I had to live with the common people.

Stendhal in his later years affirmed what Jean-Jacques Rousseau, though the vagabond son of a Swiss watchmaker, had also expressed when he said: "I love the people, but at a distance." The impressions he gathered at the Jacobin Club of Grenoble stayed with him and lent ambivalence to his rebelliousness, as has so often occurred in the case of ardent revolutionaries sprung from the more favored classes. But then news would come of fresh victories for republican arms over foreign powers besieging the Republic. His father and Aunt Séraphie would set to lamenting, and he would feel his distaste for the Jacobins effaced once more.

Dutifully he attended mass, which was sometimes held behind closed doors and blinded windows, in private homes, during the days of the Terror. Because they were forbidden he enjoyed these secret ceremonies, feeling himself moved by the solemn sound of church bells, or the image of Christ in sacred paintings—the aesthetic side of the Christian religion—but his faith departed from him.

Only once, in 1797, did a touch of the old fervor return, when his sickly, "sour-faced" aunt Séraphie reached her end. Henri, then fourteen, and fairly godless, threw himself on his knees "to thank God for this great deliverance." It was perhaps the last time he ever permitted himself prayer. In any case, he already enjoyed a vastly increased personal freedom. The year before he had entered the Central School of Grenoble, one of the new free public schools established throughout France by the Republic. Thus he escaped at last from the suffocating family circle; and it was as a revolution in his life, the beginning of that personal liberty he longed for.

4

Early in 1795, following the adoption of the Constitution of the Year III of the Republic, a new law for public education was promulgated which established a lay school system replacing the Jesuit or Church-dominated *collèges* or grammar schools of France.

The opening of these schools in the principal cities of France during 1795 and 1796—when the Terror had ended, and Robespierre was dead—was attended with great democratic celebrations in honor of Reason and Liberty. In Grenoble, Dr. Henri Gagnon, reconciled to the republican order of things, served as chairman of the school board. He gave an opening-day address, in 1796, in which he declared that the new generation was to receive a truly public instruction, and was to be educated "in accordance with ideas of republican virtue." The free-thinking followers of the Encyclopedists who had devised the new program, for the first time in France—while eliminating religious instruction—stressed the sciences, mathematics, physics, and chemistry, above instruction in ancient languages and rhetoric. Children of all classes were encouraged to attend and learn to be free men who could think for themselves.

Henri Beyle, enrolled in the Central School, when just under fourteen, thus was directly affected by the far-reaching moral and social upheaval which uprooted the old system of instruction. Though it was to be a transitional process—Napoleon annulled the law in 1802—his education in the Central School marked more deeply than ever the cleavage between his own revolutionary generation and that of his parents. While they, at heart, belonged to the old regime, he belonged in the most militant sense to modern youth.

The school was installed in a picturesque group of old Jesuit buildings at the edge of the town, which had been taken over by the government. Here he was entered in an upper grade and played in the company of boys of his age, among the children of peasants as well as nobles—those of them, at any rate, who had refused to emigrate from France. It was not only a new, democratic experience, but also an intellectual excitement. For example, one of the best known of his masters, Dubois-Fontenelle, prided himself upon being an anti-clerical ideologue. In his lectures on literature and world history, openly and with a sort of pompous eloquence, he espoused a materialistic philosophy, supported by many citations from the writings of John Locke, Condillac, and Helvetius. Instead of learning to write tedious Latin verses, Henri absorbed all sorts of skeptical ideas which, to his delight, utterly refuted the pious dogmas of his family. According to the plan of instruction fostered by the utilitarian philosopher, Destutt de Tracy, one of his courses, conducted by an unfrocked priest, was in logic and ideology. It was designed as a preparation or "general grammar" of scientific thinking, and at an impressionable age provided Henri Beyle with an intellectual discipline which he used ever after to rout the spokesmen of orthodoxy, superstition, and all "useful falsehoods."

For three years he also studied literature, reading voluminously all the classical French poets, but as is suggested by his earliest journals—those of 1800 that refer back to his school days—forming his own independent judgments. Perhaps it was not quite true, as he says, that at fourteen he disliked Racine, then the idol of all men of letters. But the manner in which Racine accepted humiliation at the hands of Louis XIV, and remained the subservient courtier, undoubtedly created prejudice in his republican mind. However, it does seem that when his professor attacked Shakespeare, in accordance with current notions in France, as a sort of accident in literary history, a "drunken savage," Henri felt himself "secretly blushing." From the age of fourteen he and a school friend of his, Louis Crozet, read Shakespeare to each other with delight—though in the pallid translation of Letourneur.

More than anything else, he loved mathematics and excelled in it as few literary men have done. In an age when artillery and engineering predominated in war, when the brilliant young General Bonaparte attributed his spectacular victories in Italy to his training in mathematics, it was fashionable to be a mathematician. Later, Henri Beyle would say that he studied mathematics with ardor because of its "clear definitions . . . excluding all *hypocrisy* and *vagueness*, my two pet aversions." At fifteen and sixteen he was possessed by the dazzling idea of escaping from Grenoble and going to the Ecole Polytechnique in Paris, the great school for officers, that had been founded by the Republic at the same time as the Ecole Normale.

> I used to imagine that the higher mathematics, those that I had never studied, dealt with all, or almost all, aspects of things, and that by proceeding to their study, I should arrive at a knowledge of *all things* that was certain, irrefutable, and demonstrable at will. . . . I said to myself: mathematics will get me out of Grenoble, out of that sickening morass . . .

At the school he was taught by Dupuy de Bordes, who had instructed Napoleon in mathematics at Valence. But to Henri Beyle, who had already read D'Alembert's inspiring article on mathematics in the Encyclopedia, Dupuy seemed too old and slow-witted. Meanwhile he had heard much favorable talk of a man in Grenoble named Gabriel Gros, a young scientist, who did private tutoring in geometry and calculus. Without the knowledge of his father, by obtaining a small additional allowance from his devoted great-aunt Elisabeth, he arranged to take special lessons, after school hours, with Gros.

He was a stout young man with blue eyes and blond hair, and his manner was full of enthusiasm, energy, and joviality. Though he was one of the leading speakers in the revolutionary party of Grenoble, and his name was not unknown in Paris, he lived in a modest furnished room, in the poorest quarter of the town. No celebrity attached itself in later years to this local notable who passed his life teaching in the provinces and died relatively young. But Henri was to perpetuate him in his memoirs as "the incomparable" Gros, the model of the "pure, disinterested democrat" of his time, indifferent to money, passionate for the spread of knowledge, ardent in the defense of the Republic. Interrupting his lessons—on which occasions he would scrupulously refuse the fees of his pupils—this young Jacobin would inveigh against the fanatics of religion and caste who plotted to "stab liberty to death"; he urged his pupils to strive toward "great and useful things"; to arm themselves well with knowledge so that "men of good will and energy may with firmness defend our rights and complete our tasks."[3]

"With Gros," Beyle wrote later, "I felt the heavens opening up, I saw at last the reasons for things. . . . It seems to me that he transported us directly to the frontiers of science, face to face with the difficulties to be conquered, the veil to be lifted." Whereas with his family, Henri showed a mania for argumentation, in this man's presence, he was silent, awkward, feeling something akin to adoration. "I was with him, as with all those whom I loved too much, ever tongue-tied, stupid, motionless, unamiable, and sometimes even offensive, through the very force of my devotion and self-surrender."

[3]P. Arbalet cites public speeches of Citizen Gros, dating from 1799, at the time when Henri Beyle, aged sixteen, studied under him. *La Jeunesse de Stendhal*, Vol. I, pp. 292–93.

5

The transition to that happier state of freedom and experience of the real world that he had so long desired was like all great adventures not without its pains and contretemps. "Everything was a surprise" in this new life at the school, among his contemporaries. He had grown up in seclusion, with older people and two little sisters, whom he used to torment a good deal. His ideas of friendship, honor, chivalry were all preconceived, or drawn from books, and full of strange illusions. Though he had longed for companions of his own age, he found himself at first shy and them far from the "noble" or "charming" friends he had imagined. On the contrary, they were selfish little brutes.

To his classmates he was an odd-looking boy, with a very solid, stocky figure, a big head, a mop of black hair, and short legs. He usually wore a long gray coat, reaching almost to his feet, and so they nicknamed him *La Tour Ambulante* (The Walking Tower), because of the effect he gave as he moved swiftly along inside his big coat. At first he was aloof in manner; so he was left out of the games the other boys played, which almost broke his heart. They teased him; he would grow angry and reply with his sharp tongue, unthinkingly uttering words that earned him hard blows. But as he grew accustomed to his schoolmates, he stopped playing the little prince, showed himself as aggressive as the others, giving as well as receiving punishment.

There was a big, awkward peasant boy in his class, named Odru, and Henri joined with the others in making fun of him, one day drawing a caricature of the boy and the ill-fitting clothes he wore on the board of the drawing class. Odru called Henri a vile name, and Henri slapped him, whereupon the other boy, when his back was turned, pulled his chair out from under him and threw him to the floor. On the spot, Henri, with his fine notions of honor, challenged the other to a duel with pistols. It was agreed to meet outside the gates of the city that afternoon; seconds were chosen, and the whole school, which had quickly learned of the affair, proceeded to the battleground.

Somehow Henri and his second obtained a huge pistol, some eight inches long; the other boy was also armed, and they milled about the fields outside the town walls with a crowd of two or three hundred persons following them, shouting, arguing, hilariously offering advice. The seconds delayed everything by their long disputes; Henri, growing more and more apprehensive, became fully convinced that the other boy "hated" him and intended to kill him. Finally they descended into the town fosse, and measured off the paces. Henri remembered afterward that he had not had time to feel fear up to the last moment, when they faced each other. His adversary was to fire first, by agreement. "Now is the moment to be brave," he told himself. Deliberately he fixed his gaze upon a queer, trapezoid-shaped rock far off in the hills, and waited impassively.

What happened then? As often, in the fragments of his recollections of early boyhood, he admits honestly that his memory breaks off. Doubtless older persons rushed in, stopped the first of Henri's "duels," and sent the boys home. Possibly the pistols were not even loaded?

Returning home, he told the boy who had acted as his second how badly he had been frightened and also how he had prevented himself from showing fear while Odru sighted him. The other boy scolded him severely, saying: "You ought never to admit a thing like that." But Henri was astonished at the reproof. He believed that he had maintained himself firmly, despite all the horrors that a lively imagination suggested. "During the two hours that that procession of two hundred scamps dragged about after us . . . what terrified me most was the thought of being brought home on a *ladder*, as I had once seen poor Lambert brought back." It was typical of his self-conscious, analytical character that as a boy of fifteen, and ever afterward, he always asked himself whether some action had been as courageous or as pleasing as he had hoped or calculated it should be. Had he been a hero? Or a fool?

Gradually he made close friends among the apt students in the school, and even assumed a certain dominance over them. Whether it was through his prowess as a scholar, his readiness of speech or stronger personality—he was both exalted and resolute in manner—he knew how to attach kindred souls to himself most powerfully, so that as one of them wrote in a letter, "they desire your happiness as much as their own." Among his friends was Félix Faure, son of a government official, who rose to be a magistrate and peer of France. Another was named Plana, and came from Turin; as a mathematician he surpassed even Beyle. There was also Fortuné Mante, like him a precocious *philosophe* and radical, his alter ego, whom Henri credited with "genius." And most notably Louis Crozet, also the son of a lawyer, a small boy with fine eyes and animated face, though unfortunately pock-marked, who was the youngest, but the most bookish and brilliant of all of them, proficient both in the sciences and literature, destined to become one of France's leading engineers. Crozet, whom Henri loved best of all, was his lifelong confidant and, like his little cousin Romain Colomb, whom he had befriended during the Reign of Terror, almost Henri's devoted slave. The striking thing about his friendships was that they endured for decades, or for life, unless fate or distance parted him from them.

They were terribly old and grave for their years. They read much the same books together, they reasoned earnestly about all things. In short they were the youths of the new generation which grew up during the years of Revolution and war, civil and national. As Sainte-Beuve describes the group of Chateaubriand's friends (a decade older), they were, when scarcely out of childhood, censorious toward their elders, solemn and stiff-necked in their manner, eager to debate all the mysteries of life before having lived. Their parents and the older generation that preceded them, accustomed to the gaiety and amenity of life under Louis XV, they tended to condemn as "frivolous." Ardent followers of Rousseau as they all were, they swore to be virtuous and democratic and irreligious. In those years when history was a mighty drama, their eyes followed the changing stars of the Republic's great men: of Barnave of Grenoble, beheaded in the Terror; then of Danton, Robespierre, Carnot, and Bonaparte. Exchanging confidences concerning their ambitions and early disappointments, these romantic friends contemplated the unknown future toward which France marched, and asked each other anxiously if the occasion would not come for them also to be great men and heroes.

One of the fancies of Henri and Louis Crozet was to be utterly "natural" with each other, even "severe" in speaking the truth, as befitted honest revolutionaries. They submitted their first literary productions to each other: at ten Henri had written a play, which has disappeared; at fourteen he had begun another, inspired by much reading of Molière, which was never to be finished. Great things were expected of the young Beyle by his comrades, for in addition to his talents was he not heir to a substantial fortune? But intrigued or fascinated as they might be, they knew already how mercurial he was, how shifting his moods. As one of them, François Bigillion (who was to die young), wrote him after a night-long discussion: "For you, Henri, everything is either happiness or misfortune. . . . Your imagination carries away your reason." And how changeable was he! "You have reflected deeply, but following other minds, for with each new book you alter your way of thinking. But are you a man of virtue, are you loyal to me, your truest friend?"

It would be misleading to assume that Henri and his friends were eternally solemn and doctrinaire. True, they were ready to die for the Republic and for liberty. But they were not above a lively escapade, and Henri was often their ringleader.

One night Henri and three other companions crept through the bushes of the Public Gardens and suddenly—though the barracks of the National Guards were but a few yards away—fell upon a Tree of Fraternity that had been set up there that day with great ceremony. They overturned it, riddled its placards with bullets, then fled through the streets with the Guards at their heels, thinking an insurrection was being attempted. A tree dedicated to Liberty they had left unmolested.

As he grew strong and broad of shoulders, the young Beyle took to hunting in the hills outside the town. His father forbade this, therefore the pleasures of the chase were secret and seemed all the sweeter, though killing game always troubled his soul with a sense of guilt. A crusty old caretaker at the farm had trained him to be a good shot. In early spring, rising before the dawn, he would be off after foxes and birds, under a beautiful moon and warm breeze, along the wild Drac valley and the hills of Sassenage, where his ancestors had lived for centuries. "I used to dream great dreams, wandering rifle in hand among the vineyards and plantations. . . ." Then, after tramping in the woods for hours, there would be the sudden movement of the bird flushed, his shot, and the thudding fall of the game.

He was much given then to romantic posturing, like a character out of Corneille's *Le Cid*. Arriving at the farm he would hand his game to the dour caretaker, saying in lordly tones: "There, Barbier, your pupil has shown himself worthy of you!"

6

Henri and his friends spoke endlessly of women and love. Each of them, he recalls, tried to convince the others "that he knew the world well, knew women, and so on—our principal fatuity in school days." But each, in almost every case, had almost nothing to boast of, save the secret sorrow of some unrequited passion.

Grenoble indeed offered green pastures to a youth reaching the age of gallantry. Opulent and pleasure-loving before the Revolution, it resumed its libertine ways—once the pall of the Terror had lifted—

with greater emphasis than before, during the years of the Directoire, when all France seemed to be trying to forget its recent nightmares.

Even the modes reflected the new spirit of the times: the women dressed in flowing "Roman" garments that exposed their arms and shoulders and nearly all of their bosoms; the dandies, gotten up like peacocks, in embroidered coats, with ruffles, jabots, immense green cravats, and rare knotted walking sticks, quite justly came to be called *les Incroyables*: the Incredibles. From the windows of his grandfather's house looking on the Public Gardens, Henri, the curious adolescent, could watch the Incredibles strutting up and down the paths under the great chestnut trees, preening themselves before the coquettish and scented ladies seated on the benches. At St. André's Church on Sundays the loud buzzing of flirtation and gossip never stopped even during sermons. Then there were innumerable parties and balls among the comfortable class, with their dances and charades, offering easy occasions for the women to grow yielding and accessible to their gallants, and to treat the marriage bond lightly, since their husbands asked so little of them.

Grenoble's pleasure palace in those days was undoubtedly the Opera House, where Henri from the age of fourteen was a steady habitué of the pit. Here the provincial Don Juans, all perfumed and bedizened, came but to "adore" and ogle the actresses from Paris. Here his rakish uncle Romain, and even Dr. Gagnon before him, had earned their local reputation for gallantry, the science of which they each tried to impart to Henri.

By 1798, in his sixteenth year, he was a solidly built youth, with a big head, a ruddy face and very long black hair. His brown eyes were full of fire, his mouth sensual, but thin and well shaped; but his nose was nothing to look at, very prominent, thick and aquiline in form, and it worried him endlessly. With his big body and short legs, he would have looked, as he himself feared, "like an Italian butcher boy"—were it not for his small feet and his fine, delicate hands, with their slender fingers that sculptors sometimes enjoyed modeling. His skin, he often remarked, was white and sensitive as a woman's: the least blow bruised it; a scratch gave intense pain; clothing tormented him.

"I feel myself made for love," he would say. Erotic dreams, even of his aunt Séraphie, whom he hated, haunted him.

At the age of twelve, his eyes used to devour a certain well-formed nun whom he would see every day during walks with the Abbé Raillane, until that stern mentor noticed and changed their route.

Though the animation of his eyes and facial expression made him attractive in a way, he had been told too often that he was homely. Clearly enough, in his memoirs, he alludes to the "feeling of inferiority" that grew fixed in him in youth.

His uncle Romain would say to him: "My boy, you think you are pretty clever, you are bursting with pride over your success in mathematics; but all that is as nothing. In this world one advances himself only through women. . . ." But since he was not handsome, his uncle predicted, "your mistresses will leave you." What a sad thought to start life with! To prepare him for these great troubles, Romain Gagnon instructed him as follows: "When such misfortune befalls you, you suffer most from the feeling of being placed in a ridiculous position. . . . The first twenty-four hours after being abandoned, you must make a declaration of love to another woman; even if she is nothing better than a chambermaid."

But in his first "love" all his uncle's various counsels of sang-froid or resourcefulness were forgotten.

To hear the opéra-bouffe music, and none too magnificent, that was offered at the Grenoble Opera House became a passion with him, and absorbed his entire allowance. Thus it came to pass that he saw Mlle. Virginie Cubly, a slender, languid chanteuse with a weak voice, playing in a comic opera by Gaveaux. "She was young, and rather tall and thin, with an aquiline nose, and graceful figure . . . but had a serious and somewhat melancholy countenance," as he describes her. "I felt a tender interest in just gazing at her. Soon I was desperately in love. . . ."

She was an actress, a *princesse lointaine*, from a distant mysterious world that he longed to know. Merely to think of Mlle. Cubly made him happier; the complaints of his family became indifferent matters to him, because "love" made him more indulgent and just!

He was troubled because the young blades of the Opera pit ogled her boldly, and spoke of her familiarly as "la Cubly." Cautiously he inquired if she had admirers or lovers, but heard only gross, mocking oaths. Finally he worked himself up to the point of finding out where she lived, "morally one of my bravest actions." It was on the Rue des Clercs; and he would pace up and down this gloomy street for hours, hoping for a glimpse of her.

One morning, walking alone in the Public Gardens, concentrating his thought upon her as always, he saw her at last at the other end of the square walking along the parapet by the river, toward the terrace where he stood like one frozen.

Long afterward he set down his recollections of the scene in the style of a precise geometer, one of his habitual mannerisms: "She was proceeding from the point L. . . . I almost fainted, but finally took to my heels, along the parapet, on the line F., as if the devil were after me." He had not even been seen by her. But then she did not know who he was.

At the end of the season Mlle. Cubly left Grenoble, and Henri was overcome with despair. Finally he confided the story of his "folly" to one of the simplest of his young friends, François Bigillion, who accurately observed that Henri "had known love only as a poet. . . . Your sensibility is always mixed with folly." But "real love" would change him, his friend thought.[4]

The Bigillions, peasants enriched by the Revolution, stood a little below the Beyles in the Grenoble hierarchy; Henri's grandfather mocked at them; his father and aunt forbade him to play with their children. Naturally, he came to the Bigillions' house in secret every day, ate a snack with them, and met his friend's fourteen-year-old sister, Victorine. He could remember Victorine long afterward for her gentle and maternal spirit; and her "budding breasts," a little exposed by her summer costume, which he also shyly admired. "But I was ravaged by the departure of Mlle. Cubly, and did not fall in love with her." When he told of his troubles with his father and aunt, she would say: "But you are a bad boy!" However, he heard in later years that Victorine used to say that Henri's wit made one forget his ugliness; and that she had pined for him a little.

Against misfortune in love, as with other kinds of adversity, it was his methodical habit, even in boyhood, to fortify himself through mental distraction. With Mlle. Cubly's departure he applied himself to mathematics with a sort of frenzy. In his second year at the Ecole Centrale he won first prize in belles-lettres and honorable mention for drawing. In his third and last year he obtained the first prize in mathematics for each half term. His cousin Colomb had the impression, perhaps exaggerated, that after a time no one dared compete against Beyle. But even his father was struck by his intelligence, and sometimes boasted about him. The school records comment upon "the precision of Citizen Beyle and the quickness of his calculation," especially in oral examinations.[5] School prizes then were awarded with much cere-

---

[4]Arbalet, op. cit., I, 371–72.

[5]R. Colomb: *Notice biographique*, p. vii.

mony at civic festivals, and Henri was quite carried away with his triumphs. Was there ever such a brilliant young man in all Grenoble?

In the spring of 1799, after his name had been posted up as first among those students who had prepared themselves to enter the Ecole Polytechnique in Paris, he walked among the trees of the Public Gardens with several friends, drunk with glory, his mind playing with the future. Rather grandly and sententiously, yet in melting mood, he said: "At such a moment one could forgive all one's enemies."

He was resolved to escape at last to the larger stage of Paris, from that Grenoble he detested as "the lowest indigestion." (Alas, his severe-faced father and aunt had not introduced him to the good and merry company which led so many others to sing the praises of his native city.) Though his father, like many Dauphinois, feared the "new Babylon" that was Paris, and fretted at giving the boy of sixteen money to go and live there, Henri's record as one of the cleverest young men of the town, his prowess as a mathematician, made it inevitable (as his admiring teachers urged) that he seek a higher instruction than the provinces could offer. Somewhat reluctantly it was agreed that he should enter the Ecole Polytechnique in the autumn of 1799 and prepare himself for a career as an artillery officer or a military engineer.

In advance of his departure his grandfather and father sent letters to influential friends and relatives in Paris introducing Henri as the prodigy of Grenoble's Ecole Centrale. Even his father was struck by his eloquence of speech, especially when he wanted money to buy some toy or trinket. Hearing him describe the thing, the father would sometimes actually give him the sum he wanted with good grace, though afterward he would complain that he was being plundered.

Before leaving Grenoble, Henri went for a last visit to the farm at Claix and wandered through those vineyards and groves where he had first read Rousseau and Shakespeare—who was so often associated in his mind with the expression of a pure, unspoilt joy. While his eye hung upon the windings of the Isère in the rich green plain below, or upon the long sunset, flaming orange and violet above the peak of Voreppe, his thought soared into the future that promised to be as glittering as it would be different from the past; impetuously his imagination rushed forward, excited always by immense pleasures or evils anticipated.

As long afterward he imagined the reaction of Julien Sorel in *The Red and the Black*, he took new breath in the presence of these mountain heights. "They depicted the position that he burned to attain in the moral sense." Perhaps like Julien he too watched a hawk, moving in immense circles above him, envying those easy and yet powerful motions, "that force and that proud isolation." Such was the destiny of a Napoleon. Would it be his own someday?

One can scarcely overstress the formative influences, in Stendhal's case, of his boyhood years, which his memoir has rendered so particular and so decisive. He was already old, in the sense that he was full of subtleties and calculation; the spirit of reason was remarkably strong in him, and his mind loved to work with "systems" for seeking happiness, or hoodwinking his parents, or demonstrating courage, or even conquering women.

But he was also much more innocent of experience, much younger —he was on the average two years younger than his classmates—even than other youths of sixteen. Though born into fortunate circumstances, the long years of alienation from his father had given him the sense of being a "lost child"; terrible fears and doubts of himself habitually assailed him and the illusions of his unbridled imagination, the power of his unpredictable sensibility could in a second sweep away all his finest schemes. His cagey father noticed this division in his character and remarked that "if he ever learned to subordinate his folly to his reason he would become a most successful man."

On a morning of autumn rain, his father, uncle, grandfather, and his cousin Colomb all accompanied him to the Public Gardens, where he boarded the diligence for Lyons and Paris under the care of a friend of the family also bound for the capital. Chérubin Beyle, usually so reserved, suddenly showed that he loved his son in his own fashion, for he broke down and wept as he embraced him. "The only impression that his tears made upon me was that I found him very ugly," the son wrote ungratefully in reminiscence. His mind was full of the plays that he would write for the Paris theater; also of the actress he would love and who would be as beautiful as Mlle. Cubly.

CHAPTER III

Alone in Paris

Other people could not help Julien; he was too different.
—Stendhal: *The Red and the Black.*

AS HIS diligence journeyed northward across France the mind of young Beyle was in such a state of tumult that he remembered almost nothing of the sights he saw, nor any incidents of this six-day voyage, his first outside the native province. Save that at Nemours, on the fateful 18th Brumaire (November 9, 1799) he and his companions heard news that the Directory had been overthrown that day by General Bonaparte, who proclaimed himself Consul of the Republic. The idolized young general would then be "king"—this was the only thought that came to him upon this truly world-shaking event. He arrived in the capital the following day and was deposited by his traveling companion at a small hotel in the Rue St. Dominique.

It was one of the oldest quarters of the city, the once aristocratic Faubourg St. Germain, in which he found himself, and quite near the Ecole Polytechnique, where he was to study. But the old mansions of the rich, surrounded by their high walls, were now shut up, and looked not only cold and unfriendly, but dilapidated. Paris had been much battered by recent insurrections and street fighting, and at the turn of the century appeared more slatternly than in many decades. Still its irrepressible citizens tried to celebrate the newest turn of events—they had been celebrating in most libertine fashion, under the Directory, since 1794. Crowded theaters and public pleasure gardens flaunted their seductions at the youth fresh from the provinces. But Henri Beyle was one of the few young men who did not join the revelers.

The first sight of the vast city of gray stones made his heart sink.

After Dauphiné the surroundings of the capital seemed to him ugly. There were no mountains! And in the public gardens the shade trees were all pruned.

Paris had been his supreme objective. To reach it he had studied mathematics night and day so that he might be admitted to its great scientific college. He had fancied that he would plunge at once into the most brilliant social life, that he would promptly enter upon the career of a Don Juan, as pictured in the books he had read. Instead, he felt a wave of disappointment sweep over him. The muddy streets, the crowds of people who stared at him indifferently, the rich in their fine carriages passing rapidly by, made him feel himself at a loss, even afflicted him, as he recalls, with a sense of "deep grief."

He set to walking about the city alone, observing all that he could, always "the passionate dreamer, gazing at the sky and on the point of being run down by some cabriolet." After a few days, on the advice of students from Grenoble who were at the Polytechnique, he moved to a cheaper room in a lodginghouse on the Esplanade des Invalides, in the same neighborhood. The room had but one small window, set so high up in the wall that he could see almost nothing through it. He would return from his walks and sit here beside a little iron stove eating his dinner "alone and abandoned."

To be sure, he paid some calls upon relatives, as advised by his family. One of these was Noël Daru, a native of Grenoble and his father's cousin. This man of sixty had been prefect of a department in the South of France, had held other high offices in the government and been close to the mighty Talleyrand himself. He had been poor, but had sailed through the dangerous rapids of the Revolution most skillfully, indifferent to the passions of parties or doctrines, while using his office to accumulate a great fortune. Henri called upon him in his house on the Rue de Lille, at the corner of the Rue de Bellechasse, and was politely received. In fact too politely. Mme. Daru was kind, though very dignified in manner. But Monsieur, a tall, distinguished-looking man with a big nose and a cast in one eye, struck Henri as having a rather false tone. "He received me with speeches about his affection and devotion for my grandfather, which made my heart sink and struck me dumb."

The youth of sixteen and a half had seen little of society outside his own hearth, having been taken to visit at most two or three of the frowsy old families of Grenoble who were his father's clients. Although he wore a fine new frock coat of olive green, with a broad velvet collar, he felt himself a rustic. And then these Parisians and their numerous grown children were so knowingly and coldly polite that he was put out of countenance, became awkward and tongue-tied. Dinner at the Darus' was a gloomy affair, filled with long silences while everyone waited for the despotic old Daru to say something. These silences made the usually animated Beyle wretched. "I never opened my lips," he declares.

He had thought himself a mixture of Rousseau's Saint-Preux and Valmont (the Lovelace of the *Liaisons dangereuses*), and that only opportunity had been lacking to him. But now he felt himself "in every respect inferior and gauche in this society that was so gloomy and depressing. . . ." He was especially shy with the women of the Daru family—there were six daughters, three of them married. Measuring himself against Daru's very gracious and fashionable younger sons—one of whom, the future Count Pierre Daru, was to become quartermaster general under Napoleon, while the other, Martial, also an officer, was one of the most elegant dandies in Paris—he felt all the more keenly his own provincial uncouthness, his clumsiness, even his ugliness. He thought he saw this mirrored in the veiled pity of their eyes, the slight curl of their lips. For the first time he became conscious of his southern accent.

He believed himself always "not *clever at the practical details of life*." In Grenoble his aunt and her friends the priests used to talk of how they deceived or hoodwinked people into doing what they wanted. But he would rather be cheated than dispute over twelve sous' worth of firewood. His glimpse of the real world, in the salon of his rich and successful relatives in Paris, suggested at once that he might never learn how to manage this world for himself. All sorts of doubts assailed him, even concerning such fixed objectives as the study of mathematics and science.

"So this was the Paris for which I had longed so much," he exclaims. This was the brilliant Paris of which he had read in *The Secret Memoirs* of the famous wit, Duclos, published after the Revolution.

He walked the streets, hoping that perhaps by chance he would come upon some lovely lady whom he would rescue during a carriage accident. "I told myself . . . 'We would adore each other; she would understand my soul.' I would say this to myself two or three times a day, especially at nightfall, which is for me still a moment of melting tenderness. . . ."

He knew what the nature of his frustration was, for he defines it in his honest and naïve terms: "It was a heart to love me—a woman—that I lacked."

Nor was it for want of money; his father gave him an allowance, ample then, of 150 francs a month. Why then did he not go and do as he did later, when he was fifty, and "hire a pretty girl for a gold louis in the Rue des Moulins"? But prostitutes filled him with horror. The young students in his lodginghouse who told him loose stories exaggerating the corruption and greed of such women made him frightened and sick. "They used to tell me about the *pierreuses*, at two sous—the girls on the stones, two hundred yards from the door of our wretched house."

Stendhal has also confessed that as a schoolboy, before coming to Paris, he shared "a bad habit" with his schoolmates, though not to excess. This also deepened his timidity.

Alone, not a little homesick, without a confidant or friend, the youth who had conceived such large ambitions and pleasures for himself, passed through a violent nervous crisis, the crisis of adolescence, at a time when he had important decisions to make with regard to his future career. The entrance examinations for the Ecole Polytechnique, for which he had so painstakingly prepared himself, took place ten days after his arrival in Paris.

Suddenly he resolved not to appear for those examinations, and sat in his room, as the final day passed, enjoying a feeling of relief. Several other Grenoble students whom he had surpassed in mathematics entered the school without difficulty. But during these days of storm he felt only that he was "afraid" to go on with his mathematics, that he hated the thought of the Polytechnique and its discipline or routine. Once the term began it would be too late to enter for at least a year, perhaps forever.

In a second visit to his relative, Daru, he was obliged to admit that he had not presented himself for the examinations, and was not even preparing himself for the following year. The severe old man addressing him as "Monsieur," and with a politeness and restraint most annoying to Henri, urged that an explanation was due on this point. It was a most "terrible" interview, Henri felt. He thought there might be pitfalls in everything the adroit old ex-prefect said, from which he would be unable to extricate himself. Yet he defended himself stoutly. At one point he remarked: "My family leaves me practically free to judge for myself what course I should take." The old man observed in a meaningful tone: "That is all too apparent!" Now speechless and sullen, Henri wondered what he could have meant by these words? M. Daru's very circumlocutions made him suspicious.

How could he explain to this detestable old man that he had really come to Paris in search of "Art and Love"? That he had the intention of writing comedies like Molière and winning a beautiful mistress who was an actress? (Alas, where was she?) Better to be silent before such a horrid man who was undoubtedly an "enemy" at heart. When, a year later, he began a journal, one of the first entries he made was:

Be mistrustful of people; the average man deserves this; but at the same time take care to keep them from perceiving this mistrust.[1]

It was in this manner that he dealt with old Daru. Early in life he learned to be secretive about his deepest interests. His one confidant was his sister Pauline, to whom he wrote divulging his real hopes and plans, but often closing:

I beg you not to show this letter to anyone, because of the feeling I have that it will seem ridiculous to cold, dull souls.[2]

Mathematics had been but an instrument to him, a means of leaving Grenoble forever—which was perhaps divined by his father when he wept at their parting. Now that he had "Paris" he no longer needed "mathematics" which had served as an arm of defense against his father. Curiously enough, Chérubin Beyle never pressed his son to return to his mathematical studies, perhaps hoping that he would after all be saved from military life and would one day return to take his hereditary place as a procurator and advocate. Possibly also, as the son suggests, his father did not think about him much, except when he was near by.

In his lonely ramblings about Paris, he had one day entered a bookstore and purchased a recently issued work entitled *The Art of Comedy,* by Cailhava. Had he not planned to be a playwright? He sat in his room and studied this dull manual diligently, for, owing to his education, his spirit was methodical. But he also loved music—he had studied the flute for some time in Grenoble—and went often to the opera. And he asked himself whether he should not perhaps try to become a composer of operas rather than a playwright? Yet he wrote nothing.

He moved, these days, in a fog in which reality seemed to have dissolved his passionate dreams; round and round in his head went the ideas "comedy" or "opera" as in earlier times the ideas of "mathematics" and "Paris," or "priest versus love," or "father versus patriotism" had haunted him. He was not yet seventeen. He searched for ways to

[1] *Journal,* Vol. I, July 17, 1801; Divan ed.

[2] *Correspondance,* Vol. I, p. 19, Divan ed., To Pauline Beyle, Aug. 1800

happiness. "But where is happiness, then, to be found?" he asked. "Everywhere I went I carried with me my terrible disappointment."

And yet he was aware of his superior sensibilities and the fineness of his sentiments, upon which was grounded some vague conviction of a "right to happiness" such as all the young followers of Rousseau then shared.

"Dare I say it?" he recollects with delicious and self-deprecating wit. ". . . *I was a poet,* or very near being a poet in 1799. . . . All that I needed was a chimney through which my 'genius' might escape." The chimney may do as a very happy and effective bit of symbolism.

The first days or weeks of the unknown provincial youth who comes to Paris are usually hard enough. Stendhal, with his intense sensibility, describes himself as bewildered. His very brain seemed "clouded," and he did not know what was tormenting him, though his recollections point to the causes of his anxiety shrewdly enough. Before coming to Paris he had been made unhappy chiefly by those "twin devils," his father and Aunt Séraphie. But now the frustration was of another sort: "*I was perishing of constraint, disappointment and discontent with myself*. . . . It was the unceasing consciousness of the things I wanted to do but did not know how to achieve." He adds: "It must be admitted that my fall was great and terrible." And in the summing up makes the heartbreaking statement: "*I had no trust in anyone.*"

Walking in the mud and rain of Paris in December 1799, while experiencing a terrible *détente,* a letdown of all his keyed-up nerves, he suddenly felt himself feverish and went to bed. What seemed at first like indigestion soon turned into a severe case of pleurisy accompanied by high fever. A charlatan of a doctor who was called prescribed draughts of a black medicine that did no good. The Darus, hearing that the boy was sick in his lodginghouse, sent their own doctor to him; then had him moved to their home and placed in a comfortable room overlooking a garden. For three weeks he lay dangerously ill, sometimes delirious, and was told later that he had been heard challenging "anyone who made fun of him for not entering the Ecole Polytechnique." January 1800, the beginning of a new century, had arrived before he was on his feet again.

2

The young Beyle perhaps saw society, in his first view, as with the optical distortion created by peering through the neck of a bottle. So he would philosophize afterward. Yet few men suffered so severely in adolescence from the form of neurosis that we think of as afflicting modern man, especially in the comfortable or bourgeois classes. Stendhal shows us perhaps more vividly than anyone who ever wrote his confessions how much he felt himself alone and "persecuted." But this obsession, rendering him even more self-conscious, observant, and introspective than ever, was of the kind that seems to have produced some of our greatest writers—"the good neurotics" as Proust called them. Men with exasperated nerves, perverse or even impotent, they have nevertheless, curiously enough, been the most marvelous listeners and observers, always feeling themselves surrounded by secret enemies, living whole lifetimes in an instant, bearing their destinies in their hands at every step.

The real world, then, was not as he had fancied it; like the other romantic sufferers since Rousseau, he cried inwardly for love and understanding and got none. His sensibilities were outraged. But unlike the other members of the romantic generation, Stendhal reacted strongly against his own Rousseauism. He was after all a youth with a mathematical mind and an ideologist to boot. Even as a schoolboy at Grenoble he had already read Helvetius, the materialistic philosopher, who in his most famous work, *De l'esprit*, had written: "Society pays for that which it sees." And so he declares that even in his youth he managed to avoid behaving like the complaining Tasso, or the melancholy Schillers and Chateaubriands, who were forever crying out against the world for the "injustice" done them.

> The difference between me and those self-important idiots *who carry their heads about like the Blessed Sacrament*, is the fact that I have never believed that society owed me anything at all. . . . I have never had the idea that men were unjust to me. I regard as supremely ridiculous the unhappiness of all our poets who ruminate on this idea. . . .

After he had recovered from his illness, he continued to live at the Darus' and began to study methodically the arts that would presumably advance him in society. He took lessons in dancing; also, later, in declamation (to improve his accent); and with a friend of the younger Darus practiced fencing. Still he was always heavy and slow-moving.

The Daru brothers decided to take up their bear of a country cousin and tame him. He was escorted to the theater and invited to their parties; he played charades and rhyming games with the Daru ladies in the evening, went for carriage rides or visits to the Louvre in the daytime. Pierre Daru, about fifteen years older than he, then a high official in the War Ministry, was also a literary man who had won some note by writing satirical and didactic verses "in the classical style of 1700." Noticing that Henri Beyle seemed to have read a few books, he took the youth to the meetings of a literary society over which he presided. There Henri heard Pierre Daru read his own verses with intense earnestness and self-importance. Henri kept his own counsel; his own more "romantic" tastes in literature were at complete variance with those of his cousin, and he refused to imitate or approve of him. He entertained himself "by admiring the bosom of Madame Pipelet" who was to be the future Princess Salm. Meanwhile he kept his opinions and intentions to himself.

It was Pierre's younger brother Martial Daru whom he really desired to emulate. Martial was a handsome fop who had the Parisian knack of always speaking lightly of the gravest subjects. In good society and to his friends he showed charming manners and had, indeed, a very kind heart that would never permit him to harm anyone. But with women he invariably adopted an air of easy familiarity often resembling brusqueness, as if he had known each one of them all his life. Henri now put Martial Daru in the place formerly occupied by his uncle Romain as his mentor in gallantry. He tried to dress and carry himself like Martial, who, at twenty-two, had had as many mistresses as he had years. He told himself that he should act upon the maxim that the other had adopted: "In this world one gets nowhere without women."

His progress as a man about town was slow. True, he was able to attend a few tedious soirées at the homes of ladies who were friends or relatives of the Darus. Their elder daughter, Mme. Cambon, discerned something in him and pronounced him "odd but not undistinguished." There was a cousin of the Darus, Mme. Rebuffel and her pretty daughter, aged twelve, who lived close by in the Rue de Lille and received him often. This lady was separated from her husband, but amused herself nonetheless; and Henri reported in a letter to Grenoble: "Mme. Cambon reigns over the empire of wit as Mme. Rebuffel over that of the senses."

Another friend of the Darus, Mme. Cardon, had been a lady-in-waiting to Marie Antoinette, and delighted the young Beyle with some uncensored memoirs of the court and the journeyman locksmith who was Louis XVI. But though he sometimes talked well, "without foolishness or overexcitement," on the whole he felt constrained even in such congenial surroundings; he had the egoistic adolescent's notion that everyone's eyes were always fixed on himself.

Why, he wondered afterward, did he cease to visit these people?

Why, he asked himself, did no one tell him to choose a salon, go there every Tuesday, if that was the regular day, and make it his business to be charming or, at least, pleasing to all he met? With the favor of an attractive woman, and aided by two or three other salons, he might after ten years get to be a "somebody"; he might gather in all that he desired. Instead, he missed all the openings that presented themselves and nothing came easily to him. He must always "conquer at the point of the sword."

Moreover, living with the Darus, who so kindly protected him, was something of a trial. He was obliged to dine with them every day, and the ceremonious and conventional atmosphere at the table froze him to silence, when he longed to spread life and animation among the company. It needed only that old M. Daru utter some words about religion and some pieties on the great principles of morality, and Henri felt himself "slain" on the spot.

Then the voice of that "terrible old man" would address itself to him in particular, inquiring politely if he had made up his mind about the Ecole Polytechnique or any other project. The Darus, of course, communicated with his family in Grenoble; they knew of his prizes at school, and thought it a pity that he should waste his talents in idleness.

One day the old man took him aside and said to him, "My son will give you a place under him at the Ministry of War." Henri Beyle was so surprised and confused that he did not remember to thank Daru.

Pierre Daru at thirty-three years of age was in effect the deputy quartermaster general of the army which Napoleon was then secretly preparing for a second campaign in Italy. In a vast room with gilded panels at the War Ministry, the younger Daru toiled night and day; Napoleon roared at him, and Pierre Daru, in turn, roared like a bull at the people who worked under him. At night, very late, he would return with eyes swollen and red from overwork; yet despite his extreme fatigue, in the company of his family he would be self-possessed and gracious.

Henri now became one of the seven hundred clerks who worked for Daru; he had reason to hope that he would soon be appointed a deputy commissary of war, like young Martial Daru, and sport a charming red uniform and a gold-braided hat. All day long he sat at a desk in the office of the War Ministry writing letters for Daru, according to instructions, which he turned over to him for his signature. Daru bore down hard upon his assistants. Soon Henri was infected with the general terror of the "wild bull," and his fear of a blistering reprimand from his chief never left him, though he was more kindly treated than others. It was his spelling that provoked the worst wrath of Pierre Daru. One day he wrote *cella* instead of *cela!* His chief became a "volcano" spouting insults. Thereafter he tried to approach the great man through an intermediary, who was his private secretary, rather than directly. "Daru was in mortal fear of Napoleon, and I was in mortal fear of him," he observed. It was all so much like Picard's theory of ricochets, he adds.

Next to him worked an ambitious young man, older than himself, who was already an assistant commissary of war. He too pretended to be an amateur of letters. But when Henri remarked that he disliked Racine as a subservient courtier and admired Shakespeare, the older man heaped ridicule upon him as well as on Shakespeare. The dispute over the English poet reduced the youth to tears, and thereafter he maintained a dignified silence toward his colleague.

The days passed, he worked hard, trying more and more to imitate the tone of Pierre Daru in the letters that were given him to write to the clothing officer of the 7th Light Horse, or to the pay officer of some other regiment. Yet he seldom seemed to please his exacting chief.

As he worked at his first job, that winter of 1800, he suffered from confinement. All that he could see out of the window near him was a long courtyard with two rows of closely pruned lime trees denuded of leaves. What a poor sight, when he thought of Dauphiné and the farm at Claix! Inwardly he wept for himself. Paris had meant a career, freedom, the enjoyment of brilliant society, Art and Love. The season advanced, and the small lime trees outside had tiny buds. But he stared at them disconsolately, thinking of a large lime tree at home, a favorite spot, under which he used to pass water. "*And is Paris nothing but that?*" he asked himself so many times, even when he was very young; is it only *that?*

Spring came finally, and the lime trees outside the window were in leaf at last. He writes: "I was deeply moved; I had some friends in Paris, after all!" Every time he went outside to pass water under those lime trees, he felt his soul "*refreshed* by the sight of those friends."

CHAPTER IV

First Voyage to Italy

> Knowledge and improvements are to be got by sailing and posting for that purpose; but whether useful knowledge and real improvements, is all a lottery.
>
> —Sterne, *A Sentimental Journey.*

I WAS dying of fright; but had prepared my soul to make the supreme sacrifice. No dangers now could have power to stop me." Though booted and spurred, armed to the teeth with pistols and a big saber for his first day's operation as a subaltern of dragoons under the banner of Napoleon, it was his horse that had given him a great fright. The spirited bay assigned to him had not been out of the stable for many weeks, and flew off not into battle but literally in all directions the moment Beyle mounted him.

The scene was indeed a peaceful one, far from the front, outside the city of Geneva, where Beyle had gone to join the reserve troops of the Army of Italy. But alas, his father had always forbidden him to ride a horse, and as his horse abruptly left the road and galloped wildly across the rough fields, and as he knew not what to do with the bridle, he saw himself falling, gave himself up for dead at every bound, while hanging on for dear life. With his large behind jolting madly in the saddle, he was absurd, yet brave.

But soon a mounted orderly came in pursuit, drew up and called out: "My master wishes to speak to you." He pointed to an officer who had halted along the road not far away. At once Beyle grew suspicious and fingered in his portmanteau for his pistols—he could hardly manipulate his big saber. The officer, despite a friendly grin, looked very much like a blackguard.

All his life, Beyle confesses, he was like a restive horse "who does not see things as they are, but shies off constantly at imagined obstacles or perils. The good side of it was that my courage usually rose to the test and I proudly faced the greatest dangers."

Approaching the officer with some difficulty, he said sternly: "What is your business with me, sir?"

The man pleasantly enough introduced himself as a Captain Burelvillers of the cavalry, and said that he had been given instructions by someone (doubtless at the order of Pierre Daru) to look after the young fellow who was leaving Geneva that night. He then set to work showing Beyle how to hold his bridle and saber, how to ride his horse downhill and uphill, and how to keep a checkrein on his own excitable humor.

However, Beyle was a dragoon in Napoleon's army, something every boy in France dreamed of. He was as mettlesome as his horse and could not calm himself easily. At Lausanne, when a Swiss officer to whom they applied for lodgings refused them in surly fashion, Beyle at once became choleric, drawing his sword as if to attack the man. Captain Burelvillers quieted him down. Later that evening he asked Beyle if he knew how to use his saber, and to his surprise the youth admitted that he had had only two or three lessons in fencing with the light épée. The captain swore and remarked that the Swiss, who seemed well armed, might have killed him with one stroke, at which Beyle seemed but little concerned. At the first halt along the road, the older man dismounted and taught his companion how to be on his guard, how to thrust with his saber—"otherwise," he said, "you will be spitted like a hog."

They rode on southward mile after mile, Beyle, a happy young madman, observing everything with keyed-up senses, and everything new to him. The scene became grander and wilder as they mounted the roads leading to the high Alpine pass that the van of the Army of Italy had already crossed.

In great secrecy, during the spring of 1800, the plans for the second conquest of Italy had been completed. Henri Beyle's cousin, Pierre Daru (one of those indefatigable young administrators who built Napoleon's empire), after outfitting and provisioning the new army, had departed for Italy in April, bearing the title of inspector of reviews. As an afterthought, for he kindly kept his eye upon his odd young relative, he ordered him to join his staff. The commission of second lieutenant in the 6th Dragoons was obtained for Beyle, but he was assigned to the service of supply headed by Daru.

The boy of seventeen, hesitating not a moment, left Paris on May 7, 1800, journeying by carriage to Geneva, where the mysterious "army of reserve" had been based. It must be remembered that Citizen Bonaparte still spoke of himself as merely the "chief magistrate of the Republic"; that he issued clarion calls to the Revolutionary soldiers of France to resume the fight against the implacable enemies of liberty, Austria and England; that he exhorted them to spread the blessings of free institutions into lands of feudal darkness, while winning glory upon the field of battle and occasionally also a modicum of loot.

Like nearly all of French youth, Henri Beyle was filled with the sacred fire that had propelled the hungry, ill-nourished soldiers of the Republic, once before, in 1796, into those fertile plains, those great cities and rich provinces of northern Italy. Though he had thought his first object was to furnish his head and cultivate his sentiments, and thus become infallibly a great dramatic poet, he also reasoned that in order to become that one must have experience of life. Like Goethe before him, and Byron and Heine after him, he longed to see the Italy of Ariosto, the Italy that Rousseau had sung, as a land of eternal summer and treasure-laden cities.

He said to himself:

> I must *live*. I considered myself like Calderon serving his campaigns in Italy . . . a curiously detached being, part of the army, yet chiefly bent on observing, so that later I might write comedies like Molière . . . I asked *only to witness great events*.[1]

That this was no afterthought is shown by his earliest letters to his sister Pauline, in which, at this very season, he urges that we must observe and think for ourselves, resisting the opinions of our elders, who apparently seek to fill us with wrong ideas so that we may be deceived and robbed of happiness. One of the first entries in his journal is:

> Let us hasten to enjoy ourselves, for our days are numbered, the hours I have spent heaping reproaches upon myself have, nonetheless, brought me nearer to death.[2]

But to travel in freedom, seeing the world from the high road, made him "intoxicated with joy," though in Grenoble and Paris he had thought he would never laugh again. Of the first journey to Italy, he wrote: "Here begins a period of perfect enthusiasm and happiness. . . ."

---

[1] *Vie d'Henri Brulard*, II, 289 (Divan ed.)

[2] Letter to Pauline Beyle, Apr. 18, 1800; *Journal*, I, p. 27, July 12, 1801.

In the environs of Geneva, while waiting for the horse that was to carry him precariously over the mountains, he ran to see the house where the romantic and solitary wanderer, Jean-Jacques Rousseau, had been born. He pushed on along the lake to Vevey, which had been described with such deep emotion by the author of his favorite novel, *La Nouvelle Héloïse*:

> . . . Suddenly I heard the majestic tolling of a church bell ringing at full peal from a hill above me, about a mile away. I climbed to the church, I saw the beautiful lake outstretched at my feet. The sound of the bell was an exquisite music, which gave an accompaniment to my ideas, coloring them with the sublime.

Stendhal's memoirs rarely have lush descriptions of his pleasures; it is as if he shrinks from defining them. How find words to express my ecstasy at such a time and place? he seems to ask, and then passes it over briefly. For how can one communicate the joy of living itself? In later life he has a horror of the overemphatic, à la Rousseau; and it is only rarely that such a passage occurs as this describing his joy in seeing Lake Geneva in 1800: "the closest approach I have made to *perfect happiness.*" And then he adds, "For such a moment it is worth while to have lived."

2

For many days before he departed from Geneva, the main French forces had been moving forward to the St. Bernard Pass, by whose sudden crossing Napoleon dumfounded the enemy. The Swiss had told Henri how arduous this passage was, but in his mood of dedication and rapture, this had merely made him more restlessly "gay." The big, choleric officer who rode beside him seemed vexed by his high spirits; Henri could not talk of poetry to him; his fine phrases and fancies only met with rebuffs from the older man.

Part of an unending column of men and cannon, they climbed into the highlands; the road became a mere track, the land barren, then covered with melting snow that was slippery underfoot. They rode in mist and penetrating cold. Here and there a dead horse caused his own mount to rear suddenly, or as loose stones rolled under hoof, almost to fall. The captain swore and beat his horse over the head. Beyle was bold on horseback, but kept asking himself nervously: "Will I get myself killed? Will I be killed?"

They reached the Hospice of St. Bernard, where they were given bread, cheese, and wine by the monks; then began the long, winding descent, always more perilous than the climb. The cannon carriages must be eased downward slowly, with immense effort to hold them back; the horsemen were ordered to hold their bridles with but two fingers, ready to leap from the saddle as they rode along the edge of abysses. Two days were passed in the mountains, then the air grew softer as they reached the foothills on the Italian side.

"Is the St. Bernard no more than that?" Beyle asked the captain. The older officer swore at him for a rascally young blower.

As a boy he had thought of the republican soldiers as modern knights who must be as chivalrous as the heroes of Ariosto's epic of the days of Roland. But the soldiers accompanying him or passing him on the way back seemed rough or villainous fellows. Those on foot looked with eyes of hate at the mounted ones, and when they pitched camp at night, Beyle had to watch sharply for prowlers. Were these the heroes he had imagined? His cicerone, Captain Burelvillers himself, as he gathered, had almost been cashiered for misconduct.

On the third day in the mountains the growing sound of cannonading, echoing strangely in a deep ravine he skirted, and becoming steadily louder, filled him with a wild emotion. They approached Fort Bard, which held out long after the main French army had by-passed it, and descended to the plain. At Napoleon's order, a rough detour had been constructed for the use of the artillery at night, while the infantry and cavalry passed it under fire in the daytime.

"This is dangerous now," Beyle said to himself. He stood on a ledge with the captain and a few other men, who declared that the enemy were plainly sighting them from their fortifications some four hundred yards away. Was he not frightened now? the captain asked. In answer he stepped out to the edge of that shelf of rock in order to be more exposed. "When the others continued their march, I loitered there for a few minutes longer," he relates, "in order to show my courage." Courage, he thought ever afterward, was the fear of being ridiculous or cowardly in others' eyes.

This was his baptism of fire, for the cannon balls were ricocheting about the site, albeit none too menacingly. "It was a sort of maidenhead I lost there that concerned me no more than the other kind," he wrote. His only difficulty, as an unskilled rider, came from the rearing of his horse at every shot and shell. That he was not pretending or boasting in those vivid, closing pages of his memoirs, written so long after the event, is proved by a letter he wrote on June 29, 1800, to his sister in

Grenoble, saying that the difficulty of the passage of the St. Bernard had been "wonderfully exaggerated"; that there was not a moment of danger, but that it made "a truly astonishing spectacle . . . it was sublime." It is likely that Napoleon, in his reports, deliberately magnified the hazards of the crossing of the Alps in order to establish a legend which the pious type of historians has preserved—though Beyle's posthumous memoirs were to refute them.

When they reached the Italian side at Aosta, and he was well out of danger, he said to himself once more that night: "Is it nothing but that?" So this was what was meant by going under fire?

Then and later the accounts given of the preliminaries to the great Battle of Marengo, outside of Milan, pictured the troops singing as they struggled to move the heavy gun carriages, while bands played brave music. It was the movement of heavy artillery that alone made Napoleon's expedition more notable than those of Hannibal, of the Romans, and the Lombards later. But the young Beyle saw little romance in the business, neither in 1800 nor, in retrospect, in 1839, when he wrote his famous description of the Battle of Waterloo. His letters to his family described the campaigns he participated in with an air of detachment that in his journals approached boredom. This tone of disillusionment, especially with his unheroic comrades, has been attributed by commentators to the fact that he necessarily marched in the "fog of war," often in the rear with drunken stragglers and shifty sutlers and camp followers. But the tone of his afterthoughts, as of his first impressions of Napoleonic war, has always seemed one of singular candor and objectivity to men of military experience, who, like him, recalled asking themselves in the midst of an engagement: "Is this a real battle?"

Yet as he rode down the Aosta valley to Ivrea, a border town of some ten thousand population, graciously encircled by mountains, his attitude changed sensibly. There was a quantity of wreckage and dead horses underfoot, but he had eyes only for the warm green tint of that valley and the brightly colored houses of the town yonder, and said to himself: *"I am in Italy!"*

Even in that small border town the native passion for music had brought forth a little opera house which Beyle promptly visited. Though it was a shabby place, and the prima donna had a front tooth missing, the evening was one of the most memorable of his whole life. He experienced what he terms a "divine happiness"—for he heard for the first time a performance of Cimarosa's *Il Matrimonio Segreto* sung by true Italian voices. The sweetness and the tenderness of Cimarosa's melodies refreshed his soul; he wept and felt once more a rapture such as he had known only on the soil of Rousseau at Lake Geneva.

His first introduction to operatic music in Italy, reinforced by his later opera-going in Milan, confirmed a lifelong passion for music. His taste was in some ways retrograde, being limited mainly to vocal music, but music answered a deep need in him; he could never have enough of Paësiello, Pergolese, and later Rossini, and above all of Cimarosa, the "divine Cimarosa" and the laughter and tears of his *opera buffa.* He had not found happiness in Dauphiné or in Paris; but in Italy he had found a music that spoke to his soul. To have crossed the Alps and been under fire weighed as nothing in his memories against hearing *Il Matrimonio Segreto.* Perhaps, he thought, he should have abandoned the gross profession of arms and dedicated himself to melody and harmony. "To live in Italy and hear this music became the basis of all my planning," he declares.

But there was more and stronger music awaiting him as he rode southward. The subaltern of dragoons descended at last to the lush green-and-yellow plain of Lombardy, under that violent blue sky, while the late Italian spring assailed him with its blazing heat. On the edge of the horizon he could see, like a cooling thought, the high, snow-covered Alps, now fifty miles away, forming a majestic amphitheater that enclosed the great Po Valley and the plain surrounding the capital of northern Italy. He could see the immense cathedral spire and the marble palaces of that storied city glittering from far off.

How fine it was to be young, mounted on a spirited horse, and riding with an army of conquerors upon a splendid city that was not merely to be captured, but to be "liberated" also, as the young First Consul announced in his spirited bulletins. At this moment the cold damp nights in the mountains, the weariness of the long journeys, the debris and the corpses, were all forgotten, as the youth of seventeen stared in complete enchantment at what he always believed then and forever after was "the most beautiful spot in all the world," the great good place he had sought. The luxuriant plain of Milan at the foot of the Alps, and the cool blue lakes in the marvelous wooded foothills to the north was Italy to him, appearing as a divinely beautiful mistress to whom he would plight the only constant love of his life.

3

On the 2nd of June 1800, the endless columns of Napoleon's army began to roll into the beautiful metropolis of northern Italy day after day. On the third morning of that triumphal march into the undefended city, Henri Beyle too rode in, to be welcomed as one of the conqueror-liberators, and with true Italian fervor—illuminations, fireworks, and music. The miracles of the Revolutionary soldiers, he declares, had aroused the slumbering folk, and they received the ragged French with open arms, "a whole people mad with love." Beautiful women rushed forward to kiss them; the young men now abandoned what was formerly their principal occupation, "writing sonnets upon handkerchiefs of rose-tinted taffeta," and embraced a new and more passionate way of life that broke with the old despotism and its ancient superstitions. Thus Beyle wrote nearly forty years later, in those vivid opening pages of his novel, *The Charterhouse of Parma*, which had nothing to do with the story, but served only to commemorate the scene of his own entrance into Milan.

The scene in reality was somewhat different. The effusive Italians had learned a hard lesson two years after the first French invasion in 1796, when the retreat of their liberators had brought back the Austrian military rulers, and thirteen months of thoroughgoing German repression for all who had espoused the cause of liberty. Their hospitality to the returning hordes of Frenchmen who had clambered over the Alps again was at first tinged with anxiety, as they wondered what new misfortunes to expect—until the day of Marengo, June 15, 1800 when all of northern Italy lay open to the young Napoleon. Just returned from the field, the great captain showed himself that very night in a box of the vast Scala Theater. Henri Beyle, accompanying his chief, Pierre Daru, who delivered reports to Napoleon, saw him here for the first time, while thousands in the theater acclaimed him madly.

Then there was revelry and frenzied joy unconfined among the people who no longer doubted that they were liberated. The opulent Milanese now threw themselves into a round of festivals and balls celebrating their freedom, also banishing their anxiety over the heavy costs of the invasion and its attendant social revolution. (This assumed, sometimes, accents of passion and vengeance that sent priests or nobles flying to the mountains.) The music, dancing, and laughter that filled the handsome streets and palaces of Milan after the Battle of Marengo festooned the memories of Beyle ever afterward, and were associated with the most joyous and enthusiastic time of his youth. In *The Charterhouse of Parma* he would associate these recollections with the first invasion in 1796, which he could not have witnessed, since he was then in Grenoble, a schoolboy of thirteen.

But he was young enough in June 1800, and his enthusiasm was genuine enough, so that later he could speak with knowledge of the high emotion of those historic hours when the Republic still lived, when France was still the center of a world in which its unloosed energies radiated liberty, when

> . . . an enthusiasm for republican virtue, conceived during the years that were not far removed from childhood, engendered an immense disgust for the behavior of the kings against whom we were fighting and . . . gave to many of our soldiers of 1794 the conviction that only the French were enlightened beings. In our eyes the inhabitants of the rest of Europe, fighting to hold on to their chains, were either pitiful imbeciles or rogues who had sold themselves to the despots waging war against us. . . . In those days all were dominated by a profound feeling of which I no longer see any traces. The reader must realize that, if what the books say is true, in 1794 we had no religion of any kind; all of our deep, inward sentiment might be summed up in this single thought: *to be useful to the fatherland.*
>
> And all the rest, clothing, food, promotion, were as nothing to our minds. Since there was no society, the desire for *success,* a dominant motive among the people of the present day, did not exist for us.
>
> Walking through the streets, our eyes would fill with tears when we saw an inscription on the wall in honor of the young drummer boy, Barra [who chose death rather than cease to beat his drum in warning of a surprise attack].[3]

The patriot and revolutionist of seventeen, who played his small part in that "army of youth" that brought liberty in its train, was dazzled by all that he saw in Milan: its smoothly paved streets, its spacious residences and palaces, mostly in the regular classical style of the seventeenth and early eighteenth centuries, seemed more imposing than in any other city. At the Porta Nuova, Martial Daru, the young brother of his chief, had found him in the hour of his arrival, and welcoming him warmly, conducted him to the lordly old Adda Palace where he was to live and work temporarily in the service of General Pétiet, the paymaster of the Army of Italy. Here he was lodged in a most beautiful bedchamber and came to work in a vast high-ceilinged salon, whose windows opened on ornate balconies overlooking the busy Corso, on one side, and a stately courtyard on the other. The Adda, headquarters of the rulers of the new "Cisalpine Republic," was at the edge of the city, near the elevated Corso, where the fashionables of Milan rode every afternoon in their carriages, to take the air, look at the country and the mountains far off, then return at sunset to sip ices on the terrace of the splendid café on the Corso.

In endless delight, Beyle, a budding connoisseur of architecture and

[3] *Napoleon,* Vol. II, pp. 7-9 (Champion ed.).

painting, rushed about to gape at the Cathedral of Milan, whose spire towered some 350 feet overhead, or to visit the Church of Santa Maria delle Grazie, whose adjacent convent held Leonardo's "Last Supper," the Bréra Palace with its rich galleries of paintings, the Ambrosian Library, and finally the huge baroque Scala Theater, then the pride of Milan, and to Beyle the shrine of the Italian music he loved above all other music.

The warm-blooded Milanese, despite the distractions of war and revolution, continued to be impassioned music lovers, knowing the scores of the operas of Paësiello and Cimarosa which they heard over and over again, encouraging the actors with shouts or sobs of pleasure, or censuring them angrily until, one might say, they participated as actors in each performance. Beyle, attending the Scala every night, caught their fever for *opera buffa* in earnest, and remained a musical maniac all his life. The imposing ballet of the Scala was also something that endlessly pleased him, the like of which he had never seen. Within the semicircle of that lofty hall, with its five tiers of candle-lit, silk-curtained boxes, he would sit by the hour, lost in a voluptuous and sentimental rapture that the Italian voices never failed to evoke.

Soon he noticed that the Scala was the very center of social life, a sort of public salon for all the fashionable world of Milan. No woman who was in vogue would fail to appear there every night, mounting the grand stairway to her private loge in the company of eight or ten admirers and guests, while the town gallants thronged the broad foyer to ogle them. For without waiting to grasp the full import of Revolutionary ideas, the charming ladies of Milan had adopted the republican or "Roman" costumes that so freely revealed their arms and breasts. The full-bosomed Milanese belles seemed to his eyes the most beautiful women of the world, and their inviting and facile manners aroused the most pleasurable anticipations. Moreover, it was the young French officers who, by right of conquest, invariably escorted them, sat proudly beside them in carriages, acted as their faithful *cavalieri serventi*. Perhaps the Italian lovers and husbands were vexed; but many, on returning to their homes, found their women in the arms of French officers, who sometimes drew their swords to turn them out of doors. Others shrugged their shoulders and consoled themselves by sharing with wives and sweethearts and sisters the rich trinkets that the French plunderers distributed with prodigal hands. Indeed some of the ladies of Milan, according to one diverting legend, could not quite remember who the fathers of their children had been, but tenderly named them after the French regiments that had been quartered among them at the time! The morals of Milan had long been of the comfortable kind; a lover was expected to show jealousy, but a husband never!

Henri Beyle, dressed in the uniform of a dragoon, with a long green cloak, and helmet with black plume of horsehair, accompanied his swaggering young fellow officers to balls and dinners as well as to the opera every night. He studied Italian, which he began to master quickly. Besides these enjoyments, several short journeys made during military missions in the environs of Milan, to the blue Lake Maggiore and the "perfumed" Borromean Isles, convinced him, as he wrote his sister, Pauline, at the beginning of his stay, that he had found all that he desired on earth gathered together in one spot.

His companions were older than he. Second Lieutenant Henri Beyle watched admiringly while his relative, Martial Daru, so elegant and so lightheaded, gathered up the prettiest women in the town. His other friends, the two sons of General Pétiet, were scarcely less fortunate; while even a plain fellow like Lieutenant Louis Joinville, a young friend and colleague at the Ministry of War in Paris, acquired for his mistress a tall, buxom, dark-eyed beauty who looked as if she had stepped from one of Leonardo's paintings. Her name was Angiola Borroni Pietragrua; she was the wife of a shopkeeper, but she was madly in love with young Joinville, and thought not at all of concealing it.

For the women of Milan were as brave as they were merry and audacious in speech. Of one it was said that she dressed like a man in order to run out at night and climb a ladder to the room of her lover who lay ill and needed her. Of another that even in old age she would point to her still beautiful shoulders and exclaim: "Ah! The King of Naples used to rest his head there." Even during dinners at General Pétiet's (who became Minister Extraordinary at Milan) the wine flowed so freely that the guests sometimes ended by falling into each other's arms. But Beyle remained timid, effaced himself. "I felt too much pride to make advances to anyone; and spent my days in an extreme *attendrissement*, full of a wistful melancholy . . ." he wrote in his journal, during a later visit, in 1811.

He was only seventeen, unaccustomed to society, worried about his unique and worn-out uniform, in which he feared he cut but a poor figure. Besides he was still innocent. He longed for a woman who would love him with a great passion and for his superior soul. The ladies he met and danced with were polite and obliging enough. But one must go forward to meet them. When, to overcome his own timidity, and in imitation of his older friends, he tried to play the bold cavalryman, to "pass himself off as a roué"—a role that did not suit him, try as he might—he found that he did not advance his cause. He convinced no one and gained nothing. Was it because he was awkward, was it that he was "ugly"?

He still had more of Saint-Preux than of Valmont in him; for, as he wrote later of this difficult time:

> No one took pity on me, and none came to my rescue with a charitable counsel. Thus I passed the two or three years when my temperament was most ardent, *without women*. . . . I was devoured by sensitiveness, timid, proud, misunderstood. . . . At eighteen, when I adored Mme. P[ietragrua], I lacked money and had only one uniform, sometimes rather patched up here and there.
>
> I watched Joinville, Mazeau, and others succeed; I saw them do things that I felt I could do better; they were happy; had mistresses. I did not stir; I waited until some romantic chance, like a carriage breaking down, should introduce my heart to some understanding soul.[4]

Two years *without women*? In that climate, amid extreme summer heat—"at that period of full youth," with only "sighs, tears, *élans* of love"—while merely hoping that some "true friend would throw me into the arms of some woman!" The brief *Journal of Italy*, written in 1811, is somewhat fictive on this matter. It is corrected by the later *Life of Henri Brulard*, which tells us candidly:

> I have forgotten to say that I brought my innocence with me from Paris; it was only at Milan that I was to rid myself of this "treasure." Amusingly enough, I cannot remember distinctly with whom I did so.
>
> The violence of my timidity and of the experience has absolutely killed my recollection.

How can one recall the moments of utter folly and self-abandon, the moments of supreme happiness and sorrow of our youth? he asks repeatedly. "One cannot see clearly that part of the sky that is too near the sun," he argues. But perhaps the man of such sharp memory did not want to remember what happened? And when one is young, "and has a great thirst, what does it matter where he quenches it?" he would say.

The truth was that he suffered during those two years because he had no *love*, but not because he was without women. The truth was that his boisterous friends did throw the novice of seventeen into the arms of some bought girl in some dim-lit bagnio in Milan on a night of late June or July, several weeks after his arrival. It was the vulgar and rather dreadful outcome of the adventure that prompted him to

[4] *Journal*, IV, 245–47.

leave it as something vague in his memory. For many years Beyle had a hearty distaste for prostitutes, and his first encounters gave him good cause.

A fragment in rather poor verse, one of the few he has written, celebrates one dark lupinarian night in which he and two companions precipitate themselves upon two poor harlots. It is a scene of mad brawling that is terminated by the arrival of the local police, who show themselves indulgent to the French officers. The time is given as Messidor, Year IX (July 1801) a year later than the first and more decisive of his adventures in bordellos, but is doubtless little different.[5]

It was at this time, probably in July 1800, that he first met Angiola Pietragrua, the mistress of Lieutenant Joinville, whom he thought so beautiful that he followed her with longing glances. With her great, prominent black eyes and "majestic shape," she seemed to him the very model of the "ideal woman of passion" who was to be found perhaps only in Italy, and notably among the Lombards of Milan. She paid no heed to the plump and homely boy; she had Joinville and perhaps other lovers of higher rank than his, a poor subaltern's.

In any case, Beyle suddenly found himself confined to his bed, suffering the pain and fever that the French call the Italian Disease and the Italians call the French Disease. His quarters were now in the Bovara Palace, and his friend Joinville, fortunate possessor of the superb Pietragrua, kindly came to look after him in his sumptuous bedchamber there. With his pale face, growing beard, long, curly hair, Joinville told him, he "looked like a sick lion."

His fellow officers tried to cheer him up by assuring him that he was not the only one—but this hardly made him less lonely, disconsolate, and poxed. Nevertheless he received good care according to the medical lights of the time, this consisting in heavy allowances of mercury that brought a fairly effective cure, though bearing hard on his kidneys.

Writing to his sister, on September 28, 1800, he shows that his love of Italy has suffered a temporary relapse at this time, one of the few of his entire life, for he tells her now that it is an "accursed land" which

---

[5]De ses pâles flambeaux la lune vagabonde
Eclairait Brescia et tout le reste du monde,
De onze coups égaux les clochers résonnants
Appelaient au combat les fortunés amants.
Dans le chemin obscur nous marchions en silence,
Nous allions au bordel chercher la jouissance. . . .
—*Mélanges littéraires*, I, 353–54, Divan ed.

he longs to flee. He hints at the experience of "great passions." The passions, declares the philosopher of seventeen, "may bring us a few moments of true happiness, but with how many terrible moments one must pay for them."

The two years of impotent tears and sighs to which he alludes afterward in his *Journal of Italy* are an exaggeration. The allusion was inspired undoubtedly by an enforced continence that he suffered for several months. But soon he was up and about, his mind cheerfully absorbed in a new plan: that of becoming a great military strategist, or at least a general.

4

Ambition possessed him in 1801, at the age of eighteen. How could one look at the careers of young men like Bonaparte, or Carnot, or the dashing Murat, and not be ambitious in those hell-for-leather days? More than any man of letters of his time, Beyle left the study, for which he was well suited, and went posting about the world, a world made turbulent by social revolution and war. He was, to be sure, an odd and bookish dragoon. In his portmanteau he carried a traveling library consisting of volumes of Homer in translation, Virgil, Horace, Racine, Molière, Boileau, all of which he read and reread. Also an obscure work on the art of comedy; and, befitting his liberal principles, Condorcet's *Progress of the Human Mind*. But somewhere along the route he acquired also a copy of Turenne's memoirs of his campaigns in the seventeenth century, and now read this constantly. The great marshal of France, by his clear, calculating mind, appealed to him as the master of military science par excellence. Studying the battlegrounds of Lodi and Arcola, he constantly measured the achievements or maneuvers of the brilliant Bonaparte against the standards of Turenne, whom he preferred as the superior general.

He was usually in the rear of the battle front, thanks to the surveillance of Inspector General Pierre Daru, for he was thought extremely young for an officer even in those days. His first provisory commission, confirmed in September 1800, attached him to General Headquarters at Milan. Then came a vacancy in the 6th Dragoons to which he was assigned officially in late October, after the Battle of Lodi. But Daru, who hoped to find a post for him as an aide-de-camp of some division—which Beyle earnestly begged for—detained him for a time in his own commissary department, where, as he reported in letters, the youth "scribbled and scrawled faithfully."

The 6th Dragoons, under General Brune, hurled back the Austrians in the campaign on the Mincio River, but Henri Beyle was not there in December, as his friend and first biographer, Colomb, thought he was. Nor did he charge any Austrian batteries. Instead, avoiding his regular regiment, except for very brief visits, he pulled wires at headquarters in Milan to have himself appointed aide-de-camp under another general named Michaud. On New Year's Eve of 1800, he fought a duel with Lieutenant Augustin Pétiet—perhaps for fruitlessly annoying Pétiet's mistress, though he tells us little of this—and suffered a slight wound in the calf of his leg that kept him abed a few days. Finally General Michaud, thanks to the recommendation of Henri's friend, Lieutenant Joinville, invited him to join his staff as aide-de-camp, Michaud believing that this would please the powerful Inspector General Daru, then absent from Milan. When Daru returned, he found "our young man" had flown without his permission. What made things worse was that Napoleon had lately issued a stern order requiring that all General Staff officers and aides be chosen only from those who had three years of combat experience.

Second Lieutenant Beyle had the qualities of a fine officer, it has been observed. He was capable of a cold courage, and showed a spirit of fatalism in time of danger; he was quick-thinking and energetic. But he detested the life of a subaltern at an army camp, drilling his men, living by rote, and he used all his adroitness of mind to shirk it. His letters home are one long lament at the ignorance and "bestiality" of his fellow officers. What he wanted was to be the adviser of some general, and he found Michaud a crude but brave and genial fellow. General Michaud enjoyed his company, took him hunting, sent him on liaison trips to Brescia, Verona, or even as far as Florence, which was most amusing and improving for Beyle. When objections were made at headquarters at Beyle's irregular change of assignment, the general said: "I like little Beyle, he is very clever. I want him very much to have the commission as aide-de-camp, though he is too frank and outspoken."[6]

However, Pierre Daru, his powerful protector, ordered him to his own regiment, the 6th Dragoons, intending perhaps to work things out in good time and with more regard for regulations. But the young Beyle held him at arm's length by writing him long letters full of arguments. To win delay he pleaded illness as well. He also wrote to his grandfather, Dr. Gagnon, in Grenoble, begging him to intercede with

[6]Stendhal: *Journal*, I, p. 9.

Daru. In reply to the good doctor, Daru wrote, in June 1801, that he found it "scarcely proper that a young man . . . admitted into a regiment through favor should have the idea of being discontented with the post assigned him and ask for another the next day. . . . He is very stubborn and for six months all my efforts to persuade him to rejoin his corps have been of no avail." He promised to do what was possible to help the boy, but added that "he must permit himself to be led."[7]

But this was precisely what Beyle did not wish. In his journal, on June 4, 1801, he wrote: "I have no counselor or friend; I am weakened by the duration of my fever; but I am determined, convinced, that by dint of perseverance and boldness, I shall succeed in becoming aide-de-camp to General Michaud. Then I shall owe this success, like the others, solely to myself." He told himself that he must work unflaggingly to develop his talents. His whole idea now was "to study and imitate Turenne."

He served eight months under Michaud, during which he probably witnessed the action before Mantua and the capture of that stronghold. His commander liked him so well that he later signed several letters or certificates attesting to his aide's prowess in various battles which later scholars believed Beyle could not possibly have participated in, according to the dates and itinerary indicated in his letters.[8] These certificates moreover were written in his own hand, though signed by the general. If they had the purpose of advancing him either in office or right to pension, they suggest a touch of the unscrupulous that accorded well with that time of violence and plunder, but not with the texture of Henri Beyle's later character.

High-willed, independent, he journeyed on horseback over most of northern Italy, often alone, armed to the teeth against peasants, who, often as not, turned into guerrillas or bandits. Violence and death were rampant in this stricken land, as so often before and since, and man's life was held cheap. An experienced assassin, he learned in Brescia, could be hired for four ducats. The ruin and ignorance that he saw, he attributed to the long oppressions of tyrants and priests which, he was convinced, the liberal ideas of the Revolution would banish forever.

"All our evils are born of ignorance," he wrote in his journal sententiously, for he observed and philosophized much: ". . . Almost

---

[7]Chuquet: *Stendhal-Beyle*, Appendix, 483–84.

[8]P. Arbalet: *La Jeunesse de Stendhal*, II, 152.

all the evils of life are born of our false ideas of that which we experience. To know men deeply, to judge events soundly, is therefore a great step toward happiness."

Withdrawing into himself, out of dislike for his companions in arms, he occupied his mind not only with military tactics but returned again and again to ideas for comedies that he would write in the future. "I believe that I will accomplish something one day in the theater," he told himself. He also wrote notes on tactics useful for conquering women, as methodical and mechanistic as those on military science. One of his fellow dragoons had told him of his own tested method of overpowering women who tried to resist him, and Beyle noted this information gravely in his journal. But his own disposition, he remarked on December 10, 1801, was "to inspire a woman with a high idea of my own lights, as the surest way to lead to the end in view." Yet when the opportunity presented itself, one must be bold in the strategy of love, like a good general. "Heroes have their moments of fear, cowards their moments of courage, and virtuous women their moments of weakness. It is a great art to know how to judge and seize those moments." But would this yield him "victory" over one like Angiola Pietragrua?

More and more his thoughts of love and pleasure assumed the generous shape of that black-eyed Milanese belle. Before leaving to join General Michaud's corps, he had paid her a visit together with several other French and Italian admirers. They had been standing at the balcony of her house looking at a parade of French troops, whom Beyle then expected to join in the field. "Alas," he said to her with a heavy sigh, "tomorrow I too may be but a corpse on the plains of Mantua." She barely noticed his words and their note of despair, their appeal for pity. Second Lieutenant Beyle, whom they nicknamed the "Chinaman" because of his fat cheeks and small eyes, was a nobody, and La Pietragrua, according to gossip, had more profitable friendships.

To attract her attention, Beyle grew desperately gay, and made advances more open than before. "But Beyle, what is the matter with you? What do all these things you are doing mean?" he remembered her saying to him.

In September 1801, stern orders came bidding him to proceed without delay to the post of the 6th Dragoons, stationed then in a small town in Piedmont. Bowing at last to authority, he returned to Milan, en route to Piedmont, and bade good-by to the "majestic" Gina, as Mme. Pietragrua was called, and the Scala Theater. The music he heard this last time deepened the ardor of his feeling for her. How much he would have longed to stay with her, to love and be loved—instead of proceeding to Turin and France. Surely, as he liked to believe, such a woman would have helped to "form" him at that impressionable age. With such help as hers—which he felt necessary to a man of sensibility—his character would have been a happier and worldlier one, and might not have had "that core of sentimentality which is chiefly useful to art."

The years of feeling himself inferior, for want of money and uniforms, and disappointment in the race for woman during his first Italian journey—to which the discomfiture of the pox also contributed—made him believe himself unlucky, made him wary and mistrustful of life in the midst of his strongest *élans*. Suffering in youth rendered him as self-conscious as a Laurence Sterne in the presence of his emotions, but gave him—in his own words—"an inexhaustible fund of sensitiveness."

"The woman I loved . . . had other lovers," he wrote reflectively upon revisiting Italy many years later. "But she would have preferred me, I used to say to myself, if my rank had been equal to theirs."[9] Once in France he thought of Italy with longing, because Gina dwelt there. He vowed to her, if not fidelity, then "a sort of constancy." "Not being able to win the love of Mme. Pietragrua, I entertained myself with all sorts of fanciful dreams conceived in her honor, in one of which I imagined myself returning one day as a colonel, or enjoying some other superior station, above that of a mere employee of Monsieur Daru, then embracing her and melting into tears."[10]

---

[9] *Vie d'Henri Brulard*, II, 320.

[10] *Journal*, IV, 241–42, 245–46.

CHAPTER V

The Apprentice Bard

Madder than ever he began to study to be a great man!
—Stendhal.

BY MID-APRIL 1802, he was back in Paris, following a furlough of three months in Grenoble and his sudden resignation of his commission. The bookish young dragoon was quite the Man of Experience at nineteen. But he had literally been made ill by doing garrison duty in a camp in Piedmont. "It seems that my principal malady is boredom," he wrote in a letter from his camp. His fellow warriors he found utterly wanting in "sensitiveness," and indeed little more than imbeciles or plunderers. They must have been astounded at the quantity of books he carried in his portmanteau. For after a season or two of soldiering, books were his only solace; he was quite convinced that he was made to be a philosopher, a dramatic poet, a Don Juan—anything but a general.

Grenoble revisited seemed smaller and meaner than ever after Milan. True, he had been homesick, and longed to see his grandfather and especially his sister Pauline, now a high-spirited young lady of sixteen, with dark hair, a pretty oval-shaped face, and an eager mind. Pauline loomed large in his life; she was all the family that he loved, for Dr. Gagnon was very old now; she was his confidante and fellow conspirator; at his order she read the same books that he read. It was she who brought Henri's requests for money to his father, when he feared to present them.

No, save for Pauline, he did not find in the bosom of his family the affection he pined for. Trade was booming now and his father was utterly "obsessed" by his farming experiments. He notes in one of his journals:

> Sunday I arrived at my grandfather's at one o'clock for dinner. From that moment to the end of the meal they did not cease to groan and lament. *This is not family to be desired* [sic] *is Pauline's advice.*[1]

Meanwhile the problem of the son troubled the father's prudent soul. Surely Henri's character would be blighted if he wandered about the world as a soldier. The elder Beyle pressed him to give up such ideas. "My father promised me an income of 3,000 francs a year if I would resign," Henri wrote in his journal after his visit to Grenoble.

But though Chérubin Beyle plunged into large speculations in land and sheep—he borrowed as much as 400,000 francs from money-lenders for such purposes—he delayed giving his son funds that were due him by his mother's will. Pauline in her letters testifies that when she, as intermediary, came to her father to seek money for Henri, he spoke only of the business debts he owed. This though she knew that he had just received a big sum for the sale of lands. "Your father," she wrote, "cares more for merino sheep than for his son." Henri found it, as he said, easier to come to Grenoble than to leave it.

Yet he was decided not only to leave Grenoble but the army as well; and an added, more romantic reason for this step is given in one of a series of Last Testaments he wrote, this dated 1828, in which he declares: "I came back to Grenoble from Italy, fell in love and, without reporting to the Minister of War, followed Mlle. V., whom I loved, to Paris."

Susceptible Henri! On his return as a sort of martial hero to his townspeople he had been invited out a good deal, and so had called at the home of Jean-Joseph Mounier, Grenoble's famous deputy to the Constituent Assembly, whose son Edouard was one of his former schoolmates. Now Edouard Mounier had a sister named Victorine who was quite pretty, and after his amorous disappointments in Italy, Henri craved an object of love. He heard her play Haydn at a musicale, and his heart was stirred. Though he was never permitted to speak to her alone, his eyes hung upon her; he knew himself at once in love, and with a great love.

But that spring, in 1802, M. Mounier, with his family, moved to Brittany, where he assumed the office of prefect of Rennes. At once Beyle, obtaining six hundred francs from his father by the most impassioned appeals, departed for Paris, which was much nearer to

[1] *Filosofia Nova*, p. 193; dated summer of 1803; partly in Beyle's English.

Rennes. Yet the Mouniers never bothered to invite the young Beyle to visit them, and Rennes was after all over two hundred miles from Paris. Henri could not even see that proud brunette, Victorine. Therefore he made a great business of cultivating the friendship of Edouard Mounier (whom he really disliked as a vain young upstart). To him he wrote most feeling letters which he hoped Victorine would read. Indeed he adopted the highly ingenious device of writing his letters so that they might be read by two persons, each of whom would understand them differently. "The insight which love gives to a heart," he remarks, "permits it to divine the hidden meaning of the most trivial phrases." He spoke of his war experiences, his early and quite vague sorrows, his high ambitions, and his longing to be loved by a beautiful and tender woman. These were the most polished of his early letters and precisely imitated the melancholy style of Rousseau.

"I have wandered at the will of all the passions which have agitated me one after another," he writes, in 1803. "I have but one left which occupies me entirely." Sometimes he wrote with ecstatic longing for a pure and good woman, for whom, he assured Mounier, he would gladly kill himself. For each man of feeling, he said, there was a woman who was "unique," and though she might be reserved in manner, out of virtue, her rare glances always revealed her true sentiment. Before such a woman the boldest man might be timid and "the fine phrases die upon his lips." He concludes: "Write me often: good hearts are so rare they should be close to each other." That sentence, surely, was aimed at Victorine.

Sometimes he spoke of his little triumphs in Paris, and boasted of "conquests." Then, in fear that he might have gone too far, he retracted, saying: "I may have delivered myself of a few outbursts of vanity—like other young men, or acted the fop. . . . But you do not know me if you think me merely a vain fellow."

However, nothing that was said or unsaid in his letters brought a sign from Victorine, who never appeared to notice his mooning glances, and whom, to tell the truth, he saw only on two or three occasions. Perhaps his charming letters were not even submitted to her inspection.

His fine phrases, like kisses in the air, simply disappeared in the drawer of Edouard Mounier's secretary. It was as if Henri Beyle declaimed before an empty theater whose mocking spectators had quietly stolen away.

This was but *un amour passager*, though it was two or three years a-dying, and in the interim always hovered in back of his mind. Yet he enjoyed it so, at this period. Victorine was his "chimera." When he was alone in his little room, or when the music he preferred moved him, he would think of her and of love. ". . . I give her a name, yes, a physiognomy: I speak to her sometimes, but she does not reply, and like a child, after having kissed a doll, I weep because she does not return my kisses."

He thought once of simply going and asking her to be his wife. "But I am too young and restless to be a good husband," he told himself in the next breath. He had promised his father that he would not marry until he was thirty, and this was one pledge that he himself really desired to keep.

2

That he should humor himself with a cerebral love affair, a thing of mere literature, was entirely in character at this stage, when he was but nineteen or twenty, and which he later called the "most exalted period" of his life. It was a time of intense self-instruction and unwearied self-analysis, without literary circles or masters to influence him, without elder friends to counsel him.

After returning to Paris he lived in a small attic room, on the sixth floor of a house in the Rue d'Angivillers that faced the great colonnade of the Louvre. His father gave him 150 francs a month, then a quite adequate income for a young bachelor, though his purchase of hundreds of books distressed his family and often put him in straits. To his father he was simply a "wild young fellow"; to his grandfather he seemed but to be living "the life of an artist in Paris." He saw none of his influential relatives—Pierre Daru washed his hands of him after his resignation from the army—save the jolly coxcomb Martial Daru, whom he intensely admired for his smart dress and his success with women. In imitation of Martial, he clothed himself as fastidiously as he might, considering his small budget, and went to the theater and opera, or sometimes to the salons of one or two older ladies, like Mme. Rebuffel, with whom he felt most comfortable. But for the visits of a few of his student friends such as Fortuné Mante and Louis Crozet, who were completing their course at the Ecole Polytechnique, he lived much alone.

Sometimes he awoke at six in the morning and began to read and study. In the afternoon he walked back and forth in the Tuileries Gardens, and on several days a week took lessons in English from an

Irish friar whom he called "Father Jakey." At night he sometimes read again or wrote in immense notebooks, one a journal of the commonest things that happened to him, another a journal of *Pensées*, or ideas and reflections, and finally a manuscript which he called *Filosofia Nova*, a title half Latin, half Italian, in which he set forth, in the aphoristic manner of the eighteenth-century writers, the system of thought that was to complement or support the system of his art.

This "mad" period lasted about three years; it was filled with inward drama and excitement. Later he never ceased to wonder at how happy he had been, though poor, unknown, having but few friends, eating little, while studying or writing twelve hours a day. He had looked forward to such an opportunity for schooling himself, according to his own lights; he had promised it to himself when he lay sick and bored in the camps of Italy.

Beyle often insisted in later years that his intellectual formation was more or less complete at the age of nineteen or twenty, that for the rest of his days he drew upon the ideas he had formed in early youth, merely perfecting or extending their application. Since he made his literary debut late in life, when nearly forty, and with works that seemed (especially to posterity) unusually distinguished for their originality and independence of thought, his claims have often been flouted. Yet the publication of his youthful notebooks, more than a century after they were written, has borne out his assertions; the youth of twenty was clearly father to the brilliant social moralist and critical thinker of forty and fifty—though his contemporaries were, of course, to know nothing of his youth, and to depreciate or condemn the writings of the older man.[2]

"If only someone had told me then to write every day . . ." he exclaimed regretfully in old age, thinking of the time "lost" in his youth. He too might have had his volumes of "youthful indiscretions" to live down. Instead he had been seduced, as it were, into abandoning the effort to grasp at the substance of writing—by completing his first fragments—in favor of a search for the spirit or general principles or laws that must underlie such expression; and eventually he had been drawn into a ceaseless testing of those principles, as fascinating as it was exhausting.

[2]How decisive was this phase of his life only became known when the publication of about three quarters of his private papers and journals was completed, during the 1920s and 1930s, in the Divan edition, thus far seventy-four volumes, edited by Henri Martineau. In the early Stendhal "revival" of 1880–1900, only a small portion of his journals and letters were printed in fragmentary form; the *Pensées*, including the *Filosofia Nova*, did not appear until 1937.

Ambition goaded him. He ruminated in his journal:

> Since love as I conceive it cannot make me happy, I begin to think of glory; I long to walk in the path of that generation of great men who, builders of the Revolution, have been devoured by their own work.

He had the will to glory; and he believed then that "if a man wills strongly and constantly enough he can attain any goal." Strength of will and concentration removed even the element of chance in such an affair, he ruminated, so long as one knew what road he must take. On February 28, 1803, he asked himself:

> What is my object? To acquire the reputation of the greatest poet in France, not by intrigue, like Voltaire, but by meriting it; hence study Greek, Latin, Italian, and English. . . . Enough to fill up a long life.

While in Italy, he had had an idea for a play which he entitled sometimes *Letellier*, sometimes *The Two Men*. But he did not know how to write plays. Therefore he began to read Laharpe, that academic critic and historian of literature whose texts, then so widely adopted, expounded the beauties of the great seventeenth-century dramatic poets, Racine, Corneille, and Molière. He read Laharpe and also attended the old man's lectures at the University of Paris, although he soon became convinced that Laharpe's taste was unsure. Since he admired Corneille, he read him until he knew *Horace* and *Cinna* by heart, not to speak of *Le Cid*. He read Racine, and the plays of Voltaire, especially studying *Zaïre*. But over and over again he read the comedies of Molière, whom he had disliked in boyhood, but now adopted as his favorite satirist.

His first intention was to discover an *ars poetica* by saturating himself with the works of these celebrated dramatic poets, and then to body forth great plays. At this period, and for over a quarter of a century longer, the drama was to be written in verse, the classic French hexameter, and observed the three unities of time, space, and action. It was to remain classical—or "pseudoclassical"—also in the restraint with which passion was represented, and with which (as in Racine) effects of the violent or the irrational were deliberately avoided.

Desiring to master the portrayal of character, and inspired by the charming portraits of La Bruyère, he would sometimes spend days on end writing "characters" together with his friend Louis Crozet; then he and Crozet, both strong dialecticians, would compare or criticize each other's portrait of the same personality.

Since he possessed wit he promised himself that he would write, not tragedies, but comedies. And like a good general, he spied out the ground in advance:

> When I wish to ridicule something in a comedy, I must first construct the canvas in which I desire my characters, amiable or comic, to appear. Then seek the circumstances most likely to render the ones most amiable, the others most ridiculous. Everything must be subordinated to the principal character, and to his dominant passion. I must begin by choosing and sublimating this leading character; then the other characters who help to bring him out. Then the circumstances of the action (or plot). Then write the scenes. . . . And correct, and *tutto é fatto.*

This is a good enough summary of Molière's technique; it all seemed so simple that he needed but to begin. But as soon as he began to write his verses, he was in deep trouble.

"*Eight hours to write one line!*" is one exclamation of anguish found in his notebooks. Doggedly he wrote a few score verses, and still after weeks and months had not one act done. But his temperament was never suited to verse, least of all the regular and stilted verse then in vogue; in his bald verses, all finesse of thought, the more delicate shades of emotion which his analytical mind tended already to search out, were distorted and lost. After grinding out a hundred laborious lines he stopped.

Meanwhile he had been reading Shakespeare, and in English. Though his grasp of the language may at first have been small, his notes of 1803 and 1804 show how freely he appreciates the naturalness, the verve, and the "comprehensive soul" of the Elizabethan dramatist. Shakespeare's plays, he came to believe, were "like nature." He told himself: "Imitate Shakespeare, or rather nature." It was the beginning of treason to the ideal of the classical drama for which he was so little suited.

A growing disillusionment with the "noble" style of Racine and the other writers of the Golden Age of Louis XIV is traceable in his notes as early as 1804 and 1805. The conviction came to him that the old poets wrote in this manner because they were "courtiers"; theirs was a "monarchical" literature, subserving a great tyrant. He even discerned a "tone of inferiority" in Racine. Now he, Henri Beyle, a modern man, whose life was shaped by the French Revolution, living (still then) under a Republic, must seek another style and form, one that was more truthful and free, suited to the new democratic age. Indeed the play he struggled to write was intended to present two characters in conflict, one symbolizing republican ideas, the other, monarchical doctrines. He felt the need for a realistic drama, even for a new language. In Racine many words of common usage were suppressed, or paraphrased in poetic locutions.

"One may create for oneself a very bold language, using words that no one has dared to employ, after having taken care to prepare them," is one of the thoughts struck off in his notes for the *Filosofia Nova.*

How pallid seemed the verses of Voltaire also, and how artificial his plays beside those of the English poet! His remarks on Voltaire, whose imitators still dominated the theater, are telling:

> The chief defect of the heroes of Voltaire is that they seem to be saying always: "Look, I am going to utter a fine phrase; look, I am going to do a brave deed." But in nature the true hero does his brave deeds without being aware of how brave they are.

He reads a new novel, *Delphine,* by the celebrated Mme. de Staël, and thinks he would like to write his first book in this medium: but he is aware at once of her weaknesses, and even considers writing to her about them:

> There is a way of moving the reader by showing the *facts, things* themselves, without discussing their effects. . . . This manner is entirely lacking in Mme. de Staël; her book shows a great need of moments of repose. . . . In other words she is too didactic—moralizes too much—whereas Shakespeare, while pushing some scenes to the heights of terror, knows how to bring in moments of relief and contrast, as in *Macbeth,* when Duncan enters and, at a moment of supreme terror, alludes to the beauty of the night in the castle, the birds . . .
>
> And with what felicitous strokes Shakespeare paints his woman figures, Ophelia, Desdemona, and above all Imogene! . . . What profound knowledge of mankind in him! O divine Shakespeare, yes, *thou art the greatest Bard in the world!*

The novel then was an underdeveloped medium in France, as compared with England; its practitioners, like Mme. de Staël, wrote chiefly, in the form of letters, more or less concealed autobiographies in close imitation of Rousseau's *La Nouvelle Héloïse.* Now the young Beyle had schemes for a form of writing that would represent human character and passion with increasing realism. Around this time, in 1804, the newspapers were full of the plot of General Moreau's faction against Napoleon, which the Consul's secret police had successfully exposed, and everyone followed the trial of the conspirators. One of Beyle's notes runs:

> I must always remember the argument of the Moreau trial in which the style of speech is not elegant, not even correct, but always perfectly intelligible, and showing the desire of each witness to be understood.

His writing must be "full of details" as was Shakespeare's, instead of being vague or "overemphatic" like Rousseau's. Replying to a letter from his sister Pauline, who had given him some account of the life she led now at a *pension* for girls, he expressed a desire for more specific information that would "help me to know woman. I count on you, I need examples and many facts. . . . Send me the facts, the *facts!*"

Another of his ideas, but one he never carried out, was to write a sort of "slice of life" by setting forth the exact, almost mechanical record of some individual's actions and thoughts, just as they occurred, during twenty-four hours of his life. (The notes for this project clearly foreshadow that which James Joyce completed over a century later in his *Ulysses.*)

One day in 1804, on receiving news of the death of the elder Daru, he went dutifully to attend the funeral services of his late host and protector. The house was full of priests, and thoughtfully the youth scrutinized the "base and, sometimes, even wicked physiognomies of the priests, the best of whom had a sodden look." In this hour of death, effects of supreme comedy were to be noted, if one could only examine deeply enough the real motives and passions of these people. "To be the greatest poet possible I must know man perfectly," he reasoned. In order to write dramas that were painted after nature, in order to portray characters, "one must observe the passions of man as he is. And to observe the passions it is necessary to know what truth is."

Thus was he logically driven to a search for first principles, for the "new philosophy," and in effect the new psychology that he needed. "*Chercher le pourquoi des choses qui arrivent, nous mènent à trouver les choses qui arrivent.*" In seeking the "why" of events would he not come to understand the events themselves?

For two years or more the self-training to become a "great dramatic bard" is in reality suspended in favor of the study of philosophy, physiology, and psychology. At the end of 1804, we find him spending many of his nights, not at parties and balls, but at the Ecole de Médecine, reading the still unpublished treatises of Dr. Cabanis on "the instincts which flow from the interior of the body to the brain."[3]

[3]*Journal,* II, p. 10; Jan. 24, 1805, p. 17. Feb. 5, 1805. Cf. also *Filosofia Nova,* p. 153 ff.

3

"Style is the secondary affair of the poet," he wrote in his notebooks, and it is a characteristic thought. To be a great writer one must have ideas, he would always say, in short, a philosophy of life through which one looked at the world; essentially the knowledge of man. "The art of writing French sentences so that they show most exactly and clearly characters and events" was important, but must wait until he had found his bearings, captured his "truths."

"It was necessary to do this work," he explained to himself, "in order to write good plays. Since we see the world and men only as our sensations record them in our minds" (according to John Locke) "therefore," he reasons, "we must know this mind . . . must know the mind and the passions."

How much the eighteenth-century reasoning spirit dominated Henri Beyle is clearly shown in the notes for the *Filosofia Nova*, which furnish a complete history of his mind during these formative years, from 1802 to 1806. He might be interrupted, swept up by the turmoil of Napoleonic world war, victimized by his own unsatisfied passions, but when he would have returned to himself, to write again after a long span of years, he would still be the man of the eighteenth-century Enlightenment, with the same stubborn convictions formed in his youth.

For his mind had been deeply molded by his education at the Ecole Centrale in Grenoble during that transitional phase of five years of the Revolution, when the school system was dominated by the doctrines of Tracy, "the last of the Encyclopedists." In his obscure rebellion against his father and the ideas of authority that oppressed him, how he had welcomed the materialistic instruction he had received, the "general grammar of science" that he had been taught. He had read the free-thinking Helvetius' *De l'esprit*, the *Logique* and *Traité des sensations* of Condillac, and Destutt de Tracy's *Idéologie* at intervals since leaving school—but now he reread them as if with a violent thirst, and set down his findings in an incomplete, unordered, but essentially consistent "system."

Taking his point of departure, like the later Encyclopedists, from the empirical or sensualist school of Locke and Condillac, Locke's great French disciple, he held that all our knowledge comes to us through the senses, and that there are no "innate ideas." Thinking was feeling; and our judgments were derived from associations of thought that were determined by experience. The paramount thing, then, putting it simply, was to cultivate the faculty of sound judgment, and to carry on the logical classification of experience through exact observation and analysis. With Helvetius and Condillac, he believed that the role of reason was limited to comparing our sensations and classifying them in a logical order; he also accepted their positivistic belief that this logic of experience permitted man to triumph over nature.

This mechanistic system, which opposed metaphysics and spiritualism, and directed men to experiment, to reason inductively about all things by means of the positive sciences, was the essential message of the Enlightenment. With utilitarian modifications it was to be revived in the mid-nineteenth century, and again in the twentieth, under the guise of pragmatism, which explains why Stendhal's attitudes still appear so "modern." To this materialistic system, in its simple form, he clung all his life.

In the field of ethics he also fervently accepted the sensualist-utilitarian view that men's motives of behavior were determined by self-interest, and by the pleasure or pain they experienced. Their prime object was "the pursuit of happiness," a theory imbedded even in the political constitutions written in the eighteenth century, and forever on Henri Beyle's lips. But happiness for society as a whole—"virtue"—resided in achieving "the greatest good of the greatest number."

We must note, however, that his scientific positivism was modified or even contradicted by the residual influence of Rousseau, who preached the "return to nature," and the fulfillment of man's natural passions. Henri Beyle too, always haunted by Rousseau, the opponent of the materialistic *philosophes*, wished to undergo great experiences, surrender to great passions, but also, calculatingly, to control them! There were conflicts and contradictions within him, as a consequence. It is questionable whether he ever fully rationalized the problems raised by the opposition between individual and collective (social) happiness. These contradictions remained to be resolved in the form of his life, as it unfolded, and in his art.

But meanwhile he perceived that success for him would lie in developing to the utmost that power of analysis that was so strong in him almost since childhood. He was determined to observe men and events without prejudice and with a wholly scientific detachment. He would be enabled by this method to avoid the pitfalls into which, he believed, "priests and charlatans" always led us, tear away the veils of ignorance, and so triumph over life's hazards—even the difficulties of art.

It happened thus that in early youth Beyle sensed that one of the great concerns of future minds was to be the study of human behavior: psychology. Through fate or chance he was to by-pass the renewed interest among his contemporaries, at the turn of the century, in metaphysics, inspired by the German transcendental philosophers. Ignoring Kant, he was to pursue his explorations of psychology as far as possible, so that long after his own time his ideas and discoveries would meet again and join with the stream of modern thought at the end of the nineteenth century.

His point of departure in the field of psychology was given by the writings of Dr. P. J. G. Cabanis on neurology, and also of the earlier Condillac, who had conceived of the "man of clay," of the mind as a blank statue upon which the impressions of experience are stamped one by one. Reading the early psychologists stimulated him to attempt independent experiments of his own. In 1804, he writes in his *Filosofia Nova*:

> I must seek to develop my powers of analysis. It will be a great step forward for my mind. I shall have the benefit of analysis when I ask myself: what is man? what is vanity? what is laughter? what is hunger? what is remorse? And I shall be able to answer exactly.

All his life, as he said in retrospect, was spent in contemplating these same problems, these "five or six truths."

At this period, his one intimate attachment was with his sister Pauline. Almost daily he wrote her long letters, sharing his intellectual discoveries with her, attempting to counsel and educate her. Thus if she reported that their young cousin, Gaëtan Gagnon, whom she had in charge, refused to do his Latin lessons, Henri immediately tried to apply his scientific methods to the problem.

Gaëtan is a glutton, he points out, therefore let Pauline punish him by giving him only soup for supper; when he has learned his lessons a little better, she may add a dish of good vegetables; when he earns an especially good report he is to have a slice of roast lamb. Through his new "ideology" might not a dunce like Gaëtan perhaps be turned into a veritable genius? What then might one not accomplish for oneself!

Many ideas for new experiments are thrown pell-mell into his early notes: one is to segregate a chosen boy or girl child in a cave and observe the growth of experience and reason in such an innocent being. Still another, long in advance of the future science of anthropology, was to study the life of primitive savages in distant lands, in order to bring light upon the customs and habits of civilized man himself.

One of the cherished projects of the young *philosophe*, at this season of his life, was to control the education of his charming sister Pauline, who was then about eighteen, and his fervent disciple. Here was a rich field for experiment! Like him, she suffered from the oppressiveness of the narrow little family circle—and he wants her to be happy, strong, and free, as he hopes to be. He wants her to leave off knitting stockings and cultivate her mind as well as any man by studying all the sciences—for he was an early feminist.

"It depends upon us," he wrote her, "to know how to be happy in this abyss into which we have been flung. . . . In general all evil comes of ignoring the truth, all sadness, all disappointment from having expected of men that which they were not in a position to give us." "We who have the inestimable fortune to be passionate beings must try to uproot those passions which we probably can never satisfy."

At his bidding, poor Pauline struggled to read (in secret) Bacon, Locke, Hobbes, Tracy, Montesquieu, and Rousseau; her remarks upon these books, written in a childish hand, and in spelling as bad as his own, were sent to him regularly, and received his correction. The lonely young man also sent her his notes in the form of letters:

> Here are four pages of philosophy that I have just written on letter paper instead of putting them down in my notebooks. You would do well to keep a copybook and copy my letters into it. . . . Do not lose them; they will be useful to both of us, for they will provide a history of my mind. . . . I often fear that I may die before having given you [the fruits of] my experience.

He wished her to shun all superstition. "One must never repeat any opinion, even if it were the Pope's, without having examined it." To believe what one's neighbor told one was to remain a booby. Of religious faith there was no question, "it is utterly useless except for fools." Most men had some interest in deceiving us if they could; we must discover what their interest was.

The question of love and marriage also comes up. Surprisingly enough, Henri advises:

> For the sake of your happiness it is necessary that you should not marry a man with whom you might be in love; here is the reason: all true love comes to an end, and the stronger it is, the more quickly it is finished than other forms of love. After love, comes disgust; nothing is more natural; then each avoids the other for some time. . . . But if people are married they are obliged to live together. . . .

He therefore counsels her to avoid disillusionment by contracting a reasonable marriage with some prosaic soul, of whom she expects little love. (He amplifies in a subsequent letter: "a good and rich man.") Once married, he advises, "you must play the hypocrite." This will permit her a fuller freedom, even to take lovers, if she is discreet enough to deceive society. For while society censures the conduct of young girls, it is indifferent to their behavior after marriage.[4]

What advice from a youth and brother of twenty-one!

Poor Pauline strove as well as she could to become a good *Beyliste.* At one time she tried to run away from her family, though her poor attempts at winning freedom terminated in a town only ten miles from home, and she was quickly brought back. Even her brother was a little alarmed at this escapade. But in the end she married an excellent fellow, one of the rich Périer family of Grenoble, and became most devoted to him, heeding less and less the devious counsels of her brother. And after the early death of her husband, she would even return to her religion, to her brother's lasting regret. His affection for her continued, but he no longer trusted her, and seldom saw her in later years.

4

The youthful notes and journals, now compiled in over a dozen volumes, teemed with original ideas and divinations set forth without order, though following a sustained thread. It was indeed a time of intense fermentation, even of mental intoxication, one might say, out of which not one complete piece of writing emerged. "I waited for inspiration," he explains. When his search for first principles and certainties exhausted him he sometimes sought worldly distractions, though hardly often enough at this period.

From 1802 to 1805, Henri was stage-struck as few other men have been. Whenever he could afford it, he haunted the pit of the Théâtre Français, and also its stage door. One day Talma, the little man who throned over the French stage for forty years, passed close by him as he left the theater. Beyle stared at him in wonder. That night he wrote in his notebook: "I was near enough almost to *touch* greatness and glory!"

The theaters in those days, following the Directoire period, were still unruly and ill-smelling milieux, and their devotees had need of a

[4] *Correspondance,* Vol. I, 202–3 (June 1804); Vol. II, 234–37.

strong stomach. The turbulent crowd came armed with food and brandy, and during the play ate, drank, and jabbered, or roared its approval, or jeered and whistled—while in the entr'acte young bawds walked up and down the aisles plying their ancient trade. But Henri Beyle forgot all else as he swooned with delight at the charm of a Mlle. George, just then making her debut. Earlier he had been conquered by her older rival, Mlle. Duchesnois, who enchanted her audiences by her violent and torrid acting. Though Mlle. Duchesnois looked not unlike a gargoyle, he was enraptured when, in April 1804, a friend actually presented him to her in her dressing room, and he gazed at her from close by, while she was nonchalantly disrobing herself.

One of the noted critics of that hour, J. L. Geoffroy of the *Journal des débats*, had slated her most severely, and hearing her complain of this, the young man gallantly offered to come to her defense. During several days he labored to compose an elaborate letter, which he brought in fear and trembling to the great newspaper office. A week later, he dared to call upon Mlle. Duchesnois again and tell her of what he had done. But she had forgotten his name! Was he "Monsieur *Lebel*?" she asked. Moreover the *Débats* never printed his letter. He was deeply hurt. Nevertheless he vowed that he would make his mark in the world of the theater. Glory, and even gold, beckoned there; for the royalties of a dramatic success, he calculated, might bring an author as much as 6,000 francs a month.[5]

But though his feeling for the drama was strong, the moral philosopher far outweighed the prospective bard in him, in those days. In order to write comedies he must ask himself first: what is *laughter?* A baffling subject that had puzzled some of the sharpest-witted cogitators, from Hobbes to Bergson and Freud, in our own day. Soon Henri was spending his days and nights in the Bibliothèque Nationale reading Hobbes, and after "sweating blood" devised his own definition (which foreshadows remarkably some of the views of modern psychoanalysis):

> Laughter is an impulse of vanity produced by the sudden awareness that comes to us of enjoying some advantage when compared with the weakness perceived in another person, or which we ourselves formerly shared; for we laugh at the follies we committed last year.

But he was dissatisfied and explored the question further for many days and weeks without tangible result. As he pondered the psychological mechanism that created effects of the comic, comedy itself de-

[5] *Journal*, I, 125; P. Arbalet, *Stendhal au pays des comédiens*, pp. 50–65.

parted from the five-act play that remained before him, with its first scene still unfinished.

Meanwhile the fact that his projected play was to have a young republican as its hero created further perplexities. He believed himself a stanch Jacobin and republican, in the old Roman manner—and the times were already changing under his very nose. Like other young Frenchmen he had admired General Bonaparte as the "savior" of the French Revolution, the embodiment of its military necessity. But the First Consul had transformed himself into an imperial despot, in 1804; he had even moved into the Tuileries Palace with his wife Josephine de Beauharnais, who now played the empress. Walking in the Tuileries Gardens one day, in 1805, Beyle muttered to a friend of his: "That palace weighs upon my shoulders." There was no sign as yet of his later cult for Bonaparte as the supreme model of human will and energy.

In 1804 one of his friends was a student from Grenoble named Joseph Rey, an ardent Jacobin, who after 1815 was to join in an insurrection against the Bourbon monarchy. Another of his friends was the philosophical Fortuné Mante who, according to one of Beyle's secretive notes in the *Filosofia Nova*, "involved me to some extent in the Moreau conspiracy." The plot to overthrow Napoleon in favor of General Moreau was a serious business, uncovered and ruthlessly punished in 1804. If it were known that he was involved—it could not have been very deeply—the young Beyle might have gone to a dungeon, like others, if not to the guillotine.

His "new philosophy" was fashioned not for an authoritarian state but for a democratic society. He believed that the age in which he lived, that of vast social revolution and civil and foreign war, was the most stirring epoch since the days of the Roman Empire, and worthy of a great literature and epic poets. This was true, but it was also an uneasy time in which to create enduring works. The literary artists were still to wait a generation longer for perspective permitting them to function; they had accomplished little in the "silver age" since the 1780s, and, as Beyle waited for "inspiration" in 1805, there was another turbulent decade to be endured before Waterloo.

He soliloquized in his notebooks:

> The true comedy of a republican people would be that in which one mocked incessantly at the customs of kings and courtiers in states that were not republican.
>
> . . . Molière is the man who saw better than others the vices which oppose the spirit of society, and he combated them with ridicule. Today we need a

poet-philosopher who attacks the vices which arise from the character of society itself; this poet would find a host of characters who were unknown in the time of Molière.

I must show that [lay] education can do everything for men, tending to make them truly honest; whereas, on the contrary, a religious education tends to produce knaves and weaklings almost invariably. I must defend philosophy and cover with ridicule those who attack it. That is the goal I propose for myself. Therefore my comedy will last as long as men are divided between religious and lay education; even after the final victory will have been gained, men will regard my work with gratitude as one of the means which assured it.

The foregoing reflections date from his journals of 1806, at the end of the period of three or four years of lonely self-cultivation I have described. By then the establishment of the Empire, the coronation of Napoleon, and the "alliance of all the charlatans," as Beyle phrased it, had already taken place. The times were turning corrupt.

No, it was scarcely a propitious hour for a bolder nineteenth-century Molière to show himself. Even before Napoleon became Emperor, Beyle had moments of pessimism. On May 3, 1803, he had written in his journal:

I feel that the time has passed for being a republican; this need not interfere with my plans for glory and ambition, but I must do nothing that would obstruct them.

But by the beginning of 1806 he felt he had reached an impasse. In the first place he had begun to study the technique of poetic drama; then in the second place he had felt that he must provide himself with "the scaffolding of ideas" upon which literature must be built. This in turn brought him to a state of extreme tension, now exalted, now fatigued and harrowed by doubts. Was it not possible that error dogged him at every step?

Living alone, pent up in his room all day with his books, he felt himself sometimes turning "gloomy and wild." And he had scarcely begun to live; he had never tested the force of his ideas in life itself. One of his warning reflections reads:

I am over twenty years old. If I do not make my way in society, if I do not seek to know men by experience, *I am lost*, I know men only through books, and there are passions which I have seen nowhere else. How can I paint them? My pictures will be nothing but copies of copies.

He attempted to concentrate all his thoughts upon some image of perfect happiness that his *Filosofia Nova* would systematically render attainable—Italy? Victorine?—until he felt terrible pains in his head, and giddiness assailed him.

Late one night a fearful thought came to him: "With my inward faculties and senses so ardent and so painful, *it is very possible that I may go mad.*"

He writes another sentence in the notebook open before him, and the pen drops from his hand in weariness and torment: "In that case, I beg that I should be taken away to Claix [his father's farm near Grenoble]. It is only there that I may be healed."

CHAPTER VI

Mélanie: Or the Search for Love

In those days . . . I was in love with love.
—Stendhal

FROM those too rarefied zones of speculation he periodically retreated, to rest his aching head, to take stock of his true situation in life. He felt certain of his own nobility of soul. But this did not mean that he must remain bitter and lonely. "Philosophy is the art of rendering us happy," he would say. Hence, "avoid the misanthropy that ruins the works of Rousseau." To enjoy people, to expand in good talk, to bring pleasure into every circle one entered, was also a part of his faith.

Thinking of the imbalance that excessive mental strain produces, he remarks:

> When I shall make my debut in my playwriting career, I must continue to cling to Martial Daru and his opera girls, in order to eliminate entirely that air of inferiority which, since Racine and Boileau, the literary art has always given to its practitioners as figures in society.

There must be opera girls as well as Art.

A "good day" for him was one after which he could record in his diary: "I spent the morning in fruitful labor . . . and enjoyed the most agreeable society in the evening."

But there were times during his intellectual frenzy of 1804 when he allowed his affairs to run down badly. At the small hotel where he lived that year he owed money for his lodging; his tailor came to dun him every morning; his shoes were so broken that he caught a cold after stepping into puddles of water in the street. Indeed he was forced to refuse an invitation to dinner, because he would have been obliged to escort a lady and her daughter home in a carriage and he lacked the two francs to pay for it.

And he loved fine clothes; he had an eye for fashion, and was the slave of its every caprice all his life. Since he was not a pretty fellow, he must be elegantly clad, and only then would the fire of his glance, the expressiveness of his physiognomy offset his homeliness of face and form. How could one appear in good society, how test one's systems upon men and women, without clothes and money?

At the thought of his wounding poverty, Henri would frequently burst into the fiercest imprecations against his father, in his letters to his sister, or in his journals. Even in the raffish salons of the First Empire he felt himself cutting a poor figure, thanks to his worn suit that was of last year's mode. And because his father, that man of money in Grenoble, retarded the payment of annuities due him from the Beyle and Gagnon patrimony, he was driven to borrow money. His father, he wrote in unphilosophical terms such as few sons have ever used, was a "scoundrel," a "bastard," a "murderer"!

When at last money arrived for him, he would furbish up his small wardrobe, don a large silken cravat, a close-fitting coat, and broad yellow nankeen trousers, and saunter forth, preferably in the company of the admired Martial Daru. Martial affected a bored and languid manner, and Henri, aping him, would walk up and down the Tuileries Gardens preening himself before the ladies sitting on the benches, who, he was certain, esteemed them both as a fine pair of coxcombs. The effect is carefully entered into his diary:

> March 17, 1805: I looked superb; my hair done in thick black curls, my face fine; cravat, jabot, two vests—superb; breeches of cashmere, good shoes.
>
> It is one of those days on which from the physical point of view I was at my best. I had the noble and assured carriage of one who figured in the best society.

Thus self-conscious to the point of narcissism, plagued by an inferiority complex, fantastically dressed in the very height of the florid male styles of the First Empire, Beyle stepped out to conquer society. He did not visit the newly married Pierre Daru, recently made a count of the Empire, but with his younger brother Martial went to take lessons in elocution from a retired actor named Larive. In a mixed company consisting of aspiring actresses and middle-class ladies, Henri aroused a certain interest because of the fire with which he read Molière.

A friend of his also brought him one day to meet his intellectual idol, Count Destutt de Tracy, the friend of Lafayette and Thomas Jefferson. Descendants of Scottish *émigrés*, the Tracys had been distinguished soldiers and courtiers under the old regime; but the count had joined forces with the Revolution, spent most of his great fortune in philanthropies, and now, as a man of fervently liberal doctrine, was in deep disfavor with Napoleon, who spoke of him and Mme. de Staël with infinite contempt as "the ideologues."

Destutt de Tracy, a small, gray-haired man with a fine head and distinguished bearing, received his young admirer with great kindness. But the nervous Beyle was so confused at meeting the man he esteemed above all others that he spoke too eagerly, with too much emphasis, and left a very poor impression. Afterward, pondering over that first visit, he said to himself: "In seeking to please people too much, one pleases them less."

Wherever he went he examined himself as in a mirror, while attempting to divine his companions and seeing always too much and too little in them. In truth the newly made barons and nabobs whom he met were but bourgeois (Balzac's "beasts of prey"), thrusting themselves forward ruthlessly and cynically in that time of social upheaval and quick profits. Men feared and hated each other, and constantly sought to push one another aside, he remarked. "In this nation vanity reigns everywhere and out of 100 persons 98 have no other passion," was one of Beyle's early judgments. He must therefore use flattery as an instrument. But gross flattery would fail of its purpose, proving nothing. It was not enough to tell another man that he was "great," but by one's manner of listening to him, by giving him opportunity to shine, one must show that one rated his importance as highly as did he himself. "There," Beyle told himself, "is the true theory of flattery . . . the ability to be a good listener."

His objective was to apply his *Filosofia Nova* to the test of experience. Constantly he examined and analyzed his conduct for his own instruction. He told himself that he must seek to be "natural" while "taking care not to show his true feelings." He must also avoid being too bold and cutting, which sometimes frightened people the first time. "We must judge our conversation by the effect it has on others and not by its contribution to our own self-esteem," was another shrewd observation.

It was knowledge of the world, knowledge of human motives, that he must master in order to win the race for happiness and glory. But though he scanned faces and probed the words he heard constantly for hidden meanings, he often sensed that it was to be a difficult process, more difficult for him than for others.

> In the knowledge of men it is finesse I lack most. I know well that a certain passion P has an effect P^1; but I do not know yet how to recognize in the individuals I meet in society the passions that animate them. Besides, my damnable mania for trying to glitter leads me to be more absorbed in leaving a deep impression of myself than in divining the motives of others. I spend too much time watching myself to have the time to observe the others.

Little by little, he came to believe that he was learning to glitter easily, to play upon people's vanity and lead them by the nose. His daily sorties from his study, to go out to dinner, to take walks, to appear at some bourgeois soirée, were absorbing and elaborate experiments in social diplomacy. To his little sister in Grenoble he confided that his social life was becoming a whirl of elegant and improving entertainments. "I am up to my neck in intrigue!" he exclaims in an access of self-importance.

He was so keen and yet so gullible, so logical and yet so timorous—sage and coxcomb at once. And it would take so long for him to ripen.

2

But what of love, surely the *grande affaire*, or at least one of the twin objects (with ambition) of his vast intellectual field maneuvers? "At twenty," runs one of those notes he called, like Pascal, *Pensées*, "I feel myself strong and well made for the pleasures of love." The image of Victorine Mounier, his "Héloïse," returned to haunt him in his study; he recalled her dark hair, her eyes, her particular, slightly mysterious smile—it seemed to have a touch of sadness—and he wept at the thought that he might never see her again. "What has she done that I should love her so much? She smiled upon me one day in order to have the pleasure of avoiding me the next." Elevated souls, he reflected, must nearly always be unhappy in love, since they constantly ignore the obstacles opposing their felicity—in this case "considerations of money and respect for age," he reminded himself, thinking of his father.

However, there were no obstacles barring him from the favors of a somewhat older belle, the "excellent and pretty" Mme. Rebuffel, a relative of the Darus, who had hospitably opened her home to him since his first visit to Paris in 1799. Separated from her husband, she lived with her attractive daughter Adèle, who was fourteen in 1802, in a house neighboring the Darus' on the Rue de Lille.

Henri, who came every two weeks to call on them, infected these two ladies with his passion for recitation, and soon they spent their evenings reading Corneille together with other visitors, evenings at which Henri charmed everyone with his fervor and his fine, ringing voice. The little Adèle was a vivacious coquette who flirted outrageously with every man who came to her mother's soirées. In corners, in window recesses, she exchanged kisses with Henri too, and even gave him a lock of her hair as a keepsake. But while Adèle was extremely *piquante*, it was her mother who, shortly after the youth had returned from Italy, extended kindness to its ultimate limits.

One night in 1802, at seven o'clock, he goes to see Mme. Rebuffel. Her husband is there and leaves in a short time. Promptly Henri goes to bed with Mme. Rebuffel. "*Je fouts Mme. R. depuis le commencement de Fructidor* (August 18, 1802)" runs one of the more explicit notes in his journal, where, for discretion's sake, the names of ladies are either in initials or altered.

"I had the need to give my heart to someone," he noted in 1803, "for I was very romantic at that time." In Grenoble his family now heard that a wealthy "Mme. de Neuilly" entertained him, and had even offered him a bequest of money, which he had refused. But was this affable woman of thirty-five a fitting object of romantic passion? He himself hints that he used to play the rough-handed cavalryman with her, as she afterward gently complained. It was her daughter that he itched for, Adèle, who by the age of fifteen was a budding hussy; and she, who had eyes to see all that went on, teased him, by showing preference for one or another of the young men who called.

Determined to seduce Adèle also, he deployed all of his "ideological" arsenal. She talked like a grown woman—for the times, before the coronation, were still emancipated and quasi-revolutionary—and he took many little liberties with her, as was customary then. In his journal for September 9, 1802, he speaks of a most curious experience with Adèle, revealing how complex, shadowy, and suggestible was his sexual character.

One day he took her to Frascati's Gardens to watch the fireworks, which he loved to gaze at all his life, as something of superhuman beauty. Fireworks always seemed to him a symbol of priapic force in eruption. In an ecstasy, Adèle leaned against him, embraced him. "Never shall I forget that moment, watching the fireworks at Frascati's with Adèle," he wrote again, most feelingly, thirty-three years later in

Henri Brulard. It was one of those moments of "perfect happiness," fleeting, ecstatic, which he believed it was his affair to seek constantly, though but a show of rockets and Roman candles and the pressure of a young girl's arms were all that it embraced.

Nothing came of his elaborate attentions to the girl, though in a supreme effort to conquer her he several times ventured to tell her all sorts of salty tales, closely watching the effect. Perhaps he might have had her then, he sometimes thought. But suddenly his often uncertain amorous courage was severely shaken by overhearing her speak to someone else as if she had already "marked him [Henri] for marriage!" He also learned, through a confidence of the more artful Martial Daru, that Adèle had already yielded herself to him, though she was barely sixteen in 1804. (Henri verified this himself, two or three years later, when Martial, on the eve of his own marriage, hastily entrusted all the letters of his "twenty mistresses" to Beyle for burning.) To Henri, her continued resistance to his own importunities was all the more tantalizing, though he guessed at her motives.

One day, at the Rebuffels', he passed the door of her boudoir as it stood, by chance, ajar, and, placing himself behind it, watched Adèle combing her hair with slow, deliberate motions. For a long time he stood there silent, fascinated, studying her face reflected in the mirror, forgetting all other interests in favor of his characteristic role of "observer of the human heart." It was like gazing through a window at someone ignorant of one's intruding presence, and he saw an Adèle utterly different from the sweet and ingratiating figure she habitually presented in the drawing room: one in whose face cunning and coldness were marked—"an absence of all tender passions, even cruelty."

That evening his talk was most scintillating for the very reason that he felt he cared nothing for her; and his words often had double meanings seemingly addressed to the mother, who slept with him, but aimed at the daughter who tormented him.

The "campaign" for Adèle, he was forced to acknowledge, was, then, "a serious defeat," whose lessons were to be patiently and self-critically examined—a defeat which jeopardized his presumably infallible system. Bravely, in his journal, he summed up the record of his errors. There were moments when he might easily have scaled those breastworks, if he had only been daring enough. "There was that kiss on the stairway . . . The salacious stories also took effect. There were twenty-four hours when I was not bold enough, and all was lost. *Above all I should not have talked so much.*"

He had talked as if he were a roué, a further fragment of confession reveals, and yet knew himself profoundly timid with women. "She believed I was what I pretended to be, and she was disappointed in her expectations. . . . By being more natural, I should have pleased her." But his system still stood, he assured himself, since it was his own weakness and poor judgment in applying it that had been at fault.

The designing girl soon afterward contracted a rich marriage with the son of one of Napoleon's powerful henchmen, General Pétiet, and this too caused the memory of her to rankle in Beyle's heart. Seven years later, meeting Adèle with her husband in Florence, he was ready to believe that her mere presence spoilt the charm of the beautiful Tuscan capital.

3

Upon the rapidly moving film of his mind the image of Victorine now came forward again, effacing that of the blowzy Mme. Rebuffel and of her too artful daughter. In a candid moment Henri Beyle confided to his sister that he had "had all the women one could possibly have had" at his age, twenty-one, which may have been a sizable exaggeration. But had he known great passions? "The passions will come," he assured himself. "I regret only one: perfect love."

What he longed for was "another Pauline," for his sister then affected him much like his memory of his mother, whom she resembled. "In Italy I knew a woman named Angelina [Pietragrua] whom I loved beyond all expression. She had exactly your character."

Why was there no one in Paris to whom he could say truly: "I love you!" All that he held dear, for the instant, was in Rennes, some two hundred miles away; and suddenly the thought came to him that he might travel there in disguise and, without compromising her in any way, feast his eyes upon her. Perhaps, with much astonishment, she would notice him spying upon her from behind the trees, yet only she would know he was there. It was a wholly romantic enterprise that he played with in his mind, but did not carry out, perhaps because of the matter of one hundred francs needed for coach fare. Instead he continued to write letters to her annoying brother, letters aimed like showers of arrows at his distant princess, though unaware of how or where they fell.

Those letters go forward every few weeks in 1803 and 1804, giving a rather rose-colored picture of his social and literary life and an often melancholy accounting of his finer sentiments. No news of her comes in the stilted letters of her brother; no sign from her. Then at last he learns that the Mouniers are to come to Paris and his journal turns feverish with excitement.

"I have seen Héloïse once more!" is the entry for December 9, 1804.

His imagination moved always in advance of events with the speed of a typhoon—but how often with him reality itself sank far below his magnificent expectations. Where was the access of tenderness he had expected, if not of Victorine, then of himself? It was she who came to the door to receive him when he called on the Mouniers. He spoke but a few polite, perfunctory words: "I have the honor to salute you, mademoiselle. Is Edouard in?" She made him a reverence, answered in the affirmative, and fled. He could scarcely have had time to look at her, and afterward wondered if it were true, as his friends declared, that she was not pretty, she was even too fat! He remembered only that she wore a pink straw hat with a ribbon under her chin. "By my dramatic system of *maximums*, I should have seized this moment to show her the love I feel," he thought too late. The reception given the madman by young Mounier and his father, the senator, was coolness itself.

By his own military calculations this should have been but a "preliminary battle" leading to the grand engagement. Now in his journal this most scientific of lovers drew an elaborate map of the "battleground" to be fought over, a chart of the house in which the Mouniers were stopping, of its rooms, stairways, entrances and exits through which he would give battle. Going further afield, he haunted the theaters, searching for Victorine everywhere with his lorgnon.

At length he screwed up courage to write her one letter directly, then a day or two afterward (January 14, 1805), a second amplifying the first. The first of these letters took four hours to copy. It was written in printed characters on vellum paper, during most of two days. He was certain that what he had written was "overdone," blown up with fine phrases and too mundane for the ideal passion he entertained. It was a word painting of "the great love that only great souls could possess for each other." It ran:

> I imagined all the joy that such a character could give me. . . . Before seeing her, all my hopes of happiness were concentrated in this ideal character which I figured for myself for three years. Seeing her, I love her as *happiness* itself; I apply to her this passion which since three years has become a *habit* with me.

He waits, noting the hour at night, and saying to himself, "My fate is being decided." But he hopes that Victorine will not be able to resist his ardor and "the goodness and honesty" of his nature. He recalls to himself, as he broods alone, the traits of his own "great and virtuous soul," his intellectual powers which permit him to discover promptly the insincerity of men beneath their pretense of good nature, his scorn of mediocrity—which has already earned for him the reputation of a Machiavelli among feeble souls like his uncle Romain. No, she cannot refuse him. "*The air is charged with love for me!*" he whispers to himself.

Then, much like Rousseau, he imagines himself by the side of his "Héloïse," replying to her question: "What are you?" The words tumble forth in reply as in imagination he casts himself at her feet: in his soul (though soiled perhaps by a few vices) she will see the noblest passions at their maximum, and love for her will share its empire with love of glory, and even surpass the other's share. "And I dare believe that at her feet I shall show my love in a manner worthy of her, and myself, in traits of an immortal beauty."[1] So Rousseau had written:

> I was intoxicated with love without having an object: this intoxication enchanted my eyes. . . . I saw my Julie in Mme. d'Houdetot and soon I saw nothing but Mme. d'Houdetot, clothed in all the perfections in which I had just decorated the idol of my heart.

Mme. d'Houdetot was not fat, but she was pock-marked!

It was at this period of strain and fatigue, corresponding to the crisis in his literary-philosophical studies, that he feared he might be going mad.

Secretively he scrawls in English almost illegible, incomprehensible phrases like: "*He shall be the better of men if you shall give me your sister.*" And: "*The beloved does not reply. I shall write after day.*"

Silence without echoes. Only once again did he see her, by chance as she rode by in a carriage, while he walked in the Tuileries Gardens with a beautiful young woman by his side. Startled, he gave her only a cold, almost imperceptible bow of greeting, and in a moment she was gone.

He had taken up the study of elocution in great earnest under the veteran actor Larive, and later under another and cheaper master known as Dugazon, who had many stage-aspiring pupils. Not that he designed to set his own chubby figure behind the footlights, but some doctor had warned him he might soon "perish of melancholy." More

[1] F. C. Green in *Stendhal*, p. 43, has pointed to the exact parallel between Beyle's language and that of Rousseau's *Confessions*, Book IX.

than most men he knew intuitively the value of distraction, and his zest, his love of people, his boundless curiosity, ever bubbling up again, led him to embrace his "distractions" with the same ardor as his "ruling passions." So with these séances of elocution, at which he felt himself, at least, close to people, able to speak to them, even embrace them, while reciting his roles, instead of exhausting himself endlessly in the "search for new truths."

Wrinkled old Dugazon, said to have been the fiercest of Jacobins in the days of the Terror, was a merry old soul, very free in his manners and gestures, still fond of pretty women. The several young ladies who came to the salon of Dugazon to improve their dramatic talents seemed to the young men who came there for similar, or less clearly defined, purposes, rather the facile type. Dugazon was forever making leering jests or passes at the ladies, which they accepted with great good nature; and the lessons, to say the least, were easygoing. There was a touch of the pander in him, too.

Beyle noticed first a young Mme. Mortier, and remarked to himself: "I am sure I could *have* her." Then too he met a young woman who bore the stage name of "Louason," but whose real name was Mélanie Guilbert. She was tall, thin, and blond, and had an air of melancholy grace that made her seem very attractive. In the rather broad comedies that Dugazon liked to rehearse, Beyle found himself kneeling before Mme. Guilbert, gazing into her great blue eyes, seizing her hands with ardor, even kissing her, while the smirking Dugazon coached them.

"Now remember," the old man would say to her, "you mustn't give yourself just for a new bonnet." And Mélanie Guilbert would laugh gently and modestly. His young fervor in acting his parts made quite an impression on her, Beyle was ready to believe. He wondered if he could not "have" her too?

On February 3, 1805, he writes in his journal, ever by his side:

> I escorted Mélanie Guilbert to her house. I almost feel the desire to attach myself to her; that will cure me of my love for Victorine.

Immensely naïve and self-deceived as he is, his psychological acumen is nevertheless a continual surprise. No word of reply has come from Victorine, and so, sensibly enough, he seeks what the French call *un amour de consolation.* The little "Louason" seemed a charming thing; he might enjoy with her the sweets of happy love, at least during the season of spring, up to the time of his annual departure for Grenoble. But to make him truly happy, he reflects, "she must have a soul." Did she have a soul suited to his own refined sensibilities, he wonders?

There was the great question! For who else had a "comprehensive soul" like his? His speculations continue:

> Would she fall in love with me? With the brilliance that I have in conversation, would I please her? *A future young dramatic bard with a future young actress.* [In English.]

4

Pausing on the brink of the precipice, he asked himself what goals he pursued: did happiness consist in finding The One Woman or The Great Love? A Victorine, an Angiola of Milan? Or was this but a false path to be avoided in favor of the road to glory, like Homer's? Still a third course, forcibly suggested by his worn shoes and scanty wardrobe, was proposed by his good friend Mante, the *philosophe*, mathematician, and would-be banker. The coming century, Mante held, would witness the triumph of commerce, and Henri tended to agree with him, despite his own aristocratic and Castilian sentiments. Since the autumn of 1804 (at the time of the "short peace" of Amiens), Mante and he had been drawing up plans to undergo an apprenticeship in trade, perhaps at the growing commercial port of Marseille, then after five years, to form their own bank and enjoy an income of ten thousand francs a year. Beyle sometimes sat up for hours at night scribbling long tables of figures in his journal to demonstrate how 24,000 francs obtained from his patrimony might bring back 180,000 francs in six years, by trading into Pondichéry, for instance. Thus mind triumphed over matter and piled up great hills of golden louis; these in turn would mean a competence, freedom, time for philosophy and for love. "For the first time in my life, I feel a desire for money," he wrote at this season. But the imagined business combinations were postponed for the moment, as the immediacy of Mélanie Guilbert banished them from his mind.

On that afternoon of February 3, 1805, when he had first accompanied her home from Dugazon's, it must be added that he had also visited her apartment, and had a first tête-à-tête with her. She told him that she had already appeared in small parts, but was now seriously preparing for her debut at the Comédie Française. If refused entrance there she was determined to take an engagement at the theater of some large town in the provinces, like Marseille, with the hope of returning later to Paris. Their talk was animated, and Henri shone a little as he delivered himself of some pleasantries on the way of the world and on love, yet with some fineness of sentiment. He felt afterward that he had advanced his cause perceptibly. Mélanie seemed most serious about her profession. Perhaps she was not a facile woman? And had he left her with the idea that he was a roué, a reputation that he sedulously spread here and there—when he knew himself all tenderness and passion and timidity? "Rousseau has given me *the loving character and great loves,*" he wrote in his rather wonderful mixed English and French. "If I have not *the most understanding soul,* I am all passion." He wanted a great love. "I was in love with love," he said afterward.

Was this possible with a Mélanie? His first impression was skeptical. There was a young German student named Wagner also studying elocution at Dugazon's, and he too dangled after Mélanie Guilbert. Moreover he had a little money and often took her to the theater. Beyle pondered: "Perhaps Wagner *has* 'Louason,' whom I have refused." All the ladies who came to Dugazon's were doubtless facile—but had he as yet refused her?

Then, four days after his first walk alone with Mélanie, he went to the Comédie Française, and saw Mlle. Mars, the rising star of the day, in a rather licentious comedy called *Les Folies amoureuses,* by Regnard. His eyes roved the theater for Mélanie, who had told him she went there almost every night. For her sake he had gone to the expense of buying a ticket for the orchestra, he now admitted to himself, disbursing all of four francs out of his small hoard, instead of two, the price of admission to the pit. But neither that night nor the next was she there, though the potential rival, Wagner, whom he shadowed, was on hand.

His thoughts were concentrated upon the young actress with large, innocent blue eyes, and three or four times a day he changed the plans of strategy that he was constantly devising. One was to offer himself as her mentor, freely teaching her all that he had learned of dramaturgy, leading her by constant rehearsals to the expression of the greatest passions, making her perhaps the greatest actress of the time. For though he was but plain, red-faced, and stout, he was a bard, and by reserving for her the leading roles in the plays he was to write he would be worth infinitely more to her career than a Wagner!

Now he was on fire. The twin passions of jealousy and desire raged within him as he sat alone in his room, pining for Mélanie, seeking to forget her, telling himself even that he had begun to "hate" her. Very easily he transported himself into what he called "a state of maximum passion," and this in itself, he hoped, qualified him to become an artist of large scope.

One of the decisive phases of the infection that touched him, described in his own book, *De l'amour,* published many years later, is the first awareness of jealousy. For who feels jealousy over the possession of something he doesn't want?

A week after his first tête-à-tête with Louason, he saw her again alone. Once more he had gone to Dugazon's, this time carefully gotten up in his one new coat of bronze-colored velvet. His air was self-possessed and yet sprightly, so that he appeared quite the amiable man of good society whom everyone enjoys.

She came in while Beyle was reciting from Molière's *Le Misanthrope: "Il faut parmi le monde une vertu traitable . . ."* and he looked at her meaningfully while he intoned these lines concerning the need for a "manageable virtue." He was fully aware that he was delivering himself, this time, with the utmost verve and "superb bearing," that his rich voice (for he had a most agreeable voice) rang out steadily until it could have filled a theater.

"What fire he has!" said the smirking old Dugazon to Mélanie.

And she remarked thoughtfully: "Yes, he certainly has a great deal of that."

But the next day when he saw her at Dugazon's she was cool and indifferent to him. At once he plunged into speculation upon the possible causes of this. On the one hand she had seemed a little indisposed: was it *il marchese?* On the other hand she seemed to enjoy the attentions of still another new rival. It was his own friend and model of worldliness, Martial Daru, who had also come to Dugazon's that day for exercise in elocution; and he had taken notice of the blond young actress. Playing opposite her in Racine's *Mithridate,* the handsome Martial permitted himself the utmost liberties. He gave her warm embraces; in witty imitation of a character in a recent popular comedy, he kept whipping her lightly with a riding crop he carried—in short, as Beyle observed with coldly jealous eyes, "handling her like an actress one had possessed, and scarcely restrained by the proprieties owing even to the drawing room of a Dugazon."

And while Mélanie defended herself not too overtly, but with an air of good-humored embarrassment, their vicious old prompter danced about, making sport of them. But Henri was not amused.

Enflamed by suspicion, he seized the first occasion to whisper questions to his friend, who whispered back: "No. She has got the c——. Do not kiss her."

"I knew it," said Beyle gloomily. (How easily gossip in those circles turned into defamation.)

Escorting her home again that afternoon, Beyle's manner was aloof. His suspicions spoilt everything. She also spoke few words. And those she spoke troubled him, giving him cause, as he felt, for deeper doubt and suspicion of her character.

Passing before a shop window, she called his attention to an embroidered robe spread forth there, saying: "It is remarkable with what art they display things in Paris." A little further on she stopped to examine two hats shown in the window of a millinery shop. Was it because she was looking for presents? Was that the sort of woman she was? Did she want only money of him? Inwardly he groaned, watching her coldly, pondering every word she uttered. Instead of mounting the stairs to her apartment that day, he left her abruptly at her door.

He was most wretched that night, and his journal is full of brooding over what he should have done about the "two hats." He assailed and defended her; but again the shadow of horrid suspicion, the Iago in all of us, blotted out all hope. From the apex of joyful expectation he was flung into the pit of despair, yet did not cease to long for her most pathetically.

"I shall blush, on reading this journal a year hence," he ruminates, "at knowing that she is nothing but a tart."

Yet despite his dark misgivings as to her character and even the state of her health, he returned to walk home with her, climbing to her little drawing room a second and third time. He had made "plans" to assail her by a series of systematic attacks, for he was determined to seduce her in the style of Valmont, the calculating hero of *Les Liaisons dangereuses.* Dominated as he was by self-love, fearing life's dangers on every hand as much as he longed to brave them, he was to be always the eternal strategist in the game of life and sex, always armed with his systems, prescriptions, stratagems, and nearly always, comically enough, fated to lose his weapons, and his plans, midway in the contest.

He must borrow money, he told himself, buy new clothes (a black coat and cashmere breeches), dress with exquisite care, and present himself as the very figure of a man of the world. He must be debonair and witty, yet by the resourcefulness and eloquence of his speech convey undertones of deep sentiment that gave irrefutable evidence of the "greatness of soul" underneath the surface. Mélanie knew nothing of Shakespeare, for example. Well, he would open her eyes to the value of the English genius and by his instruction aid her to climb toward the heights of dramatic art. Then, as she grew more sensible of his worth and her need of him, he would suddenly turn and pay attentions to Mme. Mortier (who, he was certain, pursued him), or to her young daughter Felipe, who also studied dramatics. Thus he would lightly strike the chord of jealousy, pause, then strike it again later. All these stratagems, *sans blague*, are clearly written down, in pages upon pages of those journals of 1805 in which he communed with himself restlessly night and day.

The second time he called, he found three other guests present, including a white-haired old man named Blanc de Vaulx whom she treated as an old intimate. Who was Blanc? A new obstacle? Did he *keep* her? Beyle held himself in leash. They went out and walked in the Tuileries Gardens, and she politely asked Beyle to walk ahead of them so that she might discuss some private business for a few minutes with Blanc. Beyle was furious; when she returned to walk with him again and took his arm he unburdened himself of all sorts of pleasantries aimed at the other man, until she protested gently.

But on the next occasion they were alone together. Previously he had talked much about the dramatic art; but now, after two weeks' acquaintance, speaking with a controlled lightness and polish (as if, he thought, in a comedy by the popular playwright Fleury), he made her a little declaration upon his "way of love." Then he described, as if in hypothesis, what he "would like to be for her."

They grew tender, she seemed touched, and with a dreamy look spoke of her past, unfolding the story of her life. She was, according to her own report, a rather genteel demimondaine. Born the child of middle-class parents, in a small town in Normandy, seduced by a vicious relative while still a young girl, she had left home burdened with a natural daughter whom she loved and provided for. She was twenty-five, three years older than Henri. Coming to Paris, she had determined to study for the stage, first under the celebrated Mlle. Clairon of the Comédie Française, then under Dugazon. Even her friends, by her account, now seemed to him persons of worth, M. Blanc de Vaulx being a government official and amateur dramatist who helped her with her investments, for she had some funds of her own.

As she discharged these confidences her eyes grew moist and she seemed to look at him with a kindling warmth. He had kissed her fully twenty times, and she had defended herself not too well. But this meant little enough, according to the manners of that day which used every pretext for dalliance.

With increasing intimacy they called each other Henri and Mélanie. Beyle asked her if he talked too much. "Let us choose a secret sign that you are to make, when I bore you," he proposed. She said: "Oh yes, indeed," with almost too much promptitude. It was agreed that it was to be the question: "Is there a ball tonight at the Opera?" He pressed her to tell him if there was someone she loved; she replied, no, then, "Well, yes"—looking at him warmly—and noticing his excited expression: "Ah, no," again, modestly dropping her eyes. All this done with so much grace and charm, all the arts and the delicacies of a clever woman of Paris, such as one never met in the provinces. "Oh," he cried to himself, "I begin to be accustomed to happiness." He added: "I do believe that she loves me."

But what of the vicious rumors concerning her character and condition? Could they be true? He rushed to see Martial Daru and asked him where he had learned such things, and if he was certain. His friend seemed puzzled and annoyed. No, he really knew nothing of the matter, but had simply warned Henri that "she *might* possibly have the c——."

The scales fell from his eyes; exalted by hope, he told himself that the pursuit of happiness was overtaking its goal. In his journal he noted the date—it was a Tuesday—and wrote, in his methodical way: "I will have her on Friday."

But on his third visit, he found the same friends of the other day in her drawing room. Mélanie, to his annoyance, spent much of the time in a corner of the room in whispered conference with Blanc de Vaulx, while Henri walked up and down discoursing before the rest of the company, one of whom, a journalist or writer of sorts, had questioned him upon Italy. He felt himself superbly dressed, and so thoroughly did he have his role in hand that he believed his ugliness "had never been more completely effaced by the expressiveness of his physiognomy." Italy and the poetry of Alfieri, which he quoted copiously in Italian, was a subject upon which he could glitter. As he held his little audience, he watched Mélanie and Blanc out of the corner of his eye, sometimes directing looks of contempt at the old man, sometimes pretending to give all his attention to another lady who had come in during his monologue. Observing Mélanie covertly, he had the feeling that when Blanc said certain things to her which he could not overhear, "the whole expression of her mouth changed . . . grew coarser."

At length Mélanie came to him and whispered: "What right do you have to *hate* Monsieur Blanc?"

"Because I do not like his eyes," he blurted. But recovering his composure, he moved off to flirt with the other lady, and set the other men laughing with his sallies. One of them, a man of letters evidently, began to quote a passage from Racine depicting the solemnity of death. And Henri, who thought the hour had come to make his exit, exclaimed with a comic urgency: "Why, sir, you terrify me so greatly with your reflections upon death that I now take to my heels." And with this he seized his hat, saluted everyone, and in a sort of breathless haste, rushed out of the house, banging his head against the door as he left.

"A perfect firebrand!" he heard Mélanie say, after she had closed the door.

But he was certain that it was one of the finest days of his life, that he had exploited his talents for conversation and social diplomacy to the uttermost, and that Mélanie was dazzled.

"All the world's a stage," Shakespeare had written, and he reflected to himself that he had played superbly upon that stage while improvising the lines of his own play. He had been "at one and the same time, author and actor"—Molière plus Talma!—thus enjoying the comedy of life at its very best terms. This reflection is as good a key as any to the narcissistic youth, forever playing out his imaginary dramas, not only speaking his lines but even serving as his own prompter.

After waiting for three or four days, during which interval the effect of his brilliant performance in Mélanie's salon was intended to sink home, he called on her again at an hour when she was usually alone. Under his arm was a copy of *Othello*, the reading of which would sweep aside her last defenses.

The maid came to the door to tell him that her mistress had just gone out. Two hours later he knocked at her door again. Again the maid told him with a knowing look that Mlle. Louason was out. The next day, and the third day, there was the same closed door.

Suddenly he felt all his finespun plots for gulling this woman, all his rakish schemes, fall to the ground. Plainly she had ordered her door closed to him. Had he offended her? He reviewed all his recent behavior, though his brain whirled. Everything now led him to believe that his stratagems had been inept, that he was far less brilliant than he had supposed. When he had glared at M. Blanc, and revealed his suspicions, her eyes had seemed to say calmly: "It is not what you suppose." And earlier his manifest irritation when she had looked at those two hats in the shop window? Ah, those *two hats!* If only he had had the few louis to buy them for her and be done with it! Alas, how inexperienced he was, and how dearly this cost him! For now he confessed: "I desire only the happiness which I may enjoy through the love of Mélanie. All else means little to me."

For a whole day he walked the streets of Paris, driven by a truly Shakesperean passion, now cursing and raging at himself, now melting with the tenderest longing for Mélanie, while looking for her everywhere. That night, at the Théâtre Français, he finally caught a glimpse of her as she was being handed to her seat in the parterre by two cavaliers unknown to him. She saluted him with what seemed but "cold formality." Passing through the crowded foyer at the end of the performance, she bade him good night with a coolness of manner showing, as he could only conclude, "that she wished to break off relations with me."

That night, and the two following, he did not sleep. "I lived through more in one day than in two months," he noted, and like a brave scientist, added that his "only compensation had been the chance to observe his own feelings." On two of these nights he stayed with his devoted friend and literary collaborator, Louis Crozet, in fear of being alone, in fear that he might end his life. To Crozet he explained only that he was "in disgrace" with the person he loved most in the world; and his friend was so touched that he loaned him eighty francs, and took him driving. Later Crozet declared to his "too sensitive" friend that on observing Beyle's storms of passion he had been cured of the desire for a similar experience.

But on the morning of the third day, when he expected to see her at Dugazon's again, he was able to rally his spirits—a striking sign of his moral courage at an hour when he was truly haggard with despair.

It was as if he were drunk or giddy: he pretended to be the gay dog, kissing her warmly, in greeting, as if nothing had happened—for the other pupils and the master had not yet come in—and invited her to go driving with him that afternoon. Later, in the carriage, he asked for an explanation, and she said she had had no idea of severing their friendship.

"But that greeting, so cold and polite?"

"How do you expect me to greet you—before all those people?" And besides, she had been made weary by her companions. It was he who had seemed cold when she tried to catch his eye at the theater.

An immense weight dropped from his shoulders, and he felt as if a reprieve from a death sentence had been granted him. Mélanie was simply more worldly, more unfathomable in her moods, than he had fancied, and he a fool. "I have always *felt* more than I *perceived,*" he would say. A mere shadow, a half-open door, always suggested some enemy lurking, and he would make as if to draw a sword and attack at once, like the immortal knight of Cervantes having at windmills.

5

"You have much wit, you can go far," Mélanie told him. "You have a great deal of fire and a great soul. But," she continued gently, "you must use more finesse in your raillery. You are sometimes too cutting."

He was delighted and exclaimed to himself, "Ah, she wishes to educate me, to lead me by the hand!" Touched by her greatness of soul, he promised to improve himself under her guidance. "I would rather please you than all others," he murmured, thinking of her at night. "Tell me what I should be, and I will be that."

That Mélanie was truly a good soul, and of gentler breeding than he had realized, was shown by her growing attachment for the youth who was but a poor student, usually with only one good suit to his name, and often in debt. His gifts to her were the walks they took in the Tuileries Gardens together, and his talk about the plays he would write, in which she would appear in the principal part, his Mlle. Clairon, his Mlle. Mars!

Still he could not entirely forego his little tricks: he would pose as the knowing young rake. One day they were walking together in the Tuileries, Beyle clad in his best velveteen jacket and she, leaning affectionately upon his arm, in a long white dress, with a charming bonnet, garnished with roses, and tied with a pink ribbon under her chin, making quite a picture. It was at this moment that Victorine Mounier, who had never answered his burning letters of love, rode by in an open carriage. Surprised, and also pleased, he gave her a stiff bow. Who was she, Mélanie asked curiously? That fashionable young lady was one of his recent "conquests," he boasted. Later, he wondered how this brazen falsehood had escaped him, as he painstakingly recorded it in his journal. "A pleasurable wave of vanity" had overwhelmed him—because Victorine had seen him with his blond actress.

But Mélanie told him that he was a young dog. When he vaunted also his affair with an older woman and her daughter, she exclaimed, "What libertines you men are!" And he replied: "You do me too great honor!"

"If women were not coquettes, then men would make them so," she said.

"If men were not coxcombs, then women would make them so," he said.

But Mélanie protested at the "irreverent and heartless tone of your young men of fashion"—pointing to the example of the fop, Martial Daru—and he respectfully agreed, changing his tone.

He was so grateful only to be with her that his advances became more guarded and subtle. Instead of speaking of his adoration directly and boringly, he tried to seize opportune moments, as one day when she read to him in her charming voice. "Even if one were not infatuated with you, one would become so on hearing you read." This was better than a bald compliment; and she plainly liked it.

"I read her soul like a book, every day I read it better," he thought now.

From the moment when he had suffered the fear of losing her she occupied all his thoughts, and by the power of self-delusion that infatuation brings, he ascribed to her every beauty, every grace, while ignoring her flat bosom, her frequent weariness of spirits, the trace of disappointment at the corners of her mouth.

Their tête-à-têtes, their evenings alone together, as they grew more intimate, were entrancing to him, banishing all care, all dullness. One night, returning from the theater, she made him a little midnight supper of fried potatoes and wine, which they consumed peacefully together, holding hands before the fireplace in the little salon. All his days Henri remembered the blissful serenity of "that evening of *pommes frites!*"

On occasion he even came into her boudoir while she was changing, or dressing her blond hair, and he would gaze at her as she sat smiling dreamily into the mirror, half disrobed. He would pretend not to be looking at her, while timidly paying court.

But still he hesitated; something held him back. "I should have seized the chance when she seemed most melting," he would say to himself repeatedly. "I am too chaste with her on those occasions. Always the Saint-Preux. . . ."

It must be explained that early in their friendship, she had told him with infinite tact and modesty, without even saying it in so many words, that she was devoting all her energies to her stage debut, and did not wish to have a lover at this period for fear of becoming *enceinte.*

For her sake he vowed even chastity, temporarily resisting all opportunities. There was, for example, Mme. Mortier at Dugazon's, who seemed to throw herself at his head. Henri could tell her all sorts of *polissoneries,* and she would only laugh the more. In return she told him the story of how her innocence had been ravished. He put her down in his lists as a strumpet: "I could have had her a thousand times, but 'pon my honor, it is impossible." It was the time of his maximum passion for Mélanie.

His impatience mounted steadily. He must somehow come to conclusions with her. "Be strong—the hell with everything—and go straight ahead," he counseled himself. Yet he recognized that "it is she who must help me to win her, or some favoring opportunity."

One day he came in and found her dressing, her hair in paper curls. She seemed melancholy, wearing almost a pout of disappointment. Her funds, she told him, were running low, they were half gone, and she had decided that she dared no longer wait in Paris in the hope of winning a minor role at the Comédie Française. She was about to take an engagement at Marseille that offered her a leading part, although the thought of leaving Paris and her friends for an indefinite period brought her to the point of tears.

He had been telling himself of late that he must be bold, at all costs. Now an inspiration came to him: a journey to Marseille with her would fit in with his business projects! His friend Mante had already left for Marseille and established himself in trade there. Why could he not go there if he wished?

And so he told Mélanie that he could not bear life if she departed from Paris. He was resolved to throw up his preparations for a career of letters, abandon his brilliant social life in the capital, and follow her to Marseille, there to accept some humble place in trade, but at least to remain at her side.

At these words Mélanie burst into tears, his journal for April 8, 1805, relates:

> She turned her face away from me, toward the window, to conceal her tears, and wept for joy, wept at my kindness. Then she asked me to fetch her handkerchief. . . . She wept a long time.

For she had not dreamed that Henri would be so good to her. Later he wished that he could have found "sublime words," like Rousseau before his beloved countess, for such a moment, in which they fell into each other's arms and wept together.

He promised further that, if her plans for the theater failed, he would "go and live with her in the country, in whatever corner of France she chose"; he would live with her and her daughter, and would be father and mentor to her little daughter. They laid plans together and then wept and kissed each other again, until Henri went home as if walking on air.

That night, however, seated at his writing table, he recorded everything with his customary honesty toward himself. On the one hand he congratulated himself upon the lucky turn of fortune that had won the promise of Mélanie's heart. But, on the other hand, he noted coldly, how deceitful he had been:

> I did not tell her that it was my plan, all along, to go to Marseille, but rather that if she went there, I would follow her and sacrifice Paris for her sake.

6

At dawn of the 8th of May 1805, in that month which the French still called by the lovely name of "Floréal," the two lovers proceeded with their baggage to the long, echoing court of the Messagerie, at the Rue Montmartre, whence the heavy stagecoaches departed for all the towns of France. The coachmen roared out the names of their destinations, orange girls and flower girls called out their wares, passengers disputed with one another as they crowded into the dark coaches, laden with bread, cheeses, tobacco, umbrellas that nearly put out your eyes, and cotton bonnets to wear on their heads against the dust of the road. Arm in arm, Henri and Mélanie, elegant as ever in her long robe, long gloves, and pink-ribboned bonnet, pushed through the crowd and clambered into the big coach that smelled of harness and horses. Soon they were off, jolting along on the road running southward to Lyons.

In the week before they had left, Henri Beyle's emotional temperature had risen to fever pitch. The journals, so rare a document of a singular man's inner life as they have been, now become a prolonged internal monologue by the Observer of the Human Heart, poised before the adventure he had longed for, yet attempting to anticipate everything, planning night and day. Among the most commonplace facts of his daily life, the bill for his laundry, the food he has eaten, the obscene jests of his companions at dinner, the girls he has pinched during the day, all methodically written down, there are also the inebriate calculations of his future profits in trade: 24,000 francs invested in cloth to be exported to India, adding up to the miraculous total of 180,000 francs in so many years, finally to 300,000 and more!

He marks down the grand strategy of the approaching campaign. "*To write the plan of conduct and say that to nobody . . .*" he notes in his private English. "And to follow it from point to point to Marseille, carefully establishing the ideal goal that I desire to attain." And what a plan, what a goal! To leave Paris all populated with complaisant wenches, and fly four hundred miles to Marseille for the sake of a Mélanie Guilbert. He was all rapture and all calculation. It came to him even then that his "habitual state of reflection was not in accord with that of action"; that even in a love affair he saw the end before the beginning. Yet this was his way, and made the commonest events of his existence indelible moments of pain or pleasure that less conscious beings might never know.

They would be voyaging three days together on the road to Lyons, where it was agreed that he would leave her temporarily to connect with the diligence for Grenoble—to replenish his funds—while she continued to Marseille and awaited him there. His concluding thought was:

> *If I have not Mélanie* [on] *the way, I shall ever be unhappy with her. But in the contrary case, I shall be the happiest of men to Marseille.*

When they parted at Lyons, on the 11th of May, Mélanie was tired, pale, indisposed; her mouth drawn in that expression of disappointment already habitual with her, though she was but twenty-five. She was harrowed by anxiety about her approaching stage debut at Marseille. Henri too was despondent.

Nor did the visit en route to his paternal city improve his humor.

That he was sick to see his father, the sour-faced old lawyer, went without saying. His idea that he should draw part of his future inheritance, a sum of thirty thousand francs—or even nine thousand francs, as later reduced—and invest it with his friend Mante in a wholesale-grocery establishment in Marseille caused his father to lift his eyes to heaven and groan. The giddy youth who had gone off to be an engineer, an officer, a playwright, now had the whim to be a *grocer*, to handle casks of wine and olive oil with his fine white hands! He, a Beyle of Grenoble, close to the nobility of the robe, to become an *épicier*—how vulgarly the word rings in French to the higher-bourgeois ear!

The weeks passed, even two months, while Henri, scarcely concealing his bitterness at his father, waited to receive money and be on his way. Only his adoring sister Pauline grasped the magnitude of his banking plans, or knew of his prodigious "conquests" of women, past and future.

Future? Even the possession of Mélanie was still in doubt. That first journey together into the springtime of France, in Floréal, had been, in truth, but a tormenting fiasco. She had resisted his most pressing attentions, pleaded a "headache," accused him of embarrassing her by his indiscretions before the other travelers, even used a separate room at the inns where they stopped. And she had wept as always. Doubtless the time, the tides, and the moon, the prosaic and humiliating accidents of nature and woman, had conspired to postpone the long-sought "victory."

Now he was full of gloom and, as usual, of suspicion. Was she but a coquette without passion, who gulled him? Was she waiting for him impatiently in Marseille, as her letters insisted, or in the arms of another?

A letter from her in June showed her full of anxiety as she rehearsed for the première; "she longed to be surrounded with affection during this time of trial," and closed by begging him "to make a wish from afar for her success." But the news that followed the opening night was dark, and gave him pause. Press and public were so cool as to appear almost hostile, though she continued to play. She now urged her Henri to hasten to join her in Marseille and even accused him of indifference or lightness, such as she had suffered at the hands of her two former lovers.

His replies were full of reproaches, even of despairing accusations of unfaithfulness on her part. Jealousy, always strong within him, afflicts him now; and the letters that pass between them, full of mutual reproaches and laments, are scarcely those of happy lovers.

But his good friend Fortuné Mante, the philosopher-financier, who was always "calm, gracious and loyal," intervened to write him: "Calm yourself, too happy fool. Mélanie loves you and loves you dearly, I can assure you." She spoke only of him, waited only for him.

At long last, Henri won permission to establish himself in Marseille. It was arranged that he serve an apprenticeship in trade as a clerk to a respectable merchant named Meunier, recommended by Mante and well known to his own family. His remittance of 150 francs a month was to be raised to 300 for the time being.

In the great heat of midsummer, on July 22, 1805, he hurried to take the diligence that brought him to the Rhône River boat for Marseille, where he arrived only three days later; for, as he said, "love had given him wings."

Mélanie was at the dock to meet him the afternoon he arrived, and that night he saw her play the leading lady in a comic opera, though he makes no comment in his journal upon her playing. His discreet friend Mante had seen to everything, even a room adjoining Mélanie's in her small hotel, in the winding, shabby Rue Sainte, back of the

Grand Théâtre, where she played. *Enfin!* During the morning hours of the following day, the young Beyle clasped the slender Mélanie in his arms. His journal in his hermetic English bears only a bald notice of this consummation:

> July 26, 1805: *I see her in her chamber at eleven o'clock of the morning.*

In after years, turning over his papers, as a man of age and wisdom, he used to remark that he had never been able to find words to describe the supremely happy moments of his life, but could only write with exactitude of the disappointments he had suffered. For too often one fell into exaggerated and false phrases, such as littérateurs currently abused, and instead of recapturing the "frenzy of happiness," one killed its very memory by speaking of it.

A sense of taste and good form enjoins him to be silent even in those intimate journals destined originally only for his own eyes. When, in old age, he attempts to write of such experiences in his memoirs, in *Henri Brulard,* he finds himself checked, and interrupts his recital forever:

> Has the reader ever been madly in love? Has he ever had the good fortune to pass a night with that mistress whom he has loved most in his life? Upon my word, I cannot go on.[2]

[2] *Henri Brulard,* Ch. XLVII. In this closing passage he speaks actually of another episode. But in 1814, reading over the passage in his journal of 1805 concerning the reunion with Mélanie in Marseille, he adds a footnote: "These recollections are dull, because I did not describe the happiness of August, 1805 to February, 1806, for fear of spoiling it." *Journal,* II, 365. Because he waged incessant war against "hypocrisy," rhetorical or intellectual, Stendhal was to appear pre-eminently the writer's writer. His standards of "sincerity" demanded restraint in the expression of his strongest emotions. "I do everything possible," he wrote, "to keep *cool,* to impose silence upon my heart. . . ."

CHAPTER VII

The End of Innocence

HIS happiness overflowed as soon as he was reunited with Mélanie; as he wrote his sister, he felt himself walking on air, like a disembodied spirit. Even a month later, in September, he speaks as if his very happiness *frightens* him. "I am tenderly loved by a woman with whom I am madly in love. She has a beautiful soul."

They walked together by the sea—which he had never seen before—they walked by the sea at night, sat down arm in arm, listened to the waves, watched the sailing boats glide out of the bay, and saw the stars disappear behind the looming bulk of the Château d'If on its islet of rock dominating the harbor. They went for picnics up in the hills, and Henri with delight watched Mélanie bathing in the little brook named L'Huveaune, and remembered the moment in all its detail thirty years after.

"She is a very beautiful woman, with a severely Grecian face," he wrote in a letter to his sister, "with immense blue eyes, and a body full of grace, though somewhat thin."

Like any married couple they lived at first a life of quiet domesticity. They would retire to their rooms, then at the sound of a discreet knock on her shutter, for which Henri listened, he would join her.

They dreamed dreams together now. In a few years he hoped to be established as a rich banker in Paris. Then his sister Pauline might come and join them and "their" child. For, by one more of his little subterfuges, he permitted his sister, and through his sister, his grandfather, to assume that the little girl (who was boarded near Paris) was the child of his union with Mélanie. Not only did he promise eternal devotion to Mélanie, but her child was to be educated by himself; in the event of his early death, his fortune was to be willed to Mélanie and her daughter.

Grandfather Gagnon himself, remembering his own gallant youth, was intrigued by reports of Henri's romance in Marseille, and wrote him sound advice about bringing up his daughter, "that poor child who had not asked to be born." Let her be reared, he said, as a simple working girl so that she might be spared the disappointment of learning one day of her natural birth.

As Mélanie revealed herself to him, he was convinced that she was a most beautiful character. When she spoke to him in confidence of the two lovers who had preceded him, and her sufferings at their hands, he was ready to believe that she was more sinned against than sinning. Her frail health also troubled him, as he wrote to Pauline, October 9, 1805, and he begged his sister to write a friendly letter to his mistress:

> What a woman! She did exactly what you wanted to do; she left her parents like ——, though not for a major love. At that moment society ceased to protect her; she found herself in conflict with the most degraded souls; day by day they tried to ruin her character. She had an old coquette for her mother, and her father a selfish debauchee. . . . Imagine the suffering of her tender soul which could weep all day at an unkind word. . . . Then, after struggling for five or six years against her evil destiny, she went into the theater.

Pauline, the little bluestocking who still shared all Henri's outspoken beliefs, wrote Mélanie a charming letter full of grace and warmth, at which both she and Henri were moved to tears. Pauline too made a will in favor of his "daughter"!

He had come to the colorful, bustling port of Marseille to study commerce now and become a banker instead of a general. Despite the renewal of war on the continent after 1803, Napoleon gave the most vigorous encouragement to industry; iron foundries, cloth mills, and banks, driven by the new steam power, multiplied and flourished. Had not the neighbors of the Beyles, the Périers of Grenoble, become one of the foremost banking families of France? Indeed the Périers even financed the house of Meunier at the Vieux Port of Marseille, where Henri Beyle was now employed as a clerk.

Was it a dishonor to be a merchant's clerk? In Marseille, he reported, "everybody was a clerk, everybody was in trade." He kept books, carried on correspondence, or weighed and measured stores of soap, hemp, and liquor at the docks. It was dull work; yet he cheerfully bore the discipline of his employer, "a pious hypocrite" who helped him to understand his father better. Inwardly he groaned as each morning began, but told himself that commerce "is useful because it forces me to suffer for eight hours the stupidities of men."

In the evening he dined out with Mélanie, his friend Mante, Mante's mistress, and assorted notables of the Marseille theatrical and commercial world. These were amusingly gross people with whom he played cards or went to balls or the theater. Presumably they lived but to eat and fornicate. Beyle followed his old habit of writing pen portraits of them in his journal, especially of one who impressed him as inordinately vulgar and crooked, a stout man who prospered by stealing the food of the prisoners in the town jail.

Against some of the Marseillais, Beyle was sometimes compelled to defend his Mélanie almost by main force. An aged officer, who made proposals to her, he prepared to challenge to a duel, which was fortunately averted. The presence of a discreet elderly protector in the background, the prefect of police, who had an important voice in the affairs of the old opera house and was said to have won Mélanie her contract, also caused some rumor-mongering, and aroused Beyle's intense jealousy.

Three months or so after their union, the lovers suddenly had an unhappy scene, Henri in a rage, Mélanie weeping and confining herself to her room all day. When in Paris he had been suspicious that Mélanie was contaminated, or gave herself to every man who approached her; now a morbid jealousy preyed upon him quite tragically.

After their quarrels came reconciliations, and renewals of tenderness and *volupté*. But by February and March 1806 their affairs were going badly.

The tightening blockade of the French ports by the British fleet after Nelson's victory at Trafalgar in October 1805 brought a stagnation of export trade that no one seemed to have foreseen. Meunier's business as a commissionaire was closed down by March 1, 1806, like many others, and Henri was out of work. The slump in trade also brought misfortune to Mélanie's theatrical company in the shape of dwindling audiences.

She had made no strong impression upon Marseille by her interpretations of Racine and Voltaire. Though Mlle. Louason was credited with good diction, her spirit of restraint earned her the disapproval of the local public, which craved fire and brimstone in the theater. At the end of February, the Grand Théâtre closed down for want of popular support. It was a calamity that Mélanie had feared since the beginning of the year, when she first spoke of returning to Paris and seeking another engagement. Full of anxiety as she was, fearing for her health and the future of her child, she wept and complained more than ever, and her lover too grew darkly despondent.

Mélanie, as he described her in his letters to his sister, had been "wounded by life." Parents, lovers, career had failed her and she by now had reason to doubt the constancy of Beyle. Her habitual anxiety, her expression of melancholy, which at first had seemed to him her greatest charm, making her a tragic heroine pursued by fate, ended by wearying him, for his was a lusty temperament that fed upon laughter as well as tears. "If only she would not tyrannize over me and complain always," he said to himself. Where were those "transports" of emotion that made life worth living? He had sought "grand passions," but found instead vexation and boredom.

When he tried to interest her in the books he was reading, he felt her indifferent to them now. One day in the spring of 1806, he was able to write in his journal: "I begin to find Mélanie stupid." How changed was his state of mind from that of a year ago when he had wandered the streets of Paris in love with love!

In reality their situation had become untenable with the collapse of Mélanie's hopes in the theater—from which she had counted on 6,500 francs per annum—and also of Henri's vague banking plans. They had set off from Paris full of wonderful anticipations. But now Mélanie scarcely had funds to permit her to return to Paris and wait for new openings, and he could help her but little. He was never ungenerous with his money; what small sums he received he turned over to Mélanie. But his father always delayed things tormentingly. In his wretchedness of soul, disappointed in her, disillusioned in himself, he now wrote to an old school friend named Plana, asking him to send some poison. His friend, however, only replied with strong words advising him to calm down, and he heeded them.

Poor Mélanie! Though she had seen much of the baseness of men, she had once more shown herself too trusting or too optimistic and literally thrown herself away for a *bonnet*—exactly what the cynical old Dugazon had counseled her not to do. When she declared that she would leave Marseille for Paris at the end of March, he told her that he had decided to stay on, endure her departure, and await events. For his own future plans already excluded her.

What could he do? Follow her about from town to town, wherever she found an engagement, living in an unnatural idleness—for she offered, on at least one occasion, to share whatever she had with him

—while waiting for his own fortunes to improve? Yet of the plays he thought to write, he noted: "I strain myself all day to do two lines." No, life with Mélanie could not further his own ends; she was like an "ivy" attached to the weak tree that he was, and "needed an oak." Besides he was once more occupied with such worldly ambitions as he had formerly scorned. He was "tired of love," he wrote to his friend Crozet. In his heart Mélanie's greatest rival now was ambition. "I ought to have been the happiest man in the world through love," he wrote as early as January 7, 1806. "It seems utterly extinct, and little by little I feel myself possessed by ambition, frantic and even furious. It shames me to think of it." His years were passing; he was at the age of a man and yet had advanced himself toward no object. This at a time when, after the epoch-making victory of Austerlitz, Napoleon poured the looted treasure of half of Europe into France, and when Beyle's young contemporaries, one after another, partook of the banquets of glory and loot and power that now regaled imperial Paris. His cousin Pierre Daru, now Count Daru, had become chief commissary or quartermaster general of the whole Grand Army that had just crushed Austria and would tomorrow invade Prussia. To the favorites of the Emperor or his powerful lieutenants whole conquered provinces were thrown to be ruled and to be enjoyed. Would there not be prizes for him, too?

On March 7, 1806, Beyle's friend Félix Faure (the future peer of France) wrote him:

> And you, my dear Henry [*sic*], do you stay on at Marseille, ever faithful to your bank? Have you no desire to return to the capital, and seek your fortune there again? The whole complexion of things is greatly changed; everything is accomplished through favor. . . . Your relatives, the Darus, seem destined to go to the highest stations. Are you not tempted to attach yourself to their fortunes?[1]

A little earlier he had, according to his own counsel, chosen his part. In the classic way of so many other young bourgeois he had concluded that the little woman was a burden which he had best abandon. As he watched her sad preparations to leave without him, he detected in himself emotions "of the profoundest disappointment, without despair, and dejection or disgust, without a trace of energy."

He accompanied her to the diligence on March 1, 1806, and wondered if he felt only "friendship" for her. The moment of departure, it was true, plunged him into a somber distress. There was a last de-

[1]P. Arbalet: *Stendhal épicier*, p. 220.

spondent talk of meeting soon in Paris. But, he writes, "immediately after her departure, I felt joy in my liberty. Some weeks later, a little regret. . . . *Ecce homo!*"

Thus disentangled, he thought he must turn again to the systematic cultivation of his mind, his character, his "genius." Instead, in his distress of soul, he plunged into a round of dissipation, gambling, wenching, even heavy drinking of rum and punch, not common with him, in the company of his rather crapulous Marseillais friends and their fleshly women. A few nights after Mélanie had left, he slept with one woman, the vulgar consort of a local tradesman. Then, on the next night but one, with her maid, named Rosa—in the shadowed doorway of a house on some narrow, ill-lit street of Marseille—he made, as Shakespeare would say, "the beast with two backs." But one could take neither ease nor joy in these sudden, stealthy orgies, from which he would return, as he himself acknowledged, sick to his stomach with disgust.

2

In his commonplace book, called *Pensées*, there occurs at this time the citation from Voltaire's *Oreste:*

> My innocence, at length, begins to weigh upon me.

Henri Beyle's age of innocence may be said to have ended at approximately the time of his rupture with Mélanie Guilbert. Not because of the evil that Mélanie wrought—she was a good enough soul, though a little battered by life. It was because of the weakness or evil, so to speak, which he discovered in himself. Later he would boldly investigate to learn if he was truly evil or not. But at the time when he lingered on in Marseille for three months, melancholy, disillusioned, indolent, his mind, as honest and alert as ever, took careful inventory of the wreck of his self-esteem, and of the collapse of ever so many castles in Spain.

He had held the Socratic axiom that "virtue is knowledge." He had told himself that to experience great passion, to know a great love, was more important than money and rank; hence to live with a pretty actress was an end-object outweighing promotion of the military or social kind. Yet now he knew that he had driven Mélanie away, that he had found her a tiresome burden. When she wrote appealing to him to hasten to join her in Paris, he, who butted every night with the commonest wenches of Marseille, wrote her letters accusing *her* of unfaithfulness to him. It was a sort of recipe against self-condemnation.

"Ah, my friend," she replied, "you know that my heart is too full of you ever to belong to another, but I have reasons to have my doubts on your account!" But he replied only after six weeks, in an evasive, and, as he himself admitted, unfeeling manner. His promises to help her and even her daughter were put out of mind utterly. His own friend Louis Crozet accused him of being cruel and faithless.[2]

A little over a year before, watching the coronation ceremonies in Paris, he had looked with disgust at the Emperor—"smiling only with his teeth like an actor"—as the new Caesar, and termed his accommodation with the Pope an "alliance of all the charlatans." He had felt a bad taste in his mouth, which he "rinsed out" by reading Alfieri, the revolutionary Italian dramatist.

Now he sat writing letters to Count Daru (whom he heartily disliked) and his brother Martial, begging them to find him some place in the imperial service. If they would but try him he would be ready to work ten hours a day. When the Darus, who had been offended at his quitting the service and their protection without consulting them, were slow to reply, he wrote penitent letters to his father and grandfather, begging them to intercede for him before the almighty officeholders in Paris.

It was at this time, in 1806, that he decided to abandon one of his current, unfinished, projects: a satire of Napoleon. It would of course be a bar to the ambitions that now obsessed him and for whose sake he sometimes felt "equal to the greatest crimes and the greatest infamies."

He was bidding adieu for the time being to the bard and the philosopher in him. For a long time he had been educating himself, in a singularly independent and irregular fashion, to be sure, yet with immense efforts at honest self-knowledge. The world was again filled with the alarums of war, the shrieks of the victims, and the ecstatic cries of the new conquerors. The escalator of the new social order was moving the old rulers downward while new groups and classes floated upward to the heights, among them many of Henri's bourgeois friends and relatives, the Faures, the Périers and the Darus, the real winners of the French Revolution. He pined to join their procession.

Like others who had been precociously brilliant and self-willed in childhood, he had remained a child too long. All his Systems based on

[2] P. Arbalet, *Stendhal épicier*, pp. 191–92.

books had been routed in the test of experience. Not that he would ever abandon Systems and Logic. But he must recast them to meet the exigencies of life itself.

At last, he believed, he was "de-Rousseau-ized." The three months of dissipation and indolence in Marseille were also a season of intellectual crisis, with bouts of long reading and writing of some very fruitful notes and new maxims. He still read books, but now it was Machiavelli:

> April 1, 1806. I began to read *The Prince*, a good remedy for that instable sensitivity which makes me like a woman, and is disguised only by my facility for reasoning.

Machiavelli and the renewed reading of history were to be antidotes to that too innocent "enthusiasm" which so often had misled him, as well as aids to a future officeholder. At heart he disliked Machiavelli; but his intuition in associating the tactics of the Corsican military captain who triumphed over Europe with the ideas of the Florentine philosopher of power politics was sound. Machiavelli made wars of conquest appear virtuous. Perhaps, Henri reasoned now, the benefits of the French Revolution would be extended by France "to Naples, Germany, Spain, and Portugal, countries grotesquely ruled by superstition." And during the violent birth labors of the new order, Beyle willed to climb to the top, seeking power, wealth, happiness. "In truth, the only good is that which is successful," he wrote to Pauline. "The true talent is to succeed, though chance plays a large part in such affairs."

He felt himself on the road to being cured of "certain presumptions." He must think now about "harshness and realities." An admixture of cynicism altered his moral ideas, though it would be incorrect to assume that he was ever wholeheartedly a "Machiavellian" or a cynic in the conduct of his life. In the end he would show himself too intelligent to embrace individual cynicism, which even the ancient Epicurus did not believe in, any more than the modern Nietzsche, but remained rather a Stoic, in the Greek way, and a humanist.

He wrote in his journal:

> A man must heal himself of enthusiasm for the happiness that he lacks.

He even hardened himself against disillusionment:

> I have noticed that all men believe themselves more or less *unfortunate*. Yesterday three persons told me they were the "unhappiest beings in the world."

> . . . The average man must learn to bear six or seven disappointments every day.
>
> One must choose his work in accordance with his "ruling passion" (after having carefully determined what that is) and avoid changing occupations.

Beyle's own ruling passion was now ambition. To further it he had some sardonic reflections upon how to use his fellow men:

> When I meet a man, ask myself what he wants of me, not "what do I feel about him?"

At the end of May, three months after Mélanie's departure, the prodigal son returned with chastened spirits to Grenoble, where he experienced a partial reconciliation with his father. But Chérubin Beyle was as chary as ever about giving him money, except in small doses, though he promised to devote larger sums to furthering the practical career of his son in the public service. Henri's visit to Grenoble was merely a halt for provisions, while en route to Paris. The way to his return there was paved by a letter of June 1, 1806, to the younger of the Darus, now an intendant general. It was a letter written in the tone of the most exquisite friendship:

> You know, my dear cousin, that I would prefer a thousand times to sit copying newspapers in your office rather than enjoy some position at 6,000 francs a year that was a hundred leagues removed from you. But do not think it is Paris I long for; it is the life of the Casa d'Adda (in Milan), the kindnesses with which you overwhelmed me, and the hope of being able to acquire a few of those qualities which make you loved by all who surround you.

Careers might be open to talent in the age of Napoleonic bureaucracy, but it was nevertheless true (as Félix Faure had written) that "everything is accomplished through favor." It was even more true, as Beyle would later say again and again, that "in France one can reach everything by pleasing women." Martial Daru, of course, led to his brother, the Count Daru. But the handsome Countess Daru was even more potent.

CHAPTER VIII

Ambition and the Countess

He sinned against the principles of Beylism.
—Stendhal.

HOW different was his state only a year after he had quit Marseille and Mélanie, how much higher stood his own self-esteem! Yesterday he had but one pair of boots and an ill-fitting frock coat which he declares "tore my soul." Today he wore the blue and gold-braided uniform of a commissary of war of the Grand Army, and was installed in a palace as intendant of Brunswick, the veritable ruler over some 200,000 Germans.

"Here I am a *somebody*," he wrote his sister. The Germans bowed and scraped before him, addressing him as *Monseigneur*. Even French officers approached him as *Monsieur l'Intendant*, and generals solicited his favor. "I write letters," he adds, "lose my temper at my secretaries, go to formal dinners, ride horseback, and read Shakespeare."

Arriving in Paris in July 1806, he had danced attendance upon the Darus—decked out in new clothes, changing his cravat and shirt every day, and playing at wearying games of cards, but convinced, as he said, that "upon these miseries everything depends." Four years earlier, Pierre Daru had married an heiress, Alexandrine Nardot, a native of Nantes. Though her husband had spoken to Mme. Daru of his young cousin as a "wild fellow," and she had heard much of his scrapes in Italy, she had received Beyle with great kindness. He in turn paid marked attention to the buxom young matron, whose warm beauty David has caught in one of his best portraits. She had thick chestnut hair, large, even brown eyes, a plump round face, with a pert nose, a charming mouth, but a stubborn chin.

He had seen Mélanie again in Paris, visiting her discreetly every two weeks. But at length they had quarreled bitterly and she had gone off to Naples with a company that was to play at the court of King Joseph Bonaparte.

Henri's eyes, however, hung upon the vivacious Countess Daru. Earlier she had written in reply to an appeal by letter that the count could do nothing for him. But now she found him a man of wit, whose sallies sometimes brought a gleam of approval even to the eyes of her dour husband, and his luck turned. On October 16, 1806, two days after the Battle of Jena, that brought overwhelming defeat to the Kingdom of Prussia, Beyle left for Germany with Martial Daru, whom he served as a deputy commissary of war.

Across the flat heaths and sandy plains of northern Germany, a subject land filled with confusion and despair, he rode in the rear of the Grand Army, until, by stages, he reached Berlin, where, on October 27, he witnessed the triumphal parade of Napoleon and his troops. How submissive the Germans were! "They could have killed him from any window," he remarked, watching them stand in sullen crowds but two yards from the Emperor on his white horse.

With the younger Daru, he was assigned to serve at Brunswick, where his cousin acted as intendant, supervising the finances of the little state and levying tribute upon it for the Empire. When Martial was called to other duties, Beyle himself in 1808 succeeded to his place.

Each day he rose early, was shaved by his German barber, then plunged into administrative labors that occupied him for some six hours until three o'clock. He carried on a large correspondence with the Quartermaster Department of the army, oversaw the accounts of the duchy, heard petitioners, answered complaints, aided in the dispatch of supply convoys passing through Brunswick. Then, his work done—for he moved quickly and performed the labors of two men—he would take tea, or sit reading in the handsome English gardens that had been planned for the Duchess of Brunswick.

In his leisure time Henri Beyle observed and cultivated the Germans among whom he was installed as one of the smaller satraps or assistant satraps of the Napoleonic regime. By disposition he was an eighteenth-century cosmopolitan, holding that the differences between races derived from the material conditions of geography, climate, and historical customs. The machinery of empire, extending its rule through blood and iron, brought both political subjection and social and legal reorganization to a Germany which, long divided into scores of principalities, seemed to Beyle to have slumbered in feudal darkness. The Germany of ancient Gothic towns and villages, so little changed, with their crooked streets, and old wood-and-plaster houses with high, pointed roofs, the servants and peasants still wearing ancient costumes and livery, all this was a full century away from Paris, so greatly transformed by the Revolution. Napoleon overturned their kingdoms and principalities, moved duchies such as Brunswick, where Beyle served, into new kingdoms such as Westphalia, spread civil rights and his modernized code of law—yet inspired an intense nationalism, like that of unified France, hitherto almost unknown to the Germans. After the Battle of Jena, the *Tugendbund*, the new patriotic "league of virtue," agitated the population, causing insurrections to flare up behind the "liberating" armies in twenty different towns. Popular insurrection, which had been the ally of the French revolutionists in earlier years, became their enemy in Germany.

Beyle has described the causes of this awakening of insurrection. "I too had the sacred fire in those days," he told his friend Prosper Mérimée later. "They sent me to Brunswick to raise an extraordinary tribute of five million francs; and I was almost destroyed by the rising of the mob. . . . The Emperor asked who was the official who had done this—and said 'It is well done.' "

Mérimée perhaps reported the affair incorrectly, and it was related by Henri Beyle twenty years after the event. Actually it was his superior, Martial Daru, who, while heading the occupation forces at Brunswick, raised the levies, with considerable mildness and diplomacy for which the Germans later praised him.[1] There was, however, a real uprising in Brunswick on September 4 and 5, 1808, in which Beyle was in danger, and behaved not only with a coolness of spirit that was one of his "ideological" rules, but also, as he writes in a letter dated September 12, 1808, with not a little gallantry.

The disturbance started when a French officer issuing from the theater had a dispute with a German civilian, drew his sword and killed the man. An angry crowd pursued and beat the Frenchman, who was narrowly rescued by French guards and removed to the town hospital, which came under siege. Going out that night, a night of brilliant moonlight, Beyle saw the crowds and heard the people along the street cursing him as a *Verfluchtete Franzosen*; soon blows rained from every side upon his embroidered hat. He was trying to reach the hospital at the end of the street. Suddenly a platoon at the other end opened fire, and the unarmed civilians ran in panic or fell to the ground. By his side an old woman fell dying, "her hands crossed over her stom-

[1]Chuquet, *Stendhal-Beyle*, pp. 93–4.

ach and . . . pierced like Our Saviour's." A beautiful young girl of eighteen sank at his feet trembling and weeping. Fearing that she had been shot, he felt for wounds, then lifted her up reverently and carried her to a protected doorway—thinking always of Sganarelle bearing away the swooning maiden, in Molière's play, and kissing her as he goes. The girl came to, thanked him and, after making a profound reverence, flew off. Then Beyle, amid new fusillades, made his way to the fortified hospital, which was under his jurisdiction, and witnessed the prompt pacifying of the populace by means of reinforcements arriving on the scene. He tells the story lightly in the letter to his sister, without vaunting his part. Yet it is a characteristic episode in that he shows none of the hate and fear of most of Napoleon's soldiers, but rather a humane solicitude.

Later at some battlefield in Austria, he stood brooding over the freshly fallen body of a handsome young enemy soldier, lying with his face toward the French lines. The German's expression seemed to him "dreamy" and tender. In his journal (in which, out of precaution, he now made but few entries) he wrote a compassionate tribute to this symbol of "German courage, faithfulness and goodness."

Truly the times did not favor cosmopolitanism. Yet Beyle, as always moving intellectually against the currents of his time, voyaging with open mind across all of Europe in the next seven years, from the English Channel to Moscow, was reinforced in his cosmopolitanism, and became one of the earlier breed of "good Europeans."

It would be incorrect to say that he liked Germany or the Germans. He made only a feeble effort, during two years at Brunswick, to study the language with a tutor, who coached him respectfully in the morning while he was being shaved. But his knowledge of German literature, then just closing a cycle of glory, remained superficial. He told himself he was done with things like Goethe's *Sorrows of Young Werther* as he was done with Rousseau. The plays of Schiller touched him only a little; the German romantic philosophers he broached, but soon threw aside as "barbarous." In any case he detested metaphysics and spiritualism alike.

But on hearing from Count Daru that Napoleon had recently given himself the benefit of an audience with Goethe—the one after which the Emperor said: "There is a man!"—Beyle was full of envy. Sovereigns, he reflected, and men in high office also, had obvious advantages over other mortals in being able to "escape boredom by communicating at will with great minds."

But leaving aside Goethe, Schiller, and Kant, the German people lived in an abominably cold and wet climate; they ate heavy food, black bread, sausages, sauerkraut; they drank beer, schnapps, and an incredible "champagne" made of white wine and gooseberry jelly! They slept in mountainous eiderdown feather beds that suffocated Beyle, so that he preferred to roll up on the floor in his cloak. Climate and food therefore made them cold in manner and slow-witted, he thought. After one of his humorous sallies in a company of several educated Germans, Beyle noted: "It took a quarter of an hour for four of them to understand my little jokes, the kind you hear more of in one evening in Paris than in a whole month in Germany."

Moreover, they were subservient by habit and tradition and bowed low before titles or uniforms. Beyle sent to his father in Grenoble for a seal having the Beyle family coat of arms, an affair of three silver stars and three silver roses set in a blue field. He now adopted the *particule* and signed himself Henri *de* Beyle, declaring that "these follies are of great importance to the Germans."

On the other hand, these industrious, conscientious Germans who seemed to him so heavy and graceless were an earnest and enthusiastic folk, free of most of the vanity that he considered the curse of the French. They were sincere, unashamed of their sentiments, full of honesty and kindness (then!) and loyalty—these qualities, he said, were "perfectly German"—and they maintained themselves thus, difficult though it was, "even in dealing with the French."

Some reflections upon Germany that he wrote ten years later (in *De l'amour*) were based on his sojourn there from 1806 to 1810, and touch upon the metaphysical and religious side of this people: the Germans were not a "reasoning" people, he maintains:

> The young Germans whom I met . . . are educated by a system that pretends to be philosophical, but which is really nothing but poetry badly written and most obscure, yet, from the moral point of view, approaching the highest and holiest sublimity. It seems to me they inherit from their middle ages . . . a strong disposition to enthusiasm and good faith. . . .
>
> Luther once made a powerful appeal to their moral sense, and the Germans fought each other for thirty years on end to obey their conscience.

Sometimes he spoke of Germany as "the land of imagination and philosophy." But his most penetrating and still timely observation was:

> The difference between the Germans and all other peoples is that they become exalted through meditation instead of calming themselves.[2]

[2]It is a truism among modern historians that French imperialism in 1806, conquering a divided Germany at Jena, awakened the slumbering beast of nationalism. Thenceforth the nation of "poets, thinkers, and musicians" was ready for a Bismarck and the mock-Napoleon, Hitler.

He made a friend of the learned, wealthy Baron von Strombeck, assessor of the Aulic court at nearby Wolfenbüttel, who often invited Beyle to his château and wrote of him as a young Frenchman of "scientific culture and the greatest vivacity and ingenuousness." He also met the Von Bülows and even the Wolfenbüttels, descendants of the ancient rulers of Brunswick. The Germans found him so sympathetic that on one or two occasions he was invited to late supper parties where no other Frenchman was permitted to appear. Thus he was able to observe the noble and wealthy class, and especially their women, whom he termed blond, well formed, endowed with the fairest complexion in the world, but generally wanting in "temperament." Whereas for French and Italian women life began usually *after* marriage, German girls, once married, subsided into virtuous dullness and simply bore children. In courting their ladies German lovers used no subtlety, no double-ententres, no "transports," but only hung about them like spaniels, gazing with lovesick eyes.

For his own amusement Beyle one evening determined to make violent love to one of those Brunswick beauties who looked to him like an imitation Greek statue—"perhaps without a soul?" Deliberately, and in the presence of her dumb, devoted fiancé, he assailed her with his attentions and compliments, until the German swain was reduced to despair.

But soon he warmed to the chase; his eyes haunted the graceful figure of this young girl, Wilhelmina, or "Minna" von Griesheim, who was the daughter of a German general. She was coquettish, high-spirited, and plainly *did* have a soul, for, long afterward, he wrote in his memoirs of "the blond and charming Minna . . . that soul of the North, such as I had never seen in Italy or France." Minna played Haydn and Mozart for him, she danced with him, but made it clear that her hand was pledged to a young German who had the honorable intention of marrying her.

And what were Monsieur *de* Beyle's intentions?

"Will you receive me after you are married?" he would whisper to her.

"Oh, that will not take place for a long time," she would reply brightly.

Beyle exhausted himself in efforts and stratagems calculated to move her heart. He had a mania for holding hands, or even more, during carriage rides. "What prudent subterfuges I resorted to in order to pinch the hips of Fräulein von . . . !" his journal records on July 4, 1807. He would ravish kisses from her stealthily when he met her alone on a stairway. Once he pretended to be dropping out of the race and tattooed the hips of another young woman, a Fräulein von Treuenfels. Yet nothing availed.

He knew a few "delicious moments" to be treasured in his memory, but admitted: "I do not know why she [Minna] makes me pay so dearly for anything she gives me." He thought that he inspired in her a touch of "amorous ecstasy," by his declarations that he loved her desperately, that he would stop at no sacrifice, no folly for her sake. Yet she was his match, German or not, and while permitting herself to be entertained, held him off skillfully.

Describing the German way of love, ten years later (for this subject was always one of overweening interest to him during all his continental voyages), he wrote of an affair between a "Captain Salviati" (really Beyle) and a German belle named Minna. The "Minna" he speaks of here might perhaps permit herself to be seduced, but once in love she was equal to a tragic fidelity; instead of laughing over the misadventure as a French or Italian woman might, she would take it hard:

> On a journey to Brocken this truly beautiful young woman had leaned upon his shoulder while sleeping, or feigning to sleep; a sudden jolt threw her into his arms, he caressed her body, but she withdrew to the other side of the carriage. He reflected: she is not impregnable, but he believed that on the morrow she would kill herself for her fault. It is certain that he loved her passionately, that she loved him too, that they saw each other often, and she was without reproach; but the sun is very pale at [Brunswick], the province is minute. . . . In their most passionate tête-à-têtes Kant and Klopstock were always present among the company.[3]

Minna, who became known in German annals for the beauty she preserved even in old age, as for the romantic attachments she inspired, forgot Beyle, and knew nothing of his later career. He set her down as one of the twelve women who had most fascinated him. But as the spring passed and summer approached in 1807 he was forced to admit that science had helped him little. "In all humility the adventure with Minna was a lost battle," he concluded somberly. "Must learn not to waste time."

On hunting trips which he took with the Baron von Strombeck, he sometimes stopped at an inn in the country, and distracted himself by a casual debauch with some flaccid chambermaid. In the autumn of that same year, he also formed a discreet connection with a certain

[3] *De l'amour*, Chapter LVIII.

Fräulein Knabelhaber in Brunswick, who was the kept mistress of a rich Hollander residing there.

It was his maxim that we must seek new passions when the old ones could not be satisfied.

"I have cured myself of my love for Minnette. I go every three or four days, for physical needs, to Karlotte Knabelhaber. . . . I am very pleased with myself over this," he notes, November 7, 1807.

Yet Minna, or Minnette, was all to him. The very sky seen a year later at sunset after a storm over the Rhine valley reminded him of her smile, and he wrote: "Germany will always have the face of Minnette for me."

2

After the overthrow of Prussia, the later defeat of the Russian armies, and the peace of Tilsit, Napoleon must needs deal again with Austria. From Silesia and Poland to Spain and back to the Danube Valley, each victory was more costly, and each led the great military dictator to new wars. The obscure commissary of war was therefore pulled hither and yon by these sweeping movements. He made swift carriage journeys to the Ministry of War at Paris, or to Hanover and Berlin. On more than one of these he passed the little Prussian town at the Elbe that was the birthplace of Winckelmann, the great historian of art and antiquities in Italy. From its resonant German name he undoubtedly drew his so mystifying pen name: *Stendhal.* In December 1808 he quit Brunswick and went to Strasbourg, called there by the order of Count Pierre Daru, who assembled all twenty-eight commissaries of the Grand Army to organize the service of supply for the new campaign in Austria.

Napoleon said of Daru: "He has iron in him." He worked for the hardest taskmaster in the world, preparing medical, engineering, hospital, munitions, and food supplies to the last detail, often working fifteen hours a day, sometimes going entirely without sleep. Beyle, whom he liked to berate as a "harebrained fellow," had shown energy and intelligence in Brunswick, supervising the fiscal affairs of the little state all by himself during his second year there; and he was recommended for promotion by the stern Daru. Though destined to fight behind the lines, in the Danubian conflict of 1809, and therefore despised by the combat officers, Beyle was regarded by his superiors as a resourceful man who could "brazen" his way through almost any emergency. Work was piled on him: he must ride hurriedly here and there, to wrest food and fodder from the infuriated peasants; he must improvise a hospital for this division, an artillery park for another division. Sometimes he went without sleep for three days on end, until finally he sank under a table on a heap of straw, at some village inn along the road, unconscious of the fact that an officer, covered with bloody wounds, lay dead beside him.

Then Daru himself would come thundering up, wake him, and order him and his assistants off to the next town to commandeer new quarters and supplies for the moving mass of men.

For his own part he always preferred peace to war. But since it was plain the war must continue, he reconciled himself to the excitement of constant change, the lure of new adventures and opportunities offering themselves from day to day. War he saw in its appearance of infinite, yet organized, confusion behind the lines of Napoleon's armies. But he saw it with a detached and considered spirit such as he used afterward to describe Waterloo with such original effect, though he was not even present on that historic occasion.

From Ingolstadt, as they advanced toward the fields of Wagram, he wrote letters picturing the "queer disorder that war produces" in the shape of debris everywhere upon the site of yesterday's battle: shoes, helmets, clothing, straw, broken carts, wheels, and always pieces of paper scattered in all directions. There were soldiers who rode past him, singing on their way to battle; there were others who rode back, silent, wounded, solaced by priests. Curiously enough there were also wagons carrying strolling players who followed the army at their own risk, entertaining them when they bivouacked at night.

On May 3, 1809, he writes from Wels, in Austria:

> I really felt the desire to vomit while riding through Ebersberg [the scene of a bloody clash] and seeing the wheels of my carriage cause the entrails of poor little chasseurs, half burnt, to fly up all around us. I began to talk to the other officers in order to distract myself from this horrible sight; as a consequence my comrades believe I have a heart of steel.

He jested, he chattered as they rode through those burning villages, over bridges blocked by mounds of corpses, while the other officers turned pale and fell silent or crossed themselves. But despite his outward composure he begged his friend Faure to send him some book which would absorb his imagination, such as Chateaubriand's newly published *Les Martyrs*.

As always he felt himself alone. "My fellow officers esteemed me but disliked me," he remarks. And he in turn detested the swaggering swordsmen, the colonels of twenty-five or thirty, whose physical courage he held cheap, while he felt himself bored and victimized by their "childish" talk. "Posterity," he said, "will never know the follies these men committed when off the field of battle." They were but "loud-mouthed" fighting men, he was convinced, who hated anyone who dared to *think*. "A wall of bronze raised itself between them and me."

But at last they entered Vienna, which to Beyle meant music, inward contentment, and well-being. He fell ill, as a result of exhaustion and exposure, and at Martial Daru's invitation spent some days recuperating at the beautiful castle of Laxenburg in the suburbs. But he was able to return to Vienna to attend the solemn funeral services for Joseph Haydn, who, amid the disasters that had befallen his country, had lately given up the ghost. The tribute of Mozart in his famous "Requiem" opened to Beyle new resources of beauty, a rich consolation for present ills.

Ancient Vienna contained all the amenities of civilization, and to Beyle looked almost as beautiful as Milan. The young officers of Napoleon's army, after the horrors and sufferings they had endured, as earlier in Italy, took over the proverbially merry women of Vienna by right of conquest. In this the young Beyle was little different from the others.

But the future philosopher-novelist pursued happiness with a more conscious and experimental craft than his contemporaries, compiling as he went the most candid, the most precisely documented of journals. Unfortunately the journal of his years in Germany was lost, and with it the full story of Minna von Griesheim. By the time he reached Vienna the pace of his life had grown so furious that his entries are made sometimes after lapses of six months. From passages in his letters and from brief allusions long afterward we learn that there was a certain "Babet," or "Babette," who entered his life at this period and became the center of a raging drama of passion.

Was it with Babette that he remained for a long time shut up in the empty rooms of a great castle? Or was this the experience of a comrade officer? Was it over Babette that he fought the second of his duels with a fellow officer, to which he also referred vaguely? He speaks of having committed the folly of sending a sumptuous gift of flowers openly to a woman he admired in the presence of her official lover, a colonel of artillery; hence the duel. In the same summer of 1809 there is mention of an illness, an illness that perhaps did him little honor.

On August 6, 1809, he writes to his sister that a "horrible gloom" weighs him down. "The object of my passion is almost entirely lost without my having derived the slightest happiness. . . . Besides the matter of a little sickness interposed to prevent me from profiting from her inclination." He recovers and walks in the beautiful Prater; the operas of Cimarosa and Mozart's *Don Giovanni* also serve as restoratives. Finally he vows that to "soothe himself" he will, in two weeks, "pursue another passion." Soon the second of the two objects of his heart possesses him exclusively. This was a truly ambitious, a most daring enterprise.

3

Two years before, when Beyle was still stationed at Brunswick, the Countess Alexandrine Daru had arrived in the city and made a brief halt overnight while en route to Berlin, where she was to join her husband. How beautiful, how imposing, how French she had seemed, even in her traveling garments. To Beyle, *grande dame* that she was, and ornament of the hastily concocted court of Napoleon, she fairly glittered in the depths of melancholy Germany. And he who already owed so much to her favor looked up to her humbly, much as a courtier does to his queen.

He had made every preparation for her comfort at the best quarters in the town.

"Come, my dear Beyle, let us converse together," she had said, as if she thoroughly enjoyed talk with him. And he who feared that women did not always enjoy looking at him exerted himself all the more through the power of the word. Her manner was affectionate, almost bordering on tenderness.

At dawn the next morning, like a gallant young commissary, he journeyed on horseback over thirty miles along her road to arrange for the protection of her convoy, the provisioning of her horses and guards, until the next fortified place was reached. On his way back he met her on the road and she descended from her carriage to take refreshments with him at a wayside tavern.

She was most grateful to her *cher cousin* for his many attentions, and he was so happy that he could scarcely say a word to her. "Our eyes spoke," he thought.

Perhaps, she suggested, as they parted, that he might come to Berlin and entertain her there too? But the count brusquely ruled that duty forbade such a mission for his subordinate.

He had seen her once more the following year, during a journey to

Paris, when her husband was still abroad. He had come to her drawing room, dressed in the height of fashion, looking like one of the Incredibles. Had he not been told even in his childhood that one accomplished everything through women? Napoleon had recently reorganized his government under a Council of State, with numerous masters of request assisting the councilors and some three hundred auditors (or secretaries) attached to its ministries. Beyle was aflame to be appointed to an auditorship, which might open the way eventually to a ministry. Eight thousand francs a year! The thought of such promotion, he confessed, "left me without repose for three whole days and nights together." He might, one day, use his wits to "manage" the powerful Daru, perhaps even become the confidant of Bonaparte himself.

On learning of his designs the countess assured him that she would plead his cause before her husband. But on the next visit there were many other elegant young men in her drawing room. She spoke to him briefly, and gave her attention to others whom he felt inferior to himself in character and wit. Such were women of society, such were the humiliations of a courtier.

But now, a year later, in September 1809, she appeared in Vienna and took Beyle for her cavalier. Count Daru toiled night and day with the Emperor over the details of the peace and his approaching marriage with the Archduchess Marie-Louise of Austria. Thus it was Beyle who rode everywhere with her to see monuments, churches, and castles in the beautiful wooded hills outside of Vienna.

What a woman! How zestful, how brimming with energy. At the Leopoldsberg castle she insisted upon climbing all the long way up rickety old ladders to the topmost turret, while he panted after her, exclaiming over her audacity, longing but not daring to dally with her. And once more her humor with him was affectionate. He had the air "of one who loves timidly without hope of reward"; she, of one "who wished to draw him into a closer circle of familiarity." She inquired after his health, even teasing him about the belles of Brunswick. He strove to be all polish and courtliness; but also wished that he knew how to achieve that "tone of gallantry which permits one to say everything, since nothing has the air of being said seriously." When they were alone together she melted a little more; when she descended from her carriage he held the lovely woman in his arms for an instant, and that, as he notes with a sigh in his journal, gave him "no little pleasure." Often, he thought, their eyes spoke "as in novels."

Finally she approached the limit of confidence. She told him her story, which was the story of her marriage. Even at nineteen she had grown tired of balls and parties and the frivolity and cynicism of young men. So that "when one man [Pierre Daru], was pointed out to her as having a certain age, indeed almost twice her own, she chose him." She did this with the idea that marriages of inclination are unhappy. "I did not want to marry someone I loved."

In a mood of reverie and self-confession she also admitted that "she had never known love. . . . Perhaps happiness lay there. This notion was fortified by her curiosity." And Beyle promised himself to stimulate this curiosity.[4] Alexandrine had borne her husband four children, but up to now, he surmised, had known none of the pleasures of the soul, and only perhaps the pleasure of the senses.

As she went on to speak of her passing youth—though she was but twenty-seven—of her preoccupation with family and social duties, Beyle was beside himself with hope. To his mind, often so self-deluded, yet also so penetrating, her remarks revealed that she did not love her now middle-aged husband. And how could she love that oxlike man, who worked night and day and gave so little thought to the uxorious amenities and refinements that meant everything to Beyle?

They were often alone together, and though she was guarded in tone she grew more tender than ever. He had many opportunities to "attack," but was, as ever, timid, ever "in love with love," fascinated by the process of the campaign itself, and all too much disposed, as he later realized, "to pause at each step and examine or enjoy his situation." To hand her her gloves, to have her return them to him to hold for an instant, to play with them, caress them as if they were her hands, then return them smilingly, and kiss the hand she finally offered as they parted—all this was heaven to him.

It was noticed how he squired her about, while Count Daru was busy in the council room of the Emperor. Soon his fellow officers in Vienna credited him with occupying the status of the official lover of the Countess Daru, and in his fatuousness and vanity he thoroughly enjoyed the discreet compliments they paid him under this head.

Was it a proper thing to do, to seek to steal the heart of his chief's

---

[4]These observations are set down in that strange fragment of analytical recollection entitled *Consultation pour Banti,* which he dictated in utmost confidence to his friend Louis Crozet, in Paris, in 1811. It was a "scientific" and "ideological" record of his campaign for Alexandrine Daru (who is listed under many different disguises: the Countess Palfy, the Duchess B., Madame Z., in order to confuse any stranger finding his private papers). *Mélanges intimes,* I, pp. 66–9, Divan edition. At this point Beyle also makes the further reflection: *foutre avec plaisir d'âme et plaisir des sens réunis, jusqu'ici elle n'a guère eu que le plaisir des sens.* The rites of love must be performed, he suggests, "with pleasure of the soul and all the senses combined" and not merely "pleasure of the senses alone."

wife? He felt a profound antipathy to Pierre Daru, always behaved with reserve toward him, feared the lash of his tongue, hated his maxims as he did his conventional literary tastes. And if he felt attracted to Alexandrine, beautiful, womanly, high-willed, "born to rule"—hence so appealing to his masochistic tastes—it was true also that he was consumed by "a frenzy of ambition." He must win the countess, gain her influence, become a member of the Council of State, wear a cross of honor, enjoy at least a baronetcy and a prefecture. To his father, whose fortunes had also improved, he wrote mentioning his hopes for advancement and demanding ever larger sums of money—as much as six thousand francs a year, to be raised by anticipating his entire inheritance—so that he might be enabled to live in a style fitting his ambitions. The erstwhile stern republican even besought his father to purchase a noble title for him. Before leaving for Paris, Alexandrine promised again that she would do her utmost to win him an appointment as auditor.

She left Vienna late in November 1809. As she stepped into her carriage she had tears in her eyes, which he fondly thought were for him. She bade him adieu as her "dear cousin" and kissed him before all the company. Though she wore a veil, he felt the kiss was given with all her heart.

For two months longer he remained in Austria. His quartermaster duties took him for a brief, enchanting tour to the rich, vine-clad plains of Hungary, where he gathered grain for the occupying armies. But in February 1810 he was back in Paris at last, and flew to Alexandrine's. Her gift to him, bestowed with shining eyes, was the news that his appointment as auditor was definitely promised in the highest quarters.

4

"Nothing is lacking to me," he wrote his sister, shortly after being confirmed in his new office, August 1, 1810. As one of the three hundred auditors whom Napoleon had selected from lists of the most talented and deserving young men in France, he served the Council of State. He now entered that hierarchy of five or six hundred top officials through whom the Empire was ruled. This made him, as he assured his family, *un grand personnage*, and brought the comfortable salary of five thousand francs a year. It had been awarded him at the climax of a furious social campaign during which he saw to it that good reports and praise of him came to the Count Daru from every side. But in addition to his secretarial post, he was given the office of *adjoint*, or assistant to the intendant general of the imperial household (in effect, aide to the grand chamberlain) who was Count Pierre Daru. In November 1811, Daru rose even higher, to become Secretary of State. Beyle's second function brought him an added six thousand francs a year, and its duties were pleasant enough: the care of the furnishings, tapestries, and art objects in the Emperor's palaces; and under this head, the executions of the orders of the Empress Marie-Louise. He also sometimes assisted the grand master of ceremonies, the Marquis Louis-Philippe de Ségur, that pompous aristocrat who went over to Napoleon. In a letter of 1810 he remarks:

My office is in a superb suite in the Palace of the Invalides, overlooking its gardens and even the forest of Meudon to the east of Paris. The official duties of my post can be discharged in about ten hours a week.

But as if all this were not enough, he now pestered his father to advance him additional sums of money for living expenses. In confidential letters to his sister he prompts her to play upon his father's pride, to paint a dazzling picture of the advantages of rank and power he may gain by further augmenting his social position:

Speak to our father, so that he does not break my neck *by covetousness. Rouse the vanity, the overruling passion of our French. . . . Speak to self-love and vanity. . . . I understand very well that my conduct appears very singular eyed from the province, but speak* . . . repeat my reasonings in twenty different ways. . . . *Rouse, rouse, rouse the vanity!*

The reasoning was that he needed six or seven thousand more than he earned, so that after a year or two of his novitiate as auditor, he might become a mighty prefect at thirty thousand a year!

At length, by signing a contract with his father for the partial entailment of his estate, Henri Beyle obtained the necessary sums, though the baronetcy waited. Promptly he established himself in a fashionable apartment in the Rue Neuve du Luxembourg, and acquired a cabriolet, two horses, a coachman, and a manservant. He even installed a cheerful little opera girl in his apartment, a Mlle. Angelina Bereyter, who was to be his humble concubine. She sang for him from his favorite composers, Mozart and Cimarosa; she made him a fire, warmed his bed, and at midnight always had a cold supper of roast partridge and champagne ready for him when he returned from his social calls. What could be more perfect?

Report of Henri *de* Beyle's "magnificent career" and of his brilliant style of living spread as far as Grenoble. His very bourgeois brother-in-law, François Périer-Lagrange, who had lately married Pauline, rolled his eyes and lifted up his hands in dismay when on a visit to Paris he saw Henri's spanking horses and cabriolet, his engravings and rugs, his sumptuous breakfasts at the Café Hardy. Henri would change his orders repeatedly, roar at the waiters, send things back. "Quite a coxcomb," muttered one of the waiters in Périer's presence, and Henri, overhearing it, was highly pleased.

Only a short time before, in the autumn of 1808, when in Paris on a brief mission from the German front, he had pointed out to Félix Faure, as they strolled in the Tuileries Gardens, how markedly the tone and manners of the capital had changed from those of republican days. Paris was indeed the "new Babylon." With a knowing eye, Napoleon lavished titles and favors upon each brigadier general; he also established the Legion of Honor for the regiments of bureaucrats who labored for him. While the soldiers enriched themselves with the spoils of conquered lands, the bureaucrats at home plundered the public purse, as Beyle himself later describes the scene in the illuminating social notes of his unfinished biography of Napoleon. In a golden horde they thronged to the banquets of the newly made marshals, dukes, and ministers, the peasants of yesterday, lording it in their big mansions. They came also to the balls at the Emperor's palace of St. Cloud, peacocks in gold-braided uniforms and tight-fitting breeches, wearing all their *cordons* and crosses, while their ladies appeared by their side in a *grande décolleté* which passed all previous bounds.

Beyle, with his sharp eye and his mania for observation, attended many of these "brilliant soirées," including mask balls at which the Princesses Caroline Murat and Pauline Borghese danced in the scant costumes of savages, with handsome generals clad lightly as Greek gods or Roman slaves. He watched Prince Metternich paying violent court to the Queen of Sicily, or the snobbish old Marquis de Ségur, his chief at the Council of State, attempting vainly to do his part as grand master of ceremonies and elevate the lax tone of the imperial court. Affected in speech and crushing in manner, this aristocrat, who had been ambassador to the court of Catherine of Russia, impressed him as a "Lilliputian" in the uniform of a minister. "Was this empty and trivial man, with his mind 'a labyrinth of pettiness,' the great diplomat, the famous historian of Frederick II?" he asked himself. His notebooks of this period were filled with mocking sketches of the characters he saw, studies that he hoped someday to complete.

He himself came splendidly accoutered to these functions; he had a bright eye, a good leg, and also wore the extremely snug breeches that were in vogue in a period marked by the nineteenth century's last flare-up of color and suggestiveness in male costume. One of his notes concerning a court lady with whom he danced reads: "My white breeches have great effect upon Mme. Boucher. . . ." Other more or less noble ladies, though in their middle age, often regarded him with the beady eye of the nymphomaniac. Still others, noting the sprightliness of his talk, boldly invited him to call upon them. "With your talents," said one of these, "I will *teach* you to advance your career. Alone, you will fall and break your neck." She had beautiful arms, but was nearly sixty. Was it of her that Beyle told the story of a woman of the court who in old age accepted as her lover a hideously ugly man? When her friends protested and asked her why she gave such a man her favor, she replied: "Yes, but I have taken him for his *mind!*"[5]

The cosmopolitan Baron von Strombeck, his hospitable friend of Brunswick days, arriving in Paris in 1811, gives objective evidence, in a letter home, of the high influence at the court already enjoyed by Beyle, when still in his twenties:

> My friend Henri de Beyle [*sic*] Inspector General of the Crown Palaces and auditor to the Grand Council, received me as I would have hoped, and presented me to his friends and relatives, notably Pierre Daru, member of the Grand Council, who exercises an immense influence. It was my friend Beyle who insisted also on having me presented to the Emperor, assuring me, and he was quite right, that I would enjoy the remembrance of having seen Napoleon all my days.[6]

Few men loved society more than Henri Beyle. At this period he had open to him the salon of the Countess Daru, his good genius. He was likewise an habitué of another equally fashionable salon, that of the Countess Beugnot, wife of the Minister of Finance, an accomplished matron of middle age, who possessed learning and wit and happened to have as her official lover a merry friend of Beyle's named Pépin de Bellisle.

In these days he read few books and wrote little even in his diaries. "I have no ideas any more," he said to himself. His plan to become a

[5] *Souvenirs d'égotisme*, p. 143. This brief fragment, written in 1831, has numerous notes on the Empire period, which Beyle intended to expand in his *Napoleon*.

[6] C. Simon: *Souvenirs de Strombeck et de Spach sur Stendhal*, p. 6.

"bard" was indefinitely suspended. At times he might reproach himself for passing his days and his evenings "with the poor rich, gathered together without loving each other and without gaiety or wit." Yet the next evening he would bubble with joy at being invited to the salon of Mme. Sophie Gay or at meeting beautiful women like Mme. Récamier, or Mme. Tallien, widow of the great Revolutionary leader, who had figured in the colorful memoirs of Marmontel.

He became worldlier and more libertine, spoke of his own talent for affairs, pushed for an official career for which he felt himself more and more suited. Yet he felt always the need, not of some common woman to entertain him, but of "a mistress whom he could love." And why not the most brilliant, the most remarkable of women? With longing eyes he looked always at his countess, asking himself: "Does she love me?"

One day in the spring of 1810, walking with the Count Daru and the countess in the park at Longchamps, he remarks: ". . . *In the middle of the walk a glance of love.*" And this even though her husband walked by her side. Her tone also, as he confides to his journal, now has "no trace of superiority, but is that used by persons who begin to love each other."

Throughout 1810 the affair drifted along while Beyle warily watched for the opportunity to bring his siege to a victorious conclusion. On several occasions he was invited to visit Mme. Daru at her country villa of Bècheville near Meulan. Usually the host himself was away, but there was other company, including two lady companions and two other young men who were, like Beyle, nominally "pretenders" or aspirants to the countess's affections. Playing uncle to her four children, reading them nursery tales or telling them hilarious stories of his own invention, he would send them into gales of laughter, which pleased her. When in the morning she put on a new white dress—a fresh and beautiful thing, "which perfectly delineated her form, and was so short it revealed her feet!"—he was sure it was for *his* sake. She wore a bouquet of roses, and he would finger it ecstatically, until she gave him a quick reproving tap on the hand.

One warm night in June 1810, they all went in a party to visit the site of Rousseau's last retreat at Ermenonville. There was much pleasantry after dinner at the inn where they put up, when Mme. Daru, reclining luxuriously on a sofa—with Beyle beside her, holding her hand, covertly caressing her leg—teased him pitilessly over his pretended passion for a Mme. Genêt who was one of those present. Beyle, who was in rare form that night, went up to Mme. Genêt and gave a wild and lifelike imitation of an old and too familiar lover, which kept the party in high spirits. "The tone of our little circle was very gay, in fact perfect, and verged on carefree voluptuousness." Bidding him good night as if she were highly pleased with him, the countess gave him a "good and *suffientemente saporito* kiss," which set him dreaming of love and the blue islands in the Lake Maggiore. He was sure he might have "had" her that night if he had but been more "enterprising," and if the other two ladies were not there.

At dinner one evening someone was describing how attractive was the new lover of a lady well known to those present, and Alexandrine Daru interrupted breathlessly to ask: "Is he young? Is he amiable? Is he witty?" And Beyle flattered himself that she had *him* in mind; for did not her most persistent admirer have exactly these three traits?

When he saw her in company she was approachable, and led him on before the others as if it were a game. But the next time he saw her alone she would be silent, constrained, even cool in tone. Walking with her in her garden, he paused at one point, took his cane and traced the letter "A" in the gravel path. She merely laughed dryly and walked on.

At this juncture he recalled the advice of worldlier men than he, and determined to try *un petit froid*, or a little coquettish coolness, himself. He affected indifference to her, arrived late for dinner, and bore her reproaches calmly. The plump little *chanteuse*, Angelina Bereyter, who waited for him at his house each night in the winter of 1811, helped him to maintain his composure before the countess.

Had she heard of his mistress? In Paris everyone gossiped infernally. There was even talk now of having Henri marry an heiress, Jenny Leschenault, with a fortune of 800,000 francs. It was his friend Félix Faure who had lately brought forward this proposal; and his family warmly seconded it. But the idea of binding himself in marriage filled him with horror. "*She is a nullity,*" he wrote his sister in English. "*The heart is for nothing in this affair.*" His heart pined for Alexandrine, who showed but mounting reserve and coldness toward him in the spring of 1811, a year and six months after the pursuit had begun.

Angelina Bereyter, to be sure, was all tenderness; but in her arms every night he soon wearied of the pleasure she gave, and remarked that he was often "compelled to think of another. . . ."

One spring morning in 1811 he lay abed late, after Angelina had left him, brooding. It was the morning when the long-awaited birth of Napoleon's heir, the King of Rome, was announced and church bells tolled solemnly all over the city, a sound that always induced reverie and melancholy in him.

What was he becoming, he asked himself? He had "leaped into the midst of the great rout" that danced to the tune played by one imperious man in the glittering capital of pleasure that was Paris. His democratic beliefs were submerged. He was growing stout, surfeited, and often asked himself if "physical contentment alone did not now deaden a great deal of his imagination?" Of his opera girl he wrote: "One hundred and twenty nights *without love!*" Perhaps his youth was passing early, a consequence of too prolonged pursuit of physical pleasure. Where were the *great moments* he had counted upon? "Is it then utterly impossible for me to fall in love again? So young, must I renounce the heart?"

The skirmishing with Alexandrine must give way to more decisive measures. On one recent occasion he had even felt that she looked at him mockingly, as if aware of his constraint and embarrassment before her.

"*Virtue is ridicul . . .*" he had written at that time in his queer code. "*. . . She thinks me restrained by somewhat . . .* but I must have her understand that it is not out of respect for her but solely out of the fear *di non esser corrisposto.*" (That is, of not being loved in return.) For how large a role was given to pride in this most dangerous game he was playing. She was the wife of one of Napoleon's most powerful lieutenants; he must have her. She was pious, the dutiful mother of five children (by 1811), with a reputation singularly unblemished; he must have her. He urged himself to be bolder; yet the fear that a final crushing rebuff might send all his dreams and hopes of advantage tumbling about his head held him back.

5

Analysis and, above all, logic were everything to Beyle even in love, as his friend Prosper Mérimée later pointed out. "By dissection one spoils the most beautiful woman," he himself had written on June 7, 1810, in his journal, yet he must dissect.

Tormented by doubt, he finally went to his old friend Louis Crozet one day in April 1811 and opened his heart to him. He described his uncertainties and self-questionings and asked his friend to advise him as to what course it was best to follow, what tactics he must use.

Like Beyle, Crozet was an impassioned ideologue and dialectician, and devoted to what they both called the new principles of "Beylism." Both of them agreed, therefore, that in the interests of scientific truth and right judgment, they should hold a *consultation*, a conference or inquest, over the whole question, examining all its pros and cons, all possible alternatives, and all the evidence concerning the persons involved. In a spirit of complete detachment, they would search for the correct solution of the problem. Not for a moment did they consider, for instance, the feelings or rights of the husband in the case, who had done so much to befriend Beyle. Beylism took no account of husbands.

Crozet asked questions; Beyle made answer, and both were written down by Crozet, who, entering fully into the spirit of the thing, acted as judge and attorney at once. The *procès verbal* or proceedings that compose the *Consultation en faveur de la Duchesse de B. pour Banti*, done in Crozet's hand, remained hidden among Beyle's posthumous papers until they were unearthed and published almost a century later. What seemed at first a most puzzling piece of legal fiction was finally understood as giving light upon the workings of Beyle's mind and his relations with the Countess Daru, nowhere else so satisfactorily explained. It is by all odds one of the most curious documents in all the history or literature of love.

Beyle (Banti) testifies for and against himself; he makes full confession of his feelings and motives. And whatever decision they may arrive at, he is determined to abide by it and follow the course indicated.[7]

The "judge" (Crozet) proceeds to question the man who, as a precaution, is named in the document, "Banti." Methodically, the inquest is divided into various heads such as:

Should Banti have the Duchess or not?

"Banti," in reply, reports all details of the family background, education, and interests of "Madame de B." She is described as being wearied by the pleasures of wealth, social position, and court life, which she has enjoyed since the age of nineteen, when she was married. She longs for new and real sensations to occupy her mind and heart; her whole appearance, her vivacity, her *embonpoint*, all sug-

[7]Like many of his posthumous and private papers, this was in no sense intended for publication, but exemplified his principle that we could best study ourselves by examining the intimate record of our lives as moving from point to point in time. The journals and the *Consultation pour Banti* were written therefore only for his own *future* guidance. Cf. *Mélanges intimes* I, 49–96, Divan ed. (First published by C. Striyenski, in *Soirées du Stendhal Club*, Paris 1904.)

gest a warm or passionate nature. She has been reared in the most pious manner, by a cold and narrow-minded mother, for a life of responsibility and virtue, but much is lacking to her. Her husband, "Burrhus," a man of great power, is overburdened by work, avoids society, provides her with little entertainment, perhaps gives her little pleasure. With age he has grown sluggish and dull-witted, thereby opening opportunities for "Banti." The *procès verbal* runs:

> CROZET: What is her idea of Banti? What would she think of him for having shown ingratitude toward the "duke"?
>
> BEYLE: She thinks of Banti as a man who has experienced and inspired the most violent sentiments, and *whom no feeling of fear or duty can withhold from seeking the satisfaction of his passions.*
>
> CROZET: Would she hold Banti for a long time?
>
> BEYLE: Too long; under existing conditions of society he is the only lover she can take. He has reached this advantageous position by family relationship and four years' effort.
>
> CROZET: Would she be jealous?
>
> BEYLE: One would think yes. She would be aware that he has had many women, and recall her age and children.
>
> CROZET: Would she feel remorse?
>
> BEYLE: It is probable that she would feel a sense of guilt for having yielded to him; and would reproach herself if he deceived her or left her later.
>
> CROZET: What of her husband? Her influence over him?
>
> BEYLE: He has simple bourgeois tastes. He is afraid that his wife may be unfaithful to him, and that this may become known in Paris. But as he is warned that a young wife must have some distractions—lest she form "dangerous habits"—he appears reconciled to having her entertained by young admirers such as his cousin. . . . It is not the horns of the cuckold he fears so much as scandal.

Thus, solemnly, the conclusion is reached that: "a lover is necessary to her happiness."

But the next question earnestly propounded by Crozet is: "*What are the advantages for him in seducing Mme. de B.?*"

The answer as given by the methodical Beyle, point by point, here summarized, is: (1) he would be "following out the inclinations of his character"; he would terminate the ceremonial form of their relationship, and end his own constraint or repression; (2) he would "win great social advantages"; (3) he would pursue further his study of the human passions upon a higher plane; (4) he would satisfy "honor" and pride, for "it would be fearful for him to see another person take the place which he had not the force to win. . . . If he does not have Mme. de B. he will reproach himself all his life."

A footnote appended to this document in Beyle's hand concludes with the decision:

> The best counsel:
> Attack!
> Attack!
> Attack![8]

Here we have the young Beyle, all "sensitivity" and yet all savant passion for formulation and analysis. As with Banti, so it lies in his character "to see always in imagination the end of a love affair even before its consummation." Few men ever lived who brought so vast and comprehensive a strategy to the lists of love. But with so much foreseen or elaborately prepared for, the occasion for surprise was diminished, the dangers of anticlimax augmented.

6

In the last week of May he journeyed to the château of the Darus, where he had been invited once more to spend a week. His spirit was reflective, watchful, ready to seize upon any opening, but determined not to "force events." He found the countess, her aged mother, and a companion and confidante, Mme. Dubignon, on hand as usual when he came.

The decisive scenes that followed, Beyle, always addicted to the terms of military science, defined in his journal as "The Battle of Bècheville." He had two nights of insomnia, most uncommon for him. On the second night he paced up and down in the park of the château, watching the moon set behind tragic clouds. He told himself:

> The army I command is filled with terror and considers the undertaking beyond its force. This is what I told myself, with bitter rage, at a quarter past eleven on May 30, walking alone in the garden, after everyone had gone to sleep. Thick clouds passed over the face of the moon, and I considered their movement and thought of the charming mythology of Ossian to distract my mind from the discontent I felt.

At the thought that his suit might be rejected, he was ready to blow out his brains. Yet he rallied his spirits and put up a brave front. It

[8]This footnote to *Banti* was actually written eight years later, in 1819, on the occasion of another great amorous enterprise, but there is little doubt that it was the consensus of the "court" in the case of 1811 also.

came to him that the best plan would be to make his declaration in a manner that avoided the overly serious or tragic. By using humor or a casual tone in speaking of his passion, he would run less risk of incurring Alexandrine's ill will.

Walking up and down with her in the garden after breakfast, the next morning he began to speak in a rather sprightly way of the question of his proposed marriage with the heiress Mlle. Leschenault (whom he had not even met). It was as if he merely sought her counsel as a wise friend. Alexandrine then gave him a charming little sermon on the obligations of a husband who has entered upon the wedded state. But as they returned to the house, she seemed strangely moved, lowering her head so that he could not see her eyes under her large straw bonnet. The children pounced upon him for stories; but as he played with them, he watched her sitting in a corner, her face turned to the window. She seemed pale, her eyelids were lowered as if with the effort to hold back tears. "*I believed to see in those tears an evident proof of her love for me,*" he wrote that night in his journal.

But a little later, while talking with her companion, Mme. Dubignon, he received quite a shock. He had alluded, at one moment, to his own "spirit of enterprise," and this woman who seldom smiled had suddenly burst out laughing at him; then, as suddenly, tried to look serious again. At once he suspected that they had already exchanged confidences about his *want of enterprise.* He grew sad and thoughtful, and inwardly vowed that he must overcome his own "bashfulness" at all costs—he used the English word, which appealed to him as most fitting to his case.

The next day Alexandrine looked pale and weary. In the salon she took up her harp and played and sang a sad air: "It Is Too Late. . . ." The expression with which she sang moved him. While singing, she looked at him fixedly. "The last couplet almost caused me to avert my gaze, so striking was its application to our case." It was a new turn of the knife in the wound, and he felt he must declare himself, come what might.

That second morning, for the day of "combat," he had put on his best striped trousers, on which she complimented him. They walked together in the English garden, while the companion, the grandmother, who was also present, and the children accompanied them at a distance of some fifty feet to the rear. As they paced back and forth, Beyle told himself under his breath that when they reached a certain point, which he considered "B," at the opposite end from "A," he must speak out or kill himself. With a great effort he said: "I may seem like a fool, but in truth I am not happy during this visit at Bècheville." She, pretending to believe that this was owing to his new matrimonial problems, began to speak of them: "Some marry for love, some for ambition. . . . Do you really know this young woman?" But he, vehemently interrupting her, exclaimed that he thought nothing of the heiress, but only of his passion for Alexandrine, for whose sake he would abandon any marriage.

"You feel only friendship for me, while I love you madly," he blurted out.

Thus the battle was engaged: he seized her hand and even tried clumsily to kiss it. She replied that he must not think of such things, but must look on her only as his affectionate cousin and friend. He then declared that he had loved her for eighteen months, had striven to conceal it when they were in Paris, and even tried not to see her, but could bear it no longer. Her evident trouble, her emotion increased. Almost in tears, she said that she was already an old woman, with numerous children, and that she must never think of such things. "Alas," she exclaimed, "young men make such declarations to ladies only in order to go about boasting among themselves that they had done so." Vehemently he denied any such dishonorable intention, but she repeated that she abhorred scandal and gossip and up to now had kept herself "intact." And he, as she implied silently, had the reputation of a rake.

The other two ladies and the children now rejoined them; and Alexandrine, avoiding his gaze, took her two children by the arm, almost leaning upon them, as if she felt weak. In silence they returned to the house. Watching her, he felt as if "she surrounded herself with her children like a rampart"—and there were already five!

After the "Battle of Bècheville," though he continued to hope that he might still wrest something from defeat, their friendship underwent a dying fall. Alexandrine was the victim of a stupid and religious education, he thought; he should have given her long ago the right books to read; should have striven to improve her mind in the desired sense. Yet she was intelligent and discerning enough; she read his wayward character, his dubious motives only too well. When, a few days later, in Paris, he seized a favoring moment to whisper to her again: "I love you," she said almost without hesitating and with a searching look: "It is not *I love you,* but *I love.*"

The last hour at Bècheville had been sad. He had called for his carriage, then felt a longing to stay on. But at the appointed hour a servant came to announce: "The horses are harnessed." And Beyle sprang up with a laugh: "Everything's done!" He explained in the privacy of his journal: "I felt the need to laugh, because I felt such a strong desire to weep." Accepting a cousinly kiss at parting, he rushed away on the road to Paris at high speed.

The formidable Pierre Daru, for all his long absences from home or late hours, had ended by becoming suspicious of his young cousin. Sometimes at table in Paris his impassive gaze was fixed heavily upon him whom he thought but a young fool and rakehell, and he remarked, one day: "One must admit there are some people who have a great deal of cheek."

Was this for the benefit of Henri? Napoleon's powerful Secretary of State could certainly have broken young Beyle's career with a word. But he was a man of character who, it was said, did not fear to speak his mind plainly even to the victor of Austerlitz. He showed no overt fear or jealousy of Henri, but invitations to dinner were spaced at longer intervals. When the young auditor asked permission for a leave of two months, ostensibly to visit his family at Grenoble, but, as Daru knew, really, in order to make a journey to Italy, the leave was quickly promised him for August 1811.

Had not Alexandrine told him that her husband, though he worked night and day, took time to read all the letters that came to her; that he watched over everything lest she make some "compromising step"? And Beyle had written all sorts of follies, he realized, such as the following piece of rhetorical gush:

> In your presence I suffer the most strangely mixed feelings: sometimes the keenest pleasure, at others, hatred of myself, revulsion at the absurd role I play in your life, and my inability even to be away from you for long intervals. . . . Alone with you, I lose all my self-possession and am able to say nothing, whilst you refuse me everything, even your hand. . . .

It was like Rousseau at his worst, or like the *Sorrows of Young Werther,* in his own cool judgment several years later. He added as a footnote to the whole affair: "*This fellow* [meaning himself] *should be thrown out of the window.*"

Even his marriage project had fallen to the level of comedy. When he wrote a letter finally to Mlle. Leschenault, it was, by some misunderstanding, her mother, a middle-aged widow, who replied, thinking the offer was for her, and politely declining!

While he continued to whisper his undying devotion to Alexandrine, he also took the most brazen liberties with the more frivolous young ladies he met at her house. "Novelty may be a great recourse," he reflected; "I must give myself to it."

The stimulation of the moment came from a young girl of sixteen, a niece of Pierre Daru's, with whom he carried on the most lecherous dalliance under the eyes of Alexandrine Daru and of her mother as well. The girl seemed fascinated and followed him about, but he himself grew disgusted at such "microscopic adventures." He notes also: "She has neither wit nor teats, *two great wants.*"

That summer of 1811, he suffered with the sense of the "emptiness of ambition." "There is no object that holds me captive," he confesses. Was ambition and success nothing but this? Life in Paris was merely a round of vanity. Had not even his passion for his "Countess Palfy" been tainted with thoughts of career and social ambition? Some months before the time of his departure for Italy, he had seen Martial Daru again in Paris. This handsome and amiable young man of thirty-three was now a baron, enjoying, since marriage, some eighty thousand francs a year, as well as the highest office that so shallow a person might win. Yet he seemed "the unhappiest of men," Beyle notes in English, for having been so foolish as to stake his life *"in the ambition—advice to you, young auditeur."*

He lived now only in anticipation of his return to Italy, the mirage of his youth. Wiser and better armed for this second pilgrimage, he would know how to approach the well-being and liberty he had seen there. For this tour he laid serious plans to study Italian art and antiquities; perhaps even to write a book upon this subject, which engrossed him more and more as a result of his experience with the art treasures of the imperial household.

Before departing at the end of August, he had a last melancholy tête-à-tête with Alexandrine. She seemed in a more melting mood, for it was his last day in town, and urged him to postpone his journey a little in order to come to the country again and enjoy the festival of the wine harvest at Bècheville. His face clouded over at this, despite the warmth of her invitation.

Rather theatrically he replied that "the voyage to Italy was as a dagger in his heart." But she said: "It is easy for you to remove this dagger by giving up the Italian journey." Whereupon Beyle, attempting for one more time—as they had been doing lately—to turn the knife in *her* side, answered: *"It is the fear that I may not be permitted to leave that fills me with chagrin."*

That remark, he felt, scanning her expression, went all the way home.

But it was high time to end the contest of vanity that too often passed for love, he believed, in polite company in France. The real position of Henri and the countess is plainly revealed in the fragment or draft of a letter included in that part of his journal for 1811 that is so voluminously devoted to the "Countess Palfy." It reads:

I must absolutely make this journey. I love you passionately; and you do not want to love me. Besides, your husband gives me black looks, as I noticed last Sunday. I may not be able to see you so often in the future, which would give me the greatest sorrow. Perhaps my absence will help to arrange things, and upon my return he will be willing to see me again.[9]

---

[9]This passage from the *Journal* (Vol. IV, p. 198) touching on his visit to Alexandrine on August 29, 1811, is preceded, however, by a statement that is plainly intended to throw intruding readers off the track: "And from the [Countess Palfy's] house I went to see Mme. de C. to whom I said the following words. . . ." There was no "Mme. de C." and her name is invoked as usual merely to hide the real person's identity. Stendhal was much afraid of the secret police of Napoleon, who, under the orders of the redoubtable Fouché, heard all, saw all, knew all. The consensus of modern researchers, based on the far more complete journals published by Stendhal's modern editor, Henri Martineau, is that the passage above explains the disappointing outcome of Stendhal's suit. This disposes of M. Chuquet's charge, made thirty years earlier, that Stendhal was a "treacherous ingrate" and seduced his benefactor's wife, though he certainly intended that. There are also many other private allusions to his "defeat" by Mme. Daru, in his private papers, which tend to remove all doubt as to the outcome.

CHAPTER IX

Gina: The Italian Interlude

AS HE went to take the diligence, early in the morning of August 28, 1811, the young lawyer Félix Faure and his "little angel," Angelina Bereyter, accompanied him to see him off. Angelina, who was genuinely fond of him, shed honest tears that splashed upon the planks of the bridge on which they stood waiting for the carriage. But at last he was rolling swiftly southward toward Italy, always in love with voyage, the rattling wheels and drumming hoofbeats a favorite music, the changing sky, the horizon undulating past his window a balm to his ennui.

During the hard journey of ten days or more through Burgundy and the Jura foothills, and via Geneva to Milan, he told himself that he was returning at last to the blessed land of his youth, "where my character was formed." In Milan, among the good fat Milanese whom he held to be the most "natural" people in the world, he had felt the utmost freedom. He had learned their native *arte di godere,* their art of playing with life in tranquillity; in Milan he had been madly in love, and "in love with its music, amusement, and its very free morals." In short, he had found, at a most impressionable age, that the *pursuit of happiness was truly possible.*

"I feel myself an Italian at heart," he wrote to his sister, September 10, 1811, "ready to commit assassinations, though of course that sort of thing scarcely happens any more in Italy."

The diary of his second journey to Italy, in 1811, is written in a more finished style, and with more nuances, than anything that has gone before. The literary man stirs a little. Up to now we have had the advantage of guiding ourselves by an unsparingly candid and genuine diary of a man's mind, but which was never intended for publication. The journal that he at first entitled *Pages of Italy*, however, appears to have had some thought behind it of eventual publication as a romance in the form of letters, like Mme. de Staël's *Delphine*. He began to rewrite it two years later as the pretended travel memoirs of a French officer who, fed up with life in Paris, goes to Italy, mother of the arts, to seek beauty and love in their highest forms. It promised to be the most charming of Beyle's early literary experiments.

But soon the habit of unmitigated truthtelling and realism that is native to him takes the upper hand. The diary becomes too utterly self-revealing, as will presently be seen; and the actors in the little romance too easily recognizable, while his interest in inventing or disguising real persons or experiences is as yet undeveloped. Once more we have no mere literature, but the dissection of the man, as he is, with the romantic epidermis removed, like an anatomical chart in a surgeon's room.

Even before he reached Italy his mind played already with the heroine of his projected romance, that Angiola or "Gina" Pietragrua, whom he had not seen for nearly ten years, yet whose name returns to his letters or journals at least once a year as the "ideal," the archetype of the woman of passion. How long he had thought of her! In his sentimental exaltation he exclaimed to himself: "For ten years I practiced fidelity of a sort. . . ."

When he was a poor young cavalry lieutenant, he had not succeeded in attracting her attention seriously. But he had dreamed great dreams, had promised himself to return someday as a colonel, in a splendid uniform; then go to her and ask for her heart. And now he was passing rich, the equal of a colonel or more, his pockets full of gold (three thousand francs), attired in long, tight breeches, superbly tailored coat, frilled shirt, and huge cravat—every inch the snob of the First Empire.

In his diary he disguised the lady's name as the "Countess Simonetta." For him every woman was a countess. The name, however, may have been suggested by his reading of the classic memoirs of Charles de Brosses of Dijon, an eighteenth-century traveler in Italy, who speaks of a Countess Simonetta of Milan in 1740 as having been famous for the "kind reception she gave to Frenchmen. . . ."

Arriving in Milan at six in the evening of September 7, 1811, he went rambling through the streets, then to the broad Corso on the old ramparts of the town, which he used to frequent Sundays with the crowds promenading in carriages, then to the Scala Theater—for him the sanctuary of true music—where he always wound up each evening. He saw persons he remembered in its boxes, as merry and loquacious as ever. Where in the world could one find people so natural in tone yet so perfectly dignified as the handsome Lombards of Milan? Did any of Napoleon's generals love music as did the Italians, and speak of it with such *brio*?

Life here was an *art*, he always insisted. Perhaps it was their civilized libertinism, persisting from the eighteenth century and the Renaissance, persisting despite an omnipotent Church whose religion they practiced but no longer really believed, that strengthened Beyle's love of the Milanese? Here, he told himself, one might enjoy society at its most pleasing terms; here one could study the most agreeable qualities of the Italian soul. Whereas the French, he constantly reflected, lived only in fear of *ridicule*, and thought only of their vanity, Italians spoke from the heart, with warmth and gaiety. Two French bourgeois, meeting and talking together at the Café Foy in Paris, would each narrate something pleasant that had happened to himself, while the other would listen perforce with an impatience he could scarcely conceal—up to the moment when he could launch into one of his own stories without thinking any further of the other man. Too often among the French, "conversation . . . was the armed commerce of two vanities."

The Italians disdained concealment, and honored those who obeyed their great passions. Did not Gina Pietragrua, in seeking to pay a compliment to a certain romantic artist in Milan, once say of him: "He is a truly *dangerous* man!" In other words, she revered him as a man who put no bridle on his emotions.

In one of the tiers of boxes he espied an aging lady, though still lovely, whom he recognized as Signora Lamberti, one of the belles of 1800, known to have had King Joseph Bonaparte as her lover. She still reigned over her friends and lovers, the gentlemen of Milan, who, all through the performance, chatted or sat down to supper, or moved from box to box, as if in a public drawing room.

The comic opera and the ballet performed here might seem "indecent" to music lovers in other lands. But to him this Italian genre represented the most perfect taste. The suave Italian voices brought a "wave of tender memories" crowding upon one another; he felt his heart "too full and was almost on the point of tears."

The next day he hastened to the shop of Gina Pietragrua's father, Signor Borroni, near the Piazza del Duomo, and, in fear and trembling, asked for the daughter! Happily he was made to wait for some fifteen minutes and had time to compose himself a little.

I saw a tall and superb woman. She still had something of the majestic in her eyes, expression, brow, and nose. I found her cleverer, with more majesty and less of that full grace of voluptuousness. . . . She did not recognize me. That pleased me. . . . I introduced myself as Beyle, the friend of Joinville.

"Oh! *Quegli è il Chinese!*" she exclaimed to her father in Milanese dialect. "The Chinaman" was one of the nicknames given him by Lieutenant Joinville, her former lover.

She remembered him well now, she said, as a young blade. He began by jesting about the great "weakness" he had felt for her in those far-off days. They stood on the balcony upstairs for a while, alone together, and now he spoke with more earnestness. His weakness, he said, was a fixed passion; he showed that he had remembered the most trivial things she had talked of ten years ago, and she exclaimed twice in utmost surprise: "But why did you not tell me then?"

At this point a Venetian gentleman arrived, one whom Beyle took for her official cavalier, and, anxious not to overstay his time, he politely took his leave. At the door she asked him to kiss her good-by, inviting him also to come to her loge at the Scala that evening. In her open, laughing way, before the rest of the company, she promised that she would have much to tell him about the intervening years and the many follies she had committed.

It flashed through his mind that perhaps he might put her on his list as a *passade*, in the short week of his stay in Milan. She had grown fat, but was more seductive than ever.

He bought a cane, something to occupy his hands and keep him from clasping them behind his stout hips like an old papa. Thus armed, he felt five years younger, "very much the man of the world who knew women." Twirling his cane, he walked to the Brera Museum and the Ambrosian Library; he visited the churches, looked at paintings, and felt art and beauty entering through all his pores. The Leonardos and Correggios too made a noble music for him.

That night he paid only a brief visit to Gina and her cavalier in her loge at the Scala, but the next day he went driving with them, and she gave him most of her attention, constantly took his arm, and followed everything he said with the liveliest interest. She questioned him closely about his work and his office, and he, speaking like a man of consequence, managed to be vaguely impressive.

Her glances grew tender; at nightfall, parting quickly to meet again at the Scala, they squeezed each other's hand. Passion flamed in Beyle as he walked the streets restlessly, waiting to meet her. As he felt his infatuation waxing, at once a sensation of fear assailed him: What was she? "I do not entertain great hopes of pleasure in the arms of Mme. Pietragrua," he told himself. Were it best to leave Milan promptly?

He was almost gloomy during his brief visit to her box that night. Perhaps his doubt and his rage at himself were inspired by little incidents he noticed at the Scala. On the one hand the Venetian diplomat who was always near Gina freely came and went, leaving him but few moments for a tête-à-tête. And her other companions took great liberties with her. "I saw that she feared lest I form a poor opinion of her because, while speaking to her, with sweeping gestures her friends would sometimes seize her by the knees. . . . Taking me aside, she explained that she would seem silly or prudish if she objected to such peccadilloes." And what of the Venetian gentleman? He seemed irritated, perhaps jealous. Would Beyle have to fight a duel with him too? His eyes had darted jealous looks at the Venetian; and in a whispered colloquy, she denied that he was her lover. Her glances grew torrid. He was falling in love with her, and it literally frightened him. Leaving her, he went to the parterre to stand there and watch her from below, but to his grief was unable to see her.

For effect, he avoided her all the next day while he walked about alone, brooding. Doubt, excitement, fear, as always, flung him into a dark humor. But on the following morning he dressed himself with utmost care and proceeded to her house.

"My mood was tender and I was disposed to make a fine declaration of my sentiments," he relates. But—oh distressful anticlimax!—Madame was out, and he had to wander disconsolately through Milan's galleries till three o'clock in the afternoon, when she returned and he saw her alone.

By then he had mastered his emotions only too well. The whim seized him—as a device to cover his timidity?—to make his declaration in tones of the utmost coolness and reason. Strange man that he was, he spoke of the overpowering inclination he felt in terms that were almost formal, as if discussing a matter that required only common sense. He had felt unhappy yesterday, he explained, at the thought that his feelings were perhaps not returned, and considered departing from Milan earlier than he had intended.

Surely he was but jesting or making sport of her, she said. But at his more and more vehement assurances she grew pensive and sighed: "Oh, how I wish it were true!"

The business of being self-possessed and sensible was now dropped by mutual consent. Melting little by little, they began to thee-and-thou each other. He reminded her that he had thought of her for ten years and recalled again all sorts of little things about her that he had kept in mind despite the accidents and distractions of continental war, the separation in time and distance. He drove that point home: "Ah, to find you again, to see you again after ten years!" And she: "It is almost like a novel!"

The other day, in hearty Milanese fashion, she had asked him to kiss her when he took leave. But now, when he tried again, she resisted, saying archly: "Receive, but do not take."

He did not ravish kisses of her, but they caressed each other more and more fondly, until she, with tears in her eyes, exclaimed: "Oh, go, go! I say that you must leave, for my own peace of mind; else tomorrow I shall not have the strength to bid you to go."

But now two visitors arrived; though Beyle, unnaturally flushed, was vexed at them, he mastered his feelings and spoke with learning and amiability of philosophy and art, which pleased Gina and impressed her with his force of character.

Upon leaving her, he wondered if there had not been "a great deal of politics in her conduct." How "reasonable" she had seemed! Did she feel what she said, or was she a coquette, a designing and knowing Italian woman? In any case, he had gone forward, having wrung from her a frank statement of her affection for him, as a small commitment.

2

Beyle was not only sentimental about Gina refound; she gave him an authentic shudder. There was something "majestic" about her person, her brows, the sculpture of her face and aquiline nose; there was something "terrible" about her dark, flaming eyes, "like those of a Sibyl."

Like Alexandrine Daru, she seemed the type he always admired: full in figure, possessed of boldness and vivacity, woman enough to overwhelm the timid, self-conscious, hypersensitive lover in him.

But Gina lived in storm. Sometimes, as he told her, she almost frightened him. Once, it was said in Milan, a disappointed admirer fired a pistol at her, fortunately with poor aim. When the police came to question her, she had denied it "with a joyous sang-froid."

Angiola Borroni Pietragrua was thirty-four in 1811 and, far from being a member of the upper class in Milan, was the daughter of a shopkeeper. At an early age she had married a little government clerk named Pietragrua, and had a son of sixteen. Her sister sang at the Scala Theater, and Gina herself moved in a circle that was more or less bohemian or *demi-mondaine* in the easy way of Milan, a city less licentious than Venice. (Most of the pious aristocrats of northern Italy, in those revolutionary and Napoleonic days, had long ago retired to sulk in their villas in the country, or shut themselves up in their town palaces, avoiding society.) Nor did her parents or husband seem to oppose her rather glittering mode of life, filled with admiring Italian and foreign gallants, artists, musicians, diplomats, and savants, who gathered nightly in her box at the Scala. But rather her family seemed reconciled to taking what comfort and nourishment they could from these circumstances. To Henri Beyle it seemed that they received him with marked courtesy. There was the little husband, but in Milan jealousy was decried as ridiculous in a husband, and was only permitted to the lover.

She told him the touching story of her affair with his friend Joinville, of their violent quarrel when he accused her of infidelity, of his departure, and her pursuit of him as far as Paris, accompanied only by a maidservant. This tale was intended to demonstrate how madly she loved Joinville, for on her return, worn by the arduous voyage and her too great emotion, she had been so ill that her life was despaired of. And before Joinville, there had been the famous French painter Antoine Gros, who had lived in Milan for a time. But of these four gentlemen who now danced attendance upon her every night at the Scala, which was the favored one? "I myself?" Alas, he reflected somberly, "more than one has been forwarder than I in her affections." Yet after only a week he assured himself that he was steadily overtaking the other admirers.

Desire for her overpowered him. He determined to shorten his intended tour of Italy, so that he might pass a month with her in Milan. In that case, she had promised, she would close her door to her friends, permitting them to see her only at the Scala—and as she said this her eyes were "full of flame."

But a still, small voice within him said: "She is too reasonable about all this."

The day after his proposal she made a rendezvous with him alone for two hours in her apartment. Once more they debated the question: Should he leave Milan or stay? And while according him the softest kisses, she exclaimed: "You must go, Beyle—go, go, go!" Sorrowfully he agreed, but at once spoke of his determination to return and stay permanently in Milan. She was touched, and soon they fell to embracing and kissing each other with even greater ardor than before. But maneuver as he would, he was unable to win still greater liberties. Or as he records it in his journal: ". . . She had tears in her eyes, abandoned herself in my arms, *ma nel mezzo de piu teneri baci, elle ne voulait jamais me permettre de lui donner un baiser sur la cuisse.*"

"What is to prevent us from going further? Is this the way to take leave of each other? We are losing our heads more and more!" she exclaimed. And, penetrated with admiration for her strength of will, he submitted. "I recognized the presence of a superior reasoning power in her," was his afterthought.

Another week passed while Beyle dangled fretfully about her in the company of four other suitors. But she told him that she was weary of her gallants, that she loved the French—had she not often manifested a taste for them?—and that he had more wit than all the others.

"*I was, I believe, in love,*" he wrote in his journal on September 2. The more convinced of this he was, the more jealous he became. He prowled about, watching for her carriage. At moments his eyes filled with tears; or, at others, he raged at himself, so that once he smashed his new cane against the pavement. Like an Italian lover, he left secret letters for her, tucked away in her divan, on leaving her parlor.

The time beyond which he could no longer postpone his departure for Rome was fast approaching. Two days before he was to leave, Gina made an appointment to meet him secretly, wearing a veil, and to drive out into the country with him. She did not come. In despair he wandered about the city all that afternoon looking for her, for her family knew nothing of her whereabouts. That evening, to be sure, he found her again at the Scala. His face was like a cloud; but she was full of warmth, gave him a couple of her flaming looks, and managed to whisper that she had been forced to miss their rendezvous in order to hide her movements from her husband, who was now filled with a terrible, a most Italian jealousy! Who knew? The little Signor Pietragrua might kill her, Beyle, or himself, with a stiletto! At thought of the fearful dangers they ran, Beyle felt himself more madly in love than ever. Moreover, she made a rendezvous with him for the morrow at her home, and did this with the tenderest glances.

The next morning at ten he proceeded to the Via dei Meraviglia, where Gina lived, and waited, by arrangement, at the little church down the street. He held his watch and paced back and forth restlessly, a stout young man clad in impeccable striped trousers, his thick fringe of whiskers carefully brushed, but his hands and cane nervous, his eyes rather wild. From her window she saw him pacing slowly back and forth down the street and, after tormenting him for a full twenty minutes, she gave him the signal through the persiennes, discreetly.

Leaving Milan by a private coach on the next day, his mood was most reflective. The notes he wrote in his journal were brief:

On the 21st of September at half past eleven, I gained the victory I had so long desired.

Nor had it been easily won, but only after "a most serious moral struggle" in which, as a last resort, he had acted "as if at his wit's end and almost in despair. . . ." Perhaps he had threatened to kill himself, for was he not an Italian at heart?

He noted that he had worn the same striped trousers as on the day of the "battle" with Alexandrine Daru. But it was on his suspenders that he wrote the memorable date: September 21, 1811. As he would say in later years, how much pride enters into love!

There are some touches of disappointment, there is a longing for a greater intimacy to come in the few lines he adds concerning the denouement in Milan:

Nothing is lacking for my happiness, unless it be that which gives contentment only to a fool, of its not being a victory. It appears to me that the most perfect pleasure is attained only with intimacy; *the first time* it is a victory; in the *three* following one acquires intimacy. Then comes perfect happiness, if the woman in the case have wit and character and one loves her.

But you know well that that *one* is myself, at twenty-eight.

How often Henri Beyle exclaimed to himself in surprise: "What! Is it no more than that?"

3

Beyle was undeniably one of the first and most enthusiastic of the nineteenth-century tourists; indeed we have it on good authority that he introduced that word to French usage. As his coach rattled away over the powdery road, bordered by stately chestnut trees, that led to Modena and Bologna, he felt himself growing more Italian by the hour. He had Vasari's *Lives of the Painters*, the travel journal of De Brosses (*Lettres écrites de l'Italie*), and the great volume of Winckelmann, the learned native of Stendhal, Prussia, who, with such fervor, had advertised to the eighteenth-century world the Greek and Roman antiquities of Italy. And like Winckelmann, like Goethe, and like the English poets who came several years after him, Beyle was resolved to feast upon the classic ruins and monuments, the Renaissance architecture and paintings that crowded this sunlit land. Now he recalled to himself with some anxiety that he had tarried too long in Milan, that he had scarcely a month left to visit Florence, Rome, and the other fabled cities, and furnish his head with their treasures.

At Bologna he saw palaces full of "grandeur and dirt"; he visited the ancient university and also the Ercolani galleries, where the paintings of the melancholy Guido Reni, of Guercino, and even of the Carracci spoke to his soul. Then he took the road to Florence over the rugged Apennine passes, from which he had astonishing views of "the green sea of the Lombard plain."

In Florence he put up at the Hotel d'Ingliterra, and after taking a bath, made off at once to the church of Santa Croce to see Giotto's frescoes. "*Mon dieu, que c'est beau!*" he exclaimed. For a long time he stood before the tombs of Michelangelo (then in the Santa Croce), Machiavelli, and Alfieri, deeply moved at the thought of these three great dead. "It gives one somewhat the desire to be buried," he reflected. He looked even longer at four Sibyls by Volterrano, and, with tears filling his eyes, stood for hours before a painting of Limbos, which he believed to be by Guercino, then one of his favorite painters. Later that day he was told by his guide that the picture was really by Bronzino. It was all a mistake. "This made me very angry," he says. Bronzino was utterly unknown to him, and he had stood some two hours admiring the work because he thought it was by Guercino!

But despite such contretemps, despite his want of knowledge, Beyle for days lived in a joyful trance while he haunted the Uffizi Galleries, the Pitti Palace, and the richly endowed churches of Florence. He had only his "sensitiveness" to guide him. He judged but "the expression, the imagination, the naturalness" of pictures. But this, surely, was enough; and he felt himself all the closer to the Italians of the Renaissance, closer than Winckelmann "who did not regard nature," but only the classical concepts of the Greeks. Later he became even more hostile to the teachings of the man whose birthplace, nonetheless, he had the whim to take for his nom de plume. For, ignorant though he was of art, he aspired to be nothing less than a French Winckelmann, providing a history and guide to his beloved Italy. This was the newest of his literary projects, competing with the still incomplete play, *Letellier*, and a little book on Haydn he had begun in Vienna.

Approaching Rome on September 28, 1811, when still many miles away in the hills below Viterbo, he had his first glimpse of the dome of St. Peter's, whose façade, when it came into view, disappointed him. He admitted that he had perhaps no feeling for architecture. But the ruins of the Colosseum made a powerful impression upon him. Where St. Peter's and its colonnades seemed too ornate, this great theater, he remarked keenly, seemed to possess a profoundly utilitarian order and simplicity. "What men were the Romans! Always they worked toward the useful, never anything without its reason."

It is doubtful that Beyle, at this period, saw the art collections of Rome save with a hurried eye. He met his old friend the Baron Martial Daru, then stationed in Rome on diplomatic business, and through him was introduced to fashionable Roman society. Every day for a week he attended balls and symphony concerts. A meeting with the popular sculptor Canova, who now filled Italy's cities with his neoclassical monuments, was also one of the high points of the tour.

Rome, overshadowed by the pomp and ritual of Mother Church, was never as sympathetic to the impious Beyle as less priest-ridden and more animated Milan, for him the true capital of the Italians. Though he was repeatedly warned that murderous bandits lurked on all the highways outside of Rome, he hurried on to Naples, where other French friends, such as the Vicomte Louis de Barral of Grenoble, and still more picturesque adventures awaited him.

The journey southward was rough but without untoward incident. With his friends he visited the Grottoes, the Sibylline Baths, the Temple of Apollo, the ruins of Pompeii, then wound up breathlessly at the famous San Carlo Opera House, which pleased him more than everything else.

Naples in 1811 is described by him as a weird bedlam, inhabited by "demons" who shouted at the top of their voices day and night, in the streets and in the cafés, in a dialect he could not understand. The quays along the beautiful, curving bay teemed with wild, ragged *lazzaroni*, beggars, each armed with a dagger, who pursued him step by step, making fantastic gestures and outcries for alms, or pretending to throw themselves under the wheels of his hurrying carriage.

While he crammed sensuous and aesthetic impressions into his notebooks, these were accompanied with general reflections upon human morals and society that were inimitably his own, pure "Beylism," and which gave such high value to his later travel journals.

Naples and Sicily suggested to him the effects of unbridled religious superstition and clerical rule persisting far beyond the point of usefulness. Hence this was a land without hope, without ideas, without liberty. The populace delivered itself to pleasure with furious appetite. In this suffocating city the people ate heavily, drank bad wine, lusted, prayed, and gave alms freely to the beggars who thronged the streets.

The women, he was told, usually had two lovers: one rich, to sustain the other chosen out of sentiment or passion. Assassinations, for which Italy was celebrated, were common enough here, but were generally committed to satisfy vengeance or jealousy. On the other hand the cafés served delicious ices. Naples, moreover, was a center of art and music; it had inspired the poetic librettos of Metastasio, as well as the music of Pergolese, Paësiello, and the "divine" Cimarosa, whose operettas one could hear to better advantage at the San Carlo Theater than anywhere else.

He would fain have stayed; but interests of a less erudite character sent him hurrying northward again after a week. He rode not toward Milan and Gina, but to the city of Ancona, where the program he had arranged in advance in Paris called for a rendezvous with still another charming Italian lady named Livia, of whom Gina doubtless knew nothing.

During the war in Austria, two years earlier, he had met her in Vienna. When her husband, a colonel of the French Army, died in battle, he had tried to comfort her; but before the chord of sympathy that he had struck could be played upon sufficiently, she had been forced to leave for her native Ancona, earnestly bidding him to visit her.

The tall, dark-complexioned young widow was astonished and happy to see him again. Her father, with whom she now lived alone, hospitably invited Beyle to stop at their home. But Livia was sad and bored. Walking with her by the Adriatic shore, he studied her profile, half hidden by a large hat, and saw a resemblance in type to Gina Pietragrua. But this very recollection proved that he could be no mechanical Casanova, no heartless collector of seductions, but remained rather the dupe of his own heart, unswervingly pursuing his ruling passion of the season. Livia seemed inviting enough to his habitually bold advances, but her kisses were not as warm as the other woman's, he coolly estimated. Instead of knocking at her door that night of October 19, 1811, he sat by a candle writing in his comical English:

> *I have find her much below my ideas . . .*
> *I could have her in two or three days but I not desire her.*
> What I desire is to see my Angelina again.

Marking her down on his list as a technical "conquest," he departed —to her profound disappointment, he believed—and rattled away westward in a hired coach over the mountains to Milan, which he reached after three days of back-breaking travel. He had "burned" to see La Pietragrua, and for her sake had literally passed over the treasures of Rome, even the beauty of Ancona. Gina was absent from town, he learned at once, and had gone to stay at a country place near Varese, about six hours north of Milan.

He had already journeyed almost the length of the Italian peninsula, and climbed the Apennines to find her. Forgetting Paris, Emperor, worldly ambitions, he pursued only the all-important enterprise of love. For in those days he glowed with youth, energy, and courage, and was certainly not the man to be daunted by a little matter of six hours' ride over mountain roads. Blithely he continued in her trail.

4

As he rode northward in a little coach, the alpine scene became grandiose; he passed rich forests of chestnut that changed into pine in the highlands, from which vistas of the chain of deep blue lakes, Varese and Maggiore, could be glimpsed from time to time. The thought came to him that he would gladly resign from his position and stay forever in this magic spot.

He read Ossian as he rode, and felt this mystic poetry suited well the majestic environs and the mood of storm in which his own soul was enveloped. At the town of Varese, he stopped and engaged a horse to climb the rest of the precipitous path to Madonna del Monte, the little village clustered about a church on a high rock, four miles away, where he believed Gina awaited him.

But, to his consternation, the first person he met as he reached the single street of the village was none other than his inamorata's husband, who greeted him with bleak formality. Beyle had been making up speeches all along the journey, but when he saw Gina at her lodgings and tried to kiss her, he was sternly rebuffed. One must be careful here in the mountain village. And did he not know the dreadful things that had happened during his absence?

Full of fear and contrition, he listened as she poured forth a long tale of the jealousies and suspicions he had aroused by his compromising behavior; her husband was wrathful; her other cicisbeo had bribed her chambermaid and learned the secrets of their clandestine rendezvous.

Beyle was alternately terror-stricken and ravished. Their danger was mounting hourly—such was love in Italy!—but what frightened him most was the thought that he had incurred Gina's anger. He had asked her to receive his mail for him, and she had read a recent letter from his friend Félix Faure, in Paris, that sounded as if he had learned of Beyle's design, well in advance, "to place La Pietragrua on his lists." She now rose to heights of injured pride and looked as fearsome as she was enchanting. Beyle's proposal to visit her stealthily in her lodgings that midnight was scornfully rejected, and he himself was dismissed from Madonna del Monte.

In his distress, ready words had failed him. Down the mountainside he went therefore, to expiate by spending the night alone, a few miles away, at an inn in Isola Bella, one of the most beautiful sites in the Borromean Isles on Lake Maggiore. There, the next morning, seated on a little terrace commanding an entrancing view of blue water and snow-covered mountains appearing through the mists above, he composed a tremendous letter of apology, in which he explained that nothing injurious to her honor had been intended in his earlier remarks to Faure about her, but only the expression of his hope and passion of ten years. The letter was that of an unhappy repentant lover, written, he assured himself, "in a firm style," worthy of the great moralist, Duclos. After forwarding this elaborate literary production (unfortunately lost to us) by messenger, he spent the night reading Ossian's *Fingal*, while rain and storm hammered frantically at his island refuge.

With hindsight, we may now judge that La Pietragrua had been willing to give a fleeting favor to her French admirer departing from Milan. But discretion and her "angry husband" (who seemed polite and harmless enough to Beyle) ruled that her Frenchman was a fellow who traveled too far and fast, here today, gone tomorrow, hence a doubtful prop in a precarious world, and must not be permitted to disturb her more permanently profitable arrangements with the reigning *cavaliere servente* or cicisbeo, who was perhaps the Venetian gentleman or another.

The day after the storm was as pure and calm as a relenting woman. His hopes reviving, the much distracted Beyle now conceived of a new folly which he sets down in his journal in full detail—and in all humility.

Returning to Gina's mountain village that night, he hired a *portatina*, a little canvas-covered sedan chair—for another squall of rain had come —and with the aid of two porters had himself carried to the inn at Madonna del Monte where he expected to stop. He thought the inn was at the opposite end of the village (which had but a single narrow street) and that he would quietly enter the place from that direction without passing the Pietragrua lodging. But by error, in pitch-darkness, the porters proceeded by a path that passed the house where Gina stopped, lighting their way with huge torches. And there in the open door of his house stood the cuckold himself staring at Beyle, illuminated as upon a stage, while from darkened windows the whole village, full of mirth and excitement, watched the torchlight parade that he had intended as a maneuver of supreme stealth.

It was a terrible moment. He relates: "I made myself as small as possible [*Je me fis le gros dos*] inside the sedan chair, and my ridiculous disguise was not detected by anyone save Gina, who, a few moments later, went with her son to my quarters to leave a little note for me."

In this she informed him that he could not slip into her room, as he had hoped, thròugh the adjoining room, as two nuns had been lodged there for the night. But she was really quite ravished by his wild antics —it was the sort of thing that pleased her—and promised that she would do her utmost to meet him at his inn at midnight.

The plot was thickening! But at midnight came a fresh billet countermanding the earlier one, and brought by her son of sixteen:

> Midnight. The jealousy of my husband is fully awakened. Prudence, and prepare to leave tomorrow not later than seven o'clock.

Zounds, Beyle's very life was in danger! He left in the early morning for a tour of the lake, and returned at night, in deepest secrecy. But again her boy was there with a message, saying: "There is no hope for tonight," and that she would be at Milan the next evening. Worn out by all his coursing to and fro, Beyle curled up in bed with his volume of Ossian, consoling himself with the thought that he could have done no better, since the two nuns in the next room would have robbed him of all peace of mind. But before dozing off he asked himself: "Are those two nuns real beings or phantoms of the imagination?"

At any rate Gina was showing unmistakable signs of melting. Her mercurial changes of mood were an eternal wonder and torment to him. She had punished him enough for his presumption and now, meeting him in Milan, on October 29, 1811, took him again to her generous bosom. But not before administering one more spirited reproof on the score of that detestable and labored letter of apology he had written her from Isola Bella.

"Would you have written a letter like that to me," she asked, "if you were truly unhappy?" And he was forced to admit, in his journal for October 29, 1811, that she had been most discerning. He must learn to avoid sentimental rhetoric and use the accent of life.

Nor was the course of their love smooth. The porters who had carried him to Madonna del Monte had informed her husband of his arrival, and he, it was said, grew furious and furiouser. Their rendezvous thereafter were cloaked in profound mystery, she appearing in a veil, he in a costume that disguised his appearance. After changing carriages several times, he would join her in some obscure street in back of a café.

"Our love is persecuted on all sides," Beyle exclaimed to her in grief.

"It is just like a novel!" Gina declared in rapture.

But he felt, he loved, he lived—not like the men of overcivilized and dull Paris—but in the cape-and-sword world of Benvenuto Cellini and Aretino.

Sometimes his belle would be strangely elusive. He would wait for her, bitterly counting each minute, only to trudge home alone. But a message would reach him that night: "I love you more than my own life, but fatal circumstances made me late at our rendezvous, and when I arrived you were gone."

Despite periodic and most puzzling interruptions—usually attributed to the "vengeful" husband—they found their way into each other's arms frequently enough. Happiness waxed with increasing intimacy, as Beyle had reasoned. and as he recorded in his diary with mathematical precision:

> Milan, Nov. 2, 1811: Unquestionably the most beautiful woman I have ever possessed, and even seen, is A——, as she appeared to me tonight, walking in the street, by the light of certain shop windows. I do not know how she happened to say, in that most natural air which so distinguishes her and without any vanity whatsoever, that certain of her friends had told her that sometimes she made them afraid. It is true. She was most animated tonight. It seems that she loves me. *Yesterday and today, she has had pleasures.* . . . In the rear of the coffee shop, her face, half lit with a suave harmony, was terrible in its supernatural beauty! . . . With her brilliant eyes that read all one's soul to its very depths, she seems like some sublime sibyl.

She spoke sometimes of quitting Milan and following him to Paris. In the emotion of parting, when the extension of his leave expired, he promised her that he would obtain a diplomatic post in Italy and soon return.

On the return journey to France, he felt that he had at last known "feelings of greatness." In that season in Italy he felt that his knowledge of the art of life had measurably advanced, and that Italian national character, social habits, and environment had everything to do with his education. Italy therefore became one of the cornerstones of Beylism. Others, including eminent Italian authorities, might protest forever that he invented an Italy of his own fantasy ("Stendhal's Italy," they would call it) and one that was grounded in the libertinism of a

Milanese strumpet. Yet he would hear none of these objections. As one of his autobiographical fragments records:

> . . . old age is repelled for ten years. I felt the possibility of a new happiness. All the springs of my soul nourished and strengthened, and myself rejuvenated . . . I know the land where one breathes a *celestial air*, and whose existence others may deny, but I set myself like flint against them.[1]

He even believed, at this point, that he had reason to compliment himself upon the soundness of the Systems he followed in his pursuit of happiness. Several times during the anxious contest for Gina Pietragrua he had thoroughly enjoyed the evident discomfiture of his Italian rivals and the spectacle of their jealousy. That they or numerous other explorers had gone before him in these smiling pastures was a thought that did not present itself strongly to his mind at this happy time. Even a slight suspicion of the husband, that he himself expressed in his journal on October 29, 1811—"I do not believe he has the honor of being jealous"—was dissolved in the wave of self-contentment upon which he rode back to Paris.

---

[1] P. Arbalet: *Journal d'Italie*, pp. 299–300n.

CHAPTER X

The Retreat from Moscow

> One must shake up one's life; else it corrodes us. . . . To fall asleep with one's character is to be in the anteroom of death.
>
> —Stendhal.

ARRIVING in Paris, on November 27, 1811, he was in high spirits. But his increasingly abbreviated diary informs us: "The next day a lost battle." There is no further explanation. This time the "battle" seems to have been concerned with his ambitions.

Beyle has made candid admission of the fact that from 1806 to 1814 he was "wholly dominated by ambition." He could not have ridiculed vainglory so fiercely in later life, had he not surrendered himself to its empire so passionately in earlier years. Precisely what worldly baubles he bargained for, at that moment in 1811, are not easy to enumerate. For three years, since his campaign in Austria, he had been asking for a cross of honor, such as hundreds of others got from the Emperor, and which he prized, in cynical spirit, as a useful article of commerce. Very likely also he asked for a diplomatic post in Italy, at Rome, Florence, or even Milan. The business of transporting certain art treasures of the Vatican to France had been recently brought before the intendant of the imperial household, in which he was a high official; undoubtedly he would have liked to head such a mission (which would have permitted him to rejoin Gina at an early date), but nothing came of it. Indeed he found himself subject to severe official censure.

He had extended his leave of absence by over two months, and tried to conceal the fact that he was in Italy, instead of Dauphiné, by having letters readdressed to Paris and using a pseudonym in signing his letters, a habit that became a mania with him. In Rome he had failed to pay his respects to the omniscient French director of police. Now he found on his return all sorts of angry notes from his superiors. He suggests a stormy scene with the sharp-tempered Daru, in which he himself did not keep his *sang-froid*:

> Not only the minister under whom I serve [Champagny] seems irritated, but also the minister who likes me [Count Daru] seems disgusted with the business of protecting me. In the midst of all that, I failed to receive an honor which I thoroughly merited and which had kept my ambition alive for three years. . . . My reputation for being a *wild fellow* is augmented. . . . I shall have to go to a hundred dinners in silk stockings, with beribboned fools, and play five hundred games of whist with old women in order to win forgiveness.

To regain lost ground, he had recourse at once to the Countess Daru, but found her door closed to him, evidently at the orders of her husband. By the agency of Napoleon's famous secret police, everything that Henri Beyle had done in Italy, including the story of his Italian mistress, was known to the imperial government, hence to the Secretary of State and his wife.[1] When at length by earnest pleadings he persuaded the Countess Daru to open her door, even to invite him to dinner again, he found her reserved; her husband for a long time addressed not a word to him. And the countess, who had done so much to advance him, felt her worst doubts of his character confirmed. "The love for Palfy [Countess Daru] is dying," he notes in March 1812.

Returning to France from Italy, he wrote in a letter of December 6, 1811, that it was as if one had spent the evening at a delightful ball, a scene of voluptuousness and grace, lit with a thousand candles, then suddenly issued forth at midnight "into a thick fog, a night of rain and mire."

The darkening times were reflected in the increasingly serious mood of the men around Napoleon, as 1812 opened. Pierre Daru once more assumed the task of provisioning the Grand Army in advance of its secretly planned march into Russia. Napoleon's continental system, like that of the Third Reich which so closely paralleled it more than a

[1]A prosaic report of the French secret police in 1814 has come down to us, describing Henri Beyle: "He is a fat fellow, born in Grenoble, thirty-one years of age. . . . He seldom goes to salons . . . but attends the theater often, and always lives with some actress. When he is not in service, he works four or five hours a day at some historical compilations and notes on his travels. . . . He never misses a performance of the Opéra Bouffe, spends all his evenings there, or at the Théâtre Français. He takes breakfast every day at the Café de Foy, dines at the Frères Provençaux restaurant, buys many books, and comes home every night at twelve." P. Jourda, *Stendhal raconté*, 19–20.

century later, was constantly threatened at its eastern and western extremities. In Napoleon's case, not only England fought on tenaciously from the seas, but Spain was a bleeding wound. To dispose of the fanatical Spanish guerrillas, and finally of the English who stood behind them, he must first turn upon Russia, whose pact with France in 1807 had been an uneasy truce, grounded in fear, during which the two great adversaries secretly prepared for the renewal of conflict.

"Up to now, I had rejoiced in the French Revolution for the sake of the marvelous institutions it had introduced, veiled though they were by the clouds that followed its irruption," Beyle had written in 1811, while voyaging to Italy. But an intelligent traveling companion on his journey, a Milanese nobleman of liberal views, had pointed out to him that the liberties which "Maximus" had promised Italy were not yet accorded, and he was led to admit to himself that liberty under the genius of autocracy was perhaps a chimera. "For some time I have had the vague notion that [the Empire?] has banished *allegria* from Europe for perhaps a century." There was gloom in war-weary France in the winter of 1812, not in anticipation of incredible defeat, but at thought of the costs of new warfare upon a grandiose scale. Early in 1812, Beyle, close to the court, knew of the preparations being made by Daru.

He need not have forsaken his comfortable administrative post at the court. Yet he volunteered for active duty in the field. What restlessness, what wanderlust seized him? Ambition, the hope of winning new distinction through active service and overcoming his momentary disgrace, were among his motives. He admits to being surfeited with life in Paris. "One must shake up one's life . . ." he would say. He had participated in the conquest of northern Italy, witnessed the entrance of Napoleon into Berlin and Vienna later, and still, as he wrote to a friend, felt the unquenchable thirst "to see," to be present at great events such as he now suspected were preparing themselves. It is evident that he also had the idea of making somewhere, during this long voyage across Europe, a goodly detour that would permit him to revisit Milan and his luscious "Countess Simonetta." He whispered to himself: *"I will see again my dear Italy. It is my true fatherland."*

How long would the distant adventure in Russia take, he wondered? "Four months—or two years?" he writes, in a letter written July 27, 1812, while en route to the front. Why should he have entertained even the slightest doubts, felt by so few then, concerning the terrible, swift conqueror who had always previously won his objective, and now marched at the head of a Gargantuan army of some 640,000 men?

He had persuaded Daru only with the utmost difficulty to have him transferred for the time being to active service with the commissary staff of the Grand Army. In July he was given the mission of bearing important documents and portfolios from the ministries in Paris to Napoleon, then at Vilna. At an interview with the Empress Marie-Louise on July 23, 1812, he received messages, letters, and parcels to bring to her husband, then left Paris in a light swift barouche, laden with baggage.

2

The most unsedentary of men of letters, after twenty days' ride, reached the front on August 14, 1812, two days before the Battle of Smolensk. He served as a full commissary, assigned to securing provisions and quarters for the army. The work behind the lines promised to be not too hazardous; Beyle told himself that his chief profit would lie in the opportunity to observe soldiers and officers in action and apply the tenets of his philosophy to classifying them.

The Russians willed otherwise. Reaching Krasnyi on August 14, he saw such confusion in the rear as never before in Napoleon's campaigns, he relates. In the crush on the road he was compelled to leave his carriage behind and push forward on horseback for five days as far as Smolensk, where he found Daru and his staff at dinner, following the bloody battle. But as they ate, the Russians, pursuing "scorched earth" tactics, set fire to the old city, and Daru's men, including Beyle, were driven out of their quarters by the flames that reached them. They ate little that night and fell asleep in such refuge as they could find, with their heads on tables, or outstretched on the floor.

These troubles were but a foretaste. In a journey of more than two hundred miles over the lonely steppes, from Vilna to Smolensk, Beyle had seen only a few sullen peasants. The fanatical patriots had denuded the land of provisions as Napoleon advanced, and the problems of Beyle and his fellow quartermasters grew worse as the invading horde penetrated into the heart of Russia. Beyle struggled against an initial disorganization that seemed endemic in this campaign. Weariness often overwhelmed him. In this strange and inclement land, fifteen hundred miles from Paris, he felt like some "exotic orange tree withering away for having been transplanted so far from its native habitat." He was also depressed on learning that his carriage, full of money, personal baggage, and books—military documents he kept on his person—was irretrievably lost somewhere in the rear. Bookish warrior that he was, he had counted on having his books as a consolation for the long Russian winter.

As danger mounted, Beyle, besides writing in his journal, began to give details of his experiences in letters sent to his friend Félix Faure and to the Countess Daru. It was a precaution against his possible death in Russia. He tells little of the fighting advance to Moscow, or of the Battle of the Moskva (Borodino), but remembers only riding in to Moscow on September 14, at one o'clock in the morning, in the rear of the army, with the convoys of the quartermaster staff. Part of the city, the old bazaar, or "Chinese" quarter, near the Kremlin, was already ablaze as they entered; but Beyle and his colleagues merely jested over that, for it was not believed the fire would spread beyond control. Calmly they set about choosing one of the city's numerous palaces as headquarters for Daru's organization.

En route to Moscow, near Smolensk, Beyle had come upon a piano in an abandoned house, and induced one of his companions—one who "had an ear for music as I have for the mass," he said—to play Mozart for him. The piano moreover was out of tune, yet music was something he needed and must invoke in the face of war's barbarity. From Moscow he wrote: "It seems that I am to pass the winter here; I hope that we shall have concerts." Plays also would doubtless be performed at the court of the Emperor.

To Beyle, the ancient capital of Russia seemed an oriental pleasure city. "Though unknown in Europe," he writes in a letter of November 20, 1812, "Moscow had six or eight hundred palaces such as one may never see in Paris. Everything here was arranged for the purest voluptuousness, the buildings being painted in the brightest colors, and containing furniture from England, statuary, pictures, charming beds, sofas of the most ingenious shape." He surmised that there were in Moscow a thousand nobles and merchants of immense wealth, who, living under a despotism, had no other resource but pleasure seeking.

However, the comforts he envied were not to exist for his entertainment. As he went to bed that first night in the palace of Count Saltykoff, a relative of the Czar, alarms were being given throughout the doomed city, whose residents had already been evacuated by the Russians. Yet he snatched some sleep, until he was waked early in the morning at the orders of Daru and told to seek headquarters for the commissaries elsewhere. A heavy pall of smoke filled the air so that it was hard to breathe. In the street outside, French soldiers and his own servants were busy looting wine, silks, money, from houses about to take fire. They were already drunk and fell to brawling. Beyle was forced to draw his sword to separate the looters.

With the fire spreading rapidly over one side of the city, he ordered the soldiers under his command to carry out stores of flour and fodder from the buildings and load them into wagons. In a letter of October 4, 1812, he relates:

> The soldiers made believe they were being very busy, they had the air of working hard, and in reality did almost nothing. It is thus that they carry on everywhere and all over the army; and this causes trouble.

The soldiers preferred to burden their vehicles with looted silver and linen instead of flour! Thus, in his hurried observations on the scene, Beyle made clear to himself the cause of the Napoleonic debacle, and contributes his clear evidence to the mass of often conflicting accounts of the 1812 invasion.

That day there occurred a strange bit of private drama ordained by the long arm of coincidence. Beyle had gone with his comrades to take refuge in a large club building near the Saltykoff palace, when a tall woman rushed up to him at the door, threw herself at his feet, and begged his protection. She was Mélanie Guilbert, his beloved of Marseille, eight years ago. Having gone to play in Italy, she had met a Russian nobleman named Barkoff who helped her to fulfill her dearest wish, which was to be married.

Beyle, in uniform and plumed hat, conscious of how changed was his state, was aware that the situation was "of the highest ridiculousness." Yet he took her under his wing, placing her, a fat Russian lady companion, and two weeping children in his crowded carriage, while he walked behind. In her exclamations of gratitude, he had time to notice, "there was not a trace of the natural" in her; she was ever the actress.

The procession then set off; but several times they found their route blocked by sheets of flame. Eventually they made a half turn and avoided the fire to reach the outskirts of the city. There new commissary headquarters were set up in the villa of Prince Rostopchin, the fervent governor general of Moscow who led the people to set the torch to the capital and even to his own property. There had been moments of fear as they rode or walked slowly between flaming buildings while sparks showered upon them. But Beyle, who showed himself a man of steady nerves, remarked in the letter he wrote on October 4, 1812, that there was really no great danger inasmuch as the city then was burning only on one side. "Our movements were imperiled only by extreme tendencies to disorder."

Besides, he had rallied his spirits by doing a little discriminating pillaging himself: a few precious books, consigned to the flames, had been snatched by him from the mansion he had occupied, among them a volume of Voltaire, and one of Lord Chesterfield's letters, a most improving work to read at such a crisis.

The whole day was passed in the struggle to extricate men, horses, and supplies from the fire. At night, from the marble villa of Rostopchin, two miles outside the city, he watched "the most beautiful conflagration in all the world, forming an immense pyramid which, like the prayers of the faithful, had its base on the earth and its summit in the heavens." All the luxurious pianos and sofas and marble Psyches of the red-tinted mansions of ancient Moscow were being consumed. "And above that pall of smoke and flame the moon suddenly rose."

By an erotic predisposition Beyle had always felt a thrill at the sight of flame or fireworks. And now, though sick and weary, he stood lost in rapture at that spectacle of superhuman, irruptive force, until he became aware of his fellow officers jabbering or making vulgar comments that wounded his sensibilities.

"It was a most imposing sight," he relates briefly, "but I should have preferred to be alone, or at least in the company of people who had the wit to appreciate it. Instead, what spoiled the whole Russian campaign for me was to have gone through it with men who would have belittled the Roman Colosseum or the Bay of Naples."

For some time he had been working twelve to fourteen hours a day despite a stomach disorder and a toothache. For all the debonair tone he affects in his letters it is plain that his heart is oppressed as he watches the carnival of drinking, looting, and destruction. Amid scenes of orgiastic horror, the soldiers struggle with each other for bottles of brandy, money, and movables, which they bear away in overburdened carts or on their shoulders. His personal servant, he notes in his journal, is drunk like the others and cannot be controlled or disciplined. "I saw new proof of the want of character in the French," he comments. The "veneer" of civilization fell away. As he wrote somewhat later, on the road back, to his friend Faure, "I saw things that a sedentary author would not have seen in a thousand years."

His attention had been so distracted by his duties that only hours later did he realize that Mélanie and her party had disappeared from view, nobody knew where. (Four weeks later, when he had leisure again to reflect and remember, he made anxious inquiries concerning her and learned that, by some means, she had made her way to St. Petersburg and eventually, after long delays, to Paris. From what she had told him she had been unhappy with her Russian husband too. Solicitously he wrote from Moscow, on October 15, to friends of hers in Paris, offering his aid and the use of his home.) But soon he was engulfed in the unearthly disasters that overtook the armies of Napoleon and, while he fought only to survive, the image of Mélanie, like so many other apparitions of that nightmare season, was blotted from his mind.

3

The fire of Moscow burned for five days. On the 20th of September, the French forces re-entered the city of charred ruins, four fifths of whose dwellings were razed and of whose monuments only the churches and the walled Kremlin remained. Henri Beyle did not witness the lugubrious occupation of the eyeless capital, for during a week he lay sick at the commissaries' headquarters outside.

Napoleon, the man of iron will and uncanny intelligence, now showed signs of increasing degeneration. Beyle's letters were to be used as objective documents by later commentators, Russian as well as French, proving that Napoleon violated his own rules of success. He "corrupted the moral character of the army" by encouraging looting, and then hesitated to impose the harsh discipline always previously used. The earlier journals of Beyle give evidence of the enthusiasm with which the Italians welcomed the French as liberators and reformers. But in penetrating the frontier of Russia, Napoleon refused to consider freeing the serfs of the border provinces, the Lithuanians and White Russians, who might have fought under his banner, as Eugene Tarlé, the Soviet historian, has pointed out. For the first time also, the Emperor, previously so thorough in obtaining intelligence and in organizing supply service, seemed uncertain of the conditions that faced him, puzzled as to the enemy's intentions, full of hesitation over his next moves. The Russians, rallying under the aged Kutuzoff, concentrated reinforcements east of Moscow and made threatening moves on the northern and southern flanks of the French, while the Czar in St. Petersburg made no reply to suggestions of peace. Meanwhile, the first frosts of early October gave their warnings, and Napoleon gave thought to improving his supplies. Then Henri Beyle, recovered from his illness, was called before the great man in the Kremlin together with other commissary officers to receive detailed orders. Sometimes he placed the scene of his interview in which the Emperor addressed him personally at the Kremlin, sometimes at another site outside of Moscow. On this occasion, at any rate, he was able to make close personal observation of the man who still then seemed to him the supreme master of logic, the mathematician in the sphere of action—

> whose sagacious and glittering mind saw in every question aspects unnoticed by others, whose speech abounded in barbed words and picturesque images that seemed all the more striking because of the occasional incorrectness and foreignness of his language.

To Beyle was assigned the task of raising "an immense amount of food" to be held in reserve, in the region of Smolensk, to which he proceeded with an armed convoy and three million rubles. With a long baggage train, some cavalry, and fifteen hundred wounded men, he left Moscow on October 17 for the journey to Smolensk. Two days later the main French army began to move out of Moscow to fight Kutuzoff's menacing forces at Malojaroslavetz; then, after this costly engagement, broke off to begin the retreat Napoleon so belatedly ordered.

Beyle, who, with most others, still believed that the Emperor intended to march upon St. Petersburg, had his difficulties en route to Smolensk. At sunset each day the Cossacks in their rear would begin their harassing raids. The journey of only 240 miles lasted three weeks, and one night the French all gave themselves up for lost, being attacked on all sides by what seemed superior forces of Cossacks and peasants. The wounded officer in command ordered his men to lighten their baggage and prepare to range themselves in a hollow square and fight their way out the next morning. "Although I had retained much hope," Beyle wrote to Mme. Daru, "like all the others during that night, I rendered up the account of my life." Ruefully he reproached himself for having pursued his ambitions as far as the boundless and inhospitable plains of Russia, and also "for not having had the wit to tell you how much I am devoted to you."

But at dawn, armed to the teeth, they marched forward into a dense fog in which Russians were nowhere visible, having disappeared as mysteriously as they had arrived. Beyle minimized the alarms as "ridiculous"; but the Russians had captured their food, severe frosts had come, the wounded died in great number every day, and the others were forced to live on a few potatoes with army biscuit.

After November 9 Beyle ranged about between Smolensk and Bobruisk and other towns, vigorously gathering up stores of flour and distributing bread, "so infinitely precious under the circumstances." Napoleon, he said, "expects miracles of us." Daru afterward complimented Beyle in the name of the Emperor and promised him a decoration. But the whole plan of retreat was one of inconceivable folly, since the French forces marched over territory they previously devastated, instead of seeking another route.

The first phase of the retreat, up to the crossing of the Berezina River, saw no suffering because of cold, Beyle relates. The weather indeed was rather mild, although they felt the want of food keenly. Later, in December, came the fearful cold. Throughout the first phase of the homeward journey, while order was still preserved, Beyle, at any rate, behaved with unusual firmness. On one of the worst mornings endured by the now ragged Grande Armée—according to a story retold later by Prosper Mérimée—he turned up at Daru's headquarters for orders, carefully shaved and perfectly groomed in his only uniform. Count Daru, an old veteran who showed an imperturbable *sang-froid* himself, exclaimed: "Beyle, you are a man of stout heart!"

The passage of the Berezina by pontoon bridge was begun in good order on November 26, though Russian horsemen harried the congested column from both sides. It was on the following day that Beyle arrived in a carriage, bearing with him a wounded fellow officer named Bergognié. Panic was gaining over the fleeing French; horses and vehicles rode over those who had fallen on the bridge—for the rear guard was soon to be withdrawn. But Beyle, overcoming the objections of his companion, drove downstream to a ford which he had been told was perfectly passable and rode across without trouble. The wounded officer later told Mérimée that he owed his life to the coolness of Beyle.

In the days that followed he lost all but the clothes he wore and lived on bread and water. After fifty days on the road to Vilna, what was left of the French force was so wretched in appearance that old friends failed to recognize each other as they met on the road. Many of them, struggling on to die in the snow, with their pockets full of gold, did not behave well in their last extremities. He too felt himself reduced to the level of the beast when, one lucky day, finding a heap of potatoes, he knelt and prayed before it. At fortified Vilna the survivors used the frozen corpses of their comrades to fill breaches in the walls.

On one day that he recalls as being December 4, 1812, the cold seemed twice as intense as before, and everyone had a look of madness. In such a moment one thought only of the danger and not of pity for others. Suddenly he himself felt as if he were about to faint, but by a supreme effort roused himself and bent all his will upon lashing his carriage horses forward, gaining several miles and reaching the head of the column he was traveling with. Thus he was one of the first to arrive at the next town, Maladechno, where he found three fresh horses; and this alone enabled him to reach Vilna alive. After a brief halt there he hastened to Königsberg, where he was nearly drowned when the sledge he rode broke through the ice of the Frisches Haff.

"I saved myself by force of will, for I saw many around me give up hope and perish," he wrote in a letter from Königsberg, December 28, 1812. Later he added that "logic" also helped, since he had his favorite maxims always ready for any emergency; while others hesitated, he always appeared with his mind composed and with a plan of action that he followed. Nor did he ever believe for a moment that he would die.

At Königsberg, he recovered health and spirits; hearing a Mozart opera "superbly sung" aided greatly in the process.

He had lost all his baggage, including the manuscript of a projected book, and the extensive journals written in Russia and in Germany. Only a few graphic letters he wrote remain to give direct evidence of the retreat from Mascow.

"The interior of souls that I saw in the retreat disgusted me forever with the armed imbeciles who compose an army," he wrote afterward. He thought that "the pleasures of the snow in Russia" must have numbed all passion in him. Even Italy and Gina seemed only chimeras now. A month after reaching Königsberg, he was in Paris again, just thirty years of age, but prematurely gray. "The only nice thing about it all was that it made me thin," he laughed.

4

As the retreat from Moscow marked the ebbing tide of Napoleon's fortunes, so did it mark the beginning of the retreat from glory, or ambition, for Beyle.

After his first month in Russia, he had written to a friend in Paris:

> How man changes! That thirst I once had to see everything is all satiated; since I saw Milan and Italy, all that I see repels me by its ugliness. . . . Sometimes I am at the point of tears. . . . In this ocean of barbarism not a sound that speaks to me! Everything is gross, vile, stinking, from a physical and moral point of view. . . . Ambition means nothing more to me; the bluest cordon would not be recompense for the mire in which I am buried now.

And in a letter from Moscow there was the sentence, like a reminder:

> *Think of amusing yourself, life is short.* Drink in the pleasures of Paris, like the deer quenching his thirst.

He returned to the old rounds in 1813: the dinner parties with bachelor friends, the soirées at Mme. Daru's or the Countess Beugnot's; then to the plump arms of Angelina Bereyter at midnight. Even Mélanie was back again that fateful season. Yet all this helped not.

Something had died in him during those months of horror and suffering that were to have been his payment for new promotions and new glory. His faith in the Napoleonic system, in his own fine schemes, even in the value of the society ornamented by the Darus, was dying.

He had coveted rewards like the other members of the army of functionaries serving Bonaparte, and felt he had thoroughly earned the commendation of his superiors for his services. When, on March 19, 1813, the *Journal Officiel* listed the names of men now being advanced in the public service, thirteen new prefects were named, and he not among them; he also found that two of his young "acolytes" in Russia, the two auditors who had served under him, had been raised to the office of *maître de requêtes*, a degree higher than his own secretarial office of auditor at the Council of State. He who had performed such important and hazardous missions in Russia had been passed over in favor of others who had stayed at home. And the Darus seemed to offer only scant encouragement to his hope of being appointed as a subprefect in Rome, or to a prefecture even "in some hole with six thousand inhabitants." Indeed Mme. Daru seemed positively cold to him, which increased his gloom. "Leaving her house, I felt my ambition declining," he writes on March 18, 1813. "All at once I saw that the great places were unattainable for me."

Failure of promotion he tended to associate in his mind with his renewed "disgrace" at Mme. Daru's. A great lady of Paris giveth and she taketh away. For it was largely her personal favor that had permitted his swift climb in the Napoleonic hierarchy.

But early in April came news of the resumption of war, after an armistice, between reviving Prussia and France. Once more Napoleon, with unflagging energy, raised an army of 200,000 men, though France (and Europe) still mourned the fearful man-power losses of 1812. Then, despite the ominous pressure of Wellington in Spain, the Emperor hastened to Saxony to make head against the combined Russian and German onslaught.

Beyle was recovered in health, but like his compatriots extremely war-weary when orders came on April 15, 1813, to report for service, as commissary, with a division on the Silesian front. Soon he was pounding along across Germany on the road to Dresden. Rage was in his heart. "I am going to be turned into a barbarian . . ." he told himself grimly. "A barbarian, lost to the arts!"

5

He was by now thoroughly sick of war, "soused, begging your pardon, like a man who has taken too much punch and feels obliged to vomit it up."

Inwardly rebellious, melancholy as well, he nevertheless used his eyes during this campaign in Saxony in which Napoleon, at bay, turned fiercely upon the Allies gathering at the borders of his shrinking Empire. At Dresden, Beyle joined the main body of the French forces, as usual riding in the rear with trains of supplies, engineering equipment, and baggage carts.

"There I was," he relates, "comfortably installed in an elegant coach, while traveling in the midst of the complicated movements of an army of 140,000 that was driving back another army of 160,000, with accompaniment of Cossacks on the flanks."

He had come to despise militarism; many of the heroes of the war in Russia were but "scared chickens" to him. Without being insensitive to the dramatic events he witnessed, it was nevertheless, as Mérimée remarks, their bizarre or grotesque effects that he enjoyed commemorating. The unexpected and the comic always caught his eye as well as the moments of horror. His determination to write was repeatedly frustrated, yet he observed, gathered precious experience. As Pierre Martino has written of him:

> The existence of most of our men of letters, his contemporaries, was passed before a writing table, in parlors, in the circles of literary men; whereas a bitter

sense of experience, a brutal candor, a harsh vision of life springs everywhere from the pages of Stendhal, even from his first works; he feels a need to compensate for his own memories . . . after so much suffering and so many approaches to death.[2]

In June 1813, during the brief armistice following the fierce conflicts along the Elbe and Spree rivers, Napoleon redeployed his forces for "aggressive defense," and established various centers or strong points with an intendant supplying the needs of each army group stationed there. Henri Beyle was named by Napoleon intendant of the fortified city of Sagan, in Silesia, to which he was proceeding with a supply column when attacked by a raiding party of Cossacks on May 24, 1813.

His description of the affair assumed a certain notoriety many years later, when his friend Mérimée retold it in his own words as an example of the clownery that also marches in the paths of glory. The long supply train, guarded by "fifteen hundred French soldiers," his tale ran, entered a ravine road near Reichenbach, in Saxony, when it was suddenly attacked in the rear by "five or six" young Cossacks, none of whom appeared over twenty years old. (Beyle sometimes changed this to "twenty-two Cossacks.") The officers and soldiers were instantly thrown into a terrible panic, he declares, and gave the alarm of an ambuscade by thousands of Russians. Some of the soldiers did nothing, others took to their heels. The fat Beyle, unarmed, with only one boot on, started to decamp, carrying the other boot under his arm. Only two gendarmes in the rear guard showed some firmness. While the Russians detached the quartermaster carriages of Daru, and rode off with them, these two stopped in their flight and used their muskets. One fired at the Cossacks; the other, with the best intentions in the world, fired at his fellow gendarme's horse, killing it and bringing the other man down. The single hero of the affair, however, denied that he had done anything to deserve glory, fearing that anyone known to have participated in a rout would be ordered executed by Napoleon.

This affair, which Beyle in later years enjoyed recalling, with many adornments, at the time, led to an investigation, in which he gave much soberer testimony. There had been signs of a mutinous disposition among the troops, as well as of panic, he charges in his formal declaration, dated at Görlitz, May 24, 1813. Serious reflections are also made on the combat officers in command. Actually there were only

[2]Martino: *Stendhal*, p. 40.

150 guards (not fifteen hundred) and 110 of these were unruly German conscripts from Westphalia.

It was significant of the renewed passion for detail now shown by Napoleon that he caused the commissary Beyle to be brought into his presence at his provisory headquarters near Görlitz. While the great man, standing by a window, listened with frowning mien, barely looking at him, and nervously turning the metal lever controlling the shutters, Beyle made his verbal report. "I had a long conversation with His Majesty," he wrote to his sister a few days later, on June 9, 1813. Afterward, in his unfinished study of Napoleon, he remarked in his dedication: "Sire, do you remember the soldier who took you by the buttonhole at Görlitz? . . ."

The Emperor disciplined the officers involved, and the incident was hushed up for the time. Its importance lay in its hint of the increasing disaffection of the German allies in the army, the last of whom, Saxons and Bavarians, finally changed sides at the great battle of Leipzig, in October.

A few days before his meeting with the Emperor, on May 21, 1813, Beyle had witnessed from close by what military authorities have considered one of the most brilliantly engineered of all Napoleon's last engagements, the Battle of Bautzen, which was marked by most complex and skillful maneuvers, though the French were too weakened to follow up their victory over the allied German and Russian armies. Others have written of battles as if they could be everywhere in the thick of the fight and also at headquarters observing a chart and receiving the dispatches of couriers. Beyle, looking on calmly from behind the lines, nevertheless gives his impressions as the combatant receives them, amid the haste, the interruptions, the disorder of real battle. It is the "fog of battle" that he describes, honestly and realistically, in his brief diaries of 1813, as in his later word painting of Waterloo (which was based on his view of Bautzen).

He was not always in time for the battle itself, owing to his quartermaster duties; but now he pushed forward, driven by curiosity, along with some staff officers. A French division at one flank had been surprised and driven back, and there was Napoleon himself riding up, and black with wrath; Beyle could see him grimacing and swearing at some of his generals who were ordered to return to the charge:

> We reached a little knoll covered with blocks of broken and scattered granite; to the right we saw our mounted scouts very close to us, and we were about to withdraw after fifteen minutes' conversation with our post commandant, when

suddenly we perceived a great movement of cavalry, and His Majesty coming behind us, on the left. We went back; everyone was preparing for battle; the troops headed toward the left, following the movements of the Emperor, and other columns swung to the right toward wooded hills. I had a great deal of trouble in inducing those mean little souls (my fellow officers) to come out and see the battle. We were able to distinguish Bautzen perfectly from the top of the slope against which it is situated. We saw very well from twelve to three o'clock. The pleasure consists in one's being somewhat moved at the certainty that something one understands to be terrible is going on before our eyes. The majestic sound of the cannon contributes much to this effect. The sound is entirely in accord with the sight. If cannon produced the sound of a whistle it seems to me it would not cause so much emotion. . . .

He describes the final advance of the troops of Marshals Oudinot and Macdonald, driving the Allies across the Spree River, while the enemy resisted with stubbornness, his sharpshooters firing from above a tileworks in the valley. Someone points to a "hollow square" forming itself in the distant background. But how can one be certain, Beyle asks? "One sees a great deal with the imagination" during a battle. Perhaps it's only a hedgerow?

Even these casual notes have the quality of the highest accuracy. They indicate the brilliant military innovations Napoleon used in his later phase, when the Allies were already accustomed to his earlier tactics: the dependence upon cavalry and advance guards in the opening stage of battle to engage the enemy and hold him in position; the formation of the *bataillon carré* or massed reserve in the rear, ready to maneuver in any desired direction and strike the mortal blow.

At Sagan, serving under General de Latour-Maubourg, Beyle ruled like a "king" over a fortress city, administering the "government" as well as the supplies for the military garrison. "I reign," he wrote in a letter of July 1813, "and like all kings sometimes yawn a little." The work was strenuous and performed during long hours, with a few clerks and assistants. But typhus raged in Silesia and Saxony, four hundred persons being stricken in his small city that summer, and the intendant too finally sank under its contagion. Soon he was so weakened by prolonged fever that he felt himself as near death as he had ever been during the retreat from Russia. After nearly four weeks of fever and delirium, a replacement was found for him, and he was permitted to move back to Dresden for further medical treatment.

On recovering a little strength, he dragged himself to the opera in Dresden, where the music he most craved, that of the "divine" Cimarosa, was being played. The consequences were a relapse into delirium. "I weep and laugh alone in my room over mere nothings," he wrote while he lay convalescing. Permission was now given him by Daru to return to France for several months, and he arrived in Paris in August looking extremely pale and almost thin. But he did not stay there, for his longing was to return to *mia cara Italia* whose warmth alone, he believed, might restore his shattered health. While the Duc de Cadore, his superior in Paris, amiably looked the other way, he made off for Milan, which he reached on September 7, 1813.

6

It was raining as he arrived; yet from the moment when he glimpsed the famous cathedral spire his fever left him, he felt warm again. "Italy," he said, "renders me more like *myself*."

Two years had passed since his "victory" over the sibylline Gina. He did not hasten to her, but permitted three days to elapse before he called. In the period since he had left Milan she had written him twice, urging him to return, and he had not even answered her. A cloud had passed over their love.

In the fragments of his journal that survived his stay in Moscow, in 1812, he related that by chance he had encountered his old comrade in arms, Louis Joinville, the former lover of Mme. Pietragrua. It was their first meeting in many years, and though Beyle liked Joinville, he was always prone to a quite Shakespearean jealousy. He could not but remember that Joinville, a genial but prosaic fellow, had *possessed* her before him, while he, a callow youth of seventeen, looked on enviously. Joinville spoke of her in Moscow as an *ordinary woman*, not given to fidelity. A few words of gossip exchanged in Moscow, added to reports that reached him later in Paris, made him think perhaps to close the chapter, leaving the perfect happiness of his Milan adventure untarnished in his memory. In his present state of broken health he almost feared the renewal of his old passion for her.

Yet the rain stopped, glowing skies soon returned, the jovial Milanese friends who, he wrote, "have loved me all these twelve years" refreshed his spirits. His mood of "melancholy indifference" dissolved as he walked in those picture galleries he loved, or drove out into the lush countryside neighboring Milan. On the third day of his visit, he sent her a message, the answer to which he read with great relief. No, she was not alienated from him; she was ready to receive him again. As a signal, the window of her house would be open a little the next morning.

They saw each other again, she dropped some tears, looked dramatic and "sibylline"—so that he wished she might be painted on the spot by some skilled artist in all her Italian beauty—and speedily they were reconciled. It was she who pardoned him—was he not a wandering lover who had journeyed a thousand miles away and answered no letters? Their first interview extended itself for eight hours!

September 15, 1813: I must admit however, to be truthful, that I do not feel the intoxication of 1811. My health, though recovering, has improved slowly, and then the effect of novelty and ten years' separation were not present [this time]. But I have reached, it seems to me, that second period *of love* where there is growing intimacy, mutual confidence, and naturalness.

She had a way with her. His apprehensions, his vague suspicions were banished for the moment.

Yet his mind could never rest; piercing regrets and jealousies goaded it awake again and again, turning upon itself, probing itself with an unsleeping eye.

September 25: In the midst of my transports, I was suddenly stopped short by a sterility and a desolating sense of cold, whose cause I suspected was the following:

She had too much feeling to be severe in the choice of the lovers who pleased her (Joinville and myself). It was not by their merits but by her own sentiments that she was moved. As to my jealousy over that, in order to cure myself of it, I must consider that she might well have reason to feel jealous of [Mélanie], and yet how wrong she would be.

But the Othello-like emotions, the doubts of his own adequacy, the fear of new rivals return again and again. Surely, he tells himself, he should be content, and he recalls Beaumarchais' dictum: "In every form of possession, ownership is nothing, enjoyment is everything." And Joinville had thought Angiola but an "ordinary woman"! Which proved only that Beyle had far more sensibility.

Then, like the youthful Faust, he would console himself, seeking to forget all but the illusion of the moment: "No, love is a fortunate fever. Nothing remains when it has passed. Must I, then, feel wretched at having meant no more to her than Louis Joinville?"

Her movements remained as mystifying as ever to him. She would be forced to leave on hurried journeys, warning him not to follow her but to remain in Milan lest he awaken the wrath of her little husband.

Yet after she had been gone a week to some refuge in the mountains, Beyle perceived that her husband was still in Milan.

Why did she not write him? "Has she another lover?" was his tormenting thought. He must perhaps follow them and kill the other man. But instead, he had the notion to take a journey to Venice so as to feed her jealousy or suspicion. For a week he loitered in the Piazza San Marco, or dreamed of her by the Grand Canal in moonlight, then returned to Milan to find, surely enough, an urgent note calling him to her side.

"*Sono felice*," he writes briefly in his journal, for she enchants him again. Though she appears at their assignation wearing a heavy veil, "she is more beautiful than ever"; and he adds in English: "Yesterday true proof of Love." He is ready to do her bidding in every regard. If she needs money for her sudden journeys he gallantly gives it to her. If her son of sixteen must voyage to Lyons to study there, he furnishes three hundred francs for the cost of the trip, and letters of introduction. He submits himself, determined to live, to live with passion and then to forget. For as he reasons in his journal: "Is it your business to describe your life or to live it?"

But while the still convalescing Beyle sighed or tossed in the buxom arms of Gina in his beautiful room on the old square of Belgiojoso, Europe thundered with the Battle of the Nations at Leipzig. The Allies then pushed as far as the Rhine and threatened the borders of France herself, while the Emperor issued his last calls for the defense of the fatherland. At Milan, still a dominion of Napoleon, terror spread at the rumor of approaching Austrian and Russian troops, and Gina and her son took refuge in Pavia. He writes, October 27, 1813:

> In view of the bad turn of affairs in France, I am leaving. . . . Have been sleeping with all my arms beside me. . . . There is a sort of panic in the city. The appearance of two Cossacks would cause everyone to flee Milan.

Out of the vortex of continental warfare, he had stolen a few hours of love and also some hours to write more chapters of the *History of Painting in Italy*, which was to him more important than any martial career.

7

In the national emergency that existed at the end of 1813, Napoleon dispatched senators and councillors of state to their home districts as extraordinary commissars, authorized to raise home guards, arm them, and direct the defense of the country. With them went auditors, or secretaries of the Council of State, who acted as their aides. To Grenoble, commanding the Isère Valley, the Haute-Savoie, and the Simplon and Leman passes over the Alps, was sent the aged senator, Count de Saint-Vallier, and with him as his deputy, Henri Beyle, who, it was thought, would function most effectively in his native town.

Beyle had been expecting promotion to a prefecture in Le Mans or Toulouse in reward for his arduous services in Russia and Germany. The thought of returning to the "general headquarters of pettiness," as he called Grenoble, filled him with pain and indignation, which he vented one day before Mme. Daru, his patroness. And she exclaimed: "If not for this cursed invasion, you would have been made a prefect in some great city." Even before he departed for Grenoble, his sister Pauline, a woman of sound judgment, warned him that this mission might turn out badly for him. "She saw well the character of the dung heap into which I was falling," he remarked later.

He rode into Grenoble by diligence on a moonlit night, January 6, 1814, sore at heart, yet busily turning over in his mind all the measures that must be taken for the defense of the region. Without joy he met his father, whom he nowadays privately called "my bastard." He disliked his father because he always whined about his extravagance. He would have disliked him, if it were possible, even more intensely, had he known that Chérubin Beyle had mortgaged away almost his entire patrimony, for the sake of his own extravagant speculations. His sister Pauline he still cared for, and he also enjoyed her vivacious companion and confidante, whom he called "Mme. Derville" (after whom he undoubtedly modeled the character of the same name in *The Red and the Black*). But aside from the walks he took with these two ladies, and the companionship of his old school friend Romain Colomb, now also a government functionary, he had no amusements in Grenoble. For the sake of peace of mind and solitude he soon decamped from his father's house and rented a furnished room in the center of town.

During the next two months, as conditions grew tense, Beyle was constantly absorbed in the administration of the Seventh Military Division, as it was styled. Urgent decisions had to be made, conscripts must be rounded up and armed, conflicting orders were to be worked out, proclamations and appeals issued to the Dauphinois. All this was done in the name of the aged Saint-Vallier, but in reality it was his deputy, Beyle, according to the eyewitness Romain Colomb, who wrote the necessary public papers, countersigned them, and acted for the old senator. As the Austrians began to penetrate the pass leading from Geneva to Chambéry, Beyle, accompanied by Romain Colomb, went up to the mountain fortifications at Carouge to supervise the disposition of the defending troops and the conduct of their commanding officers. Night bombardment made it impossible to sleep; lack of supplies, the discontent of the population, the bitter quarreling among the officers, made him wearier still.[3]

That in this dark hour he behaved with his usual energy is shown by an official report of his chief, Saint-Vallier, in which a request was made for the decoration of his deputy. "Monsieur de Belle [*sic*] is all alone with me," runs the letter, "worn down with fatigue by working night and day; he has also given other notable services which entitle him to the regard of the Emperor. If these decorations [blue cordon and Cross of the Reunion] were sent to me, I think it would produce a good effect."[4]

Though weary of war and taxes, the Dauphinois fought bravely again in these final hours of invasion. The fathers of Beyle's school friends, old men of seventy, rallied to the colors, and came to him to offer their old swords and fowling pieces. The tight-fisted peasants brought gifts of wine and bread to the conscripts. Crisis and panic were dealt with in all-night councils over which he presided effectively as the Austrians approached the Grande Chartreuse and Lyons. He himself was carried away by patriotic ardor in this heroic season of his life when, as chief of staff to the septuagenarian Saint-Vallier, he virtually commanded the defense of two hundred miles of France's mountain border, almost the last front to capitulate.

"It was the moment in his life that was noblest," remarks Chuquet, usually his severest critic, "and of which he has told us least. In all his voluminous self-confessions there are only a few words on this assignment, and these speak of his vexation and disgust at his townspeople."

The difficulty was that he worked, fought, and issued decrees among the folk who were not impressed by his splendid, gold-braided quartermaster's uniform, but remembered him as an odd, "wild young fellow" of whose misdoings and scandals local gossip delighted to prattle. Moreover, he had acquired certain pretensions: at some stage of his career, when he had administered large towns in foreign lands, his superiors had used the form "*de* Beyle" in addressing him, and he him-

[3]R. Colomb: *Notice*, pp. 29–30.

[4]Chuquet, *Stendhal-Beyle*, p. 139.

self used it in signing public documents. It was a display of vanity such as he often decried in his French compatriots. Now his sharp-witted townspeople knew that his father's title of *noble* was non-hereditary, and to make sport of his little pretensions they defaced some proclamations he signed as "de Beyle" that were posted on the walls of their city. Colomb recalls that they did so with insulting or even obscene remarks.

His eyes were everywhere. He raised money, ammunition, reluctant conscripts from an exhausted population. Using the arts of diplomacy, he went even to the priests, whom he always believed disloyal, and persuaded them to preach rousing sermons when the people seemed increasingly disaffected. During the nights of danger, when news came that Chambéry had fallen, he showed the calm of a man who had passed through many trials, a *sang-froid* in accord with his "logic." Meanwhile the local luminaries, prefects, and mayors, with whom he labored, irritated him to the point of savage mockery—but only in the privacy of his letters and journals. His disappointment at the delay in receiving recognition for his services, as requested by the commandant at Grenoble—on this point he himself was supremely vain—also made him almost physically ill.

With the consent of his chief, he departed for Paris bearing military dispatches, though well aware that the capital itself was about to fall. Ostensibly his object was to lay a report before the Emperor and appeal for reinforcements. He also pretended that, in the emergency threatening the dynasty, his presence in Paris as inspector of the Crown furnishings might be required. In truth he was fed up to the depths of his inconstant soul. Nor must the little matter of the defaced bulletins, by which his thin-skinned dignity was attaint, be forgotten.

En route to Paris he was forced to detour to the west of Orléans, already taken by the Russians in late March 1814. "At Orléans, he despaired for his country, which is to say for the Empire [that] had eclipsed the fatherland!" reads one of his numerous brief Testaments.

He arrived in Paris on March 29, in time to see the Empress and the infant King of Rome leave the Tuileries palace, while the Senate debated over the demand for the abdication of the Emperor. He wandered the streets, observing how silent, weary, and apathetic the people seemed, while the ponderous imperial dynasty and all its "insolent agents" were being swept away. He saw old men and women weeping, as reports of the Emperor's capitulation came. Yet in the Tuileries Gardens he heard young Parisian fops, who looked as if they had never done any fighting, laughing and jesting lightly over the reverses in the national fortunes. He himself, proceeding to the boulevards, gazed in a sort of stupor at the heights of the Montmartre, whence the brisk sound of the last musket fire could be heard, as the Russians fought their way into Paris. But he had seen so much of this sort of thing!

CHAPTER XI

Escape to Italy

> In that period . . . I felt that one had the chance of showing some merit only through being oneself, while to succeed in Paris one needed, above all, *to be like the others.*
>
> —Stendhal

I FELL with Napoleon in April 1814," Beyle tells us in *Henri Brulard.* "I went to Italy to live. . . ." The year 1814, year of the collapse of the Empire, marked his own fall from a life of high favor, he was fond of saying afterward. "Choking with scorn," he had watched the Bourbon king and his retinue of émigré nobles and priests ride into Paris at the invitation of the foreign conquerors. Then the lights went out over France; then began the reprisals against the Bonapartists and the partisans of the French Revolution that by 1815 recalled somewhat the Terror under the Republic. The cowards and turncoats now hastened to sign an oath of allegiance to the restored Bourbon king, eager but to be "pardoned" and retain property, emoluments, and place. Henri Beyle, who had reached a fairly high rank in the Napoleonic hierarchy, chose instead to take flight from a society plunged into reaction. Abandoning all his previous advantages of public office, even refusing important posts offered him under the Bourbons, he embraced a life of obscure poverty, a self-imposed exile in Italy. In July 1814, three months after Louis XVIII had been established on his throne, Beyle quietly slipped out of Paris and hurried to Milan, where he lived for long years as if determined to have nothing to do with his native land.

Was there ever a greater piece of folly? All his friends and relatives stayed in France, simply changed their allegiance, and flourished as before. No one threatened Henri Beyle, as no one molested Pierre Daru. All he needed to do was to wait for things to blow over in order to win some sinecure in the public service again. But to leave one's country out of "disgust" and "indignation" was unheard of.

Yet such is the story as he has told it, and upon this *beau geste* is built the legend of Stendhal's flight toward liberty that has adhered to his name and glory. It was, in former times, something of a scandal in the history of French letters. For how few great French writers have had the folly to exile themselves voluntarily from *la grande nation,* to quit the comforts of the City of Light for some obscure provincial town or some distant wilderness? In the nineteenth century only the poet Rimbaud was to insult French tradition and French parochialism so rudely.

"Accustomed as I was to Napoleon"—and "I who always adored Napoleon"—are some of the phrases he used in his memoirs to convey the scorn he felt for the men of the Restoration. His friend Count Beugnot, for instance, who had switched over to become prefect of police under Louis XVIII, offered him the task of provisioning hungry Paris in 1814, but he refused it, according to his own account. However, such an offer could not have been made unless he had signed the oath of allegiance, as so many of Napoleon's officers did. Now recent scholarship, since 1890, when *Henri Brulard* appeared posthumously, has easily unearthed the document containing Henri Beyle's oath of allegiance to the monarchy, dated April 19, 1814. Also evidence that before leaving for Italy he made some efforts to be returned to the public service, by obtaining letters to Talleyrand and other dignitaries.[1]

Was he, then, by his self-willed exile a heroic enemy of royalism, or only a "disappointed office seeker," as the detractors of Stendhal have called him? His own accounts, usually so unsparingly honest, are contradictory or confusing on this point. In Stendhal's behavior nothing is simple.

It was certainly not as a romantic partisan of Napoleon that he took flight. His cult of Bonapartism does not seem to have been so strong in 1814 as it became long afterward, when the great man was dead.

His cousin Colomb, who was with him in Paris in 1814, declares that Beyle surprised him by showing actual pleasure at the downfall of "the despot who had stolen France's liberties." Moreover, the Bourbons began by establishing a constitutional monarchy, in imitation of England; and Beyle, according to Colomb, actually showed a certain contentment with these "semblances of liberalism." When Napoleon burst forth from Elba and landed in France again early the following

[1]A. Chuquet, *Stendhal-Beyle*, Appendix, p. 513; Farges, *Stendhal Diplomate*, p. 255; cf. also *Correspondance*, Vol. V, Letter of July 18, 1814.

year, Henri Beyle did not move to join his banner. On the historic day of Waterloo he was in Venice, in the arms of the voluptuous Gina.

Before he left for Italy, he wrote his sister Pauline, on May 7, 1814, a letter pointing out that he could no longer count on living in the style to which he was accustomed. "To live here in poverty is impossible for me, connected as I am, almost exclusively, with rich people. . . . I am going to sell everything and leave Paris forever." Thus pride also entered into his calculations.

Yet the more we examine it, the more does Beyle's "escape" to Italy seem an honest and courageous action, one that does him great honor and that has had a profound influence upon his intellectual followers.

This fateful decision was long prepared: to understand it we must go back nearly two years to the time when he was in Moscow and his letter of August 24, 1812, which showed the extent of his alienation. He had by then consecrated long years to ambition, denying his own political Jacobinism and his own moral philosophy which bade him always: "Be thyself!" Ambition had led him to the nightmare horrors of the invasion, plunged him into an "ocean of barbarism." He himself acknowledged, as he wrote to his friend Faure, having committed a "sin against *Beylism.*" Instead of devoting himself to music, to writing, to love, to the forthright quest of happiness, he had betrayed himself. He had hoped that Napoleon was the agency by which the work of the Revolution was to be accomplished: the destruction of feudalism. In the words of Chateaubriand, Napoleon had seemed "like Mahomet with his sword and Koran, marching with arms in one hand and the rights-of-man in the other." But the sword of the modern Caesar, whom Beyle had served up to 1814, had become a law unto itself. As he said later in one of his memorable phrases: "The saber kills the spirit."

What he saw in France, as he watched the return of the old order, and waited in antechambers for some official appointment, undoubtedly offended all his old liberal anti-clerical feelings. The stupid aristocrats of 1789, "thirty thousand nobles who know nothing," had returned and their priests were everywhere. A pall of gloom hung over Paris; the age of cant had begun. He would have to bend his knee, pretend that he never thought or said anything against them. "In April, 1814," he wrote in one of his Last Testaments, "when [I] considered the Bourbons, [I] had two or three days of black humor."

He could have stayed on in this "fetid mud," hiding his feelings. His father, who had come out again as an Ultra-Royalist, was now in high favor, and was made deputy mayor of Grenoble and decorated by the King's brother. Beyle's friends were ready to help him as a man who merited honors for his war service and whom it would be useful to attach to the new government. But he did not like to wait upon the great persons who must be seen; they were "not amusing" to him. And though his friends believed in his abilities and urged him to wait, what he wanted most of all was to "be himself again," and bid farewell at last to ambition, farewell to all sorts of illusions. For you do not win office in the public service, you do not contract a rich marriage, or advance in the salon or literary world by going to bury yourself in some province in Italy.

As he wrote the Countess Beugnot, on August 29, 1814, he felt "a sharp pang in his heart on leaving Paris and those scenes which call to mind the most charming illusions, but which were after all only illusions. . . . I left on horseback in the morning, alone, and rode for two or three leagues through a silent forest, a good occasion for reflection. I saw again that I had cherished only illusions. . . ."

He had sold his horses, carriages, and furniture, announcing that he intended to retire and live in Italy on five francs a day.

Colomb, who saw him off, commented shrewdly: "Perhaps he saw in the change of his situation only a natural means of freeing himself of all shackles and leading that cosmopolitan life to which he thenceforth abandoned himself without restraint."

He had waited almost too long; half his life was spent. "Rome, Rome is my fatherland," he exclaims. "I burn to depart."

It was on July 20, 1814, that he left for Milan.

2

Stendhal, we must always remember, was a figure of transition, who had sprouted between the end of the eighteenth century and the coming of the industrial nineteenth century. How much history he had seen, how many dynasties had risen and fallen even in the first three decades of his life, whose most impressionable years were spent amid the violence of revolution and continental war. It is because he is a transitional thinker, a hybrid of the eighteenth century's rationalistic and revolutionary enlightenment, and the romantic philosophy that was soon to react against the commercial nineteenth century, that Stendhal is so appealing to the men of our own troubled epoch.

The times in which he lived retarded his artistic development, but made him history-minded. Dimly at first, later with great exactness, he grasped that the nineteenth century had begun in 1814–15. The man,

Napoleon, whose power he said could be likened only to Caesar's and Alexander's, had fallen with a crash that resounded throughout the world. What was the meaning of such a world event? And what meaning or direction could there be in such a life as his own, so much at the mercy of events?

He came to Italy, or rather "escaped," as we say nowadays, in order to win time to think and to live. He was by disposition and conviction a sensualist, questing systematically for happiness. And in Italy he had found more physical well-being than anywhere else. Each escapist—and Stendhal was one of the earliest and most conscious of modern escapists—must find his own earthly paradise; Stendhal's was Italy, as it had been Goethe's a generation earlier, and soon afterward became Byron's and Shelley's.

Increasingly he had felt irked and frustrated by French society of his time. He had struggled too long over his cravats and waistcoats to go to evening parties and sit beside old ladies or government ministers who bored him. In Italy, this essentially solitary man, who was forever escaping from something, had found a society that gave him a sense of ease and asked little of him.

Soon after his arrival he wrote:

> In this century that is so vulgarly comic and hypocritical (this age of *cant*, as Lord Byron calls it) the extreme candor and good nature I have perceived in the circles of the noblest and richest people of Milan has impressed me so deeply that I have formed the idea of establishing myself permanently in this country.

He flattered himself in believing that the men and women who were his friends in Milan, whom he saw every night at the Scala, were persons of the most distinguished society; in fact they were bohemian in manners and liberal in politics, which in those days meant secretly revolutionary.

How often he praises the liberty and the "naturalness" of the Italians. Like Rousseau, who influenced him in spite of himself, he desired to escape from conventionalism and, in his own way, effect a return to nature. But Stendhal's "noble savages" were the Italians, especially those of urbane Milan, much to the surprise of the Italians themselves when later they learned of his theories. To be sure, the Milanese were not in any sense primitives, as were the wild Sicilian beggars he had seen in Naples: rather were they the children of an overripe civilization, who still retained the refinement and wisdom of life of their golden age four centuries earlier. Nor had subsequent invasion or foreign oppression changed them, he held; it had but rendered them all the more devoted, as if in compensation, to social amenities and pleasure seeking.

Since the sixteenth century, thanks to foreign despotism or clerical tyranny, it had been dangerous for Italians "to think . . . or to speak out one's mind." Hence they had learned by instinct to speak with infinite grace. Nor did they live "in fear of dying of hunger," like the English, or of "hellfire." Nor were they ruled by their terror of appearing ridiculous, like the vanity-ridden French.

Perhaps it was all his romantic illusion—*Dichtung* rather than *Wahrheit*—that he had rediscovered in 1814 a humanistic Italy little different from the cinquecento, whose "art of life was more favorable to happiness" than that of other lands. Nevertheless he believed with all his heart that now, as in 1500, the Italians were both more civilized and closer to nature than others. In their midst he felt even his wickedness dissolving. Hence he belonged here and not in France: "The true fatherland is the land where one meets people who like us and are pleasing to us."

Even after an uninterrupted stay of three years he was able to write in 1817: "If a man have a heart and a shirt on his back, he should sell his shirt to see Italy." As if transported by his Italomania he continues:

> I experience a sensation of happiness at my sojourn in Italy which I have found nowhere. . . . I feel a magic in this country that I can scarcely define: it is like love; and yet I am not in love with anyone. . . . Often, late at night, returning to my house in [Milan], passing those great portals, my soul obsessed by the lovely eyes I have just seen, looking at those palaces in dense shadow, their masses outlined in the clear moonlight, it happens sometimes that I am choked with joy and exclaim to myself: "How beautiful it is!" . . . How well I have done to come to Italy.

These reflections are from *Rome, Naples, and Florence* (1817), the witty and philosophical travel book written in celebration of his return to his chosen fatherland, which, as it was a hymn to Italy, was an unsparing polemic against France. In one of the more significant of his generalizations upon Italian folk psychology, expressed almost in the terms of modern psychoanalysis, he sets forth the justification for his "escape": "A people is only happy when there are no more conflicting interests dwelling in its heart than are necessary to the maintenance of its well-being." As with nations, he implies, so with individuals, who must also seek an end of conflicts in themselves.

In more than one sense did he resolve conflict within himself (at least for the time being), for on returning to Milan he was reunited with his "majestic and voluptuous" Gina.

But Italy was also the mother of the fine arts. He felt himself enveloped still in the atmosphere of the Renaissance; he drank of the sacred fount of Europe's culture! The very palaces of the old quarter of Milan, at the Piazza Belgiojoso, seen in moonlight, recalled to him "the feudal ages, with their bloody conspiracies and gigantic passions." He desired now, in the repose he had so long sought, to explore as far as possible his own impressions of art and music. His newly won leisure he could use to indulge his "egotism" to his heart's content, savoring it, inspecting it incessantly. With relief, he opened his old notebooks and favorite volumes, that he had dragged with him through half the Napoleonic campaigns, and began to write. And as he lived in his reveries, eternal *flâneur* that he was, he could saunter about under a smiling blue sky, "setting off each day in search of the special category of beauty to which he felt responsive upon waking up." Should it be the Brera Galleries, where he might gaze at the Correggios? Or once more Leonardo's "Last Supper"? Should it be an opera of Mozart at the Scala, or a dinner of cutlets and wine with Italian poets and musicians? Or an assignation with Gina? To Stendhal all the conditions favorable to fullness of living and hence creativeness were present in a Milan of crooked, winding streets, ancient gray palaces and churches, a Milan that was the Italian capital of music and literature, and not yet transformed into one of the world's marts of commerce. He had escaped from the hypocrisy and conventionalism he cursed in French society; sometimes he thought he had escaped from the onrushing nineteenth century itself.

Those seven years, from 1814 to 1821, in which Beyle lived in or near Milan, like a "ruined French gentleman," years exclusively occupied with love, and the arts, and writing, marked the flowering of his original talents. The impoverished ex-soldier, ex-career-official, ex-dandy, was turned into the Stendhal we know. Italy helped him "to be himself."

His purse was meager now: he had a *rente*, inherited from his mother's estate, of 1,800 francs, expectations of soldier's half pay amounting to 900 francs, and annuities of 2,000 francs or so contributed by his "miserly" father with increasing irregularity, until by 1817 they were stopped. In short he had eight or ten francs a day to live on. Yet poverty was no disgrace in Italy, he reported. He could live in Milan at a third less than in France; and there were hundreds of Italian noblemen who lived on less than he. Thus he was able to rent charming rooms in the Corsia del Giardino, in an old and fastidious quarter of Milan, rooms that gave a spacious view of gardens, trees, and sky, and of those adjacent late-Renaissance palaces where dwelt still the descendants of the mighty Sforzas and Viscontis of the *quattro-cento.*

Poor though he was now, compared with his position at the court of Napoleon, he could study or write in the morning, saunter about in the afternoon, visiting bookshops or churches full of art treasures, or sip ices at a café terrace in the open air, while gazing at Gothic spires or baroque palaces or even the snow-tipped Alps in the distance, a cool white thought on a burning day of July. And at seven-thirty in the evening to the Scala for only thirty-six centimes—the cost of admission to its pit—or, on festive occasions, for two francs in the parterre.

The historic Scala, the largest theater in Europe, save for the San Carlo of Naples, and in its baroque way the handsomest, was always for Stendhal the headquarters of music. Within its lofty horseshoe of candle-lit loges and balconies, he sat with streaming eyes listening to the first act of a Cimarosa, a Paësiello, and now a Rossini opera; then he watched the elaborate Italian Ballet served as an entr'acte, with sumptuous costume and scenery and almost ritual dance; afterward the second act of the *opera seria,* followed by a short act of robust *opéra comique,* with effects of the grotesque and salacious succeeding the sentimental, so that everyone who had wept out his eyes might go home convulsed with laughter. Night after night in the warm bath of this animated multitude of two or three thousand that laughed or groaned in unison, cried out praise or blame without restraint, between gulps of ices or wine or a throw of the cards, Stendhal sat entranced, reveling in his own emotions as they rose or fell with those true and suave Italian voices.

Three times a week, issuing from the theater at midnight with his Italian friends, Henri Beyle would go to the home of the beautiful Milanese chanteuse, Elena Vigano, daughter of the most famous ballet master of the age. The "mad" Nina, as she was called, was a pupil of Rossini and one of the finest sopranos in Italy. And though she had already performed that night at the Scala, she would, merely for the pleasure of her friends, sing seven or eight airs, sometimes as many as a dozen—while Beyle reveled in delight upon a soft sofa. To be exposed to his favorite vocal music in such intimate circumstances was for him a joy without end.

Musical maniac that he was, he desired now to pay tribute to this art, which he would have longed to grace as a composer. Like painting and poetry, it was one of "the resources open to unhappy hearts," he remarked. He had wandered so long in the wake of Napoleonic battles, with his baggage of unfinished literary projects, his unslaked thirst for opera, that more than almost any other man he knew the cost of revolution and war.

When he learned of the outcome of Waterloo, he made the reflection that seems so heartfelt, that "now at last young artists would no longer need to die for their country unheard."

With the coming of peace, he had taken up, not his old, oft-interrupted play, nor the half-complete history of Italian painting, but an essay on music he had planned ever since he had witnessed the funeral rites for Haydn in Vienna, in 1809. His musical education was imperfect; he hardly knew how to read notes, having only studied the flute in his boyhood for a short time. His passion for Cimarosa and Paësiello would scarcely be shared by modern music lovers. Yet all his life, as Romain Rolland has said, he lived in a sort of "musical mist." Music, he declared, was "the language of the aristocracy of the heart." He traveled about the world "in order to enjoy the *sounds* played upon his soul by strange mountains and people." To have heard Cimarosa's *Matrimonio Segreto* was to him a greater achievement than the two bravest things he had done in his youth: climbing the St. Bernard Pass with Napoleon's army, and coming under fire for the first time. And from the palace of St. Cloud he had raced twenty miles in his carriage one evening to hear this opera again in Paris, an extravagant journey for those days. But in his little book on contemporary music, *Haydn, Mozart et Métastase,* he speaks less of the frothy melodies of Cimarosa, and pays his respects to the more advanced orchestration of Haydn and Mozart. He would weep endlessly over *Don Giovanni* and over the now comic, now tender music of *Cosi Fan Tutte.* Mozart he always associated with melancholy, and his tears pierced Beyle's soul—"like a serious and often sad mistress, whom one loves because of her sadness."

In 1812, Giuseppe Carpani, an accomplished Italian musician who lived in Germany, had already published a book on Haydn, called the *Haydini,* with some notice of Mozart as well. Beyle had read this with relish while in Milan, and made copious notes on it; on Metastasio, the eighteenth-century Italian improvisatore and composer of famous cantatas, still regarded in his country as one of the wonders of the ages, he found information elsewhere. In his enthusiasm he likened Metastasio to Shakespeare and Virgil. Besides drawing upon Carpani's book, he drew many ideas from his nightly talks with the Milan music lovers, whose favorite operas were soon to conquer all Europe.

It was in Paris, from May to July 1814, that he wrote, or rather compiled his book which appeared as: *Letters Written in Vienna, on the Celebrated Composer Joseph Haydn, Followed by a Life of Mozart and Some Considerations on Metastasio and the Present State of Music in France and in Italy*, by Louis César Bombet. It was printed in Paris in December 1814, at the author's expense (about 3,500 francs), and put on sale in January 1815, a dark season in France. Notice the pen name. Henri Beyle never published anything under his own name, according to a custom that was more prevalent in the eighteenth century than later. During the time of Napoleon, he had formed the habit of signing even his letters with pseudonyms such as: *L. Roux, Chapuis, Col. Favier, Fauris Saint-Bard, C. Simonetta, C. F. Ravet, aîné, Lunenbourg*, and scores of others.

The *Haydn, Mozart et Métastase* is a slight book done in the form of letters and in the aphoristic style of Montesquieu, whom Beyle so much admired. The author pretends that by "some happy chance" he had made the acquaintance of Haydn—a complete fiction—and determined to write letters about him to a friend, which the friend persuaded him to publish. He confesses: "I was tempted to become an author and see myself in print while living." He himself, in one passage, admits that his work is merely a piece of hasty compilation.

Back in Milan, Beyle was in high spirits as his book made its appearance in France. It would fill a void in letters; it would introduce Mozart, still too little known to France, and herald the coming triumph of the Italian school. The discussion of musical taste in France and Italy was a sharp polemic aimed at the French. Many digressive passages, moreover, were his own independent reflections upon the concept of ideal beauty, or aesthetics, upon romantic and classical art, and upon Shakespeare, still a subject of heated controversy in those days.

But the book was scarcely noticed in the French press, though it was seriously reviewed in England. Up to the time of Stendhal's death it sold less than two hundred copies, a poor sale even for those days of relatively costly books and small publics. What was worse, he had the humiliation of seeing, printed in an Italian journal some six months later, a long letter by Carpani, the author of the *Haydini*, addressed to "Louis César Bombet" and denouncing him as a plagiarist. Later, this letter, with its long citations of plagiarisms and sworn testaments by authorities that "Bombet" had never known Haydn, was published in Paris also, in the newspaper *Le Constitutionnel*. The offended author wrote that he would have ignored the plagiarism by this fledgling French writer who borrowed others' plumes for his first flight, were it not for the statement in Bombet's book that it was written as early as 1808, four years before his own work appeared, making out Carpani himself to be the plagiarist!

The truth is that Beyle had borrowed from Carpani, without acknowledgment, about two thirds of the factual material for his piece on Haydn, and most of the biographical facts about Mozart. To be sure, he had added many of his own ideas, and numerous technical errors as well, as Carpani enjoyed pointing out. In praising Mozart and even saying a good word for Beethoven he diverged from Carpani. Those passages which have been marked out as purely Beyle's have considerable charm. Hence it is the greater pity that in his eagerness to "see myself in print" he gave a personal example of the lax literary morals of his time. Plagiarism was all too common then; and a legitimate authorized compilation would have been ill regarded. Beyle said at the time that if he had brought out his book as a translation, as he first intended doing, no one in France would have bought it. His folly lay in trying to pose as an authority on music rather than admit himself a mere acolyte. It is a paradox that the writer who was to be esteemed above all others in his time for originality began his career with a piece of plagiarism.

The exposure in the press humiliated him, though it aroused little interest. But as a hoax, or out of sheer brass, he addressed a letter to *Le Constitutionnel* that he signed "H. C. G. Bombet," pretending to be the brother of the accused author, and laughing off the charges of Carpani in a most flippant tone. Some facts, admittedly, had been borrowed, but had he not the right to do this, like Molière, who said: "I take my property where I please"? Besides Carpani was dull, while "Bombet" was "full of grace and wit." In short Beyle, in disguise, defended and even praised his own work![2] Later he was a little ashamed of the whole affair, and pointed out that he had not signed his name to the book and had lost money on it.

3

Milan and its great open salon at the Scala Theater meant music, but also, what was not less absorbing to him, friendships, and good

[2]Introduction by Romain Rolland to *Haydn, Mozart et Métastase* (Champion ed.); also *Correspondance*, IV, p. 365; Sept. 26, 1816 (Divan ed.).

civilized society in which he could endlessly observe, or himself enter into, the Italian game of "playing" with life.

In *Rome, Naples and Florence,* the book which so faithfully reflects his mind at this period, he relates:

> In Paris, each time you present yourself to an intimate friend, you must break the surface film of ice, which has formed during the last four or five days that you have not seen him; and when this operation is happily terminated and you have regained intimacy and contentment at last, at the peak of your friendly intercourse, midnight strikes, and the mistress of the house tells you it is time to go. Here, at the loge of Madame L., we would begin by staying in the theater until one o'clock; we continued our faro game in the well-lit box a long time after the hall was emptied and the spectators gone. Finally the porter of the theater came to warn us that one o'clock had long struck; solely in order not to separate, we went to sup at Battastino's, the caterer to the theater, and did not part from each other until daylight had come. I had no close friends in this circle, and yet those evenings of unaffected charm and happiness will never vanish from my memory.

What he loved to watch for in human intercourse, he relates, was *le divin imprévu,* the "divinely unexpected" in thought, or turn of speech, or human gesture.

But in Paris even the company of a pretty woman might pall on him after he had come to know her well.

> And if as was often unfortunately the case she happened to be well bred, then I would be reminded at once of my family, of the upbringing of my sisters, and could foretell every one of the woman's gestures and the most fleeting nuances of her thought. It is that which has made me often prefer low company, where one finds more of the unexpected. . . . Think of my delight at finding, in Italy, what none had informed me of previously, that it was precisely in the best company that one found the *unexpected* most often.

Though a foreigner, Stendhal was most cordially received by the literati of Milan. Chief of these was Count Ludovico di Breme, who (under Napoleon) had been almoner to the King of Italy, a tall, thin young man with noble features and the pallor of a marble statue. Naturally Stendhal was introduced to him in someone's box at the Scala. Di Breme was the editor of the newly established review *Il Conciliatore,* representing the new romantic literary school. He had beautiful manners, but like his compatriots was capable of a furious eloquence, or a fierce, moody passion when aroused. Around him were grouped the already famous poets of young Italy, such as Monti, Silvio Pellico,

Grossi, and Manzoni, who was already likened to his great model, Byron. Through Di Breme, Stendhal also met Giuseppe Vismara, the ardent revolutionary, who became his close personal friend and confidant.

Little wonder that he felt at ease in this circle of young men, as he entertained them with his endless "inside stories" of the court of Napoleon, or tales of his youth as a soldier of the Republic. They liked him because, besides being romantic poets, they too were devoted Jacobins; they had generous passions, and dreamed of liberating their country from the yoke of foreign conquerors. Actually they spoke little of politics, for there were too many (Italian) spies of the Austrians listening eagerly; yet they conspired, they schemed—up to the days of the abortive insurrection of 1820–21—to bring forth a *Risorgimento* of national unity and democracy in Italy. Most of them were poor, but their gifts of friendship were rare.

Grossi was a simple clerk, yet esteemed by all the town because of his poems in the Lombard dialect. The ill-fated Silvio Pellico (whom Europe would remember later for his tragic prison memoirs) lived on but one hundred lire a month, earned as tutor in the household of some rich friend; and the worthy Count di Breme paid for the publication of his books which were then the glory of Italian letters. Stendhal declares (in *Rome, Naples and Florence*):

> In Italy art is ill paid, but they talked for a whole month of Pellico's *Francesca da Rimini*. . . . Literature in Italy will never become a vile trade that a Monsieur de V—— [Villèle, Prime Minister of France under Louis XVIII] rewards with places in the Academy or the censorship bureau.

"Romanticism is all the rage here," wrote Stendhal to one of his friends in Paris. "I too am a wild romantic, that is to say, I am for Shakespeare against Racine, for Lord Byron against Boileau."

Milan was assuredly the Mecca of many distinguished foreign travelers besides Beyle, for one day in the autumn of 1816, Lord Byron himself arrived, with his whole menagerie, including his dogs, horses, and monkeys, his friend Hobhouse, and his Italian secretary, Dr. Polidori, who, Beyle suspected, quietly carried on in Italy as his pimp.

Byron, the first poet of Europe (which read him in a stream of translations), the champion of liberty, the conqueror of woman!—all Milan was aflutter at his coming. Beyle saw him for the first time at the Conte di Breme's box in the Scala. "Full of enthusiasm, forgetting the proper repugnance that every man of pride should feel in meeting a peer of England, I asked M. di Breme to introduce me to Byron," he relates. In a letter to Louis Crozet the following day, October 20, 1816, he writes:

> I dined with a handsome and charming young man with the face of an eighteen-year-old, though he is twenty-eight, the profile of an angel, and the gentlest manner. He is the original of Lovelace, or rather a thousand times better than the talkative Lovelace. When he enters an English salon, all the women leave on the instant. He is the greatest living poet, Lord Byron. . . . Greece is to him what Italy is to Dominic [Stendhal].

At that dinner the poet Vincenzo Monti was also present and, following a discussion of modern Italian literature, was besought by Byron to recite some of his poems, which he did *con brio*. The author of *Childe Harold* listened intently, and Beyle, observing him, felt that "his habitually haughty look, such as a man wears when repelling some importunity, and which rather diminishes the beauty of his magnificent countenance . . . vanished and gave way to an expression of absolute joy. . . ."

The admiration of the pudgy, side-whiskered Frenchman was obviously not reciprocated at the outset. Beyle, who when with strangers was usually reserved in manner, began by committing an indiscretion. On one of his first evenings in Milan, Byron, leaving the Scala, remarked that he intended to walk home across the city, instead of using a carriage, and asked Beyle (who spoke English of a sort) for directions. At this, Beyle forgot his reserve so far as to show concern over Byron's lameness, the distance to be traversed, the ever present danger of footpads, and urged that he take a carriage. But he regretted these words the moment they were uttered, for the English poet, extremely sensitive on the score of his lameness, drew himself up and said with exquisite politeness that he had not inquired whether the journey would be fatiguing or dangerous, or how it should be made, but had simply asked for directions.

Beyle's first feeling toward the idolized poet had been of "tenderness mixed with timidity." He had felt himself "ready to kiss the hand of Lord Byron." Now he swore to himself that he must avoid further rebuffs. When next they met, Byron had learned what all Milan knew: that Beyle was an ex-officer and secretary of Napoleon who had survived the horrible retreat from Moscow. Now it was Byron whose curiosity was piqued; it was he who urged Beyle to narrate some of his remarkable experiences in Russia and his personal impressions of the Emperor, while Beyle, wishing to pay off the conceited aristocrat, allowed himself to be pressed for a long time before he consented to unburden himself.

Napoleon was a favorite subject with both men. Soon they were walking up and down together in the immense, deserted foyer of the Scala, while the music came to them from a distance, engaged in what Beyle termed "the finest conversation in all my life." The Frenchman had feared that Byron was, like most Englishmen, prejudiced against the French as well as their Emperor, which was partly true. At moments Byron appeared to envy the mental brilliance or genius credited to the Man of Destiny. "Curiously enough," Beyle recalls, "it was not the despotic spirit in Napoleon's heart that offended the young English lord." Yet their talk was animated, for Stendhal was always ebullient in conversation, and Byron was a "volcano" spouting ideas. "Whenever this strange man was strongly moved . . . and spoke with enthusiasm, his sentiments were large, generous, noble, in a word, on a level with his genius."

Sir John Cam Hobhouse, in his memoirs of Lord Byron, records some of the more curious things the French traveler related. Napoleon is shown in the retreat on foot instead of being mounted on his white horse—when the ice was too slippery for riding—and bearing his white baton in his hand, the "white stick" which in the old French proverb is an omen of misfortune. Throughout the period of the Russion invasion Beyle describes him as being distrait and apathetic, sometimes signing orders or decrees with some strange name, instead of his own! But his sadistic qualities are also noted: during the Battle of Borodino, as he sat on a knoll, he received with extraordinary callousness the news that his commanding generals had been killed, one after another, saying only: "Very well, go away now," or: "Well, run along there."

Hobhouse goes on to say: "I have every reason to think that Beyle is a trustworthy person, he is so reported by Breme. However, he has a cruel way of talking, and looks, and is, a sensualist."

Beyle, aware no doubt of how much cant there was after all even in these two liberal young English lords, and offended at the pharisaical questions coming from Byron (of all men!) concerning French "immorality," did his best to explode petards under them. He said that Napoleon, in his opinion, far from having been a cruel man, as Byron supposed, was not cruel enough. This was one of his characteristic jests: the pretendedly serious notion that cruelty must always be thoroughgoing rather than partial, if used at all. Hobhouse, with a touch of pious horror, quotes him as saying: " 'Napoleon had the

Bourbons in his hands and would not do away with them.' Beyle alluded to poison." Ah, poison! A wholly Italian fifteenth-century idea, worthy of the Borgias.

Like other eyewitnesses, Beyle testifies to the great natural intelligence of Byron when he was being himself and not the pretentious descendant of Norman conquerors and Scottish kings. His observations on philosophy and literature, upon utilitarianism and logic, impressed even a Stendhal both by their thoughtfulness and sincerity. But on occasion the handsome poet would turn silent and moody; he would stare about him wildly, or seize his head in his hands as if he suffered a tremendous headache, forgetful of the company, thinking only of the terrible scandals about him that raged in England, of which Milan knew nothing as yet. Puzzled by his violent changes of humor, the group at the Scala sometimes conspired to tease him especially on the subject of his rank. They were republican in their sympathies, and quickly noted the contradiction between Byron's professed hatred of kings and his frequent references to his patrician birth. Beyle in particular was capable of the sharpest mockery of the nobility of blood and on one occasion joined with the others—who were secretly Carbonari—to such effect that Lord Byron suddenly rose up from his chair, evidently in a cold fury, yet controlling his expression, and stalked out of the loge.

Beyle measured the amazing arrogance in Byron and said in later years that he and the author of "Don Juan" could never have been close to each other. "He lacked plainly any real experience of men, and his pride, his rank, his fame had always prevented him from treating them as his equals," Beyle judges. Too often Byron would play the misanthrope, convinced that "all who surrounded him were occupied with him, and sought to arouse his jealousy or deceive him." But was he not also a man of energy and courage in action? Beyle continued to admire and defend him—until Byron began to write in more classical style.

Byron, on the other hand, though declaring that he detested all authors, undoubtedly relished the conversation of the stout and ugly little Frenchman as one of the "human curiosities" he had met. After 1818, Beyle made no further effort to see Byron, who resided mostly in Venice and Leghorn, but the English bard read his books with great interest. Several years after they had first met, in 1822, he wrote Beyle a long and friendly letter, recalling their mutual friendships and experiences in Italy.

Meanwhile, in visiting the picture galleries of Milan, Byron had the advantage of having Beyle accompany him as his cicerone. It was on such an occasion that he spoke in confidence of his recent visit to Mme. de Staël in Switzerland, where respectable folk had snubbed him, and of his grief at the calumnies spreading in England. In his *Rome, Naples and Florence,* Beyle came gallantly to the defense of the man who was being then denounced as a monster of immorality, calling him the "pleasantest monster I have ever met," and lightly mocking at the "Hebraic" prudery of the English middle classes who condemned him for "doing what all rich young men do," that is, living with actresses and suchlike.

A famous courtesan of the early nineteenth century has written in her memoirs of an interview with Lord Byron in which he questioned her concerning the "Baron" de Stendhal. Apparently he complained because the other criticized his aristocratic attitudes while himself playing at being a baron. But Beyle, he said, was "a clever man, even original, which is something rare among authors who are men of society."[3]

But plainly Byron suffered from a delusion of persecution, as Beyle could judge by the way he sometimes went about grimacing and muttering to himself. His great error lay, as Beyle shrewdly remarks, in trying to be at one and the same time an English aristocrat and a great poet. When Byron made repeated complaint of the persecutions he suffered, his French friend gave him a quite original piece of advice on how he might spare himself the petty hatred of the English bourgeoisie, and yet leave himself free to follow his own great designs: namely, he should pretend to die, and, with the help of a few friends, stage a bogus funeral. After that, under some name unknown, he could go and live wherever he pleased, let us say, in Lima, Peru. But at the time of his real death he could leave a message to the public as follows: "The Lord Byron said to have died thirty years ago is really myself. But British society appeared to me so stupid that I simply left it behind."

It was an ingenious scheme—worthy of a man who used three hundred nom de plumes and himself often felt the breath of persecution. But Byron, fearing that his leg was being pulled, drew back and said acidly: "My cousin, who will inherit my title, would owe you a warm letter of thanks."

[3] D. Gunnell, *Stendhal et l'Angleterre,* p. 58.

4

Music, friendship, cosmopolitan conversation flourished in the luminous "beehive" of the Scala Theater. But above all these things in interest for Beyle were the women, the so luscious Italian, or rather Lombard, women who came every night to their loges and, while the music played, openly, without thought of concealment, carried on their love affairs under the eyes of the whole town. The women of Italy, he informs us authoritatively, were—and, it is said, still are—the most intensely feminine of all women. "In France, the women look at each other; in Italy, they look at the men." Brought up in convents to the age of fifteen, they developed perforce "souls of fire, and loved madly"—not their husbands, of course, but their lovers. Nor did this create the least unpleasantness or scandal, for according to Beyle:

> At the Scala a woman's reputation was made or broken; it was made when she had her lover escort her to her box; broken when only a servant or her husband accompanied her.

The happy lover would pass four or five hours thus in the most complete and tender intimacy with his mistress, discoursing upon his lawsuits, his English garden, his horses and hunting. The husband was never expected to show jealousy—that is, after the first two years of marriage, as Beyle was informed. But why, then, should one be jealous if one were not in love?

In his private letters, as distinguished from his travel book, Beyle extolled even the native courtesans, as well as the demimondaines at the theater. When his good friend "Nina" Vigano, known for her mad escapades, went to Paris to sing, he introduced her to a friend there with the recommendation (written in English): "*Contrary to all the women of this country she has never took a penny from her lovers.*"

Like a born novelist, he loved to listen to the endless tales of their adventures and intrigues; and, from some of the aged belles of Milan, even the enthusiastic, detailed description of the attributes of their famous lovers. How candid they were!—and yet so unfailingly capricious, so full of the *unexpected*. In his essay *On Love* he declares:

> To coquette with Italian women is my supreme pleasure. It is said that a confirmed intriguer loves intrigue for its own sake and not in order to attain some definite objective. It is thus that I loved to enter into the secrets of Italian women; the most *womanly* women in the universe.

Those secrets, those intrigues would furnish him with a treasure store of dramatic and fictional material. But the best intrigue of all, more instructive by far than any he merely heard of, was the one he lived through with the stately and pneumatic Gina Pietragrua.

Naturally upon arriving in Milan in the summer of 1814 the thought of Gina was foremost in his mind. To him she was ever a figure out of Leonardo, with great blazing orbs for eyes and a melancholy smile hovering mysteriously at her mouth.

But how would the unpredictable Gina, she who was all flame and pride and so quick to anger, receive her worn, far-wandering lover? During the year of tumult and horror that had passed since he had last seen her, he recollected, to his own surprise, that he had not even answered her two last letters. He returned, as if with passion spent, feeling himself "cold and dead, like a man of sixty." But the first sight of her served to banish anemia. She understood what he had endured; she pitied him. She took him back.

But now, it was plain for her discerning eye to see, her clever Frenchman no longer boasted the impressive rank and income of the year before. This was decidedly a problem. Soon all sorts of delays and obstacles were interposed between their irregular rendezvous. It was required that he show the most cunning discretion. For the French, after 1815, were in deep disfavor in Milan, Gina earnestly assured him. The Germans of Austria once more were in the saddle, and Beyle was suspect as a Bonapartist. Her husband, moreover, had grown "jealous" on hearing of his return, and her other admirers were no less suspicious. At length she begged him for the sake of her peace of mind, her honor, her reputation (which one would have thought so adjustable), to leave Milan for a space of two months and wait at Genoa, until political and domestic conditions could grow more composed. Perplexed because she vowed that she "loved him better than all other men" and yet sent him away, also pleased that he must front so much danger, he submitted to her will and set off upon a leisurely tour of Tuscany and Parma. When he returned to Milan, as agreed, in mid-October 1814, he met her secretly at a little church.

But once more she played the same tunes over. She stormed and wept, reproached him for having delayed writing to her, and, charging him with being a man of ambition who would forget his poor Italian mistress the next time he returned to Paris, went so far as to propose a rupture of their friendship.

"She looked very pretty in her black veil. And did not say what she had to say, without great pain," he notes in his journal, October 16, 1814. Nevertheless she made an appointment to visit him in his quarters the next day.

Henri Beyle, the indefatigable observer of the human heart, was baffled by the thickly tangled problems woven into his own life by this woman of passion. The idea that his presence was not wanted filled him with such despair that he asked her if another *cavaliere servente* was not hovering behind the scenes. In a stormy interview, Gina upbraided him for his "bloodsucker-like jealousy," and exiled him again, commanding him this time to go as far as his native city of Grenoble. It was midwinter, he protested; the passes of Mont Cénis were deep in snow.

Gina rejoined severely: "A man who was among the conquerors of Moscow should not be afraid of a little cold."

Sadly he heeded her once more and rode northward toward France, which he had no wish to see again, in late December; but at Turin he stopped and quietly made his way back to Milan, where he remained in seclusion for a few days.

How exacting was the Italian way of love! Gina was all caprice, all summer lightning, and in her presence boredom, at any rate, was banished. He felt himself "so torn by the storms of a great passion," he relates in his journal, "between December 22, 1814, and January 6, 1815, that I was on the point of bidding good night to the company." The arsenal of Logic was exhausted, his dialectics helped not. When all seemed lost, he who was so profound in divining the motives of others thought of a last expedient, and by applying what he called "the genius of the former Mr. Lovelace," for the moment, restored a measure of calm to their relations.

By strident calls upon his family at Grenoble, and by making a partial draft against his expectancy, he was able to scrape together a goodly heap of gold pieces, a matter of three thousand francs, which, in the summer of 1815, he turned over to his adored "Countess Simonetta." Gold was the saving genius of Lovelace, in the last resort, and warm Italian smiles lighted up the moral darkness into which he had been plunged.

He announces himself happy again in the spring of 1815. His plan, with which she appeared to fall in, and which provided some discretion for their connection, was to remove to Venice, that pleasure city which Beyle loved next to Milan. In a rather large train, which included her fat brother, her son, her servant, and, oddly enough, a middle-aged banker who now appears on the stage, they journeyed in two carriages to Padua, then by the mail packet down the Brenta to Venice, which they reached in July.

Here, Beyle found warmth, wine, good and cheap food, auburn-haired girls, the Grand Canal and its gondolas, the Piazza San Marco in moonlight—"the gayest city in all Europe"—and he was in funds for the moment. Moreover he had his heart's desire, which was to have Gina by his side without the need for concealment.

But soon—at this *comble* of his happiness—jealousy and strife divided them. Why did she insist, after a time, that they live in separate hotels? And what was that dreary old man, the banker, doing, staring at her mournfully while they dined together at a restaurant? "Was he jealous? Did he have the right to be so? Or was it but an expression of disappointed hope?" Bitter scenes took place between them. Gina might be a soul on fire, but her importunities were not of the passional kind, his diary shows.

> July 17, 1815: She pretends that she *makes me a great sacrifice going to Venice. I was very foolish of giving her the three thousand francs which were to pay for this tour.*
>
> July 19, 1815: The question of two hundred francs. Bitterness when *money* is spoken of. Dominic always seems the dupe. . . .

Alas poor Dominic! Political economy, day by day, embittered the love potion he drank. For he remarks on July 27, 1815:

> *I have had her* . . . but she talked of our financial arrangements. There was no illusion possible yesterday morning. Politics kills all voluptuousness in me, apparently by drawing all the nervous fluid to the brain.

Distracted in Venice, he learned belatedly that Napoleon, who had landed in France from Elba, had met catastrophe at Waterloo, June 16, 1815, news of which reached him only three weeks later. The fate of his country had been decided for long years, supreme humiliation had come to France, while he, in enchantment, tossed in the arms of his Italian Circe.

"For the first time in my life I felt a wave of patriotism," he relates. "The cowards!" he exclaimed to himself. France had lost everything, even honor. He did not mourn the French of today, but "what they might have become fifty years hence." But then, what had he done to aid his admired Emperor in his supreme gamble? He did not act or fight; nothing mattered to him now. He said: "I am merely a passenger on the boat." The truth was that Gina did not let him leave for France.

In the autumn they were back in Milan, but once more their movements were cloaked in utmost secrecy, so that he alternated between explosions of sheer joy and tormenting periods of melancholy solitude, sometimes illuminated by sudden and terrible suspicions that made him burst into savage laughter at himself.

In Milan he was required by her to take rooms in an obscure suburb of the city and see her only under circumstances freighted with mystery. When she would accord him an assignation (as he told the story to Prosper Mérimée, years later in Paris), he would put on a disguise, envelop himself in a long dark cloak, and depart in the dead of night, changing carriages several times in order to throw presumed spies off his trail. Arriving at the house of his mistress, he would be admitted by a chambermaid who had long enjoyed their confidence.

All went well for a time, until the chambermaid, quarreling with her mistress, or won over by the money of Beyle, made a startling revelation: Madame's husband was not jealous at all; she demanded all this mystery in order to prevent M. Beyle from encountering a rival, or more properly speaking, one of his rivals, for there were numerous ones, and the maid offered to prove it to him.

Somberly he agreed. The next day he arrived in town at an hour when he was not at all expected, and hidden by the chambermaid in a small closet adjoining his lady's boudoir, "*he saw with his own eyes*, through a keyhole, the treachery that was being done to him, only three feet from his hiding place."[4] It is a memorable picture that the malicious Mérimée leaves us in a privately printed memoir of his corpulent friend Beyle, the calculating Lovelace and the eternal observer of the human passions, wedged in a cabinet and with an eye frozen to its keyhole, staring and staring. It is a picture of a sorrowful experiment by a natural genius of psychology upon his own illusions and vanities, commemorated also in a scabrous portrait by Félicien Rops for connoisseurs of scatology. What a price to pay for the truth!

"You may think perhaps," said Beyle, "that I rushed out of that closet in order to poniard the two of them? Nothing of the sort. It seemed to me that I was present at a scene of the most terrible buffoonery, and my sole preoccupation was to restrain myself from bursting into laughter, in order not to spoil the mystery. I left my dark closet as quietly as I came in, thinking only of the ridiculous side of the adventure, laughing to myself, and also full of scorn for the lady, and quite happy, after all, to have regained my liberty. I

[4] P. Mérimée: H. B.: *Notes et souvenirs.*

went to a café to take some ices, and there met some acquaintances, who were struck by my gaiety and my distracted air: they told me that I had the appearance of a man who had suddenly come into an inheritance. Even while talking with them, the irresistible desire to burst out laughing came over me repeatedly, and the image of the marionettes I had just seen kept dancing before my eyes. Returning to my room, I slept as usual. The next day the spectacle seen from the dark closet had ceased to appear to me under its comic aspect. It seemed to me sordid, vile, and sad. Each day the image became more and more sad and odious. And each day thereafter a new weight was added to my unhappiness. During eighteen months I remained stupefied, unable to write, think, or speak. . . . I felt myself oppressed by an unbearable sense of evil, without being able to explain to myself what I was feeling. There is no greater unhappiness, for it robs one of all energy. After that, recovering a little from that crushing depression, I felt a strange curiosity in ferreting out all the infidelities committed against me. It hurt me fearfully to know of them; but, at the same time, I took almost a physical pleasure in imagining all the details of her numerous betrayals. I avenged myself by persiflage directed at her."

Despite his jests about his cuckoldry, the shock of the affair did permanent damage to his *amour-propre*. Eternal dupe that he was, he had finally discovered what all Milan knew. Though Gina, as he remarks, seemed greatly affected by the rupture of their relations, and came to him to beesech his pardon with streaming eyes, he would not relent. "A man can never pardon an infidelity in a woman," he always insisted, faithless though he was.

But he consoled himself by saying "that La Pietragrua was a strumpet, but *a sublime strumpet, like Lucrezia Borgia!*" That she strove to win him back is evidenced by a note he scrawled under the date of October 10, 1815, on the margin of a volume of Molière he often carried with him:

> *Reconciliation and I believe last time.* The visit at the Brera Museum together with General —— disgusted me once and for all. . . . I did not see her for six months afterward. Then I regretted that I was no longer in love with her. She has treated me like Turenne [whom she deceived earlier in favor of Stendhal]. *She has five or six* lovers.[5]

She must have come to see him one day in October at one of his regular haunts, in a gallery of the Brera Museum, where he used to stand for hours, gazing in anguish at the celestial pictures of Correggio, his favorite painter. In his sorrow art and music were his solace.

Gina knelt before him and wept and implored his forgiveness.

[5]Henri Cordier, *Stendhal et ses amis*, p. 51.

"I had the ridiculous pride," he related to Mérimée, "to repulse her with disdain. It seems to me that I can still see her clinging to my garments, and dragging herself after me on her knees all the length of a great gallery. I was a fool not to pardon her, for assuredly she never loved me more than on that very day."

CHAPTER XII

The Italian Years: Happiness Through Art

> Dear unknown friend, surrender yourself freely to the arts. Their study . . . will bring you, out of the depths of your miseries, a most splendid consolation.
>
> —Stendhal, *Histoire de la peinture en Italie.*

IT WAS not quite true that Henri Beyle, after his own amorous Waterloo in 1815, spent eighteen months in a stupor of grief. Slowly the broken pieces of his self-esteem were mended. But that his "march toward happiness," for which he had felt himself armed with the most complete set of rational maxims any man ever set off with, should have ended in such a signal defeat inevitably had a cautionary effect. Like a brave scientist he swallowed his humiliation, charging his losses to his fund of experience. For several years thereafter he showed enough prudence to avoid the exposure of his too susceptible heart. He became more solitary than before: that is to say, even when in the company of friends or social acquaintances whom he enjoyed, he exhibited his true feelings rarely, and wore a somewhat mocking smile, a characteristic expression that became a fixed habit and part of his physiognomy. In short the man of superior quality and sensibility defended himself against the world and the wounds it might inflict upon his pride. He tended to use a certain deception, a certain hypocrisy toward society, concealing his true motives, and even his originality, under pleasantries and commonplaces, or sometimes even silence.

In the absence of love, there was always the resource of the arts. "No happiness without work," he would tell himself. Hence he read much and wrote five or six hours a day. "Lacking any serious occupation, after 1814," he reported to a friend in Paris, "I write, but as one smokes a cigar, to pass the time." In his introduction to *The History of*

Painting in Italy, he states that after taking up the study of painting, solely out of boredom, and in a highly methodical way, he found to his surprise "that it brought a balm for the cruelest disappointments." In writing of the great painters of the past, he was "amusing himself by threading pearls."

Thus Beylism, like Grecian stoicism which, after all, it greatly resembled, abounded in recipes against melancholy or loneliness and in compensations against life's misfortunes. For example, one could turn to books—"a storehouse of happiness, always safe, and which man's ill will can never steal from us." Confronting poverty, Stendhal wrote: "People think they have done all the harm possible to a man by reducing his income, let us say, by six thousand francs a year. But if the man love books and have a good stomach, he can be happier than ever for all that. . . ."

In June 1810, he had written some advice to his sister Pauline, who declared herself unhappy, advice which he followed for himself:

> One may find happiness in one's stomach, in love, or in the head; with a little good sense, one may take something from each of those three kinds of happiness and make oneself a pleasant lot that is immune to the cruelties of men. . . . Here is the picture: in the morning read a book which brings some sentiment into play; by three o'clock make some necessary visits; dine voluptuously, carefully, tranquilly; in the evening spend some time with women who are amiable, and avoid like the pest the conversation of men full of bitterness, vanity, and the dark side of life, etc.

Assuredly this is not the program of a pessimist, but of a man who rebounds after the buffets of fate, and loves life with every fiber.

Ever since his vacation in Italy in 1811, he had planned writing a sort of manual of the history of Italian painting which was to serve as a vade mecum for himself, heightening his own enjoyment of the great works that, lying on every hand, made the pleasure of living in this golden land all the richer. He was methodical, always the "ideologue," as when he had learned by heart the doctrines of Cabanis and Tracy; but such a methodical attack, he found, far from spoiling his pleasure, increased it. Where he had once enjoyed pictures painted on fans, or really liked only one or two Raphaels seen in the Louvre, reading of the life and thought of the painters opened up for him a knowledge of the many different schools of art, discovered for him painters he had not enjoyed before, gave him a thousand fruitful subjects for reflection. He read of course Vasari's *Lives of the Painters*, but the Abbé Lanzi, an eighteenth-century historian of Italian art, was more complete and, partly in order to improve his own Italian (which he found still deficient), partly for his own education, he had begun to translate Lanzi, as early as 1811 and 1812. Within three or four months he had done Lanzi into French, in abridged form, and also filled a dozen large manuscript books with outline notes on the leading figures of Italian painting since the Middle Ages. Part of his notes he took with him to Moscow in 1812 and lost in the great retreat. But after working at the project in a desultory way during the next two years he took it up in earnest in the autumn of 1815.

It was not only that he sought forgetfulness of present ills, but that he was spurred on by the hope of completing a modern work on Italian Renaissance art that would both fill a real need and help ease his straitened circumstances. Throughout 1816 he toiled steadily at his history until he had finished the equivalent of two volumes on the Florentine School. This manuscript he sent off to Paris to be printed early the following year. (There were to have been four more volumes on the other Italian Renaissance painters according to his original plan, later abandoned.)

In his youth he had studied drawing; and in Paris he had attended art classes. But though he drew hundreds of little sketches on his manuscripts while he wrote, he showed no particular gifts for the plastic arts. The clue to his deepening interest in the arts seems to lie in his growing disposition to solitude at the time when he became a wanderer. For painting is best enjoyed alone.

At first he enjoyed travel to hear the "sounds" of strange lands and peoples, mountains and valleys. He preferred so much to enjoy his sight-seeing alone that he said even the company of the friend he most admired, Louis Crozet, would have spoiled things for him. "My happiness consists in being solitary in the midst of a great city, and passing every evening with a mistress," he writes in Venice on July 17, 1815. "Venice perfectly fills these conditions." But it was not often his luck to be with a mistress every night, and his extremely modest budget would not have permitted it. More usually he was alone, or among strangers with whom his relations were perfunctory, but, as happened in Italy, genial enough. When the terrible news of the capitulation of France after Waterloo reached him he relates in his diary: "In order to console myself for this great misfortune that has befallen human civilization, I went out and made a tour of Venice." And earlier, after the Moscow campaign, in 1813, when he was melancholy and sick, he went to Dresden and its Royal Galleries there to enjoy "the arts and solitude."

Soon the enjoyment of these solitary promenades was augmented by his growing interest in history, his sense of the past, whose great monuments everywhere surrounded him. In Florence he had been "moved to tears" at finding himself at the tombs of Machiavelli and Michelangelo. The Leonardos in Milan, and the Correggios, recalled to him the golden age of Renaissance Italy, the fifteenth century. This led in turn to his absorption in historical and aesthetic speculations. What constituted the beautiful? What were the conditions that made for beauty? What brought about the Renaissance in Italy? If he found a great picture in the street would he pay attention to it? A well-known Milanese painter kindly gave him a long list of artists whose works he must study. Very docilely he copied down the man's recommendations that began with Raphael and Correggio and went on to the Carracci. For he was but a novice then and followed the judgment of others. Like most students of art in his time he passed over the pre-Raphaelites, Cimabue, Fra Angelico, Botticelli, and Mantegna.

The *History of Painting in Italy*, in the restricted form Stendhal gave it, is mainly an adaptation of the long history in five volumes and 1,900 pages by the Abbé Lanzi whose work was issued between 1788 and 1790. Approximately two thirds of Beyle's book follows the old Italian scholar, even slavishly imitating his deficiencies of taste, as they appear to modern students of art. Beyle's "compilation" involves liberal borrowings from other, older sources such as Vasari and Mengs (on Leonardo), as well as the recent lectures of Sir Joshua Reynolds, and the studies of Giuseppe Bossi (a contemporary painter and student of art history) of Leonardo's "Last Supper." The book is skillfully fused of borrowings from all these earlier biographical and critical studies, to which are added his own highly personal reflections and digressions amounting to a third or perhaps only a fourth of the two volumes. Beyle's original contribution consists of most of his introductory discussion of Italian history in relation to its arts, his much admired 100-page study of Leonardo—Lanzi contained only twenty pages on this theme—and most of the reflections in his second volume upon the concepts of ideal beauty, and of antique and modern canons of taste. But even the study of Leonardo, who held such great attraction for him, owed much to the writing of Bossi, who died in 1815, five years after Lanzi. And so, once more, playing the dilettante, he opened himself to charges of plagiarism.[1]

Moreover, he invited suspicion when he incorporated in his book eyewitness descriptions and comments upon pictures he could never have seen, since they were in the Hermitage of St. Petersburg, which

[1]P. Arbalet, *L'Histoire de la peinture en Italie, et les plagiats de Stendhal*, p. 193.

he had never visited. The speed with which he wrote also renders him suspect. Though he had lost a great part of his manuscript in the retreat from Moscow, he was able to complete most of his two-volume work in five months, since the major part of it was translation.

Yet after weighing carefully the exposure of his plagiarisms by Professor Paul Arbalet, one tends to conclude that the modern scholar has stated the case too severely. This lifelong Stendhalian, like Taine himself, does homage to the originality compounded here with more or less uncalculated literary felonies. In those early years as a would-be author, when he was fired with the ambition to launch himself quickly in the republic of letters, Beyle had had no literary apprenticeship, no scholar's discipline. For almost a decade of his young manhood his only school had been the Napoleonic war front. The drudgery of historical research—as when in 1817 he contemplated writing a twelve-volume study of Napoleon—always frightened him. Though he was only a brilliant dilettante in fields such as music and painting, he loved to wear the garments of learning, as he loved clothing of the latest mode. Bookish man that he was, his happiest definitions and phrases often (though not always) came to him as embellishments of others' words. Even as late as 1820, he could write in a letter to a friend in Paris, in admiration of some newspaper article he had read: "*It is pure Stendhal!*" and add that he would gladly "steal" it if need be. "For, if my own books become known in 1890, who will care about the grain of gold I had found in the mud?"

But if he had lived in our own age of compilers, the readers of his two first books would have been able to distinguish promptly what was his, would not have needed to learn from literary detectives what was borrowed. It would be more fully evident that, despite its incompleteness and its borrowings, his *History of Painting in Italy*, which was substantially the first expression of his true personality—most of it written in 1811 and 1812—contained ideas that were almost too original or too "revolutionary" for his time.

2

Confining ourselves to that which was "pure Stendhal," the first thing that strikes us in the *History of Painting in Italy* is his rationalistic approach to the subject of aesthetics, in which so much vagueness had ruled. A follower of eighteenth-century positivism, he remained outside of the currents of thought in France and Germany at a time when Catholic mysticism dominated one country and transcendentalism the other. His favorite philosophers, Montesquieu, Condillac, Helvetius, and the "last of the Encyclopedists," Cabanis and Tracy, had attempted to apply scientific criticism to social institutions: law, government, and education. It was Beyle's intention to complement their work by using their methods of observation and analysis in the field of the arts—later even in that of love! Here, as in other fields, it was the destiny of this obscure exile to hand on the torch of the Enlightenment at a time when the rationalistic tradition was in danger of dying out.

As always before and after, he was ideological. That is to say, like Condillac and his followers, he considered human ideas as merely so many different types of original or transformed *sensations*. And it is because he clings to this sensualist philosophy that he appears so close to modern theorists of aesthetics. In setting off for Italy in 1811 he reminded himself that he must observe the following points: (1) The state of the land and the climate; (2) the character of the inhabitants; (3) its painting, sculpture, and architecture; (4) its music. Here, of course, we have the inception of Taine's theory of the determining influence of climate, race, and milieu (in the sense of historical-social environment) upon man and his civilization.

"I wanted to do a history of Italian *energy*," Beyle said after he had written his book. In her art was the key to the understanding of Italy. The production of monuments of art was to him the highest form of energy, rivaling, but also linked with, the achievements of the Napoleons, past and present. "Stendhal was the first man," according to a thoughtful German commentator, Weigand, "who conceived of art as the flower of an entire culture and who pointed to the climate and the moral customs of society as the source of origin of artists."[a]

It is in this deterministic spirit that Beyle begins his study of the Italian painters by an introductory discourse on the geographical, historical, and social conditions under which the great schools of painting were born. The city-states of medieval times, he points out, acquired a wealth and leisure unequaled in those days. In feudal Italy, the Church as an institution was predominant, and the arts were captured

[a]Wilhelm Weigand, *Stendhal*, p. 128; concluding volume of the Georg Müller edition of Stendhal's *Gesammelte Werke*, Munich, 1925. The idea of treating cycles of culture as an ensemble, an organic unity of climatic, racial, and social-institutional forces was to gain wide support, after Taine discovered Stendhal. Taine applied this idea in his *History of English Literature* (1863), in which the record of literature is used to demonstrate the true folk character of the English people, and the "meaning" of their history. Stendhal's methods were also used in Taine's *Origines de la France contemporaine*.

first of all by religion—or "by the priests." The great painters therefore expressed reality as they saw it through their religious faith. But the Italians of that era, "full of energy and passion," lived in a smiling climate that contributed to their love of pleasure. After the end of the wars between Guelphs and Ghibellines, their cities began to fill up with art treasures. The despots themselves enjoyed embellishing their tyranny with a glory that derived from the encouragement of the arts.

The artists, then, freely expressed the "virtues" of their society, as exemplified in its religious-political institutions and the individuals who headed them. Ardent creatures that they were, the Renaissance Italians loved and hated greatly; they risked their lives, sated their passions, killed with ferocity, and afterward prayed like superstitious fanatics, "freely delivering themselves to their highest exaltations." To understand their Ghirlandaios and Leonardos you must understand Machiavelli and Benvenuto Cellini; you must admit, as Beyle declares, that "Caesar Borgia was the representative man of the fifteenth century."

For Beyle there is chiefly erotic appeal in the Madonnas of Raphael (!); in the frescoes of Michelangelo he sees principally the effect of veritable terror, the genuine fear of hell; in the others, superstition and fantasy, violence and voluptuousness.

But if it is the complex of the geographical, racial and social milieu that determines the character of a cultural development, such as the cinquecento in painting—if the art of Leonardo, Raphael, and Michelangelo stems from the turbulent historical period in which they lived, with its particular religious concepts and way of life—then how idle and wrong it is merely to copy or imitate their works, or for that matter those of the classic Greeks. The widely accepted notion that either the Greek sculptors or the Italian painters after them had discovered absolute models of "ideal beauty" that must be imitated forever, as Winckelmann stated, was an absurdity. Beauty and the taste for it were not immutable, but eternally changing and relative, depending on race, geography, and human institutions. Stendhal thus prepared the way for the romantic revolt against the pseudoclassical academicians of his time, the school of David. Like Mme. de Staël and other proponents of romanticism, he held that in each age and society artists must strive to discover and represent the "genius" of the civilization in which they live.

The real value of Beyle's fragmentary *History of Painting in Italy* resides in its long introduction, which contributes so much to our understanding of the origin of nineteenth-century ideas. Where he copies the older Italian historians of art, incorporating their prejudices and errors, his "history" brings us little that is new. But in those digressions and general reflections that are everywhere interlarded in this ill-ordered work he often writes with the insight of critical genius. As if he were a man of the twentieth century, he gropes for a social-historical approach to culture. And despite his posing, and his evident ignorance of the painter's craft, the sum of his reflections is an audacious polemic against the reigning schoolmen of art. His tribute to Michelangelo, for example, does him great honor still, for the painter of "The Last Judgment" was still in disfavor among authorities upon art when he wrote it. Certainly he was one of the first to liken Michelangelo to Dante, saying: "The proud and masculine genius of these two men is absolutely the same." To the young Eugène Delacroix, who was beginning his rebellion against the tyranny of neoclassicism, Stendhal on Michelangelo offered "a fragment of genius, one of the most striking and poetic I have ever read."

What he asks—and his thought has become so widely accepted as to seem commonplace now—is that artists must strive to be as modern, as contemporary, as were the great Greek and Italian masters. In opposing Winckelmann and his later followers who held that the classical Apollo of Belvedere, image of harmony, ideality, and "calm serenity," was the supreme model, Stendhal argues that the ancient Greeks were simply expressing their vision of reality in accordance with their religious superstitions and social customs. "Their gods had . . . the particular virtues in credit among their people and age: to wit, strength and prudence." "But they were in no sense," he remarks shrewdly enough, "like the idea of the ancient Greeks entertained by professors who sit in a library thinking about the 'Grecian ideal' "; in their savage way of life, they must rather have resembled "the North American Indians hunting in the forests along the Wabash." He adds: "I would like to see the veritable Achilles of the Trojan Wars appear suddenly in the midst of [those professors'] lectures; I am sure he would give them quite a scare." He was to return to the charge against the classicists later on, in another field, that of literature.

It is notable that, like a faithful materialist, he throws off rich suggestions for the analysis of aesthetic experience, a labor that was to occupy the psychologists of the century that followed his. The enjoyment of beauty, he holds, is not "in the mind," as Kant believed, but is *pure emotion.* And in the closing section of his book there are daring *aperçus* that seem to forecast clearly what the direction of the new nineteenth-century art and literature must be if it were to respond to the profound changes in society that "our glorious French Revolution" had wrought:

> The enjoyments of modern man demand of the arts that they . . . speak to us again with the power they had under our belligerent ancestors. . . . It is difficult not to see what the nineteenth century seeks: a growing thirst for strong emotions is its true character. . . . It is passion itself that we seek. It is therefore by a painting, exact, and yet inspired, of the human heart that the new century will distinguish itself from that which preceded it.

Some fifteen or twenty years before romanticism belatedly conquered France, this was accurate prophecy of the direction Delacroix, Géricault, and Courbet would take, as well as Balzac, Hugo, and Stendhal himself.

3

The manuscript, completed at the end of 1816, was published after long delay, in July 1817, by the bookseller Pierre Didot, in an edition of 1,000 copies. The delay was caused by the fact that Stendhal sent the book chapter by chapter to his friend Louis Crozet, who emended its "imprudences." For numerous passages showed too plainly the cloven hoof of the freethinker and Jacobin. Yet after Crozet's revision Stendhal added still more indiscretions, in which he referred to the conveniences of clerical corruption in Italy, and treated religious art with high irreverence. The title page named the author of the work simply as "Monsieur B.A.A."—which some have construed as meaning "*Beyle, ancien auditeur.*"

Soon the novice author was excitedly urging his friends in Paris to see to it that his book was reviewed. Louis Crozet, the engineer and man of letters, though having no large influence over the public, finally did write a review for the small *Moniteur universel*, in September 1817, in which he managed to be both friendly and reasonable. Following this there was no further comment in Paris until early the following year, on March 9, 1818, when the powerful, conservative *Journal des débats* published a long and enthusiastic commentary upon the book as filling an important need and being both original and "complete." This review was written also by a friend of Beyle's, Joseph Lingay, a journalist of shifty, yet amusing character, who worked for many years as a ghost writer for the cabinet ministers of opposing parties in France.

But three days later disaster befell the new author. On March 12 the editors of the *Journal des débats* executed an about-face—certainly an extreme measure—by publishing a second article reviewing *L'Histoire de la peinture*, while repudiating the previous one by Lingay, as "an abuse of confidence." Now they denounced the book in the most scathing terms; it was called extravagant and absurd, "teeming with irreligious statements and immoral insinuations." The sad thing was that Stendhal had taken the trouble to insert a number of "passports," as he called them, sentences intended to ingratiate the censors. He had assured his readers that he himself "earnestly respected the Holy Book"; and that, having been "much buffeted by revolutions," he was no longer a "republican rascal." But these rather jesuitical efforts to appear *right-thinking* helped not. It was as if his identity were known. This castigation, coming to a hopeful young author at an early phase of his career, greatly embittered him.

What was worse, only 284 copies of his book were sold in the next seven years. Though he tried various expedients to spur the sales of his books—even, sometimes, reviewing them himself in obscure literary journals, such as *Galignani's*, issued by the old English bookseller of the same name in Paris—he was ignored. He sent copies of his book to Sir Walter Scott, Goethe, and Premier Decazes. It would have made him happy to know that the aging Goethe read his books with enjoyment and said in the *Conversations with Eckermann*: "This man knows how to use others with skill and make their ideas his own. . . . He attracts, he repels, he interests, he vexes us; and so . . . I read him, put him down, and take him up again, unable to let go." Yet no sound, no cheering word came to him. And so he abandoned the plan of writing four more volumes, though he carried his projected dissertations on Raphael, Correggio, and Guido in his head. Perhaps also he shrank, as he hints, from the rigors of "that cruel discipline without which one cannot penetrate so vast a subject." The French, he complained, were "monsters of vanity and gossip" who could never be made to understand art. Besides, he reflected: "It is trivial to pass one's life in describing how others were great."

The *History of Painting in Italy* had been a labor of love; no other book, he has related, cost him such agonies in composition, augmented toward the end by "forty or fifty days and nights of coffee drinking." It had been so long delayed in the printing that his next work, *Rome, Naples and Florence*, followed it on the stalls of Paris by only two months, in September 1817. This travel book was a quite different affair, a wholly informal potpourri of Stendhal's memoirs, reflections, and travel notes, as well as notes on the architecture, painting, music and moral customs he had studied in Italy. Though intended as a travel guide, it was more nearly the travel diary of a philosopher, filled with miscellaneous gleanings from his own journals of earlier years and even with his notes on crime stories reported in the press. Its informality gave ample scope to Stendhal's wit, his undisciplined talents, and his inexhaustible intellectual curiosity. Here we have the true Stendhal, the *raconteur* and aphorist, no longer constrained by his duties as a historian. It is significant that this book is the first to be signed by his Germanic or Viking-sounding nom de plume of "*M. de Stendhal*, former cavalry officer." It was his third pseudonym (undoubtedly inspired by the memory of the great German art critic, Winckelmann) and was retained because of the relative success won by this unpretentious book.[3] The "Baron de Stendhal"—for so he was called by courtesy—was foreign-sounding, resonant, and mystifying; it suited the cosmopolitanism of a Frenchman who lived in Italy by choice and used a Teutonic nom de plume.

I have cited freely from *Rome, Naples and Florence* in the preceding chapter, in describing Stendhal's sentiments toward an Italy as yet scarcely touched by the movements of the industrial revolution. Even today the book has a flavor as distinctive as Sterne's *Sentimental Journey*. One travels with the irrepressible Stendhal through city after city, stopping at dusty inns, visiting all sorts of ruins and monuments, meeting uninhibited travel companions, going to the opera, and listening, so to speak, to his conversations upon nature, man, and the mutations of history.

His mode of travel and investigation is highly original too:

> When I arrive in some city, I ask a friend (as soon as I have made his acquaintance), who are the dozen richest men in town; who are the twelve most beautiful women; and who is the man most disliked (who can have me hung if he wishes); then I associate myself with the man who is most decried, then with the pretty women, finally with the millionaires.

One of his favorite devices in a strange town was to go to a bookshop, buy some books, and solicit information about the town. From his early days he also had a way with him when dealing with wild-looking coachmen or ragged peasants, and learned something of their dialect.

Despite the book's discursiveness, it pursues a number of dominant themes: (1) life in Italy is "closer to nature," a Rousseauist valuation;

[3]Following a French edition of five hundred copies issued in London in 1817 by Colburn, there appeared an English translation, in 1818, entitled *Rome, Naples & Florence, Sketches of the Present State of Society, Manners, Arts, Literature, etc. in those Celebrated Cities*, by the Count de Stendhal.

(2) the quest of happiness, which is increasingly lost sight of in the countries to the north, is still possible here; (3) these observations lead him to a sustained polemic against the society of his own country, in which, he holds, "character" has declined since the days of the French Revolution; (4) in the Italy of 1817 he insists upon seeing the persistent traits (or their residues) of the people who brought about the Renaissance five centuries earlier, though on this point the Italians themselves strongly disagreed with him. He saw them still as creatures of impulse, brimming with undiluted love and hate; even their cities still were jealous of each other as in no other country. It was his theory that though the Italians had long languished under foreign despots, and suffered the oppression of the corrupt clerical police, they had learned how to make all sorts of subtle moral adjustments permitting them to survive essentially unspoilt: whether by paying bribes to the bishop's mistress, or pretending to serve the foreign rulers. They remained essentially children of pleasure. Though they might profess Christianity, and serve Mother Church, the people of the Papal States especially, Stendhal insisted, were pagans under the skin.

Studying the great Cathedral of Milan, he recalls that Gian Galeazzo Visconti began building it in 1386, after he had poisoned his uncle Bernabo, the former ruler, and taken power. "Doubtless he built the cathedral in order to appease the Virgin Mary," Stendhal observes. The present relations of the subject Italians to the Austrian despots and their spies and censors remind him of the moral finesse of Machiavelli. For he quotes the Italians as saying: "To serve the King (Austrian or Spanish) is pardoned, because he pays. But to serve him zealously is considered *infamous*, because he is our enemy."

Italians had felt deeply and spoken freely in the fifteenth and sixteenth centuries; and they were really no different today. "All of present-day Italy," he said, "is an outgrowth of the Middle Ages." It was a judgment dictated by his convictions concerning the material force of climate and historical environment; one worth pondering still in the atavistic decades of the twentieth century that produce a Mussolini modeled after the *condottieri* of old times.

And outside of Italy, he asked, did anyone know what politics really was? "Politics," he said, "is the art of getting people to do what you want without money or violence."

This is not to say that the spirit of criticism flagged in Stendhal. At times his notes become an essay in folk psychology that appears well in advance of its age. The Italians are lacking in wit, because instead of conversation being an art with them, as in France, it is a means to an end: the satisfaction of passion. Unlike the German, the Italian is indifferent to metaphysics; and as against the Englishman, he is accustomed to leaving questions of individual conscience to his priest—for "personal examination leads to reasoning," which is frowned upon. Jests offend the *amour-propre* of the Italian, who is serious when in love; for six months the vengeful Italian will remember a slighting word. Nor is he without vanity of a naïve sort, for once, when Stendhal mocked at a recently installed public monument in Milan, he saw that his friends were made angry; he had offended the "patriotism of the anteroom," and perceiving this, feigned a headache and hurried away.

Finally he moans over the appalling ignorance, decreed by the "Jesuits," who had condemned Rome and all the region south of the Tiber to "three centuries of childhood," and forced the workingman to live on alms. "To think is dangerous," he said. "One may make love in any way he pleases; but to jest about religion is dangerous." Stendhal's analysis of the character of the various Italian cities, so different from each other, is still illuminating, though much of his description has value chiefly as a historical document.

Yet, as the infatuated lover attributes every perfection to his inamorata, so Stendhal in his enchantment with Italy clung to the conviction that he had rediscovered the Italy of the ruthless, magnificent, and voluptuous Medicis and Sforzas. Were not the young Italians, whom he saw every night in Milan, already busily plotting an insurrection that would liberate and unify their country? The love of liberty smoldered in their breasts, though every means was taken by the authorities to discourage it. Napoleon, when told by the citizens of Brescia that their people loved liberty more than other Italians, had said mockingly: "Yes, they speak of it to their mistresses." But many young Italians repeated the phrase of the patriot, Pietro Massirili: "The more unhappy Italy is, the more faithful to her I shall remain." In his revised edition of *Rome, Naples and Florence*, (1826), speaking much more openly, Stendhal prophesied a national insurrection whose date accurately enough he named as *circa* 1845.

Italy appeared at first blush to be unhappy and stagnant; but though repressed by their police, the common people repeatedly burst forth in acts of individual passion; for a scudo, or a crown or two, their *bravi* could kill without remorse; for bread or love the peasant of Sicily would commit a "beautiful crime." Under this head Stendhal collected a store of nerve-tingling anecdotes, and, in his admiration for the unexpected or unpremeditated act, went so far as to utter praise of those who committed *des beaux crimes*.

"When I am waylaid by highway robbers who fire at me, I always feel a great anger at the government, and at the local curé. As for the bandit, I like him because he is energetic and amusing." The bandit, too, embodied a variant of the Napoleonic ruthlessness and energy he extolled. He said also: "Only the common people possess the energy to obey their passions." After clipping stories of recent crimes from the French newspapers, he remarked further: "The best characters in France are to be found in the galleys." These were strong words, intended to shock and infuriate, openly hinting at a cult of violence.

But Stendhal had a good deal of *blague* in him; and in what we now consider the Shavian manner, loved to set off petards to startle his readers. At any rate, he himself indulged in no crimes; few men observed the peace more scrupulously than did this retired veteran of Napoleon's campaign in Russia. Nor was he the man to follow his own realistic prescriptions for the seizure of power, or of its modern equivalent, money. On the contrary, his wisdom bade him be content with living in a provincial city on a budget of five or six francs a day.

On beginning his self-chosen retirement as a scholar and impoverished gentleman, he had written to a friend in Paris:

> Well, Italy pleases me. I pass each day from seven to midnight hearing music and seeing two ballets; the climate does the rest. . . . You find me mad; but what would you have me do? All that is worth the trouble, in this world, *is the self*. The good side of a character like mine is that I take a retreat from Russia like a glass of lemonade. Blame yourself, my amiable friend, if I have spoken so long of the *I*.

This forerunner of the Good Europeans has grasped some of the great secrets of history and power; yet, modern neurotic and intellectual though he is, he prefers to live alone with his ego in a furnished room, and speculate upon them in his head. His spirit of discrimination and self-criticism forbids him to use his own doctrines as dogmatically as his later admirers of the most diverse schools, determinist, socialist, individualist, and fascist, would use them. Taine, the liberal, Nietzsche, the iconoclast, Zola and Léon Blum, the socialists, and Count Gobineau and Charles Maurras, the philosophers of fascism, all were to find nourishment in his writings and claim him for their own. Yet, in truth, he does not belong to them or their systems, but is himself.

Besides, he had a healthy fear of the police. As he himself admits, he deliberately interlarded in his text all sorts of transparent pieties and bromides which were designed to appease the censors. He claimed that he was "no dog of a liberal," and with respectful doffings of the hat to Louis XVIII allowed that constitutional monarchy was the best of possible governments. Jestingly he remarked: "To have a republic we must begin by making our country an island."

These were the "passports" by which he hoped to escape censure or suppression, always a likely possibility in the days after Waterloo. From Paris, his printer had written warningly that he must be careful to "cut out anything that may bring us into trouble with the law and goes beyond the bounds of liberalism. I want no difficulty of any kind with the authorities." Thus the pretended pieties jostled strangely with provocative or subversive reflections, a condition that rendered his manner of writing all the more intriguing to the initiated who understood the secret. Moreover his "Beylisms" were wrapped up with many pages of practical travel information, hastily culled from old Italian guidebooks, sometimes none too accurate, which lent the book a modest and useful air.

4

To his delight the travel book sold well enough to bring him a few hundred francs in royalties. Though it was barely mentioned in France, it enjoyed the honor of a long and favorable notice in the *Edinburgh Quarterly Review*, the most influential literary and political journal of the age. Perhaps Stendhal's searching criticisms of French national character commended him to the English, for his earlier books were more hospitably treated by them than by his compatriots. Also, his ill-concealed anti-clericalism and liberalism was much relished in the great English reform quarterly. As if to repay the compliment, Stendhal with his first royalties purchased all the back numbers of the *Edinburgh*, dating from 1802, a considerable expenditure. It was in a sense also a tribute to the nation of freedom, whose advanced system of government had been celebrated by Voltaire and Montesquieu.[4]

Through a young English friend named Edward Edwards, the rather rakish brother of the scientist, Dr. Edwards, who resided in Paris, Stendhal was able to arrange for publication of both his book on music and his travel book in London. It was in order to conclude these arrangements that he set off in the company of young Edwards, in August

[4]The *Edinburgh Quarterly Review's* commentator on French books apparently recognized the author of *Rome, Naples and Florence*, the "Count de Stendhal," as the "B.A.A." of the *History of Painting in Italy* and did not neglect to twit him upon his obvious plagiarisms from the *Edinburgh* itself in the earlier book, while praising him for his verve in the later one.

1817, on his first journey to the land of Shakespeare, Locke, and Byron.

England, and especially London, made a deep impression upon him. But as much of the time of his visit was spent in drinking brandy and roistering with Edwards, his ideas of the country were less distinct than on subsequent, longer visits, during which the cosmopolitan Stendhal acquired a more intimate knowledge of English literary and political movements.

On his return he spent but a few days in Paris and as little time in Grenoble, before hurrying back to Milan, which, after his brief look at the world outside, he felt more than ever to be his true home. With him he brought back his sister Pauline to spend a few months in his company in Milan. She was in mourning, owing to the recent death of her husband, and Stendhal, who loved her alone among the remaining members of his family, his grandfather and great-aunt having died, thought to distract her from her grief. At Grenoble, however, he had received bad news: his avaricious father was in debt to the extent of 250,000 francs; most of the Beyle patrimony was hypothecated, and Beyle, père, was all but ruined by his frenzied speculations in land. From now on, Stendhal understood, he could look to his "bastard" for but little financial help, and must live on his meager 2,400 francs a year and what he could earn in addition by writing. Thus far he had lost rather than gained money by his books.

He was more determined than ever to remain in self-willed exile. Some two years earlier, in January 1815, word had come to him that Mme. Alexandrine Daru, his "Countess Palfy," had died of a sudden illness at only thirty-three. "What terrible news the press brings me," he wrote his sister. "She was, after you, the best friend I had in this world." With Alexandrine dead, he had less reason than ever to return to Paris. He always disliked thinking or speaking of death, and he mourned her silently, like a stoic. A little later, after the Battle of Waterloo, he wrote in his journal: "I will not return for a long time to a country that is without liberty and without glory."

The Great Revolution was being undone; for cowards and hypocrites were in the saddle. Napoleon languished in St. Helena—he who despite his evil "personal rule" had wished "to cure all of us of eighteen centuries of Christianity and feudalism." Under the Empire, though too many citizens had thought only of honors and baronies, the social gains of the Revolution were consolidated; the freed peasants and new middle classes were secure in their title to land and property, while the nobility was dispossessed and no one thought of the priests. But now, he feared, the lights were being extinguished all over Europe, or as he phrased it: "The party of the candle-snuffers triumphs." Everything that would be done in France for years to come would be in the line of candle-snuffing. He watched while dull-witted aristocrats and superstitious priests, in the name of a Charter that enfranchised only 200,000 Frenchmen, ruled France, "with their sole legislation the fear of hell." From all that he heard, he felt himself fortunate in having missed the White Terror of 1815.

But if reaction triumphed in France, its rule was relatively enlightened when compared with that authoritarian darkness in which the rest of Europe was engulfed after the Congress of Vienna. For Prince Metternich's obsessive dread was of a "new 1793," with the people coming out into the streets again. In Austria, most of Germany, and the Italian states, thousands of police spies watched over everyone and gathered immense dossiers for Vienna, noting what men read, wrote, or said to each other. Under Napoleon's "Cisalpine Republic," Italians had known a decade of relative progress and personal liberty. But by 1819 they seemed thoroughly cowed, as did the Germans, by censorship of university and press, which, Stendhal was convinced, the Jesuits mainly directed. Indeed, all Europe lived in a nightmare of fear. Liberals and reactionaries both lived in fear, the former dreading unjust imprisonment, the latter a return of popular revolutions and "Men of Destiny." These developments the exiled Stendhal pondered in solitude; they were the subject also of much of his private correspondence, for throughout his life he showed the liveliest interest in the questions of politics and power, in the movements of world history, such as he himself had witnessed, whose broad currents sweep through his books.

At this period, after Waterloo, one might say that Stendhal went "underground" in Italy, as men would take to the "underground" more than a century later in the odious times of Hitler, Mussolini, and Marshal Pétain. Indeed the parallel between the generation after 1815 and the dark epoch of France's defeat in 1940 is so salient that it is not surprising to find young French writers and leaders of the underground Resistance movement in the 1940s reading Stendhal again with almost religious fervor; for countless pages of his novels, essays, and particularly of his autobiographical and epistolary writings breathed an intellectual revolt that was subtle and resourceful as well as stubborn. By reading him one became schooled in the art, the technique of secret resistance as practiced in an earlier time, under the authoritarianism of Catholic royalists. He was libertine and skeptical—often to the limits of cynicism—but in the end he showed a rare courage: that of being honest with himself.

This extreme intellectual honesty—the most admirable trait among the mixed elements of his nature—led him to oppose, with the utmost tenacity, the moral tendencies that were officially in favor and more or less *de rigueur* in his time. Thus he was like a lonely and lost figure who had lived on beyond the eighteenth century whence he came, a century that had believed in Reason. Indeed if ever there was a symbol of a "lost generation" it was the ex-commissary Beyle, who had survived the retreat from Russia with Napoleon, now, as a secret Jacobin, hiding himself in Italy during Metternich's Age of Darkness, and waiting for the world to return to the beliefs that others termed "outmoded."

Could he, should he have yielded to the spirit of the times? The arrogant Chateaubriand, champion of legitimism and Christianity, dominated letters in France. Joseph de Maistre, the ardent Catholic polemicist, filled men's minds with hatred of the Revolution and of the evils it had wrought. France was given over to "the men in black"; for the Congregation, that mysterious and powerful secret order, directed by the Jesuits, watched over education, the press, and literature. Meanwhile, in Italy also, men who loved liberty, such as the Carbonari, were forced to meet together secretly in the depths of the forests—hence their name of "Charcoal Burners." Society lived in fear, fear even of ideas. Men intrigued and denounced each other to gain favor; conspiracy and counterespionage created a world of cape-and-sword that would have been comic if it were not so depressing.

All this Stendhal watched with a heart full of scorn. He loved liberty and, he declared in letters to his friends, could not live without it in a degraded France where he would be made "to tremble every morning in fear of being suppressed by some new decree." As he had written in an unguarded page of his *History of Painting in Italy* in 1817, "monarchical government crushed the souls of artists" in former times; and now "ideas were the bogey of the party in power." Moreover society in France was plainly decaying, for the energy unloosed by the Revolution and Bonaparte was sacrificed by the aristocrats, those men of "cold, dignified, and polished emptiness," who were trying to return to the ways of Louis XIV, "the king of fools."

What would he be doing in Paris, where conformity and cant spread like a leprosy, and false dignity frowned upon wit or merriment? "To succeed in Paris, one needed above all to be *like the others.*" One would have to be as dull as they and bend the knee, and his knee was not "supple enough." The condition was precisely that described later in his first novel, *Armance*, in which the hero, repeatedly warned to be silent when he attempts to speak his mind on divers public questions, exclaims in despair: "Alas, do not reproach me for the greatest of my misfortunes, *that of being obliged to lie every day!*"

At the thought of returning to Paris, Stendhal said: "The enormous hypocrisy that will be necessary is what fills me with despair."

His friend, Joseph Lingay, who as a political journalist earned the large sum of twenty thousand francs a year by selling his talents to both sides, laughed at all of it, and spent his money in royal dissipation. But though Stendhal is often termed a cynic, he wrote protesting against the cynicism of Lingay, the ghost writer, to still another friend who had also accepted a high place under the Bourbons and whom, by indirection, he also reproached. Should one be content "so long as he was paid? Was it to be each for himself . . . the reasoning of a Talleyrand?" No, Stendhal was convinced that such moral hypocrisy would end by depriving a man of his capacity even to reason correctly. His reasoning, he believed, was founded upon the long-run truth of the principle of *salus populi*. "In this century, to combine the honors of virtue with the pleasures of vice is impossible."

To be an author, a professional author, in the dubious manner of many of his contemporaries was not possible. "Now, I have always fulfilled my mission, which is not to speak as an author," he wrote in a letter of December 1, 1817. "The trade of author seemed to me degrading, or rather degraded. . . . In my fall from greatness, I had my pride, a stubborn pride which neither prayer nor fasting could banish." He must remain, then, an amateur, writing for his own pleasure. "I write in order to drive away boredom in the mornings. I write *what I myself think, and not what is thought.*"

Stendhal's intellectual life during the long years in Italy after 1815 is mirrored in a series of "underground" letters, among the best that he wrote, to his old friend Louis Crozet, and particularly to a new friend, the Baron de Mareste, a very clever man who shared both his passion for Italian music and his interest in politics. These letters are a full and brilliant commentary upon popular movements in Italy, Germany, and France, and have the interest of a singularly vivid historical document. What is more, they are letters written in great secrecy, and in a secret lingo or code of his own, devised with the evident purpose of throwing spies and censors off the track. Not only do they give a rich and intimate record of his mind, but they reveal the little daily shifts and stratagems by which he survived his Dark Age.

In his *Rome, Naples and Florence*, he describes a certain Milanese lady, and relates how before a mixed company she spoke freely of her love affairs, though in remarkably indirect or veiled terms. And this leads him to exclaim: "Oh, if there could but be a secret language of the heart." Now, with infinite precautions, he himself fabricated a secret language in which he could give and receive intelligence of political affairs. By inverting words, twisting them into strange anagrams, mixing them with English and Italian terms (also anagrammatized), he arrived at one of the weirdest jargons there ever was, the jargon of *resistance*, which, curiously enough, French writers would use again under Papa Pétain a century later. For example, when he wished to speak of kings in French he would use, instead of *rois*, an abbreviation of the English "kings," "K——s," depending upon it that his clever friends would puzzle such things out. Names were always given in anagram: *Zotgui*, for Guizot, *Rièpre*, for Périer, *Bertlu*, for Lubert. Some of his typical cipher code follows:

> *Téjés* = *Jésuites*
> *Prs*, *or Trèpres* = (*Prêtres*; i.e., priests)
> *gionreli* = *religion*
> *Kainesrépublis* = *républicains*
> *votdés* = *devots*

Other terms such as *noblesse*, or *aristocrates*, he translated into English as "the blood." He dated and postmarked his letters falsely; he signed himself with a thousand different pseudonyms. This secret jargon became a mania that clung to him all his life. Feeling himself insecure, watched by spies continually, he used even the trick of inserting pious and Ultra-Royalist phrases into his letters in order to baffle those who might open his mail, and urged his correspondents to do the same. His handwriting itself became impenetrable. And what is both comic and pathetic about the whole business is that his "secret" writing could not but arouse suspicion, which would lead to the deciphering of his facile code by the use of a little English. This rigmarole of secrecy—the sport of Stendhalian scholars today—was in truth no protection, but the sign of a state of mind that never left him, a sense of danger and alienation and persecution. That it was no protection is shown by the fact that the secret police both in Italy and France had complete dossiers on Henri Beyle and "Stendhal" also, and were quite aware of his true opinions.

In this acrostic of pieties and misspelled words there were clear enough allusions to the fact that he trusted neither the lying press of

France or Italy, but often depended for information upon English tourists arriving in Italy, or on the news in a small newspaper from Lausanne, Switzerland, "a hole where a little freedom vegetated." Italy, he declared, was being rendered treacherous and knavish by papal oppression; "I dare not speak of the intrigues." German students were rioting in 1818, because no constitution such as was promised them was forthcoming. And, quoting Gray's "Elegy," he relates that the "village Hampdens" were at work all over Europe; that he has been reading the unpublished manuscript copy of a new book by Destutt de Tracy on representative government, which is to be published in English by Tracy's friend Jefferson. There he hinted was his own democratic credo, and he signed himself "Th. Jefferson" by way of disguise!

Imbedded here and there in these letters were some truculent statements:

> A collection of bayonets or of guillotines can no more stop the movement of public opinion than a collection of gold pieces can stop the gout.
>
> The shepherd . . . can never convince his flock of sheep that his interests and theirs are identical.

Also some prophecies: that "curious things will happen in France . . . probably toward 1830"—this in a letter of December 21, 1819.

"Liberty for *all* Europe by 1850," he ventured boldly. (The "Red" revolutions were to arrive in 1848.) Meanwhile, he vowed to himself that, come what might, he would be faithful to the party of progress. "Writers are the hussars of liberty," he wrote bravely in 1817. "And always in action. Sometimes they retreat, but only to advance again."

Even in Italy, he notes, those who hold power "are forced to avert their eyes as they walk the streets, to avoid looks of scorn from the common folk at every step." Most men nowadays only feigned obedience to regimes that none believed would last long. If the friends of liberty could only hold out, all would be well; time was on their side.

Hope rises in the heart of Stendhal, and also a subdued fear. In Milan, in 1818, he could hear the young men of the Carbonari buzzing everywhere with their conspiracies, their plots for an insurrection. Stendhal himself, though full of misgivings lest his cherished creature comforts, his music, his women friends—all that made for happiness—might be forfeited in the event of disaster, was drawn, nevertheless, ever closer to the circle of the revolutionaries. What drew him helplessly into this net was, once more, love: the love of a noble and courageous Italian woman, perhaps the deepest he ever felt.

CHAPTER XIII

Metilda: Or the Anatomy of Love

Love is a precious flower; but one must have the desire to pluck it from the edge of a precipice.

—Stendhal, *De l'amour.*

SINCE 1814, Stendhal's literary and musical friends had never ceased their highly vocal plotting for Italian insurrection against foreign rule, under the leadership of Count Frederico Confalonieri, one of Milan's leading nobles and a ringleader of the secret society of the Carbonari. In the north, Lombardy and Tuscany were to be induced to rise against the Austrians and join with independent Piedmont; in the south, Sicily was to take up arms at the same time, so that the peninsula would be aflame from one end to the other. Though disappointments were piled upon disappointments, and betrayals as well, the ranks of the conspiring patriots steadily swelled. By 1818 and 1819 the polite circles of Milan were alive with intrigue, and there was hardly an evening at the loges of the Scala Theater, Stendhal declares, when the conversation did not turn upon the great event all awaited, or when it was not repeatedly hushed at the entrance of a spy known to be in the pay of Austria.

It was the time of the romantic revolution in literature also. When Stendhal's literary friends, who were of the circle of Ludovico di Breme, launched a new review in 1818, they announced that its purpose was to "liberate" literature from the tyranny of classicism. But *sotto voce* they always added that it was no less their purpose to liberate Italy of its Austrian garrisons. And as they were romantic in poetry, so in their politics. For it was chiefly the young nobles and the educated middle class who rallied to the red, blue, and black banner of the ritualistic Carbonari, while, plainly enough, the impoverished masses ignored the call to rebellion. For these reasons, it has been remarked, Lord Byron, who was still living in or near Venice, distinctly preferred the charming Italian variety of revolution to movements of the English radicals at home; whereas Stendhal, though swept along by his intimate friends among the Carbonari, such as the immensely enthusiastic Giuseppe Vismara and the poet, Silvio Pellico, gave them his sympathy with marked reservations.

"I dare not tell you of the plotting that goes on here," wrote Stendhal in his "underground" letters to his friend Mareste in Paris. What he had seen of men who wielded power ruthlessly in republican and Napoleonic days convinced him that the Italian enthusiasts were too "vague" in their plans and too given to verbal indiscretion. Quite conceivably their design might miscarry and he, the foreigner in their midst, would be blamed. "The police can do anything with me here," he said, for he was suspect as a godless Frenchman who had served the "antichrist" Napoleon. Besides, Lombardy enjoyed an honest if vexatious rule by the Germans, in comparison with neighboring Modena or Venetia, and far better than the Papal States in the bonds of the Vatican's crooked police.

The men of Milan, like those of sedate Florence, he thought, were prosperous, comfortable, and paunchy fellows, addicted to music and to pleasure, and would never fight seriously. "Their tongues are liberal, but *the heart wants a little,*" Stendhal remarked after learning a little more of insurrectionary strategy.

These prophecies of gloom were to prove accurate enough, but when, in the spring of 1818, his friend Vismara brought him to see the beautiful Countess Metilda, at whose apartment in a battered old palace of the Piazza Belgiojoso some of the principal conspirators regularly foregathered, he was ready to champion Italian liberty with all his soul and without reservations of any kind.

Despite his claims to the contrary, he had up to now met only a few representatives of good society in Milan. The Countess Metilda, a young woman of twenty-six, was a descendant of an old and wealthy family named Viscontini, and was married to the Polish General and Count Jan Dembowski, formerly in the service of France. While the others present talked politics, Stendhal had eyes only for her, for she seemed to him one of those Lombard beauties whom Leonardo had painted in his charming Herodiades. She was tall, dark-haired, with a delicate aquiline nose whose curve harmonized most gracefully with her finely shaped head. Grave and proud in manner, her smile, though decidedly melancholy, had great finesse. "It was with a deliberate slowness" that she turned to look at one with her large, dark eyes, the enchanted Stendhal said, "as if she knew in advance that nothing she regarded would render her happy again." Yet there would also be moments when she seemed on fire with enthusiasm for some ideal or cause.[1] That she ran some danger in associating herself with the revolutionary plotters, and that Milan gossip censured her for her indifference to convention in some regards, but added to her perfection in his eyes and set him dreaming of a happiness lately lost to him. For his heart had been arid; he had suffered from loneliness since the break with Gina.

Metilda Viscontini had been given in marriage to Count Dembowski, along with a dot of 150,000 lire, when she was barely sixteen. Her husband, twenty years older than she, soon showed himself not only brutal but faithless. After several years of suffering at his hands, the young woman displayed enough spirit to leave Milan of her own accord and go abroad with her two young children, residing for several years at Berne, Switzerland. Since the most celebrated of Italian poets, Ugo Foscolo—Italy's "Young Werther"—also was exiled then in Berne and paid her court, Milan society said that Metilda had left, not to escape the cruelties of her husband, but to live with Foscolo. "Though she had had but one lover, she was publicly dishonored," Stendhal relates—not because she stood accused of having been someone's mistress, for that was common enough in Milan, but because she had left home and husband and lived alone abroad.

Certainly Foscolo had the reputation of a Don Juan; he was also a patriot leader and had suffered greatly for his political beliefs. It was in this guise that Metilda admired him, as his biographers have shown; for both his private papers and poems alluding to her tell the story of an unrequited suit. Yet sympathy for the exiled revolutionary, then living in great poverty, led Metilda to aid him and to devote herself thenceforth to the cause for which he fought.

It was only late in 1816, after having gained a separation agreement from her husband, that she returned to Milan to live in an apartment of the old family palace on the Piazza Belgiojoso, only two minutes' walk from Stendhal's quarters then in the Via Andegari. She lived apart and went out little, aware of society's scandalmongering. As she had known how to resist the tyranny of her husband, and wrest her children from him, so now she resolved to help resist the oppressors of Italy, whose plight was as unhappy as her own. Soon the Austrian

[1]Stendhal: *Mélanges littéraires*, Vol. I, p. 19 (*Le Roman de Métilde*).

espionage system reported this independent and cultivated young woman to be one of the souls of the insurgent movement in Milan.

Stendhal, in a passage of one of his later travel books, describes her (under a disguised name) as having a "noble candor" and an eloquence of expression on the score of her sentiment for Italy, so great as to "cast a spell over all those who surrounded her." Since the time of Alexandrine Daru's ascendancy, he had known no woman as innately refined and high-minded as the impetuous Metilda. This idea of her was to be borne out subsequently by the firmness of her behavior in the hour of crisis; the Italian women, Stendhal insists, often exceeded their men in courage. Oh, if something of this warmth of devotion could be turned toward himself!

After meeting her for the first time in April 1818, he was absent from Milan on a journey lasting three weeks, but thought of her constantly. On his return he haunted her door, in the company of other admirers or fellow plotters. In imagination he magnified every virtue and every feature of her beauty; and, constantly occupied with the memory of her glance, her gestures, her tone of voice, he would feel, when waiting to see her again, something akin to a "frenzy of nervous agitation." Every moment he would look at his watch, and feel delighted if ten minutes had passed since he had last looked at it. Then, at length, the hour approached when he could see her again. But once in her presence he would be so shaken and full of dread lest he make some wrong move "*in the great combat* that was beginning, in which every word or gesture counted in the balance," that he would fall silent, and appear embarrassed or timid. His inward tumult was so violent that it seemed to him "the eyes of all who were there must read the love in his eyes." Then out of fear of being silent, he would sometimes burst out in a spate of words that he did not even believe in, and could even less defend or explain. "The number of foolish things that I said during two years . . . in order not to be silent, throws me into despair when I think of them. . . . For when the too ardent interests of his passion are at stake, the tender and proud soul cannot be eloquent in the presence of the being he loves; the thought of possible failure appears too terrible an evil to bear."[2]

In other words, his emotions had "crystallized" about Metilda Viscontini, to use the terms of that curious, methodological treatise, or anatomy of love, *De l'amour,* which Stendhal, inspired by her, wrote in 1819.

Once more he became a man of action, trusting to the poetic im-

[2]*De l'amour,* Ch. XXIV ("Lisio Visconti").

mediacy of the deed, advancing, skirmishing, and chattering all the while. Since his diary stops at this period (perhaps out of political caution), we must reconstruct the grand lines of the "combat" for Metilda from those specimens of "sensitive passion" given in his treatise on love, which so unmistakably illustrate his problem and his drama.

It was always his conviction that the language of love has many tongues, first of all the eyes. While he discoursed or was silent, his eyes spoke to her incessantly. Even in a gesture of salutation, not only his warm glance but the pressure of his uncommonly small and delicate hands could communicate artfully with a woman whose heart was on the alert. Yet Metilda, in response to his compliments, maintained only a melancholy reserve.

Stendhal himself was in his thirty-sixth year when he met Metilda, though you would scarcely believe it from the eternal buoyancy of his feelings. Just as you would scarcely believe that this red-faced, thick-shouldered, round-bellied dandy, looking like a stout shopkeeper, was constantly absorbed by "ideal love" and by "passional love."

On one of their first meetings, he spoke about the different attitudes that people held toward love at various stages of life: as in youth, in ripe age, and in old age. In response to these *démarches,* she explained to him in her grave manner that since some years ago, "despairing of society and, almost, of human nature . . . she had renounced the hope of finding what was needed for her heart." Age and experience since then had but fortified these views.

But he replied by advancing the opinion that the first love of youth was not the stronger but the weaker form of love, whereas passion felt in the years of ripeness could be more desperate, more absolute than all that had gone before.

> METILDA: But it is when the imagination of a young girl has not been crushed by some unhappy experience in the fire of first youth, that she may associate the most ravishing images with some man. . . . Later, deceived by her lover and disillusioned in all men . . . mistrust clips the wings of her imagination. No matter who it is, though it be some prodigy, she will never form so entrancing a picture of him as in the first instance.
>
> STENDHAL: No, madame, the presence of mistrust, which did not exist at sixteen, but gives a deeper color to this second, this later love. In the first flush of youth, love may be like a torrent that sweeps all before it. But at twenty-eight, if a woman be an understanding soul, she knows that if there is any happiness left

> for her, it must be sought in love. Hence there arises in her poor, torn heart a terrible combat between love and disillusionment. The process . . . is slow, but the love that is the outgrowth of this cruel ordeal is a thousand times stronger than that of sixteen . . . much less a thing of pleasure and far more passionate.[3]

Thus they fenced with each other, though his mood was earnest enough, and he constantly asked himself: "How can I please her? How can I make her love me?" While it seemed to him that she, mistrustfully, thought: "Is he not merely playing a game in telling me he loves me? What sort of character is he? How can he guarantee the loyalty of his sentiments?"

But the veteran of Moscow was ever a man of courage. Much as he feared the outcome, he told himself that he must "attack." Or as Mérimée quoted his advice to young men:

> "When alone with a woman, take five minutes to prepare yourself for the prodigious effort of saying: 'I love you.' Tell yourself that you are the lowest coward if you do not say it. . . . One must always attack. One succeeds once out of ten times. Let us say once out of twenty times. Is not the chance of being happy worth the risk of nineteen affronts and nineteen humiliations?"

Yet this was no routine engagement of a hardened campaigner. Sometimes when he thought he spied her white satin hat approaching at the end of a street, "his heart stopped beating and he was obliged to lean against a wall in order to sustain himself." The day came, after he had been seeing her for five months—not five minutes—when, despite his terrible apprehensions, he brought himself to make the avowal of his feelings. Afterward he could never remember whether he was too ardent, or too reasonable, or spoke foolishly. The gist of what he said was that they were each superior souls of the same stamp, made to understand and love each other in the face of the world and its opinion. As a man of honor he declared that he loved her with the most selfless passion, and was ready to sacrifice his very life for her. On this occasion again, he tried to banish timidity by "playing the bold dragoon," seizing her hand, implanting burning kisses upon it.

But the net effect on her was one of revulsion and anger. How absurd was this talk of "ideal passion" in this fat Frenchman whom local scandal associated only with the Ninas and Ginas of the Scala Theater! Instead of giving the impression of one penetrated by ideal-

[3] *De l'amour*, Ch. VIII.

ism, he seemed rather to be wanting in delicacy, a man who, by his brusque approaches, showed expectation of an easy conquest. And she, who was now, as it seemed, concerned about her social position, had no wish to be compromised by this homely roué. With cold wrath she forbade him to speak to her of "love" again, and showed him the door.

Autumn had come to Milan. Stendhal, a broken man, crept from the old Viscontini palazzo in a cold, driving rain:

> I went out in the rain, not knowing what would become of me. My apartment, the one I inhabited in the early days of our acquaintance when I used to see her every evening, became unbearable to me. Each picture, each piece of furniture reproached me for the happiness I had dreamed in their presence, and which I had lost forever.

He walked the streets for hours, being unable to sleep. "In despair at the unhappiness to which love reduced me, I cursed my existence." He trudged through the town until chance, if one could call it that, brought him beneath her window, and then stood

> with eyes full of tears fixed upon that window. Suddenly the curtains were parted slightly, as if someone were trying to glance out at the street, then closed an instant later. My heart underwent the wildest commotion and, scarcely able to stand up, I took refuge under the portico of a neighboring house. . . . Could it have been her hand that moved the curtain?[4]

2

After this stinging rebuff, that would have meant complete rupture for a man of weaker kidney, Stendhal went on a lonely journey to the beautiful mountain town of Varese, and from there, on November 16, 1818, wrote Metilda a letter asking her forgiveness and declaring that he could not bear the pain of absence from her. Nor could listening to music or gazing at Alpine scenery console him, but only the thought of returning to Milan and finding a letter from her:

> For I count enough upon your mercy to believe that you would not refuse me a few lines, to you a matter of such indifference—to a heart in despair, so precious and consoling. You should be too certain of your absolute power over me to permit yourself for a moment to be withheld from replying by the fear of appearing to encourage my passion. I know myself; I love you for the

[4] *De l'amour*, Ch. XXXI, "Extrait du journal de Salviati."

rest of my life; whatever you may do will not change the idea that has seized me, the idea that I have conceived of the happiness of being loved by you and the scorn I feel for all other forms of happiness! In short I need, I thirst to see you. I believe I would give the rest of my life only to speak with you for a few moments of things that are utterly indifferent to me.

Adieu, I leave you, in order to be near you, closer to you, to dare to speak to you, with all the abandonment, with all the force of the passion that devours me.

HENRI

Closely besieged by such appeals, Metilda relented and permitted him to see her at intervals spaced regularly two weeks apart, and usually in the presence of others. In *De l'amour,* Stendhal sets forth as a "scientific" document the journal of a "young Italian gentleman of 'Bologna' named 'Salviati,' who has recently perished of unrequited love for a lady named 'Leonore.'" In the memoir of Salviati, which tells us how, at one period, his lady restricted his visits to her to but once a fortnight, it is not hard to discern the masochistic emotions which Beyle, in Milan, endured under similar severities:

> Those visits so rare and so much desired brought an access of folly. . . .
>
> To begin with, the thought of the hour that would end the visit was too much present for me to derive pleasure from it. One talked a great deal without remembering what one was saying, often seeming to contradict oneself. . . . The effort at self-possession is so arbitrary that sometimes I seemed to speak with an air of coldness. Love hides itself by its excessiveness.
>
> Away from her the imagination had conceived the most delightful conversations. . . . But, as one approached the terrible moment the fever began and redoubled.

As soon as he enters her parlor, he is tormented by the fear of committing some breach of taste and bringing new punishment upon himself. Desiring to speak to her, he is forced to be silent; longing to look at her, he averts his eyes. And if another is present, some dull fellow telling an interminable story, "the poor lover as if in fear of losing the least of such rare moments becomes all ears. This hour that he had visioned as promising so much delight, passes like a streak of lightning." No slightest detail of what goes on is lost to him, and yet though the others are making only a casual visit, he feels how much he alone is unaware of the ordinary facts of her daily existence, and has become as a stranger to her he loves. "Finally he leaves and, as he coldly bids her adieu, suffers the frightful thought that he will not see her again for *two whole weeks*; and wonders if he would not suffer less for never seeing again the woman he adores."

Such was Stendhal's way of love, the masochistic way, and he has commemorated it not only in his treatise, but in his novels, especially the great unfinished romance of *Lucien Leuwen,* in which the hero is also reduced to seeing his lady every two weeks. In his conscious mind, he would like to be a Don Juan, or at least a Valmont, equal to attacking systematically and conquering swiftly. Subconsciously, however, as in his childhood, fear and masochism always possess him; and like the heroes of his fictions, his spirit yields weakly before high-willed women, and all sorts of castration complexes afflict it. In *De l'amour,* Salviati is described as telling Leonore that self-denial and sorrow over her severity only make his love grow stronger; and she shrewdly comments that that is "a *feminine* sort of love" in a man.

But Salviati reflects:

> Even the asperities of the woman one loves have an infinite grace not to be found in the most pleasing moments with other women. [!]

In the same essay occurs that beautiful, reverberant epigram of Stendhal's that so perfectly summarizes his fear-haunted attraction to Metilda Viscontini:

> *Love is a costly flower, but one must have the desire to pluck it from the edge of a precipice.*

This, as the Freudians say, is an exact *erotization* of fear.[5] But though fear often disturbed his potency, love was no less deep and powerful in Stendhal than in the still more timid Jean-Jacques Rousseau whom charming women also adored with a maternal passion. On the contrary, like Rousseau, Stendhal believed that his melancholy "and sensitive" way, (e.g., effeminate-masochistic) was the higher, the more refined way of love, the love of modern man, burdened by his knowledge, his doubt, his imagination, his neurosis. Thus no athletic Hercules, nor mechanical Casanova, ever wrote of love with such *eloquence* as these two weak reeds, Rousseau and Stendhal.

But to relieve or escape from the pain and fear that always accompanies love in his case, Stendhal writes down the memory of his feelings and experiences, and the analysis of those experiences. He suffers, but also reflects and observes; he is passionate, but also cerebral. He tells us in *De l'amour* that such confession is a device for

> gaining wisdom by being one's own confidant. Write this very evening, under concealed names, but with all characteristic details, the dialogue that you have

[5]Cf. Edmond Bergler, *Talleyrand, Napoleon und Stendhal,* (Vienna, 1935), a somewhat "speculative" study by an extremist follower of Freud.

just had with your beloved and the difficulty in which you find yourself. In a week, if you are still in love, you will be another man; and then, reading your own consultation, you may give yourself some good advice.

He had no thought of abandoning the chase. After a time it dawned upon him that Metilda had been given a bad character report of him. As her companion she had always with her an older cousin named Mme. Traversi, a woman of wealth and social position, whom he thought "horribly devout" and narrow. Mme. Traversi, he was convinced, who strove to protect Metilda in society, disliked him and warned her cousin to shun the immoral Frenchman who, it was rumored, on leaving her house each night repaired to taverns with harlots.

Once at a great ball in Milan he had stood in a window recess watching Metilda as she danced with another man. Gazing at her silently, his eyes had grown moist with tears. Then he suddenly became aware that Mme. Traversi, standing near by, was staring at him and at Metilda, watching them both with a curious smile. At length she came to him and spoke some words, but he was so confused that he continued to look only at Metilda and ignored the older woman. Whereupon she suddenly seemed to blaze up with anger, and turned from him with an expression of intense hatred, as if resolved to punish his presumption at staring so longingly at Metilda. From that day when he had offended her, it was his fixed idea that she was his sworn enemy.

To convince Metilda of his good faith, he led an exemplary life, lived alone much of the time, even took a vow of chastity! One day the saucy "Nina" Vigano, descending the grand stairway of the Scala with a queue of admirers at her heels, hailed him as he leaned against the balustrade. "They say that you are in love with me, Beyle," she sang out gaily. "Is it true?"

"They are mistaken, madame," he answered coolly and without kissing her hand. He knew the news of this bold action would reach Metilda. But he never could come again to the house of the merry Elena Vigano.

Hearing such reports of him, Metilda, he hoped, would change her tone, soften a little, and his life would become radiant, the sky would take on a new color. He felt himself even filled with a spirit of charity toward all men, made better, more tolerant, more "the virtuous Roman" by her smile. But two weeks later, on his next visit, she might be indifferent and cold and the sky would darken once more.

He had only two or three confidants in Milan, of whom he loved the warm-natured Vismara best; and this friend would say to him:

"Ah, my dear comrade, I see that you are busy again with your follies. I urge you once more to drop the affair. Cease to love a woman who cannot love, who is nothing but selfishness, who with her ideas of constancy will never care for a man who is one day in Milan, tomorrow at Naples. Besides it has been reported for some days that she is interested in G. . . ."

Stendhal would burst into a rage, but his friend tried to console him:

"My poor madman, why do you not make some other choice? You have the 'Countess' K[assera] who offers you and everybody else her heart. You have Ninetta who treats you with distinction. . . . Do you think this is some ordinary woman? . . . Mere gallantry has no power over her. I tell you she is the haughtiest little soul in all M[ilan]."

He waited, hoping against hope. Often he drew little pictures of pistols on the pages of his manuscripts. He said: "If some assassin had shot me in the head with a pistol, I would have thanked him before I expired."

3

In April 1819, the thrilling North Italian spring returned once more; the great Lombard chestnut trees blossomed and scented the air; hope rose again in the heart of our melancholy Lovelace who, though approaching his middle years, miraculously preserved himself from the chilling reason of age.

A year had passed, a year punctuated by fortnightly ordeals of anticipation and regret, and his principal affair in life had not advanced perceptibly. He was not finally dismissed and he was not accepted, though he began to suspect that only Metilda's stubborn pride steeled her to hold him off. But perhaps this pride could be worn down slowly if he showed the patience of an angel.

And yet, wonderful to relate, great love made Stendhal more *angelic*, as he himself now admits. Only the year before he had felt sympathy and affectionate friendship becoming more rare, life being passed in cold relationships, "in which one proceeded with yardstick always in hand, measuring ideas of interest and vanity." When still in his thirties life had seemed bleak, and the tender parts of his soul sterile, petrified. "Yet in the midst of this arid desert, love caused a fountain of emotion to gush forth, fresher and more abundant than that of first youth."

This love of his ripe years revivified him. "Like some social eruption such as periodically shakes society from top to bottom, renewing and reconstituting the world upon a more reasonable basis, so love renews and retempers a generous character."

Had he not shown during long months how selfless was his devotion? In a note found on the flyleaf of a book he was reading at this time he wrote wistfully: "She has the pleasure of feeling that there is a man, not odious to her, who takes the most passionate interest in the slightest things that happen to her." Love, in short, had made him a good man, and he felt her esteem for him rising, for she spoke more kindly to him nowadays. "She addressed me precious words. . . . I left her drunk with joy."

Yet at the next bimonthly meeting her humor would be altered; she would, as he sadly complained, even watch for the hour when he must go, as if its approach gave her relief. Once she even said: "I did not know you would be so hard to discourage."

Never had he assailed so difficult a woman, and the more difficult she made herself, the more he loved her. The process held him enchanted. On the margin of one of his books he wrote: "Always a little doubt to calm; this is what gives life to passionate love."

After visiting her he would write her letters steeped in humility and exposing the man he was, true to nature. Metilda had left Milan for a journey of five weeks, and recommended that he pass the time by returning to France for a visit. He answered:

> No, I could never consent to place mountains between you and myself. But can I hope, by force of love, to reanimate a heart that cannot be dead to this feeling? Yes, I fear I am ridiculous in your eyes; my timidity and my silence have bored you, and you take my arrival at your house as a calamity. . . . When you said with the accent of a truth profoundly felt: "Ah, *so much the better that it is midnight, at last!*" should I not have realized that you would be pleased to be rid of my importunities . . . and sworn never to see you again? But I have courage only when I am far away from you. In your presence, I am timid as a child, the words die upon my lips, I can only gaze at you and admire you. Must it be that I should feel so inferior to myself and so dull?

Yet, though she had given him no sign of relenting, one of his Italian friends, doubtless Vismara, reported that she now spoke very pleasantly of him before others. "*She is yours,*" the other man had whispered, "now are you going to do your part?"[6]

[6]Letter of June 24, 1819, *Correspondance*, Vol. V.

But what would he do during the forty days of her absence? He sat for hours *"thinking ripely and profoundly to M.,"* one of his autobiographical notes informs us in English. The countess had left Milan on May 12, 1819, to visit her two sons at a seminary in Volterra, a goodly distance away. In her absence he felt the desperate courage to follow her there. It was a most perilous thing to do. Yet in love one must be brave: "Attack! Attack! Attack!"

Two weeks after she had gone, he suddenly took the coach to Genoa, then boarded the coastal boat that ran down to Leghorn, and from there climbed to the desolate sun-baked hill town of Volterra, after a hard journey of over two hundred miles.

On June 3, a stout stranger was seen sauntering about the ancient Etruscan city, a man wearing green glasses. Metilda saw him in the main street, but thought nothing of the matter. But at dusk, strolling with an acquaintance he had made in the little close at the edge of the town, he removed his colored glasses. At that moment Metilda, in the company of two other persons, passed by, gave him a startled look, and continued on her way without saluting him. That evening she sent him a note, addressing him as "Monsieur" and berating him for having followed her to Volterra and compromised her by hanging about the park where she walked every day.

He hastened to place a letter in her hands, begging her forgiveness and giving his oath that he had taken no premeditated step in following her, but only obeyed his fantasy, since passion made him no longer a reasonable being. He had come to be near her, incognito; hence the green glasses. And he had removed them at nightfall only to avoid suspicion. In this letter of June 8, 1819, he earnestly defends his character, saying that his Italian friends who have seen him every day for five years in Milan will vouch for his sense of honor. He concludes:

> I have had only three passions in my life: ambition, from 1800 to 1811; the love of a woman who deceived me, from 1811 to 1818, and for a year this one. . . . Love me if you can, divine Metilda, but in the name of God do not scorn me!

He did not preserve his incognito long, for he was not unknown in these parts to various persons who had met him in Florence or Milan. Thus it happened that after three days had passed he was invited by the rector of the seminary of Volterra to a little reception which Metilda also attended. It was a most uncomfortable evening, whose unpleasantness he tried to banish by posing as an antiquarian and talking at great length on the Etruscan ruins of the region, so that he ended as usual by falling into vehement arguments with everybody and incurring the displeasure of Metilda.

What was worse, there was present a Signor Giorgi, a handsome and noble Italian, upon whose arm Metilda leaned, as he remarked to himself, with an air of great intimacy. "Alas, virtuous women are as much cheats as the other kind," he reflected bitterly.

On the following day he paid Metilda a visit in the garden adjacent to the school, was coldly received and as coolly dismissed. Hastening off to Florence, he sent her more despairing letters, making the humblest apologies for his behavior. Her reply, after more than a week's delay, indicated a complete rupture:

> Sir, I do not wish to receive any more letters from you and I will not write to you. I am with perfect esteem, etc.

With this note she returned two of his letters unopened. His renewed appeals were moving: "Though I hope no more, the only part of the earth where I can be least unhappy is near you." She answered by citing a line of verse that he himself had previously quoted as illustrating the distance separating Italian and French character: "*Trop d'espace sépare Andromaque et Pyrrhus.*"

But if they could not be united, neither could they be long separated. By stubborn petitions Stendhal won a pardon, and restoration of the limited privileges he had enjoyed before.

4

Returning to Milan at the end of July, he found that nine letters had come notifying him of the death of his father, Joseph-Chérubin Beyle. He felt a wave of emotion, unmixed with filial tenderness, but more like deliverance.

In August he was in Grenoble, on the other side of Metilda's mountains, busy straightening out the tangled affairs his father had left. The long years of absence had frozen hatred in Henri's heart for his parent, whose letters to his son in themselves give evidence of his unloving and hypocritical personality. "All that the most profound and most implacable hatred could devise against a son was attempted by this father," he wrote to Metilda at this time. He inherited, not 100,000 francs as he had hoped, but chiefly debts and litigation. The wealth of the Beyles in land and houses was gone, and the discovery that he was left comparatively poor came with a great shock. Chérubin, the avaricious speculator, had lost on every side, in land, in sheep, in vines, and so had betrayed him. After legal suits that lasted for years, Stendhal raised enough to pay his considerable debts, and in addition realized a sum of about thirty thousand francs, paid him in several allotments. This capital he drew upon year by year to augment his small annuities of 2,400 francs—until one day he found it all gone. But in the meantime he was able to visit Paris for a month to see the latest plays and operas; then he hurried southward again to Milan, at the end of October 1819, to place himself once more at the feet of the reluctant Metilda.

After having chastised him enough, so that he threatened to end his life, she always readmitted him to her presence in the status of an unhappy friend. Although she made plain that she was not in love with him, he perceived that she obviously delighted in hurting him. He would never forget how, in the course of a quarrel, she once, "red with anger," confronted him and cried out at "those letters you *dared* to write me." To such a measure did he associate the image of her with asperity and cruelty that, in later years, when journeying through the Jura Mountains and gazing at their frowning horizons, he would be reminded of the visage of Metilda in anger, and tremble anew.

Only in Italy, Stendhal claims, could love be pursued with such prolonged fidelity, for three, five, or twenty years. Night after night, when this was permitted him, they would sit together like old friends in the parlor of the gloomy Viscontini mansion, feeling a profound intimacy yet also a terrible barrier.

Metilda—like the character of Mme. de Chasteller in *Lucien Leuwen*—was proud and intensely religious. Stendhal himself tells us that she felt herself "highly dishonored" by her misfortune in marriage, and that "the women of good society in Milan avenged themselves upon her for her superiority over them." With the aid of the Baroness Traversi, she was now gradually winning her way back into the society which had cast her out.

She acted as one wounded by life and believed she could depend on a man like Beyle only to injure her again. He had the *esprit raisonneur* of the French; he was faithless, and made mock of many things, even of the patriots and their schemes for insurrection. His extreme self-consciousness, his want of Italian sweep and emphasis suggested an insincerity of sentiment against which he often vainly defended himself.

One day Metilda told him the story of an affair between two well-known persons in Milan, and commented, in conclusion: "*Think* of her situation: every night, her lover, leaving her house, went off to see some street girl!" He realized afterward that this little moral sermon was intended for his own benefit. For in effect, every evening after depositing Metilda at the door of her cousin Mme. Traversi, he went to spend the rest of the evening in the company of the "Countess" Kassera, Milan's light-o'-love. "And out of stupidity . . . I refused, on one occasion, to become the lover of this young amiable woman, in order to merit, in the eyes of the Lord, the love of Metilda." This was a second sacrifice for Metilda, counting the chanteuse, Elena Vigano.[7]

Sometimes he suspected that her intense social prudery and coldness was but a trick to raise the price of the treasure he sought. But the problem of her health, which began to fail toward the end of 1820, also played its part. Her chest pained her and, like all tubercular persons, she feared the early death that was to be her lot, and this also strengthened her resolve not to yield to him. When spring returned he would note, in his mixed jargon (now on the margin of some book he read): "*Very in love*, February 5, 1820. . . . March 14, the first fine day of the year, *I see her before my window*." And whenever she melted and smiled upon him, he would be transported with hope. But later, he would have occasion to admit: "This cruel woman is *enraged* at me, that is the word her friends use." It was his "one enemy," that "fury," Mme. Traversi, wanting in youth and love, who had wrought this mischief.

Stendhal's long, stern pursuit of happiness in the shape of Metilda reached what he picturesquely termed "*le dead-blank*" at the end of 1820, although it had often touched a low-water mark during the preceding year. After long delay, since 1816, he turned again to his writing, that solace he had used before to repel dull care and the "vapors" of melancholia; his mind, his memory, and his pen were to him as a *laterna magica* with which to light up the darkest hours.

5

One evening in November 1819, he had the idea of writing the story of his love for Metilda and sending it to her. But after a dozen pages were done he threw this aside. Seven weeks later, he marked December 28, 1819, as "*Day of Genius*." It was the day when the idea came to him, not of going on with the romance of a Polish officer exiled in Bologna, a tale too revealing by far, and perhaps offensive to Metilda,

[7] *Souvenirs d'égotisme*, pp. 35–6, Divan ed.

but of writing a philosophical discourse on love that centered upon a new idea, a significant psychological discovery that had come to him during the recent years of trial.

"All my life has been spent in considering five or six ruling ideas," he was to conclude in the *Henri Brulard.* In 1803, when he was twenty, he had written a fragment called the "Catéchism of a Roué." In 1816, writing one of his numerous Last Testaments, he had offered to provide money at his death for an international prize for the best essay on the nature of "love, ambition, hate, laughter, tears, friendship, terror, happiness." By disposition he was a moralist and psychologist; that was why, in earlier years, he had always abandoned experiments with plays or prose romances in favor of the essay of ideas. What he planned now was to be a "scientific" study, such as had never been undertaken before, analyzing the "disease" called love.

Everyone had written of love, from the classicists to Rousseau and Benjamin Constant. But what was it? In those earlier romances a person was either "in love" or not. Yet no one had deliberately set about analyzing love as reasonably as men dissected a specimen case of yellow fever.

Stendhal's favorite philosophers of the sensualist school, Condillac and Helvetius, had stopped their investigations short of a rational analysis of this passion. To Helvetius it was but sensuality refined; to Tracy, who came after him, it was "friendship embellished by pleasure"; but aside from some brief utilitarian reflections on marriage and domestic life, the late eighteenth-century materialists, such as Dr. Cabanis, held that what was called love "does not enter into the plan of nature," and was only a product of a complex and artificial civilization.

But Stendhal for years had been obsessed by the concept of an all-pervading, "passionate love," that made him, of all men, temporarily chaste. Helvetius and the other positivists, he concluded, were "cold" men who had never understood the "ardent soul," which he now proposed to dissect, and thereby create a new ethics of the passions. The originality of Stendhal as a thinker had long consisted in his attempt (exemplified in his life) to use the strategy of the eighteenth-century rationalists in that uncharted, instinctual region called "happiness." Now he would bring the methods of the rationalists to bear upon the passion of love. But in attempting this, as Léon Blum has said, he was inspired, not by the materialistic *philosophes,* but by their great intellectual opponent, Jean-Jacques Rousseau.

Was not Rousseau, whom Stendhal read devotedly in boyhood, under the lime trees of Dauphiné, the great expounder of passion and enthusiasm? Stendhal, perhaps unwittingly, returns to the influence of the man of intuition as he analyzes the psychology of the passions. His terms are mechanistic, being borrowed from Helvetius and the physiologist Cabanis, but his perspective is, as we would now say, naturalistic. Thus he combines in himself, in his method and his writing, "the two opposing currents of thought of the eighteenth century: that of rationalism and of intuitive-romanticism. . . . This contradiction is the real key to Beylism."[8] One might add that this apparent contradiction is what makes Stendhal so curiously contemporary.

In Stendhal's somewhat incomplete system of philosophic hedonism, the passion of love is seen as the supreme source of happiness; it becomes the highest form of energy, an *élan vital.* "To love is to feel alive, to have strong sensations," he wrote in his treatise.

It was on that "day of genius" in December 1819, that he thought of the idea of the *"crystallized branch of Salzburg."* This was the parable of the rotten bough of a tree that had fallen into the depths of a salt mine near Salzburg and which in time had become entirely covered with beautiful sparkling crystals, and remained so forever. Such, he said to himself, was the process of love! *Crystallization.* It was a process by which the imagination of the lover attached all sorts of illusions of every perfection to the personality of the beloved, while his own self-interest became purified, his ego itself identified "incurably" with the person loved. Stendhal then analyzes the gradual steps of this *crystallization,* or falling-in-love process, in an orderly way; and the opening section of his book, as we now have it, contains the core of his thought. Rediscovered, after long neglect, by modern readers, the term *crystallization* became part of the French language.

His definition of the process of love has endured as a contribution both to psychology and to aesthetic theory:

> Near the salt mines of Salzburg, a leafless branch falls into the depths of one of the mines; two or three months later it is found with its tiniest twigs, no bigger than a titmouse, entirely covered with an infinity of sparkling diamonds. One can no longer recognize the original branch.
>
> What I call *crystallization* is the operation of the mind that draws from everything around it the discovery that the beloved object has new perfection. . . .

Stendhal's idea has the added value of epitomizing romantic aesthetic doctrine in his time: just as there is, for the romanticist, no absolute

[8]Blum: *Stendhal et le Beylisme,* pp. 177–79.

artistic or literary canon of beauty, so there is none in the case of feminine beauty. Beauty is relative, it is the illusion produced by time and circumstance, "the collection of all the satisfactions and of all the desires that have been formed successively with regard to the object of love," Stendhal wrote. He adds: "in love one no longer sees things *as they are*," and the statement is still valid. One may fall in love with a homely or even a blind woman, one may love without physical satisfaction and gain happiness nevertheless.

Belated ideologist that he was, Stendhal believed in a mechanistic science of human ideas that were so many transformed sensations. The rigid categories in which, like Cabanis, he classifies human love as falling into four different types, and the process of falling in love into seven emotional stages, have an amusingly antiquated and arbitrary character.

Quite solemnly he postulates his four ways of love:

(1) physical love
(2) love through taste
(3) vanity-love
(4) passional love

The first is the simplest: "meeting a fresh young peasant maid while hunting in the woods"; the second represents a higher stage of affinity among civilized persons through the appeal of taste; the third, he charges, is primarily the French manner of love, embraced for the sake of social pretension; the fourth type, passional love, is to Stendhal by all odds the highest and strongest form (that which he feels for Metilda Viscontini as he writes).[9]

His seven stages of love are divided as follows: (1) admiration; (2) the beginning of desire; (3) hope; (4) inception of love; (5) the first *crystallization*; (6) doubt (and/or jealousy); (7) the second, or final *crystallization*, the confirmation of love. These divisions are certainly suggestive, though they seem rather pedantic. Stendhal himself later

[9]Since *De l'amour* is also an exposition of ideology, Stendhal adopts Dr. P. J. Cabanis's theories, in *Du Physique et du moral de l'homme*, of six different types of physiological temperament, classified as: the *sanguine*, the *bilious*, the *melancholy*, the *phlegmatic*, the *nervous*, the *athletic*. Thus his own four types of love may be multiplied by six types of temperament, making twenty-four varieties. These may vary materially in different types of society—of which there are six: Asiatic despotism, absolute monarchy, constitutional monarchy, aristocracy, republic, and revolutionary state—making in all 144 different types of love! Such are the mathematical fantasies to which the ideology of the 1790s might lead one. It is only fair to say that Stendhal himself drops his pretensions to a logical treatise, and soon proceeds to the real matter of discursive reflections and observations on human nature.

demonstrated in his novels other varieties of love, such as the love that comes of long friendship, or love from need of consolation, or the coldly cerebral love (of Mathilde de la Môle in Volume II of *The Red and the Black*).

But after discouraging his readers for a few pages, at the beginning of the first book, by his "mathematical" categories of passion, Stendhal plunges into a series of sparkling observations and aphorisms upon the only love that matters to him, the love of great passion. For, besides being a work of ideology, *De l'amour* is a piece of confession, somewhat generalized to be sure, but none the less searching and profound, in which Metilda might easily have recognized the heart of her French admirer laid bare.

Irreligious man though he was, he seemed to understand full well the value of the confessional therapy sixty or seventy years before Freud. His confessions are neatly inserted into his philosophical discourse as the "Journal of Salviati," and the "Journal of Lisio Visconti" (both representing himself), but offered blandly as "scientific" documents, or specimens, taken from cases of superhuman passion. As scientific evidence they give promise of the master of romantic and psychological fiction that is to come. They sing also of Italy and its passional customs as Stendhal sees them. Finally, in honor of the man of sensibility, they celebrate that timid and tremulously masochistic love of which Stendhal, in particular, was an adept. But what is even more significant is that the author ends by exhorting us to seek the highest, the most "spiritual" forms of love and—in contradiction to the materialism he seems to embrace elsewhere—condemns love that is dictated by vanity or mere physical pleasure.

Vanity-love is epitomized, in his opinion, in the court life of the 1760s in France. The stage settings for its games of gallantry are by the soft-tinted Watteau and Fragonard. But its true character is represented, in the words of Chamfort, as "The contact of two epidermises and the exchange of two fantasies." Thus Stendhal, in illustration, gives the anecdote of an old nobleman who tells an aged marquise that he has long adored her in vain. To which she laughingly replies: "Ah, *mon dieu*, why didn't you tell me before? You would have had me like all the others!"

Physical love, dictated by vanity, he declares, is the tradition of the French eighteenth century handed down from generation to generation. Thus, even in the nineteenth century, he says mockingly: "To a bourgeois a duchess is never more than thirty years old."

Similarly he condemns the physical love of Don Juan, with whom he always had not a few secret ties. Such love, he holds, is based on an overweening interest in strategy and tactics, as in military campaigns or in the hunt, or at the gaming table. Don Juan accepts no obligations; "he takes and pays nothing." To him woman is but "a machine for joy"; her desire for equality he spurns, seeking only to dominate and deceive, enjoying even her misfortunes. In youth this may do well enough, but by the age of thirty Don Juan (with whom Stendhal holds an imaginary dialogue) confesses that he feels himself an old man, remarking: "There are not twenty different types of women, and when one has had two or three of each . . . then satiety begins." Even the melancholy sorrowing Werthers, novices who see life only through illusion, are happier, Stendhal judges, for "the misery of inconstancy is boredom."

It is passionate love, profoundly interwoven with the sense of beauty —"the promise of happiness"—and the best music, painting, and literature, that Stendhal establishes in the center of his moral-aesthetic system. For he refuses to consider love as part of the system of nature, or purely as nature's scheme of reproduction as so many other philosophers have done. Great love is, to him, the fullest realization of the ego, *"the wonder of civilization."* The attainment of complete self-surrender in passional love is then his higher law of human happiness, which "great souls"—Stendhal's Happy Few—may alone fulfill. Though of course not the first French moralist to hold such a view, Stendhal certainly approaches more closely to the conception of Freud's imperative libido than any of the other older writers. Love as pure "act," as the highest expression of man's energy, to which the arts and the beauties of nature contribute their harmonies, seems to transcend all other forms of action. It is well to consider this point in weighing Stendhal's resemblances or differences from the later Nietzsche. It provides also a key to the meaning of the surprising denouements of his novels.

With such convictions, reinforced by the ideologic-utilitarian dogma that "man is not free to avoid doing that which gives him most pleasure out of a number of alternate actions," Stendhal proceeds to a vigorous polemic against the social prudes and the church. These are the liveliest and most amusing parts of his book. It was a time when cant and respectability were being revived in France under the restored Bourbons and when a forbidding religious piety was being imposed upon the continent under the powerful Metternich. Queen Victoria, born this very year, 1819, was still in the offing. How much moral suffocation the nineteenth century might have escaped if men had listened to the counsel of the too obscure Stendhal upon sex and marriage!

He inveighs against that Christian morality now being restored to favor which sets up "the fear of hell" in order to constrain people to a "prosaic virtue." Thus a good woman might resist a devoted lover "solely in order to avoid being fried in a caldron of boiling oil in the next world," an absurd situation in which a vat of boiling oil becomes the "rival" of true love. "Prudery is a form of avarice, the worst of all," is one of his telling sentences. Paraphrasing Chamfort, Stendhal declares: "No true union is forever legitimate save that which is ordained by a true passion. A woman belongs by right to the man who loves her and whom she loves more than life itself." (Some of these shafts are certainly directed at Stendhal's reluctant belle.) In this vein, this early feminist goes on to propose complete moral liberty for women, as well as a fully masculine education for them. If women studied mathematics and the sciences, he argues—somewhat selfishly—they would not prefer a handsome fop in a uniform to a man of intelligence who had a plain face (!). Marriage he decries, saying, "It is the priest who is the fertile source of all vice and misfortune afflicting our modern marriages," since he renders liberty impossible for young women before marriage and excludes divorce afterward. Then, not too jestingly he adds:

> It is a much greater violation of modesty for [a young girl] to go to bed with a man whom she has only seen twice in her life, after three Latin words uttered in a church, than to yield herself to a lover she has adored for two years. But I am speaking an absurd language here.

Though *De l'amour* is in no sense an orderly treatise, its seminal qualities appeal to us on every page, especially in the first short book, written in Milan in 1819–20. (Later, after holding the little manuscript by his side for two years, he casually added Book II, a compilation of historical material on customs of marriage and love in various periods and climates, and divers reflections on social morals, intended to make his small book more vendible.) Stendhal's analysis of the emotions of modesty or shame, or of pride, or of the various emotional states through which lovers pass, seems as pertinent as anything that appears today in our learned quarterlies of psychology. It is impressive also that Stendhal showed his deep interest in the science of man, before anthropology was officially born, under the aegis of Darwin, by throwing off the proposal that "we ought to establish an academy at Philadelphia (under republican freedom) devoted solely to gathering materials for the study of man in his savage state, and not delay until those curious tribes are extinct." What is most important is his underlying thought ("naturalistic" or "pragmatic") that we should pursue the examination of the passions of man, i.e., his psychology, in systematic form, and that we are capable of arriving at some exact and at least workable knowledge in this field. A "logic" or rationale of happiness, he asserts, is discoverable and we must seek it.

6

The best of his little book *On Love*, part philosophy, part autobiography, at once pedantic and paradoxical, was completed in the spring of 1820, when the growing popular unrest and rumors of an impending revolution in Italy interrupted him, and he was forced to put it aside. (In any case he showed it only to his friends and feared that he would be forced to publish it privately.)

There was no question of where Stendhal's sympathies lay. The police in Milan, who were carrying out widespread arrests, knew well who he was and what he thought. For on July 12, 1820, in one of his "code" letters to a friend in Paris he reported that the pro-royalist French consul had spoken ill of him to the authorities:

> *Je suis inquiet* because the Con[sul] of Mi[lan] has said that I am a pernicious liberal *et l'on a su que Dominique avait* made the P[eint]ure. *Le Prince* has spoken of Stendhal.

Spies shadowed spies; everyone feared being denounced by his neighbor; and Stendhal feared most of all being clapped into a dungeon, which was what happened to some of his friends.

Whatever his sympathies, he had grave doubts about the seriousness of the young Italian revolutionists, whom he described as full of talk and "vague aspirations." In his letters during the autumn of 1820, time of the "terror," he reports accurately that the masses were not following the nobles and bourgeois who led the Carbonari. Somewhat earlier he had promised himself: "On the eve of the assassinations I shall skip the camp." The philosopher of energy, the admirer of Danton, Napoleon, and Lord Byron (who was at the moment engaged in a comic conspiracy of arms smuggling for the Carbonari at Ravenna), would lend no support to the revolution that was at hand because he was convinced that it would be squelched and would merely disarrange his earthly paradise.

His Italian friends were familiar with his spirit of contradiction and persiflage. The Milanese conspirators, he would argue, knew nothing of the rigors of national or civil war. And even if they succeeded in constituting a republic, would it help make them happier? The Americans had a republic, he would say, but because of their climate, doubtless, were unhappy and thought only of "dollars." Did Philadelphia possess the music, culture, and good society of Milan under its German tyrants?

Yet on the next occasion the roguish Stendhal would exclaim at the vexations he suffered from the police, and cry that he longed "to have eight thousand francs a year" so that he could "go and live in Philadelphia for six months under political freedom." But as life became grimmer his paradoxical sallies, which the slower-witted Italians never relished, brought him under suspicion by both sides.

On July 23, 1820, he reported to his friend the Baron de Mareste in Paris:

> My dear friend, the worst misfortune possible has befallen me. Jealous people have circulated the rumor that I am here as an agent of the French Government.
>
> For six months now this is what has been going on. I noticed that several persons avoided greeting me in the street.
>
> For what would this Frenchman be doing here? The Milanese *bonshommes* will never understand my philosophic life, and that I live here on five thousand francs better than I could live in Paris for twelve thousand.

Word had come that he was spoken of as a "spy" in the service of the French Government. He found himself excluded from certain houses.

On March 10, 1821, there was an uprising in Turin, and the next day Victor Emmanuel, King of Sardinia, abdicated, to be replaced by the presumed liberal and nationalist, Charles Albert. Fighting also broke out in Naples where the Carbonari, resisted at first only by troops whose commanders were secretly allied to them, opened what seemed a successful struggle for a constitution. Similar, though much weaker, manifestations of unrest in Milan were met by the Austrians with vigorous measures of repression. Count Confalioneri and the poet, Silvio Pellico, were arrested, tried secretly, and sentenced to death—though this was later commuted to imprisonment for a long term in the dreaded Spielberg fortress, the usual fate of conspiring liberals caught in Metternich's net. Stendhal's friend and confidant, Giuseppe Vismara, condemned to death *in absentia*, fled abroad. Finally his beloved Metilda was called before the secret tribunal sitting in

Milan. The leader, Confalioneri, under the relentless examination of his military judges, broke down, confessed, and compromised his comrades. But Metilda Dembowski, under examination, bore herself with heroic firmness and betrayed no one.

Meanwhile Stendhal, who had been closely associated with the condemned lawyer Vismara, and Pellico, secretary of the Carbonari's Milan "executive," had been given quiet but clear hints by the authorities that he would do well to depart from Italy.

On April 1, 1821, he wrote his friend Mareste in Paris (more or less in English):

> I believe, my dear friend, that I have took *la plus pénible résolution* in all my life, that of coming back to Bruxelle's Hotel [Paris]. . . . I will have only three thousand for the remain of my life after this year. . . . I shall make my enter in Lutèce, somewhat in May.

He had cleared himself of all suspicion before Metilda who, whatever she thought of him, knew he was no spy; but time had brought no solution of the "dead-blank." Her appearance in his life and his passion for her had indeed been "a great misfortune" for him, as one of his Italian friends said. But now he could not even play with the hope of winning her.

He had waited in Milan with the sense that future happiness existed but a few steps from his house—if she would utter the word and give the smile she denied him. (He did not know that she was ailing and would be carried away suddenly only two years later.) But now Milan was sad; the opposition was crushed, his friends imprisoned or fled, and it was time for him to go.

We see him always in the posture he has described, in *De l'amour*, of one of those devoted Italian lovers, standing in a street of Milan at night in the rain, silent, rigid, watching her window, then mad with excitement seeing the curtain stir—was it her hand, or only the wind? Returning to his melancholy quarters, he would be unable to sleep, sitting in long reverie, sometimes thinking of death. At length, unlike any lover, Italian or otherwise, that ever was on land or sea, he takes his notebooks, or some scrap of paper, and describes his emotions, precisely, coldly, setting down some "true fact" after nature![10] For his task of self-observation is never done.

Despite his follies and ecstasies, Stendhal is never far removed from the discipline of the true scientist when his mind turns from passion and begins to reason.

[10]Etienne Rey, preface to *De l'amour*, p. xcix (Champion ed.).

He refused to believe that she did not love him.

"After three years of intimacy, I left a woman whom I loved and who loved me, and yet who never gave herself to me." Years later, in the salons of Paris, where he shone as a wit, he would feel moments of *attendrissement* and think of "my poor, sad, and lonely lady in the depths of Romagna, who loved me and would not admit it, and whom I was never to see again." These three years of combat between pride and hope were nevertheless precious memories to a man whose imagination always cherished the poignant hours of his life.

"When will you come back to Milan?" she asked him when he came to bid her good-by.

"Never, I hope," was his reply. These were the last words spoken between them. She was silent, and gave him only the inscrutable, finely melancholy smile of her dark eyes and the corners of her mouth, such as one sees in the women of Leonardo.

CHAPTER XIV

Return to France

LEAVING Milan early in June 1821, he went by carriage to Como, with many a backward glance, wondering if he had the strength to go forward over the mountains, and how long it would be before he retraced his steps. It seemed to him that he "died many deaths" with every mile he journeyed away from that city where he had desired to end his days. Like Mr. Shelley (whom he had met in 1818), he breathed only in sighs. "Ah, in that last hour . . . a single word of hers might have changed my life."

When, a few days later, he was proceeding on horseback, in the company of a courier, over the barren St. Gothard to Switzerland, he still hoped that some misstep would carry him over a precipice. At night, when he wrote in his notebook, he would again draw little pistols on the margins of its pages. Often he thought of blowing out his brains, but feared that he might merely wound himself and not die. "It also seems to me that it was political curiosity that prevented me from finishing things." Persistently he awaited a new revolution that would sweep the stage. Perhaps in 1830, he told himself, perhaps even sooner, liberty would come, and even a man like himself with a mortally wounded heart might find some ground for hope again.

That politics was always important in Stendhal's life is shown even in this crisis. As with heavy heart he crossed the border to Switzerland and reached Altdorf, near Lake Lucerne, he asked for the statue of William Tell, the rebel leader of the Swiss patriots. "Although people who write under the ministerial censorship in all lands pretend there never was such a person, I am a great admirer of William Tell," he says. But all he found was a hideous stone monument with the figure having a skirt that was very poorly draped. "There, I said to myself, with a soft melancholy, overcoming for the first time my dull despair, there is what becomes of the most beautiful things in the eyes of gross creatures. Such thou art too, Metilda, in the midst of the salon of Mme. Traversi."

On June 21, 1821, he arrived in Paris and stopped at the little Hotel de Bruxelles, at 47 Rue de Richelieu, which he had frequented on previous visits. To its proprietor, a former valet at the court of Louis XVI, named Petit, and a most excellent and discreet character, Stendhal turned over the last sum of money he would have for a long time, some three thousand francs. He got a receipt for it—which he promptly lost—and then walked over to the nearby Tuileries Gardens, where in youth he had been wont to parade like a coxcomb. There he sat alone plunged in long reveries.

What would he do in Paris now? How would he amuse himself? Society here lived under false lights; it was without energy or naturalness. Besides, he had little money now and at first desired to avoid his former friends, who, he was sure, would snub him. Time, which he had spent gracefully in Italy, now weighed him down. In his brief, casual memoir of this stay in Paris, from 1821 to 1830, *Souvenirs d'égotisme*, he recalls:

> In Paris, in 1821, Sundays were really dreadful for me. Lost among the great chestnut trees of the Tuileries Gardens, so majestic at that season of the year, I thought of Metilda, who ordinarily spent the summer days at the country villa of the opulent Traversi, that sinister friend who . . . persuaded her that she would be completely dishonored if she took me for her lover.

He was nigh on forty—yet there he was still wondering what he was to do with his life. Incessantly he asked himself: was he a failure, a success? Happy or unfortunate? His life, in fact, was a prolonged youth, it has been remarked. Long after other men grew rigid in habits, established in their homes, firmly set upon the middle course of a middle-class existence, he was still adrift, without roots, without career, without a fixed circle of friends, without even a permanent address, only a hotel or a furnished room. "I am but a passenger on this boat," he would say repeatedly.

He lived only to realize the dreams he had conceived in youth, and yet perceived more than anyone else the lapsus between dream and reality. To realize, in the ripe years of manhood, the dreams of youth, is how a poet has defined happiness. These dreams in Stendhal, with all that they imply in disillusionment and frustrated ambition, were prolonged during his entire life without ever being realized. His private life is a long-continued youth, which he has described, or rather confessed, in his work with a devotion scarcely diminished by experience or age. Neither he nor his heroes could ever adjust themselves to a society that had once more become temperate and orderly, and where one advanced oneself only through the hierarchy, whose political intrigues themselves had grown tedious.[1] No, the bourgeois careers and fortunes were not for him! The days of revolutionary or military exaltation were gone—yet hope and imagination still pursued them.

He had dreaded the return to France. There were perhaps only two or three other periods of his life when his spirits sank so low as at the time of his involuntary departure from Italy, in 1821. Then, like the stoical fellow he was, he came to himself by degrees; Paris caught him up again; divers adventures and friendships distracted him; and renewed activity, literary, social, and amatory, that was in accord with his own canons of success in life, helped to repair some of the ravages done to his self-esteem.

Though at first he had heartily wished to be alone, by dint of much walking the streets he met his old friends one by one and was persuaded to visit and dine with them. His boyhood friend, Louis Crozet, whom he admired as a man of superior character, was no longer in Paris, separated from him by a wife who seemed jealous of their affection. But he saw the Baron Louis Adolphe de Mareste, who shared his love of Italian music, literature, and liberal ideas; Lingay, the cynical journalist who had so many amusing stories to tell of the cabinet ministers he subserved; Romain Colomb, that wise and temperate counselor; Poitevin, a gambler and Beau Brummell, who advised Stendhal upon fashions in dress; Di Fiore, a tall, handsome Neapolitan nobleman, who had once been condemned to death as a revolutionary conspirator by the King of Naples, but escaping to France, and changing his citizenship, served as an official in the French Foreign Ministry. Finally he saw again Count Beugnot, whose wife presided over one of the most entertaining salons in Paris. The Beugnots had treated him in former years as their protégé. Kindly they took him back to their hospitable hearth, which he noticed was now also graced by their charming daughter, the Countess Clémentine de Curial, whom he had known since she was a girl of fourteen.

Stendhal, with his fringe of black side whiskers, was an outlandish figure to the ladies of the Beugnot circle: ex-soldier, official of Napoleon's court, wanderer in Italy, author of anonymous books. These women who, save for Mme. de Curial, were middle-aged, retained some

[1] Blum. *Stendhal et le Beylisme*, pp. 19–20.

of the license and frivolity of the eighteenth century and evidently made efforts to divert him from the mysterious sorrow that haunted him. They spoke with worldly insouciance of their love affairs. One, for example, told of how she entertained two lovers, one in town and the other in the country, in the summertime. When her young nieces asked her to explain what love was, she said: "It is a vile and evil thing, of which chambermaids are sometimes accused, and when found guilty of it, are dismissed."

But Stendhal no longer enjoyed even such free talk, so dark was his mood; and he would retreat to the garden of Mme. Beugnot's château at Corbeil, to sit alone, turning over the pages of his book, *De l'amour*, which he was now preparing for the press.

Although he was animated as ever in conversation, he behaved with reserve. His intimate friend Mareste saw him twice a day for seven years; they discussed every subject under the sun with the utmost fervor and agreed about almost nothing—though Mareste, who gained some reputation as a wit, was known to have plagiarized the *bons mots* of his "Mephistopheles," Stendhal. Yet for all their intimacy, Stendhal told little of himself and was firmly convinced that even old friends like Mareste and the "bourgeois" Colomb could never possibly understand him. Each day he went through the same routine with them:

> Rising at ten, I repaired at half past ten to the Café de Rouen, where I met the Baron de Mareste and my cousin Colomb. The trouble was that these two persons understood absolutely nothing of the theory of the human heart, or of the portrayal of the heart in literature and music . . . which for long years had been the most interesting subject for me. . . .
>
> After having partaken, at the Café de Rouen, of its excellent coffee with two brioches, I accompanied Mareste to his office. We strolled through the Tuileries and down the quays, stopping at every stall that had engravings. On leaving Mareste, the dreadful part of the day began for me. In the heat of that year I would go and sit under the great chestnuts of the Tuileries. I would reflect: "Since I cannot forget her, would it not be better to kill myself?"

He would read a volume of Shakespeare, and often find himself interrupted by an apparition hideous to him:

> Again and again, the fat King Louis XVIII, with his eyes like those of an ox, his carriage slowly drawn by six stout horses, would pass by, a sight that particularly filled me with horror.

Then at five o'clock, still avoiding his lonely hotel room, he would hasten to the restaurant of the Hotel de Bruxelles, where Mareste, returning from his office at the Prefecture of Police, somber, weary, and bored, and one or two bachelor friends of Mareste, such as the jovial manufacturer, Lolot, would join him for a meal. Often they dined at the epicurean restaurant of the Frères Provençaux; then afterward again went to a café.

But though he passed his days for years and years with these friends, he hid his heart from them and spoke gaily or with a debonair indifference of all things. The friends he made were vastly amused and intrigued by him, and most loyal, yet the man of wounded sensibilities writes in his *Souvenirs d'égotisme:* "The worst of misfortunes, I cried to myself, would be that these men who were my friends, who were so cold, amongst whom I was going to live, might divine my passion, and for a woman whom I had not even possessed!" Whatever circle he appeared in, he felt himself alienated. Consequently he assumed every possible mask that might serve to conceal or protect him. He posed as dandy, roué, and fine talker: "I returned to Paris, which I found ugly, and insulting to my grief, with the one idea, not to be *divined.* . . . It was thus that I became a *wit,* something I would have scorned in 1818, in the days when I loved Metilda."

2

Stendhal's bachelor friends were fun-loving men whose vulgar habits and vices suited his desperate humor. This was so gloomy, he recalls, that in 1821 it gave him "a rather comic virtue; that of chastity." Sensing that he was unhappy, his friends strove to distract him; and one day, against his own wishes, he was induced to attend a "delightful dinner party with girls that Lolot arranged in his honor."

This rich manufacturer of pottery had talent and experience of such things; for part of his wealth had been invested in the establishment of a certain Madame P. in the Rue de Montmartre—which Stendhal himself in after years earnestly recommended to visitors arriving in Paris for its reasonable fees and services. It was here, in a private room at Madame P.'s, that Stendhal and his three middle-aged friends came one night for an ample dinner with many bottles of champagne. When they had finished and sat back at their ease, the duenna suddenly ushered in a remarkably young, pretty, auburn-haired girl, clad in the simplified costume of Lady Godiva, whom she presented to them as Mlle. Alexandrine. This was Lolot's great surprise for his friends. (The girl, Stendhal assures us, was the toast of the boulevards for a year, after which she began to look a little hard.)

Stendhal's spirit, like that of the other men, had been one of ribald merriment up to this point. But when he retired with Alexandrine, he found, to his own great surprise, that the beauty and modesty of this young hetaera touched him deeply, and that he had no heart for the adventure. What followed was a "complete *fiasco*," much like the famous episode of Rousseau's visit to a Venetian harlot described in his *Confessions*. But Stendhal relates that he was haunted by the thought of Metilda, and overwhelmed by a feeling of sadness. Soon after he returned to his friends his contretemps was known and commemorated with shouts of laughter that continued for long minutes. "Those gentlemen tried to make me believe that I was dying of shame, and that it was the unhappiest moment of my life. I was simply surprised and nothing more." It was thus that he acquired the reputation of a *babillan*, as the French term for an impotent male then was; this fine reputation, he relates, was mischievously spread by his three friends, and clung to him until some years later when quite different reports of his "deeds and gestures" circulated in Paris.

It was perhaps in honor of this misadventure with Mlle. Alexandrine that Stendhal, who was still occupied in 1821 with his treatise on love, added, in the way of an appendix, a now celebrated chapter on fiascos. His candid examination of this vexing problem, based as it was on firsthand observation, still seems a most useful analysis of false shame, the sense of inferiority and of the sexual inadequacy accompanying mental stress. He writes:

> If the soul is occupied in feeling false shame and in overcoming it, it cannot have pleasure. Pleasure is a luxury; to enjoy it, it is necessary that one's sense of security should not feel itself running any risks.

He also reports that he once catechized five handsome and apparently virile young men, of whom four admitted that at some point, especially in the first opportunity with the "most desired mistress," they had experienced some trouble of this sort. The fifth man, by his answers, seemed to Stendhal either wanting in sensibility or a blower. Citing Montaigne, who devoted a most charming and discerning essay to this same subject, Stendhal observes sagely that: "The idea that this misfortune is extremely common ought to reduce the danger of it."[2]

[2]Because of his own unflinching honesty on all such questions Stendhal has been subjected to some unwarranted suspicions on the part of literary scholars who, upon superficial evidence, have made reflections upon his potency. This old canard, also stimulated by the subject of his first novel, *Armance* (1827), has been revived recently in an essay by William Troy, in the *Partisan Review*, January 1942. The clinical study of the Austrian psychoanalyst, Edmond Bergler, is obviously much nearer the truth in characterizing Stendhal as a man both obsessed by sexual passion and ridden by his anxieties on this score, hence periodically depressed or "disturbed"—but no more than this. Care-

Still low in spirits, and seeking distraction, Stendhal, in August 1821, set off on a second voyage to England. What he hoped for was to place the English Channel and the acting of Kean in Shakespeare between himself and thoughts of Italy.

His first journey to London, in 1817, in the company of that intoxicated young English soldier and journalist, Edward Edwards, had provided him both with some striking impressions of England and some curious adventures which in the afterthought of his *Souvenirs d'égotisme* are confusingly merged with the impressions of his second journey, in 1821.

It was probably on the first occasion, in 1817, that he met Edwards at Calais and while waiting for the Dover packet spent two wild days guzzling ale with him in all the low taverns of the port. At the beginning of this nightmare interval Stendhal found himself eating and drinking in some pothouse with Edwards and several other men, including an English sea captain. In high spirits, Stendhal, with much fervor and emphasis, told some of his favorite stories, presumably of adventures with women, to which the English sea dog began to take exception, in surly fashion, as so much boasting. "I replied to him quite merrily and amiably," Stendhal says.

But on the next morning, when his head still ached with the effects of the heavy English ale, young Edwards in a serious vein proceeded to give him some lessons in British etiquette, which, he pointed out, had been gravely violated. The captain had been insulting, and Stendhal, far from laughing the matter off, should have called him to account, like a gentleman.

Always meticulous about his "Castilian" sense of honor, Stendhal felt mortified at his error, and, though suffering from a fearful hangover, set off with Edwards to find his man and challenge him. They searched all the bars of Calais, and meanwhile imbibed brandy instead of ale. Edwards, overcome with compassion for his French friend, now disputed with him over the right to deal with the offending stranger. Did Stendhal think he could use pistols or the *épée* in such a case? Impossible. "Each nation," he stated, "had its own manner of fighting. Admittedly our English way is baroque," but since his corpulent friend

---

ful study of the twenty volumes of his correspondence, diaries, and memoirs shows voluminous and precise evidence opposing Professor Troy's thesis; some testimonial letters from his mistresses are also to be found among the Stendhal Papers, at the Library of Grenoble, which permit no doubt on this score. Dr. Bergler, although fully recognizing the powerful, occasionally moody, attachments Stendhal felt for certain women, goes on to characterize him in extreme Freudian fashion as "unconsciously masochistic" and a "suppressed homosexual"—the last a rather gratuitous and too loosely used diagnosis that adds little to our understanding.

knew absolutely nothing of the manly art of pugilism, Edwards demanded the privilege of knocking the enemy down for him.

This new problem led to such high wrangling, continued from bar to bar, that they almost flew at each other's throats. Stendhal roared that he must deal with his man himself, with pistols or fists. Then they resumed the long chase. "Two or three times, I felt my hair rise," Stendhal recalls, "for I believed I had recognized the captain. Afterward, I realized that the affair would have been difficult for me without Edwards." But fortunately the captain had disappeared forever.

On first arriving at Brighton, in 1817, this England seemed nothing extraordinary after the Bay of Naples, yet Stendhal had felt overwhelmed by a wave of tender emotion at touching the soil of liberty for the first time. Here, he remarked, one could not be arrested merely for reading a book, and even a workingman (though often hungry) had the right to a fair trial. The manners of Londoners seemed rude after Paris, but though he shrewdly observed their shortcomings and national vices, their air of being free men living under a constitution and a free press was beautiful in itself to him.

Stopping at the Tavistock Hotel fronting on Covent Gardens (during both visits), Stendhal immediately plunged, as if with relief, into the immense gray anonymity of the London streets, and walked for hours on end, pushing as far as Chelsea, whose old rose-bowered cottages charmed him, and Richmond Park, from whose heights he viewed the expanse of London on one hand, the green fields and ancient trees of the suburbs on the other.

The spread of heretical and Whiggish ideas at this period, the heyday of Jeremy Bentham, appealed to him strongly after the years of living on the continent in Metternich's authoritarian darkness. Through Edwards, one of the Happy Few who had read and admired Stendhal's writings, he was able to meet the publisher Colborn and arrange to contribute articles regularly thereafter, from Paris, on letters, music, and art to Colborn's *New Monthly Magazine*. Later he also contributed to the *London Review*, the *Westminster Review* and the *Athenaeum*, an activity that not only kept him in closer contact with English literary movements than almost any other French writer, but also gave him a small living amounting to one hundred pounds or so a year.

But while he noted that the English had less vanity and more energy than the French, he remarked acidly that "democracy did not work effectively for two thirds of the English people." The full sweep of the revolution of steam power already made England more modern and grimier than France. Wages were low, and a slump in trade after the great war made thousands ragged and hungry. Driven by hunger, he said, the English worked too hard, had no leisure, and always hurried through the streets as if they were unhappy and worried. A born mimic, Stendhal imitated their manner and felt that this gained him consideration. The weather, moreover, was so damp and foggy that it made men "bilious"; Stendhal insisted he once saw a man in London, perhaps in a drunken rage, smash a shop window with his fist for no reason at all—something that could only happen in the English climate. On the other hand, he felt compensated by the vast steaks and the "thirty-pound sides of roast beef" that were set at his table, and with which "one drank hot tea, so that those raw viands were cooked in one's stomach!"

He did not call on Lord Brougham, the great Liberal orator whose acquaintance he had chanced to make in Milan, nor upon that much-traveled celebrity Lady Jersey, nor Sir John Cam Hobhouse, Byron's friend, also known to him in Italy. To one who asked him why he did not go to them, he remarked that he had known them too little, and had heard that "English travelers were subject to loss of memory after re-crossing the Channel."

Class feeling, he perceived, despite the democratic constitution in force, was if anything stronger than in Bourbon France; the whole society was "stratified like the rings of a bamboo cane," and each individual examined his fellow to see if he was trying to climb into the class just above his own. He remembered always the envious air with which a bank official, through whom he ordered a ticket one day to Almack's Ball, remarked to him: "I have been trying, sir, for twenty-two years to get into that ball which you will see in an hour from now!"

But seeing Kean in *Othello* at the old Covent Gardens Theater was worth the whole journey to him. Night after night he haunted the theater or the opera (to hear Mozart), usually in the company of his friends Lolot and Mareste, who, shortly after his second visit to London, joined him for a summer's vacation. However, when there was no play or opera to be seen, things were terribly dull for the three French tourists. The few middle-class English persons to whose homes Stendhal was invited seemed to him usurious and narrow-minded; their women were ugly and drank hard.

On arriving in London, Lolot had engaged a little valet to attend to their personal wants at the Hotel Tavistock; and Stendhal, who was always sensitive to the caste feeling of the English, even in the servant class, found the man a trial because he had a sour face and looked down his nose at the queer Frenchmen he served so submissively. One day, in a temper at this valet, Stendhal delivered a vigorous harangue upon the starvation of the British working class, the long hours they labored, and the grimness of their life even compared with the lot of ignorant Italian peasants. These, he held, toiled in leisurely fashion, knew how to be happy in their rags, drank good wine, made love, and had some religion, at least, that gave them the fear of God, etc., etc. Whereupon the little cockney showed signs of mental distress and protested that his national honor was insulted.

As if to mollify him, Stendhal then explained that he and his comrades were accustomed to enjoying pleasant company and were profoundly bored in London, especially when the theaters were closed. At once the valet, perhaps misunderstanding things, assured them that he would attend to their wants himself, and warned them to trust no one else, lest they be robbed. He left the room and soon afterwards returned to report that they were to go the following night to an address on Westminster Road, where they would be certain of cheerful entertainment.

Sensing that a gallant expedition of some sort was in prospect, Stendhal made some inquiries and was informed that Westminster Road was lost in the distant, poverty-stricken suburbs of London. "Do not go there," his informant warned him, "it is a snare." Surely some ruffianly pander would murder these ignorant Frenchmen. The enterprise gave promise of being either dreary or costly.

But the next evening the theater was closed again, and Stendhal said to Lolot: "We are strong men, we have arms." He and Lolot, who was a big man, set off in a cab, armed to the teeth, while the little Baron de Mareste, in terror, stayed at home. Soon they were riding in the outskirts; it was nightfall; there were no more houses, only an unpaved country lane. After what seemed hours their coachman stopped at a tiny cottage. Stendhal thought he had never seen anything so small and poor. He had expected to see some horrid old wenches welcome them, but instead three timid and very pale young working girls came out and politely invited the strangers in.

The drawing room had some worn old furniture that looked so diminutive, so much like that of a doll's house, that the big Lolot and the fat Stendhal feared to sit down. Everyone looked embarrassed. Finally, Lolot asked to see the garden, a tiny plot ornamented with a washtub, a brewing vat, and other domestic objects. Discouraged, Lolot whispered in French: "Let's pay them and clear out." But Stendhal felt the poor lasses would be humiliated. "Their poverty, all their little pieces of furniture, very old, but quite clean, had touched my heart," he says.

They sat down to tea, and in his poor English Stendhal began confiding to the young ladies their absurd fears of being robbed and murdered. After a while Lolot marched upstairs with one of the girls, while he retired with another, a chestnut-haired Miss Appleby, whom he already regarded "as a sweet, long-lost friend, refound after a long absence." She was startled when she saw the stout, black-whiskered Frenchman calmly discard a dagger and brace of pistols from his belt and lay them upon the dressing table; but soon recovered from her fright.

The next morning they felt so pleased with everything that they sent their valet, who had called, to fetch Mareste, and also some champagne and cold meats. The young ladies had never seen such fine things, and went into quiet transports of delight. Thereafter, shunning the sad strumpets who patrolled the Covent Gardens foyer, Stendhal and his friends spent every evening, when there was no other entertainment in London, in the tiny cottage on Westminster Road. He began to cheer up decidedly, and confesses: "It was the first real and intimate consolation for the misfortunes that poisoned all my moments of solitude."

But, in December, the time came at length for him to return to Paris —his friends Lolot and Mareste had gone back many weeks before. As he said good-by to his humble little mistress of Westminster Road, Stendhal was touched almost to tears by her pleas that he take her with him to France. She would work for him, eat only potatoes, and cost him little, she urged. For a moment he was sorely tempted to heed her. But all his life he had felt an aversion to fixed attachments. Even having his sister Pauline with him in Milan for a season had proved to be a trial, and he had soon parted company with her. It was in observance of the needs of his "egotism," which imposed solitude, as well as unshackled personal freedom, that he left behind him his poor English girl who, he admitted, might have brightened many a dark hour.

He never saw her again, though he sought her on later visits; and the pages in the *Souvenirs d'égotisme* that speak of her have the strange melancholy of De Quincey's story of his search for the poor street girl, Ann, whom he loved and lost in the teeming labyrinth of London. It was over ten years later, in 1832 (while living again in Italy), that he wrote down his recollections of this journey in fullest detail. This unrevised fragment of his memoirs is at once artless in its candor and extremely rich in that self-observation that accompanied his most commonplace adventures. To know himself and thus to know man was after all his principal business in life. It was his justification for living as a truthful and free *égotiste*—a word that Stendhal helped to fix, in his own sense, in the French language. "Egotism that is *sincere* is a way of painting the human heart, in the knowledge of which we have made giant strides since 1721," he remarks in his *Souvenirs.* "One may know all except himself. . . ." To be sure, his great experiments in "egotism" did not prevent him from using people whom he met with an exquisite and old-fashioned courtesy.

It is with a generous compassion that he recalls the lost Miss Appleby, fixing her as a symbol of the starving masses in London in one of the blackest periods of human exploitation. The French, he said, had at least buried their dead after Waterloo and in some wise sought happiness again. But the English who had conquered them were being conquered themselves by giant industry, which degraded their lower classes and already extended its squalid blight throughout their green land.

One day, just before his departure from London, he read that a mass hanging of eight criminals was to be performed in public early the next morning. Feeling it his duty to witness such an affair, he asked to be awakened in time by the hotel clerk, but then, out of tender-heartedness, canceled his order. The incident, however, gave him cause to write some lines of strong denunciation of England's ruling hierarchy of land and property owners:

> In my eyes when they hang a robber or murderer in England, it is the aristocracy that sacrifices a victim to its need for security, for it is the aristocracy that has forced these people to be criminals. This truth, so paradoxical today, will doubtless seem but a commonplace in the days to come when my babblings may perhaps be read.

3

In the early 1820s, no artist of the theater enjoyed a greater international fame than the Italian chanteuse, Mme. Giuditta Pasta. A native of Como, trained at the Scala Theater in Milan, this small, plump Lombard woman had reigned in Paris for some ten years, thanks to her authentic singing and acting of the new Italian operas, whose great popular vogue she fostered. Having met her in Milan, Stendhal at once went to call on her in Paris, and to his delight found her established in the midst of a whole colony of Milanese music lovers. He asked for news of his friends, and though he dared not mention Metilda, sometimes heard them speak her name. To come to Mme. Pasta's was for him the next thing to being in his beloved Milan. Though they played the same game of faro all night, he enjoyed sitting with them in a happy reverie, while winning or losing his thirty francs.

Soon he came every night, for his admiration of the dark-eyed La Pasta was intense. He considered her to have a greater talent for tragic acting than Talma himself, the favorite artist of Napoleon. And she, in turn, showed a fondness for the Italophile Frenchman who knew all the repertory of the *opéra bouffe* and spoke in Milanese dialect.

> Out of habit formed in youth . . . I would have liked her to fall in love with me, for I felt the highest admiration for her. I see now that she was too cool, too reasonable, and not caressing enough for our liaison, if it had come to the state of love, to have continued. It would have been but a *passade* on my part; she, rightly indignant, would have broken with me.

As usual he outlined, in imagination, the end of the romance before it began.

But though he did not win her love himself, he was able, by chance, to direct it, benevolently enough, to another man. One day in 1822, at the table d'hôte of his hotel, he met an interesting stranger who, like him, was an exile from Italy. He was a tall, elegantly dressed Belgian officer, named Micheroux, who had been for a brief time Minister of War to the King of Sicily. Now, as he told Stendhal, he was utterly ruined and considered shooting himself. To cheer up the unhappy stranger, Stendhal brought him one evening to his Milanese friends. Soon afterward, to his surprise, he found Micheroux a fixture in the jovial circle of La Pasta, indeed he quickly became her *cavaliere servente*. Presumably, Stendhal reflected, Micheroux's taste in music had won greater approval than his own. Noted for her charities, La Pasta had a husband, a mother, children, relatives, all living with her; but in the generous manner of the Italian theater folk, she now added the ruined Belgian to her large retinue, and installed him in a room above her apartment, on the third floor of the Hotel Lillois.

Stendhal, also longing to take shelter under all this Italian joviality and warmth, then moved from his own hotel to the Hotel Lillois and took a room next door to Micheroux's on the floor above the chanteuse. For years he held the status of a friend of the family, an equivocal but assiduous fourth member of this triple household, whose paterfamilias interested himself only in saving the money earned by his wife. Stendhal joined happily in their talk of music and Italy, or their games of faro; he paid his court in the debonair Milanese way to La Pasta. The official lover ended by being vexed at him, but Stendhal chose to be patient and hold his ground.

"Things cannot go on like this—it makes no sense!" Mme. Pasta must have thought often. Yet it went on. Night after night, for years, he frequented this music-loving circle, to which many French celebrities also came, until gossip spread about Beyle's peculiar relations with La Pasta. They were in truth harmless, and those of a "liaison of friendship"—as Stendhal has gone to great pains to testify—friendship grounded on his admiration for the simplicity, naturalness, and great art of Mme. Pasta. Poor and unhappy, often obliged to sign notes for his card debts, he felt himself truly at home in this salon, especially late at night, after quitting some respectable soirée whose hostess would never have come to the home of the actress.

At this period, he also came regularly, once a week, to the salon of the Countess de Tracy, whose learned husband he so fervently admired. On one occasion, happening to arrive there in a new and elegant suit, he overheard someone say: "Oh, Monsieur Beyle has a new suit; I suppose La Pasta has come into an inheritance."

That was a remark that wounded him to the heart, made by some gossip who had spied upon him. It was in order to clear La Pasta and himself before posterity that he later gave his account of her singular household in his *Souvenirs d'égotisme*.

In truth his outward constancy to La Pasta during five or six years served but to shield from the world the secret affair he carried on, from 1823 to 1826, with another and very different lady. After his return from England, when visiting his old patroness Mme. Beugnot, he frequently met her vivacious daughter Clémentine de Curial. More and more often, as he relates, "I enjoyed looking into the fine eyes of the Countess de Curial; but in my stupidity I went no further. I did not ask myself: why does this young woman look at me so?" Once, in 1823, he overheard her mother teasing her: "Your eyes fix themselves upon Beyle; if he had a taller figure he would have ventured to tell you long ago that he loves you."

Clémentine de Curial, then a comely woman of about thirty-five, had been married, rather unhappily, to an aristocrat, Count de Curial. She was grief-stricken by the death of one of her two daughters in 1823, when Stendhal first began to look at her with admiration. But in addition, her husband had had the cruelty not only to beat her when he was in a temper, but to prefer her servant maids to herself. In revenge she took a lover, of whom Stendhal knew nothing at the time.

Her husband, though he lived apart from her, continued his persecutions, sometimes threatening to kill her and her lover.

Meanwhile she had shown increasing attention to Stendhal; ruddy and rotund though he was, and bewhiskered, she appreciated his nimble wit and "comprehensive" soul. It was she who pursued him. When, in the autumn of 1823, he went off on another journey to Italy (avoiding Milan and its sad memories), he wrote Clémentine a letter from Rome, December 3, 1823, declaring that for her sake he "almost regretted the mists of Paris." His letter was full of charm, but its tone was still formal.

That Clémentine was shapely and attractive is reported by that connoisseur of woman flesh, Mérimée, who met Stendhal at this time. He describes "the charming Mme. de C.——" as being "in the prime of her beauty" when his older friend became wildly infatuated with her. However, Napoleon, according to legend, had other views. Seeing her one day at his court, he asked her for her name and, on learning it, observed maliciously: "I should have recognized you by your nose which is so much like your father's!" The prefect, Count Beugnot, had bequeathed his daughter a nose that was nothing if not prominent. Yet how little this mattered to the man who, according to young Mérimée, "was never seen save in the state of being in love or about to fall in love." Beauty, as he wrote in his treatise on love, was relative, the product of illusion, "the promise of happiness."

On returning to Paris in the spring of 1824, he besieged her stoutly. She invited him to the dinner parties she liked to give for numerous guests, and he, who could be so *spirituel*, pretended to be impassive or indifferent to the company, presumably because he was overcome by his passion for her. On one occasion he went out and walked alone in the garden of her mansion, counting the moments and the leaves of the trees. Then, when she came to him, he "attacked," that is, made his declaration. To his delight, his proposal was received with pride and joy. She had loved him for two years, she confessed. A letter of his, dated May 18, 1824, shows him prowling about Clémentine's home, pretending to be prudent, but writing her of the "extreme emotion in his heart" felt merely at approaching her house. And in his habitual romantic style he begins again with the business of secret signals:

> A little sign at the window of the boudoir where you stood this morning, for instance, the persienne half closed, or the jalousie lowered, would indicate to me that I could enter freely.
>
> If I do not see this sign that you are alone I shall not knock, but shall return a quarter of an hour later.

In a fragment among his papers the note has been found: *"May 22, 1824, cured."* He was cured of Metilda, but the passion for Clémentine, or "Menti," as he called her familiarly, was a fever violent enough for any taste.

4

They were no longer young, he over forty, she thirty-six, but flung themselves into each other's arms with all the more ardor. He was made happy at discovering again the gusty passion he craved and which alone made life worth living. Menti, for her part, found M. Beyle a strange and fascinating man, for she was intelligent and high-spirited too. In the voluminous letters she wrote him she protested that she was a good woman who never pursued any man but always fought against temptation as long as she could. She had taken her first lover in a spirit of vengeance against her husband, but later, disappointed in him, suffered from deep remorse. So with Stendhal: once she had yielded to him, she desired to surrender, to sacrifice, to submit herself to him in every sense. He had exacted the promise that she would be "sincere" with him, and she was. But once having "fallen," she suffered remorse once more; she repented and wept stormily; then, recovering her spirits, strove to show her lover still greater devotion.

And he would write to her: "I love you so much, I am so devoted to you, that I feel I must write, since I can tell no one else of my love." It was in the early phase that he wrote also:

> When I see you three days together, my angel, it seems that I love you more and more. . . . *Mon Dieu!* How happy I was yesterday! . . . If we passed a week together, I do believe we would end by never separating from each other.

She loved him exuberantly and wrote him 215 letters in two years, or one every three days. "Tell me, sir, how we can arrange to see each other before Monday, if only for ten minutes; because, if I were to leave for the country without hearing you say *I love you* it would be a sacrifice beyond my power." It was important for him that unlike other women she thoroughly enjoyed his "originality," as she termed it, his humor, his fantasy. After her husband and lover number one, she found a sensitiveness in Beyle that delighted and surprised her. Outwardly he might look the ruddy-faced butcher, but how fine and delicate were his hands, for example.

Clémentine's education had been interrupted during the Revolution by years of exile and her orthography was turbulent, her epistolary style sometimes too robust. On August 10, 1824, she wrote: "Your little note of Saturday made me tremble with pleasure just like that which I feel when your pretty hands go wandering over my old hide." Sometimes it seemed that he taxed her very health, which she thought failing, and she said she would like to pass entire months by his side merely listening to him, talking to him and "without according you anything at all. It is only then that I would consider myself truly loved."

He pleased her, she added in a note in July 1824,

> not because it was shown to me that you are the possessor of those robust merits which generally accompany broad shoulders, but because at certain moments you have a grace, a tenderness. . . . As to *tours de force* of a certain kind, I profit by them, but do not esteem them alone. . . . It seems to me, I must say, that I felt myself turning a little cold because you were too sublime in that regard; it was too vulgar a manner of proving your tenderness.

And to this he replied apologetically: "Could it be that my cursed originality gave you false ideas of my [want of?] tenderness?"[3]

In the summer of 1824, their passion was at its full noon, and Menti herself shrank at nothing. Despite their efforts to hoodwink family and acquaintances, the husband was made suspicious by the assiduity of Beyle, whom he found too often present in his house whenever he chose to come there. During the hot days of summer Clémentine would go to stay at her château at Mouy, near Andilly, on the Seine River. Following her minute instructions, Stendhal would pay her secret visits. He would assume a disguise, would take a carriage from Paris and, in darkness, ride full-speed to her château, where he would arrive after midnight. And Mme. de Curial proved herself as audacious as any heroine of a novel by Stendhal. Once when unexpected guests arrived—perhaps her husband—interrupting their assignation, she hurriedly led him down to the cellar, removed the ladder by which he descended, and shut the trap door. There in a dark, romantic cavern the enraptured Stendhal remained for three whole days imprisoned, nay entombed, while the madly devoted Clémentine prepared food for him, lowered

[3]The letters of Clémentine, in the Bibliothèque de Grenoble, dispose of the myth that Stendhal was inadequate, in the manner of Swift. When, after his death, his cousin and literary executive Colomb went over his papers, he never ceased to marvel at how the homely Beyle had gathered in so many "countesses" and women of rank, as he wrote to Crozet. (A. Cordier: *Comment a vécu Stendhal*, pp. 138–48.) Beyle preserved over two hundred of her letters; his executor destroyed almost all of them (as she had requested), but preserved those which had notes in the hand of his friend and literary idol, and summarized the contents of others that marked the course of their liaison.

and raised the ladder so that she might come to him secretly, and even, in order to attend to his wants, brought down and then emptied the "pierced chair." Alone in his prison, or cave, Stendhal lived only for the transports of love, like his imagined Julien Sorel and Fabricio. Menti was "sublime," he wrote afterward, when she came to the cellar at night.

By August 1824, danger threatened them. To his worldly friend the Baron de Mareste, Stendhal wrote: "I must consult you about a *husband*; I fear that I may have to fight one of the Knights of St. Louis." But there is no further mention of this danger, and it is presumed that the anxieties of the spouse were allayed.[4]

"There must have been great passion on both sides to make them take such great risks," the sober Colomb observed, as he edited the old letters of his friend. The Curials were both aristocrats and royalists; exposure of the affair at this period of extreme Catholic reaction, under Charles X, would have precipitated a great scandal, and a duel to the death. But if whipped-up passion always accompanied Stendhal's affairs of love, so the storms of morbid pride, jealousy, and wrath were never far behind.

After but a few months of intimacy these two vehement natures flared up in furious quarrels. They had pledged that they would be candid and sincere with each other at all costs. It was thus that she came to confide the story of the lover who had preceded him and whom, she assured Henri, she had not seen in six months. But the man lived near her still, in the country, and Stendhal was overcome by a quite Shakespearean access of jealousy, insisting that she had deceived him and still did. Appearing at her dinner parties, he would be somber and rude to her guests, his eyes probing them bitterly one by one to see whom she favored. Finally he began to break engagements with her, leaving her in torment at his behavior.

Tenderly though she loved him, she found him "bizarre," or evasive, and breathed the suspicion that after leaving her he frequented low company. There were always rumors in Paris also concerning Stendhal and Mme. Pasta, and Clémentine would exclaim: "Go, run to her arms —I hate La Pasta!"

"My dear friend," he wrote in reply to her reproaches and doubts, "do not have the slightest anxiety. . . . I love you passionately. . . . This love perhaps does not resemble that which you have seen in society or in books. I would like it to resemble only that which is ten-

[4]Cf. Stendhal, *Théâtre*, Vol. III, *La Gloire et la bosse* (Divan ed.), in which allusion to this episode is made in the fragment of a play.

derest." He had his faults, he admitted, but he was free and "Italian," he cared nothing for the opinion of his neighbors, and must remain so.

In the autumn of 1825, after little more than a year, there were renewed quarrels; she was losing faith in his profession of love for her, and found him escaping from her when she needed him—perhaps to street girls? On October 11, 1825, she says: "Physically I have no need of a lover, it is even dangerous for my health, but I feel the desire and the need of being loved." A month later she declares that she has suffered greatly at his hands and absorbed some rude lessons. Her Henri had brought "only trouble and misfortune," and she was determined to be finished with him. But soon they were together again, tormenting each other as before.

Clémentine complained that he used her with a "calculated cruelty," as subject of his experiments or "systems." Had he not written: "When one has to deal with a princess, or a very rich woman, one must beat her often or love will become extinct." And Clémentine was, if not a princess, a countess and passing rich.

The storms and stresses through which they passed in 1825 and 1826 were so trying that Stendhal often remarked later that he knew more sorrow from love than pleasure. Their drama is mirrored in a long letter of uncertain date, perhaps even as early as 1824, written at a time when he had left her in a rage, though he was to come to dinner that evening.

Almost unintelligible through grief, and her spelling and punctuation more turbulent than ever, she writes:

> You are frightful to me—you who have had a hundred mistresses—have you the right to treat me so? . . . You have used me so abominably that I am scarcely able to receive the company at dinner . . . at a time when forty persons are waiting for me at table you cannot wait but must turn the knife in the wound. Your love is the most fearful misfortune that may befall a woman. If she should enjoy happiness you would take it from her. If she had health you would destroy it. The more she loved you the more barbarous and cruel you would be. When she tells you that she adores you, then you begin your "system" with which you refine her sufferings more than she can bear.

Despite her wild spelling and grammar, Clémentine is nothing if not keen, for she shows that she understands her man. She knows that he "enjoys all the pain" he causes in her; and that "it would be mad to expect anything but pain" from him. She speaks of him also as "that fat man whom I liked to believe good," but sees now that he is bent upon making her suffer at all costs. Nevertheless she cries out in her pride: "Your ferocity shall not enjoy the evil you do me."

Then she confesses also that it is a consolation to write to him. And in the manner of one of Shakespeare's authentic heroines she exclaims: "And yet I love you still I love I love you—but oh do not believe me I no longer love you so much my reason tells me. I am sure I shall cure myself of this mad passion. . . . It must be a great pleasure to detest a man who has done one such great wrong."

Little wonder that Stendhal cherished this letter, penetrated with understanding of his own troubled personality and a testimonial of unfeigned and natural passion, that he later blotched with his tears. For he wrote at the head of it: *"Sunday. Tears and true tenderness, alas! I write this October 11, 1826, after my great misfortune."*

In the summer of that same year, she seemed to fear that her lover had presented her with a contagious disease. If this proved true she would never see him again—"adieu, wicked libertine"! At other moments in the autumn of 1826, she thought she was *enceinte* and promised that she would kill herself. To escape from torment, she prayed that she would have the strength to put herself to sleep "with the gas of sixpence worth of coal."

Perhaps her accusations wounded or enraged him. *"I was very near of pistolet,"* he noted in his peculiar jargon. On the other hand his suspicions fixed themselves upon a rival, General de Caulaincourt (it has been assumed), with whom a duel almost resulted. He therefore determined that he must fly from her, or be separated for a few weeks, and therefore made a third journey to London. One of his very secretive autobiographical notes runs:

> *The most sensitive misfortune of his life.* Left Boulogne June 27, 1826; storm at San Remo.[5]

Another of his brief *Notices sur M. Beyle,* dated April 30, 1837, relates:

> During this trip to England [in the summer of 1826] he was abandoned by this last mistress C——; for six months she loved [another?]. . . . He was terribly unhappy and left for Italy.

He tried to forget her, but fifteen years later he could still write in *Henri Brulard*:

> What chagrin she gave me when she left me! The surprising victory over Menti did not give me a pleasure equal to one hundredth part of the pain I felt when she left me for Monsieur de B.

[5]Stendhal, *Mélanges intimes,* II, p. 90. Mme. de Curial had gone with her husband for a short time to San Remo.

While some have held that it was Stendhal who left his Menti, and that he used the impulsive woman too cruelly, there is no doubt possible, after his repeated and bitter allusions, that she chose a successor to him. Besides, the discovery of additional letters of hers has shown this aristocratic adventuress of love—true to the period of Mary Godwin Shelley and George Sand and Lady Oxford—as proceeding from one lover to another, year after year, ever repentant, yet falling again. As she had zealously deceived her husband, so, after Stendhal ran away to England, did she resolve to desert him for another.

Alone in his hotel at Covent Gardens, he thought that he would die of this great trial of love which had been equaled only in the time of the dead Metilda. Metilda had "surpassed all the others in the Spanish nobility of her sentiments," but "Clémentine exceeded the others in spirit."

Was he not an eternal innocent, like the Vicar of Wakefield, he asked himself, perennially led astray by his impetuousness and always gulled? This was truly one of his heaviest "defeats."

His wounds healed, though very slowly. As he had sought Clémentine in compensation for the lost Metilda, so now he looked for another love of consolation. Yet long afterward, when he was almost in old age, at fifty-three, he would try most earnestly, though vainly, to win her back. After a decade of separation, he would still wonder if he was not still infatuated with her, and—though she was no longer young herself—he would feel as emotional about her, perhaps "as much in love with her as in the first days, in 1824."

Though no longer lovers after 1826, they became reconciled enough to remain good friends, and corresponded with each other freely, especially after Stendhal returned to Italy in 1830. Clémentine's profuse and breathless confidences, touching on all sorts of private and political scandal, even the intimate details of her love affairs, must have given him much cause for vexation. Yet he bore with her. Their friendship continued; and she often turned to him for his *doctes conseils,* in the complex game of her life. And he, with endless curiosity and goodwill, listened and gave counsel; for he was at heart a novelist.

CHAPTER XV

The Wit of Paris

> Beyle whose piquant vivacity perhaps no one can render . . . used to conceal his sadder feelings under the cover of his pleasantries, and he never seemed so merry as on days when some misfortune had befallen him.
>
> —Virginie Ancelot, *Les Salons de Paris.*

HUMOR, especially humor of the ironical sort, is the defensive weapon of men who have felt themselves ill-used by life. To shield their wounds, to hide the sense of inferiority which life, in some wise, has stamped upon them, such saddened men habitually seek to divert or distract their fellows by their follies, or to ward them off with their barbed laughter.

When he first returned to Paris, after his long sojourn in Italy, Stendhal was so determined not to be "divined" by his friends that he appeared to them but a gay dog who mocked at everything men held sacred. But several years later, in 1826, under the stress of accumulating misfortune, at the hands of Mme. de Curial, his grief was so great that he attained a state of mad gaiety. It was then, he confesses, that he acquired a reputation that he would have despised in former years: the reputation of a wit. His wit soon brought him a measure of social fame. Though his writings were still little read, Parisian hostesses competed with each other to win his regular attendance at their soirées; a half-dozen writers of memoirs, during the 1820s, recorded his anecdotes and epigrams.

He had frequented the salon of the philosopher and educationalist, Count Destutt de Tracy, since the early days of the Empire, when the count's liberalism brought down upon him the condemnation of Napoleon. The Countess de Tracy, moreover, a beautiful, white-haired woman of sixty, had in earlier days discerned a "spark" of something in M. Beyle. She encouraged him; he "loved her like a mother," and returned to her fireside toward 1822.

But instead of remaining shy as he had formerly been in the presence of the distinguished company that came to the Sundays of the Tracys —usually including General Lafayette and the statesman-author Benjamin Constant—Stendhal began to speak out on everything under the sun. He would contradict, shock, or rail at his hearers. This was all the more diverting, inasmuch as Tracy himself was in manner distinctly a man of the old regime, despite his leadership of the liberal opposition. Small, graceful, erect, and always elegantly dressed in black, the philosopher would stand by the fireplace of his parlor conversing with his guests in cool and measured speech. A green visor that Tracy always wore to shield his eyes accentuated the air of cold and virtuous liberalism that Stendhal came to associate with him.

"And what is your profession, pray?" a guest at Tracy's once asked Stendhal.

"Ah, I am simply an observer of the human heart," he replied. The man took fright, assumed that he might be a government spy, and abruptly retreated to a distant corner of the salon.

Stendhal found these people, whom he once esteemed so highly, ponderous in their thinking, overly prudent or well-bred in their liberalism, ignorant of the fact that "two and two made four," and too effete to act with boldness and energy. In their midst, he, with his huge head and ruddy face, his piercing eyes and shaggy black hair, stood forth like a wild Jacobin. Their solemnity exasperated him to utter phrases that irritated and scandalized them. One day Tracy and another man asked him what his political doctrines were and what he would do about the Royalists who had returned to France. Stendhal, for the benefit of these genteel liberals, declared that if he were in power he would "exile all the returned émigrés to three or four departments of the Pyrenees Mountains, and have them surrounded by a cordon of troops. . . . Those who tried to get out would be pitilessly shot."

Tracy and his friend were plainly frightened at the violence of his spirit, and grew more so as he went on to expound his ideas on the men of the *ancien régime* and the French Revolution. The aristocrats, he held, had only shown "the courage of sheep," going to the scaffold with graceful manners, but without the boldness to fight for their system, which had collapsed through their own weakness. On the other hand his admiration went out to the ruthless leaders of the French Revolution; they were plain men, but they were "heroic." Danton was "colossal"; he stole a little, but he and Carnot saved France from becoming another Poland, overrun and partitioned by its enemies. Carnot himself had erred later in being too humane. The men of the Convention, especially its extremists in the Committee of Public Safety, who wielded the guillotine so freely, were also heroes and men of energy in his eyes. "Only the lower orders of the people," he would exclaim, "are still capable of energy and passion"; only a poor man was ready to commit a crime or "throw himself out of a sixth-story window." The aristocrats and the rich "thought only of polishing the mahogany furniture in their parlors," which were as dried up as their own souls.

Such sentiments, at a time when most enlightened thinkers hoped that there would never again be another Terror, were calculated to horrify his listeners. "The face of M. de Tracy and his friends grew longer and longer," Stendhal relates in the *Souvenirs d'égotisme*, as he went on with his "doctrines," and it was plain to see that they thought him a most unfeeling or immoral man.

"I was either a monster of immorality or a god to my acquaintances," he remarks.

But one day a handsome young woman, overhearing his audacious harangues at the Tracys', showed intense admiration and declared that she thought he was a real "Huron," one of those wild Indians (in Voltaire's novel of that name) who were lost in an overcivilized society. "Then she added: 'I want to say something to you in private.' Passing into a corridor where we were alone she suddenly gave me a kiss full on the mouth, which I returned with ardor. The next day, as it happened, I left Paris on a journey and the affair went no further."

Gradually, over the years, the Tracys grew cool toward him—though this did not stop him from visiting them each week for nearly a decade. However, in retrospect, his estimation of Destutt de Tracy was diminished, if just; he is represented, in Stendhal's reminiscences of the 1820s, as falling considerably short of the stature his enlightened doctrines promised. An even more malicious portrait is given, in the *Souvenirs d'égotisme*, of General Lafayette, the lion of the Tracy salon and "hero of two worlds," who was now in his late sixties:

> He was a tall figure of a man, and his large frame was surmounted with an impassive, cold, insignificant face, much like that in an old family portrait, while his head was always covered with a wig of short, unkempt hair. This man, always dressed in an ill-fitting gray suit, and leaning upon a cane, would enter the salon of Mme. de Tracy, who always addressed him as "*mon cher Monsieur*" in a swooning voice. . . .

Washington's gallant comrade in arms certainly throned it here among the "stupid and fawning" politicians of the anti-Royalist party, buzzing with their plots for an uprising. He was polite and easy with his followers, "but polite like a king, mind you." Idolized champion and symbol of democracy that he was, he remained, nevertheless, a simple and unaffected man, unspoilt by public use. "To be successful today as a political leader, a certain immodesty and downright charlatanism is necessary," Stendhal remarks; yet Lafayette was above that, and so merited forgiveness for the intellectual weaknesses he so plainly revealed. Stendhal enjoyed watching this Great Figure of History. Often, while his associates filled his ears with political twaddle, the shadow of polite boredom lay on his empty face—until some charming young thing of eighteen with bare shoulders and bosom came tripping into the salon, when his blue eyes would light up and he would suddenly rise from his chair to wander after the lovely shoulders, leaving his aides gaping in the middle of a sentence. "In spite of his years, and without caring what anyone thought, M. de Lafayette at the tender age of seventy-five (really sixty-nine) had the same faults as I had," Stendhal notes contentedly. "He was chiefly interested in pinching the behind of some pretty girl . . . which helped him pass his old age cheerily, to the great horror of all the middle-aged women present."

The Tracys, in the early days of their friendship with Stendhal, introduced him to Mme. Cabanis, the widow of the great physiologist he had long admired. In her salon he met the naturalist Georges Cuvier, who also became his friend. One day he heard Cuvier discussing the unscientific fear and disgust that is inspired by vile and ugly insects, and how one might conquer this unreasonable feeling by concentrating upon their ways of gathering food, or reproducing themselves, and classifying them according to their differences and resemblances. Thereupon Stendhal had a great idea: "Why not do the same thing with human beings, in order to overcome one's loathing of them?" Thus he could be patient even when his passport and baggage were being examined by some idiot of a customs official, absorbing himself in studying the abject creature, in order to learn what species of the crab family he belonged to. Stendhal used to repeat this maxim in company, with meaningful glances toward those persons whom he considered chuckle-headed or otherwise odious.

Mme. Cabanis' little parlor was always overheated by a "hellish" fire, and Stendhal, suffocating, was soon driven forth, never to return. But he had met there also the learned Claude Charles Fauriel, esoteric philologist and historian, who had once served as a secretary to Napoleon's police chief, Fouché. Fauriel, too, was "no charlatan," for he told Stendhal some authentic tales of the art of love among the Arabs, which were put to use in the appendix of *De l'amour*. Through Fauriel he was introduced into the home of the Mlles. Clarke, two spinsters who received many literary celebrities, such as Victor Hugo, Sainte-Beuve, and Augustin Thierry, the romantic historian. But one day at the Clarke home he ventilated his theory that when a man fell in love with a superior woman, richer or more aristocratic than himself, "he should beat her up now and then" in order to keep her interested. At this the young historian, Thierry, berated him as a vulgar fellow; Stendhal answered by calling him a "Jesuit," and left the place, never to return.

He also knew the Count Appollinaire d'Argout, an old colleague among the officials attached to Napoleon's Grand Council, who turned his coat and became a peer and minister under the monarchy. Stendhal's close friend the Baron de Mareste was related by marriage to the Argouts, who might have done much to further Stendhal's career. But in this ultraconservative household his chief sport was to exhibit his irreligion shamelessly. In ribald fashion he mocked at the Archbishop of Paris, who was the confessor of the Countess d'Argout. He had a goodly store of godless sayings, such as:

All religions are founded on the fear of the many and the cleverness of the few.

Ah, I know the Jesuit well. He says: "Do all that you like in youth, enjoy yourself, provided that you confess all your little sins to us. And when you grow up and have some power in the state, let us direct it for you."

Irreligion is a bad thing for young girls because it might prevent them from finding a husband. One must agree that if God exists it must seem pleasant to him to be honored for such reasons.

Our somber and lugubrious churches were invented by swindling priests who wanted to enrich themselves by frightening timid people.

The only excuse for God is that he doesn't exist. . . . If I ever met him I would be quite surprised, and I would have some fine things to say to him if he let me get a word in. [Skeptic that he was, he suspected God was as garrulous as himself.]

What sort of a God is he who invented the scurvy and plague, who sets up all sorts of snares for me, hurling me into this world so that I might catch the pox and all that?

On the other hand, like Voltaire, he thought it might be safer if the servants and the laundresses were believers. He said: "I feel very religious when it seems to me that some of my shirts are missing!"

Sometimes to amuse his friends (at Mme. Pasta's) he would tell his own version of the Creation, with his eyes rolling, and most expressive mien:

> God was a busy mechanic, and very clever; he worked night and day at his trade, said little, and invented all sorts of things, now a sun, here and there a comet. They said to him: "But you should write down the formula for your inventions so that they won't be lost." "No," he answered, "nothing has reached the point of perfection that I am seeking." One fine day he suddenly lay down and died. They ran out and looked up his only son who was studying with the Jesuits. He was a gentle and studious lad who did not know two words about engineering. They took him to the workshop of his father and said: "Well, get to work, you have to run the world!" He was highly perplexed: "What did my father do?" he asked. "Oh, he turned this wheel and that, he made things go this way or that way. . . ." The son took the wheel and the machine began to go—in reverse!

He needed only to exhibit a little of his regular stock of impieties at the salon of the Countess d'Argout, and one of the shocked ladies present would cry out: "Madame, tell Monsieur Beyle to be still!"

Thus he lost ground in high places, and narrowed the chances of his return one day to some sinecure in the public service. But he spared himself the madness of ennui, and his sayings echoed about for a time. Looking back on these days, after long absence from Paris, he once wrote to a friend: "I do not regret my lost opportunities." What if he had had ten thousand francs more a year, or were honored as an *Officier* instead of a mere *Chevalier de la Légion d'Honneur?* "For the sake of such ambitions I would have had to do degrading things. . . . I would have had to think up three or four platitudes each day to please the right people!"

2

Up to the age of forty, Henri Beyle, the veteran of Napoleon's campaigns, the traveler and man about town, was quite unknown as a man of letters. He was almost twice the age of the eager young men, such as Victor Hugo, Alfred de Vigny, and Sainte-Beuve, who were to represent the new postwar generation in literature, and quite removed from them in his ideas, when he returned to the Paris scene from Italy in 1821, with his little book, *De l'amour*.

He himself had feared that this book, which he then and always considered his masterpiece, would interest no more than "a hundred readers . . . those who have feeling and are without moral cant, whom I desire to please." In fact, only three hundred copies were printed (of which half had the chapter on "Fiascos" emended, so that he might present them to ladies he knew without giving them cause for alarm). His preface to an alleged "second edition" struck a pessimistic note, while apologizing for the formlessness of the book:

> The author, returning to Paris after a long voyage, believed it impossible to obtain a success without degrading himself before the journalists. Now when it comes to low conduct, one should reserve that for the prime minister. What is called a success being out of question, the author has published his thoughts exactly as they came to him.

But his worst fears proved optimistic when, years later, inquiring at his bookseller, he was informed that only seventeen copies in all had been sold. "One might say that this book is sacred, for no one will touch it," the man added.

It was a soundless literary fiasco.

What hurt him most was the fact that his friends, with only one or two exceptions, heartily disliked the book. Mérimée called it "horribly obscure" and "ill-written"; its mechanistic terms, applied to a subject like love, seemed offensive, and dated the author as an amateur who clung to the "old-fashioned ideas" of the Encyclopedists. No reviews appeared save one or two brief notices stealthily written by Stendhal himself in the obscure English literary journal issued in Paris by the bookseller, Galignani, and they helped little.

"Well, there is nothing to be done about it, the French are too vain to read me," he wrote to one of his women friends. He also jested about the whole edition having been used as ballast for a schooner voyaging to America. However, his *amour-propre* as an author was deeply injured. It is at this period that he begins to entertain the strange idea, which becomes an obsession, that his writings will only be enjoyed "in fifty or a hundred years." What served to harden his conviction was the undeniable fact that the booksellers clung to unsold copies of his books and, as with the passing years they grew scarce, exacted an ever higher price for them. His observations were not welcome to the critics of the great press or to the schoolmen of his time, but during the 1820s his book *Rome, Naples and Florence* commanded the respectable price of forty francs (eight dollars) in the bookshops. In *Henri Brulard* he describes, quite in the style of his own anecdotal conversation, how outlandish his writings appeared to a contemporary public figure who had also won literary distinction of a sort, his own relative Pierre Daru:

> It was a matter of surprise to Count Daru that I was at all capable of writing a page that might give pleasure to anyone. One day at the bookshop of Delaunay (who told me about it) he purchased a little book of mine, which, because it was out of print, sold at forty francs . . .
>
> "What! Forty francs?"
>
> "Yes, my lord, and it would not matter to me at all if you decided not to take it at this price."
>
> "Is it possible?" exclaimed the Academician, raising his eyes to the heavens. "This child, as ignorant as a carp!"
>
> He was quite sincere. The men of the antipodes, regarding the moon when it is only a crescent-shaped quarter to us, say: "What brightness! The moon is at its full!" So the Count Daru, member of the French Academy, associate of the Academy of Sciences, etc., etc., and I regard the heart of man and nature from entirely opposite points of view.

But by 1823 Stendhal emerged a little from the obscurity that covered him. At this time the controversy over classicism and romanticism was at last beginning to absorb literary France. In a Paris theater recently the unruly spectators had actually fought with the police over an English troupe's production of a play by Shakespeare—though hatred of the English conquerors and of the Holy Alliance had more likely inspired the riot. In the salons he frequented, Stendhal came vigorously to the defense of both the English and his "god," Shakespeare, who was still officially considered a barbarian on the French side of the Channel. And in March 1823, he published his pamphlet *Racine and Shakespeare.* Though not a solemn or a scholarly or even an original work, the publication of this manifesto was to assume historical importance as marking the official beginning of a Romantic School in French literature—so long foreshadowed, yet never formally launched.

The great value of his brief pamphlet, aside from its lively and ironical argument, resided in the fact that he focused the whole discussion upon its true issues, as Mme. de Staël had not succeeded in doing in her earlier book on German romanticism. He named the two opposing idols of literature and asked in effect: "Shall we follow Racine or Shakespeare . . . in attempting to write interesting tragedies for 1823?" Racine, he declared, had written pompous tirades in rhymed hexameters "for the enjoyment of the snobbish court of Louis XIV." Must French dramatic authors continue to imitate his tone and ideas a century and a half later? The French Revolution, the Republic, and the wars of the Empire, more stirring than those sung by Homer, had shaken the very foundations of society. The new age awaited its new dramatists. "Never has a people experienced more rapid and sweeping changes than those of 1780 to 1823, and yet they want to give us the same literature . . . the characters and forms that were enjoyed in 1670."

Canons of taste and form were not immutable but eternally changing, in accordance with historical and social conditions, he urged, as he had written almost ten years earlier in his book on Haydn. Like the young Italian poets whom he had seen launching their own romantic movement in 1816 in Milan, he desired that literature should cease to imitate classical models and be "modern" and "free." (His Italian friends, such as Pellico, now languishing in a dungeon, had wished also that romantic literature might incorporate within itself a movement of political liberation, and this thought underlay Stendhal's pamphlet too.) But how could one paint the soul of man, and his great passions, if one followed the pseudoclassical rules of that Johnson-like pundit of France, Laharpe, or wrote with the "*extreme dignity*" that was fashionable in Racine's day?

Whereas Racine conceived of his dramas as *poems*, Shakespeare had made the drama rich in action. Shakespeare was "closer to nature," and while violating all the rules of literary pedants, created characters of flesh and blood. Like him the playwrights of the nineteenth century must consign the classical Greek unities of action, time, and scene to the rubbish heap.

Stendhal included some extravagant or deliberately provocative statements in his pamphlet; he called Racine France's greatest literary idol, a "craven courtier" who wrote mere declamations, in which a father, even when beside himself with emotion, never failed to address his son as *Monsieur*. Unjustly he ridiculed the use of rhymed verse in drama as a device for concealing the foolishness of the author (*une cache-sottise*), or for aiding the memory of actors and public. Later in the nineteenth century, despite the rigidity of tradition in the theater, the French were to turn to the Beyliste prescriptions for a realistic drama in prose—something almost unthinkable in 1823.

Racine and Shakespeare bristled with what now appears, after generations of tedious literary debate, brilliant common sense, but at that early date in France seemed paradoxical, and even subversive. Assailing the French Academy (when it was not yet a traditional sport to do so) he wrote:

> The French Academy has taken the resolution never to admit into its midst any man of letters who is soiled with the heresy of *romanticism*. This explosion of temper has been most useful to the romanticists. A dominant trait of the French people is mistrust; it needs only that a doctrine be protected by the government or by persons in authority and it becomes suspect before the public.

He also gave a searching, coolly logical definition of romanticism that the new literary school was to treat as a piquant jest, but which still appears tremendously relevant:

> Romanticism is the art of presenting to the people literary works which, in view of the existing state of customs and beliefs, afford them the utmost possible pleasure.
>
> Classicism, on the contrary, presents the literature that used to give the utmost possible pleasure to our great-grandfathers.

Sophocles and Euripides, he said, were romantic in their own time; but today they were classical. "To imitate Sophocles and Euripides today, and to pretend that these imitations will not cause the French people to yawn, is to be classicist." For that matter, even Racine and Corneille were "romantic" for their time. Stendhal, in other words, demands that we be *modern* at all costs and not imitators of antique models.

It was, of course, not the first time that such counsel had been given. The English had been debating these questions since the 1760s, when Samuel Johnson championed Shakespearean drama. The German critics, Lessing and Schlegel, had assailed French classicism and called for scenes of bourgeois life. Nor must Diderot be forgotten.

Yet so tradition-bound was French literary taste that Stendhal's pamphlet, in its first version of 1823, had the effect of a brusque challenge. The future heroes of romanticism, such as young Hugo, were still writing verses in honor of the birth of a crown prince, pleasing to the Academy, the throne, and the altar. But the "Baron" de Stendhal threw a stone into the quiet pool of literary discussion, which thereafter rippled into angry wavelets of controversy.

It was difficult to know whether the "Baron" was to be treated seriously, or as a man who tried to amuse himself by breaking icons in public. As Taine wrote long afterward: "His talents and his ideas were premature, his admirable divinations were not understood, any more than his profound sayings so casually thrown off, or the astonishing justness of his perception and his logic." What fooled most people,

Taine points out, was that while speaking his mind so shrewdly, he preserved the exterior of a conversationalist and man of the world.

Yet the younger men began to pay heed to him. One of the new and important journals launched in 1824 began to support the literary romanticists from the start, and called attention to the wisdom of Stendhal's pamphlet, remarking also that the writer, "though gifted with enough originality and critical perception to win fortune for three or four authors," persisted in appearing under divers mystifying pseudonyms and avoided literary glory.

Now his ideas echoed a bit in Paris. What was more, the pontifical Auger, member of the French Academy, who had formerly served as a government censor, thought the situation serious enough to warrant a formal, ex-cathedra denunciation of the new romantic "sect." On April 24, 1824, he gave an address in which he attacked Shakespeare, Goethe, and Lope de Vega, and declared that romanticism was a "foreign" and chaotic cult that had no rules and no ideals.

This was, in effect, a police measure. As if in answer to Auger, romanticism began to show its political colors with the founding of *Le Globe*, by Dubois, in September 1824, as a literary newspaper dedicated to liberty in society as well as the arts. Censorship and political repression had redoubled in severity after Charles X, the soul of the Catholic reaction in France, succeeded his brother to the throne. Manuel, the liberal deputy whom Stendhal had met at Tracy's, was expelled from the Chamber for speaking in praise of the French Revolution—an event that stirred all France. It was then, early in 1825, that Stendhal returned to the attack upon the French Academy and the classicists, who stood so close to the throne. Adding ten letters on romanticism and classicism to the earlier pamphlet, he published them together as a second, augmented edition of *Racine and Shakespeare*. The new material was more polemic than ever, but what all of Paris's literary salons laughed over and remembered was the opening sentence, addressed to L. S. Auger, his opponent, who was one of the Forty Immortals.

"Neither you nor I are known to the public, M. Auger . . ." Stendhal began. But though few persons read the works of the "superannuated" Academicians—as few as read his own writings—the issue was important enough to be explored further.[1]

---

[1]The second, 1825, version of *Racine and Shakespeare* contains some amusing dialogue between an imaginary classicist and a romanticist under the heading: "What is Romanticism?" But also, following his old habit of "taking his property where he pleased," he included a free translation or paraphrasis of some five pages of Samuel Johnson's Preface to his edition of Shakespeare's plays

The battle for romanticism now was on in earnest. Stendhal's youthful friend and disciple, Prosper Mérimée, published his first romantic plays, *Le Théâtre de Clara Gazul*, in 1825. Victor Hugo, whom Stendhal had called the poet laureate of the political retrogrades, in the following year swung over to assume leadership of the Romantic School by virtue of his preface to *Cromwell*. In 1827, Cavé and Dittmer produced the nightmarish *Soirées de Neuilly* and dedicated it to the "Baron" de Stendhal. Then followed Dumas' melodramatic *Henri III* in 1829, and Hugo's epoch-making *Hernani* in 1830—and the battle was won.

It was not the romanticism Stendhal had wanted that triumphed. The rhetorical extravagance and bombast, the "Gothick" settings, the exaggerated melancholy and sentimentalism of the Hugo School in the end wearied and vexed him. He was present at the turbulent première of *Hernani*, but his heart was elsewhere, and he applauded only with his finger tips. "He had dreamed of the drama as a mirror of the life of the past and the present . . . full of strong emotion, but true, precise, and penetrating . . . in which the movements of the human heart could be exposed under circumstances chosen for that purpose." He wanted men who were observant and analytical, not poets, given to new kinds of tirades and indifferent to the truth or to his theories of human psychology.[2]

Although Victor Hugo "liberated" French verse, Stendhal still condemned its use in drama and, as Hugo justly remarked, "blamed the tools rather than the workmen who used them." Hugo saw Stendhal as "an enemy of poetry." There was a schism between Stendhal and the Hugo School. When the two men were once brought together in a parlor by a mutual friend, that of the Misses Clarke, as Sainte-Beuve relates,

> they were like two alley cats from opposite sides of the gutter, on guard, their fur standing up, and approaching each other with infinite precautions; Hugo,

(London, 1765). In this passage the question whether the playgoer can follow with any credulity the shifts of scene, as from one continent to another, or the break of years in time between acts, is logically worked out by Stendhal, in close imitation of the reasoning of Johnson. Johnson, it will be remembered, wrote that the playgoer, like the reader of a book, whatever illusion he may feel, does not believe he is seeing the real action, and so is not disturbed by change of time and scene. Miss Doris Gunnell, in *Stendhal et l'Angleterre*, pp. 340–51, gives the parallel passages, revealing the plagiarism of Stendhal, done in French with his usual verve. The more the pity, as *Racine and Shakespeare*, by its original passages, could have aroused sufficient interest without resort to plagiarism. Since Miss Gunnell's researches in 1908 no other cribbings have been detected in this work. This was the last instance of any serious plundering by Stendhal, who, after 1825, devoted himself principally to fiction.

[2] P. Martino: Preface to *Racine et Shakespeare* (Champion ed.), Vol. I, p. cxxviii.

frank and broad in spirit, realizing that he had to do with an enemy of verse, of the ideal and of the lyric; Beyle, sharper in tone, irritated, and less generous in spirit.

He continued upon his solitary way. *Le Globe*, the organ of the literary and political romanticists, said of him in 1825 that he was like an advance skirmisher in letters, "always eager for battle, pursuing, harassing the enemy wherever he appeared . . . in every engagement [he] brought victory for the cause he defended." But soon his contribution to the romantic campaign was overlooked. At heart he believed himself "the initiator of the new theater," but ended by detesting the historical dramatists he had helped to introduce in France. Reflecting his own feelings, his friend Mme. Jules Gaulthier wrote him in 1832:

> It was you who created romanticism, but you created it pure, natural, charming, amusing . . . and they made of it a howling monster. Create something else.

3

Stendhal's influence in the republic of letters during the 1820s was pre-eminently personal and worked by word of mouth through a small circle of friends. As Sainte-Beuve was to say long afterward: "He was a critic, not for the public, but for writers and artists themselves." Toward 1825, at the time when "all Paris" was repeating his gibe at the Academy's spokesman, Auger, a little band of his followers used to meet with him regularly in the afternoon at a café terrace near the Palais Royal, and after taking refreshments there they would go on to some restaurant of note, such as Tortoni's, for supper. They talked long and well, it is said, and never got drunk.

Most faithful of his disciples in those days was the short, thickset, pock-marked Baron de Mareste, a man of society and a wit in his own right. Soon there was a third figure always accompanying these two:

> A poor young man in a gray frock coat, who had a snub nose and was quite ugly. There was something brazen and most unprepossessing about him, young though he was; one felt this in his small, cold, impassive eyes and his malicious manner.

Such was Stendhal's first impression of Prosper Mérimée (then twenty or twenty-one), the young friend whom he would enjoy and admire above all others. For the craftsmanlike Mérimée, more than any other writer, met the test of Stendhal's critical standards that demanded a realism and stylistic restraint not yet in popular favor. It was thanks to Stendhal's strong influence over him in early youth that Mérimée was to separate himself from the official Romantic School. But in a passage written after knowing him for ten years, Stendhal keenly observed (in the *Souvenirs d'égotisme*) how much this clever and polished youth surpassed him in sheer egotism, reinforced by a quality of coldness of which others, notably Mme. George Sand, also complained. He wrote:

> I am not so sure of his heart as I am of his talents. . . . His mother is very clever in the typical French manner, and has a most reasonable spirit. *Like her son she seems to me capable of feeling a tender emotion once a year.*

Stendhal, Mareste, and Mérimée, wary though they were of each other, were such close cronies that soon they became known in Paris as "a diabolical trinity." In those days, according to Mérimée, Stendhal took a certain pleasure in showing himself rather worse than he was, a sort of "monster of immorality," while the impudent young Mérimée, a good foil for his wit, seldom failed to spur him on. This group was often joined at dinner by a Dr. Koreff, a mysterious Russian of international social celebrity, who was believed to have acted sometimes as a spy; also by the younger Ampère; by Eugène Delacroix, who was to become the greatest painter of his age; and, toward 1829, by the angelic-looking boy poet Alfred de Musset. Still another familiar in this circle was Victor Jacquemont, a handsome young giant, who was already famous as a naturalist and an explorer, whom Stendhal loved not only for his many talents, but as a paragon of energy and courage.[3]

The gatherings of Stendhal and his young "apostles" were occasions for rousing argument upon all subjects. The older man, as Mérimée has related, would expound his "systems," contradicting everyone and everything, yet with a forthrightness and sincerity that won over those who thought he aimed merely at paradox. He would insist that his young friends read Montesquieu and the later eighteenth-century materialists. He urged Mérimée to beware of "overemphasis" in his writing, and to seek to be objective at all costs. "I desire to be remembered for my ideas, not for the language in which I clothed them," he would say. "To be a good philosopher one must be dry, clear, with-

---

[3]Victor Jacquemont was fated to die young, while exploring the Himalayas in 1832, leaving chiefly his admirable travel letters.

out illusions. A banker who has won fortune has something of the requisite qualities . . . the faculty of *seeing clearly things as they are.*"

One trait that endeared him to the young men whom he favored especially with his friendship was his frankness and lack of vanity about his own writing. He would send them his manuscripts and ask for their severest criticisms, then discuss them in lively fashion, but without any resentment whatsoever, as if their strictures had to do with some other writer's work. For in the long run, did it matter if they disagreed with him?

"Praise is a certificate of resemblance," he remarked. Another of his sayings was that "anyone who follows the trade of 'putting black on white' must neither be surprised or hurt if he is sometimes called a fool."

That young firebrand among painters, Delacroix, who was also about half Stendhal's age, spoke of him in his journal as a man who often indulged in wild talk. Yet he listened sympathetically not only to the older man's advice on women, but to Stendhal's reflections on painting, and always remembered his counsel: "Do not be afraid to work on the grand scale."

Though he was a man of violent emotions, as Mérimée pictures him, Stendhal always pretended to be guided solely by reason and the rule of logic. Mérimée could never forget the special emphasis with which he would hammer out the word (in French) in its three syllables: LO-GI-QUE! When Mérimée on one such occasion quickly reminded him that he had just told of how a woman who had loved him passionately in former years had lately refused to see him again and asked what reason or "logic" there was in her behavior, Stendhal replied: "But her conduct was, after all, quite reasonable. She formerly liked whist, now she does not like it. Unfortunately for me, I still love to play whist."

He had maxims for every occasion. One was: "Never repent of any folly you have committed." To provoke or amuse his companions he had pejorative nicknames for the accepted masters of literature and learning. Chateaubriand, the mystical defender of Christianity, he called "the Grand Lama." Of Bossuet and his noble sermons he said: "His writing is humbug that takes itself seriously." Since he disapproved of the German transcendentalist school of philosophy, he would rail at their French spokesman, Professor Victor Cousin: "Except for Bossuet, Cousin is the cleverest dealer in serious humbug." Lamartine he characterized as "Lord Byron done up in French paint"; and Joseph de Maistre, the eloquent Catholic pamphleteer, as "a scoundrel who writes well." And when someone once praised Goethe's *Faust*, he argued: "Why enlist the aid of the Devil in the little business of seducing a village seamstress?—which we all did when we were twenty."

In literary debates, he would assail Racine, declaring that he was wanting in *local color* and "details." But Shakespeare also had this defect, he was reminded.

"Ah," he would exclaim, "but Shakespeare knew the human heart far better. There is not a passion, not a feeling that was not painted by him with admirable truth and in all its fine shadings. The lifelikeness and individuality of all his characters places him above all other playwrights."

Mérimée and other chroniclers agree that Stendhal did not seek to shine in large gatherings, but rather more modestly, in smaller, more congenial groups of eight or ten persons, usually after midnight, when most of the company had departed. "Then was the hour of triumph for him," as Sainte-Beuve also relates, "at table with his friends. What tempests, what outbursts of laughter, or anger, or verbal wrestling bouts, inspired by his conviction that 'nothing is so pleasurable as to speak out some hearty insults among friends.' "

Colomb declares that despite the great changes in French salon life he brought back "something of the atmosphere it formerly enjoyed. . . . He succeeded in making conversation general, a difficult art almost entirely forgotten whenever three persons come together nowadays."

Nor was he ever brutal in his mockery, but when opposed by some dolt or pedant, he would amuse all who knew him by putting on his silkiest manner and most honeyed tones, leading the man on until—at some offending platitude—he would turn upon his fool, and catch him in his own trap. The flavor of his talk, Mérimée said, was something impossible to recapture, though his letters have much of it. One observer of the time said that "Stendhal never knew what it was to prepare his thoughts; while talking he invented everything . . . and constantly turned up with unexpected ideas that could not possibly be the result of study."[4] But sometimes, after he had talked himself out, and feared he had made too much noise, he would say apologetically as he took leave: "Ah well, one must pay for one's ticket of admission."

Sainte-Beuve and Mérimée, both reckoned as the two most malicious men of their literary generation, testify to the gentleness of Stendhal's character as a friend. He repelled the advances of some who sought

[4] C. Striyenski, preface to *Souvenirs d'égotisme*, xvii, 1892 (first edition).

his friendship, he offended or mystified others; yet, as Sainte-Beuve declares: "How much this man who passed for a wicked character (to those who did not know him) was loved by his friends! How much thoughtfulness he showed them, and how generous was his soul!" And the cool Mérimée, who would later deny what he had learned from his master, added: "Good faith was a marked trait of his character. No one was ever more honorable or loyal to his friends."

By 1826 his weekly calendar of social appointments was all filled up, and Stendhal gives his program as follows: "Tuesday at Mme. Ancelot's; Wednesdays at Baron Gérard's; Saturdays, Cuvier's; Sunday afternoon to Delécluze's; Sunday night, the Tracys'; and in addition, three suppers out each week at the Café Anglais, and I am *au courant* with all that is talked about in Paris!"

He would go forth each day, all two hundred pounds of him, a gentleman of the old school, but dressed always in the very height of fashion. As his cousin Colomb relates:

> Having preserved to an advanced age the affectation of passing for a man of some fortune, Beyle professed an absolute submission to the laws of *fashion*. So different from others in all things, he nonetheless approached the vulgar on the one point: of *fashion*. No one followed more slavishly the thousand changes of this foolish Parisian deity. He devoted all the resources of art also to correct or conceal the wrongs that nature had done him, and the ravages of time. Thus even at fifty-nine Beyle coifed himself like a young man. His head, denuded of hair, by dint of a large wig, offered the aspect of an almost irreproachable *chevelure*. Thick whiskers extended themselves in a long fringe round his face, and under his chin. Need I add that hair and beard were dyed a deep brown? Then, with a cigar in his mouth, his high hat lightly tilted over one ear, a cane in his hand, he would mingle with the dudes of the tavern and the Opera. His sensitiveness about everything that made up his toilet was extreme; a reflection, however slight, on the style of his suit or trousers, would cut him to the quick.

For what was better for one's sense of inferiority than to be superbly tailored, and to be able to enter a crowded room with a hero's ease?

In his most worldly tone, Stendhal tells us (in the *Souvenirs d'égotisme*): "I do not remember who took me first to the home of M. Delécluze. . . ." Etienne Delécluze was perhaps the foremost art critic of the day, who long reigned at his post in the all-powerful *Journal des débats*. "He asked to meet me," continues Stendhal, "and I was taken to his place on a Sunday, at two o'clock, the so awkward hour at which he received. He presided over his little academy on the sixth floor of a house . . . replete with engravings and curious objects of art."

At Delécluze's attic chamber, above the roofs of Paris, in the old Rue Notre-Dame-des-Champs, Stendhal would meet with a distinguished circle of literary men, artists, and scientists; and, sitting before a small fire, would begin to function, as Sainte-Beuve says, "as the trumpeter and vanguard leader of the new literary revolution." It was here that he first read aloud the second version of his *Racine and Shakespeare.* Delécluze, who lampooned Stendhal in his rather dreary memoirs, pictures him as usually beginning his discourse by telling some salty story gathered from the greenrooms of the Paris theaters, in order to attract the attention of his hearers, all exclusively masculine. This done, he would launch into his habitual argument against the pedantic and the fraudulent in literature. To imitate the trappings of Racine and Molière, he would say, was like trying to wear today "the black wigs and the embroidered coats of the marquis of 1670 that cost five thousand francs. . . . We need a new form of tragedy in prose. . . . We must use the *art* of Shakespeare and not imitate him."

Delécluze made complaint that Stendhal rather forced things in trying to amuse or provoke people and, in general, acted "like that corsair of old legend who, dining at a tavern with some sluggish Flemings who said not a word and fell asleep, discharged his pistol under the table in order to dispel their apathy." Despite his immense girth, says Delécluze, he seemed to want to dance all the time.

But Stendhal, in the *Souvenirs d'égotisme,* had the last word on Delécluze. Though he felt that the man arranged good parties and knew the art of leading general conversation tactfully, he termed him a "Boeotian" who, in character, was much like the Vicar of Wakefield. As to his famous collection of art objects, Stendhal remarks acidly:

> He had the pettiness of a typical bourgeois. If he bought a dozen handkerchiefs for thirty-six francs in some shop down the street, he would insist that his handkerchiefs were of an unequaled rarity and that nowhere in Paris, at any price, could one find their like.

So much for the reigning art critic of the day.

That Stendhal could be deliberately profane or bawdy was well known. To shock persons who esteemed what they considered patriotism, and what he called chauvinism, he would repeat stories of the Napoleonic campaign that reflected his own ideas of martial heroism and eloquence. He enjoyed telling of how once, during the retreat from Moscow, when he was with a detachment that was surrounded by the

Cossacks, and all the French gave themselves up for lost, he heard the aged commander make an appeal to his "brave soldiers" to rally their spirits for battle the next morning, somewhat in the following terms: "You lousy, stinking rabble! You will all surely be rotting corpses tomorrow, because you are too f—— cowardly to pick up a musket and use it!" These words, he claimed, produced the desired effect.

Admirer of Napoleon though he was, he would say: "I don't care a damn if I am 'conquered.' " Or: "What difference does it make to me if Saarlouis is no longer French?"

But his humor could also rise to effects of the most delicate irony, like his finest prose. In order to confound some people whose extreme piety in religion annoyed him, this hardened atheist would sometimes pretend to be more orthodox than anyone else; he would defend the Inquisition itself, and argue that tolerance was absurd:

> What! When an unfortunate creature is about to bring down upon himself centuries of horrible torture, at the bottom of a caldron of boiling oil, should we not try to spare him all that, by putting him in prison for a few years, or even give him a little pain for a brief hour by building a little fire under him in some public square! Ah, what cruelty there is in not being cruel enough!

Though he spared no one in his conversation, he could be keenly hurt when others misrepresented or spoke ill of him. "I am only a playful young dog, yet the others *bite* me," he once complained sadly to Mérimée. He was not aware that he often took the stronger bite, Mérimée adds.

The Baron Gérard, a hugely successful academic portrait painter, was also very fond of Stendhal, whom he met at Mme. Pasta's, and invited him to the large midnight parties he gave on Wednesdays. Stendhal enjoyed his parties and balls, but correctly called him a "brazen charlatan" as an artist, and predicted that he would be quickly forgotten by posterity. At Gérard's, however, he met the excellent Mme. Virginie Ancelot, wife of the popular playwright, Jacques Ancelot; she too was renowned as a hostess, and was herself a successful playwright. But though she enjoyed talking with him, she did not invite him to her home at first blush, because she noticed at once that "he was full of contrariety by nature and by design."

But one day he remarked: "I know why you never ask me to your Tuesdays; it is because you receive Academicians, and so you cannot have me." Whereupon he was pressed to come the next day, and agreed, upon the condition that he might announce himself not as Henri Beyle, but under one of his many pseudonyms.

The next morning, as Mme. Ancelot related, she received by messenger "a copy of a work on Haydn, by César Bombay [*sic*]."

> Very early, on the evening appointed, when only a few had arrived as yet, Monsieur "César Bombay" was announced, and I saw Beyle enter, looking chubbier than ever, and saying:
>
> "Madame, I have come too early. It is because I am a very busy man ordinarily; I must get up at five o'clock in the morning, visit the army warehouses in order to see if my furnishings are all there, for, don't you know, I am a supplier to the army of cotton stockings and caps! Ah, what fine cotton caps I make! That is my great role, and I must say that I have suffered for it since my earliest youth, and nothing has enticed me from this honorable and lucrative occupation. Oh well, I've heard that there are artists and writers who win a little glory for their pictures and books. Bah! What is that compared to the glory of dressing and capping a whole army, so that its soldiers can be spared suffering from cold heads and feet?"

Thus the "stout Mephistopheles"—as Adrien de Jussieu dubbed him—continued to hold forth breathlessly, giving no one else a chance to speak, while he told how many pennies of profit he made on each cap and how he overreached his rivals in trade. "When I used to improvise," Stendhal himself recalls, "I would run wild." His host and hostess, stifling their laughter, were forced to escape into an adjoining room until other guests arrived who, recognizing the pretended provisioner of socks and caps, put an end to his mad charade.

Mme. Virginie Ancelot, a large and bosomy woman of most amiable disposition, soon became a devoted friend of Stendhal, who, accompanied always by the little Mérimée, attended her Tuesday soirées regularly for many years. Her husband was one of the Forty Immortals, her home was a very den of Academicians, and she herself, always deep in their electoral intrigues, even helped to "make" Academicians. Yet she cheerfully tolerated the *boutades*, the hoaxes, and the pranks of Stendhal, not to mention his "stubborn prejudices."

He made people laugh, and it was impossible even for prudes to resist him. But sometimes he would be vexed by pretentious people who plainly disapproved of him, and he would turn upon them. It was thus that one night at the Ancelots', meeting that old bluestocking Mme. Sophie Gay, and her poetic daughter, Delphine, he suddenly burst into a speech so strange and absurd that the two ladies thought his reason had flown from its chambers and in great fear made off as soon as they could. The beautiful Delphine Gay, who was, incidentally, one of Victor Hugo's muses, on becoming the Baronne de Girardin, rose to be a social dictator of Paris, and maintained perhaps the most imposing literary salon of the day, from which Stendhal was of course rigorously excluded.

Mme. Ancelot not only accepted but warmly encouraged him, and in her recollections (*Les Salons de Paris: foyers éteints*), declared that none equaled him for piquant vivacity:

> Beyle was moved by anything and everything, and within a few minutes experienced a thousand sensations. . . . It is impossible to give a complete and just idea of his originality and his sallies. . . . Sometimes the debonair mockery of Mérimée, to be sure, recalled him to himself; but, after being held back, his wit would bubble up anew, more vigorously and more brilliantly than before.

The two guests were scarcely reverent toward their host and his "epic" tragedies, now utterly forgotten, and spoke no less lightly of their hostess, whom they liked to describe as a rather blowzy and too eager Diana, forever pursuing them or other celebrities. "Ancilla"—so they nicknamed her—"had two large squashes decorating her chest," according to the heartless Mérimée, and "sometimes adorned the brows of her husband with something more than the laurel wreath of poetry." Sainte-Beuve adds that Virginie Ancelot had a whining voice and gave him the effect of "an old, yellowed sirup, too long forgotten in its flask—phew! I would rather take vinegar a thousand times!"

In his somewhat compromising recollections of her (published posthumously in the *Henri Brulard*), Stendhal pays her a doubtful compliment, saying: "If I am not mistaken, wit nowadays takes refuge in the salons of ladies of light morals, such as Mme. Ancelot, who has not less lovers than Mme. T——." But years later, when he was far from Paris, he wrote her in a most affectionate tone, calling her his "tenth Muse," and declared that he pined for her hospitable hearth, adding: "If I could but come to your Tuesdays, I would be as happy as a newly elected cabinet minister."

Thus in his ripe years Stendhal found ways of enjoying civilized society and diverting himself from spleen—and in Paris, metropolis of the absurdly vain French. He who had come to the great capital as an awkward provincial, now presided over five or six of its salons, as an acknowledged master of general conversation, which still flourished as an art in the 1820s and 1830s. The Noble Savage in him was being tamed. He himself went so far as to say that he had learned how to find happiness in good society, which for him consisted in a salon having a small group of persons, "where all the women present have had lovers, the conversation is gay and anecdotal, and a light punch is served at half past twelve."

He may have remained at heart always "the Milanese"; Sainte-Beuve even thought that by staying too long in Italy he had lost the thread of ideas in France. Yet who was ever more French in the best sense of the word, in clarity of thought and sharpness of wit? That Paris conquered him, that he made a partial conquest—the most intangible and fleeting of conquests—or at least left his mark there, is shown by the testimony of numerous memoirs in which, thirty or forty years later, he was recalled chiefly as a figure of the old salons of the 1820s and 1830s. Sometimes he is remembered as a source of amusement, sometimes with disgust as "that monstrous cynic," or "the fat Machiavelli."

Yet literary fame continued to evade him. Few took him seriously as an author, and this was of course one of the secret sorrows that he concealed by his periodic fireworks in conversation. It was in alluding to his ill-regarded books that he used to say, half in jest, half in earnest: "Literary fame is a lottery. . . . I am taking out a ticket in a lottery whose winning number is 1935." This atheist certainly believed in immortality!

How well the amiable Virginie Ancelot understood him is shown by the reflection, in her memoirs, that Stendhal "always concealed his sadder feelings under the cover of his pleasantries, and never seemed so merry as on days when some misfortune had befallen him. Then he would vent himself in verbal sallies that were as full of wisdom as of folly!"

He did not use his social connections as a means to advance himself, though he loved the gossip he heard and gathered it up eagerly for his unsigned articles in English magazines on current books, plays, and paintings. By means of this hackwork, of which Paris knew almost nothing, he was able to survive the collapse of his private fortune. He did not deliberately try to shine, but to amuse himself and others. The presence of a fool or a bore made him freeze up, and he would fall silent, refuse to play or even take flight. Mérimée thought him utterly without patience or tact on this score, and said Stendhal considered dull people the next thing to criminals. He enjoyed repeating the *bon mot* of his friend the Baron de Mareste that "bad taste leads to crime." Then he would add: "Life is too short, and the time we waste in yawning can never be regained."

CHAPTER XVI

"*Armance*"

HE WROTE every day, no matter how often he went out; he wrote constantly, voluminously, though few men liked what he wrote or the way he wrote it. Travel books, histories of art, biographies of musicians, pamphlets, essays followed each other; finally even a first novel, *Armance,* came from his pen in 1827. His books were largely ignored or lightly treated in the press, enjoying either a poor or mediocre sale; yet he continued to write, for few authors ever wrote so much for the sheer joy of writing as did Stendhal.

Had he become successful, writing would have become a trade and perhaps a burden, until the hand at the pen, as Rimbaud wrote, were no better than the hand at the plow. But there was no nonsense about abandoning literature in Stendhal. "I write for my own pleasure," he repeatedly remarked, "as one smokes a cigar," or "to distract myself in the mornings" (*pour me désennuyer les matins*). Since his writings gave so few people pleasure, assuredly he wrote but to please or relieve himself. Since literary renown was so uncertain and speculative —"a lottery"—he wrote mainly for his own amusement, playing to his heart's content with the kaleidoscope of his thoughts. It was not art for art's sake, but for the health of his ego. Hence the extraordinary intellectual honesty of his writings, a quality noticeably wanting in the Chateaubriands and Mme. de Staëls of his time, but recalling rather the haunting Pascal, whom Stendhal read and admired more and more, and even thought he resembled a little. The least of his books, travel guide or compilation, had the merit of being an intimate and unfeigned *conversation,* full of humor and wisdom of life, insatiable in its pursuit of those general moral ideas that may be discovered through the intense observation of man and his world. This was true even of a potboiler he chanced to write in 1823. At this time, when the composer Rossini was taking Paris and London by storm, Stendhal quickly turned his versatile hand to getting up a little biography of the young prodigy of romantic music.

In January 1824, his *Vie de Rossini* was published in Paris; it had been preceded the year before by an English translation published by Hookham, in London, under the title, *Memoirs of the Life of Rossini*, by the "Author of the Lives of Haydn and Mozart." Since the appearance of this biography coincided with the world-wide ovations then being given to the young Rossini's operas, it proved to be one of the few books of Stendhal that were timely, and enjoyed a moderately successful sale, bringing him fifteen hundred greatly needed francs.

Though rambling and discursive in form, the book was nevertheless a more genuine contribution to the knowledge of modern Italian music and to the improvement of contemporary taste than his early work in this field. Moreover, it was based upon his personal acquaintance with Rossini—which he rated one of his great experiences, like meeting Napoleon, Byron, and Canova—and upon his own authentic collection of anecdotes of Rossini's life and work, gathered both in Italy and at the informed salon of Mme. Pasta.

He wrote of course as a subjective music lover, rather than as a musician, but one who knew deeply the lore of certain departments of music, such as the eighteenth-century Italian *opera buffa* and *opera seria,* and the traditions of the theater that nourished a Rossini. His subject gave him opportunity once more to pay tribute to the Italy that he loved, to describe its theatrical and bohemian world, to compare its moral customs with those of France, and finally to deal many a neat thrust at classical pedantry in music, as he had done in the lists of literature.

Stendhal's interest in Rossini also marks an advance in his musical taste, for the young nineteenth-century composer reflected the influence of the great German musicians and their richer orchestration. It is noteworthy also that Stendhal, flying in the face of French musical prejudices, even pays modest homage to the "moody" genius and "almost mathematical harmonies" of Beethoven, around whom so much controversy still raged. Rossini was a most fortunate character for the biographer; from a childhood of poverty he had swiftly advanced himself, by the vitality of his musical genius, until the great "lottery prize" of fame fell to him while he was still a youth. With Italian gusto he lived and loved and worked, composing so rapidly—

twenty operas in a few years!—that he once admitted that he "copied" his own earlier work. Rolling about in bed, eating four meals a day, guzzling wine, the handsome Italian giant in twenty minutes could turn off an overture that was to be immortal, and this while a dozen men and women friends invaded his quarters, laughing, shouting, and gesticulating. Such was the picture Stendhal gave, and one feels that Rossini might well have posed as an Italian model of Beylist success in the pursuit of happiness, were he not so gross in his appetites that Stendhal himself appears shocked at him. After describing in some detail Rossini's heartless treatment of his mistresses, his biographer concludes regretfully: "He knows nothing of the grand passions."

The book is so full of digressions that it would scarcely pass for a biography by present-day standards. The author himself suspected as much, for he avowed—paraphrasing Aristophanes—that he chose willfully "to let his thought fly like the winged insect one tosses into the air, with a string attached to its leg." There is in this book not a great deal less about Stendhal in Italy than about Rossini. Yet for all that, and despite what Hector Berlioz, his fellow Dauphinois, later called its "irritating stupidities," the book that happened to be the first biography of Rossini is a contribution to the history of music.

Rossini himself, and his more fanatical admirers, soon disavowed it as unauthorized, ill-founded, and scarcely doing justice to its subject. Yet amusingly enough, just as Stendhal earlier had pillaged other authors, so now, for the sake of its authentic gossip and anecdotes, his *Rossini* was pirated in foreign countries and extensively plagiarized by other writers. Meanwhile, inasmuch as the appearance of the book in France helped to reveal his own personality—"full of verve, originality, and wit" as one reviewer remarked—and it enjoyed a small commercial success, it removed something of the stigma of failure that was attached to his efforts as an author.

It was time, then, that he turned his hand to a freer and more creative form of literature. For twenty years he had yearned to write a play that would actually be produced, and clung to several fragments of first acts that were never completed. Now, in 1826, encouraged by the two editions the *Rossini* had reached, and the good reception also given a second, expanded edition of *Rome, Naples and Florence*, he undertook to write a novel. This was after his rupture with Clémentine de Curial, his third journey to England, and his return to Paris in the autumn, when to distract his mind from reverses in love he concentrated with all his will upon a new literary project.

The fashion then was for historical romances, à la Walter Scott, with suitable descriptions of ancient castles and characters in medieval costume. Perhaps a variant of the Scottish-made historical romance even more favored in France during the 1820s was the "Gothick" novel of Mrs. Ann Radcliffe and "Monk" Lewis, with its trappings of funereal ruins and moonlit horror. As Stendhal remarked at this time, "a great host of littérateurs are concerned with exalting Sir Walter Scott [whom he himself long had enjoyed]. . . . The dress and the copper collar of the serf are much easier to describe than the movements of the human heart. . . ." For his own part he thought such works as Charles Nodier and Alexandre Soumet were producing were fit only for servant maids. He said also: "I abhor physical descriptions; the trouble I have in doing them prevents me from writing novels." But if one created the drama of true human characters, and rendered their *minds* in conflict with the institutions and traditions of their age, would this not be more rewarding than those false tapestries of ancient times?

As writers went, he was old, nearly forty-four, when he came to write his first novel. His beliefs were fixed; he had lived, observed, reflected much. Almost every inclination of the novelist had been shown in him, though perhaps he had long considered himself primarily a *philosophe*, an essayist on man and morals, like Montesquieu. Yet his essays, such as *De l'amour*, and his travel books, were like cargo vessels carrying many an illustrative anecdote or tale, with its pointed moral, each of which might have been the starting point of a whole novel. Only the mechanics of the novel were unfamiliar to him.

It was in Stendhal's character that, in his first trial, he should attempt to swim against the stream. To his bookseller, with whom he corresponded on the subject of his plan for a novel, he wrote that it would treat of "present-day morals." The setting of his first novel was not of the thirteenth but of the nineteenth century. It was called *Armance, or Scenes of Society Life in Paris in 1827.*

Armance appeared in August 1827. Just the year before there had been much gossip in Paris concerning an anonymously published novel entitled *Olivier*, whose hero embodied a certain type of sexual abnormality. This scabrous novel (whose authorship was traced to Henri de Latouche) intrigued Stendhal, and he himself adopted the *tares* of its hero, though in no sense its plot, or its ideas. The singularity or perversity of his own hero, like that of the original *Olivier*—the name even became a byword in Paris for some years—appealed to him as having a symbolic value that would lend significance to his novel. In his deliberately mystifying preface he spoke of the moral purpose of his book, described it as a *mirror held up to life,* then broke off with a puzzling allusion to its singular theme.

Stendhal's hero is the Viscount Octave de Malivert, a twenty-year-old youth, sole heir of an ancient and noble family. He is very handsome, tall, and blond-haired; he is also intelligent and learned, having graduated from the famous Ecole Polytechnique (which Henri Beyle in his youth once prepared to attend). He even has a fortune of two million francs recently restored by the monarchy's Law of Indemnity in favor of the nobles, whose lands had been divided up under the Republic. Everything favors him, yet his character is strange enough to be defined as that of the "bilious-melancholy type," one of the categories classified by Stendhal's precursor in psychology, Dr. Cabanis.

Octave de Malivert, then, typifies the dilemma of the aristocrat in the age of royalist reaction succeeding the Republic and Empire. His health appears to have been delicate; his moods shift rapidly from violent gaiety to the gloom of a misanthrope who flees society. Like a dilettante he has tried a dissolute life, among harlots and criminals; then, for a time, religion; finally he has adopted the philosophy of the eighteenth-century materialists, to the regret of his pious mother. By various hints we are also told that his prevailing melancholy is due not to spiritual confusion, but to some unnatural physical affliction whose secret he will not divulge.

But gradually the sentiments of this misanthropic young man converge upon Armance de Zohiloff, the beautiful orphaned daughter of a Russian general and a French mother, who serves as the companion of one of Octave's noble relatives. She is the first of Stendhal's "ideal women"—as generous and high-spirited as she is intelligent—and in his cosmopolitan way the author makes her partly a foreigner rather than a purely French woman. The growing love of Octave and Armance is pictured step by step, as it passes through the phases of admiration, hope, misunderstanding, jealousy, and finally, "crystallization," all quite as formulated in Stendhal's *De l'amour.* But in this case the process of love is complicated by the peculiar personality of Octave.

As if against their will, these beings are helplessly borne toward each other. There is a duel, in which Octave is sorely wounded, following an intrigue by other interested parties designed to keep them apart. Finally he recovers his health, all obstacles and misunderstandings are overcome, and their betrothal is announced. But as the wedding day approaches, Octave falls into fits of dejection; it is as if some unnatural doom hangs over him; and now he regards his fiancée in melancholy silence, or now uses her with extreme cruelty. Pressed to explain his strange behavior, he cries: "The man who adores you is a monster!" In passages of soliloquy, whose psychological realism is remarkable for that time, he is shown exclaiming to himself:

> Ah, such a beautiful soul! To attach myself to her for all time, to live solely for her and for her happiness! I should love her with passion, I should *love* her, alas, I, unfortunate one. . . .[1]

Should he tell her his secret and lose her forever, he wonders? For Octave's tragedy is determined not so much by his peculiar affliction as by the obsessive idea that he must rather kill himself than reveal his secret. Thus Stendhal, in the view of the modern master, André Gide, divined the veritable tragedy of such an abnormal personality: his eternal necessity to be silent upon the nature and cause of his tragedy, to guard its secret "even if it killed him."

He had given her some inkling of his "fear" of her. "*Armance has always made me afraid.* I never approached her without feeling that I was appearing before the master [*sic*] of my destiny."

His troubled efforts to give her some hint, in veiled language, of his predicament lead Armance to believe that her beloved has been guilty of some fearful crime which haunts him. At this, like one of Shakespeare's heroines, or better, like one of Stendhal's Italian women of passion, she utters a thought as *unexpected* to her as it is to us: "I have had the idea of committing some crime equal to yours, so that you need not fear me any longer!"

The upshot is that despite awareness of his enigmatic monstrosity, and after being tormented to the verge of madness, Octave feels himself compelled to go through with the marriage ceremony, embracing his fate as in a rage of self-destruction. Their wedding takes place; on the same day they depart for Marseille, where, for a week, we are informed briefly, the young girl "finds bliss in his arms." But at the end of that week Octave informs his wife that he has made a vow to fight for Greek independence and must leave her forthwith. Despite her tears he embarks, and on the ship, while in sight of the Hellenic shore, takes poison. Before dying—I simplify the summary—he sends her the letter he had formerly intended to give her before their marriage, revealing the secret that dooms him.

The reader, however, is left with no clue to the mystery of Octave.

---

[1]In afterthought, Stendhal believed he should have written here: "And *how* would *I* be loved?"

In 1827, when the novel first appeared, it was considered most bizarre; its hero was characterized (in *Le Globe*) as a good candidate for the insane asylum at Charenton.

His trouble, to put it baldly, was that he was impotent; in other words, a eunuch or *babilan,* to use the old French term that Stendhal reintroduced. Mérimée had been let into the secret of Octave's perplexities, and in a rather scabrous letter ventured some doubts as to the technical feasibility of the honeymoon week in Marseille. He also seems to have made objection to the choice of so singular a character. But Stendhal, in salacious humor, argued that there were more *babilans* abroad in the world than people believed, citing the case of Dean Swift, of Maurepas, a minister under Louis XV, and of a contemporary they knew, whose wife Mérimée himself hopefully pursued. As to the alleged week in which Octave and Armance were married, he suggests that the hero by some sleight of hand might easily have beguiled his wife, who was innocent of exact knowledge and madly in love. Then he adds: "As for me (at forty-three and eleven months) it no longer matters. . . . I would have taken my wife to Rome. There, for a sequin or two, a handsome peasant would have paid her three compliments every night."[a]

He had intended, originally, to name his hero *Olivier* de Malivert, thus recalling the eunuch of the scandalous novel that had appeared a short time before. But Mérimée counseled him not to do this; for in France the idea of sexual impotence was still something to laugh at, and its specific introduction would have marred the intendedly serious tone of the novel. André Gide, in his preface to a modern edition of the novel, holds that Stendhal erred in not making the nature of Octave's difficulties unmistakable. It was out of a sense of artistic restraint that he left this in doubt; bold as his thought may be, he is habitually restrained in treating of the details of physical love. But he himself later realized that he had made the whole affair too obscure, for in marking his own copy of the book he indicated several places where he might have given broader hints to the reader and permitted the impotence of Octave at least to be *divined.*

But is *Armance* an unjustly neglected masterpiece, as M. Gide contends? Certainly it announces a new talent and a new personality in the novel. It is already distinguished by a spirit of analysis that sets Stendhal's fiction apart from everything else written in his time. Before Octave must fight a duel, write a love letter, or take poison, he starts

[a]Stendhal read Scott's biography of Swift with great interest at the period when he prepared to write *Armance.* He claimed that he modeled his leading characters somewhat after Swift and Stella.

with a searching examination of his conscience, in a long interior monologue which is a distinguishing feature of the Stendhal novels. (The dramatic soliloquy, now so admired in Proust, was not relished in 1827.) The study of Octave's abnormal personality and the interpretation of his passions is already the work of a master of psychology. His portrait of the charming young girl, Armance, is even more appealing and fresh; few men were to write with such knowledge of the heart of a woman as Stendhal. But despite its atmospheric qualities, the work has the mark of the amateur: its picture of the aristocratic circles of the Faubourg St. Germain in Paris, which Stendhal may have known too little, lacks those details, the "little true facts" that he himself demanded of literature. The people he lampoons and all the secondary characters are essentially cartoons. Finally, though Stendhal intended a powerful social criticism of royalist France, this intention is obscured and overbalanced by the vague circumstances of his hero's downfall and the mystery in which this is shrouded. He writes with irony and restraint, and with much wit in his satirical passages, but it is the romantic Chateaubriand, whose influence he has been vehemently opposing, whom he nevertheless still reflects. Forcibly one recalls *Atala*, with its brooding guilt and its incest theme, in reading Stendhal's somber first novel. The very selection of a tragic eunuch, despite its appeal as a novel subject for psychological analysis, throws him into the "overemphatic" romantic camp.

That the impotent Octave was designed as a symbol of the decadent ruling class is shown by Stendhal's notes on the manuscript of the novel, in which he remarks that a young member of the privileged class in 1827 "can only be: (1) a Jesuit; or (2) an officer of the guard, always on horseback and having the intelligence of his horse; or (3) sad like Octave." And Octave is made to say: "We see the absurdities of our position, and yet dare not laugh. What good is the great age of my name to me? . . . Ah how I would like to command a battery of cannon, or even a steam engine!"

But in the reign of the despotic Charles X, the constitution is flouted, the press is censored, the universities are muzzled, and the people are sullen with discontent, under the watchful eye of government spies and priests. Octave de Malivert may be enlightened, but in truth there are no more great careers open to talent. He can only wait, fully aware of the "contradictions" in society, full of regret for "that which he values," and full of fear for "that which he foresees will come to pass in the future." A new revolution? This, it is implied, cannot be avoided, though the regime of darkness may preach incessantly the advantages of birth and religion, and strive to compress and corrupt the common people "who have every advantage save that of birth."

The political tone of this novel has gone unnoticed by critics of Stendhal's time and since then. Yet those pages in which Octave's lament is recorded are most significant and, by a remarkable parallel, apply perfectly to our own age of late capitalism, when men once again with troubled souls sustain an old order, though they have lost faith in it, and in anguish await the hour when the new and the unknown forces of tomorrow are to engulf them. Octave feels that he belongs to "the losing side." He exclaims:

> "Truly we live in a city that is besieged—but the rulers of the city command us to go on as if nothing were happening and permit no one to speak of the siege. . . .
>
> "We are like the priests of the idols of paganism at the moment when the Christian religion is about to conquer all. We still persecute today, we have the police and the treasury on our side; but perhaps tomorrow it is we who will be persecuted."

Stendhal, who pretended not to be interested in economic questions, was in truth passionately interested in politics and made some uncanny historical prophecies. (The revolution whose shadow falls over this novel of the doomed aristocracy in 1827 was actually but three years away.) But as if to apologize for his hardihood, or provide a mock "passport" to show the censors, he explains that he is merely trying to be a faithful historian:

> Politics coming in suddenly to interrupt such a simple story may have the effect of a pistol shot in the middle of a concert. Besides, Octave was not a philosopher and characterized his time . . . unjustly.

But politics was always to intrude upon the harmonious music of his novels with the effect of a pistol shot.

The impotence of Octave is for Stendhal symbolic of the aristocratic regime, which he, like Rousseau, condemns as decadent and emasculated. He also assails the Restoration regime on the political level, for suppressing freedom of thought and equality of human rights. However, the polemical force of the novel is weakened by the ambiguities surrounding the hero's character and tragedy. For Stendhal it is a transitional book, whose intermittently flashing perceptions and aphorisms give a foretaste of the continuously scintillating volumes to come.[3]

Armance was scorned by the press. Its mechanistic approach to hu-

[3]A novel, a work of the imagination, is inevitably part confession. Stendhal had inserted a chapter on fiascos in his treatise on love; in *Armance* he wrote of the torments of a castrate; in the

man morals was considered repulsive by Sainte-Beuve, who reflected the taste of his period. To a friend in London, Stendhal wrote breezily on March 23, 1828: "All my friends find it detestable; as for me, I consider them crude. It is the greatest of all 'impossibilities' of love. The hero Octave is *impotens.*" Yet only Benjamin Constant's autobiographical novel, *Adolphe*, rivaled it in its time for psychological acumen. At any rate, Stendhal's lifelong inquiry into human nature was now entering upon a new phase, in which the medium of fiction was principally used for his speculations. The philosophical moralist now devoted himself to novels, though the indifference with which the public received his books really pierced him to the heart.

2

With the meager earnings from his books, and drawing also upon his own dwindling income and capital, Stendhal would set off at least once a year on long journeys by carriage and boat, usually alone, only rarely in the company of a friend. Touring in places strange to him, meeting or merely observing strange people—for he always traveled "among people"—was for him an unfailing distraction. Sometimes he would wander off for weeks, as if in a trance, until he found his purse empty, and from some roadside inn would write to Paris for money with which to return.

Thus in 1826, on his third visit to England, he penetrated as far as the Lake Country in the North, in the company of a lively young English friend, William Sutton-Sharpe, whom he had met at Cuvier's in

posthumous *Souvenirs d'égotisme* (1832) he recalled one of his own fiascos with a courtesan. These coincidences have given rise to suppositions.

Moreover, he tended to identify himself with the blond, blue-eyed Octave, for he wrote in one of his autobiographical notes: "If I had the power . . . I would change myself into a tall, blond German and parade along the boulevards in that guise."

Undoubtedly, there was ambivalence in the "narcissistic" Stendhal's relations with women, also a pronounced "castration complex," stemming from his passionate attachment to his mother and early loss of her in childhood. He was neurotic in the extent to which his potency was periodically disturbed, as he confesses; he was sensitive about his ugliness; he tended to be masochistic by the intensity with which he contemplated his disappointments with women. To the extent that he entertained periodic fears concerning his own potency (fears that were as often dispelled), the image of Octave may have suggested itself to him. In another sense, the castrate Octave is also the container of his own masochistic sufferings in love.

Had he not been in the position of a tormented eunuch with regard to his beloved Metilda for three years?

But the most significant comment to be made on all this is that of one psychoanalyst: that Stendhal's failures with women made him introspective—as he would not have been if more successful—and helped him to become a great psychologist. Bergler: op. cit.

Paris. "Conversation" Sharpe was the nephew of the wealthy, ill-humored old poet laureate, Samuel Rogers; though he practiced law, he himself had much literary taste and greatly enjoyed the mental qualities of Stendhal. It was through Sutton-Sharpe, who became his devoted friend and correspondent, that Stendhal was able finally to visit English country houses, and to be received in the exclusive Athenaeum Club in London.

His correspondence at this time is filled with keen reflections upon society in post-Napoleonic England on the eve of bloodless political upheaval. He found that superior men in England, such as that strong Liberal orator, Lord Brougham (whom he had known well in Italy), "have a most admirable simplicity and naturalness of manner. With us French, when a man has won some battle, he always feels himself obliged to strike a pose." Yet he saw that the growing wealth of England, based on her advanced manufacture, rendered her working classes "more slaves than in Morocco." Rich and poor alike must give themselves only to work, and with a sort of "Hebraic ferocity." The increasing social puritanism of the people who had cast forth Byron and Shelley also oppressed him in later years.

Although he was in no sense a social Utopian, and understood little of the Saint-Simonian movement of his time, Stendhal was led to make the observation that after 1815, in England, "the nobles and the rich of every sort seemed to have signed a definitive alliance, defensive and offensive, against the *poor people and the workers.*" Industrialism in its mighty youth, imposing the fourteen-hour day, was not a pleasing spectacle.

His next journey, in August 1827, brought him once more to Italy. Descending the peninsula as far as Naples, he crossed the bay and for the first time visited the marvelous isle of Ischia, ancient resort of Roman emperors, which he explored from one end to another while mounted on the back of a small Sicilian donkey, upon which, it must be said, his ample posteriors were bravely balanced. The vistas of the Bay of Naples from Ischia's beach elicited cries of delight in the letters of this early connoisseur of tourism. Then, after attending dinners and balls in Rome to which he was nowadays invited by English as well as Italian social leaders—Lady Devonshire and Lady Jersey as well as the Prince Borghese—he proceeded to Florence. There, armed with a letter of introduction from his friend Mareste, he called upon the poet Alphonse de Lamartine, then serving as secretary to the embassy in the Tuscan capital.

At first the thought of a visit from the reputedly soulless Beyle, as the famous poet later confided to Sainte-Beuve, filled him with apprehension, but this was soon allayed by the humor and verve of the Falstaffian figure who knocked at his door.

Stendhal himself was not a little embarrassed, because he, for his part, entertained grave doubts about Lamartine; he had often ridiculed the verses of this sweet singer as a feeble, French imitation of Byron, and felt some guilt on this score. To offset the constraint between them he decided to come right to the point and clear the air of mutual suspicion.

"They have doubtless told you terrible things about me," he said, as Lamartine recalled, "that I am an atheist and make mock of those three letters of the alphabet that spell out what is called God, and of men, as well, those poor mirrors of their God. Well, I shan't try to deceive you, it is all too true." Then, while Lamartine was left breathless, he swept on to expound his own freethinking philosophy. No, he could not believe in a just and all-seeing Providence; the whole universe was governed by chance. The only force for order or logic in this life was something called *conscience*, which might be a reality for some human creatures, or, on the other hand, only a prejudice for others. As for Stendhal, he felt in his heart that he was "an honest man," and could be nothing else—"not for the sake of pleasing a Supreme Being, who does not exist, but to please myself and to satisfy my own need to exist in peace with my prejudices and habits, and give some direction to my life and some nourishment to my thoughts."

Then he closed his introductory speech with some sound buffets for his host, a younger man by seven years: "My friend Mareste assured me that you had a thousand times more wit in person than in your books, and that you were acquiring still more as you grew older. . . . Now let us talk!"

In his literary memoirs, written long afterward, Lamartine confesses that he was disarmed by the originality and candor of Stendhal; that they grew somewhat friendly, met on many occasions in Florence, and that he often tried to use his powers of persuasion against his companion's religious incredulity. He relates: "I inspired in him some doubts upon his irreligion and he, in matters of music, art, and poetry, brought some illumination for my ignorance."[4] However, Lamartine's prudent English wife, it was reported, refused to receive the "sinister" Stendhal in their home in Paris.

On New Year's Day, he interrupted his stay in Florence to make a

[4]Lamartine: *Cours familier de littérature*, Vol. XVII, Entretien CII.

visit to Milan, which he had not seen in seven years. He had both longed and feared to go there. Metilda was dead. Yet how many and poignant memories of days and years passed so heedlessly in ecstasy or sorrow called him back! Tears streamed from his eyes, and his old Italian friends were no less effusive in greeting him on the afternoon he arrived. But the police authorities of the town, this time, gave him poor welcome. Indeed, despite his eloquent protestations and the fervent offers of his friends to give personal guarantees for him, he was ordered to leave Milan within twenty-four hours. Mérimée, Sainte-Beuve, and other friends of his liked to mock at the elaborate precautions he used against alleged spies and persecutors, or the many pseudonyms and disguises employed in his letters, as signs of mania in him; and yet, in this cruel order of expulsion, we have the clear justification for some of his obsessions.

The report of the Baron Torresani, chief of police of Milan, to the Vienna Prefecture of Police, dated January 29, 1828, tells of the arrival of

> Henry Beyle, Frenchman, January 1, 1828 . . . known as the author of an ill-famed work entitled *Rome, Naples and Florence* by *de Stendhal.* In this work not only did he unfold the most pernicious political ideas, but he also compromised the reputation of numerous persons residing in these provinces by his calumnious statements, and even had the insolence to hold forth in the most damnable manner against the Austrian Government.
>
> . . . Let me add respectfully that Beyle, during his stay of several years in Milan, made himself known as an enemy of religion, an immoral man, and dangerous to royalty, in such a degree that it is incomprehensible that my predecessors should have tolerated his presence so long . . . especially in view of the fact that he maintained close connections with our most notorious liberals.

Though he vowed that he wanted to stay merely for the sake of his health and entertainment, and declared that "Stendhal" and Beyle were not the same, the "dangerous foreigner" was commanded never again to enter the territory of Lombardy. All frontier officials were warned, and notice of the order was also sent to the imperial police at Venice and Trieste. In addition, he was "held under surveillance" during his short stay in Milan, that is, followed by spies; though this, it was reported, "yielded no evidence of any interest."[5]

Despondent, he looked at Milan for the last time, and rode northward. In March 1828, he was back in Paris, his funds utterly depleted.

[5]C. Simon: *Stendhal et la police autrichienne,* pp. 13–14.

3

In 1828 there began a most difficult period for Stendhal. Gradually, by his free way of living, dandy and gourmet that he was, he had exhausted the slender fortune he had inherited at his father's death.

For several years he had depended greatly on earnings of from one hundred to two hundred pounds annually from articles and notices contributed to various English reviews, especially Colburn's *New Monthly Magazine.* He had obtained these commissions through good friends in England, such as Sutton-Sharpe and an Irish barrister whom he called Stritch, who sometimes translated his pieces. Though his articles were unsigned, and often carelessly translated, they reflected his unmistakable personality and his prejudices; in shrewd, lively and skeptical fashion they commented upon a large miscellany of subjects, generally under the heading of "Letter from Paris," and sometimes bore down hard on the current Romantic School in the French theater and the novel—on the Lamartines and Hugos—in a way that would have caused some trouble if the author of these commentaries were known. Curiously enough, his contributions from Paris or Italy enjoyed a certain influence in England in the 1820s, where his unorthodox critical spirit and political liberalism were highly relished. We know that besides Byron, William Hazlitt (who once called on him) and Thomas Moore esteemed his work, though in the 1830s, when he became known principally as the author of certain "immoral" novels, he was ignored and soon forgotten. The best of his commentaries and sketches in the *New Monthly*, the *London Magazine* and the earliest issues of the *Athenaeum* (the French original versions of which have nearly all disappeared) have been collected and retranslated by contemporary scholars.

But in 1828, what had been a fairly steady source of income—better than most French journalists received in those days for similar work—came to a stop when Colburn, publisher of the *New Monthly Magazine,* fell into difficulties. Efforts to recover sums owed by him brought little; the other magazines used less of Stendhal's commentaries and paid much less. He was almost at the end of his rope.

In his dire straits he considered the idea of writing another Italian travel book made up of notes left over from his earlier *Rome, Naples and Florence.* It was to be, a little before Baedeker's day, a sort of guide to Rome, which, it was thought, the increasing crowds of tourists now coming to the Eternal City would buy eagerly.

Stendhal's friends were now genuinely concerned about the mood of depression that showed itself only under the surface, but never left him. It was in this year, while obsessed by thoughts of ending his life, that he wrote a whole series of Last Wills and Testaments, constantly rewriting and revising them. In principle, he approved of suicide, and was unafraid of death, though he disliked to speak of it. A debt of four hundred francs to his tailor troubled his soul in this dark hour, and he scrupulously arranged for payment by the sale of some of his books. He greatly disliked to borrow money and did so only in a small way, during this crisis, with many formal apologies for troubling his friends.

Colomb, his literary executor, relates:

> Endowed with a habitually merry humor, Beyle was subject to an access of intense misanthropy. The year 1828 is the one in which dark thoughts dominated him most. . . . I found evidence of this in four testaments written while he was in perfect health, between August 26 and December 4, 1828. In one he begs pardon for the embarrassment which he *is going to cause* me and beseeches me not to be sad on the occasion of an *unavoidable event.* In the letter of December 4, he begs me to finish the *Promenades dans Rome* myself, correct the proofs and oversee the printing already begun.

It was in this grim mood that Beyle whipped himself on to complete his second travel book, urged forward by Colomb and Mareste, both of whom anxiously stood by him. *Promenades dans Rome* was a potboiler, frankly written to gather in some "fish," which it accomplished to the extent of fifteen hundred francs when, finally, it reached the stalls in the autumn of 1829.

The work was rather planless and full of digressions, like Stendhal's earlier essays. As in all of these, the wit, the sensitive aesthete, and the passionate tourist in Stendhal make the *Promenades,* if not quite a reliable manual of Rome's ancient monuments, then something much rarer, a vehicle for the inimitable reflections, table talk, and anecdotes of Stendhal.

Before the Second World War, and its new harvest of ruin, one could journey in Italy with Stendhal most profitably, to discover not only the art treasures and relics of antiquity and the Renaissance, but that feudal Italy which he still discerned, as he insists, in the early nineteenth century. With him one could watch the wise, weary old cardinals riding by in coach-and-four, with liveried postilions accompanying them, deferentially saluted by the Swiss Guards and the populace. His book recaptures the atmosphere of an Italy that is vanished. In recalling the brief, enlightened interregnum of Napoleon and the Code Civil, how illuminating is his remark:

> During five years, 1809–1814, a strange idea spread in Rome, that it was possible to get something out of a prefect without paying his mistress or his confessor.

But after 1815 the Papal States returned to an authoritarian theocracy, its despotism suppressing individualism, crushing out even the arts which were native to the Italians in the days of the city-republics.

Stendhal was one of the first, if not the first, commentator upon Italian history to stress the great upsurge of individualistic ambition and energy in the fourteenth and fifteenth centuries, attended with the production of masterworks of art that were the natural expression of the "democratic," if strife-ridden, city-republics of those days. The violence that marked Italy's Renaissance, he reasons shrewdly, was itself the by-product of increasing learning, self-knowledge, and the passion for liberty.

But now, in 1828, as he dissects the social and political mechanisms of the Papal States, with their secret police and their well-entrenched routine of bribery, he notes how "a deepening miasma destroys and depopulates the town . . . enough grass grows in the streets of Ferrara to feed a battalion of cavalry." The workers live on alms, or, south of Rome, gain money for the payment of taxes by highway robberies. The tyranny of Metternich's proconsuls or of the Vatican police makes thought itself dangerous; yet the Italian, natural child of the sun, knows how to circumvent or outwit oppression.

"The Italian believes that to be happy in this world, one must satisfy his passions; and to be happy in the next world, one must satisfy the ritual of the Church." But the results did not augur well for the future, he held, and this, he foresaw, would be complicated further by the advance of commerce and industry, bringing new forms of oppression. With Napoleon in mind, he said in effect: "Either you must have a *successful* despot, or you must make way for democracy."

Journeying with Stendhal in Italy, one sees better the long schooling in corruption that this people has undergone. One reads him and understands more easily how an oft-betrayed Italy, old in experience, and yet eternally young and beautiful, could sink again in our own time, under the power of a modern *condottiere*, such as Mussolini, and after new debacles set off once more in search of liberty.

In the *Promenades dans Rome* Stendhal pays tribute to his Italian friends such as Pellico, one of the early conspirators of the Risorgimento, who still languished in prison or in exile. He prophesies the days of 1848–49, even suggesting the time of renewed revolt with uncanny accuracy.

Though a guidebook by intent, it is as a "journey among people," as an informal *causerie* upon the effects of environment, climate, and historical tradition, that the *Promenades* is most effective. Stendhal's general reflections on man, history, and the arts are interlarded casually among hints about the best inns or restaurants, or directions for finding the Trajan Column and the Colosseum, or among impressions of St. Peter's and the pictures in the Vatican Galleries. In its advice, as in its descriptions of ancient monuments, the book teems with errors of fact and history, confusing dates and the names of Roman emperors and popes. There is also much that is *pastiche*, borrowed from other authorities, though this seems more justified in a work that is half compilation. Yet his observations upon Michelangelo's murals were read with excitement by the romantic artists of his time, such as Delacroix. His comment upon the *Pietà* of Michelangelo is challenging still: to his mind it paints a "Promethean revolt . . . a God, all-powerful, and infinitely merciful, who permits the anguish of a human death to satisfy the vengeance of another God of infinite mercy."

Continuing his plea for a romantic conception of art, which is in truth an unremitting demand for "modernism," he points out the vital relationship between the paintings of Michelangelo, Leonardo, and Correggio, and their age, when the concept of the beautiful was determined by the social and religious forms of the Church. The modern artist in the nineteenth century, too, must be in accord with the time-spirit. He concludes with the striking and richly suggestive proposition: "To my mind, beauty throughout the ages has been the *promise of a useful character* (*La prédiction d'un caractère utile*)." Literature, too, he reasoned, must paint with truth and naturalness the ruling passions of the men of our own time and not of vanished yesterdays. (This was the preoccupation of the new novel which he was writing at this same period.)

His travel books, in short, were imbued with the belief that life is an art which is best practiced in places like Italy. As his fancy strikes him he banquets upon sculpture, architecture, or anecdotes of folk customs, and even recent crimes. To paraphrase Anatole France, these "promenades" were the adventures of a sensitive soul not only among the masterpieces of man's handiwork, but among those of nature and history.

4

He jested and laughed much in company, yet melancholy dogged him. Not only did he grieve over his fallen fortunes, he who had been one of the young swells of Empire days, but in his middle forties already felt warning signs of age. His paunch waxed; his breath grew short; the pains of gout racked him at times. And what was more, the abnegations of old age were plainly foreshadowed by a new misadventure in love dating from 1829, and a connection formed with a lady who was certainly one of the more facile muses of the Romantic School.

Her name was Alberthe de Rubempré. He had been introduced to this imposing, voluptuous, though eccentric young woman by Eugène Delacroix, who was her distant cousin. She was the daughter of a theatrical impresario who had cut quite a figure in his time and was rather a bounder. For some years she was said to have served as model for certain of the leading painters and sculptors. But besides having a form and a face, she had learning of an esoteric sort, and entertained many literary and political celebrities in her apartment in the Rue Bleue. This she decorated in somber colors, shutting out the light of day with great black curtains that were always drawn. In this singular *décor* she would sit, always dressed in black velvet robes trimmed with red cashmere, absorbed in spiritism and table-turning, looking a great deal like some alluring demoness out of Victor Hugo's early ballads.

Mérimée described her as clever, but quite mad; while Stendhal thought her one of the "least artificial" of French women. In afterthought, he added that she was also "a strumpet, like Mme. du Barry, with nothing of the sublime, like Gina Pietragrua."

His susceptible heart was touched from the first hour he met her. Soon after he resolved to "attack," and his offensive quickly gained the fortunes of love. For all of a month he was madly infatuated; but while made happy, he was also highly tormented by his "Mme. Azure," as he named the lady—because she lived on the Rue Bleue.

Soon he noticed that fidelity was not one of the virtues embraced by his romantic siren, and suspected that his forehanded young friend, Prosper Mérimée, was the newest object of her passion. Half ruefully, half in anguish, he exclaims: "I have always had a faculty for communicating my tastes in women to my friends." Alas, his eloquence sometimes betrayed him.

In despair, he pleaded with Mérimée to leave the lady to him. But Mérimée, perhaps deceivingly, replied: "I have no taste for her, sir, as I have seen her stockings falling down." Stendhal, nevertheless, was persuaded that his "Mme. Azure" preferred a man of half his age, and became quite tragic. He was then in the midst of his *Promenades dans Rome*, and his faithful friend Colomb had all he could do to sustain him so that he might complete the so necessary task.

"Mme. Azure" meanwhile continued to flourish, and some years after his stormy parting from her, Stendhal returned to her side, at least on a footing of friendship. By then she had become the mistress of another of his cronies! He relates in *Henri Brulard*:

> In 1832, I inoculated Mareste in a very pleasant manner with my love for Mme. Azure, whose devoted friend he has been for two years, and what is more amusing, he has even rendered her faithful.

A few years later, Stendhal had forgotten her real name and could only remember her as "Mme. Azure."

The new travel book was fairly successful as such things went, for its author reported that all the English tourists in Rome arrived there armed with it. But its modest royalties were exhausted by the repayment of debts. Throughout 1829, Stendhal sent piteous appeals to men in public office, begging for some small sinecure that would bring him a pittance of seventeen hundred francs a year, such as that of assistant curator of the Royal Library. Yet he was passed over.

In his desperation, in June 1829 he wrote to the Count d'Argout, his former colleague in the army commissary department, begging for his aid in obtaining a post of some kind. It was at D'Argout's home that he had once mocked at the Church and the Christian faith. Hence he writes now: "Time, *edax rerum*, has somewhat moderated my political opinions." He recalled his "fourteen years" of public service and pointed out that "foreign literature has been the preoccupation of my entire life." What he longed for was some place as secretary of a legation. But, to his chagrin, the government of Charles X, the last of the Bourbon kings, would not even appoint him a clerk in the Bureau of Archives.

There is a vague allusion in his private papers to a temporary diplomatic mission that he carried out in secret, during a brief visit to Rome in 1829, an assignment given him finally by Amedée de Pastoret, another old friend in the government, but evidently without the direct approval of the Foreign Minister, or the ambassador to Rome, who then happened to be Chateaubriand himself. A pope was being elected; Stendhal, after observing events and drawing upon his knowledge of Italian affairs, submitted a memorandum on the character of the different cardinals, of whom one, Cardinal Gregorio, was advocated by him as most suitable for the support of the French king. But his *mémoire* was vigorously opposed by Chateaubriand, who termed it the wildest nonsense. Little or no compensation, and no reward in the form of an office, came of this mission, to Stendhal's intense disgust.[6]

Did he not say often that he felt in himself, despite his fallen fortunes, a pride befitting one who was endowed to be a prefect or even a minister, sufficient sign that he recognized in himself that *esprit supérieur* which his followers in later times discerned in him? And yet he had humiliated himself to beg in vain for some small public office, of a government that in his heart he loathed. That his poverty had brought him to such shame made him detest this government twice over.

Sitting alone in his fifth-floor room in the Rue de Richelieu, he would sometimes feel beside himself with "generous indignation" at the "imbecile Bourbons" whose measures of repression against the people, against freedom of speech and thought, by 1829, made a mockery of the Charter. Did he not exclaim in the presence of conservative persons who might have denounced him, at an hour when the last direct descendant of Louis XIV was reported to be dangerously ill, "I wish that the Duke de Bordeaux would die!" But the very excesses of the King and his minister, Polignac, bred hope that a violent political overturn would soon come. As in 1814, so in 1829 and 1830, curiosity about the political future sustained him.

In these darkening days bitterness and wrath blazed in his heart as he wrote the immensely rebellious novel that was the secret occupation of his mornings and nights. How tense were the times, how raw were tempers was shown by the way in which he now broke with his old friend, the Baron de Mareste.

Mareste was then one of the highest officials of the Prefecture of Police in Paris, and so in a position to know a great deal of inside politics. For seven years Stendhal had been taking breakfast with him daily at the Café de Rouen, then would stroll through the Tuileries for an hour on the way to the other man's office, while they briskly exchanged opinions on the news of the day. Mareste considered himself a disillusioned liberal, indifferent to the work he did so long as it paid well; but now increasingly disgusted at the maladroitness of the Bour-

[6]Farges: *Stendhal diplomate*, pp. 20–29; Colomb, op. cit., p. 60. Farges' intriguing study cites freely from official papers in French Government archives.

bon monarchy, he revealed things that startled Stendhal himself. There were rumors that, in fear of a popular rising, the monarch was prepared to encourage the invasion of France by a foreign army! Such reports, perhaps unfounded, inspired Stendhal to prognostications of the inevitable and early downfall of the regime. This was too much for his friend. Mareste, who was rich, and now "clearly saw the danger to his property," withdrew his own complaints against the government, and made strenuous objection to Stendhal's "indiscretions" in the presence of groups of people in salons, such as might spread alarm or panic. The time had passed for raillery, Mareste urged; their disputes became bitter. Stendhal says:

> I had then barely enough to live on, he had an income of 22,000 francs. I felt that for some time he had been assuming a superior tone. In our discussions of politics he would say: "But you, you have no fortune."

Finally, Stendhal relates: "I came to a most painful resolution, that of changing my café without saying anything to him." He began to take breakfast at the Café Lemblin, also near the Palais Royal, and a haunt of Republicans. Thereafter he saw Mareste only at long intervals. For how could one speak freely to a friend when "*he feared only for his 22,000 francs*"? And yet he was convinced that his friend needed him "to distract him from his black humor caused by the terrible *fear of losing money*."

Old friendships were breaking up on class lines in the spring of 1830, the eve of revolution, as Stendhal came to the end of his novel, *The Red and the Black.*

He was growing old, and more than any other man he was disposed to examine himself, to ask himself constantly: "What am I? What have I been? How have I filled up my life?" And heavens, time was growing short! Who would know that he had always felt himself a "potential" Danton, or a Napoleon even, without office and without baton?[7] Like the brilliant hero of the novel he was writing, Stendhal too might exclaim: "I am a great *perhaps!*"

When, after the distractions afforded by society, travel, or love affairs, Stendhal turned to his writing, he would throw himself into his work with uncommon powers of concentration. His mind traveled fast, he pushed on breathlessly, whole volumes came from his hand in a few weeks or months. But now he wrote with all his soul, spurred by

[7]Balzac, though nearly two decades younger, also was obsessed by Napoleon and kept a statuette of him in his study, with an inscription on it reading: "What he could not achieve with the sword, I shall accomplish by the pen." (Signed) "Honoré de Balzac."

a passion that, though tinged with the bitterness of disappointed ambition, could also rise to heights of noble anger. He had lived hard and reasoned much upon his experiences. He had many ideas, a great deal to say that, as a man of the world, he often politely concealed. But now at last he confessed himself without shame or restraint; he wrote what were his secret beliefs, come what might. And it gave him immense consolation to do this. As Goethe said, to write, to create, was "a deliverance."

Long afterward he remembered the five or six months in which he wrote the bulk of this novel as a time that passed without reckoning, one of the happiest seasons of his life.

Could he publish such an icon-breaking book in this dark age of belated despotism? Perhaps France would be set free? At any rate he had written it down, and, he told himself, it was all done "for the sake of *freedom of thought.*"

CHAPTER XVII

"*The Red and the Black*"

"You are so full of odious truths!"
—Prosper Mérimée to Stendhal.

Un roman c'est un miroir qu'on promène le long d'un chemin.
—Sainte-Réal.

FOR a year following the spring of 1829, Colomb, Stendhal's faithful shadow, saw always lying on his table a large, bound manuscript upon which was written in big letters: "JULIEN." Stendhal told him nothing of this new work. But one morning in 1830, he exclaimed to Colomb, as if talking to himself: "What if we should call it *The Red and the Black* [*Le Rouge et le noir*]?" Thus it was called.

The title has puzzled his readers. But the sub-title, "A Chronicle of the Nineteenth Century," clearly states Stendhal's conception of his book as a social novel; while the phrase: "The Red and the Black," suggests its *idée maîtresse,* its ruling idea, which, as in all truly great works of fiction, epitomizes the historical era that is pictured in the novel. For the "Red" refers to the uniform of the soldier in the time of the republic and empire; the "Black" to the uniform of the priest who, in Stendhal's view, dominated society under the monarchical restoration after Waterloo. In this social history in fictional form the principal character, Julien Sorel, is deliberately choosing the black cassock of the priest in order to have a successful career, where yesterday he would have chosen the rose-colored uniform of Marshal Murat, that son of a French innkeeper, whom Stendhal once saw riding proudly into battle. The title thus suggests both the conflict within Julien, and his secret war with society. By disposition one of the Reds of the preceding generation, he parades about as one of the Blacks of the present, though he has no faith in their religion! Life conceived on these terms, both militant and calculating, accompanied by the sense of constant danger, imposes a terrible inward solitude upon such a man. It is the predestined lot, Stendhal seems to tell us, of the superior individual in a time of social retrogression.

But then, as now, society was divided fundamentally into "Reds" and "Blacks": those who believed that the progress, the liberation of man must be carried on endlessly and by revolution if need be; those who desired, above all, the conservation of the old order and the old faiths.

Stendhal was endowed with a rare historical perspective. An eighteenth-century man, he had seen the stable and genteel old regime vanish, never to return in its pristine form; he had witnessed three revolutions in forty years, and ten different regimes one after the other. It is plain that he grasped the dynamics of social change that the new industrial century had introduced. He could see, and repeatedly said, that the French Revolution was no blind accident, but a Great Divide in history, whereas the Bourbon Restoration was but a false attempt to return to the hierarchic system of Louis XIV. But transient though it seemed, he saw that a regrouping of social classes had been engineered in which, temporarily, the Church, leagued with the aristocracy of the land and with the bourgeoisie of commerce, was dominant. This balance between the ruling classes would shift perceptibly from time to time. But whatever shifts were made, the cultural environment of the new century, essentially bourgeois, though increasingly democratic and individualistic, promised to be hostile to the arts and the human values he cherished.

He recognized energy, to be sure, in the men of business; and it is significant that this man who felt himself at home in Napoleon's bourgeois empire spoke with respect of tradesmen in his novel and in his letters, though he professed to loathe money-getting. Yet he saw that this mercenary society was now a competitive battle-ground, in which men of the lower orders, inspired by education and new opportunities, struggled only for *success*.

But Stendhal could look back to a time when the idea of *success* was no problem because it was determined exclusively by one's birth and status; when religious belief was no problem because all were required to believe. Now men might pay lip service to old faiths and moral values, but these were none the less discredited. Society had become a jungle teeming with "pursuers and possessors." With lightning speed men were transferred from one class or calling to another; they passed back and forth in a desperate, hurrying throng, along unseen stairways, those social escalators that carried some upward and others downward. In this cruel stampede, it was as if only lust for money and power possessed all men, and not only the gospel of Christ but the French Revolution's doctrines of the natural rights of man were being abandoned.

But what of the generation of youth, endowed with talents and education, in whom religious dogma had been replaced by faith in a humane social ideal, in dreams—if you wish—of justice and earthly happiness? They were given books to read, their ambitions were exalted, then they were thrown into the wilderness of society to survive as best they could. The dominant theme of the novel was to be the education for life of a modern youth, Julien Sorel, as it was also to be the theme of many famous nineteenth-century novels or autobiographies of disillusionment that came after Stendhal—from Musset's *Confessions of a Child of the Century* to Flaubert's *Sentimental Education* and Samuel Butler's *Way of All Flesh*.

Are we here to triumph by force and cunning alone, like beasts of prey? Julien Sorel asks himself in anguish, at the end of his swift, tragic race. "Must one steal, must one betray?" He too sickens with "the malady of the century"; the same disease that will consume Baudelaire, and Flaubert's Fédéric Moreau (in *The Sentimental Education*), who forty years later would also find that "the happiness merited by the excellence of his soul was certainly slow to arrive." At first blush, Stendhal, by choosing this theme, seems to resemble the other disillusioned, melancholy Romantics at war with their century, and longing for escape to some more favoring or more exotic climes. However, the differences are as marked as the resemblances.

The hero of *The Red and the Black* is, in effect, Stendhal himself, hence like nobody else that ever was on land or sea. All that the ex-soldier, ex-courtier, traveler, lover, and society wit has learned of life is deposited in the imaginary Julien Sorel. He feels no vague sentiments and melancholy frustrations, but specific desires, measured almost in mathematical terms. He is no romantic fool, but reasons and examines himself at every instant of experience. He is the spirit of analysis in action; he is will, audacity, and energy, and unlike the sad heroes of the other Romantic writers, knows how to gain power, how to use it, now with ruse, now with violence. Julien Sorel *is* one of the superior minds of literature, a mask of Stendhal.

The inspiration for the story of Julien Sorel came to Stendhal from life itself, that is, at second hand, when in October 1828 he read the report of an extraordinary murder trial recently held at the Court of Assizes of his native Grenoble.

The case of the young seminary student of Grenoble, Antoine Berthet, was one of crime committed for the sake of material ambition: it fascinated Stendhal not only as a superb specimen of what he termed *un beau crime*, but as containing the moral essence of contemporary history. This youth had served as tutor at the home of a wealthy lawyer, Michout, well known to the Beyle family. Berthet had seduced Mme. Michout, while occupied in educating her children. The affair had been hushed up; he had been dismissed, and then found similar employment at the house of another of Grenoble's leading citizens, this time a nobleman named De Cordon, and had ended by seducing the daughter of this employer too! Expelled from the seminary he attended—after the scandal was exposed by a servant maid—his career frustrated, he had gone to the church which his former mistress, Mme. Michout, attended each day, fired two shots at her with a pistol, then tried to kill himself, though he was only lightly wounded.

The testimony of Berthet showed the finesse with which he practiced seduction and blackmail, it recorded his remarkable charges that these women had "corrupted his youth." In his appeal for clemency, puerile, romantic, and egotistic, he confessed that love had been *but an instrument of his ambition*, adding:

> "It is too bad that I missed the career for which I was destined. I would have made a good priest. I would have known well how to move human souls. I believe I would have been particularly skillful in playing upon the chords of human passions."

There was another famous criminal case that seemed to Stendhal no less symptomatic than Berthet's, which he discussed in a digressive passage of the *Promenades dans Rome* at this same period, 1829. This time it was a Paris cabinetmaker named Laffargue who committed a crime of jealous passion by killing his mistress. But what absorbed Stendhal, who, like De Quincey, was a student of "murder as a fine art," was the "intense exaltation" shown by this assassin when he spoke of his crime in court; he had executed it with a remarkably cold will and energy. And, while pretending to be jesting, Stendhal remarked that the upper classes of society seemed to have lost the capacity to feel great passion and to *will powerfully*, and that this was conserved principally in the lower classes. He concluded: "Probably all the great men of tomorrow will issue from the class to which M. Laffargue belongs."

It must be noted that all the Romantic poets and novelists wrote of gory crimes; but Stendhal reasoned about them coolly and, rightly or wrongly, correlated them with the stirrings of discontent he perceived in the lower classes.

In his novel, intended both as a study in the natural history of morals and as a thoroughgoing attack on the decadent society that followed the Empire and the Republic, he used the figure of young Berthet as his hero. Soon he identified himself wholly with the poor seminary student. Had not his own career been disrupted by the downfall of Napoleon, in whom he saw in retrospect the military instrument of revolution, the genius of energy, remembering less and less his despotism and immense brutalities? At various times Stendhal's sentiment toward the Glorious Emperor changed decidedly. Hatred of the Bourbon monarchy, at this period, nourished the cult of Bonaparte in many hearts and forms one of the accompanying themes of *The Red and the Black*.

For Stendhal too (like the other Romantics) believed that he had been born "too late." He had lived as a boy in the heroic days of Danton and Carnot and the Convention. He had enlisted as a soldier to fight for the overthrow of feudalism and kings. "Under the Republic we were as great as the early Romans!" he would cry. Talent and leadership and heroism had been engendered in the masses of people; this democratic trend had continued under the Consular Republic, the phase of Napoleon's career which Stendhal most admired.

But now the kings and their priests had returned; the defenders of divine right held back public opinion with bayonets. Like a leprosy, conventionalism and vanity spread through society, afflicting nobles and bourgeois alike. To him it appeared, as to the great historian, Michelet, some years later, that the Jesuits directed a vast conspiracy designed to keep the people in ignorance and submission. But nonetheless the common folk had learned much, thanks to the Revolution; irrepressible ambition and energies stirred within them. A year like 1793, which the conservative party dreaded above all things, would erupt again. History was to Stendhal's positivistic faith a series of struggles or crises, in which men sometimes retreated but always advanced again toward greater liberty, knowledge, and earthly enjoyments.

"Two hundred thousand Julien Sorels," he wrote in a letter defending his novel, conspired among the thirty millions in France who still had no right to vote, waiting grimly for their chance, and nothing could stop them. They had seen "lawyers' clerks become senators and counts of the Empire. How do you expect that they should not overthrow the regime of those loafers [the royalist monarchy]? Perhaps the Terror that will come will be less bloody?"

The Red and the Black is, in truth, strong meat. It is in one sense a sort of devil's manual of revolt, in which the weak and oppressed are shown using the arms of civilized society, ruse, against the strong. One hundred and ten years afterward, in 1940, the Resistance in defeated, occupied France, ruled by fascists, made the teachings of Stendhal and his hero, Julien, their secret cult. The time had come again, the men of the Underground whispered to themselves, when, like Julien, one must be ready to die for certain ideas.

2

The setting of *The Red and the Black* is the provincial, middle-sized town of "Verrières," situated in mountainous eastern France, near Besançon. But it is easy to see that Verrières is really mountain-rimmed Grenoble, where Henri Beyle's unhappy, rebellious boyhood was spent, and whence he escaped at the age of sixteen.

In its first half the novel's action follows the grand lines of the story of the seminary student, Berthet; its chief characters are drawn from the Grenoble families involved in that passional drama. But Stendhal superimposes the story of his own youth upon that of Berthet, and tells it with a singular vividness and sardonic humor. In the second volume, whose scene is Paris, the action closely follows the Berthet case with some variations, becoming a projection of Stendhal's own life *as it might have been.*[1]

Julien Sorel is the offspring, not of the old bourgeoisie as was Henri Beyle, but of an ignorant and avaricious peasant, a sawyer who, utterly indifferent to the signs of brilliance and sensitivity in his son, beats him brutally and drives him each day to the same chores as are performed by his rough-handed brothers. The tender protection of a mother was lost to him at an early age. At eighteen, Julien has read books far beyond his age and is a master of Latin. An honest old Jansenist priest, the Abbé de Chélan, has acted as his mentor and friend; his only other friend is a retired surgeon of Napoleon's army, a Liberal, who instills in him some of his own equalitarian ideals, and the nostalgia for the days of glory that seem in 1823, when the novel opens, to have vanished forever.

[1]Contemporary critics found the plot bizarre, and—like Joseph Wood Krutch, in his *Five Masters* (1930)—were unaware that Stendhal quite literally followed the court records of such a case.

Ardently Julien lives in the world of his dreams, from which he is repeatedly and rudely recalled by the blows of his father and the heavy burdens he is ordered to bear. Under this sadistic treatment (like Stendhal) the boy conceives an immense father-hatred; sometimes he fancies himself "a sort of foundling, hated by my father!" His fear and hate is also directed to all the other persons who may have authority over him, including the other members of the family. The cruelty of his upbringing makes him secretly rebellious, but because he is young and weak, this rebellion takes the form of *hypocrisy*. Since the other people around him are cruel and stupid, always ready to injure each other, or himself, as he reasons precociously, they merit the tactics of deception.

Like the young Beyle, Julien longs to leave his native city; "he abhors Verrières, and all that he sees there freezes his imagination." In recompense he dreams of escaping to Paris, meeting beautiful women, living a brilliant career, engaging in daring adventures. In secret he reads Voltaire and other forbidden authors. He experiences moments of exaltation; he is full of a pride and a courage that waits only for its chance.

But what career is open to him? The days of the great revolutionary captains are ended. In their place the priests seem to reign everywhere. And Julien determines to "seek his fortune by becoming a priest." Though disliking the Old Testament, he memorizes the New Testament from beginning to end, recites any part of it upon request, and manages, by his combination of precocious learning and external piety, to arouse the wonder of all Verrières. (What he really believes in is Napoleon's *Mémorial de Sainte-Hélène*, in which the victor of Austerlitz represents himself as the arbiter between the past and the future of Europe.)

From the wretchedness in which he lives he is suddenly rescued by the offer of the town's mayor, M. de Rênal, to employ him as tutor to his children. The richest man in town, Rênal, by engaging a private tutor, seeks to put out of countenance the next richest man, Valenod, governor of the town jail, who has just acquired two spanking new coach horses. After some hard bargaining between Rênal and his father, Julien is ordered to go and live at the Rênal mansion.

He is a slender, handsome youth, with delicate features and fine eyes, a compound of craftiness and innocence. His first meeting with the mistress of the Rênal mansion is a scene drawn with remarkable finesse. The self-consciousness and timidity of the boy, his awareness of his ragged clothes, his sense of inferiority, his dazzlement at the beauty of this highborn woman, and his envy of the splendor of style in which his masters live—all his mingled emotions upon entering this unfamiliar world are clearly delineated. "How happy these rich people are!" he exclaims to himself in an access of class hatred. At the same time, despite his furtive and humble airs, the boy feels a vague but powerful attraction to Mme. de Rênal, a beautiful woman of thirty, and of a distinctly maternal type. It is like the first meeting of Jean-Jacques Rousseau and Mme. de Warens, in the *Confessions.*

While he tutors the children faithfully, and feigns coldness and reserve, he plans in the most deliberate manner, step by step, to seduce Mme. de Rênal. The terrible thing is that his strategy is bound up with an ambition and a pride that seeks vengeance upon these people of superior fortune. Suffering in childhood has made Julien an "enemy of society."

The relations with Mme. de Rênal are a key to the central problem of the novel: the conflict in Julien between the motives of self-interest (ambition, pride) and the laws of passion. In scheming to seduce her, Julien at first writes out for himself "a whole, detailed plan of campaign," like a military tactician. At the beginning he engages her interest by his vivacity and wit in conversation, so that she can scarcely wait until her dull, aging husband is gone, to be with him. Then, in the dark of the garden at night, sitting with her and a lady companion, he screws up his courage to seize her hand stealthily; she removes it; he takes it again. Step by step he assails one position after another, for as the virtuous mother of three children she defends herself earnestly—even against herself. He takes one liberty after another, extends his empire over her soul.

Julien is shown, at first, as horribly afraid; "he carried his life in his hands, feeling that a single false step might ruin him, yet he is also resolved never to show fear." Gaucherie and boldness struggle within him.

It is as one entering great and dubious battle that his "attack" is begun:

> "When the clock strikes ten, I shall take her hand, or go upstairs and blow out my brains. . . . I may be crude, but I will not be *weak.*"

And after she has permitted him to hold her hand,

> His heart was flooded with joy, not because he loved Mme. de Rênal, but because a fearful torment was now at an end. . . . *He had done his duty, and a heroic duty.*

With him it is always a "duty" to run such "risks"; he believes in a system, an "ideal plan he had set himself to follow," failure of which would make him ridiculous in his own eyes, and filled with a sense of inferiority. He tells himself: "I *ought* to be stirred by her beauty; I *owe* it to myself to be her lover."

This enterprise that begins without love on Julien's part becomes one of the most remarkable love stories in all literature. The womanly nobility and virtue of Mme. de Rênal are undeniable; but passion, in its resistless growth, dissected stage by stage, until it reaches that of *crystallization,* compels her to yield to him, despite duty and the fear of hell. (Julien too, after all his subtle calculations and stratagems, is eventually trapped by the "sublime unexpected" in life which Stendhal courts everywhere.) She yields, in the face of all her terrors, when one day he tells her that he will come to her room in the early hours of the morning or kill himself. The end of this scene is a page out of Stendhal's own curious sex life. The surprise and joy he feels at possession of a woman so noble and beautiful at first unmans Julien (as with Henri and the women he loved in earlier days). "What made Julien a superior being was exactly that which prevented him from tasting to the full the happiness laid at his feet." And afterward, he asks himself: "Heavens—to be loved, is it only that?" Then, self-consciously, like an actor, or a soldier on parade: "Have I played my part well?" And what a part, Stendhal comments ironically, "that of a man accustomed to shine before women!"

The love of the youth and the older woman is strengthened by the very sense of guilt that alternates in her soul with passion. At one moment she is shown almost unable to close her eyes in sleep because of the memory of her happiness with Julien; but at the next "*suddenly the frightful word 'adultery' came to her.* All that was vilest and most debauched . . . in the idea of physical love presented itself to her imagination." Thus Stendhal notes how words dominate our emotions.

When her young son falls sick, Mme. de Rênal is convinced that God is punishing her for her transgression; her feelings alternate from pleasure to remorse, she is between "heaven and hell," and he not a little pleased because the supernatural now appears as a rival. Wonderingly he remarks: "She feels that she is killing her son, yet she continues to love me." And this, he reflects, though she is an aristocrat and he the son of a laborer. "At times their happiness assumed the physiognomy of crime. . . ."

However, since the author is anti-clerical, the child recovers full health, and the mother, too. She had all but confessed her fault to her husband; but he, stupid man, had refused to understand. It is an anonymous letter, which a chambermaid addresses to the master, that brings trouble down upon them. As M. de Rênal paces the floor during a sleepless night, the movement of his thought is rendered most brilliantly by Stendhal: Who could have dictated such a letter to him and with what object? the tormented cuckold wonders. He knew that "he had earned the jealousy and hatred of the majority of the townspeople." To reveal his secret to his intimate friends would give them nothing but pleasure. He was envied because the King of ——— had slept in his town house, and because he had made "such a splendid thing of his country house at Vergy," which had a dazzling white façade and windows with green shutters, setting all the other old gray-stone châteaux of the region in the shade.

> For a moment he was comforted by the thought of this magnificence, visible for a distance of three or four leagues.

Even in his sorrow, Stendhal shows, the man's vanity interposes, leads his fancy to wander, and the accidental image of his magnificent white mansion comes to console him.

But M. de Rênal is chiefly afraid that others will *believe* in this scandal and *ridicule* him if he honors it by dismissing Julien. In this crisis Mme. de Rênal shows a profound feminine resourcefulness by instructing Julien to produce a second anonymous letter indicating that Valenod, her husband's rival, is at the bottom of the affair, because of his desire to attach Julien to his own service. To this hoax Julien lends himself with all his "Jesuitical verve" so that the husband's fears are quieted. Nevertheless, discretion leads Julien to absent himself from the Rênal château and reside in Verrières for a week. Splendidly dressed, a local celebrity, he dines out with the notables of the place: those who flourish by stealing bread from the town prison; those who are God's bishops but live only for food and drink. Among these persons figuring in Stendhal's vigorous satire of provincial society, Julien continues to move with adroitness, a man of subterfuge, hating them, yet using his tongue to conceal his thoughts, speaking fair words and telling them only "what they would like to hear."

But Julien is not merely a perfidious fellow who turns the methods of Jesuitism against the Jesuits. His concealed hatred of these provincial nabobs, we must note, is based on close observation of their business morals—as Stendhal himself observed them in Grenoble or Marseille in earlier life. For example, a sumptuous banquet to which Julien is invited, at the house of Valenod, the governor of the town jail, is interrupted by the noise of the hungry prisoners howling and singing obscene songs in the adjacent detention house. The crooked Valenod at once sends a servant to silence the prisoners by force so that the feast may go on. "To stop them from singing!" Julien exclaims to himself. "Oh God, and thou suffereth it!" What vermin these people were; and he reflects: "The conventions are laws destined for mediocrities by mediocrities."

Yet the time comes when Julien must at last part from Mme. de Rênal and enter the seminary of Besançon to study for the priesthood. A "skeleton army of defense" composed of fifty thousand priests holds down the people, and Julien, the unbelieving Jacobin, must join them. If he should become a bishop at forty, like the magnificent and perfumed one he has met during that potentate's official visit to Verrières, he too might have 100,000 francs a year!

The gloomy opening scene of his initiation before the stern rector of the seminary, Pirard, is one of the most powerful chapters of the book, and in it Stendhal writes a bitter indictment of all such religious institutions. The description of Julien's fellow students, of the way they eat—a test of their spiritualism—of the intrigues and dissensions within the seminary and bishopric, are further occasions for polemics against the orthodox religion. Julien is "persecuted" because he is the favorite of the honest Gallican, Pirard, who is also pursued by a cabal. Julien is hated too because, try as he may to conceal it, "he still has the air of thinking." And the Abbé Pirard says: "You will always be a stranger among them."

Nevertheless he fasts and prays as hard as anyone, and shines forth as a theologian. How strong and astute he is, is shown by an examination in Latin, during which one adroit father lures him into displaying his passionate admiration for Vergil, Horace, and other profane authors. Upon demand he recites lengthy passages of their poems from memory, seduced by his examiner's apparent approbation—until the other man, suddenly changing his expression, turns upon him and heaps bitter reproaches on his head for having wasted his time in such useless and sinful studies.

Was Julien shocked or indignant at this snare? No, he masters his feelings at once, and "with a modest air, replies: 'Sir, I am a fool, you are quite right.' "

After finishing with the seminary, Julien's first appointment—thanks to the favor of the Abbé Pirard—takes him to Paris as secretary to a minister of the King, the Marquis de la Môle. The picture of this great Paris establishment, in which Julien soon enjoys a most favored position, is drawn from the period of Stendhal's own youthful service with Count Pierre Daru. The re-education of the ex-peasant now proceeds along aristocratic lines; yet, however finely polished he may seem, he remains on his guard, "so to speak a rebellious plebeian at war with society," finding no happiness in this brilliant social world, but feeling only secret scorn for it. The nobles and Ultra-Royalists whom he serves are empty-minded fops; dinners with them are tedious, full of dreary silences in which they wait for the master of the house to speak. The diplomacy, the political intrigue of their class, aimed at repressing the popular will as long as possible, is detestable to Julien, though he plays a notable part in it. More and more he is trusted by the Marquis de la Môle to carry out the most secret or delicate missions. He is promoted in rank and salary, rewarded with a cross of honor; and yet he is eaten by doubt and disillusionment, the sense of never having attained his dreams. It is still "each for himself in this wilderness of egoism that is called life." He loves no man or woman—until Mathilde, the beautiful daughter of the marquis, begins to show some interest in him.

At first, he is impressed only with her haughtiness, and tries to pique or humiliate her, but as time goes on she reveals an uncommon intellectual curiosity, becomes intrigued by the lowborn young priest, and fancies him as a man of natural force of passion "who will play a leading role, if revolution comes again." Despite her aristocratic birth and training, she too (out of boredom?) seems to long for rebellion; and soon desires only Julien, abandoning her noble fiancé and the idols of her class for his sake. For she needs "anxiety," the whip of danger to excite her.

But he thinks only that "her pride of birth would be like a high fortified hill to be captured." The stratagems of Beylism are then applied to her "subjugation." When, like one of those emancipated bluestockings who appear more and more often in the Romantic age, Mathilde, in an unsolicited letter, declares her unconditional love for him, Julien, after some calculation, determines to preserve this for future use if need be, and has the letter copied and hidden away as evidence. "It must be admitted," Stendhal observes at this point, "that the look in Julien's eyes was atrocious, his whole expression hideous. It suggested unmitigated crime. He was an unhappy man at war with the whole of society."[2]

No, he would not spare her father, who employed, trusted, and re-

[2]Stendhal, the determinist, himself admitted later that Mathilde de la Môle did not conduct herself in accordance with the pattern of social habits dominating her life, or the nineteenth century, but harked back to the "energetic" era of Margaret of Navarre in the early sixteenth century—who had an ancestor of the Môles as her lover, and coolly watched his beheading from her window.

warded him, this misfortune. He would take what was offered and so triumph over those who, though using his services, at heart always despised him as a poor abbé, and a carpenter's son.

When at length the proud minister learns from his daughter, become *enceinte*, of her guilty connection with his secretary, and that it was formed at her own wish, he is at first overcome with wrath. But, like a man of the world, he is shown recovering promptly, then even arranging for the ennoblement of Julien and an early marriage.

3

Up to now—to interrupt for a moment the résumé of *The Red and the Black*—the intrigue of the novel has seemed plausible enough, and based on credible situations and characters, saving perhaps that of Mathilde. However, the fascination of the work, in which Stendhal, in an outburst of creative force, far exceeded anything he had previously written, depends not so much upon the intrigue itself, full of novelty and dialectical brilliance though it is, as upon the profound psychological analysis that accompanies the action. And this running analysis intensifies, rather than weakens, the effect of reality and drama, adding, as it were, a new dimension. Exposing as he does the finest shades of motive and emotion, Stendhal, with his microscope, renders his principal characters more lifelike, more consistent with themselves, than any other romancer of his epoch. We have marvelous insights into human behavior in the ancient writers, in Boccaccio, Cervantes, and Shakespeare; but never, in the novel, certainly not in Fielding, or even the wise Jane Austen, do we have the psychological portrait upon such an extended scale. Stendhal was breaking new ground; one was to wait almost a half century for a Dostoevski—whose *The Possessed* forcibly invites comparison with his work—to meet his like again. Thus, at the flood tide of French romanticism, in the heyday of Dumas *père*, we have one of romanticism's innovators creating the methods of psychological realism, that appears (only superficially) to be the antithesis of literary romanticism, yet was its natural offspring.

Only one younger contemporary, Balzac, was to equal Stendhal in psychological insight, and he was not yet fairly launched upon his vast, inchoate *Comédie humaine*. But Balzac, like Flaubert after him, sees his characters always in the ensemble of their physical setting: their homes, their clothing, their appearances, all described as with a painter's eye. It is by this sensuous method that Balzac obtains his best effects of realism. Stendhal, using only the scantiest physical description, locates or fixes his characters within the pattern of their mental habits, observed by an analytical rather than a sensuous process. He peers beneath the surface ensemble; his lifelong disposition toward "coldly scientific" dissection has helped him to know what there is *inside* people that makes them different. Hence even his exceptional characters, like Julien, appear consistent and credible; so with the other "superior personalities," like M. de la Môle, or the very feminine Mme. de Rênal, or the merchants, bishops, ministers, who are all made strikingly real, by one who profoundly observed the minds of such persons.

But then few novelists, in modern times, have written with Stendhal's experience and wisdom of life behind them. Most writers do with only a few ideas, if any; not many novelists are truly intelligent, or have the intelligence of a Stendhal—certainly not a Balzac or Flaubert—so that every page he writes bubbles over with ideas.[3] For he is essentially the psychologist and moral philosopher, using the novel as the medium for his speculations, now ironical or paradoxical, now challenging by their profound truth.

Since the end of the last century the figure of Julien Sorel has become a powerful symbol for many of our modern writers; his words have been their articles of faith. Was he solely, as Sainte-Beuve wrote, the prototype of the "careerist . . . seeking only to make his way in the world, with the unique, cold passion of educated and impoverished youth?" Was he but a figure of evil, a "sinful youth," like the castaway Rousseau in early life? This was not Stendhal's idea, and we cannot understand the denouement, if we hold this view.

Clearly Julien is the product of an unfortunate childhood, feels himself persecuted, and only in self-defense becomes a calculating aggressor, eternally on the alert, fighting even against dangers invented in his own mind. Stendhal explained, in a letter written ten years after his novel appeared, that he had wished "to present a tender and honest young man, and made him ambitious, but also filled with imagination and *illusions.*" (Elsewhere he remarks that he has been much reproached for having dared to picture a character of real "energy" and will.)

Those "illusions" are important to bear in mind. But what are

[3] *The Red and the Black* either enchants its readers at once or repels them. The "fanatics" of Stendhal, during the 1880s and 1890s, memorized whole chapters of this novel and could not get Julien out of their minds. Some felt that they were never again the same men after reading the book! They even engaged in dialectical contests, questioning and answering each other in the terms of Stendhal and his characters. I speak of Paul Bourget, Maurice Barrès, and their circle of friends, in early youth. But Taine, earlier than they, confesses to having read it over eighty-four times!

they? We know that he has ideas of martial heroism, of personal honor, even of political liberalism; he is scrupulous about money, loyal in his services, and none can bribe him, for he does not really desire worldly gains. Though he can be coldly logical or "Jesuitical" toward men, those who are sincere and approach him with pure hearts, his old Abbé de Chélan, or the republican tradesman, Fouqué, can move him to tears with a word of true kindness. For he is as *sensitive* as Rousseau's Saint Preux. Constantly he asks himself, where do I belong, what will I do in this sort of world in which I have been born? And he promises himself: "I will not follow the bourgeois, middle-of-the-road way of life, I seek rather some revolutionary exaltation!" When his elder friend, Fouqué, in Verrières, offers him a profitable partnership in trade, he firmly rejects it, for the very reason that "it would lead to an assured well-being, and mediocrity," but away from "the heroic dreams of his youth." What he seeks is a life of action, danger, struggle, ambition; he is an "exalted soul." For the sake of his "ideal plan" he will deny all moral inhibitions, giving free reign to his ego. Unlike other romantic heroes, this French (and Napoleonic) precursor of Nietzsche's *Uebermensch* knows what he wants: freedom and the fullness of self-realization. "Be thyself!" is his guiding thought.

Thus in the figure of Altamira, brave Spanish conspirator, whom he meets in Paris society, he recognizes a man after his own heart (like Stendhal's friend Di Fiore, who inspired the same aphorism), and he exclaims with admiration: "There is a man who has won the only distinction which cannot be bought today—that of being condemned to death."

But then, thinking of the great and implacable leaders of the French Revolution, Mirabeau, Danton who stole, Napoleon who looted, he asks himself if moral compunctions may be permitted to arrest the march of humanity toward progress and imperil the welfare of the many. "Is it not permissible to kill two or three men in order to save four?" And turning upon Mathilde, his aristocratic mistress, with a terrible regard—this, too, thrills her—he cries: "In a word, mademoiselle, may not the man who longs to drive ignorance and crime from the earth sweep through us all like a storm, doing evil as if by chance?"

To sum up, Julien, like Stendhal, is a divided personality, perhaps the first truly split personality in the novel, it has been remarked; and the key to his character lies in Stendhal's. While being ideologistic he is "Castilian" and romantic; his "illusions" are Rousseauist intuitions or ideals. Complex, self-conscious, willful, and skeptical though he may be, he is after all but Stendhal's highly original, "anti-romantic" variant of the romantic rebel typified by Byron's *Childe Harold,* or Hugo's *Hernani.* In the end, in the supreme crisis of his life, the unconscious —as I translate Stendhal's *imprévu,* or "unexpected"—the mysticism of the deed will overthrow all that is planful and logical in his life. To solve his moral dilemmas he will destroy himself. But such as he is, amoral, in conflict with himself, filled with "dangerous thoughts," yet reaching toward supreme self-knowledge, Julien is a superior and more refined conception than the other famous romantic heroes, who, in comparison with him, were such simpletons. While they have lost favor, Julien is the fictional creation of nineteenth-century romanticism who most haunts the twentieth century. In creating him, Stendhal showed himself "the first *modern* man," as the painter, André Masson, has said.

4

But to take up the thread of the plot again, while the Marquis de la Môle, though hating Julien, arranges for his marriage with Mathilde, a blow falls that precipitates disaster. Julien had proposed to the marquis that he investigate his record by writing a letter of inquiry to Mme. de Rênal. In reply came a letter written by her hand, but copied from a letter composed by her confessor, denouncing Julien as one who seduced women for the sake of money and position. Doubtless he was repeating his misdeeds at the Môles'. The marquis, now determined that Julien must never be his son-in-law, forbids the marriage and orders Mathilde to have her child in secret. In an indescribable state of emotion, Julien departs for Verrières, arrives at the church there on a Sunday morning, and from behind a pillar fires at Mme. de Rênal twice with his pistol. The first shot misses; at the second she falls, and he surrenders himself to the police, declaring with Stendhalian precision: "I have committed homicide with premeditation. Under Clause Number 1,342 of the Code, I know that I must be condemned to death." A characteristic touch, this, bringing up *the little true fact* that savors so much of reality; and it matters little that there happen to be less than a thousand clauses in the Civil Code, so that the number given is wrong. In no less original a manner Julien, soon afterward, urges his lawyer to speak in his defense "without too many long periods," for he holds the overemphatic, inflated style of oratory in horror.

Once in prison (a place that holds a spell for Stendhal), Julien undergoes a kind of transfiguration. Remorseful and proud, he meditates, reviewing his brief, eventful life, probing for its meaning. By the catharsis of the shot he fired, ambition is destroyed in him and he prepares, as if with joy in his heart, for death. Mathilde rushes to his side; to save him, she spends masses of gold louis, seeks to move altar and throne. But he repels her, saying that he wishes to die: "Leave me my ideal life!" he exclaims; and remarks to himself: "Strange that I did not know how to enjoy life until its end approached so near."

When he learns that Mme. de Rênal was only wounded and is on the way to recovery, he is made happier than ever, but none the less resigned to death.

After having given us, in his first volume, dealing with the provincial scene, a pioneer experiment in psychological realism, a veritable slice of life created out of his own memories, Stendhal, in the second volume of *The Red and the Black*, especially its closing chapters, is less the realist and more the novelist of ideas. As in a play by George Bernard Shaw, the characters become his mouthpieces; they have been that in great measure throughout, but at the end become exclusively so. The penchant of Stendhal, as Balzac said, was for the "literature of ideas." Granted certain premises of material environment and heredity (such as Julien's peasant energy), the rest must follow a logic of "probabilities."

The prison scene now becomes fabulous or allegorical rather than realistic. Here at last, in the confining antechamber of death, the tormented Julien finds "freedom." His friends who gather to defend him, such as the liberal Fouqué, the aged Abbé de Chélan, serve as disciples to this rebellious plebeian, this antichrist, who now appears like a saint seeking martyrdom. Mme. de Rênal, whom he has subconsciously longed for, rejoins him; of course she had not been responsible for the letter dictated by her confessor. She had hoped, in transports of joy, only to "die at the hands of her Julien." And he confesses to himself that it was not the fear of death but "the absence of Mme. de Rênal that had oppressed his spirit." When she joins him in prison their love is at last openly and fully realized. The prison thus becomes a boudoir. Mathilde attempts to banish the older woman, who has made the first and deepest imprint upon Julien, but he informs her coolly that she is merely his "wife," while the other is his "mistress." However, the high-willed Mathilde also clings to him, and so he has two Magdalens as well as apostles. Everybody comes into the prison and discusses everything until his cell begins to resemble a grist mill in a small country town. Since he refuses to use some Julienesque stratagem to escape punishment—now quite feasible, since Mme. de Rênal has recovered—and instead expounds his philosophy to all his visitors, the prison also becomes a rostrum. As in the legendary trial and death of Socrates, Julien places every obstacle in the way of his reprieve. True to himself, he always says or does the unexpected.

At his trial he makes an address to the jury that is an epopee of defiance, a poem of indignation and scorn, denouncing the Philistines who judge him, and inviting them to condemn him. The prisoner's statement proclaiming himself an enemy of their caste seals his doom:

> ". . . Gentlemen, I do not have the honor to belong to your class; you see in me a peasant who revolted against the baseness of his fortune.
>
> "I ask no mercy of you," he continued, raising his voice. "I have no illusions, but see that death awaits me, and that it will be just. . . . But even if I were less guilty, it would not matter, for I see men before me who would punish and discourage forever those youths who, born in an inferior class and . . . oppressed by poverty, have the luck to procure a good education, and the presumption to mingle in what the rich call society."

Julien's final utterances upon life and death bring him to his end in brilliant style. "Tomorrow," he observes, thinking of the guillotine, "I have an appointment for a duel with a gentleman of great skill who never misses his mark."

But in those last night hours he asks himself if there is a God, and if he is the gentle Abbé Fenelon's God of mercy, or only the cruel God of the Old Testament whom he does not wish to meet. Looking back over his twenty-three years, he exclaims: "I have loved truth—where is it? Everywhere charlatans and hypocrites." Unregenerate, he concludes that there is no "natural right . . . only that of self-defense, the force of the lion at bay, the need of the hungry or the cold. . . . In short, in the beginning there was need."

His judgment of himself is significant: "*I have been ambitious; I have acted in accordance with the conventions of the times.*" The people who had condemned him were merely cheats who had not yet been caught in the act; and the chief of his jurors, Valenod, the corrupt governor of the Verrières prison, was a hundred times more injurious to society than Julien.

"This philosophy might be true, but it was of a nature to make Julien desire death," is the author's brief, parting commentary on him.

Thus the subversive Julien Sorel goes to his end, in scenes as rich in the substance of religious legend as they are "Freudian": there is the alienated libido and the expiating martyr, "in love with death";

and there is the mother fixation connected with the middle-aged Mme. de Rênal, and the return to the dark womb of earth which is the prison. Over his personality and its meaning men have debated for a century and will continue so long as youth feels its natural sensibilities outraged by the experience of the real world, and lives in secret conflict with society, giving but false allegiance to interests, institutions, or parties it secretly scorns. For are there not Julien Sorels everywhere among us in American society today, already aware of its contradictions, increasingly poisoned with disillusionment and revulsion? So long as the dilemma of Julien recurs, so long as he is a symptom of a malaise, men will remember him and study his case.

By virtue of this novel alone Stendhal has remained essentially "the man who appeals to us in confused moments, epochs of disturbed social conditions and disorder. . . . Periodically, when individual ambitions are baffled, when the historical movement of society seems deadlocked, when our young people feel that the experience and disciplines they must accept are hateful or painful, and their position in the world dubious or equivocal, at odds with society or with classes"—with the return of such Stendhalian periods, agitated, embittered, and full of clashing influences, Stendhal wins converts again.[4]

In *The Red and the Black*, the antinomy, the contradiction in Stendhal's thought becomes evident; it has troubled many of his most sympathetic critics who hold this to be one of the great novels of the ages —a "Human Comedy" not in forty volumes but in one. We have in this book the eighteenth-century rationalist, the religious skeptic and political liberal overwhelmingly concerned with the irrational and the unconscious. Stendhal advocates an ideology, a logic for the pursuit of happiness; yet his hero is shown destroyed by the unexpected or irrational, and expresses a final disbelief in the existence of any natural law. Julien, it has been said, is "Napoleon without the sword"

---

[4]Blum: *Stendhal et le Beylisme*, pp. 312–13.

It is the contention of one school of Stendhalians that Julien Sorel's life is a parable of the New Testament (". . . *Cette âme de feu, noble et généreuse*," as the author describes him). Zola, who of course was a partisan of the "Reds," found Julien "*une noble nature, sensible, délicate . . . au fond le plus noble esprit du monde. . . .*" And Léon Blum, later, added: "One seeks in vain to learn what is the crime of Julien Sorel. . . . Throughout his career, at the Rênals', in the seminary, in Paris, he acts with perfect probity, ever loyal and without meanness, never betraying a confidence. One finds here none of the cheating of Rousseau or the commonplace peccadillos of youth." And to one contemporary student, Professor Ramon Guthrie of Dartmouth College, Julien's difficulties flow from his unmitigated honesty and from his being "truly religious." To support this view Stendhal is cited as saying: "He [Julien] was a believer—what did the hypocrisies of the priests matter to him? Could they remove the power of the truth or alter the sublimity of the idea of God?"

operating in society; he has also been likened to "the romantic outlaw" of Gothic fiction. In him, it has been charged, we have "the romantic will," which is in reality "nothing but instinct parading as Machiavellian reason." This comes down to anarchic individualism, as it is practiced in the modern world. When, according to this view, his ego enters into conflict with the needs of society, he is doomed to self-destruction.[5]

But such a view ignores the validity of Stendhal's premise that society, as constituted in the industrial age since the early nineteenth century, in the first place imposes war upon the individual. The Julien Sorels are driven to fight for their existence singly or collectively because of the very absence of acceptable values, traditions, or moral codes—such as the New Humanists or Thomists hold should exist to restrict the ego and the will, though they offer nothing truly acceptable to fill the void.

But Julien Sorel is no unreflecting, hysterical hero of Byron or Musset; he is no example of a disordered, lyrical expansiveness. His faith in reason or logic remains unaltered; he sees his case dispassionately, analyzes it for us himself. The reasons for his warfare with society in his time are clearly set forth. Those reasons are still valid. In short, though Julien, like his author, has his ties with the Romantic period, historically speaking, his divergences from the typical characters of that literary era who were, after all, the products of Christian thought, are no less marked.

It would be wrong to think of Stendhal, though bound up with the Romantic movement, as one with the Byrons and Chateaubriands. Unlike them, he repeatedly declared: "I do not say that I have been persecuted by men. . . . I say that men are dominated by vanity and self-interest." The task is therefore to study these motives of interest and passion. He also wrote: "I do not believe that society owes me anything in the least. . . . Society pays for what it wants."

Stendhal's own spirit was not turned toward violence and self-destruction; ambition in him underwent the most curious lapses. The quest of happiness did not lead him to struggle for power, but increasingly toward a life of inward harmony, toward tranquillity, much like the followers of Epicurus who were Stoics at heart.

Stendhal's function was both diagnostic and prophetic; he pictures a society whose false authorities and pharisaical social code breed individual and group maladjustment. The problem of sexual therapy looms large in his thought, as it was to be central in Freud's. The problem of

[5]William Troy, "Stendhal," *The Partisan Review*, Jan.–Feb., 1942.

class hatred, the group sense of inferiority, so to speak, is equally prominent.

Though universal enough in his interests, like a Goethe or Voltaire, he offered no "complete" or closed system of philosophy, but rather a critical and suggestive one. One must not read him too literally or humorlessly where, with design, he sets off his petards to waken those of us who have allowed their consciences to fall asleep.

But in his great novel, as everywhere in his intimate writings, are scattered suggestions or proposals for that "transvaluation of values" which Nietzsche was to undertake a half century later in a wholly different spirit from Stendhal's. Stendhal's "Happy Few"—those who understand his "logic" of the pursuit of happiness—would become Nietzsche's elite of "supermen" pursuing power.[6] However, the unhappy Nietzsche (who was no Nazi, in truth, but suffered rather from the literal debasement of some of his ideas) served the same function as Stendhal, in administering a devastating criticism of our social idols and challenging us to overhaul our whole moral system, a work that is always to be done over and over again. And long before him, Stendhal had asked us, in effect, to determine what goals our ethics propose. He overturns and probes everything; and it is not surprising that Nietzsche, the real founder of modern psychology and pragmatism, read him with delight, when almost none read him, and wrote in *Ecce Homo*:

> Stendhal is one of the happiest accidents of my life . . . and is quite priceless, with his anticipatory psychologist's eye; with his grasp of facts, reminiscent of the greatest master of facts (*ex ungue Napoleoneum*).

Stendhal, however, was no mere reckless defender of the unbridled ego, or the expansive will (any more than Nietzsche later). He was, admittedly or not, *both* a follower of Rousseau, the teacher of the morality of passion and enthusiasm, and of the materialists who opposed Rousseau. Long and earnestly he expounded the rational and utilitarian theory of human morals; he proposed a "logic" of happiness and continued to urge this to the end. He was clairvoyant enough to see the unconscious, the irrational, the violent in man, and face the problems they imposed courageously—unknown areas to be explored,

[6]As early as 1817 he had dedicated the second volume of his *History of Painting in Italy*, in cryptic fashion "*To the Happy Few.*" This is the first hint of the idea of a cultured elite which, for Stendhal, included only those choice souls who understood the art of pursuing happiness. "That explains the whole book; I dedicate it to sensitive souls," he said in this dedication.

Elsewhere he refers to the Happy Few as those who "oddly enough have the habit of thinking as they read."

to be conquered by knowledge, still to be mastered today. With age, Stendhal continued to perfect the tools of analysis and judgment in himself. His reasoning upon men and events shows a marvelous discrimination and sensibility, actually balancing the demands of intelligence against those of intuition or sensibility. The irreconcilables, the contradictions in Julien Sorel are synthesized artistically in the novel. In Stendhal's own personality they are reconciled in the art and manner of his life, day by day. This is no doubt part of his enduring interest for modern man.

But even Stendhal's modern opponents testify to the "obsessive" and "terrifying" reality that his Julien Sorel holds for us today; clear evidence that the conditions making for such character are present in greater force than ever. Proof enough of Stendhal's enduring value as prophet and truth sayer.

5

When *The Red and the Black* appeared several months after the July Revolution in 1830—it would certainly have been suppressed by the Prince de Polignac if his wretched ministry had continued—excitement still prevailing in France contributed to its being neglected, though decidedly less so than Stendhal's other books. What attention it received was fiercely hostile. Jules Janin, one of the most powerful literary critics of the day, slated the book in the *Journal des débats*, calling it an "amphitheater for the dissection of moral leprosies" and a "defamation of the human soul." Yet Janin, though terming him a "cruel mocker who believed nothing and respected nothing," bestowed some indirect flattery, and predicted that the author would be more widely read in future years than in his own time. Even Stendhal's friend Mérimée refused to come to his defense, holding that the "aim of art is not to show this side of the human soul." In other words Stendhal was vigorously denounced as a moral scoundrel, but to his delight he was no longer ignored, and his novel attained a moderately successful sale of fifteen hundred copies.

He pretended to understand nothing of all the attacks on him, and puzzled his friends, now by denying, now by admitting that Julien Sorel was based on himself:

> Good heavens! [he wrote to Mme. Ancelot]. When did I ever climb a ladder to your boudoir window? Doubtless I often desired to do so, but did I ever show such boldness?

However, to that mischief-maker among writers, Henri de Latouche, he said: *"Julien Sorel, c'est moi."*

Printed in May 1830, the actual publication and sale of *The Red and the Black* was seriously delayed, up to November, by the outburst of the very revolution it prophesied.

For years Stendhal had waited for this event with impatience. In 1825, he had witnessed the funeral of General Foy, popular chief of the Liberal party, attended by 100,000 persons, who made the funeral procession an occasion for insurrectionary rioting. In April 1827, he had seen riots at a review of the National Guard in Paris, when, with Charles X looking on, soldiers cried out to him: "Down with the Ministry!" But the Bourbon monarch had fixed his mind only upon restoring the absolute rule of Louis XIV. The appointment of the reactionary Polignac as his Prime Minister in 1829, the Ordinances of July 26, 1830, finally suppressing freedom of the press, and the annulment of recent elections in order to prepare a new, more restricted electoral law were unbearable provocations that led finally to the explosion of July 27, 1830. Even the ineffable Talleyrand, who had brought back the Bourbons in 1814, was saying that they would have to be driven out again that France might have peace.

Stendhal had feared up to the last, as did even Armand Carrel, the fiery republican leader, that military force might prevail once more. But on July 27, the people pouring out into the streets with wild enthusiasm, the trees felled in the main avenues, the barricades, the steady rattle of musketry told another story. On the following climactic day, the 28th, he was in his room quietly reading Napoleon's *Mémorial de Sainte-Hélène*—as a dated marginal note of his reveals—while outside, in the center of town, near the Rue de Choiseul where he lived:

> [Page 147]: Fusillade, platoon firing while I read this page 1:15 p.m. [Page 148]: Complete *sang-froid* of the people. . . . [Page 195]: Beginning of gunfire that I hear in reading this page. Those are the Jesuits who are shooting . . . 1:45 p.m. [Page 151]: Platoon firing, very steady, now at 1:51. [Page 201]: 1:55. The firing which was in the east has passed to the south. It is less intense. Platoon firing near the Carrousel or in that general direction.

It was entirely typical of the now middle-aged Stendhal, who in youth had hankered only to witness great events or know great sensations, that he refrained from mounting any barricades, making inflammatory speeches, or using a pistol, which he handled well, but instead sat quietly reading a book. Neither great crimes (such as he pretended to admire) nor acts of heroism, such as he advocated, were undertaken by him. For him, violence was henceforth to be an exclusively literary exercise. Yet the firing brought his own liberation steadily nearer.

On the third of the "July Days," the 29th, when the armed people of Paris finally defeated the King's men, the happy Stendhal could no longer contain his curiosity, and that morning, as he tells us, went to the Palais Royal section, and there, squatting on his posteriors behind the pillars of the Théâtre Français, listened to the music of the musket balls and witnessed the final rout of the Swiss Guards.

It is my duty to add here that, undismayed by many previous reverses, our impenitent, bewigged Lovelace had recently acquired a new and youthful mistress, his eleventh or twelfth, I estimate. For one of his random autobiographical notes on the 1830 revolt tells us: "I spent the night of July 29 with Mme. G. to calm her terror."

During the 1820s Stendhal used to make the paradoxical statement that he felt himself at heart an aristocrat who "hated the rabble, yet at the same time most passionately desired their happiness under the name of the 'people.' "

But now he declared that "never in his life would he forget the beautiful sky of July 29 and the tricolor floating again above the Tuileries Palace" for the first time in fifteen years. And it was the rabble who had done the fighting! "For every man who owned a coat, ten wore smocks and were without stockings." The common people showed themselves both brave and magnanimous. They alone had courage and energy, he exclaimed once more, writing from Italy, a few months later. He was then defending his novel, *The Red and the Black*, which had been locked in the printing shop during the battle, and said:

> Look at July 1830, when ten thousand of the rabble fought, Heaven knows why! And not a Montmorency among them! Not one, and everything was going *their* way. Those people [the aristocrats] would have fought in a duel; but good tone forbade, under pain of eternal disgrace, that they should fight in the streets.

The memory of the 29th of July, he also said in a letter of August 15, 1830, was ineffaceable:

> The more one is separated by time, and looks back at the great week, as M. de Lafayette terms it, the more surprising it seems. It is like the effect produced by colossal statues. By Mont Blanc, which is more sublime seen from below, at twenty leagues from Geneva, than at its base.
>
> All that the newspapers have reported in praise of the common people is true. . . . Out of one hundred men on the 28 July, only one man was well clad. The lowest *canaille* was heroic and full of the most noble generosity after the battle.

The Bourbon king, Charles X, morosely rode off to England. The cry was for a true constitution, two chambers, and universal suffrage. "Lafayette is the anchor of our liberties," Stendhal surmised. But the King's cousin, Louis Philippe, the Duke of Orléans, was in the offing as a compromise arrangement, as he also foresaw. In any case the press would be free; his heretical novel could be published; his liberal friends would now compose the party in power. None too soon, for Stendhal's fine clothes were almost threadbare, his pockets were empty.

CHAPTER XVIII

The Consul

ON THAT tumultuous summer day of 1830 it was General Lafayette, then the idol of the republican Left, who had saved France for law and order, and from the steps of the Hôtel de Ville in Paris conferred his blessings upon Louis Philippe as "the best of republicans." Stendhal, somewhat earlier, had prophesied that in the event of collapse of the Bourbon regime, the Duke of Orléans, rich, clever, enlightened as he was believed to be, would have the ardent support of "every bourgeois with four thousand to six thousand francs a year." The Citizen King had often expressed his admiration for English parliamentary institutions; he began by flattering the republicans and choosing a government "a little left of center." Besides, Lafayette, chief of the National Guard (whose wonderfully wavering qualities were not yet appreciated), was considered the power behind the new king, and a guarantee that promises of reform would be honored.

What followed was to be most disillusioning to the little people who, as Stendhal testifies, gallantly did all the fighting in July. But what was most important for him at the moment was that the Liberals, those genteel conspirators who under Lafayette's banner foregathered at Tracy's parlor, now controlled the loaves and fishes of public offices. Joining the rush for jobs, Stendhal sent his card around, and with the "heroic" support of his own and Lafayette's friends, came out in September 1830 with something less than he had hoped for, no prefecture, alas, but at any rate a consulship at Trieste, then Austrian territory, and a salary of twelve thousand francs a year. From this he would have to deduct several thousand francs for the expenses of his establishment and staff. But whereas in 1829 he had been in despair and had thought seriously of "saying good night to everybody," the 1830 Revolution saved him from penury and made him, in truth, almost rich.

Another stroke of fortune, as he would term it, had come to him earlier that year, at the time when he was finishing *The Red and the Black*. On an evening in January, while at the home of Cuvier, the natural scientist, he had shown himself in such rare conversational form that a young Italian lady who was present was much taken by him. On leaving she had offered to conduct him in her carriage to his home in the Rue de Choiseul, and engaged him in animated talk upon Italy and love. Only a few days later, meeting him again, the impetuous young woman declared: "I love you!" She added: "I know well that you are old and ugly . . . but I love you." One day in March 1830, she surrendered herself to him without reservation or regret.

He was not merely pleased, but surprised, for he could now make no claims to youthfulness, and he noted down in a scrap of diary, "Come, jump, Marquis! Think of it, four days after forty-seven years a young girl tells you: 'I love you!' "

The lady, Giulia Rinieri, was nineteen at the time, and was of good family, being the niece and adopted daughter of Daniele Berlinghieri, who served as Minister to France for the Grand Duke of Tuscany. How serious the affair was for Stendhal is shown by the fact that he used the utmost discretion, wrote almost nothing about her, never boasted of Giulia to his friends; only long afterward did the curious Mérimée learn of his having a "rich and amiable young Italian woman" as his mistress.

These days he suffered from gout and "gravel," and began to entertain serious fears for his health. He had quite despaired of ever arousing again a genuine passion for himself in a woman he might love. Yet now in the autumn of his life came this new love of a young girl. In November 1830, as he prepared to make the long journey to the city on the Adriatic, faced with years of loneliness and boredom in a foreign land, he determined to seek Giulia's hand in marriage. To her uncle and guardian he wrote humbly:

> It is perhaps a great presumption on my part, poor and old as I am, to avow that I would consider the supreme happiness of my life assured if I could obtain the hand of your niece.
>
> The sole fortune I have is my office; I am forty-seven years old; I am too poor to be concerned with the dowry of Mademoiselle. Even if I were rich I would not be any more interested in that. I regard it as a miracle to have been loved at forty-seven. . . .

However, Signor Berlinghieri, who knew something of M. Beyle's reputation, postponed a decision, evidently hoping that his niece would soon forget her strange infatuation. Stendhal departed alone for Italy. In Trieste, he who had so vehemently denounced the marriage bond now lived only in anticipation of forming it with his Giulia. In a renewed plea, he offered to have Giulia arrange to stay with him only six months of the year, spending the rest of the time with her aged uncle, to whom she was greatly attached. Tremulously he laid plans for their marriage to be held in one of the lovely lakeside towns of the Italian Alps, his favorite retreat.

He waited. The next year, 1831, when Giulia and her uncle came to Siena, their native city, Stendhal paid them a discreet visit, remained as Berlinghieri's guest for several days, and renewed his suit, though in vain. Since he was an unwelcome and suspicious representative of France in the realm of the Austrian Emperor, his mysterious visit to Florence and Siena, in November 1831, was carefully watched by the Duke of Tuscany's police, who were in close touch with Metternich's espionage organization. Besides, the times in Italy had been threatening ever since the July Revolution in Paris; whole provinces had risen in insurrection under the Carbonari. And so the notorious and impious Liberal was once more shadowed by police spies both in Florence and Siena. Their report showed that he had called on the French ambassador to Rome, who had halted during a voyage to Paris, at Florence. Also that he had entered a bookshop, the usual haunt of subversive men, and "though there were Liberals there, did not speak to them, but only read the newspapers. . . . Nothing reprehensible had been discovered in the movements of Signor Beyle."[1] How relieved the Grand Duke and his officers would have been if they had discovered the woman in the case!

To his grief, his marriage offer was finally rejected, though in most friendly terms, on the ground of difference in age. Two years later, he was deeply chagrined to learn that Giulia had married another and younger man. He seemed fated to live out his days alone, and now entering his sixth decade, no longer enjoyed his bachelor state. Besides, Italy was no longer the paradise it had been for him in his youth. It is dangerous to retrace one's steps. The years that he now passed there were disconsolate. A measure of happiness remained (though limited), for Giulia's feeling toward him did not change after marriage.

[1]H. Martineau, *Le Divan*, Mars-Avril, 1935, presents an extract of the old police archives, which bears out Stendhal's conviction that he was often persecuted and spied upon.

At long intervals, once in a year or two, by dint of wearisome journeys, he continued to see her again secretly.

He had arrived in Trieste on November 25, 1830, donned an imposing blue uniform, with high embroidered collar and gold buttons, and taken charge of his office, which employed a half-dozen clerks and consular agents. The consulate was established in one of the handsomest villas of the port, and had six large high-ceilinged rooms. By social precedent, the French consul had the place of one of the first citizens of the town. "In the street people uncover their heads and bow to the ground before me," he reported with amusement. His duties, including the routine of issuing visés, inspection of ships, and reports on trade, afforded him at first a pleasant distraction, and he described them as on the whole a cheerful and "paternal labor."

He had desired a "warm haven" for his old age, but soon found that Trieste, represented as a place of gentle climate, suffered from the *borea,* a cold wind sweeping offshore that gave him the miseries. The vast German porcelain stove in his house overheated the place so much that he felt suffocated. Not less suffocating was the society of the provincial Austro-Italian city. Though he came armed with letters from M. Meyerbeer, the composer, to Trieste's leading hostess, a certain Frau Reyer (who was of Italian descent), and though she and other persons he met, who formed the best society of the town, received him hospitably enough each night, he grew restive. They were respectable "barbarians," he found, and so unspeakably dull; one could not flirt with their women, or venture a witticism. The port "opened on the Orient," and was filled with Slavic and Turkish sailors; the sea and the surrounding hills were magnificent; yet Trieste offered too few distractions. He was forced to dine in lonely splendor "like some great milord," because protocol demanded that he eat with none of inferior rank, "a great vexation to me!" Besides, he was well aware that he must be circumspect; his conduct was closely watched.

December 4, 1830, he wrote to the Baron de Mareste:

> I am like Augustus, I desired empire, but in desiring it I did not know what it was.
>
> I have tried not to play a single trick on anyone since I came here; have said not a word that tried to amuse; I have not seen the sister of any man; in short I have been most prudent and am dying of boredom.

The playful Stendhal was now "as cautious as Telemachus." It was hard. His letters were, as usual, written in his queer code, signed by false names and falsely date-marked. But nothing helped. Prince Metternich, who literally looked under his bed every night for wicked liberals, wanted him out.

Only a few weeks after his appointment the Austrian Foreign Ministry and the Papal Government exchanged information about him and his writings, which they easily recognized under the nom de plume of "de Stendhal." Soon a message went from Prince Metternich to Paris refusing his exequatur for this suspicious character who, only two years before, had been expelled from Austrian-ruled Milan.

The new king of France, in these grave times—when Poland, Italy, Spain, even England suffered from popular unrest—was haunted by fear of the Holy Alliance and a new invasion. Metternich must be appeased, and Consul Beyle must therefore be shifted. "I am but a bird of passage," Stendhal commented on receiving this news early in 1831.

In Paris, reaction had already begun, and the aging Lafayette was removed from leadership of the National Guard. The cautious King Louis Philippe, far from aiding the revolutionary patriots in Italy or Poland who called on democratic France for help, busily repressed riots in Lyons and Paris. The statesmen who counseled him now were conservatives such as Guizot; and a man like Beyle was something of an embarrassment. His novel, *The Red and the Black*, just then being slated in the press, was a minor literary scandal, and the learned but devout Minister Guizot spoke of Beyle, whom he had met, as a "scoundrel."

Stendhal now desired a decoration, a Cross of the Legion of Honor, in recognition of his former services to the government under Napoleon. In the manner of Julien Sorel, he remarked in one letter to a friend: "You have no idea how much superiority is enjoyed here by diplomats who are 'crucified.' " At a dinner in Trieste a pompous fool of a Russian consul had been given precedence over him, because he wore three decorations. But the French consul was given no decoration by Guizot, despite his earnest petitions. Indeed he believed that he owed his failure to win some superior place to that statesman's animus against him. A copy of *The Red and the Black* from Stendhal's own library has been found marked at one of its most heretical passages with the note: "Cost me a prefecture—Guizot—August 1830." The authorities in France, he concluded, "disliked people with ideas. Never will a government, no matter what kind it is, sincerely endeavor to protect any literature that is not dull . . . and *void of ideas.* Ideas are the bugaboo of people in power." To avoid arousing the jealousy of His Excellency the Prime Minister, himself a noted historian, Stendhal now resolved: "*I will print no more. . . .*" His novel was sought after; but cautiously he avoided having it reprinted for the time being, while he waited to learn if it pleased the Papal Government that he might be transferred to a post in Civita Vecchia.

How he lamented now that he had a father who had ruined himself! Had he known what was to come, he would have studied to become "an extractor of teeth, or a lawyer. Anything, rather than to sit and tremble for a job in which one croaks of boredom."

In the spring of 1831 came confirmation of his assignment to the little port outside of Rome, whose College of Cardinals had evidently decided to overlook him for the time being. In leisurely fashion, he rode across the Peninsula, through territory reported to be controlled by turbulent Carbonari or banditti, but without misadventure.

2

Italy was in a very interesting condition from a political viewpoint. The events of the preceding July in Paris had inspired many Italians with the idea of imitating the French, and the Romagna and Marches, the strip of Papal Territories south of Venice, were the focal point of trouble, as they were the worst-governed regions in Europe. Here the Carbonari and the liberals fought against the Papal troops, who were often aided by a hired *canaille* of hungry banditti, out for plunder, organized and uniformed by the conservative authorities under the banner of the "San Fedisti" to fight the revolutionists. Treachery, espionage, torture, and assassination also featured this intermittent civil struggle. For example, in Bologna, under Papal rule, the populace had risen in desperation and was besieged by the government troops; Stendhal was obliged to detour this place en route to Florence. The worst of the fighting, however, had taken place at Ancona and Rimini; it was put down by Austrian troops invited in by the Vatican, but when they retired, the red, white, and green tricolor was raised anew in July 1831. The Austrians prepared to intervene on a larger scale; but France, disturbed at this extension of Austrian control in the Peninsula, was at last sufficiently aroused to send an expedition to Ancona, early in 1832, ostensibly to "protect the property of the Pope."

It was a heart-stirring scene, from 1830 on, the real beginning of Italy's forty years of Risorgimento. To the observant and philosophical traveler who had analyzed the passions of men with such sagacity in his books, the thought now came that it might be a fine thing to instruct his government truthfully concerning the meaning of these events, upon which he informed himself thoroughly by friendly chats with coachmen, peasants, and townspeople on the spot. Thus he hoped to furnish sound counsel to the statesmen and help to shape, in some wise, the course of history.

From Florence, April 10–13, 1831, the consul dispatched four long letters to Count Sebastiani, Minister of Foreign Affairs in Paris, beginning:

> I do not know if the usages of the Ministry permit a mere commercial agent to present in his correspondence more than the political news of his own region. The gravity of the circumstances I have witnessed leads me to believe that it is my duty to communicate, not so much the facts, which I did not really observe myself, but the tendencies of the popular mind which may determine these facts.

He then gave an account of the plots, counterplots, and insurrections raging in North Italy. Behind his reports lay the hypothesis that the struggle for popular liberty was a ground swell which in the long run could not be resisted, but which French interest, by an enlightened policy, might turn to its own account. His analysis of conditions in Tuscany were of special significance: for one thing the Conte di Saurau, the Duke's prime minister and the real ruler of the Duchy, caught his eye as a figure of superior cunning, worthy of one of his novels. Tuscany was in a state of alarm; and Saurau, who was attached to the Austrian cause, used methods now of repression, now of conciliation. However, the alienation of the Third Estate, Stendhal said, was complete, and only genuine concessions to popular feeling could tranquillize Italy.

Stendhal's voluntary diplomatic reports were pigeonholed, and he heard nothing to indicate what impression they made. Yet three years later, in January 1834, during a journey from Civita Vecchia to Florence, he wrote further reports on conditions in Tuscany, being apparently encouraged by Count Molé to furnish them to the new Foreign Minister, the Duke de Broglie. Here he gives a lively account of the intrigues and scandals that current gossip in Florence dilates upon. In the manner of a master novelist he sketches the personalities of the Grand Duke, of his pious, widowed mother, the dowager Grand Duchess, who exerts great influence over him, of the *camarilla* of rival counselors and ministers who struggle for dominance, and the foreign interests they secretly represent. One is ambitious for popular admiration; another lusts only for women; a third is secretly liberal, but loves money above all. Perhaps, Stendhal hints delicately, something could be done in this case to offset the material advantage which the Austrians enjoy in his favor. Such a man, he says, is not open to outright bribery, but only to "presents" given, as the Italians say, *con buone maniere*. It would be dangerous to offer money to Signor F——, but his relative, the Bishop of ———, might first be reached through generous support of his ecclesiastical ambitions. "We must not forget," he remarks, "that love of money is the ruling passion of the Tuscans today." To justify these rather Machiavellian counsels, he points out that the Austrians constantly tempt the poorer Italian officials in the most vulgar manner; and concludes, in his letter of January 10, 1834:

> If the King's Government values the interest of France in achieving the principal influence in Tuscany at 40,000 francs [$8,000], I believe that, with the judicious expenditure of this sum, one might win for Tuscany the same Code [the modified Code Napoléon] now enjoyed in Naples.

In similar reports of the political situation in Rome, Stendhal gives illuminating pen portraits of the new Pope, Gregory XVI, the various cardinals, and even of their valets, who, he presumes, enjoy some influence over them. These reports are brightened by many an anecdote, told with his native shrewdness and enriched by a knowledge of Italy gathered during thirty years.

In his early years as a consul, he tried to exceed the mere performance of the duties required of him. He reflected: "In reading my letters, at the end of two or three years, and comparing them with those of ——— [the ambassador at Rome], the ministers in Paris would perhaps sense the difference."

Vain hope. His diplomatic reports (literary productions of rare worth, bespeaking the novelist and student of history) were buried. Perhaps only Count Molé, who at periods replaced Guizot as minister, saw some merit in the odd fish who was consul at Civita Vecchia. But neither hope nor promotion came of all this ingenious effort. The Stendhal documents lay forgotten in the archives for seventy years, until historians, such as Albert Sorel, unearthed them with cries of admiration. But Stendhal had learned that it profited him little to apply his intelligence to the performance of his task.

3

On April 17, 1831, he arrived in Civita Vecchia, after calling at Rome to report to the French ambassador, the Count de Sainte-Aulaire. Civita Vecchia, though the main port of entry to Rome, forty-five miles distant by road, was a sun-baked, sleeping village of seven thousand inhabitants. The climate was fearfully hot, save at the season when the sirocco blew all day and one shivered with cold. From the windows of his house, handsomely situated on a height above the port, he had admirable views of the blue Mediterranean, as well as all the harbor with its long jetty and its two towers built by Emperor Trajan guarding the entrance.

Each day he would go down to the dock to meet the incoming boats smoking a cigar while he waited there for hours. "I am the first beautiful sight that the passengers see as they disembark," he wrote to his friend Mareste. He examined ships' papers and passports, he treated the complaints of captains and passengers with benign tolerance. Under him served a staff of illiterate assistants and clerks, headed by one Lysimaque Tavernier, an evil-looking little fellow. Tavernier was part French, part Greek; he had been chancellor to the previous consul, who had discharged him after an angry dispute, warning M. Beyle not to engage him again. However, Tavernier could write legibly in French and Italian, and made impassioned pleas which won him back his place.

In February 1832, there was much ado when the French expeditionary force landed in Ancona, to remain there for many years as a check to Austrian encroachments. On March 6, Stendhal was given the mission of bringing a large sum of gold and bills of exchange to Ancona and supervising the payment and provisioning of the French military force, some ten thousand men.

Despite the confusion he found there, owing to a conflict of authorities on the scene, he completed his task with great energy. Later there were to be charges of irregularity and negligence at Ancona, some of which he himself reported, leading to an investigation that dragged through years. Stendhal was held blameless in this affair. In fact Ambassador de Sainte-Aulaire reported that M. Beyle had completed a disagreeable and difficult task with a skill that derived from his long experience as a quartermaster:

> I have been sounded out on the possible recall of Beyle from Civita Vecchia [wrote the ambassador to Minister Sebastiani]. I have answered that in spite

of my desire to comply, I would not sacrifice a man to whom I can offer no reproach for the discharge of his duties. True, Beyle is ill chosen for the local *convenances* of his office; but since he has exercised it he has committed no fault to my knowledge, and it is a testimony that I owe it in all conscience to render.[2]

It would appear that there were added reasons for the French ambassador's contentment with Stendhal, which remained confidential, and of which the consul himself never spoke. From his private letters we know that Stendhal was disgusted by the foreign policy of Louis Philippe. The French Republic had once liberated Italy, and now Italy and Poland were abandoned to despotism. "I blush to be a Frenchman!" he wrote in secret. But Sainte-Aulaire, it was said, made very plain to Stendhal the desire of the French Government that the landing of its troops must not be made an occasion for a rising of the Italian patriots against the Papal Government. In other words, the French were bringing no liberation to Italy. Now Stendhal knew personally a good many of the Carbonari leaders who were waiting to revolt in Romagna. He knew how delicate a task it would be to "explain" things to them. He was aware also that his own superiors, knowing his reputation, would be watching him closely. "Despite his liberal convictions," one eyewitness of these events tells us, "Beyle promised the ambassador that he would do his duty and follow the instructions given him." As a man of honor he kept his word.[3] It was one more "toad" that the unhappy officeholder was forced to swallow, while eating off the French budget.

Sainte-Aulaire's letter defending Stendhal suggests that the Vatican had become aware of his presence in the vicinity, and made some diplomatic inquiries about him. But somehow he was permitted to cling to his uneasy seat in Civita Vecchia, a rather forlorn figure, who was happiest when he was on leave, or when some friend from Paris wandered in while en route to Rome.

Thus Alfred de Musset, arriving one day in 1834, described him in epistolary verses as being in a charming mood:

Tu l'as vu, cet antique port,
Où dans son grand langage mort
Le flot murmure,
Où Stendhal, cet esprit charmant,
Remplissait si dévotement
Sa sinécure.

[2]Chuquet, *Stendhal-Beyle,* 197, Letter (undated) to the Duc de Choiseul-Praslin.

[3]C. Simon, op. cit., pp. 10–11.

But soon, weary of Civita Vecchia, he discharged his sinecure with far less "devotion" than the young poet imagined. Throwing himself into a carriage, he would leave his office in charge of Tavernier, and hurry off to Rome, or even, sometimes, on longer journeys to Naples, Leghorn, or Florence. Though he was always ready to return on short notice, he managed to be away from his post at least half the time, usually finding some pretext to stay in Rome, where the consul at Civita Vecchia customarily kept a lodging for his occasional use.

The proximity of Rome, only five or six hours away by carriage, was a consolation. Thanks to his respectable rank, he made friends among the Romans and their ladies, and became for years a familiar, if always odd-looking and unorthodox, figure in the social life of the Eternal City.

The fragment of a story he wrote at this time, entitled *Une Position sociale*, sketches for us the ideas and sentiments of a certain "Roizand," who, after a career in Napoleon's army, has retired to Rome as a minor diplomat. (He is so much like Henri Beyle that the differences matter very little.) Roizand's object, through following a diplomatic career for ten years, is only to "raise himself a little above poverty." (In the same tone the *Souvenirs d'égotisme* reveals that its author thought now: "It is time to finish off one's life as decently as possible.") Hope and ambition are dead, yet the scandalous reputation of a "reformer" clings to him however prudently he behaves; the only friends he attracts are "two or three young Romans who, like himself, felt some romantic curiosity about what the world would be like in twenty years." In his heart Roizand despises the new king of France who, by 1832, had shown such bad faith toward those who raised him to power. These opinions he tries to hide from the ambassador, who is an aristocrat of the most polished manners. Willingly enough he appears at parties and embassy balls, in full uniform, but moves through the crowd like a stranger, scarcely able to restrain his mocking spirit in the presence of the overdressed Roman matrons and the Roman princes in their embroidered costumes, men so small and brittle that they seem like hunchbacks. The young Italian belles, to be sure, are as alluring as ever; but now they pass the middle-aged consul by.

"I am beginning to grow old," he whispers to himself, "I am wrong not to perceive it." Roizand reflects the gloom of the author.

Nevertheless Stendhal became the devoted friend and frequent guest of the Duchesa Caëtani, a woman of cultivation, and of her two young sons, one of whom, Don Filippo, was a man of letters of sorts. Through the Caëtanis he met the Countess Cini, who was much younger and gayer, and whom he was sorely tempted to "attack," though his age, his lined face, his wild-looking reddish wig and declining health forbade. Thanks to these friends, and also to Horace Vernet, the fashionable French painter then residing in Rome, and a Swiss miniature painter named Abraham Constantin, with whom he lodged, Stendhal was given "at least occasion to chatter in the evenings." When, in addition, there were musicales, orchestra concerts, or operas to attend, Rome acquired almost the attractions of Paris. He found, also, certain aristocratic ladies of unaffected character, that is, "not educated for the *bon ton*," who appealed to him strongly; but he was forced to admit sadly that the Romans were incapable of understanding a book printed in Paris, and there were virtually none among them who could play with him "at those games of battledore and shuttlecock that are called in France *being witty*."

The rather rare visits of friends from France, such as Mareste (with whom he had become reconciled) and Mérimée, and the young Ampère, gave him his greatest delight. He took pleasure in acting not only as their host but as their guide, showing them all the sights of Rome and even of Naples. For, Mérimée said, he knew how to exhibit the local mores to his guests, how to present to them truly Italian characters, peasants, vintners in harvest time, young village maidens drawing water at the well as they had done in the days of Horace.

A distinguished Russian historical scholar, Count Alexander Turgeniev, who came to Rome in 1833, having met Stendhal in Paris, sought him out again, and walked with him about the city for three whole days. He relates:

> This brilliant Frenchman is the best of *ciceroni*, he knows ancient as well as modern Rome, and thinks out loud as he walks with me. I am indebted to him for the most exact *Aussichten* on Rome's internal situation and politics. He is not liked here because of the truths which he utters and the bright sayings with which he seasons them, but in my humble opinion it is he, at bottom, who is right.[4]

Diplomat or not, Stendhal never succeeded very well in hiding his true sentiments. As his old friend Mareste reports during a journey to Rome, in 1833:

> He is outrageously wearied by the Eternal City. He attempts to speak freely as in our salons in Paris; he argues and discourses in his usual way. The poor Romans, who have a terrible fear of compromising themselves with their amiable government, shut their ears or take flight. The interlocutor remains

[4]Jourda: *Stendhal raconté*, p. 107.

alone and does not know what to do with himself. You know that for him an audience is utterly necessary. He writes me that he is sick, very sick, has the rheumatism, and fears the cholera morbus, etc., etc., all of which means that he is dying of boredom. He has just lately sent me a thick notebook on the *pimps* of the cardinals and monseigneurs; . . . if his diplomacy exercises itself on such subjects, he must have few friends indeed here.

Another who observed him from close by was Ludwig Spach, a young German diplomatic official who had literary inclinations and kept a diary. To him it seemed that Stendhal was a somewhat disappointed man, disappointed at being misunderstood and underestimated, hence given to persiflage or bitter mockery, and even to violent and irreligious outbursts. Quite unlike a Talleyrand, he would exclaim with flashing eyes and wildly grimacing face that if he had the power to do so he would "cut off hundreds of heads." His novel, *The Red and the Black,* was condemned in good society, Spach relates, and read only in secret:

Henri Beyle—why should I hide it?—was not at all liked at the [French] embassy. His diabolical nature, which he revealed too easily, displeased people. This disguised Republican did not accommodate himself except with an unwilling heart to the July Monarchy, which he believed was transitory, and often he would take off the mask in a most naïve way. "How much longer do you believe you will be able to check the torrent?" he exclaimed one day before several members of the embassy. "You permit higher education to be spread; and a turbulent youth will cry sooner or later: 'Give us bread, gold, influence!' "

Yet Sainte-Aulaire overlooked his faults and even his frequent absences from his post in Civita Vecchia, because in the first place he was amused by him, and in the second, no one else knew Italy so well. No one else knew which bishops had mistresses, and which had business concessions for sale. And even Spach, who shows himself a petty soul, perceives that this rather coarse-looking French "Mephistopheles" had an unexpected refinement and charm:

He was one of those singular natures who, out of a sort of modesty, hide the idealistic aspirations of their souls under the mask of irony, and use raillery as an armor with which to protect their wounded hearts, always tormented by the need for love.[5]

[5]C. Simon, *Souvenirs de Strombeck et de Spach sur Stendhal,* pp. 9–13, 15.

4

From Rome, and the soirées of the Duchesa Caëtani, or of the French artist Horace Vernet, the return to the heat and vexations of Civita Vecchia was always desolating. In 1832 and 1833, the arrival of the cholera plague in Italy from southern France greatly increased his burdens. For years he was forced to impose a strict quarantine on all incoming French ships. As panic spread among the poorer and more ignorant people at his seaport and at Rome, the churches were crowded by terrified mobs, praying for their lives; and the consul sometimes came to spy upon the superstitious and too passionate folk who, herding together in church or cathedral to cry for the magic of the Virgin, made their chances of infection all the more certain. Standing behind a pillar in a Roman cathedral one day, he counted up eighteen hundred hysterical believers, some of them well-clad merchants or even aristocrats. With disgust he observed what he called "the comic spectacle of fear in all its forms," and strove to estimate exactly what percentage of these worshipers were fated to die of the plague.

But though disbelieving in incantations, he became gloomy as he sensed that the specter of the plague might well touch him too. His friends in Rome observed the depression of his spirit at this evil season, and the young German, Spach, mocks at him a little for showing fear of the cholera. But what he feared was that death in its most hideous form would come to him after prolonged torture, as was the case of four out of five who were afflicted. "Ah, such atrocious suffering, and I have always desired a swift death," he once exclaimed.

It was when he sat alone at night, in his house at Civita Vecchia, and a touch of fever or indigestion suggested the cholera morbus to his mind, that he wrote more Last Wills and Testaments, noting down briefly the principal events of his life, disposing of his property and money, giving instructions for his burial. In one of these he directed that he should be interred "beside the body of my friend Mr. Shelley," at the pyramid of Cestius in Rome—though he had only met the ill-fated English poet once or twice in his life.

In all Civita Vecchia there was but one man he cherished as his friend, Donato Bucci, who had an antique shop in which objects of art, Etruscan vases, and old books and manuscripts were bought and sold. Bucci was a sympathetic soul and possessed some learning. In his shop the few liberal persons of the seaport always gathered to talk;

Papal Government spies also came there to listen in. Suspected and sometimes persecuted by the Papal police, Bucci was a brave soul and held steadfastly to his liberal opinions, for which Stendhal esteemed him all the more. To stroll about the town each evening with Bucci and speak freely to him as his heart desired was one of his few agreeable distractions in those years of exile and solitude.

Bucci relates that on several occasions Stendhal offered to prove to him that God either didn't exist or was inexcusable if He did.

"You need not trouble yourself," said Bucci politely on one such occasion.

"Ah, my friend," sighed Stendhal, "it is too bad that you are wanting in a little religion."

"Why so?" asked Bucci in surprise.

"Because in this way we have nothing to argue about and will go walking along like two imbeciles," he said slyly.

If, on their evening walk, they passed some pitiable creature disfigured by a dreadful disease, Stendhal would remark: "There is the mercifulness of the Almighty Father." Once a hideous beggar approached him, imploring alms "in the name of the five bleeding wounds of our Saviour Lord Jesus." Stendhal flew into a fury and roared: "Away with you!" menacing the poor wretch with his stick.

Normally a most considerate and courteous man, Stendhal could be swept by ungovernable impulses. People who vexed him by repeating themselves or making the same complaints threw him into a rage, and he would do anything to avoid meeting them.

One day, as they were strolling together, Bucci pointed silently to a local character of this sort approaching along the street, a man who was in truth an inoffensive, though dull fellow. Stendhal, who had been in good spirits till then, suddenly seemed anguished, as if not knowing what to do. "Ah! we are lost," he exclaimed. "Here comes this dreary idiot to interrupt us, and there is no way of avoiding him!" When the man reached them, Stendhal assumed his sternest manner, then, before the other could open his mouth, began to abuse him so violently that the poor man was dumfounded, his knees quaked, and he soon fled. But calming down quickly, Stendhal said: "It was wrong of me to forget myself so, but as soon as I saw that fellow the blood rushed to my head."

At this period, Stendhal began collecting old Italian manuscripts, chiefly seventeenth-century memoirs, many of them never published, which in simple, unaffected style chronicled the lives and times of the successors of Cesare Borgia, and the Cenci. In these somber tales, often likenesses of the confessions of Benvenuto Cellini, Stendhal, like Jacob Burckhardt later, found "the true history of Italy" in Renaissance days, "and of the morals which formed the Raphaels and the Michelangelos, whom people nowadays so unthinkingly recommend as proper models to be imitated in academies and schools of fine arts."

For his growing collection of Italian manuscripts he spent thousands of francs. Some of them were in the Neapolitan dialect, and for their translation alone he noted that he expended fourteen hundred lire. His purpose, as he wrote to his cousin Colomb, was to translate or adapt this material into French as a series of "Roman" or "Italian Tales." It was in his leisure time, stolen from his consular duties, that he wrote "The Abbess de Castro," "Vittorio Acarombini," "The Cenci" and those other tales making up the volume of the *Chroniques italiennes,* in which the folkways of old Italy are pictured by him as a blend of natural nobility and daring violence.

And was it not still so? Had he not seen the other day, as he wrote to a friend, in the streets of Rome, at his very feet, a beautiful young girl, stabbed to death by her lover, lying in a pool of blood? Nay, he says, parodying the empurpled style of the young Hugo, "she was *bathed* in her own blood." And why? For a few lire! And one day, in Naples, he took a friend to a church to see the body of a handsome young cardinal, recently poisoned, as it was assumed, by members of an enemy faction among the Sicilian clergy. A horrid sight: "His lips and eyes," Stendhal relates, "had turned lapis lazuli in color."

One great distraction, the taste for which had been communicated to him by the learned Bucci, was for archaeological excavation, now the craze of all the tourists, especially the English. Along the beach outside of Civita Vecchia, they would go digging away for beautiful Etruscan vases and sarcophagi, or Roman statuaries, that seemingly lay lightly buried on every hand. Soon Stendhal joined a society of amateur archaeologists, purchased some small strips of land near other excavations, and either dug himself, or engaged some peasants for the task. It was to him an amusing "lottery," a hunt for buried treasure; and to his infinite delight he was soon rewarded by the discovery of an excellent Roman bust of Emperor Tiberius. Stendhal announced this with shouts of joy to all his friends in Paris, saying: "I recognized the fine eyes of Tiberius at once. He is a rare old rascal. Nevertheless he ruled for twenty-two years over one hundred and twenty million subjects. And he cost me only four piastres!"

Such were the simple distractions afforded by life in sleepy, sunbaked Civita Vecchia—save for one additional convenience described cryptically as "Signora C., at three hundred francs." For one season she figures in the scattered notes of his diary. "The Divine C.," he exclaims, "she has taken hold of me completely, and often jests about my potbelly. A splendid wench!" Flabby, fifty-year-old Stendhal is thus finally reduced to downright extravagance in seeking the bought pleasures left to him.[6]

During his many absences, his Greco-French assistant Lysimaque Tavernier usually carried on as vice-consul according to instructions left by Stendhal. For a year or two this seemed a comfortable enough arrangement. But soon Stendhal realized that Tavernier was a deeper and crookeder little man than he had believed. His private correspondence was opened and spied upon; reports of his absences were forwarded to Rome and Paris; some of his personal papers disappeared. During several stormy sessions, the consul now called his assistant to account; but unable to find any other competent person who was willing to suffer the heat of Civita Vecchia for a clerk's pittance, he ended by retaining him, on probation. The man had wailed that dismissal would mean his ruin, and Stendhal pitied him.

But later, when some act of extreme negligence on Tavernier's part earned Stendhal a reprimand from his superiors, and further evidence came to him that the little man had secretly denounced him to the Papal Government as a wicked Liberal, the consul flew into a great rage and demanded his resignation at once. This, however, led only to a fruitless contest: Ambassador de Sainte-Aulaire was absent from Rome, and was temporarily replaced by the Marquis de Latour-Maubourg, who, by authority of some new ordinance, had Tavernier reinstated over Stendhal's protests. There followed a bureaucratic tug of war that went on for years, while the treacherous underling strengthened his own position and sought to dislodge the consul.

To the kindly Bucci, who had once interceded on behalf of Tavernier, Stendhal exclaimed: "My friend, I would rather you had given me fifty blows with a stick than let me keep that infamous Lysimaque as chancellor." Bucci himself was victimized, for he afterward related that both he and Stendhal were often shadowed by police spies owing to information secretly lodged against them by Tavernier.

More than ever the place became a suffocating prison to Stendhal, and he often fell sick. This would cause him to take still more frequent leaves, during which he would escape to the cool of the Alban Hills, where the Duchesa Caëtani received him at her villa. Or he would go

[6] P. Arbalet, *Trois solitaires*, p. 184.

for long walks in "the admirable solitude of the Roman countryside, intersected by those long broken aqueducts that," as he admirably phrased it, "are for me the most sublime of tragedies."

However, the best cure for the "miasma" of Civita Vecchia was a leave of absence permitting him to revisit France. The ambassador at Rome, seeing him "mortally sick," approved his petition, and in September 1833 he was finally enabled to embark on one of the new steamers that went direct from Leghorn to Marseille in two days. Within a week or so after that he arrived in Paris again.

His sickness vanished, as he ran about to all the theaters, dined with his literary friends, and went to evening parties at Mme. Ancelot's, at the Countess Clémentine's (with whom he was on a friendly footing again), and Judith Gaulthier's, the last a more recent object of his admiration. Once more he engaged in conversations that were bouts of wit, and no mere formal ceremonies. At last he was able to "shake up the mass of ideas that congested his head" when he was too long alone. To his friends in Paris his explosive vivacity that season seemed to border on folly. But within three short months his leave ended, and in despondent mood he must ride again on the road to Italy.

However, at Lyons, where he changed to the steam packet down the Rhône, he had the great good fortune to meet up with Alfred de Musset and George Sand, who were just beginning their too widely celebrated and rather "tragic" elopement to Italy. Stendhal greatly admired the pale, blond-haired young poet, but thought poorly of the sentimental and "overemphatic" lady novelist, then at the height of her fame. She for her part repaid him the compliment; plainly enough she did not enjoy the encounter with the stout Mephisto of French letters at this trying moment, and so included in her memoirs an intimate and, for her, unusually acid sketch of Stendhal relaxing, even growing drunk and noisy.

In fairness she described his conversation as remarkable in itself, full of a grace that was in odd contrast with his gross appearance. But she goes on:

> He mocked at my illusions about Italy, assuring me that artists who came to this country in search of the beautiful were truly idiotic. I did not believe him, feeling that he was weary of his exile. . . . He railed also at the Italian character in a highly amusing way, describing it as insufferable and speaking most unjustly. He predicted that I would be unhappy, deprived of enjoyable talk and all that made for intellectual life: books, newspapers, news. I realized quite well that this was what was lacking to this charming mind, so original and so given to poses, far from friends who might enjoy and stimulate him.

> He pretended, above all, to scorn all vanity and tried to expose in each person he met any pretensions that he might destroy under the rolling fire of his mockery. But I do not believe that he is a bad man; he takes too much trouble to appear so. . . .
>
> We supped with some other travelers. . . . Beyle rose to a pitch of wild gaiety, was moderately drunk, and, dancing about the table in his thick, furred boots, became a little grotesque, and not at all pretty.

In Avignon they were quartered at a wretched inn and toured the old town together. Stendhal conducted them to a church that had an unusually large, painted wooden image of Christ on the cross, such as southern people cherish. After calling their attention to its "uncommon ugliness and cynical nudity," he burst into a blasphemous rage at the image, and looked as if he were going to attack it with his fists. The handsome, self-possessed young Mme. Sand was troubled and concludes her reminiscence of him:

> As for me, I did not regret that Beyle took the coach to continue on to Genoa. . . . We separated after several enjoyable days; but since the essence of his spirit suggested the bad taste, the habit, and the love of obscenity, I confess I had enough of him.

Once more he found himself alone in Civita Vecchia, and as he wrote to his "dear and gentle" Mme. Gaulthier, who now "reigned over his heart," the return after a holiday was all the sadder. He stared out at the eternally blue sea, asking himself: "Am I to live, am I to grow old far from my native land? . . . Am I to live and die by this solitary shore?"

CHAPTER XIX

Secret Writings

I count only on being reprinted in 1900.
—Stendhal.

ON A fine morning of October 1832, a very fat man with a very red face could be seen slowly climbing the Janiculum Hill in Rome. Finally he halted before the Church of San Pietro-in-Monterio, both to take breath and to look back at the view. It was a day of clear sunlight, one on which it felt good to be alive; only a few white clouds scudded before the light sirocco, over the distant Alban Mount. From this height, on one of Rome's Seven Hills, one could distinguish not only Frascati and Castel Gondolfo a dozen miles away, but even the details of white-walled Villa Aldobrandini, the orange groves of the Capucini Garden, and the winding Tiber down below. All ancient and modern Rome, from the Appian Way, with its moldering tombs and aqueducts, to the old palaces and churches in the heart of the city, lay before one at a glance. It was a magnificent and yet also an oppressive view; for the remains of three thousand years of history in all its ponderous ruin lay thickly gathered here. The stones of Rome look so eternal and the onlooker so mortal.

This troubling thought soon communicated itself to the lonely tourist, Stendhal, for it was he, of course, in his habitual posture of observation and reverie. "What a view!" he whispered to himself. "This place has not its like in all the world." It embraced treasures that meant more to him than all other things, the wealth created by men's hearts and minds. This very Church of San Pietro, upon whose steps he rested, had witnessed the installation, originally, of Raphael's sublime "Transfiguration," which had been admired here for two hundred and fifty years before it was removed to some dim gallery of the Vatican.

"Two hundred and fifty years," he repeated to himself over and over again. Then, with a pang, there came to him the unconsoling thought: "Ah! In three months' time I shall be *fifty*." And what was fifty years here, he asked himself, as he reflectively hummed the sad old air of Grétry's: *"When a Man Hath Fifty Years . . ."*

He thought of Livy and his Romans and of Hannibal, whose battleground he could see beyond the city limits. "Greater men than I are dead and gone," he mused none too cheeringly. "And after all I have not filled up my life so badly." But did anyone really shape his own life, did not chance direct it for him? Had he, Henri Beyle, ever really directed his life?

Sitting down on the steps of the church he fell into a reverie, as he often did, that lasted for two hours. He whispered to himself: "I shall soon be fifty; it is high time that I got to know myself." What had he been, what was he now, how did he come from there to here?

He himself, born in the eighteenth century, a son of the Revolution and the Empire, had known what he called "an ocean of sensations." He had seen dynasties come and go, and revolutions succeed each other during a span of history rivaling the most turbulent eras of old Rome. He had lived through this, felt it; he had witnessed great events and surrendered himself to life. But what would remain of all that he had known and experienced? Would he not be forgotten by men? Was he to die alone, far from his native land?

True, he had lived through many adventures and perils; he had loved fully a dozen different women; and he had written some twelve volumes. *Visse, amo, scrisse*, he summed it up in an epitaph he conceived for himself. But what would remain of it all, who would know of it afterward? He had rejected marriage and family ties; men had spoken of him as a libertine, even a "monster of immorality." But who would know the "prayer and ecstasy" he had sought in love each time, and of which he was still not cured? He had lately also enjoyed the reputation of a wit: in the travel memoirs of Lady Morgan and in the letters of the dead explorer, Victor Jacquemont, he had been spoken of as "brilliant." His oldest friends had often voiced despair at his wandering and wayward life, assuring him that he might have surpassed the greatest figures of his age if he had but *applied* himself. But who in the future would read the books he had written? And he reflected now that if he passed on to the next world (always provided there was one), and met certain great dead authors whom he esteemed, he would not be surprised if they said to him: "My poor fellow, you had no talent whatsoever."

And as for love, which had been his all-important preoccupation, had he possessed a talent for it, as he had believed? Passion had literally filled his life for years; he had made every sacrifice of worldly advantage for its sake. "But I see that I have spent most of my time in unhappy love affairs. . . . My chronic state has been that of the disappointed lover." He asked himself now, in this reverie that he records in his autobiography:

> Have I had a talent for anything? Am I clever or a failure? Have I been happy or sad? It is important to know in the end. . . . What have I really been? To what friend, however enlightened, can I appeal for knowledge?

But he had never confided his greatest sorrows or joys to any friend.

The day wore on, and he sat frozen in his reverie. But the light evening mist with its damp chill warned him at length that sundown might overtake him out in the hills. He felt harassed and old. But before he rose to go, he laboriously drew up his leg and wrote on the inside of the cuff of his white flannel trousers—they were of English cloth too, for he was dressed in the very height of fashion—the date and his age, and in a most mysterious scrawl. Secretive and suspicious man, feeling himself ever spied upon, it was an acrostic he wrote, with the words divided up so that none might understand them. It may be translated:

OCTOBER 16, 1832
IMGO INGT OBEFIFTY

That same evening, returning from a reception at the French embassy, he said to himself: "I ought to write the story of my life, then perhaps I will know what I have been."[1]

All hope of advancement in the diplomatic service to some honored and well-rewarded office gradually died in Stendhal after four or five years. That bourgeois monarch, Louis Philippe, "the crookedest of kings," as Stendhal called him, had by this time shown that he would follow only the craven policy of the *juste milieu*, save when the popular movement which had lifted him to the throne threatened to get out of hand. Then, by force of arms, he would crush it pitilessly, as in 1834. The consul Henri Beyle himself was merely tolerated as an underling in this government, so long as he behaved with discretion.

[1] *Vie d'Henri Brulard*, Chapter I. The above reflections were written in the autumn of 1832, and form the opening retrospective pages of the autobiography of his boyhood. The second chapter and all the rest were written three years later, in 1835.

In Paris, his absence from the literary scene had been noticed, at least by a few persons, some of them booksellers and editors, who wrote inviting him to send them manuscripts. To one he answered that anything he wrote would offend some group or other, and that he could not risk this while "eating off the Budget"; he would publish nothing for the next eight or ten years. To another he wrote asking what would happen if in his writings there occurred some pleasantry at the expense of men in power and "the useful absurdities" they practiced upon the public:

> One is permitted to say everything nowadays, provided one avoids mentioning this, that, and the other.

But how could Stendhal stop himself from writing?

"The real trade of my kind of an animal," he wrote to his friend Di Fiore, in 1835, "is to write a novel in an attic room, for I prefer the pleasure of writing all sorts of foolishness to that of wearing an embroidered coat costing eight hundred francs." Ah, to live even in a hovel in Paris with a table and some candles to work by! But though in Civita Vecchia he felt himself an exile twice over—first, because he did not think the "right way," and second, through having been sentenced to live out his days in seclusion—he had rallied his spirits and from the beginning of his consular employment set to work writing in all his leisure time. "Without work," he said, "the human vessel has no cargo." In solitude the last resource of happiness was one's own brain. This solitude itself strengthened his habit of introspection.

He was banished and forgotten. He was gagged. He could not print what he believed as he wanted to say it. Therefore the idea came to him that he might as well write in secret, for posterity.

Several months preceding that day of reverie on the Janiculum Hill in 1832, he had already begun a first experiment in autobiography—not counting those methodical journals of his early youth, virtually abandoned since 1816. He had decided at first to write of more recent events, freshly remembered, in the period of his life that was passed in Paris between 1821 and 1830, a whole decade of his middle years. It was his purpose to examine his conscience as it had never been done before, to "reach something *positive* that would stand *as true for a long time.*" These chapters of his later life he had begun to write almost as soon as he had settled down to the routine of Civita Vecchia, doubtless intending to combine them with memories of his earlier years. The title he chose was: "Recollections of an Egotist" (*Souvenirs d'égotisme*). The title itself is eloquent of his deep-rooted opinion of civilized society in Paris of the 1820s: "I do not believe men are wicked, I do not feel myself persecuted by them, but consider them as being, especially in France, only automatons driven by *vanity*." Modern society was for him a contest of egos, more or less masked, a proposition that Balzac also would support in the forty volumes of the *Comédie humaine*. But Stendhal insisted upon tracking down the egotist in himself. In earlier years he had boasted:

> I am not one of those who, seeing a rainstorm on a summer's day, think only of the ravaged crops, and the ruined peasants. . . . I am one of those who think: So much the better; the weather will be cooler and it will be good to breathe; I love the air when it has been swept by rain. . . . I do not consider anything but my pleasure: I accept my own being; I am the Egotist; I am Myself.

His brief memoir of Paris days would be, admittedly, a work of "abominable egotism." Reading Chateaubriand's *Voyage to Jerusalem* recently, he had noted the wonderful and unwitting arrogance with which that great man of letters wrote of everything that happened to him; and Stendhal had remarked to himself: "I have never seen such stinking egotism in anyone." What, then, excused his own variety of literary self-interest? It was aware of itself; "an egotism that is sincere," he said, became but a new way of picturing the human heart, in the knowledge of which such giant strides had been made since the early eighteenth century. Unlike Chateaubriand, he was determined to describe all his own weakness, and spare himself in no way. Thus alone would it all become worth reading for the men of 1860 or 1880, or later. The only excuse for such writing, for wallowing in one's ego, was the idea that "someday these pages would be printed, and read by some soul whom I love, such as Mme. Roland or the geometer, Gros." Those enlightened readers of the future whom he always addressed nowadays were children or even unborn. "I regard my works as *lottery tickets* and count only on being *reprinted in 1900*."

The *Recollections of an Egotist*, in the manner of a spontaneous Stendhalian conversation, or rather soliloquy, pictures his self-interested friends, his vanity-ridden contemporaries, great and small, and himself moving amongst them, skeptical, self-conscious, irreverent, yet masking an infinitely tender heart, an "impractical" or "Castilian" temperament, too often given to enthusiasm and generous indignation. Stendhal and his young disciple Mérimée vaunted their "egotism" in the 1820s, pretending always to be cold and detached, as if in protest at the hypocritical manners of their contemporaries. One follows Stendhal's movements in the memoir from the time of his retreat from

Italy and Metilda, in 1821, through the new friendships he contracts, the salons he penetrates, the bachelor dinners, the fiascos, the love affairs with Clémentine and "Azure," the journeys to England, the meeting with Miss Appleby. The narrative is carried on by means of anecdotes, character portraits, and general reflections upon manners and customs, written as if by one who looks back from 1880 or 1900. Friends or celebrities are drawn for us with brief and telling strokes; the generalizations are offered in the guise of witticisms suggesting themselves quite spontaneously—for no one wore his wisdom more lightly than Stendhal. But the overtone is far from that of a heartless egotist; on the contrary it is the warmth and vivacity of the man that makes these pages live for us.

It must be remarked that when Stendhal, on one occasion, found Mérimée going far beyond him in cynicism, he turned upon the younger man and upbraided him for his coldness and want of sentiment.

For years, out of softheartedness, he could not bring himself to dismiss the treacherous Tavernier, who rose to be his vice-consul at Civita Vecchia. Mme. Jules Gaulthier, one of the most intelligent of the women he knew at this time, on seeing a portrait of him, wrote that, despite the touch of malice that always hovered at the corners of his mouth, he was to her mind "an angel who pretends to be a demon."

The unearthing of the *Recollections of an Egotist* long afterward caused some shocked outcries that Stendhal had given us a nauseating picture of a man who was equal to the utmost baseness, proof that he had not spared himself. But the salient quality by which he has appealed to his modern admirers has been the accent of truth, so manifest in all his autobiographical fragments, the truth, unpretentious and yet so novel and surprising at every turn. He writes as if he is unconscious of any of the inhibitions of circumspectness; he writes swiftly, *automatically*, lending his statements all the more a truly confessional quality. "Often the hour deceived me: I thought it was two A.M. and saw that it was six-thirty." What he tries to conceal, or at least to restrain within decent limits, like a man of the world, are his emotions. He laughs, he mocks at them dryly, with an air of extreme detachment. Yet, despite the irony with which he regards himself, it is emotion, it is passion that so casually appears between the lines. His unaffected and almost effortless style thus achieves "the most individual tone," it has been said, "in all literature."[2]

[2]Paul Valéry, *Variétés, II*. The names of friends and mistresses were replaced with pseudonyms. Stendhal intended to revise and to add to these memoirs and have them published ten years after his death. They were not made public until 1892.

For example, in telling of the death of his old friend Martial Daru, associated with the happiest days of his youth, his feelings become a mixture of sorrow, disapproval of the man's faults, even embarrassment at his demise. These he sets down exactly, without exaggeration. Of late they had seen each other seldom. On his return from Italy in 1821 he had not called on the younger Daru, though warmly invited to do so. He relates:

> Toward 1829, the amiable Martial Daru died: he had become heavy and insignificant-looking by overuse of aphrodisiac potions, on the subject of which I had had more than one scene with him. Several months later, while I sat in my Café de Rouen, I was thunderstruck at finding news of his death in my newspaper. I leaped into a cab and rushed to number 81 Rue de Grenelle. I found a servant at the door weeping, and I too began to weep scalding tears. I felt myself truly ungrateful; and capped my ingratitude by leaving that very evening, I believe, for Italy; I advanced the day of my departure; it would have killed me to go into his house. There again you have something of the folly that made me so baroque.

The memoir breaks off with an amusing account of a literary party in Paris toward 1826. It is little more than a hundred printed pages in length. Brief as it is, it strikes us as a marvelous historical document, and has a most singular spirit and tone throughout; that of a modern man of the 1940s, one would say, observing and reporting on the manners and morals of the 1820s. Perhaps Stendhal himself became tired of its "egotism." Other ideas came to him, in the summer of 1832, for stories, even for a long novel. Nearly three years were to pass before he resumed writing the chapters of his autobiography. Rich as the *Recollections of an Egotist* promised to be, the next attempt, that started with the beginning of his life, was better still.

2

During the interval between his two serious attempts at autobiography, he had experienced one more amorous misadventure and a most ludicrous one.

This was shortly after his vacation in France, in 1833. He had taken a fancy to a young girl in Civita Vecchia, who was descended of a French family named Vidau that had served the consulate in the town for generations. Her father, however, had come down in the world and married an Italian laundress. The girl was only nineteen and he already over fifty-one; yet Stendhal had the folly to make an offer of marriage to her father through his friend Donato Bucci.

In a letter of April 15, 1835, to his friend Di Fiore in Paris, he explains that though he had once loved "*Mille ans*" (Milan) he had won only "her elder sister" (Rome) and was now after four years so tired of her that he "would gladly abandon her for a Mlle. V[idau], of whom much good is spoken." But to marry a young girl was a great problem. "What if, in plunging my hand into the closed sack, I find that I have seized not an eel, but a serpent!"

As he waited for the answer of old Vidau, who seemed kindly disposed to him, he actually began to go to church every Sunday, in order to impress them favorably. In the bargaining that went on, he declared that he asked for no dowry—there was none, in fact—but hoped only to have an affectionate wife to care for him in his last years, and intended to leave what money he had to her.

Little as it was, it would have meant much to this poor family. The young girl, like a working-class woman, went about without a hat. Her mother appeared dazzled at the opportunity.

But M. Vidau happened to have an older brother who was an aged monk, living in Piedmont, and having a competence of his own. He inquired of this brother what could be learned of M. Beyle. When, after long delays, the reply came, it was so unfavorable, spoke of the prospective bridegroom as so horrid and debauched and godless a man, that the marriage, almost on the verge of being celebrated, was forbidden. The monk had threatened to disinherit his younger brother, his only heir, if this were not done.

Stendhal was heartbroken over this contretemps, which came in the spring of 1835. It was said at the time that his chief assistant, the despicable little Lysimaque Tavernier, had spread both the evil reports of his past and news of the forbidding of the marriage. It seemed to Stendhal that Civita Vecchia had nothing else to gossip about, and people smirked at him when he took his daily walk. In his humiliation and despair he fled to Rome, hiding there for many weeks, feeling himself more than ever a persecuted man. Once more, he was convinced, the Jesuits had undone him.

Again, in a mood of melancholy reverie, he walked alone in September 1835 by the shores of the Alban Lake near Rome. His mind was fixed upon the past, and once more the idea of writing the story of his life, to be published after his death, obsessed him. Above all things, women had shaped his destiny, for love of them had occupied his life, and he reflected: "With all of them . . . I have always been as a child." And yet it was also true that "self-love, self-interest, my very self disappeared in the presence of the person I loved."

His extraordinarily vivid memories crowded in upon him as he walked. Finally he sat down upon a little bench for worshipers and, like Zadig, took his cane and traced in the dust before him the initials of those persons by whom he said "my life could be summed up." He wrote:

V.A^{x} A^{d}. M^{l}M^{e}.A.A^{ine} A^{pg} M^{de} C.G.A^{r}
1 2 3 4 5 6

There were the initials of Virginie, Angiola, Adèle, Mélanie, Minna, Angelina, Metilda, Clémentine, Giulia. He adds: "Most of these charming creatures did not honor me with their favors, but they have literally filled my life. After them came my works. The fact is that I have possessed only six of the women I have loved."

But though the role of sex is certainly pivotal in his reflections, he did not devote his memoirs to boasting about the girls he had been lucky with. What he has to say of them, except for those who were plainly strumpets, is rather restrained. The great question was:

> *Have I made the best possible use for the ends of happiness of the circumstances in which chance has thrown me?*

The other question was like that which is asked by every great autobiography or confession: will I live? Will I be remembered? Stendhal was aware of his talents. But would the world ever know that he might have been (as he had Julien Sorel say) another Voltaire or Montesquieu, or even a great man of action? The political ideas of his time, the literary fashions of his age were alien to him. Fame had passed him by. But with an eye to the "lottery" for 1880, or even 1930, he asked himself earnestly if he was not right after all, and if he might not yet win? He remarks at the beginning of his autobiography:

> I can see clearly that many writers who enjoy a great reputation are detestable. What would be a blasphemy to say now of M. de Chateaubriand, however, will be a truism in 1880.

He too might have been a "success" if he had brought himself to write and think like others. But he had been stubborn in his quarrel with his age, its fashions, conventions, and its *mariage de convenance* with despotism. At bottom he had never sold out. He could say: "I have been different. But was I not right to be so?"

If he continued to be different, opposing those who were "right-thinking" to the very end, it flashed upon him, then he would *live*. For like all those who wrote memoirs, Benvenuto Cellini and Rousseau, and even Chateaubriand, he too desired to live on, to be remembered in the days to come. He said: "Benvenuto was truthful and one follows him with pleasure, as if he had written yesterday," though his story had not been found until two hundred years after his death.

The project haunted him once more, and he resumed his autobiography—already interrupted a second time in early 1833—on the evening of November 23, 1835, never stopping for four months until he had written some nine hundred manuscript pages. In the rambling introductory remarks, he says:

> I have had a fire lit, and write this, without lying, I hope without any illusions, with real pleasure, like a letter to a friend.

Then, in addition to the idea of being unsparingly truthful, he has the brilliant notion of addressing himself exclusively to an imaginary friend of 1880 or 1930, in other words, to readers fifty or a hundred years after his time! In short, this freethinker pursues, as Paul Valéry has phrased it, "a *policy* of immortality." In his solitude, from his vanishing point in time, he strives to forecast what opinion and taste will be, and never seems to doubt his own judgment or prophecy. The world of his time is a tissue of falsehood. But with the dear reader of future times he can be at his ease, discharging his heart in confidence. For he wagers that his judgment of religious and political institutions—now censored or condemned—will be vindicated. There would be only the gap of fifty or a hundred years to bridge and then his ideas, now so ridiculed, would be universally accepted. Romanticism, Catholicism, and monarchism would be forgotten?

This was an exhilarating game, quite different from that of other autobiographers, who, like Rousseau, write an *apologia pro vita sua,* seeking to justify themselves before God and man, and really addressed to their contemporaries—even published for them. Stendhal detaches himself from his time, and makes it his consolation for present ills to address only his "friend" of 1880 (or 1930).

"What will this friend's ideas be in 1880? How different from ours?" Certainly he would smile at those who wrote only to appease "the most rascally of kings" (Louis Philippe) or the "hypocritical Tartar" (Alexander I). He addressed posterity in imagination:

> Oh reader of 1880 or 1900, you will wonder much at our behavior in 1830. . . . You will not think highly of our canons of good taste or fine style. . . . [Then soliloquizing]: This is something new for me, to talk to people whose cast of mind, education, prejudices, religion are totally unknown. What an en-

couragement to be truthful, and wholly truthful! That is the only thing that endures. . . . What a great good thing would be the memoirs of a man who had seen something of his time and was no dupe.

With complete abandonment his pen rushed on headlong in the complete silence. Hitherto he had instinctively tried to avoid conforming with the taste and the commercial standards of his contemporaries; now he wrote without even intending that his contemporaries should read him. With utmost care he hid these papers from strangers' eyes, or his friends. He wrote with altered names and many secret signs, in his own code:

The embarrassment of having some indiscreet person read my soul in seeing my papers has always prevented me since the age of reason, or rather of passion, from writing down that which I truly felt. . . . My bad handwriting will hinder the indiscreet.

His handwriting in the *Life of Henri Brulard*, as he called this intendedly posthumous work, was more nearly indecipherable than anything else he had written.

He had a plan, a frame for his autobiography, and of course exceeded it. It was his intention to write at least two volumes in chronological sequence: the one we possess concerning his boyhood up to the time of his arrival in Italy in 1800 at the age of seventeen; and a second (unwritten) dealing with his service under Napoleon, and life in Italy. His boyhood itself he divided into four periods: from his birth to the death of his mother; schooling under the "tyranny" of the Abbé Raillane; the year of Terror in Grenoble, in 1793; the phase of the new democratic Central School. But in the effort of recollection certain elements loomed larger, clearer than others. He discovered, as he probed his own memories, all sorts of things that surprised or shocked even himself, and permitted himself to be drawn on. Thus we have probably the first autobiography, partial though it is, that appears to be largely *dictated*, without interference or "censorship," by the subconscious mind.

After all he had resolved to experiment upon himself, so to speak, like a brave scientist in the unexplored field of psychology. *Ecce homo*: he would study man in himself, if only out of pure curiosity. One of his manuscript notes reads: "I have no other claim to merit than to picture faithfully, after nature, that which appears to me clearly at certain moments. I am certain of my good faith. . . . I take pleasure in writing this." The story of the boy in Grenoble, in conflict with his father and his family environment, becomes more truthful than any other such memoir because of the psychological discipline of the man of fifty-three who writes it. He does not boast of his perfect honesty, in order to deceive us: "I do not pretend to picture things in themselves, but only their effect upon me."

He takes pride in overcoming the instinct to deceive; he even pounces upon his own lies. Thus, reviewing his life in the introductory chapter, he calls our attention to the fact that in one of his first sentences, by inadvertence, he may have given the impression that he took part in the Battle of Wagram, and exclaims: "How many precautions are necessary to prevent oneself from lying! . . . No, I was not a soldier at Wagram in 1809. The reader of 1880 . . . must know that it was once the fashion to have been a soldier under Napoleon. The fact is that I was a quartermaster."

In searching his memory he finds that some events are vague; or that he is not certain whether he witnessed them himself, or knew of them by hearsay, at second hand. This he always records. The picture of the past he says "is like an old fresco from which whole pieces have fallen away." There are gaps that ask to be filled in or painted over. But no, he decides, he will not "retouch" anything, but will leave the broken fresco of the memory as it is. It is thus that he contrives to fall into deception less than other men.[3]

In this way, probing the memories of his childhood, he records his "criminal" passion for his mother, and gives us what is probably one of the first clinical reports of a mother fixation—one that Freud, reading it some seventy years later, considered a manifestation of psychological genius. Not without embarrassment did he write this passage, for he remarked he might feel himself later obliged to throw it into the fire. But in these "buried memories" he perceives the decisive childhood sexual impulses that, to the Freudians, determine the central drama of man's life.

With no less clairvoyance, looking back forty-five years, he discerns the beginning of "jealousy" and hatred of his father; describes the deepening of these feelings after his mother's death; the transference of them to his Jesuit tutor, who oppresses him by virtue of the father's authority; and finally to the King of France, whose execution he gloats over in secret. In these unretouched memories we may trace the boy's alienation and rebellion against his father from the stage of family conflict to its transference, when he joins the collective, social revolt

[3]One of his many "Notices" of his life, written in 1821, ends with the phrase: "*Not reread*, in order not to lie."

against the Father Image. The case history of the alienated boy "Henri Brulard" assumes the broadest significance as the drama of his struggle for full liberty and self-realization—momentarily reached when, at seventeen, he crosses the Alps with Napoleon's Army of Italy.

More than forty years after the execution of Louis XVI, in remembering that day, he can still burst into rage at the thought of the new king, Louis Philippe, and write:

> The death of a guilty K—— is always useful *in terrorem* to prevent those strange abuses to which such people are led by the extreme madness of absolute power. . . . Any compromise, when the safety of the fatherland itself is at stake, still seems to me *puerile*, or, I would even say, *criminal.*

Essentially the *Henri Brulard* is a bourgeois family drama of the provinces in the time of the French Revolution. To its readers of 1892, nourished upon Flaubert and Zola, it appeared suddenly, with its superb character portraits, as a work of matchless realism, surpassing even Stendhal's two great novels. The very restraint and sobriety of its style, though written in the heyday almost of the Romantic School, added to its effect of exactitude.

"Often I pondered for a quarter of an hour," Stendhal has said, "before I put down an adjective after a noun." It was not the *mot juste* he hunted, but the precise shade of thought. It was at this stage, he boasted in a letter to Sainte-Beuve, that he read a few pages of the Civil Code (Code Napoléon) every day in order to improve the tone of his writing. He felt pride when he had written a sentence that exactly conveyed his own idea, one that he was sure would be offensive to the rhetorical "giants" of 1835, the Chateaubriands and Villemains. No, he would not have his work "*well written*" like theirs, at any cost, he says defiantly: ". . . What is called *fine writing* in 1825–1830 will appear highly ridiculous as soon as France . . . will have found time to think of the enjoyments of the mind."

Of his emotions of absolute joy he said always: "I cannot describe them." He would stop short, as if in fear that affectation would intrude itself. His deepest, most genuine emotions are expressed almost involuntarily. Writing of the sorrow caused by the death of Lambert, the servant who was his boyhood friend, he remembers the elegiac music of Mozart, then the image of the women he had loved who were long dead:

> I have given myself much pain in recalling these sensations after many a year. Where is Lambert remembered today, save in the heart of his friend?

Who remembers the death of Alexandrine [Daru] in January, 1815? Who thinks of Metilda, dead in 1825? Are they not mine, do they not belong only to me, who love them more than all else, who think of them passionately ten times a week?

Rousseau's *Confessions* much earlier had lodged a great protest against the old ways of education and care of children. Stendhal's autobiography embodies, more specifically, a protest against the family institution itself, against its repressions and hypocrisies, that made his boyhood "a sorrowful drama, suggesting only suffering."

Rousseau (who had almost no family life) taught that the bonds of family must be drawn closer, that parents must show sympathy and tenderness. But Stendhal demonstrates that the problem is far less simple: only two generations after Rousseau, he dissects the troubled modern soul in all its complexity, and demonstrates how the "exceptional" or gifted child may be driven to revolt against the family. Today conflict within the family is stronger rather than weaker; the conditions of modern society seem to make for increasing breakdown. This was foreshadowed in *Henri Brulard*, which first exposed to us the neurotic personality that appears in legions in the twentieth century.

After Rousseau, the "Romantic Rebels" were given to much confession, direct or concealed. The semi-autobiographical poems of Byron, the memoirs or novels of Chateaubriand, Musset, and others, all tell us much of the conflict of youth with family and social environment. In each of these cases the alienated youth seems to ask: "Where shall I go with my ideals, in this sort of world given over to money and vulgarity? How shall I escape to the places I have dreamed of?"

But Stendhal, in those pre-Freudian times, located in precise terms the sources of struggle between the generations. His position in a privileged middle-class family resembled greatly that of youth in our century when wealth, education, and leisure—and also neurosis—would become widespread. The early loss of his mother intensified his sensibility. Thus he was able to make the story of his youth *universal* for the innumerable personalities of the modern age who have felt themselves marked by the ordeal of repression and suffering in their formative years.

Today we live among crowds of psychotic "rebels," more or less "misunderstood" and oppressed personalities. The terms of modern life seem only to have increased their numbers. And how much modern literature, in emulation of Stendhal, was to dwell upon their case! It is presented in the "cathartic" or confessional writings of Tolstoy, as in Turgenev's *Fathers and Sons*, in the novels of Paul Bourget, Maurice

Barrès and André Gide; in Dostoevski's *The Possessed*, where the terrible confessions of Stavrogin are set forth; in Samuel Butler's *The Way of All Flesh*; finally in the novels of James Joyce, of Proust and Thomas Mann.[4]

When Stendhal's posthumous autobiography was finally published in 1892, it found its place quite naturally, like his novels, among the works of the "social" novelists and dramatists of that time. Despite its *bizarreries*, its brevity, and the omission of what was to have been a summing up of his later life, the *Henri Brulard* still seems the classic study of the alienated ego of modern times. Here Stendhal, often so elusive with us, is more himself, more fully revealed than in anything else he wrote. And by its terrible honesty, this book haunts those readers who arrive at understanding of it, as only three or four of the world's greatest autobiographies have ever done.

Illness and depression at the end of 1835 caused Stendhal to break off his narrative on reaching only the seventeenth year of his life. A long leave of absence in France interrupted him further, in 1836. He wondered if he could go on in this unsparing manner; or if it could be published even after his death. Doubtless to throw suspected police spies and Jesuits off his track, he wrote in large letters on the cover of his manuscript: "*There is nothing political in this romance.*" His executors later were to advise suppression of the book, because it denounced many living persons. So it lay interred for fifty years.

3

Repeatedly in his novels Stendhal apologizes for permitting the intrusion of political questions.

But politics never ceased to interrupt the concert of his imagination with its pistol shots. In France the reaction under Louis Philippe gathered force during the 1830s. In Italy, where Stendhal lived as if in exile from men of wit and enlightenment, an abject despotism, Bourbon, Hapsburg, or Papal still prevailed. More than ever before, Stendhal, who tended to look upon himself as having been in earlier days one of the "obscure artisans of glory" under the Republic and Napoleon, felt

[4]Tolstoy, though resembling Rousseau more than Stendhal, greatly admired the latter, having discovered his works for himself long before the popular revival. But he warned his friends not to read Stendhal unless they had strong stomachs morally speaking. Dostoevski's nihilist, Stavrogin, with his *actes gratuites*, strikingly parallels Stendhal's heroes.

himself truly one of a lost generation. Nor could he gain repose by some individual therapy, a logic of the pursuit of individual happiness, so long as society itself was made horribly unstable by the continuance of unjust political institutions.

It was his occasional complaint that the enjoyment of the arts, of ideas themselves, was spoiled so long as fools and scoundrels, full of pretended "finesse and falsity" managed things so badly that they precipitated political revolutions "every fifteen years." The government of the violent Napoleon had lasted only fifteen years; that of the "imbecile Bourbons" also fifteen years. How long would that of Louis Philippe last?

Interrupting the story of his youth in *Henri Brulard,* he exclaims: "But . . . our grandchildren will have to pardon us who held the pen with one hand and the sword with the other." How much happier, he often imagined, men would be who lived under the free institutions of the future. Perhaps they would even cease to worry about politics:

> Excuse this long digression, O reader of 1880. All that I have just mentioned will be forgotten in your time. The generous indignation that makes my heart tremble prevents me from saying more. If in 1880 there will be a passable government, the rapids, the shoals, the perils through which France will have passed in order to reach that point will be forgotten; history will write only one word for the name of . . . [Louis Philippe]: *the most crooked of K[ings]*.

Politics was a means to an end—this was increasingly his opinion in later years—the end of human happiness. But how could his aristocratic prejudices be reconciled with his republican sympathies? "My parents communicated to me their aristocratic tastes and reservations," he acknowledged. "This defect has remained with me. . . . But at the same time I desire the welfare of the people passionately and believe we can only win that by settling the question of . . . representative government."

He had perceived his own aristocratic bias, and decided to make the best of it. But though his friends doubted his sincere liberalism, logic made him a "violent Jacobin, an extreme Republican." The aristocratic system was *the* greatest of all evils to him. It meant the retention of irrational privileges. What it came down to, as he brilliantly phrased it in a letter of this time, was that "the shepherd always tries to persuade the sheep that their interests and his own are the same!" But sooner or later the sheep must always be fleeced again.

Stendhal's political convictions, despite frequent changes of emphasis, were always predominantly those of radical democracy. The teachings of his admired Montesquieu, in *The Spirit of Laws,* had formed the ideas of the founders of the American Republic, and Stendhal was willing to accept this as the freest political system in the world. Often when he felt himself hard pressed by petty tyrants and police spies he wished himself "in a perfectly legal country like New York."

Toward 1814, his friend Tracy published his *Commentary on Montesquieu's 'The Spirit of Laws,'* which opposed the too great separation of powers and expressed faith in government by popular will. Tracy recommended that there be but a single legislative house, and held that the thirty years' experience of the American Republic exemplified the success of what was primarily a plebiscitary system. This book, which also reflected Jefferson's views that the least government was the best, was mentioned by Stendhal in letters to his friends as embodying his whole political faith. It was a faith that seemed all but Utopian to one who lived under the Papal government in Italy.

Though Stendhal pretended to some knowledge of economics, he really disliked the whole subject and boasts that he always left the room when people in Paris talked of it. A small pamphlet aimed by him at the Saint-Simonian or Utopian socialists, in 1825, entitled *Un Complot des industriels* ("A Plot of the Industrialists"), indicates how completely he misunderstood their purpose, which he held gave too much place to mere productive efficiency. Moreover he found the Saint-Simonians and other reformist sects doctrinaire and impractical. "Must it be my fate to pass my life between the Royalists, mad egoists in love with the past, and the Republicans, generous but tiresome fools, in love with the future?" is a statement of his own dilemma by one of the characters in his posthumous political novel, *Lucien Leuwen,* written in 1834–36.

Stendhal admired what he heard or read of the United States, but wondered if the Americans knew what happiness, music, conversation, love were? As early as 1819, in the essay *On Love* he pointed out that a Frenchman living in Ohio was sometimes forced to travel a hundred miles on horseback to find someone to talk with. He added:

> A free government is one which not only does no harm to the citizens, but which on the contrary gives them security and tranquillity. But that is still far from *happiness,* it needs that man make that for himself; for he would be a very crude soul who considered himself perfectly happy because he only enjoyed security and tranquillity. . . . [In Europe], accustomed as we are to governments that injure us, it seems to us that to be delivered from them would be the supreme good, as with invalids tormented by painful chronic diseases. But the example of America shows us quite the contrary. There the

government acquits itself creditably and injures no one. But as if fate wished to confound or deny all our philosophy, or rather expose us as ignorant of all the [diverse] elements in human nature . . . we perceive that when the evil arising from government is removed by the Americans they seem to show new deficiencies of their own. One would say that the very sources of sensibility among those people are spoilt; they are just, they are reasonable, but they are not happy.

No, happiness in the Stendhalian sense was unattainable in a land where men thought only of rich acres, or animal hides, or dollars, as Europe was already saying of the United States. His investigation into American democracy proceeded no further. But the keenest suggestion in the passage cited above is his notion that political science and political doctrinaires somehow remained "ignorant of all the [diverse] elements in human nature"—a remark that seems most timely in the 1940s.

Those diverse elements in man, enthusiasm, passion, fear, violence, constantly absorbed the psychologist in him and made him critical of conventional political doctrine, either of the Right or the Left. There were times when he, like Jefferson, thought a little violence, an occasional revolution, was good for society. When in August 1831 he saw that Louis Philippe had already betrayed the popular mandate of 1830, and still limited the right of suffrage to a tiny fraction of the population, he hinted in a letter that he desired the same fate for this king as for his cousin, Louis XVI. He prophesied "a terrible September 3d" in ten years, if not in two. Then this king would be followed "by a drunken usurper. . . . Thus the Child of the Miracle [royalism] would be undone by the mistakes of the Guizot party itself." There were bloody uprisings of the working class in the early 1830s, and a great revolution in 1848, followed, as Stendhal foresaw, by a "drunken usurper," Louis Bonaparte.

Though he was serving his king, his views were sometimes treasonable. In a letter of March 14, 1836, to his friend Mme. Gaulthier in Paris, he discussed the sensational case of the political assassin, Fieschi, who had recently almost succeeded in killing Louis Philippe at the Opera. "True, Fieschi was wicked," he wrote; "he was a man of the lower class; but he had more will power in himself alone than all the one hundred and sixty peers who condemned him to death." The consul wrote this from Civita Vecchia, just after Minister Guizot had awarded him his long-coveted decoration of Officer of the Legion of Honor. It was fortunate that neither M. Guizot, who cordially disliked M. Beyle, nor the King ever heard of this private letter.

4

If in his youth he had lived all too much for the present moment, for ambition and sensuality, so in his sedentary "old" age he lived almost exclusively in the past. Incessantly he looked backward, to dream and write the story of his childhood and youth; he reread his early journals and philosophical and critical notes of a quarter of a century ago with a melting heart; and commented in French-English upon the margin of one of his old papers:

> *Quelle difference,* his life in Civita Vecchia and his life *Rue d'Angiviller, au Café de Rouen! 1803 et 1835!*
>
> Yet, at bottom, the true preoccupation of my soul has always been the same: To make *un chef-d'oeuvre.*

O admirable consistency! In those thirty and more years, despite every temptation or interruption, he had continued the same stern chase, as unswerving as that of Captain Ahab in pursuit of the White Whale. His goal had been always the creation of a chef-d'oeuvre, a masterpiece. Yesterday it was to have been a comedy; today a novel. But always it was to have been the great comedy of himself.

Since writing *Armance* and *The Red and the Black,* he had come to believe that the novel as a medium was admirably suited to his needs: on the one hand it could be a walking "mirror" in which one reflected all that was to be seen along the highway of life (*un miroir qui se promène sur une grande route*); on the other hand it could serve as a most elastic receptacle for his ideas. Through the novel, finally, he could continue the endless and narcissistic speculations upon himself, almost his last resource against the monotony of his present existence in Civita Vecchia.

Between the two experiments in autobiography, written in 1832 and 1835, he had devoted most of two years to a new novel whose title he never fixed upon but which was to become known, posthumously, as *Lucien Leuwen.* This too was autobiography, though in fictional form. It was always the same novel, always the story of the same fellow—"bold as a dragoon, subtle as a casuist, sensitive as a woman"—who, with mere surface differences of character and origin, appears as the hero of all his novels, as of his *Life of Henri Brulard,* and even, it has been remarked, in feminine guise, in the unfinished novel *Lamiel.*

In few writers has the confessional quality been so dominant as in Stendhal. The central problem is always the same: the education of a youth for life; the formation of his mind and character under the blows of experience; his debut in modern society. Stendhal even boasts that he invents little. He may borrow an episode from the newspapers, or from history, grafting it upon the structure of his own life. As he explained a few years later in a letter to Honoré de Balzac: "I take a personage well known to me, leave him the habits he has formed in setting off in pursuit of happiness every morning, but give him a little more wit."

This time he proposed to write a satire of the social and political world, picturing the morals of the Orléans regime, as earlier he had made the Bourbon Restoration his canvas. In place of the ruthless Julien, he intended to portray in Lucien Leuwen a gentler, more sympathetic hero, as the idealized container of his own personality. If Julien Sorel was Stendhal in a mood of bitter rebellion, Lucien Leuwen was a more fortunate projection of the same character endowed with every advantage that might lead to success in life.

But he too was "born too late." Like the other Stendhalian heroes, he would have liked to figure in the heroic scenes of the Revolution; or at least to fight in the Homeric wars of the Empire. Instead, he reaches his young manhood in the prosy era of the bourgeois king, Louis Philippe. This new age of steam power and big banking Stendhal now studied with close attention.

"Society has been changing, and I am not there to see this change," he wrote at this time to a friend in Paris. During his absence Paris had become a Babylon of trade and wealth. The railroad had arrived, the large factory, the limited corporation, the big bank, the new Bourse; even the mysterious telegraph. Stendhal thought for a time of entitling his novel: *The Telegraph.* One of the first was already in operation in Paris, he learned, for secret government use. With these great improvements there had come mass poverty and frequent riots among the discontented workmen. Also the Constitution of 1830, and its representative system; but this was emasculated by the practice of large-scale electoral corruption.

The government had promised security and well-being; but they lied; they had promised liberty, and lied. Everybody lied and stole. It was a time for "charlatanism without talent," Stendhal observed. "A halt in the mud," General Lamarque had called it. Such was the age in which Lucien Leuwen had been born, though he had not asked to be born in it.

Stendhal wrote to many of his friends begging them for details or "inside stories" of political developments in France. He wanted his novel to be a documented study of the Orléans monarchy and its manners. The King himself, he learned, was the most avaricious and brazen of financial speculators. It was with the aid of a cabal of bankers that he wielded power. Stendhal would therefore have his hero born the son of a great banker who dominated the Bourse and the court. Using a striking metaphor in one of the manuscript notes written for his own guidance, he remarks to himself that Lucien is to be "a nail pounded by the hammer of his age."[5]

Lucien Leuwen is again the history of the growth of a mind that seeks "happiness" on earth, though on its highest, Stendhalian terms—a mind disposed less to action than to reasoning about such action or experience as the age accords. The hero is handsome as well as vivacious, and born to wealth, since his father heads a great banking house of Paris. Unlike Julien Sorel's parent, this father is a kindly though skeptical philosopher, who mocks at all things in *bons mots* that are repeated all over Paris, and remind us of the witticisms of the older Stendhal himself. By contrast, Lucien is romantic and idealistic. Though he is an accomplished student at the Ecole Polytechnique, he is expelled from it because of his participation in the students' republican riots. Good-humoredly his father scoffs at his political extremism; but Lucien continues to show indifference to money or practical career-making, and enters the army as a second lieutenant of lancers stationed at Nancy, in Lorraine. His thought is to acquire military experience that may be of use someday for the popular cause.

Though he wears a splendid purple lancer's uniform, and rides a superb horse, Lucien soon finds army life in the service of the banker-

---

[5]The inspiration for the plot of *Lucien Leuwen* or at least for its *point de départ* may have come from a manuscript by his friend Mme. Jules Gaulthier, who attempted to write the memoirs of a young cavalry officer stationed at a garrison town. After finding that the charming Mme. Gaulthier wrote badly, and that editing would help little, Stendhal, evidently with her permission, took up the story of the young officer himself; but, as will be seen, made it entirely his own story. Cf. Martineau, preface to the Divan edition of *Lucien Leuwen*.

In returning to the novel, Stendhal in his manuscript notes reminds himself that he must broaden his narrative, give greater attention to minor characters, and avoid having the principal character dominate the story exclusively, as in a biography. The model he tried to keep in mind was Fielding's *Tom Jones*, and he notes: ". . . Fielding describes *at the same time* the sentiments and actions of different persons, and Dominique [Stendhal] of only one. Where does the method of Dominique lead, I wonder? Is it an improvement?" (*Lucien Leuwen*, Divan ed., p. xxxiv.) It tended, by its intensified analysis, toward the philosophical or psychological genre now in vogue.

In another manuscript note, defining his working method, he writes:

> "Fix the characters clearly in mind; the action only in general outline (*en masse*); admit the details only as they present themselves. . . . Reason: because one never thinks so deeply about the details as at the moment when one writes the book. In fact, without intending to work this way, it was this method that I used for *Le Rouge*. . . ." (Notes for *Une Position sociale*.)

king far beneath his expectations. His fellow officers seem to him unthinking brutes. From his colonel, moreover, he receives a remarkable lecture on how to "think right" on all subjects, and advice that he avoid going to bookshops, or reading liberal newspapers—for he had been detected buying a book! He is also told to frequent only the most conservative society, and to go to Mass every Sunday.

But good society, so called, in the provinces, is dreadfully gloomy. Embittered at the usurping king, jealous of the new bourgeois, and living in "perpetual fear of the common people," the provincial noble, unlike the Parisian, exhibits a sort of militant dullness, and is given to "saying the same things over and over again, for three quarters of an hour, without brooking contradiction."

As for the martial career, there are no more fields of Marengo or Austerlitz upon which Lucien may advance himself by courage, because the money-minded king uses his troops only for "expeditions" against the mill workers in the slums of the cities. Life stretches out as a routine of drill grounds, barracks, and billiard games in cafés.

The future that Lucien has chosen seems only too dismal. But his father, by letter, challenges him to show that through his wit and address he may succeed even under such discouraging circumstances; and he takes up the challenge. Since Utopia appears far off as yet, he observes, and he must meanwhile live under a hypocritical regime, he too will play the hypocrite. He determines that he will allow himself, or pretend at least, to be "converted" to conservative opinion and usage. He will cure himself of the natural disgust that the nobles, officers, and priests inspire in him; he will believe everything he is told, no matter how absurd; he will "think right"; he will accept everything, even the dirty work of the army.

By this device of Voltairian satire, under whose light the social experience of Lucien Leuwen is presented, Stendhal provides himself with a marvelous opportunity to ridicule the reactionaries of his time. In Lucien's mouth the hypocritical defense of conservative ideas becomes a travesty; his imitative behavior a farcical charade. It is through this systematic parodying of conservatism that *Lucien Leuwen* assumes so much interest for the modern reader. One may imagine the same situation for a youth in rebellion against Victorianism; or today, for one who has lost faith, let us say, in "economic royalism," yet pretends, by giving it lip service, to conform to its dogmas so long as it is expedient for him to do so under the *force majeure* of hunger.

There are many pages in *Lucien Leuwen* in which Stendhal in his ironical manner epitomizes the intellectual disorientation of his age, which so closely parallels the intellectual dilemma of our own century. Lucien is shown taking part with his regiment in those "glorious expeditions" at night against weavers in ugly mill towns, that were a feature of the Orléans regime. The workers fight the troops with slop pails and rotten vegetables, since they have no arms; it is *la guerre aux choux pourris,* Lucien reflects bitterly, thinking of the soldiers of Marshal Murat or Ney fighting the Germans.

Thanks to his fine clothes and rich equipage, Lucien is able to win his way into the circles of the Legitimist nobility of Nancy. He goes to the most fashionable church in town, buys a breviary which he pretends to study, courts the bishop, reads only conservative newspapers in public. "After a while Lucien *knew by heart what he must say to them, and what their replies would be.*" Would this not be equally true today in the case of an intelligent young man, forced to frequent only the circles of our Union League Clubs in America, our conservative capitalist class of the twentieth century?

"How is it that you say things," one discerning friend remarks to Lucien, "that are absolutely contrary to what you truly believe and say to me? Are you not being rather false?"

Lucien replies (with a sort of righteous indignation): "Madame, I was thrown into the midst of the ocean. I swim in order not to be drowned, and yet you say to me reproachfully: 'Sir, you agitate your arms too much!' "

"The inconvenience of speaking out loud what he truly believed was the worst of all trials for Lucien," yet he does his best. The penalty for this life of subterfuge which he feels himself forced to endure is fatigue, boredom, a never-ending melancholy that wastes his spirit slowly—until one day he glimpses the beautiful Mme. de Chasteller. Politics is all-important to Stendhal, as to Balzac; but he also conceives of sexual fulfillment as a *sine qua non* of his ethical system: to Lucien passionate love must be "the one consolation."

In the manner of his gallant comrades in arms, he at first had thought only of adding this presumably accessible widow to his list. Before he has managed to be introduced to her—she is one of the proudest aristocrats of the town—he rides under her window on his horse, and suffers a fall. This mischance happens twice, and is one of the oft-repeated symbols of sexual timidity that occur when Stendhal writes of love. At length Lucien meets her and falls madly in love.

The Countess Bathilde de Chasteller is a woman dominated by her conservative code, by her sense of modesty, by public opinion; face means everything to her. Like Metilda Viscontini, in Milan, whom the reader may easily recognize in this great portrait of a woman, she rebuffs or torments her admirer, who pursues her all the more ardently. (One of Stendhal's marginal notes reads: "You take as your models *for love* always Metilda and Dominique.") Like Stendhal, Lucien *talks* too much when he is in love, misses his opportunities when he might have carried her away by storm, merely sits by her side adoring her, and in short, "acts always like a child" in her hands. She, for her part, mistrusts his verbal fireworks and his cerebration, taking them for insincerity. There are quarrels between them, and intervals in which they melt toward each other in deepest mutual understanding. The so difficult Bathilde, in her yielding moments, seems all the more wonderful and appealing as a woman. This extended love episode, filling most of the first volume, is a combat between pride and desire, in which every nuance of unsatisfied passion is analyzed with infinite subtlety. Indeed the dramatic weakness of the novel resides in its excessive passages of analysis, given almost without relief.

By a conspiracy of the local aristocrats and Jesuits who are interested in Bathilde's fortune, a rupture between her and Lucien is brought about. Through some scandalous rigmarole he is made to believe that she has borne an illegitimate child, and is no better than she should be. In despair, he leaves for Paris, resigning his commission, retaining only the memory of a great unrequited love for a woman who was perhaps false to him.

The provincial scenes in the first volume are remarkable enough, not so much for the visual reality which a Balzac or a Flaubert would give to them with their painter's eyes, but for the sparkling analysis used in portraying a large gallery of characters. The second volume (as we have it), where the action is placed in Paris, has still more remarkable things in it, especially for the student of social history.

By his father's influence, Lucien is appointed secretary to a cabinet minister and takes up a political career. He receives his instructions from the elder Leuwen, the banker, in the form of a memorable sermon on the art of government under a parliamentary system, one worthy of the cynical Robert Walpole. "An honorable career . . . as the fools call it," opens before him, but his father's one fear is that Lucien will not be *crooked* enough to rise to his opportunities:

In a word, *will you be enough of a scoundrel for this* service? There will be many little tricks to be played. Will you aid the minister in carrying them off or will you obstruct him? Will you become bitter like some young democrat who pretends that he can reform the French people so that they may be like angels?

The important thing is "stealing money." All governments, Leuwen *père* continues, even that of the United States, lie everywhere and always. "There are good and bad lies. The good ones are those that are believed by the little people with 250 to 15,000 francs a year income; the excellent ones appeal to people who ride in carriages; the bad ones are those that nobody believes." Lucien in short must become a rogue, that is to say, a "politician" like Martignac, if not like Talleyrand. "Leave behind you all your moral scruples you who enter here into the government, as men have left their patriotism behind them on entering the army."

Thoroughly convinced, Lucien throws himself into his new role "with all that folly of youth that is called zeal." For he seeks distraction from his grief. Dressing in sober black, he tousles his hair and tries to look "older." Nowadays the ministers are chiefly interested in speculations on the Bourse, carried off with the connivance of men like his father. "Since July 1830 the world of the Bourse has become . . . that of the ruling class, the only one possessing influence. The people of money displace the families of the Faubourg St. Germain." Lucien is assigned to support this whole system by going into the field and "fixing" provincial elections which sanction it. Such missions, especially in closely contested districts, may become turbulent affairs, with the popular party rousing the people against the "spies" from Paris. Lucien does his work thoroughly, but returns to Paris literally bespattered with mud, clods of which are thrown at his fleeing carriage by the enraged populace. And one of his assistants remarks: "Well, this is the other side of the medal! That mud they threw at us tonight is the equivalent of the dust of battle on the fields of honor yesterday." Lucien, filled with revulsion, asks himself: "How can I ever extricate myself from the mire in which I flounder?"

No novelist knew "high politics" as deeply as Stendhal. The general character of the Orléans dynasty is clearly defined in *Lucien Leuwen*, and bears a striking resemblance to the Walpole era in England, or the President Grant administration in the United States. Through the story of the elder Leuwen, working closely with the wily old king, Stendhal pictures the political divisions in the nation, the maneuvers of blocs, the financial intrigues carried on through the court, and the whole art of ruling public opinion by deceiving it.

Lucien, despite some periodic soul-searching, by his cleverness raises himself to a place of some power: in part, this results from bringing himself to make love (though he still longs for the vanished Bathilde) to a Mme. Grandet, whose salon is a political center. But in the end he becomes fed up with his own successful scheming. His intelligence itself breeds suspicion around him, and incurs the silent enmity of his superiors in the Ministry. In a long soliloquy he reviews his years of shady service, and realizes that while he has "sold out profitably," he has only duped himself, since he remains at heart profoundly unhappy, and his life appears as dishonorable as it is stupid. And could one say that he really *lived*? He existed only for the vanity of his family, "*according to their lights, not mine.*" How long could this go on, and to what end? "Is power nothing but that? This house of marked cards—how long can it stand up? Five years more, or ten years?"

As in *The Red and the Black*, Stendhal's teaching is that of Polonius: "To thine own self be true." Lucien must renew that pursuit of happiness which so often in Stendhal assumes immaterial and metaphysical aspects, even aspects of renunciation. At all events his existence must cease to be a living lie; his actions, his day-to-day behavior must achieve harmony with his "sensibility," with the beliefs he holds true, whether by his reason or his intuition. Otherwise there would be no end to "those self-reproaches which admit of no reply."

The end of volume two indicates that Lucien will renounce ambition and set off in search of Bathilde. The death of his father suddenly brings both financial and political ruin, though he feels indifferent to all that, as he leaves for Italy, where he is to serve as a secretary of legation.

Here the novel breaks off, never to be finished. The notes for its plan show that Stendhal, in his third volume, intended to reunite Lucien and Bathilde so that they might live in Italy, "the richest and noblest life possible for the French who dwell outside of France." But he laid his long novel aside, intending to return to France and seek more detailed information upon the inside politics of its period.

He entertained great hopes for this work; it was, in truth, an enormous canvas of the social scene, crowded with characters small and large, some of whom were easily recognizable as leading figures in the French Government of that time, especially the ponderous Marshal Soult, Minister of War, whom Stendhal had met. This was one of his obvious reasons for postponing the publication of the book. He had literally spared no one in the passages of satire that dealt with the public service. Then he had written it in his most precise and sober style—the style of the Code Napoléon, as he jestingly said—which would render it unpopular in a time when fashion favored the "charlatans" of romantic prose who wrote for servant maids.

Lucien Leuwen errs on the side of length, though it has Stendhal's unfailing intellectual vivacity to carry it. It would have benefited from revision, which he intended to make had he lived. It is as a novel of ideas and of satire that the book, unfinished as it is, lives for us; no other he wrote is so surcharged with his aphorisms upon war, love, religion, business, education, and politics, all seeming curiously timely today, as if written for us. In this sense, *Lucien Leuwen*, almost unknown to the English-speaking world, is only surpassed in interest by his two more famous novels, *The Red and the Black*, and *The Charterhouse of Parma*. Moreover Lucien Leuwen is closer to Stendhal's real personality than the ruthless and tragic Julien Sorel. Both Lucien and Julien lived lives of dissimulation, while secretly in revolt against the society they each strove to master; and their dilemma is akin to that of disaffected youth in our own century. But Lucien Leuwen's gentler nature, in the end, was to reject power and money in favor of love, music, and even gardening. His story is related more closely to the older, mellower Stendhal and the spirit of resignation with which he lived out his days in the service of a government he hated.

On February 17, 1835, he wrote in a small memorandum: "I shall not be able to *print it* [*Lucien Leuwen*] as long as I serve under the Budget, for what the Budget most abhors is that anyone should have ideas." He feared lest some "eunuch" of an editor might bowdlerize it.[6]

When he felt himself ill, and at the point of death, he thought of sending it to his sister. But she had lately turned pious, and he was certain that some priest would induce her to use his novel as kindling in her fireplace! Therefore he went to the touching expedient of having the whole manuscript elaborately bound, with some fifteen engravings, borrowed from an art publication, inserted among its pages. On the flyleaf he wrote:

> To fools: this stupid engraving will make this ms. worth much to the bourgeois into whose hands it may fall after me. . . . The papers may be preserved for the sake of the pictures.

---

[6]Romain Colomb and Mérimée did, in fact, bowdlerize his book, as he so greatly feared, by publishing only a third of it, as *Le Chasseur vert*, in the 1855 edition of *Romans inédits*, using the opening section placed in Nancy. The rest of the work remained unknown until 1894, when Jean de Mitty, one of the early "rediscoverers" of Stendhal, found it in the Library of Grenoble and brought out his somewhat inexact edition in two volumes. I have used the 1926 edition edited by Henri Debraye for Champion, and the Divan edition, by Martineau.

An alternate title Stendhal considered was *The Amaranth and the Black*, referring to the uniform of Lucien; another was *The Red and the White*, alluding to the contrasting republicanism of Lucien and the royalism of Mme. de Chasteller. But *Lucien Leuwen* was the title left at the head of the manuscript.

He also prepared a preface which was in effect one of his counterfeit "passports," and pictured the author as no republican, but a partisan of moderate constitutional monarchy. A final word of instruction among his papers directs his executors "to wait ten years, if the police make publication inadvisable."

The older he grew, the more wary and suspicious he became. But now what he feared most was that he would die alone on this foreign shore, where he stood each day at noon smoking his cigar, as he watched the boat from France making for port. His complaints of ill health, his petitions for a leave of absence became more insistent than ever. At last his prayers were answered in April 1836, when his friend Di Fiore persuaded the Foreign Minister, Thiers, to grant him a reprieve.

CHAPTER XX

The Eternal Tourist

ON MAY 20, 1836, Stendhal arrived in Paris, after having arranged for his temporary replacement at Civita Vecchia. "*I have looked too long at the sun,*" is one of the revealing phrases in a letter written before his departure. He had also written to Sainte-Beuve: "Italy is no longer as I admired her in 1815. . . . She is in love with the one thing she lacks." That was nationhood, unity, such as France, Spain, and England boasted. But would the "lilac robe" of state become her well? "The arts, for which she was fashioned above all, are only a *pis-aller* nowadays."

It was in Paris, as it seemed now to the habitual exile, that the arts and the amenities of life flourished. If he could have a small sinecure, say a chair as a lecturer upon art or history, which his friends now sought for him, and a modest lodging in the center of town, all his prayers would be answered and he would write innumerable stories and novels. To be able then to go to "a small well-heated salon" such as Mme. Gaulthier had, "and chatter with a few intimate friends, who regard nothing seriously save friendship and love," would be heaven itself, he avowed. Only in Paris, in the 1830s, was there conversation, and Stendhal thirsted for it.

He did not win the sinecure he craved, but something very close to it, inasmuch as Count Molé, his benefactor, once more in office as Prime Minister, had him placed on half pay, at five thousand francs a year, and given some light official tasks that required his presence in France for years. This good fortune stimulated a late blooming, a renewed happiness in a Stendhal who, though nearly decrepit in his middle fifties, immensely fat and apoplectic, was insatiable in his lust for life.

Paris had never seen him gayer, more bent, as he said, "on resisting old age." He stopped at the modest little Hotel Favart, near the boulevards, and breakfasted every day at the Café des Anglais with Di Fiore and Mareste. Tuesdays he went to Mme. Ancelot's, Wednesdays to Gérard's or others'; he now even became an habitué of the Countess de Castellane's, whose home in the St. Germain quarter was a social center not only for the leading authors and scientists of the day, but for the ministers Molé, Thiers, and Guizot. Stendhal's interest in Mme. de Castellane seemed stimulated by his desire for documentation on "high life" in Paris, which he thought he needed for his unfinished *Lucien Leuwen*. The accomplished hostess, for her part, found him charming, judging from their correspondence. For nowadays, when appearing in such company, as authoritative as it was respectable, he no longer spoke out his mind like a firebrand, but tended to listen in silence. Indeed his friends found him a greatly mellowed man. Henri de Latouche, for example, testifies that in the aging Beyle the fierce Jacobin gave way to the diplomat and officeholder: "Beyle reproached me, in his later years, for having remained younger than my age, always indignant, discontented, and republican." But others found his humor sweeter than ever before.

Prosper Mérimée, who had recently returned from a long tour in Spain, brought him one day to meet the Countess de Montijo de Guzman, who visited Paris in 1836. "A beautiful example of the Andalusian woman," Mérimée had called her; and Stendhal, having always noted something "Spanish" in his own nature, attributed to remote Italian ancestors who had once lived under Spanish rule, conceived a great sympathy for the accomplished mother of Eugénie de Montijo. In 1838 he used to dine regularly with the countess, and her young daughters, the twelve-year-old Eugénie and her sister Paquita, grew so fond of him that on those evenings they were permitted to stay up late to hear his stories.

In recollection long afterward, Eugénie declared that M. Beyle was the first man who moved her heart. He would seat the beautiful young girl in his lap and tell her of his wanderings in the army of Napoleon, and anecdotes of the Emperor himself. He also pretended gravely to be her cavalier. "When you are a big girl, you will marry the Marquis de Santa Cruz," he would say to her, with a comical emphasis upon that noble title, "and then you will forget me, and I won't love you any more." But Eugénie, who was to climb even higher than he feared, remembered him even in her old age; she kept an engraving of the Battle of Austerlitz that he gave her as a present. In 1860, when, as Empress of France, she chanced to visit Grenoble and inspect its library, she exclaimed at seeing his portrait hanging there: "Why, it is M. Beyle, who used to dandle me on his knee!"

Before returning to Madrid, the Countess de Montijo cordially invited Stendhal to come and stay with them as a long-term guest, even offering him a carriage for his personal use. But by this time he had gone back to Italy and, to his intense regret, found himself unable to accept. Eugénie continued to write to him, and in 1840, at the time of the Carlist Wars, reported sadly that these upheavals had cost the Montijo family a million reals, half their fortune. In reply he wrote on August 10, 1840, in his most bantering manner, that he thought it would be impossible to regain this vast sum, adding the advice:

> It would be best not to think of such things any more. You will have to make the same sort of effort again at forty-five, that is, at the period when the first effects of age overtake us. At such a time women buy a little English dog and talk to the dog.

Shortly before returning to France he had written to felicitate one of his literary friends, Albert Stapfer, whose approaching marriage had been announced:

> I sincerely congratulate you upon having found a companion for life. One may experience moments of vexation in marriage, but never the deep and dark dullness of the celibate!

How his views had changed! Now that he "trembled like an old man when the sirocco blew," he was firmly resolved to find a companion for the years that remained. His thoughts fixed themselves first upon the "wild and reckless" and still so adorable Clémentine de Curial who had led him such a dance ten years before. His bitter anger at her had long subsided; he had forgiven her not only for having a lover before him, but for lovers number three, four, and others besides, of whom she had written him all too freely during his absence in Italy. Faithfully during those ten years, Stendhal wrote her at least once every two months. He forgave her even her age, for she was now more than forty-five, and asked only to be reinstated as her *cavaliere servente*. A copy of one of his oft-reiterated appeals to "Menti" belonging to this period, the summer of 1836, reads:

> It seems to me that we both have a piece of road to traverse together. This road goes in about the same direction; only you are going to go farther than I. Would you deign to accept a travel companion who would serve as a sort of major-domo, charged with the care of the post horses along the way, and even, if need be, driving them?

The sad thing is that since this courier has passed a certain age at which one mounts horses with grace, his sole merit would be in sparing you the trouble of dealing with the postilions yourself.

Continuing in this sad tone, he adds with great frankness that he has not only few years, but few francs, to expend on their voyage together.

But Menti, who was then at her summer place in Dieppe, replied that "one did not light an extinct fire with embers—the embers of 1826." Her passion was dead these many years, and Henri must content himself with the place of her first and best friend.

Do not think that because Stendhal was so susceptible to women, and distributed his affection so profusely among them, that he did not suffer at this latest blow. Mérimée describes him at this period as an utterly broken and inconsolable man.

On returning from Italy he had not seen the young novelist, whom he cherished as one of the most brilliant writers of the age, until the end of July, when they met by appointment at Laon, a day's ride north of Paris. Mérimée, a skilled archaeologist, was then occupied by his official labors as inspector general of historical monuments, and stayed in Laon to make a report on its thirteenth-century cathedral.

Meeting after long absence, they had a thousand things to say to each other. All through that evening they paced back and forth in the little public garden set on a high terrace of the ancient Frankish citadel of Laon, more than three hundred feet above the surrounding Flanders plain. In the lonely darkness of that sleeping town, Stendhal talked endlessly and passionately of his love for Menti:

> He could not pronounce her name without his voice changing. . . . It was the only time I had seen him weep. An affection dating from long ago was not returned. His lady had simply become sensible, while he remained as wild as at twenty. "How can you still love me, when I am forty-five?" she had asked him. "For me," said Beyle, "she has always the same age as when she gave herself the first time."
>
> He spoke of the audacity of the woman, and the memory of it delighted him who was so prudent. Then, with that spirit of observation that never left him, he described all the smallest symptoms of her growing indifference to him. She ended by being tired even of the "LO-GIC" which he always expounded to her.

Thinking of her. the tears came to his eyes, and he cited Dante:

. . . Nessun maggiore dolore
Che ricordarse del tiempo felice
Nella miseria. . . .

But no, these beautiful lines of Dante were wrong, he contended: it was not "all the greater pain" to recall the times of felicity in the dark present; on the contrary the memory of past happiness always stayed with us as supreme consolation. "I recall that I defended Dante," Mérimée said, "but now I think Beyle was right."

However, his friendship with Menti persisted. The aging belle would come to call on Stendhal in 1837, in his quarters, then at the Hotel de la Paix, and, with a naïveté that was both cynical and disarming, seek "the learned counsel of the author of *De l'amour*," on how to win back a reluctant lover. And Stendhal, forgetting his own heartaches, would become absorbed in the intricate game of her love life, advising or warning her, carried away by that overweening passion to observe, which is the true, yet vicarious, destiny of the novelist. Gratefully she wrote him:

> You are indispensable to me; without you, I would kill myself, for it is only through depending on you and leaning on you that I can gather a little strength to go on.

Her breathless notes to him continued in this tone until she was fifty, when, her last lover having abandoned her, and feeling herself already old, sick, and at the end of her portion of love, Menti did what she had often vowed to do: she took her own life. This tragedy was to take place several years later, when Stendhal was once more far from her side and he too sat waiting silently for the end.

But in the summer of 1836, at the time that she rejected his renewed proposal, he was still very much the brave old boy and briskly rallied from defeat. With utmost pains, he dressed himself in his finest coat and richest cravat, put on his lavender, or, it may have been, his white flannel English trousers, and cane in hand sailed forth—while his friends Mareste and Colomb leered at him—to carry the "attack" to another and no less admirable and beloved lady.

"Jules" Gaulthier, his faithful correspondent of recent years, who was masculine only in name, was also no longer young. She was the daughter of the prefect, La Bergerie, whom he had known in the time of Napoleon, was married to the tax collector of St. Denis, and had three grown children. But she was still beautiful, very intelligent, and the most literary of his women friends.

"You reign over my heart," he had written her from Italy, several years before, in a letter full of genuine respect. Later, continuing his suit by correspondence, he went so far as to say: "I love you with a tenderness that increases every day." But she replied, chiding him gently for paying her what seemed merely polite compliments: "Fortunately I am as patient as a peasant woman. For have I not waited twenty years to hear your declaration of friendship? No one shall know our secret, else it would be a secret no longer, and farewell to all enjoyment of it."

Mme. Gaulthier knew him well; she had recognized the depths of grace and warmth in him. But she was resolved to set limits to their friendship, for she had had experience of the world. When she had "played safe," she told him, things had turned out well for her; but when she had ended by being too kind, too yielding to her admirers, they had "stood her up." "As you see, my sentimental life has left me few happy memories; whereas my friendships have turned out more fortunately, and I keep and enjoy them with a pleasure that far surpasses that which the fever of my love might bring."

Nevertheless, all combed, scented, and wearing his luckiest suspenders, he marched to the final assault on December 25, 1836. For two hours he sat alone with her in her little salon in the Rue d'Hanovre and breathed flame. She was gentle, but firm and resourceful in defending herself. At last he retreated, sadly baffled. And scarcely had he passed beyond her doorway, when she hastened to her secretary and rushed off a letter in terms of the warmest affection and respect, designed to soothe his wounded old heart:

> It is not to the Duke de M. that I write, it is to you, my friend, who are still virtually beneath my window. Do not regret your lost day; it must count as one of the greatest of your life and one of the most glorious for me! I feel all the soft joy of a great success. Well attacked and well defended; no treaty, no quarter, no defeat; there is glory enough for both sides. You will not deny that. . . . And I am happy, very happy, and yet I love you well, and to love is to wish what your best friends wish; my spirit has divined your virtue. Beyle, call me fool, cold female, timid idiot, your scoldings will not efface the happiness of our marvelous *causerie*. . . .
>
> Beyle, believe me, you are a thousand times better than men believe, than even you believe, and than even I believed two hours ago.

On such terms their friendship could be continued. Stendhal remained the staunch admirer of Mme. Gaulthier and to the end of his life "worked for her without pay," as the French saying goes. Her affection for him persisted long after his death.[1]

---

[1]More than ten years after that event, when Mérimée's essay on Stendhal made its appearance, the author of *Carmen* received an anonymous letter, signed only "Jules," reproaching him for his want of indulgence toward his old friend, and citing from a letter of Stendhal to the correspondent which

2

But at the beginning of the year 1837, smarting under the sting of two successive "defeats," and at an age when an old campaigner like himself should have known better than to have risked them, Stendhal found solace again only in travel, this time throughout the length and breadth of France.

Travel books, and touring also, were by now in great fashion. Charles Nodier, the romantic antiquarian, was issuing one by one his nine volumes of *Voyages, pittoresques et romantiques dans l'ancienne France.* Nodier's young friend Hugo was soon to write his highly imaginative work on the Rhine. Mérimée himself now published his essays or travel notes on the art and architecture of the South of France and other regions, written during journeys in which Stendhal, his great precursor in this field, sometimes accompanied him.

But the writings of Mérimée and Nodier were really archaeological studies; and Stendhal saw an opportunity to do something quite different: another useful and perhaps profitable little work describing a tour in France, a subject which he hoped would not embarrass his official position in the government as a novel might. "There are almost no real travel books on France, which is what encourages me to publish this," he remarks in the preface to his *Memoirs of a Tourist* (*Mémoires d'un touriste en France*). This was approximately true, since almost nothing that might instruct or stimulate the traveler had appeared since the eighteenth century, and the best of those was by the Englishman, Arthur Young, written on the eve of the Revolution.

"Never did the thirst for voyage so possess me," he remarked at this time. In the spring of 1837, he went by diligence to the Auvergne in the Massif Central west of the Rhône River, where he joined Mérimée, who was still taking notes on the ancient churches in the region. Then, at the end of May, they parted company, Stendhal journeying via Bourges and Tours, and down the Loire, to seagirt Brittany, which he had never visited. After sight-seeing at the old port of Nantes and its environs, he continued through Normandy by short rides, returning to Paris in July. In the autumn of that year he made another tour through France, going south this time to Lyons, Valence, and Mar-

contained expressions of the highest praise of Mérimée. "It was," said Mérimée, "a most ridiculous communication intended to inspire *remorse* in me. . . . But who is this 'M. Jules'?" he asked Colomb. "I never heard Beyle speak of anyone of that name."

seille. Then, early in 1838, he wandered as far as the Pyrenees and the Spanish border, and returned by a circular course through Switzerland, down the Rhine Valley to the Lowlands, and by the new steam railroad from Brussels to Paris.

As before, Stendhal's travel notes constitute no methodical "Baedeker," but rather an endless *causerie* which takes its direction from any object or incident that catches his fancy, or, stimulated by some chance thought association, digresses into folklore, art, history, politics, philosophy, or even autobiography. Yet many modern travelers would rather tour France or Italy in his company than with any other travel companion.

He gives us, of course, impressions of the principal towns along his route, and some account of their monuments and old churches, the facts of which are sometimes borrowed from earlier compilations, sometimes incorrect. But he travels with his eye upon history. A fair landscape is always like music to him; but it is all the better if, as in the Midi, it is ornamented with some relic of the Roman Empire, such as the Pont du Gard, or the colosseum at Nîmes. Hence "even the most insignificant of ancient columns has an infinite value" when viewed on such a journey. "It throws the soul into a special state of emotion. The Mozart of this harmony is Titus Livius in the Roman countryside."

In Brittany the sights and sounds, and the people also, remind him of the spirit of fanatical superstition attached to the region; he is minded not only of the bloody civil wars in the days of the Republic, but naturally of Cardinal Gilles de Retz, the "Bluebeard" of legend, whose mad debauches and experiments in alchemy terrorized the whole countryside in the fifteenth century. This inspires a long chronicle of the sinister adventures of "Bluebeard" and his execution by strangling in Nantes.

Mérimée had tried his best to impart some of his knowledge and enthusiasm for Gothic art to his friend, but it is plain that Stendhal did not share the current interest in pre-Renaissance architecture. There are a thousand Gothic churches in France, he remarks, but the deep piety, approaching "terror," that is expressed so often in their very form repels him. At the great cathedral of Bourges, he admits, the soaring nave seems to make one feel the presence of the Divinity. But this feeling of reverence, so far as he is concerned, is spoiled by his awareness of "the hypocrisy and the *political purpose* underlying all of it." He is happiest outside of the church, in the charming garden of the episcopal palace, which he describes with greater pleasure than he takes in the cathedral itself. There, on a comfortable bench, under the shade of giant trees, he sits dreaming, and tells us of his reveries.

The glimpse of an unknown Spanish lady with her retinue on a boat along the river—"a beautiful Carlist in a green hat"—may be the content of his dream all the next day. Or on another he walks with the ghosts of his loves of long ago:

> Formerly, when I was alone, I used to dream of love adventures that were romantic and sentimental rather than flattering to my ego. Since then I have become less stupid. I have learned, what most men know, that you must appeal to self-love in the other, carefully concealing the true passion you feel as if its exposure would be a serious disadvantage. . . . For, once the other person is sure of your feelings, she may think no more of granting that which you desire.

Our oft-blundering, ingenuous Don Juan is now certain that the scales have dropped from his eyes! But experience in this "warfare," wisdom of life, has deprived him of the most charming illusions:

> Ah me! I would love to become a fool and an idiot again so far as the world's realities are concerned, if I could but enjoy once more those reveries, so beautiful and so absurd, which led to such follies on my part, but which, as I journey on in solitude, furnish my head with the most wonderful memories, everywhere accompanying me, yet harming no one.

And was it not true, as his reason whispered to him, "that at a certain age, at any rate, one must not love"? No, it was a falsehood to believe this. Stendhal is incurable. "So long as one is capable of loving a woman for her person, or even her naïveté, or for her very foolishness itself, so long as one is able to cherish an illusion of some kind, one may love."[2]

The *Memoirs of a Tourist* takes delight above all in dwelling on the "little true facts" that reveal the meaning of history to us, according to Stendhal. He observes the folkways and local customs of the people in different regions and towns; he goes into cafés, shops, and inns to gather his anecdotes; he stands watching people in the streets and squares. "What excites my curiosity most is all that goes on in the streets. . . . That which fools scorn as gossip is the only history which, in this century of affectation, truly depicts our country."

A beautiful Béarnaise peasant girl, walking erect with a large basket on her head, and in the basket a marvelous peacock for sale in the

---

[2]This fragment of reverie occurs not in the original *Memoirs of a Tourist*, but in its sequel, written at the same period, and then suppressed, *Journal d'un voyage au Midi*, published only in 1937, among his posthumous papers included in the Divan edition.

marketplace, is something that catches his eye. The crowds who come each year to the fair of Beaucaire absorb him: here women of good peasant family surrender themselves to some stranger in the intoxication of the dance and the carnival, "*because* they will never see him again in their native village." At Beaucaire or Valence, after the cold winter in the North, "at last I felt I had reached the South. . . . Sunlight, laughter, and people who live for physical pleasure surround me." And in Bordeaux, one of the most truly civilized cities of France, the local arrangements of domestic life, providing a well-regulated quarter for the class of demimondaines who were the recognized mistresses of the youth of good family, recall to him the comfortable and elastic social conventions of Italy in the days before 1815.

Stendhal's descriptions of the natural beauties of France are sober, clear, incisive, in accordance with his avowed principle of avoiding overemphasis. He writes often in the casual tone of a man of the world who never seeks to dazzle the reader with purple patches, as if to say: "Look how well I write!" In his mockery of the more extreme Romantics, he is led so far as to belittle "la belle Touraine," of which George Sand had written in such lyric prose. When he comes to the Indre River, which she described with flocks of adjectives, he observes maliciously:

> It is a pitiful-looking creek, perhaps twenty-five feet in width and four in depth, meandering about in the midst of a rather flat plain, and bordered by low hills covered with some small nut trees only twenty feet tall.

Even riding down the Loire itself, he complained that its banks were monotonous, being fringed only with willows and poplars. "The interest in a certain landscape of itself is not enough," he remarks; "in the long run we must feel a moral or historical interest." Then only did a landscape become a "plectrum for the soul."

Such passages of denigration, added to the outspoken reflections on the ugliness of certain cities, such as Lyons, were calculated to bring down upon him the wrath of readers or commentators from many different parts of the country. But then, he wrote only to please himself.

In Lyons he saw mainly an orgy of silk manufacture; people talked and dreamed only of the price of silk, a sign of the sweep of commercialism, to which he gave full attention. France was changing swiftly, was becoming *embourgeoisée*. He recalled the graciousness of life under the old regime, the days of glory and disinterestedness under the Republic, and exclaimed that all men seemed to be surrendering themselves to "vile and egoistic passions. . . . I see nothing of the spirit of generosity." The enriched peasants and bourgeois "triumphed by their baseness, as a pig wallows in slime." Stendhal could not endure the battles they waged over a matter of two francs with the conductors of his diligence. "Such affairs fill me with shame, and I avert my eyes as from a hideous spectacle."

Certainly the conditions of life in France, as Stendhal recorded them, had become meaner and, for many, more burdensome than before, though the industrial revolution promised wealth incalculable. The year 1837 was one of intense commercial depression. The workers had fought hard in 1830, 1831, and 1834; but now they were starving, and did not revolt. "We anglicize ourselves, we no longer laugh," he remarks. Soon most Frenchmen, like the laborious English he had seen, would be working in shops or factories for ten hours a day and go sulking about joylessly on the Sabbath.

"It is a civilization that has lost sight of its goal," is one of his disturbing reflections. Another (in the posthumous volume of his travel notes on southern France) speaks of the sadness that afflicts him as he compares the present with the scenes he witnessed in his adventurous youth: "I feel that I have fallen upon an era of transition; and scarcely will it have run half its course, when time, which moves so slowly in the history of a people, but so swiftly for the individual, will give me the signal that it is the hour to leave." Renewing their courage, men would resume the advance again, he thought, winning more freedom for themselves. Even the arts and literature would flourish more nobly, he predicted. "Our French literature [which at present he derided] may perhaps hope for a splendid epoch of energy, when the grandchildren of those who were enriched by the Revolution will have come of age." This prophecy might be true enough (as indeed it proved to be in the second half of the century), but he, Stendhal, would not be there to witness it.

His picture of life in the provinces is as dark as the gloomiest pages of Balzac written on the same subject. France was a centralized bureaucracy, and in the country "the government *is the prefect*," a provincial satrap before whom all men bowed low. But these prefects who rule with the authority of Paris—"which the provincials hate because Parisians enjoy life and think only of their vanity"—are detestable mediocrities, who become the butt of Stendhal's satirical spirit.

In its political reflections, his last travel book was perhaps more outspoken than anything he had written before. No opportunities to tilt at the superstitions of the religious and the tricks of the Jesuits were lost. His freethinking, his Jacobinism were but poorly concealed by those occasional passages written to appease the censor, in praise of that "wise king . . . whose government interferes least with the governed, while assuring them security on the highways, and legal justice when they feel like squabbling with each other." But even such a paragraph is given away by the irony of its concluding sentence of eulogy for the regime: "And what is more, it amuses the people by giving the National Guard bright-colored, horsetail plumes to wear on their helmets."

The *Memoirs of a Tourist* gives us also an intimate and parting picture of Stendhal in his sixth decade, a picture admittedly full of "egotistical details" but also tinged with sadness. We see him posting about the world energetically in pursuit of clean lodgings, for he is a fastidious man. He suffers a little when riding on the noisy and dusty steam railroads, though he likes their convenience: "Many poor devils, it is said, are killed on them each week," he observes somberly. He also offers some remarkably prophetic doubts about the future of the iron roads, then a subject of intense speculation on the Paris Bourse: "What will become of the capital invested in the railroads if a carriage is invented that can run on ordinary roads?"

Like an experienced traveler, "avoiding noise and show," he stops always at quiet, second-class inns rather than hotels of the first class. Wherever he goes he asks which is the best café in the town, the place where the local blades and the wits foregather. There he samples the coffee and tea, but since tea is execrable in France he brings his own, sternly instructing the *cafetier* how to brew it. In Lyons, like a courageous scientist, he tries twenty-two different ways of cooking potatoes, and gravely reports upon his experience. At Bordeaux he emulates the winetasters, "artists who can detect not only the vintages, but the year of harvest." To impress a gathering of American and Parisian bourgeois at an inn in Le Havre, he orders champagne for his dinner, giving exact instructions on how it is to be cooled with cracked ice. When the ice proves to be wrongly treated, he makes a loud protest, startling the other diners, who, though they had formerly ignored him, now regard him with respect. This pleases his ego. On boats or carriages, when he finds pleasant company, he invites confidences and carries on endless conversations. When his companions appear dull, he turns up his collar and buries himself in one of the books he carries with him everywhere.

A strange, unclassifiable work, the *Memoirs of a Tourist*, as one reviewer said, was in some wise "dominated by [his] politics throughout," and tended "to create a dislike for our soil and climate, for the men and monuments of the past, as for the faith of our fathers." Stendhal had frequently compared the landscape of France most unfavorably to that of his beloved Italy, the only exception being his native Dauphiné, now rediscovered in all its beauty, and with a reverent heart. His friends and literary advisers thought that in many passages he was being imprudent. But he replied:

> What is there so imprudent in the *Touriste?* To please fools while proving to them for seven hundred pages that they are fools is an impossibility, in any case.

Only one critic, E. D. Forgues, one of the few who admired Stendhal, likened him to Diderot passing through his century, too little heeded or unjustly appraised. The others slated him in the press, though acknowledging the author's wit. But the increasing interest in *le tourisme* created a ready demand for the fifteen hundred copies of his book, which was, after all, one of the prime causes of its being.

3

One cherished literary project that Stendhal reserved for his leave of absence was that of adapting into French the collection of Italian memoirs which he had been gathering for many years. These genuine documents, he held, formed a veritable "introduction to the knowledge of the human heart." They teemed with conspiracies, robberies, rapes, and murders, often committed for the sake of ambition; they were for him penetrated still with "the fierce energy . . . the gigantic passions of the Middle Ages."

Modern Italian thinkers, like Benedetto Croce, tend to smile a good deal at the habit of most Italophiles, including Stendhal, of seeing everywhere the Italy of pagan voluptuousness, Machiavellian perfidy, and Borgian crime. Stendhal doubtless exaggerated in picturing the Italy of his time in such colors as he used; but his interpretation of seventeenth-century Italy as an era of relative anarchy and large-scale brigandage, following the downfall of most of the city-republics, scarcely errs, and was later corroborated by the more extensive researches of Jacob Burckhardt.

But whereas Burckhardt, and also the French historian, Michelet, popularized the idea that the Renaissance civilization was a "final flowering" of culture, engendered by the revival of Hellenistic learning (Humanism), Stendhal, before them, shrewdly suggested that there was a strong relationship between the whole "rebirth" of the fine arts in Italy and the social tendencies and drives dating from the Middle Ages—a view that is much closer to that of today's historical theorists. To his mind the men of the Renaissance, and even their near descendants, approached what might be called "the state of nature." They were what "noble savages" were to Rousseau, and "primitives" to aesthetes of today. Stendhal, then, saw "natural man" in the contemporaries of Lorenzo de' Medici and Leonardo. In those days society was a miracle of courtly refinement and artistic creativeness; yet the age was notable also for its excesses of lust, violence, and treachery. To Stendhal this was no paradox. He wrote in a letter of November 21, 1835:

> It was those bold morals that nurtured the Raphaels and Michelangelos whom people pretend to imitate so stupidly by means of academies and schools of fine arts. What they forget is that it needs a bold spirit to wield the brush of a master, and not that of some poor devil condemned to pay court to a bureaucrat in order to get a commission for a picture.

To the uninhibited violence and passion of the earlier Italians, Stendhal, like some psychoanalysts of today, attributes their creative genius. It was, for his time, a challenging and advanced notion, very close to Freud's idea that the great creative artist may be defined as "a successful neurotic." In the same spirit, Stendhal, so law-abiding himself, fondly regards the seventeenth-century banditti and assassins who are heroes of the tales he writes or adapts, in his volume of *Italian Chronicles* (*Chroniques italiennes*), as individual manifestations of the drive toward liberty and justice. All previous ideas about these people, as given by writers of the "melodramatic" school, are false, he declares at the beginning of the story of "The Abbess de Castro." "One may say, in general, that those brigands were *the opposition* to the cruel governments which in Italy succeeded the republics of the Middle Ages." How often they used poison or the stiletto to dispatch some petty tyrant!

In 1821, Stendhal had appealed to Sir Walter Scott by letter, urging him to turn to Italy for his subjects, and "paint a true picture of the Middle Ages. . . ." He had suggested stories based on the lives of Rienzi, Cosimo de' Medici, and others. But Scott never replied to him, though other English authors such as Byron and Shelley were already utilizing the lore of Italy with notable results. Stendhal had continued his reading and purchasing of old Italian manuscripts until this became a mania with him throughout the 1820s and 1830s. Eventually he possessed a hundred quarto volumes of manuscripts. He wrote to Sainte-Beuve, in December 1834, "I have selected that which appealed to me as revealing the human heart. . . . Their style is without pretension or noble rhetoric, and I shall translate them thus." The manuscripts themselves he desired to bequeath to a library in Paris, so that men could see that he had written the truth.[3]

In 1837, finally, he was able to make an arrangement with François Buloz, editor of the newly founded *Revue des deux mondes*, to publish these tales in his own French versions. Two years later they appeared in book form.

Each of his *Chroniques* is a drama of passional violence. In "The Abbess de Castro" the heroine loves and is loved by a brave soldier of fortune who, in an unsuccessful attempt to abduct her, kills her father, then is forced to flee for his life. She is shut up in a convent, but eventually, thinking her lover dead, becomes the mistress of the Bishop of Castro, and bears a bastard. Her adulteries being discovered, there is great scandal, and this at the moment when her first lover returns from exile to reclaim her. Though she might have escaped condemnation, in remorse, and for honor's sake, she kills herself.

"Vittorio Accoramboni" is the case of a lady who secretly poisons one husband after another, but of whom a horrid vengeance is exacted by the brothers of one of her victims. Pursued by the authorities, these murderers are only done for after a stirring, pitched battle in the streets of Venice. The other tales, which include that of "The Cenci," dominated by such subjects as incestuous passion, parricide and rape, are pitched in much the same key. In this whole collection, only the tale of "Vanina Vanini" is set in the nineteenth century. This is based on the affair of a brave young Carbonaro and a young girl of the Roman nobility who, by chance, succors him when wounded, and at the risk of her own life nurses him back to health. She loves him madly, and willingly yields the flower of her virtue to him; but when one day she sees that his heart is more wedded to the cause of Italian liberty than to herself, she betrays him to the authorities. The inclusion of "Vanina Vanini," a story presumably based upon a recent episode, among the collection of true chronicles of the sixteenth and seventeenth century, is Stendhal's way of saying that Italian "primitivism" survives in his own time, that men and human motives have changed little.

[3]They were sold to the Bibliothèque Nationale, in the time of Napoleon III, by his sister Pauline, and may be consulted there.

These stories of crime and vengeance, which Stendhal in the main adapted faithfully enough from original manuscripts, are in one sense a compensation for the very sedentary life he had led since 1814, much as in the case of our sedentary authors of crime fiction and their readers. But in a more important sense they reflect his deep interest (despite his love of reason and logic) in "primitive" passion and violence, in the "unexpected" (*le divin imprévu*), that he constantly distinguishes in the unconscious mind. His preoccupation, at this stage, is not with ideas of social order, but with the realities of instinctual passion, fear, aggressiveness, greed, lust, in individual and group, the unshrinking knowledge of which offers a challenge to our systems of ethics. The Italians of the Renaissance were, for him, men and women who developed their individualities as far as possible, defying the limits of morality and religion that had confined men's behavior in earlier times. (For this reason, Nietzsche, in imitation of Stendhal, later wrote that he wished we might become again as the men of the Italian Renaissance.)

But in this world of violence, are there any standards or code of values that may serve to defend society, in the long run, against limitless evil? To Stendhal (as for Burckhardt later) the sense of honor was a moral determinant in the Renaissance Italian when all else failed. In the long opening story of "The Abbess de Castro," approximately the size of a short novel, Stendhal, with his usual shrewdness, presents a complex picture of such unbridled conduct, yet shows the sense of honor irrevocably determining the self-inflicted fate of the Abbess. It is the same motive, that, in the guise of selfless patriotism, in "Vanina Vanini," determines the young revolutionary rather to go to his death on the wheel than accept the chance of escape which his treacherous mistress, in her repentance, offers him. The sense of honor is an enigmatic enough mixture of conscience and egotism; it is compatible with vice and maddening illusion; yet the most gifted personality, though plunged in defeat or despair, may still draw immense strength from its source.[4]

Stendhal's recurrent absorption in the anti-rational, the unexpected and the fantastic in human nature, has troubled many pious moralists. Yet what he attempted with so much insight was to introduce method

[4]Cf. Jacob Burckhardt: *The Culture of the Renaissance*, pp. 262–63, London, 1944, Oxford Press. There is great correspondence between the ideas of these two very different students of Italian history; Burckhardt expressed deep approval of Stendhal's interpretation of old Italy in *The Charterhouse of Parma*. However, Stendhal did not refer to the sense of honor as explicitly as does Burckhardt, but rather by implication.

and subject to reason these hitherto forbidden, uncharted regions of the mind. (It was a work that at the end of the nineteenth century would be taken up on a grand scale both as the field of scientists and great novelists.) Meanwhile he bids us in the *Italian Chronicles* to seek "understanding of the profound hatreds, the eternal suspicions, which gave so much wit and courage to Italians of the sixteenth century, and so much genius to their artists."

Nor was he wrong to say this, we reflect, when we think of the residual violence that has featured Italy's recent tragic history, and Germany's, under the madmen of power. Indeed, Stendhal recalls to us that a secret esteem for crime lurks in the minds of the uneducated masses, behind the façade of a policed civilization, and is linked with impulses either of revolution or of destruction and retrogression. He was of course not the first thinker to make such observations. From Stendhal and Freud (both essentially men of reason grappling with the anti-rational) we have received gloomy warnings of the dangers that lie in the easy assumption of an inevitable social progress. Nevertheless Stendhal—his was no "closed system," to be sure—clung firmly enough to his faith in a naturalistic "logic," a pragmatic strategy of happiness. Similarly, in his later years, Freud's dark presentiments about the future of human society were also brightened by hope for the conciliation of the ego and the collective.

The *Italian Chronicles,* besides being the most spirited of Stendhal's shorter pieces, have the added value of providing a key to the understanding of his last book, that masterwork of his ripe years, *The Charterhouse of Parma.* It was while he lived in France that he dreamed of Italy in her freshest colors. It was while he was absorbed in reading over and adapting one of his most precious Italian manuscripts, one giving the secret history of the celebrated Farnese family, that the inspiration came to him to enlarge upon this subject in the form of a novel.

CHAPTER XXI

"The Charterhouse of Parma"

SELDOM does Stendhal "invent" stories or plots; rather he takes them from newspaper reports of a trial, as in *The Red and the Black,* or from historical documents. For it is the moral ideas that these histories or plots illustrate that interest him.

For six years, since 1832, he had had in his possession a large Italian manuscript recording the rise of the Farnese family in the sixteenth century. This manuscript, he had said in a letter written at the time of its acquisition, was like a novel. "It has everything, even magic." The powerful Farnese clan, he noted, enjoyed its fortune "thanks to a strumpet, Vanozze Farnese."

In the time of the unspeakable Pope Alexander VI, she had reigned as the veritable queen of Rome, being the mistress of Alexander's favorite, the Cardinal Roderigo Lenzuoli. It was owing to her cleverness and influence that her young nephew, Alessandro Farnese, whom Stendhal considered one of the most brilliant and fortunately endowed personalities of the sixteenth century, won advancement to the highest places in the Church. But in youth the young Farnese had abandoned himself to sensual pleasures; enamored of a certain Roman lady, he had attacked her carriage escort, killed one of her servants, then carried her off to a castle, where he detained her for a month. The affair created a scandal even in those pagan days; Farnese was seized and imprisoned in the ancient Castel San Angelo in Rome. But with the aid of Roderigo, his aunt's lover, a rope three hundred feet long was smuggled to him, and he was able to escape from the tower of the great fortress, avoid trial, and live in hiding or exile. Eventually, thanks to the intrigues of his aunt, he was pardoned and even elected a cardinal while still a mere youth. This did not prevent him from forming a secret connection with still another noble Roman lady, named Cleria, noted for her great piety as well as her beauty. This union, which endured for many years, brought him two natural children. At the death of his mistress, Farnese, now in middle age, altered his whole way of life, and by his great religious devotion and diplomatic services distinguished himself as one of the leaders of the Church. At sixty-seven he was elected Pope and became known as Paul III.

Here, then, were the historical materials which, augmented by certain legends concerning other ruling Italian families, provided the grand outlines for the romance of *The Charterhouse of Parma.* The story of the Farnese family appealed to Stendhal as a perfect illustration of the art of life in old Italy whose children seemed to grow like fair plants thrusting themselves toward the sun, charged with the will to live, and the will to power.

In the scattered diaries of Stendhal, nowadays written furtively on the margins of his books, occur notes showing that even while engaged in his tour of France in 1838, he was absorbed in reading and translating his Italian manuscripts. Under the date of August 16, 1838, while studying the Farnese papers, he writes (in English): "*To make of the sketch a romanzetto?*" During the two months following he was occupied with the plan of his "little" romance.

He was now in a very happy frame of mind, in marked contrast to the sadness he felt when writing of Julien. His tales were appearing in the leading literary review of the day, the *Revue des deux mondes,* and his *Memoirs of a Tourist* had sold reasonably well. The tardy, if modest, recognition of his talents gave him hope of freeing himself at an early date from distasteful consular work. And best of all, Giulia Rinieri, his "mad virgin" of the 1830 Revolution, had returned to Paris, and, stealthily, to his arms again. He was thus able to mark one more red-letter day upon his historical suspenders: "August 3, 1838. . . . She has rendered to Dominique his friend of eleven years ago." (Actually it was eight years since he had first met her.) These autumn days of his life brought a modicum of happiness more surprising and poignant than he had ever known. It was in this mood that he began to write at top speed on November 4, 1838, continuing without a halt for seven weeks, to December 26, when the two volumes of his novel were completed!

In *The Charterhouse of Parma* the little Duchy of Parma replaces Rome: he takes the historical figure of Vanozze Farnese and makes her the Duchesa Sanseverina, or "Gina"; Cardinal Roderigo becomes Count Mosca, Minister to the Prince of Parma and lover of Gina; the handsome young Alessandro Farnese reappears as Fabrizio del Dongo, nephew of Gina; Cleria, of the Farnese annals, turns up again as *Clélia* Conti. But the singular thing is that all these characters and their adventures typifying the sixteenth century are carried over by Stendhal into the nineteenth century; we are asked to believe that the despotism and debauchery of Rome in 1500 could reappear in the little Italian principality of Parma in the 1820s. In short Stendhal reverses the procedure of Walter Scott; instead of writing really of modern people dressed in antique costumes, he writes of sixteenth-century characters and events as if they appeared in his own time.

The Charterhouse of Parma is, therefore, a sort of paradox among historical romances, and to this fact may be attributed most of the objections to the novel made by Italian critics such as Benedetto Croce, who have assured us that only "the Italy of Stendhal" is to be seen here. Insofar as the novel is a wish-fantasy, this impression is true enough: in old age Stendhal had the habit of reliving his life in dreams. He dreamed of his youth in Italy, and by a further leap of the imagination transformed those scenes he knew into those of the year 1500 when he would have desired to live.

But, it has been pointed out, in the 1820s industry and commerce already were changing Italy; popular political movements were under way, and young Italians, instead of climbing garden walls to serenade their belles, were organizing the struggle for liberation. Despotism still existed, to be sure, in various parts of the divided country, but in weakened, transitional form. Stendhal, in his canvas of "modern" Italy, it was said, ignored that which was most generous and heroic, the Carbonari, who fought for national revival.

However, Stendhal did, most patently, seek to picture the movements and forces that foreshadowed the coming upheavals in Italy. But to write with open sympathy (such as he felt) for Carbonarism, for the revolutionary movement of Young Italy, was exactly what he could least afford to do when he was still serving as a French diplomatic officer in the Papal States.

Yet *The Charterhouse of Parma* is really penetrated with the spirit of Carbonarism, the cult of Italian liberty in the 1830s. Its irony is directed unflaggingly against an outworn despotic and religious orthodoxy. The young Fabrizio is shown to be so much allured by the cause of the "antichrist," Napoleon, that he flies from home during the Hundred Days in order to take part in the Battle of Waterloo. Indeed all of the novel's principal characters are presented as extreme individualists imbued with the qualities of independence, courage, and will typical of the great Renaissance Italians. By disposition they are rebels who openly or secretly flout existing law; as Stendhal himself remarks apologetically in his preface, they all violate the criminal code in one way or another. Fabrizio is the most innocently romantic and naïve among them—but were not the Carbonari like him?

It is significant also that the climactic episodes of the romance take place in the prison of the great Farnese Tower (an imaginary edifice recalling the Castel San Angelo in Rome), where Fabrizio is unjustly incarcerated by the tyrannical Prince of Parma. These dramatic scenes in the prison-fortress were undoubtedly inspired, in part, by Stendhal's reading of his friend Pellico's prison memoirs, which during the 1830s were read all over Europe. The experience of Fabrizio thus symbolized the sufferings of the Italian political prisoners long pent up in the dungeons of the Spielberg, and clearly recalled to the many readers of Pellico that in Italy, at this period, the only place for generous youth might well be a prison dungeon. Stendhal's dedication for the second volume, as usual a little mystifying, in deference to the censorship, reads:

> By her continual outcries this republic will prevent us from enjoying the best of monarchies.

The "republic" he mentions was not yet in being.

The Charterhouse of Parma was, then, a pageant of feudal Italy in modern dress to many of its readers, especially the Italians among them. But was it the less real or truthful? It is, in great measure, thanks to Stendhal's special tactics, a profoundly "realistic" romance. Like an observant foreigner, Stendhal saw more deeply than many Italians into their own moral ambiguities, to which, in the long run, would be traceable their tragic blunders in the thirty years that were still to pass before unification came, in 1871.

But if too much of the old sixteenth-century Italy survives in Stendhal's picture—and it was that century that witnessed Italy's conquest by foreign powers and her inoculation with the habits of corruption—it is nonetheless true that he writes of his adopted land with love. For in contrast to the historical thinkers after him who worshiped the Nordic way of life, Stendhal is with all his heart a Meridional, and celebrates the way of life of the southern European, whom he honors for having produced a true civilization both in ancient and in recent times. The uninhibited "naturalness" of Italian folkways once more wins his eloquent commendation. His Italians are nearly always virile models of the passionate life, and imbued with energy to boot. The natives themselves, while flattered enough, have sometimes modestly disclaimed the virtues that Stendhal so liberally accorded them. Human traits and habits produced by climate and race are still not susceptible to exact measurement. While Stendhal could observe men and things with remarkable objectiveness, there is no doubt that, part of the time at least, he saw in sun-drenched Italy that which suited his doctrine, that which had helped him in the years of his youth to realize happiness. This novel, perhaps more than any other he wrote, was both profession of faith and confession. The impetuous, nearly automatic speed with which he wrote it—twenty to thirty pages or more in a morning—and the sense of relief and "pleasure" which, he remarks repeatedly, it gave him to do it, hints to us how much it was the work of a dream. His mind was lightning-fast. But two hundred thousand words in fifty-two days![1]

2

Over and over again, all his life he wrote the same novel. The hero, whether Julien, Lucien Leuwen, or Fabrizio, is always himself as a young man making his way through the school of experience. Each of his heroes is a youth of zeal and imagination, imagination inspired by the reading of books which have filled him with "noble illusions" about the world. Each feels himself disoriented by the defeat of the French Revolution and its popular symbol, Napoleon. Fabrizio, being a noble young Italian, is less calculating and more impulsive than Julien Sorel or Leuwen; but he too is shown to be, by force of his sensibility, sexually timid. Fabrizio, too, though held in the mold of his Italianate character, has a passion for self-analysis before action that makes him, once more, the "modern" Stendhalian man. But while Julien is tragically destroyed, his Italian counterpart achieves success, in the sense of fullest self-realization, through methods that are entirely amoral by nineteenth-century lights.

This time Stendhal was resolved to entertain the public by *narrating*, by telling a story, rather than by cool philosophizing. We must note

[1]His faithful alter ego, Romain Colomb, tells us that one day in the winter of 1839, when Stendhal was busily correcting the manuscript of *The Charterhouse*, he fell sick with gout and rheumatism, and what of pain and distress absent-mindedly misplaced a sheaf of some sixty pages of the original. As the presses were waiting, he set to work and wrote a new version of the whole missing sequence, a long chapter, which he finished in two days or so. Later, when the whole book was printed, he told Colomb about his misadventure, and Colomb relates: "I began to search for the lost manuscript, and soon located it under a great pile of papers, pamphlets, and proof sheets. Astounded at my discovery, he, nevertheless, feared to look at the original, and would not even compare it with the pages he had rewritten."

that he was writing during the flood tide of romantic prose in France, with Dumas, Hugo, Eugène Sue, and Honoré de Balzac (a Balzac still much addicted to "melodrama") as his competitors. Though Stendhal was the true forerunner of the "realistic" school, the elaborate plot of *The Charterhouse* is outwardly in the cape-and-sword tradition of the 1830s. But in examining closely the romantic properties of his novel, we perceive that in spite of them the rationale of his characters and their action is determined as by a psychologist and not by a literary romanticist. The personalities before us, in contrast with the world of voluptuousness, conspiracy, assassination, in which they move, are amazingly real, owing to the faithfulness with which the behavior pattern of each is observed. *The Charterhouse of Parma* is once more a novel of ideas.

The time of the story is the era of revolution and continental war, 1798–1825. Fabrizio del Dongo, born in the year of Napoleon's first invasion of northern Italy, is the younger son of a Lombard nobleman who brings him up in the seclusion of his country estate outside of Milan, because he is an enemy of the revolutionary French and a partisan of the Catholic-Royalist House of Hapsburg. But Fabrizio's beautiful Aunt Gina, who enjoys great influence over him, had married one of Napoleon's Italian generals and absorbed his enthusiasm for revolutionary ideas. Her nephew too becomes infected with Bonapartism in boyhood. After the defeat of French arms in 1814, the royalist nobles come creeping back to Milan; also the Austrian military rulers, the Jesuits, and all the other servants of medievalism. But during the exciting interregnum of the Hundred Days, when Napoleon suddenly escapes from Elba, to give a last battle to the Holy Alliance, Fabrizio, then only sixteen, obeys a reckless impulse and flies from his home to fight at Waterloo under the banner of the "liberator" and "true king" of Italy. Aristocratic, handsome of face and figure, artless in his idealism, Fabrizio is of course a "sublimation" of all that Henri Beyle was in youth, or would have longed to be. Like the young Beyle, he finds his father avaricious and detestable and rebels against him. His mother and aunt, on the other hand, actually serve as his confederates in arranging for his flight. The mother, however, becomes vague as the story progresses, and eventually dissolves into the high-willed but "maternal" figure of Gina, to whom her role is transferred.

The Battle of Waterloo is a digression, having little to do with the novel, and indeed takes place before its real plot begins. But Stendhal, who all his life regretted his *lâcheté* in lying in the arms of Mme. Pietragrua during that historic event, indulges in the vicarious experience of living through the great battle in fifty pages which have become as celebrated as anything in all the literature of war. In contrast with the romantic stage scenery of the rest of the novel, the Waterloo chapters compose one of the greatest experiments in literary realism, a triumph of Stendalian sincerity in art.

It seems that no one before him had the notion of describing a battle, not as if he were one of the commanding generals endowed with a bird's-eye vision and knowledge of everything going on, but as if he were a combatant, writing down only what he might have seen with the eyes in his head. The result is that original painting of the "fog of war," which Stendhal imagined was witnessed by the participants at Waterloo, based, of course, upon his own observation of large engagements on numerous battle fronts. As in a dream, or a flickering, oft-broken motion picture film, Fabrizio moves through the flotsam of the great battle, tossed hither and yon, his efforts at aggression or display of courage seeming almost comic against the confusion of the real scene. He fights, advances, retreats, gets lost, is wounded, robbed, and is both entertained and succored by the looters and camp sutlers who throng the battlefield. He wonders: "Have I really been under fire?" And like the other Beylist heroes asks himself: "Was Waterloo nothing but that?"[2]

On his return from the fields of glory to Milan, Fabrizio finds himself disinherited by his father and outlawed in his country. But he has the protection of his resourceful aunt; and, while he evades the police authorities from day to day, she bargains for his freedom. Through one of her admirers, an influential priest of Milan, Gina (who is now a widow) is able to arrange for the pardon of her adored nephew. Exiled to a neighboring city, he is to undergo a period of probation, during which his conduct must be of the most rigorous orthodoxy. It is by his spirit of independence and enthusiasm that Fabrizio has incurred the suspicion of those who rule Lombardy. Now he must win their good opinion by (1) going to Mass every day, and having a confessor; (2) avoiding persons "reputed to be intelligent"; (3) reading nothing but the official gazettes. " 'Finally,' the Canon added with a touch of malice, 'he should pay court openly to one of the pretty women of the noble class. This will show that he does not have the somber and discontented cast of mind of a potential conspirator.' "

---

[2]Military men who were present at Waterloo attested to the accuracy of this word painting. One veteran of war, Tolstoy, used its lessons to great advantage, as he acknowledged afterward, in the description of Borodino, in *War and Peace*. Stendhal's "Waterloo" is often singled out for study in comparison with Hugo's version in *Les Misérables* (incorporating the typical errors of romantic art), and with Zola's treatment of the Battle of Sédan in *La Débâcle*, modeled after Stendhal.

Fabrizio's education in conformity and virtue is now conducted solemnly enough under the eye of the clerics and his aunt. The beautiful widow, however, despite her secret passion for her nephew, is now impoverished and in search of a career herself. She is one of the great belles of Milan, a ravishing creature, all fire and wit and gaiety; but she can also *will* greatly, and exhibit a boldness in action that is reckless of moral consequences. In short, a composite of the Italian woman of destiny, with something in her of Lucrezia Borgia and Vanozze Farnese as well as that later *femme fatale* of Milan, Gina Pietragrua, whom Stendhal once loved and lost.

One evening in her box at the Scala, she meets the Count Mosca, Prime Minister and Chief of Police of the neighboring principality of Parma.

> He might have been forty or forty-five; he had deeply lined features, with no trace of self-importance, and a simple, lighthearted manner which told in his favor. He would have looked very fine indeed, if a whim on the part of his Prince had not obliged him to wear powder on his hair as a proof of his professing the right opinions in politics.

The powdered wig is of course the symbol of attachment to the *ancien régime*, the altar and the throne. But the middle-aged Mosca is quite a deep fellow: formerly a fervent Jacobin, or Italian republican, under Napoleon, and a brave officer to boot, he has ended by growing more moderate with age, and joined the party in power; but while earning the reputation of one of the most astute statesmen in Europe, he works secretly, in the interests of the popular welfare, to mitigate the excesses of the conservatives in his government. In his private conversation he mocks lightly at the dignity of his position, laughs at the prince he serves, jests about the intrigues he carries on, and strongly resembles the elderly Beyle in his role as consul to a king he despises.

But brilliant though he is, as his epigrams on history, religion, and power politics show him, his heart has always remained young. Loving Gina, he is ready to abandon all the power he holds and place such fortune as he possesses at her feet. His proposal to her—for he is married and long separated from his wife—is that they should go to live in retirement in Naples upon the moderate income he enjoys. But because he has been uncommonly honest for a politician, it is not a large fortune and offers no prospects worthy of her beauty and his talents. Perhaps this proposal is not inducement enough?

As an alternative Mosca then suggests that Gina come to Parma, where she can share his immense political power, virtually equal to that of the prince, and where the ever-fascinating exercise of such power will keep them both from being *bored.* In Parma there is a certain aged Duke Sanseverina, a man of great wealth but only recent nobility, who feels that he needs more public honors than Mosca is willing or able to grant—without certain considerations. He will persuade the old duke to marry Gina, as a formality, then leave her in his palace in Parma and depart forever to serve as ambassador to France. By this *mariage de convenance* Gina will become a duchess and be able to live secretly as Mosca's mistress, while playing a mighty role at the court of Parma. And her husband would not live forever.

"But do you know that what you propose is highly *immoral?*" she protests demurely.

"Not more immoral," he replies, "than that which is done at our court or twenty others. The advantage conferred by absolute power is that it sanctifies all sorts of conduct in the eyes of the common people." Officially no one will notice what they do, and so no harm will follow. Besides, court life is dull and has, nowadays, a most pessimistic tone. Gina will spread happiness and gaiety, a moral good in itself. She yields to him, one of her real motives being the hope of furthering Fabrizio's career, and removes to the city of Parma, where she soon shines forth as the Duchess Sanseverina.

The whole court, prince, princess, even the royal mistress, fall under her spell; the affairs of Mosca prosper, and the Opposition Party is the more easily held in check.

But what of the beloved Fabrizio? Must he live only to pass his time in cafés, ride an English horse on Sundays, and pay court to a dull mistress? What future was there now that the Revolution and Bonaparte were undone and careers were no longer open to talent? The sage Mosca points out that "though the next century will be dominated by lawyers," the young man is too noble and enthusiastic to be one of them. The army career which Fabrizio would favor would mean but the life of "the squirrel in a turning cage." Civilization, hierarchic and bureaucratic, seemed to have reached a dead end in Europe. "The main qualities required of a young man of today," Mosca reasons, "and for the next fifty years . . . so long as we are ruled by fear [for property] and religion, are those of being incapable of enthusiasm and lacking in wit."

What else was left? He must, like certain famous ancestors, take up the robe, and Mosca and the duchess would scheme to have him made Archbishop of Parma one day—the Prince Ranuccio would be persuaded to do this, since Mosca was indispensable to him.

It seemed to Fabrizio a dreadful fate to be a priest, and not a "hero." But Mosca, with deep worldliness, urges: "I do not at all intend to make him an exemplary priest. . . . He may remain as ignorant as he wishes." Was he not, by birth, a great noble?

The education of the charming Fabrizio is now continued at a great seminary in Naples, according to instructions laid down by the amiably Mephistophelian Mosca and transmitted by his aunt. He must first of all learn the "rules of the game"—the game of life, of course—and how little, alas, they seem to have changed from the time when Stendhal superbly travestied them!

> "Believe or do not believe that which you are taught, *but never make any objections.* Consider that you are learning the rules of the game of whist. Would you object to the rules of the game you are to play?"

How to succeed, how to conform, or at least how to *appear to conform,* to the opinions of those who rule society in an age of darkness, is a theme upon which Stendhal discourses with exquisite irony. Repeatedly his heroes put on the masquerade of orthodoxy or respectability the better to ridicule it. Fabrizio must believe and obey!

> "Remember that there are people who will note carefully your slightest objections; they will forgive you a little amorous affair if it is handled in the right way, but not an iota of doubt. . . . Bear this in mind at the confessional. . . .
>
> "The second rule which the count prescribes for you: if you are suddenly struck by some brilliant idea, if some crushing retort comes to you which may change the entire course of the conversation, do not give in to the temptation to shine, but remain silent; people who have finesse will see your cleverness in your eyes. There will be time to show your wit when you are a bishop."

There you have the moral subtilizations of Stendhal applied in defense of one's sensibility—Jesuitism turned against the Jesuitism with which he was at war all his life.

After three years Fabrizio returns, a man of the world at twenty-two, clad in the Purple Stockings that officially mark him as a noble and privileged member of the clerical novitiate, and destined for the higher offices in the Church. His protectors arrange for an audience with the Prince of Parma, and this too provides a scene that sparkles with Stendhalian intellectual comedy.

The monarch is no fool; surprised at seeing before him not a dull little abbé but a youth of fire and beauty, he resolves to have a little sport with him. "I think I shall play the Jacobin; we shall see what answers he will give."

He begins in the manner of Frederick the Great, the patron of Voltaire:

> "Well, well, Monsignor, are the people of Naples happy? Is the King liked?"
>
> "Serene Highness," Fabrizio replied without a moment's hesitation, "I used to admire, when I passed in the streets, the excellent bearing of the troops of His Majesty's various regiments; the better classes are respectful toward their masters, as they should be; but I must own that in all my life I have never allowed people of the lower classes to speak to me about anything but the work which I pay them to do."

Thus Fabrizio went on, parrying every effort to draw him out on forbidden political topics with reflections full of prudence and piety. Ideas about liberty, justice, or popular welfare were "infamous"; what if their application brought some material gains? Would they not end by destroying "*princes established by God*"? And of what avail were "a few years of well-being, or even a century of good fortune, compared with the eternity of suffering they ensured in the next world?"

The prince was put out of countenance and thought to himself: "There's a sly bird for you; I recognize the Sanseverina touch." For he, like everybody else, lusts for the clever Gina, and so is under pressure to show favor to her charming nephew. But if he could expose the youth a little he would have the remarkable aunt a little more under his thumb. He comforts himself by considering that, given enough rope, this clever youth, like all the other lively young men, would reveal himself at heart a follower of Voltaire and Rousseau, and so hang himself.

3

Fabrizio, with powerful support, and by his own diplomacy, climbs in the court of Parma, a microcosm of royalist society, and a mirror of the political-clerical conflict gripping the Europe of the Holy Alliance. The complicating factor is the ill-concealed passion of the duchess, now a ripe woman of thirty-five, for her young nephew. Their endless, enchanting tête-à-têtes are artless on the surface, semi-incestuous under the surface, and the meaning of this is not lost upon Mosca, middle-aged, but all somber flame for his mistress.

In one of the truly "Shakespearean" scenes in which the novel abounds, Mosca is shown pacing back and forth in the shadows of a long room, at the opposite end of which Fabrizio languishes at the feet of Gina, opening his heart to her like a child to a mother. Mosca sees the danger. He is a man of will, who has played boldly with life for high stakes, and holds to the ruthless maxim that "*the risks a man is willing to take are the measure of his rights over other men.*" He fingers his dagger, deliberating whether to kill them both and himself, but replaces it after an agonized and silent soliloquy, and hurries out with a formal "Good night." For he is also a man of measure: "I must avoid bloodshed at all costs." And young men want each woman they meet, but forget about her the next morning. He bribes the servants and pays his *sbirri* to watch them.

Fabrizio feels himself helplessly drawn by the maternal in the older woman, but is also aware of a growing sense of danger and guilt. Gina would perhaps have stopped at nothing; but in his malaise, Fabrizio takes a solitary journey to revisit his native countryside and distract his mind. He does not recognize the deep attachment to his aunt as the "great love" that he, like all the youth of the 1820s, seeks. By the shore of Lake Como, at the foot of the Alps, he wanders in a profound reverie; prowls about the château where he was born and from which he is banned; revisits in secret the church of his boyhood and a beloved old abbé who is an astrologer, and, dying, prophesies terrible dangers and adversities for his young friend.

In this so "*thickly foliated* romance" (as Balzac called it) there are continually surprising rituals and symbols, recalling ancient legends, surging up as if from the dark of the unconscious mind. Fabrizio, wandering in his native forest, that is territory forbidden him by the Austrians, determines to "reject" and never to speak of his evil passion for Gina, but asks himself if he will ever know, ever be *capable* of real love. There is the suggestion here of a hidden fear of impotence.

At one point he goes to seek a spot in the forest where his mother once planted a young chestnut tree in his honor, calling it "*Fabrizio's tree.*" To his intense relief he finds it still living and erect. The fear had come to him earlier that his father—"that stern man who had never loved him"—and his elder brother, both of whom he hates for their unnatural cruelties to him, "might have had the tree cut down." But only a single branch "broken by the wind, or mischief-makers, hangs down, all withered." Reverently he cuts it off, cleans the wound with his knife, and turns up the earth around this tree which is the image of fruitfulness, before departing on his lonely way.

This was but a superstitious folly, the author apologetically comments, yet the whole extended passage is extremely rich in symbolism and "dreamwork." Fabrizio is modern youth, in reverie in the mysterious forest of life, feeling himself persecuted by his own father, fearing for his own strength, filled with guilty longings or remembrances, "attentive ever to the need for keeping on his guard in the presence of hypocritical and dangerous enemies."

During that long dark night in the forest, brooding, sometimes weeping, never closing his eyes, he wrestles with the problems of his ambivalent relationship with Gina, his future as a priest, his doubts of himself when on the threshold of life, his sense of society's injustice and of his own privileged position. But when the night has ended, he has arrived at certain "courageous resolutions," and at last joys in the mighty dawn that pours its light down the giant spurs of the Alps and over Lake Como. He feels himself charged with "generous and virtuous sentiments . . . delivered of an enormous burden."

His solutions are "Italianate" in the Stendhalian sense: "Since my birth has given me the right to profit by those social abuses it would be an extreme folly not to take my share." Fabrizio stops thinking at a certain point, accepts life, and suffers no prolonged torments of conscience over doctrines. But one marvels at how well Stendhal, nearing sixty, remembers and understands all the dreams, the fears, the desires of the heart of youth.

On his return to Parma, Fabrizio becomes absorbed in a little actress. Her jealous lover, the clown, Giletti, encounters him by chance on a road outside of Parma and attacks him; Fabrizio, though poorly armed, kills the clown and runs off with the actress.

For a nobleman to kill a poor comedian in self-defense was then a legal bagatelle; but high politics and the Opposition Party in Parma, eager to injure Mosca and his brilliant mistress, will otherwise. Fabrizio is charged with murder by false witnesses, and his arrest is ordered by the prince, still piqued at not having had his way with the Duchess Gina. The youth is driven to flight again, and experiences some picturesque adventures, including a new though shallow amour (for an opera singer), which lures him back to Parma. Discovered in spite of an amusing disguise, he is apprehended and imprisoned in the mighty citadel of Parma without charge or trial, for a term fixed at twenty years.

As in *The Red and the Black*, so in *The Charterhouse* a prison plays a most significant part in the drama. And what a prison is the "Farnese Tower," three hundred feet high, with great windows opening upon a splendid view of life itself, for Fabrizio's keep is on the topmost terrace, adjacent to the turret in which the governor and his beautiful daughter live. The prison enters the story because Alessandro Farnese, the original model of Fabrizio, was imprisoned in the Castel San Angelo, one of whose famous inmates was Benvenuto Cellini. But another reason for it is that Fabrizio is after all the blood brother of Julien Sorel. He too must be alienated from his evil father, he too divided in his heart between two women, one older, one very young. And the recurrence of these themes is required by the "system" of Stendhal's libido, by the unconscious desires and wish-fantasies in his mind.[8]

Imprisonment was what Stendhal most feared; and though he could be brave enough in time of war, the thought of the risks he ran of being shut up in the Spielberg fortress as a liberal often made him take almost comical precautions against the police. Prison meant the end of his liberty; it meant death, and resolution. It was both feared and secretly longed for. As often as he mocked at the fear of death in others, so did his mind preoccupy itself with it, drawing little pictures of pistols on his manuscripts, gripped by the fixation of suicide and death as the "Dionysian" immolation which would finally dissolve his ego, with all its doubts and conflicts. But while unconsciously he renounces life, the ultimate prison house of death is graciously ornamented by his imagination, as was that mythical underworld to which the heroes of ancient Greek legend used to descend, and Orpheus went to find Eurydice and sing to her.

In the citadel of Parma, Fabrizio, who has been struggling for solutions of his own problems, finds a peace he has not hitherto known and a great love. In the daughter of the governor, Clélia Conti, whom he has only seen once before in Milan, as a mere child, he recognizes his long-sought Eurydice. He too, like Julien Sorel in the prison of Verrières, experiences that Dionysiac frenzy of self-fulfillment that Nietzsche would call "liberation from the *principium individuationis.*" So long as he may speak with his eyes to Clélia on her balcony, or, despite the prison bars that separate them, make ardent love to her in sign language, he will not leave his prison for any other place in the world.

Meanwhile his high-willed aunt and the resourceful Count Mosca have been moving heaven and earth to arrange for Fabrizio's escape. They convey a rope to him, and devise a system of secret signaling by a lantern in the hills to the youth up in the tower. To the anguish of his infatuated aunt, he signals back: *"I do not wish to escape, I wish to die here!"*

---

[8] "These themes . . . corresponded to strong sentiments that sought to liberate themselves: thwarted ambitions, aesthetic feelings, old fears, disgusts, obscure dreams. . . . Stendhal carried in himself a fixed image of *his hero* . . . and Fabrizio is . . . brother to Julien, albeit a privileged brother, fairer and happier." Pierre Martino, *Revue d'histoire littéraire de la France* (1930), p. 114.

To escape, live in exile from all he loves (as even Clélia urges), would leave him "unable to breathe." It were better to be poisoned by his jailers, as his friends fear is intended. This is a fate that only Clélia's courage and cleverness spares him.

It is only because Clélia, despairing of his safety, commands him to escape, that he finally makes his way down the sheer citadel walls. But feeling that she has betrayed her father in aiding Fabrizio's flight, Clélia vows before God that if only her lover's life is spared, she "will never see him again" as long as she lives.

The affair of Fabrizio and Clélia is a model of pure and passionate love, which Stendhal paints with great depth of sentiment and yet with restraint. Clélia, like Gina, is one of Stendhal's matchless portraits of women, for the understanding of whom his own sexual timidity and his masochistic penchant for feminine authority so singularly qualified him.

Prior to his escape, the indomitable Gina, with the aid of the wily Mosca, has been waging a mighty political battle to defeat the rival party, turn Parma upside down, and win the release of Fabrizio. In this mimic warfare every device of power politics is employed by both sides; newspapers are bought, the public is agitated by rumors, and poison too comes into play. At Gina's command, one of her would-be lovers, a revolutionary poet, does for the prince with a deadly potion, for Gina has given up her nephew for lost. In her frenzy, she even orders the bursting of a dam on her estate outside of Parma, loosing a flood of moderate depth upon her enemies. At her château in Sacca, she meanwhile holds a great Priapic feast, attended with fireworks, the distribution of money and vats of wine for the peasants. "Wine for Sacca, water for the people of Parma!" she cries. These episodes, extravagant though they seem, were developed by Stendhal from actual incidents in the history of the city-states of the sixteenth and seventeenth centuries; they seem scarcely suited to 1825.

At this point, the novel should have been brought to an end, whether tragic or comic: at the conclusion of Chapter XXII of the second volume. It was the opinion of no less an authority than Balzac; for, hereafter the force of the action is diffused; the principal characters seem exhausted by their passion. The heroic figure of Gina retreats into exile with that man of wit, Mosca; Clélia goes to the altar with the respectable husband chosen by her father; Fabrizio takes vows, becomes profoundly religious, and in a threadbare old cassock preaches the most fervent sermons. What follows appears to us anticlimactic after the dramatic amplitude of the prison sequence, and somewhat comic in spirit.

But Stendhal intended to write a third volume; he had a good deal more to say and, as always, it was not wanting in interest and importance. Prodded by his bookseller to shorten the novel, he "strangled" or hastily compressed what remained, to his own regret. Much of its retrospective and philosophical summation was to have been developed in that imagined Charterhouse of Parma to which Fabrizio eventually retreats, and which happens to provide the mystifying title of the novel, though mentioned only briefly on the last page.

It was the essence of his plan in this novel, which is the uninhibited realization of his own dream, that his hero should triumph over life's adversities and dangers. It was to be an illustration of his favorite thesis that happiness *was* attainable in Italy. For in that fortunate land the people were possessed still of the advantages of a form of civilization, ancient and subtile, which also wisely permitted them to live as "natural" beings in full accord with their instincts for animal pleasure. Whereas in northern Europe man, caught in the mold of modern society, showed himself already dominated by money-greed, vanity, and the fear of public opinion.

The Charterhouse of Parma, compared with *The Red and the Black,* is a work of affirmation; it is a "hymn to life"; a song of the Italy he loved in youth and dreamed in age; it is suffused with joy, and good humor lightens even its most ironic passages. While it is a beautiful pendant for the earlier masterpiece, it reflects the more resigned temper of Stendhal in his late years. He loved life with his last breath, and far from being a pessimist, was equal, up to the very end, to the most Shandean gaiety. In his swan song he gives us intimations, more clearly than before, of his challenging doctrines concerning his "art of happiness," which, now by brave defiance of the social police, now by skillful protection of the sensibility and discipline of the emotions—"distracting" if not removing life's chagrins—may lead to the full flowering of the individual being.

That such physical and moral harmonies could be achieved only in Italy strikes us as adventitious, and grounded in the accidents of his personal geography. But have not modern men continued to search for their own "Italies" wherever in the world they may be found? Has not "escapism," never better diagnosed than in Stendhal, remained a profound symptom of social malady since his time?

Both as essay in ideas and work of art his novel is a persuasive pleading for the true therapy of man as social being. Even religion is pressed into service and shown to have a vital and protective function for Stendhal's "natural" Italian. "To believe is a good thing both for this world and the next," was Gina's parting counsel as Fabrizio entered upon his clerical career. By intuition he is a believer, but it is no burden to him. The concluding moral of the whole tale is as impious as possible.

Fabrizio's eloquence and fervor as a preacher enchants all Parma, wins him the greatest honors, and draws crowds of women of the best society, who weep and swoon on hearing him. Only Clélia shuns him. At length, partly out of a presumed piety, but also out of curiosity and downright jealousy, she too comes to the cathedral. Once having heard him she promptly yields and sends him a note fixing an assignation. Fabrizio is filled with a sense of triumph; as he doffs his old cassock for mufti, and goes to her, he exclaims: "At last I am done with preaching!" But owing to her earlier vows to the Virgin (never to *see* him) and with not a little casuistry, Clélia insists upon receiving her lover in an apartment that is always completely darkened. To the public he remains a great prelate, privately he is the discreet lover. Eventually Clélia bears him a son, whom he educates to be a great lord.

When Clélia dies, after but a few years of happy union with him, Fabrizio goes to his monastic retreat at the Charterhouse of Parma, a new "prison" deep in the countryside, where he lives out his days renowned in all Italy for his virtue and wisdom. For all these personages the end comes quickly, as if they disdained to live, once the cycle of danger and passion was finished for them.

4

On reading *The Charterhouse of Parma,* Balzac said in his enthusiastic review: "He [Stendhal] has written 'The Prince of Modern Times,' the novel Machiavelli would have written if he were living banished from Italy in the nineteenth century." Other reviewers and commentators shared Balzac's view of its "Machiavellian" character without approving of the novel. They went on to point out that each of the four principal characters was essentially "immoral" or antisocial: Gina was a strumpet who exploited men's passions for her, married an old man whom she cuckolded, poisoned the Prince of Parma, and committed adultery with his young successor to win the freedom of Fabrizio, for whom she showed a guilty love. Mosca served a prince whom he despised, gave bribes, provoked public disorder for political ends;

Fabrizio lived but for his amusement and sensual pleasure, and entered the service of the Church without being truly called; while even the fair Clélia betrayed her father and broke her vow in surrendering herself to Fabrizio. At first blush their lives seem rooted in cynicism. And the public career of Mosca in particular appears, as Charles Maurras said, "a charming manual of political knavery."

In short, the rather *simpliste* impressions of Balzac (who with the publication of this novel now came forward as an unconsidered admirer and champion of Stendhal) have helped to spread the notion that in presenting characters who were "as a law unto themselves," the author had given too little thought to the opposition between unrestricted individual liberty and the general good. Some of the forerunners of modern Machiavellianism (or fascism) have used or abused his ideas: these are Count Gobineau, Charles Maurras, of the Action Française, and Maurice Barrès. Yet the Left also has cherished Stendhal as its own: Léon Blum and Louis Aragon (and the young Resistance leaders of 1940–44) have taken their inspiration from him. The modern critic, André Suarès, has named him pre-eminently the "good European" and "the poet of France and Revolutionary Europe." Each generation and each camp has used him according to its own world view, as has happened with others of the more difficult and inscrutable masters of the world's literature.

It is nonetheless true that in this novel he illustrates and defends his ethics of passion, presenting his principal characters as inherently rebels against society. In doing so, Stendhal continued the work of Rousseau, who advocated the "return to nature" and the liberation of the individual.

Born under an authoritarian regime that collapsed, and having seen later the attempts to restore that *ancien régime* in the face of all popular movements, his chief concern, during the phase of history through which he lived, was lest social institutions crush the free individual. It was to be the overwhelming concern of the great social-minded writers at the end of the nineteenth century, the Russians, Swedes, French, and English of the movement that embraced Tolstoy and Shaw, among whom Stendhal, posthumously, took his natural place.

One can scarcely leave the subject of this novel without considering further the portrait of Count Mosca. It has exerted a spell upon thoughtful readers who have seen in him the political oracle of the older Stendhal. Only a born diplomat and a profound student of statecraft, Balzac held, could have drawn such a portrait. Balzac even assumed that Mosca had been modeled after Prince Metternich himself, though Stendhal denied this. Mosca was most likely patterned after Count Saurau, minister to the Duke of Tuscany, who after 1815 labored secretly for the unification of Italy, and was much admired by the consul at Civita Vecchia for his sagacity. Stendhal explained to Balzac that he took real people and placed them in different circumstances. Thus there was actually no despotic Prince of Parma ruling in 1825—rather a mild regency government under Marie Louise, the wife of Napoleon, placed in that principality by the Congress of Vienna. The Prince Ernesto Ranuccio IV may have been modeled after that Duke of Modena, who, in Stendhal's time, prohibited the passage of diligences through his territory for fear they might become carriers of modern political ideas. But as Stendhal wrote to Balzac, his studies of high politics were really carried on at St. Cloud at the court of Napoleon I.

Worldly, irreligious, tolerant, and philosophical, Mosca is essentially an Italian Humanist of the Renaissance type, and the Humanist then was amoral by our present standards. In him Stendhal exemplifies what he has called "the ravishing happiness of power," but also its dangers, of which he is aware. (The picture of the power politics of his imaginary Italian duchy may well be regarded as a microcosm of the political activity Stendhal observed at the Grand Council of Napoleon.) Problems of the utmost complexity are met and solved with infinite finesse by Mosca. While pretending to be a conservative, he mocks at his prince, yet also serves him faithfully, for "the tradition of the courtier" is strong in him. But he stops the too frequent hanging of the revolutionary Carbonari; he ridicules the prince's inept measures of despotism. "You must either slay ten thousand people at once, or yield to the force of events," that is, make concessions to popular demands. This is a remark worthy of Machiavelli, who at any rate was systematic in his approach to the problems of power. But then, unlike Machiavelli, Stendhal's Count Mosca shows a conscience. There are things he will not do in any event, because he does not want to be afflicted with "dark thoughts," that is, remorse, in his old age. He is also bent on avoiding violence and bloodshed. To be sure, he mocks at the republicans and the doctrinaires who believe that a constitution and a representative system alone will lift mankind into Utopia. But, at heart, he is a cagey, opportunistic Liberal.

In the field of politics, as in that of social ethics, Stendhal delights in rattling all the skeletons in the closet. He stresses the atavistic in human nature; he shows us how easily men of power may dazzle and mislead the people. For did he not live and serve under Napoleon the Great? The lesson of Napoleon for him was that of the need of will and energy as well as good doctrine. The French Republican leaders were still talking of freedom and equality, quarreling with each other and accomplishing nothing—in 1799 as in 1939—when Napoleon seized his chance and made himself the "progressive" dictator of the bourgeoisie, the armed champion of their revolution. Nor can the lessons that Stendhal draws from Bonapartism be ignored by us who have seen recently how the statesmen of the world's richest and most advanced nations, while prating of their humane principles, permitted a few energetic scoundrels to win power over most of the European continent. And how much dreadful effort and sacrifice of life and treasure it would need, in the end, to repel the threat of the new barbarians.

Stendhal tenaciously believed in the eighteenth-century concepts of reason and progress, by whose lights we still struggle to advance again; but he also warns us that besides having humane ideals we must have will, enthusiasm, and energy in order to realize them. This exponent of extreme individualism, hating the reaction that dominates Europe in his time, is no political retrograde but a realistic democrat whose minimal demands are for the free press, the jury trial, a parliamentary system, and universal education. Big Government in its Napoleonic form sometimes allured him by its mastery of the realities of power, but Jefferson's maxims of liberalism had the more enduring appeal, by his own testimony. Meanwhile his satirical picture of a despot and his rule is not designed to make his readers long for the blessings of authoritarian regimes.

The setting and the action of *The Charterhouse of Parma* are romantic; the treatment and style are realistic.

Stendhal admitted that he liked his characters to be of a heroic scale and "noble." His descriptions of them are brief and without the massed detail or vivid colors of Balzacian description at its best. But, as in *The Red and the Black*, he "places" them by their mental characteristics, their habits of fearing or desiring, loving or fighting, their different ways of pursuing happiness.

Whereas characters in Balzac's novels are often represented by but a single human trait, appearing as the man of avarice, or the man of power, the man of pleasure, the "beast of prey," those of Stendhal are rounded, complex, made of many contradictory impulses.

Unlike his contemporaries, Stendhal does not rejoice or weep over his personages; he neither condemns nor apologizes for them (or very seldom), so that they seem to have an objective existence; their own acts and words speak for them.

Was he romantic or classical? Obviously he was both. By his dry wit and his restraint he often resembled the great seventeenth- and eighteenth-century French prosateurs and moralists. But, by his own definition, he was also romantic, since he wrote to please himself, or his own idea of the time spirit, and not in imitation of models approved by the Academy.

As Stendhal largely resisted the intellectual influences and fashions of his time there is something timeless about his novel. Much of *The Charterhouse of Parma* might have been written by a contemporary of Shakespeare or Cervantes; but other parts of it might have been written in 1938 instead of 1838.

His style, which was severely censured during his own epoch, was made up of short and often choppy sentences, sometimes ill-formed, sometimes monotonous by dint of repetitions of phrasing and sentence structure. But Stendhal sought above all to be clear and exact, often going to great pains to explain his thought in precise terms. He wished that his style might be neutral, impersonal, even impalpable, for he thought that an involved style that called attention to itself was an obstacle to the communication of ideas. And ideas were of paramount importance to him. In the end his great lucidity won the admiration of readers of later generations. His pleasantry about carrying over the tone of the Civil Code, which he told Balzac he read each morning while writing *The Charterhouse*, has become famous; but there is no doubt that he sought a corrective against romantic style and romantic thinking. Nevertheless, as he goes forward under the lash of strong feeling, in his last novel, his prose assumes a pace and power unsurpassed by anything written in his century. The intrigue of *The Charterhouse of Parma* is designed upon a vast scale. Yet the novelist directs the action like a general who is a born strategist of life. Though the characters, behavior, and the setting may sometimes appear arbitrary, we end by accepting them, by reading with excitement, never knowing from page to page what intellectual surprises this master of psychological probabilities will provide next.

But the success of his novels is based chiefly on their use as vehicles for his ideas. One may reread him endlessly, each time discovering new shades of thought. "Often there is a whole book contained in a single page of his," Balzac commented admiringly. His work suggests to us that we must seek to revive the novel in which ideas are dramatized. It is perhaps the only hope for prose fiction. The novelist too must be a man of intelligence.

5

Early in April 1839, *The Charterhouse of Parma* was published in two volumes by the bookseller, Ambroise Dupont. The contract brought Stendhal twenty-five hundred francs, considerably more than any other of his books, and this one was well received by the public, selling in two editions, amounting to three thousand copies. But as France began to read him, Stendhal had already left the country for Italy. This was part of the mystery that always attached to him, a mystery made up of his pseudonyms, his long absences abroad, his independence of spirit, that set him apart from his contemporaries. As Balzac wrote:

> In the world of letters, M. Beyle is not a courtier; he has the most profound horror of the press. . . . He does not haunt the footsteps of the reviewers. . . . When his books come out he is usually two hundred and fifty leagues from Paris. . . . I admire this pride of character or this sensitiveness of self-esteem.

Balzac, who had only recently begun to enjoy the success he merited, had met M. Beyle two or three times in society, before he read the new novel. Encountering him by chance on the Boulevard des Italiens, Balzac congratulated him warmly and doubtless promised that he would say something about the new book in the *Revue de Paris*. To Balzac, he seemed almost a legendary figure; his speech was full of charm and eccentricity, while "his fine forehead, his keen and piercing eye, his sardonic mouth . . . had altogether the physiognomy of his talent." The two stoutest men of letters in France approved of each other generously, but went their separate ways.

Few reviews of any consequence appeared in the press; there was danger that the book would be entirely overlooked. Stendhal's faithful cousin, Colomb, therefore earnestly besought Balzac, whom Stendhal already called "the King of Novelists," to rescue the work from oblivion. Rather late, for Balzac was much overworked, the article appeared, taking up seventy pages, in two numbers of his own *Revue de Paris*, in September and October 1840. The impetuous author of the *Comédie humaine* did nothing by halves and his long notice, with its ringing encomiums, made up one of the few literary triumphs Stendhal enjoyed in his lifetime:

> *La Chartreuse de Parme* is of our period . . . the masterpiece of the Literature of Ideas. . . .
>
> M. Beyle has written a book in which sublimity glows from chapter to chapter.

Balzac has the air of embarking on a controversy, of taking up cudgels for what Sainte-Beuve would call one of his "beloved unknowns." He tells us that he only seeks to bring fame, "to do justice to a man of immense talent," whom the public ignores and who is read only by "a few privileged beings." And is that not a good deed? he asks.

M. Beyle was "one of the superior men of this time." The picture of Waterloo, the atmosphere of Italy, the action of his romance, were all beautiful and true beyond words. The whole thing was perhaps too long; it should have been either shorter or longer, he remarks shrewdly. But what living man knew politics and court life so deeply? Who was there who could depict characters of such "monumental" size? Artlessly and generously Balzac bubbles over with his admiration, which, he assures us, increases each time he reads the novel over, and he concludes:

> It is hard to explain how this observer of the first order, this profound diplomat who, whether in his writings or in his speech, has furnished so many proofs of the loftiness of his ideas and the extent of his practical knowledge, should find himself nothing more than consul at Civita Vecchia. No one would be better qualified to represent France at Rome.

To Stendhal, who was in Italy when this article of Balzac's was sent to him in October 1840, the unstinted praise of the man who was becoming the leading novelist of his day was heady wine. It is evident that he felt quite overwhelmed, and started to write a letter of thanks to Balzac three times—we do not know which draft was finally mailed:

> I was quite surprised, sir, at the article which you were so kind as to devote to the *Chartreuse*. I must thank you for your advice even more than for your praise. You have shown a perhaps exaggerated pity for a poor orphan abandoned in the streets. I had expected not to be read before 1880.

With much humility he admits the justice of Balzac's criticisms of the length of his novel and accepts his suggestions that some of its digressions be emended. For who was a better judge of the subject than

M. de Balzac? (When, however, he came to revise his first version, his tendency was to lengthen rather than diminish it: a whole added chapter concerning the experiences of Fabrizio, after his adventures at Waterloo, and exceedingly rich in Stendhalian wit and inventiveness, is the result of this attempt at excision, and may be read in the appendix of modern editions of the novel.) But though he appreciated Balzac's advice with regard to organization, he resisted proposals for the improvement of his style.

The amusing thing was that Stendhal despised Balzac's often inflated style. In the *Memoirs of a Tourist* he had remarked, in one of his digressive literary notes, that while he admired Balzac, he thought his style (even in the brilliant *Vicar of Tours*) was overladen with phrases such as "snow is falling in my heart," and other such fine touches designed to please servant maids or provincial readers. In his letter of October 1840 to Balzac, he argues vigorously against "the style now in fashion." Nothing will induce him to write like Sir Walter Scott, Xavier de Maistre, Mme. Sand, or Chateaubriand, who, he was certain, would be ignored by future generations. No, he must strive to be clear at all costs: "If I am not clear, the world around me collapses." In a portion of his letter that was perhaps suppressed, Stendhal goes so far as to criticize and warn Balzac upon his own style and his marked tendency to overwrite.

But there is no doubt that Balzac had made him happy. No contemporary having such influence, not even his own friend Mérimée, had ever spoken kindly of his books. (Stendhal had known nothing of the great interest that Goethe took in *The Red and the Black* in 1831.) He was even in some embarrassment lest his friends laugh at the whole business as a hoax: "I wonder what faces they will make when they read this," he exclaimed.

The Charterhouse of Parma gained a moderate public success; but as its spirit and tone were utterly opposed to the current literary trend, it exerted no discernible influence at the time. Soon Stendhal was forgotten again. Even the rousing calls of a Balzac could not help him.

CHAPTER XXII

"The Difficult Passage"

MIRACULOUSLY his leave of absence was prolonged for three whole years, up to the spring of 1839, thanks to the benevolence of Minister Molé; then abruptly and painfully came to an end.

During his stay in France, besides enjoying literary dinners, going to the theater, and haunting the bookstalls, Stendhal delighted in following the great game of politics as if from the wings. Under the wily constitutional king, the tactics of parliamentary combination had become trickier than ever. With infinite cunning, the rival party leaders of the Right, Center, and Left constantly maneuvered for advantage, while the even more astute "July Monarch" played them off against each other in the interests of his personal rule. On days when important debates were expected in the Chamber of Deputies Stendhal would attend in the gallery. Thus he himself applauded the overthrow of Count Molé's Ministry, which terminated his holiday.

On January 3, 1839, he wrote to an Italian friend in Rome that a great parliamentary contest was shaping up which promised to be more amusing than the finest novel in the world. As always, Guizot, chief of the Conservative party, was pitted against Thiers, the "eloquent representative of the Center," while Odilon Barrot, the leader of the moderate Left, also pushed himself forward from time to time. Stendhal writes:

> Three thieves have combined to rob a man who is possessed of the fair diamond that is called power; once the man is down and out how will they arrange to share this diamond?

Uncertainly propped up in office was the government of Count Molé, the liberal Catholic, who befriended Beyle. A resounding attack was being prepared by the leading orators of the opposition, including the Deputy Duvergier de Hauranne, sometimes described (by Sainte-Beuve) as one of Stendhal's young philosophical disciples. With a discerning eye Stendhal points to the heart of the dilemma that has often plagued bourgeois politics, whose factious conflicts always center upon disagreements over the profits of power rather than its permanent disposition:

> Here is the funny side of the picture. . . . The attacking forces are moving to have the Chamber vote a resolution which strongly censures the policy of the Minister and may force him to hand in his resignation. The opposition cannot say plainly to the Ministry: "Instead of doing *this* you should have done *that*."
>
> For if they succeed, tomorrow they will find themselves in the Ministry and then, by the words they pronounced yesterday, will be obliged to do *that which* they themselves recommended.
>
> Therefore they must find some ingenious way of censuring the Minister violently without ever saying what *they* would do in his place, otherwise their speeches on the morrow will provide an extreme embarrassment for them.
>
> And now, my dear Count, you may understand how amusing this contest seems to a nation that is so full of wit. And especially when the leading figures are among the cleverest people in the country.

It was all too fascinating; but the attacks of the liberal opposition leaders, including his own friend, Duvergier, so hugely enjoyed by Stendhal, embarrassed the government enough to force a vote of confidence that led to the resignation of his protector, on March 8, 1839. Renewed efforts to win some office that would keep him in Paris failed again; and in June, Stendhal was forced to return to his disagreeable duties at Civita Vecchia, with Marshal Soult as his chief. En route he tarried at Florence and Siena, pleading an attack of gout. But happily the affectionate Giulia Rinieri was there to console him. Only in mid-August did he regain Civita Vecchia.

Conditions here had become even less agreeable than ever before. His detested assistant, Lysimaque Tavernier, reigning in his absence, had managed to advance himself recently to the office of chancellor to the consulate, and with the aid of the ambassador to Rome had gained the Cross of the Legion of Honor. Stendhal also found that trade had become far more active and the routine business of his office, much as he tended to neglect it, now seriously interrupted his own writing program. Defying the polite complaints of his superiors in the Foreign Ministry, he continued to absent himself as often as possible by making frequent journeys to Rome and the Alban Hills, and even as far as Naples, which he revisited in the company of his friend Prosper Mérimée in November 1839. But Mérimée, now very much the dandy, the lady-killer and the time-server in public office, irritated him by his "fearful vanity." Stendhal, it must be noted, could not abide the real cynicism of the future court favorite of Louis Napoleon. Their friendship cooled. What Mérimée later wrote of Stendhal, scarcely the loyal testimony of a disciple and friend of twenty years' standing, reflected the polite rupture that took place late in 1839.

At this period we place another amorous *passade* involving a certain unknown "Lady Earline," so named in the hermetic fragments of Stendhal's diaries. Presumably she was a respected figure in Roman diplomatic society, whether English, as the name suggests, or Italian we do not know. Stendhal studied the defences of this lady, and analyzed her as *"reservée, timide, si bourgeoise—la femme sans roman!"* Nevertheless, though he had now turned fifty-seven, he once more put on his finest sartorial armor and gallantly "attacked," that is, he made his declaration and proposals in full accordance with his precepts. He was ignominiously rebuffed.

By January 1841, his diary notes record the aging Lovelace as watching "Lady Earline" at a ball in Rome, with an aching heart. She had closed her door to him forever.

2

On returning to Civita Vecchia, Stendhal resumed his habit of writing every morning to distract his mind from a sense of loneliness and the cares of the consular business. It is evident from a letter of April 25, 1838, dated at Bordeaux, that he planned a series of novels that were to deal with the moral customs of the regime of Louis Philippe in France, and form a "history of my time," to be published only after his death. One of these, *Lucien Leuwen,* was two-thirds done. Another he outlined in the autumn of 1839, making detailed notes on its principal characters. Beginning the writing of it in October, he soon completed three hundred pages of the unfinished novel that was to be called *Lamiel.* But he interrupted it midway, and early in 1840 tried to revise and rewrite the opening chapters with great care. His earlier novels, even *The Charterhouse of Parma,* had been censured for being too cerebral. What he was concerned about once more was to "narrate an action, instead of the moral résumé of an action." Illness stayed his hand. All that we have is a strange fragment, half of an unrevised novel, and some notes that give a clue to the nature of the concluding section.

It is plain that he was influenced, at this stage, by the successes of Eugène Sue and Balzac with novels of horror or crime. "I must follow the methods now in fashion," he tells himself, "though adapting them to *my* ideas." But inevitably *Lamiel* was to carry on in the tradition of *The Red and the Black*, and the heroine, again a free soul in rebellion at the vulgarity and hypocrisy of the world, was to be the female counterpart of Julien Sorel.

Stendhal's mood darkens perceptibly in this novel of his declining years, whose tone is quite different from the tender irony of *The Charterhouse*. In the depression that followed his return to his post in the "desert," as he called Civita Vecchia, his very appearance seemed to disintegrate. Those who saw him in Rome occasionally in these last years found him fatter than before, but also more lined and wrinkled than ever. And his face was now somewhat disfigured by all sorts of muscular tics and contortions. His smile seemed more a grimace than a smile. As if aware of his increasing heaviness and ugliness, he made himself even more bizarre than before. He would laugh and mock at everything, and most of all at himself. "Well, I would rather be taken for a chameleon than an ox," he would say to explain his strange sallies. At Rome, as he himself related, he used to eat at one of the best restaurants of the town, but in old age had an infernal habit of breaking dishes, owing to his great corpulence and consequent awkwardness at the table. And so he felt obliged to pay a double tip to the waiter who served him. "Hilariously he likened himself to Philopöemen paying Mégaris the added reckoning for his ugliness, as he at Rome paid for his embonpoint."[1]

In the unfinished novel *Lamiel*, we find a striking portrait of an ugly, hunchbacked, intriguing fellow, named Dr. Sansfin, whose wit reveals him as a possible self-caricature of the author. One of his bitter sayings, reflecting Stendhal's present mood, runs: "This world is nothing but a bad comedy played without grace by heartless scoundrels and infamous liars. . . ."

Lamiel, the heroine, however, is a beautiful girl, with an oval face, fair hair, deep blue eyes, and a long chin, much like Stendhal's friend of long ago, Mélanie Guilbert. Born in the foundling asylum of a Norman village, she is adopted and reared by the sexton and his wife; but because of her remarkable intelligence she is engaged by the local

[1]Desroches, "Souvenirs Anecdotiques sur M. de Stendhal," *Revue de Paris*, Tome XXVI, 1844.

chatelaine, the Duchess de Miossens, to be her reader and companion, and takes up residence in the castle overlooking the village. Yet Lamiel is discontented and restless: she has a disposition to reason and read books; curiosity about everything dominates her; and the country nobles seem as horrid to her as the peasants. At length she falls dangerously sick, and none can diagnose her illness, until the cunning hunchback, Dr. Sansfin, is called in. He announces that her illness is simply boredom, and proceeds to "cure" her by acting as her mentor, giving her all sorts of forbidden and "immoral" books to read, preaching to her incessantly his own "terrible maxims." She must know herself and the world, casting off hypocrisies and repressions such as her foster parents and the curate believe in, or the duchess finds useful in dealing with her servants. His cure for her is the advice to "hearken to the voice of nature, and follow every caprice . . . in order to gain pleasure, the sole object of the human race." He warns her:

> "How many young girls die before reaching the age of twenty-three and then what good are all their pains, the pleasures they have denied themselves in order to win the good opinion of the eight or ten old women who form the high society of the village?"

As a parting shot, he adds that while engaged in the pursuit of happiness, Lamiel must not fail to arrange "all the necessary little subterfuges and tricks" (of hypocrisy) which will permit her to hold the good opinion of the old women who enjoy social credit.

In old age Stendhal enjoyed his youthful disciples as much as Socrates did. He delighted in playing cicerone and mentor to the Counts Cini and Caëtani, or in Paris to young Ampère and Duvergier, advising them what books to read, or even where to find a reasonable and discreet bordello. Much in the same terms as we conceive he used, Dr. Sansfin reasons with Lamiel and instructs her. In this world, he says, men are either dupes or rogues. But could Lamiel believe him any more than the others? Did not he too have some interest in deceiving her? He answers her doubts by inviting her to "test" his truths freely:

> "As I have said, being surrounded by gross creatures to whom I must lie every day in order not to become the victim of the brute force they wield, I find it the greatest boon to discover an unspoilt person filled with natural genius. To cultivate that genius and to dare to speak the truth to her is a supreme pleasure consoling me for all that I am forced to do each day to earn my living."

But what is *love*, Lamiel asks, that everyone talks about, and warns her of? "A dangerous subject," he replies, which he refuses to discuss, for he himself has elaborate plans for her: the ugly man loves her, but intrigues to have her marry the foppish son of the duchess, hoping to make her his mistress afterward and use her wealth to further his own schemes for gaining political power during a revolution.

Lamiel uses his devil's counsels to her own ends. Since she must know what love is, she walks in a strip of woods near the village—that the curé has forbidden young girls to enter—with a sturdy peasant youth. He proves to be interested only in his crops and the money he may earn; therefore she promises him ten francs, twice his daily increment, if he will show her what "love" is.

"Kiss me," she said. He thought it was almost too good to be true; she paid well and she was so pretty. She desired to be his mistress, she said point-blank:

> "Ah, that is different," said Jean in a businesslike tone. And then without transports of feeling, without love, the young Norman took Lamiel for his mistress.
>
> "Is there nothing more?" Lamiel asked.
>
> "No."
>
> "What, is love no more than that?" she asked herself in surprise. "Why then do they condemn it?" She called him and paid him the ten francs. He gave impassioned thanks. . . . She watched him go off, then burst into laughter, repeating to herself: "What! This famous love, is it only that?"

In this tone of brutal satire the story continues. Beautiful Lamiel, sufficiently armed with knowledge of the real world, seduces and marries the young Duke de Miossens, then leaves him because he is only an effeminate aristocrat. Fleeing to Paris, she deliberately lives the life of an expensive courtesan, takes a notorious gambler for her lover, and by grace of her beauty, wit, and style, becomes the toast of the demimonde.

At this point, the manuscript becomes merely a series of notes. Through their brief indications we gather that Lamiel has never known a great love, despite many trials, until one night when, lying sleepless in her boudoir, she hears a robber enter her apartment. Hiding behind a curtain, she watches him, then suddenly steps forth. He springs at her, knife in hand, ready to slit her throat. But in the struggle her breast is exposed, and he changes his mind about killing her, instead paying her attentions of another sort to which she makes no resistance. His passion and courage please her, for in tarrying he risks his very life.

"Who are you?"—"Valbayre. I make war upon society, which makes war upon me." He is a celebrated criminal, full of apt quotations from Molière and Corneille. Lamiel joins forces with him and aids him in crime, but eventually he is caught and sentenced for life to the hulks of Toulon, while she is forced to live in hiding.

The rough plan suggested by Stendhal's notes shows the Mephistophelian doctor turning up again and bringing about a reconciliation between Lamiel and the young Duke de Miossens. Several years later, passing through Toulon by chance, Lamiel sees Valbayre in chains and promptly abandons all her rank and wealth to help him escape and rejoin her. However, her criminal lover tends to kill too many people and is at last properly guillotined. Whereupon Lamiel with a rare spirit of enterprise sets fire to the Palais de Justice in Paris and throws herself into the flames!

But it would be wrong to judge a work left in so fragmentary a form. Doubtless Stendhal would have given an extensive revision to this added study of "energy" in female guise; he would in the end have eliminated many of its extravagances. The character of the diabolically ugly and skeptical Dr. Sansfin, as a caricature of the author himself playing the part of the philosopher corrupting the young, is most intriguing. From the manuscript notes it appears that Stendhal intended to deepen this character and enlarge his activities. Even so, Sansfin strongly reflects the defiant and unregenerate quality of Stendhal's skepticism in his last days.

3

A long letter of March 14, 1841, to his friend Di Fiore shows the consul in merry humor as he sits for his portrait by the fashionable Swedish painter, M. O. Sodermark, who had recently gained a Prix de Rome. "My features appeal to the painters," he observes. His head was really splendidly formed; its small, shrewd, deep-set eyes, its rounded masses and deep lines, especially about the rather mocking lips, were something to conjure with. He thought, however, that the artists did him little justice: one, an Italian, made him look like a "hard-boiled general"; another rendered him a man about town; a third made him seem "silly." But he was pleased when a famous sculptor asked for permission to model his small hands for a statue of Mirabeau.

His letter speaks also with an interest that never diminished in him, no matter how old he was, of a new contralto who had come to sing at the little opera house of Civita Vecchia, and whom he heralds as a future star of the comic opera. The whole seaport was agog over her. "But I am too 'important' to pursue Signora Mollica," he remarks wistfully. One of his young clerks was busy looking after her, a firebrand named Alberti, who had a habit of getting into mischief. A year or two earlier, on the consul's doorstep, he had stabbed one of his mistresses with a poniard for having deceived him, then threw himself on M. Beyle's mercy. What punishment would be suitable for such a crime? the consul asked him paternally. "Three months in jail," the young man promptly answered. And with great diplomacy his chief obtained a light sentence for him. In any case, he remarked, the wound had not been serious, having been inflicted in a well-defended portion of the false woman's anatomy.

The letter gossips cheerfully of local scandals, opera music, and recent exhibitions of painting in Rome—then abruptly breaks off.

That letter was not to be resumed for three weeks, until April 5, when he wrote Di Fiore again somberly: *"I too have been glued to the Unknown."*

On March 15, 1841, on the day after he had begun that earlier letter, as he sat at his writing table in his room overlooking the Mediterranean, he had suddenly felt a terrific pain in his head, then had fallen to the floor in a coma. After an hour had passed, his servants found him in his study and carried him off to bed, where he lay with his limbs and facial muscles partly paralyzed. He found difficulty in eating, drinking, and even speaking. His left leg and thigh were numb; his tongue, all thickened, seemed to fill his mouth.

He had been suffering severe headaches for some six months past. After his first stroke he recalled that four times in those recent months he had experienced sudden lapses of memory, and for six or eight minutes at a time found himself unable to speak in French. Then the words would come back; after what seemed long effort he would succeed in uttering them. Yet he had done nothing about these warning signs.

But now, under the effect of this attack, he lay more dead than alive, in the heat of Civita Vecchia, tended only by his ignorant servants. Nor did he think much of the local doctor who diagnosed his case as one of "nervous apoplexy without hemorrhage." Only after weeks had passed did he recover enough strength to make the painful journey to Rome and seek the treatment of a learned physician who served the Pope himself. This doctor bled him and ordered prolonged rest. He therefore decided to stay on in Rome, and engaged a furnished room next to that of his Swiss friend, Constantin, for he had feared greatly that he might die alone in dreary Civita Vecchia with not a single friendly soul to speak a cheering word to him at the end.

All day long he lay helplessly in his room on the busy Via dei Condotti, nursed by a fat serving-woman. At least the painter Constantin was able to look in twice a day to see to some of his wants. Though the maid quietly robbed him of various articles of clothing one by one, as he noticed, first his shirts, then his shoes, he felt too weak, too helpless to protest.

"I hold myself back," he wrote later. "I do my utmost not to ask her for those boots, since I may turn very sick in her hands. In any case, it will be better than dying alone in some tavern out in the country."

The letter to Di Fiore was resumed as soon as he had sufficient strength to write, and in it he occupied himself in noting down all the symptoms of his disease, saying:

> I observe myself with curiosity; except for my awkwardness of speech, I now enjoy all my natural faculties. . . . But sometimes I cannot bring myself to say: "*Give me a glass of water.*"
>
> . . . Four or five times a day I feel on the verge of choking. . . . A hundred times I have given myself up for lost, believing firmly as I go to bed that I will never wake up again. . . . I have concealed my illness as carefully as possible; I find that there is no shame in dying in the streets as long as one does not do it on purpose.

He bids his friend Di Fiore adieu, concluding: "I earnestly hope to come back. But after all I do want to say good-by to you, in case this letter will be the *ultima.* I truly love you and there are not so many I love. Take whatever happens cheerfully."

He was resigned to waiting for the end, and had foreseen how it would come. His friends Mérimée and Sainte-Beuve had heard him utter the wish: "To die of apoplexy in the street at some unknown doorstep!" But he disliked talk of death, holding it to be something vile and ugly. In his *Life of Rossini,* he had written: "Men will always be frightened when death is mentioned, and to speak of it will always be an act of foolishness, or a priest's trick; since death is inevitable, let us forget about it."

In the fragment of a story found in his posthumous papers (*Une*

Position sociale, dating from 1833), he had set forth explicitly his stoical belief:

> "But Madame, death is only a word, devoid of sense for most men. It takes only an instant, and in general one does not feel it. One suffers, one is astonished at strange sensations which come upon him, and suddenly one suffers no more, the moment is past, one is dead. Have you ever ridden in a boat through the dangerous rapids under the bridge of the Saint-Esprit on the Rhône, near Avignon? The passengers all talk about it in advance; they are afraid; finally they perceive the passage ahead at a certain distance; all at once the boat is seized by the current and in the twinkling of an eye one sees the bridge left behind."

After his heart stroke he wrote in the same unregenerate spirit in his letter to Di Fiore: "It is only the passage that is difficult, and this simply because of all the nonsense with which our heads have been stuffed since the age of three."

He had little faith in the doctors who gave him horrid sulphuric medicines that he was certain did him no good. He even chided his friend Constantin for his obvious and solicitous efforts during daily visits to his bedside, "to sweeten the pill." The only possible cure would be that used, several years before, by Count Molé, a leave of absence permitting him to return to France.

But the end he waited for was not to come this year. By midsummer, he had recovered to a remarkable degree and was back in Civita Vecchia again. Now he was no longer alone. Writing to his cousin Colomb, from whom he had concealed his illness, he reports:

> I have two dogs whom I love dearly: one is a black English spaniel, very pretty but very melancholy; the other, whom I call Lupetto, is coffee-colored, and very lively, very much the young Burgundian. I was so sad at having nothing to love.

By August, stout fellow that he was, Stendhal felt so much in his old form again that he surrendered himself to excesses which he himself thought he was done with forever, and in view of his cardiac condition, subjected him to the gravest risks. The result was renewed illness that made his retirement from the consular service and return to France imperative.

Yet this latest folly was not entirely his own fault, and partook so much of chance or accident that he considered it nothing less than a "miracle"!

4

He had been forced to direct the affairs of the consulate himself, until his chancellor, Tavernier, could return from a journey to Constantinople at the end of July 1841. Then he set off for Florence, perhaps with the desire to see his beloved Giulia Rinieri again, she who had made him so happy in 1830 and 1838. Oddly enough, she was gone when he arrived, and there was only the opera to beguile him. But to his great pleasure a young Italian chanteuse, known as La Cecchina, a dark and passionate beauty, whom he had met in Naples, was singing at the Florence opera house. He called on her a few times. Then the opera closed in August, yet the buxom actress still lingered in Florence, alone, bored, unhappy, perhaps awaiting a letter and money before rejoining her reigning lover abroad. Thereupon Stendhal (deserting his consular duties) also tarried a whole fortnight longer and, gallant as ever, offered his company and protection to the young woman. His random notes on this *passade* hint at a last stroke of good fortune, the "swansong" of our assiduous, though decaying, Don Juan.

One of the toasts of Naples in her day, La Cecchina was always known for her impetuous and fantastic character. Her first husband had been a French musician; but after he died, it is related, she married a young concert pianist whom she loved to the point of frenzy. When he in turn died, the strange young woman, though transported by her grief, with her own hands placed his remains in an alcohol bath "so that she might preserve him in visible form as long as possible."[2] Truly she was one of those flaming Italians pictured for us by Stendhal himself, and one is not surprised to find that La Cecchina enjoyed the fantastical old "Dominique" for all his purplish-brown wig and his facial tics. Aged though he was, old enough to be her grandfather, he was still a merry soul, and he amused her. To him this encounter was "an oasis in the desert," the desert that was now his life.

Suddenly his diary notes abound in secret exclamations of wonder and joy, as if some astonishing victory had been won. He commemorated the "miracle" in his unique gibberish on the margin of a copy of *The Charterhouse of Parma*, marking down the date as August 2, 1841. Also, on August 10, there is repetition of the "miracle," and the touching phrase (in English) : "*Perhaps the last of his life.*"

[2]R. Vigneron: En Marge de *La Chartreuse de Parme*: a propos de Madame Os. *Modern Philology*, Sept. 1944, Chicago.

Because of the great heat, we are led to presume from these scraps of allusion, the lady had received him on the first occasion while only clad in a light dressing gown. Then the temptation of the moment had overwhelmed the old gallant.[8] As if struck by lightning he was drawn toward that which a chance breeze suddenly exposed. For in his notes he seems to repeat her mild plaint of protest: "*C'est mon peignoir qui est remonté.*"

Afterwards, he expiated. Feeling on the verge of another stroke, he wrote a pathetic letter to Minister Guizot describing his grave illness and begging for a leave of absence that would permit him to consult the famous Dr. Prévost at Geneva and return to France for a rest. A month later the permission came; leaving his office in charge of Tavernier he set off via Geneva for Paris, where he arrived November 8, 1841.

Dr. Prévost's examination and treatment evidently gave him encouragement, for he came back to Paris confident that he was on the road to recovery. His letters, either diplomatic or personal, show no sign of mental deterioration at this stage. But his friends, as Romain Colomb testifies in his *Notice biographique,* were greatly shocked at the sight of him:

> Sadly I remarked the ravages that disease had left, and had great difficulty in hiding from him the sad appearance and effect he made. Physically and morally he seemed strangely broken down; his speech, once so lively, was now halting or stammering; his character was also sensibly altered, so to speak; his talk offered less of asperity or contradiction; he understood better the little duties that comported with social relations and acquitted himself more carefully; all in him seemed more communicative, more affectionate; even . . . in the direction of sociability. . . .

Yet with undiminished zest he resumed the same round of life he always enjoyed in Paris. He went out to dinner, visited Mme. Gaulthier and Clémentine de Curial, and attended the weekly soirées of Mme.

---

[8]His abracadabra-like diary runs:

> *15 Luglio 1841*
> *Klle Fauss!*
> two
> *c'est mon peignoir est remonté*
> and ten days *par le bat. B..a..t.* Le 19 I go out
> for Rome

Professor Vigneron, in his diligent study (ibid.), has suggested that *Klle Fauss* refers to that *profunda fossa* described by Petronius in his "Priapics," that *femineum barathrum* which suddenly opened before Beyle's startled eyes. (But his secretive notes leave the whole episode most obscure.)

Virginie Ancelot, his "Tenth Muse," who also had more embonpoint than before. The added good humor and patience that even the dull-witted Colomb noticed—for Stendhal always seemed to be repelling his advances—was also shown in his growing fondness for the very young, to whom he seemed drawn as if with a sense of arrears of paternal enjoyment. As with Eugénie before, so now Stendhal loved to play the genial old uncle with Louise Ancelot, his friend's fifteen-year-old daughter, whom he regaled with bedtime stories.

The girl (who was to become noted in later life for her piety and philanthropy) was then being reared in orthodox fashion at the historic convent of Picpus in Paris, and Stendhal would talk with her of all the saints whose stories she learned. But then he would always end by asking her mysteriously: "And what of St. Opportune?" There was no such saint, she would reply laughing. And he would insist seriously that there was, that she must learn all about him too. Louise, after inquiry, assured herself that his saint had never existed. Yet he would always ask her in gently bantering tone: "And what of St. Opportune?"

Louise, who also kept a diary, wrote:

> M. Beyle has come back; he has certainly grown older; if his wit has lost something, his heart seems to me to have gained much.[4]

With Mme. Ancelot he carried on some pleasantries about standing as a candidate for the French Academy. For was he not *old* enough now, he remarked to Colomb? "Mme. Ancelot . . . thinks she can have me elected." It was a way of being kind to her, for that strenuous woman was forever organizing campaigns, even one to establish an Academy for women. But Colomb could never judge when his cousin was being serious or was jesting.

Busily he made plans to resume literary work. He would be retired on half pay, would live in a fourth-floor room in the center of Paris, and still be able to eat heartily and dress as fastidiously as ever.

Early in 1842, Buloz, editor of the *Revue des deux mondes*, contracted with him for another series of his Italian tales, to be published both in that famous review and as a book, for a compensation of five thousand francs. Visibly the future prospect brightened, for never before had his writing received such public recognition and support.

Late in February he felt strong enough to take part in a large shooting party arranged by the Countess Clémentine de Curial at her estate near Compiègne. With a great crowd of guests, dogs and *valets de*

[4]Martineau: *Stendhal et le salon de Mme. Ancelot.*

chasse he rode across the fields in a train of carriages, firing away at birds they flushed, and bringing down three, for he was a good shot. But on returning from the hunt he was almost too fatigued to make his toilet for the elaborate dinner party that followed, whose gaiety, flowing wine, and hearty fare left him, he admitted, physically "embarrassed."

Fat and apoplectic though he was, on beginning his sixtieth year, he continued to frequent society and its exhausting dinners, for he had the repute nowadays of being "one of the last Frenchmen who loved conversation for its own sake." Some three weeks after the hunt at Compiègne, on March 22, 1842, he went to a large official dinner given by M. Guizot at the Ministry of Foreign Affairs. Returning at seven that evening, while walking on the Boulevard des Capucines, he suddenly collapsed and fell to the ground under a new stroke of apoplexy. People in the street carried him into a shop, then to his lodgings at 78 Rue Neuve des Petits-Champs, where Romain Colomb soon arrived to care for him.

For some twenty hours he lay completely unconscious.

At two o'clock of the following day, March 23, 1842, death came to him as he lay in his uninterrupted coma, mercifully unfelt, and in the swift, unexpected manner he had desired; he died *repentinam inopinatamque*.

His cousin piously ordered a religious service performed for him at the Church of the Assumption, but the simple burial rites at the Montmartre Cemetery were without benefit of clergy. As he had willed. a small stone was placed at his grave with the brief strange legend:

Arrigo Beyle, Milanese
Visse, amo, scrisse[5]

Mérimée, one of the three persons who made up the small funeral cortege, remembered wondering at the time if they had not forgotten or left something out. But the dead man had requested that there be no prayers said at his grave.

Few great men in history have passed away so ignored by the public.

---

[5]The famous epitaph renouncing his French citizenship is believed to have been inspired in 1836 by Stendhal's anger at the cowardly foreign policy of France under Louis Philippe. Appeasing the Holy Alliance led by Metternich, the French Government abandoned all pretense of sympathy for popular movements, as in Italy and Poland during the 1830s. Thus, this pure Frenchman, with a German *nom de guerre*, ended by making Italy the fatherland of his choice. When he died he was far more reconciled to life in France than ever before; but his executors respected his written will. Cf. Cordier, *Comment a vécu Stendhal*, pp. 65–71.

Two Paris newspapers gave brief notice of his death in obituaries of three lines; it was as if he were but a diplomat of the fourth class. One journal even misspelled his name as "Bayle," and gave his pen name as "Frédéric Styndall"—which was really the title of a recent novel by the popular serial writer Kératry. Obscurity shrouded him at once. His passing was almost completely overlooked by the literary world; only his young friend E. D. Forgues, critic of the liberal daily, *Le National*, a week after his death, protested that "one of the most distinguished spirits of the age" had gone to his grave with no more notice than some old broken-down actor.

But the public had known very little of the Observer of the Human Heart under his confusing pseudonyms. "There was silence around him, when he died . . . regretted by a few, he was forgotten by the many," Sainte-Beuve wrote a decade afterward. For years his own friends seemed to accomplish almost nothing that might help to preserve his memory. But his was a lively ghost that from the grave whispered and laughed incessantly for the "Happy Few" he had courted. Little by little his books were bought up, collected, disappeared from circulation. In due time the ghost began to walk abroad, making at first a quiet stir which steadily grew louder and ended as one of the greatest commotions ever heard in all the annals of the literary dead.

APPENDIX

The Stendhal Revival

AFTER that prayerless burial, two of the mourners present, Romain Colomb and Prosper Mérimée, taking counsel with each other, agreed to do what they could to perpetuate, nay to revive, the memory of their almost forgotten friend. Mérimée undertook to write a brief memoir or biographical study of "H.B." for which Colomb was to supply the factual material. Colomb, for his part, was entrusted, as executor, with the task of republishing as many as possible of the dead author's works and letters. The new edition would serve as a literary monument to Stendhal, erected by his surviving friends; and since there was some small public demand for a few of his books, their royalties might help to support his sister Pauline, as he himself had been doing since 1830. To carry out this trust, Colomb turned for help to Louis Crozet, the scholarly engineer and sometime mayor of Grenoble, who had really been Stendhal's most intimate friend.

Patiently these two old men, both sexagenarians, labored to promote the fame of Stendhal; for in their different manners, Colomb's unquestioning, Crozet's more critical, they were convinced that his strange genius had never won the recognition it merited. Had not Balzac written in his article of 1840 that in all Europe only some twelve hundred or fifteen hundred readers—diplomats, society men, philosophers, and the like—could truly understand and enjoy him? Crozet sometimes feared that the tendency of nineteenth-century literary taste might forbid even such a limited recognition. For in his opinion Stendhal had "too much wit"; a novel such as *The Charterhouse of Parma* was so packed with ideas as to seem fatiguing to modern readers.

Truly the prospect for a collected edition seemed dark. One of the few serious studies of his work that appeared as an obituary essay (by

Bussières) in the *Revue des deux mondes* described him as a curiosity of literature and predicted that he would have, not fifteen hundred, but "only one or two readers in each generation." That same year, 1844, another critic, Louis Desroches, in the *Revue de Paris,* though extolling Stendhal as a man of the highest intelligence, described him as profoundly out of key with his times and "wanting in the strength of character that would have permitted him to overcome his own [literary] weaknesses."

But their dead friend continued to haunt his intimates. For was there ever a man who had so much life in him? At the thought of writing his biography, Crozet, who (according to Stendhal himself) "knew him inside out," grew hopeless. Probably no one would ever succeed in telling the whole story. "He had not one personality but many," Crozet concluded. As he looked at a little drawing that had been left to him by Stendhal, done by De Dreux Dorcy, the portrait painter, he said that it was a fair likeness of *one* of his friend's physiognomies. For he had at different times quite different physiognomies.

Combing over the immense mass of his posthumous papers, in the chest he had left them, Crozet and Colomb discovered and read (with no little alarm) the "Journals" and the unfinished autobiography of "Henri Brulard." Revealing though it was, they determined that the autobiography (like the "Journals") must not be published, for it defamed almost everybody in Grenoble, even Stendhal's father, and spared only his two old friends. The *Recollections of an Egotist* was handled with the same prudence. Crozet even considered eliminating *The Red and the Black* from the Collected Works!

Yet though their taste was uncertain, devotion to their friend spurred on the two old men to long and selfless efforts to prepare Stendhal's works and letters for republication, and, despite the world's indifference, to solicit the aid of friendly authors and booksellers for the project. For all his faults, and his self-proclaimed egoism, Stendhal had been entirely honorable as a friend, their letters to each other testified. As he piously deposited De Dreux Dorcy's portrait of Stendhal in the Library of Grenoble beside those of the other notables of the old town, Condillac, Mably, Barnave, and Mounier, Crozet could not help remarking with a sigh that his friend might have surpassed them all had he willed to do so.

At last, in 1845, they induced that speculative "artist" among Parisian booksellers, Jules Hetzel, to reprint *The Charterhouse of Parma.* But the sales were discouragingly slow; and even the enthusiastic Hetzel was forced to admit that the public "seemed fiercely determined to forget the name of Stendhal." The assistance of Balzac, who contributed his long eulogy as a preface, helped not.

That same year Colomb brought out his small *Notice biographique*, which, though ill-written and even somewhat pompous in tone, has the Boswellian merit of being an eyewitness report. Mérimée, who had promised to perform this service, ended by completing only a brief essay called "*H.B., un mémoir*," a fairly malicious sketch of only twenty pages, in which he told precious anecdotes of his older friend and mentor, but carefully avoided reference to his literary productions! Concealing the influence Stendhal had exercised over him, Mérimée presented him as essentially an odd character, an amusing *causeur* and maker of paradoxes, but not as an author of any merit. This "Memoir" was published in 1850 in a private edition limited to but seventeen copies and having as frontispiece a rather scabrous etching by Felicien Rops. (A bowdlerized version of the same sketch was used as the preface to the *Correspondance inédite*, issued in 1854.)

The political upheavals of 1848–51 discouraged the reprinting of Stendhal; yet in certain select circles he was read and spoken of with intense curiosity. Finally, in 1853, eight years after Hetzel's partial failure, Colomb was able to arrange with the large house of Michel Lévy to have Stendhal's principal works and letters issued in a collected (but incomplete) edition embracing the three finished novels, two volumes of tales (including the opening portion of *Lucien Leuwen*, under the title of *Le Chasseur Vert*, the *Essay on Love*, the *Walks in Rome*, and two small volumes of selected letters. At the same time the influential Sainte-Beuve was induced to devote one of his *Causeries du lundi* to Stendhal; according to legend, he was persuaded to do this by means of a secret honorarium from the booksellers. He had known the author well, and his essay, spread over two of his Monday *causeries*, has the value of a contemporary account, though a very prejudiced one. To Sainte-Beuve, Stendhal was a wit who had provocative intellectual qualities, and who served in the advance guard of the Romantic School; but the famous critic showed a real distaste for Stendhal's novels which, as a belated convert to the Church, he termed offensive, ill-written, and mechanical. It is a sobering reflection that the man who dominated French literary criticism for forty years disparaged not only Stendhal, but Balzac, Flaubert, and even the young Zola.

But Sainte-Beuve acknowledges: "Ten years have scarcely passed and here is a whole new generation that takes up [Stendhal's] works, seeks him out, studies him from every angle as if . . . he were a classic." This is an exaggeration, but it is nonetheless true that a few of the younger literary critics were discovering Stendhal; Baudelaire, it is said, read him with deep interest; and finally Hippolyte Taine, the young historian, critic, and philosopher—in France he was to be as Huxley, Spencer, and Matthew Arnold all in one—entered the lists.

Up to the days of the Second Empire posterity had stored Stendhal in a niche of its library of dead authors, beside the late eighteenth-century moralists and memoirists, such as Chamfort and that cold and dry wit, Duclos. To be sure, Mérimée, at the conclusion of his "Memoir" had offered the hope, none too confidently, that a revival of interest might come about at some distant future date:

> I wonder if some critics of the twentieth century will not discover the books of Beyle among the rubbish of nineteenth-century literature, and render him the justice that his contemporaries did not grant him. It is thus that the reputation of Diderot has grown in the nineteenth century, it is thus that Shakespeare, forgotten since the time of Saint-Evremont, was discovered by Garrick.

It seemed most improbable that Stendhal, read by literary curiosity seekers mainly, would achieve the fame of a Diderot, despite the efforts of his friends who still survived him. But the coming of revolution shook men's minds; and one of the revolution's uncalculated effects was to produce a new intellectual generation possessed with renewed faith in science and rational progress, and so attuned to the thought of Stendhal.

In the late '40s, the youthful Taine, then a student at the Ecole Normale, heard the lectures of an obscure professor named Jacquinet, in which the novels of the forgotten Stendhal were enthusiastically recommended. Soon Taine and his fellow students at the great college, who included such future celebrities as Edmond About, Francisque Sarcey, and Prévost-Paradol caught the contagion and became fanatical admirers of the author of *The Red and the Black*. The concept of Julien Sorel appealed to their own *mal de siècle* a generation after he was created. As a fervent democrat, Taine defied the attempts of the university authorities, under the President-Emperor Louis Napoleon, to censor his thought and writing; punished and "exiled" to the provinces, the brilliant youth fortified himself by reading everything he could find of Stendhal's. His classmate Prévost-Paradol, the future literary critic, publicist, and diplomat, in 1851 joined the resistance to Louis Napoleon's *coup d'état* and went to prison for a time. Taine, more the intellectual and the bourgeois at heart, confined his own opposition to this new political tyranny to advocating the democratic, progressive, and materialistic doctrines which he espoused.

The strongest currents of thought now swung away from the Transcendentalism of the Romantic generation toward materialistic determinism. At the head and front of this intellectual movement of the mid-century stood the many-sided Taine, attacking classicism and romanticism in literature, championing positivism in the field of science, determinism in history, mechanistic sensualism in psychology. And through him not only the philosophic-moral theories but the very method and spirit of Stendhal lived again and gained an immense following. In an essay written in 1864, Taine most handsomely acknowledged his debt to the forgotten master whose books he had almost committed to memory, and whom he was determined to rehabilitate.

He had simply gathered up the ideas of Stendhal "when they were lying on the ground," he declared, and given them currency. "Stendhal taught me to read beyond the black and white of the printed page . . . and to observe the exact feelings, the movement of ideas, the states of mind" represented in old texts and memoirs that formed the true material of historians. It was to his spiritual mentor that Taine owed the idea of his famous interpretation of the French Revolution, *The Origins of Modern France*; it was from him that the concept of the inner weakness and collapse of the old regime had been taken; similarly his new interpretation of Napoleon I.

But it was in the field of psychology that the "admirable divinations" of Stendhal could now exercise an immense influence. Stendhal, wrote Taine, was "perhaps the greatest psychologist of all the ages," and had "introduced into the history of the human heart the process of science." He had "treated human emotions like a naturalist and physician . . . marked out race, climate, temperaments" and probed toward the "fundamental causes" of history and sociology. The years that immediately followed the publication of Darwin's *Origin of Species* (1859) and Taine's writings on psychology marked the turning of the literary movement toward realism and toward the narrowly Tainian doctrine of determinism that the young Zola adopted. The novel, said Taine, ought to be "*un amas d'expériences,*" which closely enough reflected Stendhal's theories. Thus one who was perhaps the most learned, or at any rate the most intellectually brilliant, man of letters of the third quarter of the century in France became a conductor for the ideas of the forgotten novelist. The historical cycle had swung away from German metaphysics to the skeptical and naturalistic ideas of the eighteenth century, of which Stendhal was a continuator. But still it was not respectable to read him under the Second Empire.

It was in 1880, when France was once more a republic, that Paul

Bourget, in the footsteps of Taine, wrote a famous essay championing Stendhal, still caviar to the multitude, in which he went so far as to declare that "there was something of Leonardo da Vinci in him." When, in the following year, Emile Zola named him "as the father of us all," the Naturalistic School in literature adopted Stendhal as its patron saint.

Now there came a veritable tug of war between various literary schools and political factions, each of which claimed Stendhal for its own. The Zola group was opposed by the "psychological" novelists of the type of Barrès and Bourget, and, later, André Gide, who with some justice claimed Stendhal to be more truly their own progenitor. (I doubt if Zola, though sincerely admiring Stendhal, understood his real tendencies, which leaned toward the novel of ideas rather than the slice-of-life; for the psychology of the Zola school is actually far simpler than that of Stendhal and treats of types, realistically observed, rather than complex personalities.)

The discovery of extraordinary literary treasures among his posthumous papers by the late Professor Casimir Striyenski, of the Sorbonne, gave strong impetus to the Stendhal revival of the 1880s. One by one, the *Journal* (1888), the unfinished *Lamiel* (1889), *The Life of Henri Brulard* (1890), *Recollections of an Egotist* (1892), *Lucien Leuwen* (1894), the notes on Napoleon (1897), and a mass of unpublished letters and miscellanies, all buried in the Library of Grenoble for fifty years, were unearthed and published for the first time by Striyenski, then by Jean de Mitty, Paul Arbalet, and other scholars. And what was surprising, these writings seemed completely in key with the works of the great literary realists and the social dramatists, French, Russian, or Scandinavian, who now engrossed the modern public.

Even dead, he was vigorously assailed by critics of Catholic faith, such as Brunetière; but his more numerous literary supporters raised him to the level of a Voltaire—who had much less wit, in reality—a Diderot, a Rousseau. To many of the new novelists, he outranked the prodigious Balzac, whom he easily surpassed in intellectual force. The self-declared "Milanese," who had censured his French compatriots more than any other man of his epoch, thus became in the end "one of the glories of France."

Bibliographical Notes

Manuscripts of Stendhal, comprising seventy-two volumes, are deposited in the Library of Grenoble. The manuscripts of the *Chroniques italiennes,* including the original Italian documents from which they were adapted, are in the possession of the National Library in Paris.

The best modern editions of Stendhal's works are: (1) the elaborately annotated Champion edition, Paris, 1913–39 (not yet complete); and (2) the Divan edition, edited by Henri Martineau, Paris, 1925–39, and up to now comprising seventy-four volumes, the most complete edition available, including "even the bills from Henri Beyle's laundress," it has been remarked. These two editions (not the only ones) have been published as a result of painstaking study of the manuscripts, often so difficult to decipher, carried on by Stendhal experts such as Edouard Champion, Henri Debraye, Paul Arbalet, Louis Royer, P. Jourda, A. Paupe, and Henri Martineau.

The bibliography of books and monographs about Stendhal and his works is vast, and in France approaches in quantity the literature about Napoleon and Voltaire. Research into every aspect of his biography and bibliography has become a mania for hundreds of scholars since the 1880s, when the late Professor Casimir Striyenski set the fashion. An extensive Stendhal literature exists in Italy as well as in Germany.

The most useful bibliographical surveys are: (1) that formerly issued at Grenoble from year to year, in pamphlet form, by the Stendhal Club (which Striyenski founded), under the heading *Bibliographie Stendhalienne,* 1928–39, Grenoble, Allier père et fils; and (2) *Bibliographie Stendhalienne,* by Henri Cordier, containing facsimiles of titles of original editions of Stendhal's works, Paris, H. Champion, 1914. Also A. Paupe's *Histoire des œuvres de Stendhal,* Paris, 1903, introduction by C. Striyenski.

A list of works about Stendhal, found most useful in the present study, follows:

ANCELOT, VIRGINIE: *Les Salons de Paris: foyers éteints,* Paris, 1858.

ARBALET, PAUL: *L'Histoire de la peinture en Italie, et les plagiats de Stendhal,* Paris, 1914. *La Jeunesse de Stendhal,* Paris, 1919, 2 v. *Louason: ou les perplexités amoureuses de Stendhal*, Grenoble, 1937. *Stendhal au pays des comédiens*, Grenoble, 1934. *Stendhal épicier: ou les infortunes de Mélanie*, Paris, 1926. *Trois solitaires; Courier, Stendhal, Mérimée*, Paris, 1934.

BALZAC, HONORÉ DE, *Œuvres complètes*, Vol. XXIII, pp. 687–738, *Stendhal* (Calmann, Levy edition).

BERGLER, EDMOND: *Talleyrand, Napoleon und Stendhal*, Vienna, 1935.

BLUM, LÉON: *Stendhal et le Beylisme*, Paris, 1914.

BOURGET, PAUL: *Essais de psychologie contemporaine*, Paris, 1899.

BRUN, PIERRE A.: *Henri Beyle-Stendhal*, Grenoble, 1900, illustrated.

BRUSSALY, MANUEL: *The Political Ideas of Stendhal*, New York, 1933.

BURGER, JAKOB: *Stendhal-Beyle und die Französische Romantik*, Marburg, 1913.

BUSSIÈRES, AUGUSTE: "Henri Beyle," *Revue des deux mondes*, July, 1843.

CHARTIER, EMILE (ALAIN): *Stendhal*, Paris, 1935.

CHUQUET, ARTHUR: *Stendhal-Beyle*, (2d edition) Paris, 1902.

COLLIGNON, ALBERT: *L'Art et la vie de Stendhal*, Paris, 1868.

COLOMB, ROMAIN: *Notice sur la vie et les œuvres de M. Beyle*, Paris, 1845.

CORDIER, AUGUSTE: *Stendhal raconté par ses amis & ses amies; documents et portraits inédits*, Paris, 1893. *Comment a vécu Stendhal*, Paris, 1900.

CORDIER, HENRI: *Stendhal et ses amis, notes d'un curieux*, Evreux, 1890.

CROCE, BENEDETTO: Stendhal, *Fortnightly Review*, Vol. III, New York, 1922.

DELACROIX, EUGÈNE, *Journal*, 2 v., Paris, 1893.

DELACROIX, HENRI: *La Psychologie de Stendhal*, Paris, 1918.

DELÉCLUZE, ETIENNE: *Souvenirs de soixante années*, Paris, 1862.

DOLLOT, R.: *Les Journées adriatiques de Stendhal*, Paris, 1935.

DUMOLARD, HENRY: *Autour de Stendhal*, Grenoble, 1932.

DURRY, MARIE-JEANNE: *Stendhal et la police pontificale*, Paris, 1925.

FARGES, LOUIS: *Stendhal diplomate. Rome et l'Italie de 1827–1842*, Paris, 1892.

FAURE, GABRIEL: *Stendhal, compagnon d'Italie*, Paris, 1931.

FINESHRIBER, WILLIAM H.: *Stendhal, the Romantic Rationalist*, Princeton, 1932.

FORGUES, E. D. ("Old Nick"): Une Erreur de nom, *Le National*, April 1, 1842.

FRANCE, ANATOLE: *Stendhal* (brochure), Abbeville, 1920.

GAUSS, CHRISTIAN: "Prophecies by Stendhal." *Modern Language Notes*, Vol. 38, Baltimore, 1923.

GOBINEAU, J. A., COMTE DE: *Stendhal* (edited by C. Simon). Paris, 1926.

GREEN, FREDERICK C.: *Stendhal*, Cambridge (England), 1939.

GUNNELL, DORIS: *Stendhal et l'Angleterre*, Paris, 1909.

HAZARD, PAUL: *La Vie de Stendhal*, Paris, 1927.

JACQUEMONT, VICTOR: *Lettres à Stendhal* (1828–32), Introduction by P. Maës, Paris, 1933.

JOURDA, PIERRE: *Stendhal l'homme et l'œuvre*, Paris 1934. *Stendhal raconté par ceux qui l'ont vu: souvenirs, lettres, documents . . .* Paris, 1931.

KRUTCH, JOSEPH WOOD: *Five Masters*, New York, 1930.

LAMARTINE, ALPHONSE DE: *Cours familier de littérature* (Vol. V, Ch. 17), Paris, 1864.

LEVIN, HARRY: *Toward Stendhal* (Pharos Number Three), Murray, Utah, 1945.

MARTINEAU, HENRI: *L'Itinéraire de Stendhal*, Paris, 1912. *Stendhal et le salon de Mme. Ancelot*, Paris, 1932.

MARTINO, PIERRE: *Stendhal*, Paris, 1914.

MÉLIA, JEAN: *Ce que pensait Stendhal*, Paris, 1938.

MÉRIMÉE, PROSPER: "H.B.: Notes et souvenirs" in *Portraits historiques et portraits littéraires*, edited by P. Jourda, Paris, 1928.

PATON, A. A.: *Henry Beyle, a Critical and Biographical Study*, London, 1874.

PAUPE, ADOLPHE: *La Vie littéraire de Stendhal*, Paris, 1914.

PINVERT, L.: *Un Ami de Stendhal: Le Critique E. D. Forgues*, 1813–83, Paris, 1915.

PRÉVOST, JEAN: *Le Chemin de Stendhal*, Paris, 1929.

ROD, EDOUARD: *Stendhal*, Paris, 1892.

SABATIER, PIERRE: *Esquisse de la morale de Stendhal d'après sa vie et ses œuvres*, Paris, 1920.

SAINTE-BEUVE, C. A.: *Causeries du lundi*, Vol. IX (301–41), *M. de Stendhal, ses œuvres complètes*, Paris, 1854. *Portraits contemporains*, Vol. IV (pp. 223–34), Paris, 1866.

SAND, GEORGE: *Histoire de ma vie* (Vol. IV, pp. 84–86), Paris, 1899.

SAINTEVILLE, GEORGES: *Stendhal et Vauvenargues*, Paris, 1938.

SEILLÈRE, E. A. A. L., BARON: *Le Mal romantique*, Paris, 1908.

SIMON, CHARLES: *Stendhal et la police autrichienne*, Paris, 1923. *Souvenirs de Strombeck et de Spach sur Stendhal*, Paris, 1925.

SOREL, ALBERT: *Lectures historiques; le consulat de Stendhal*, Paris, 1898.

SPACH, LUDWIG: *Zur Geschichte der moderne französischen Literatur*, Strasbourg, 1877.

STRIYENSKI, CASIMIR: *Soirées du Stendhal Club, documents inédits*, Paris, 1905–08, 2 v.

THIBAUDET, ALBERT: *Stendhal*, Paris, 1931.

VALÉRY, PAUL: *Variétés II*, Paris, 1927.

VIGNERON, ROBERT: En Marge de *La Chartreuse de Parme*: a propos de Madame Os. *Modern Philology*, Sept. 1944, Chicago.

ZWEIG, STEFAN: *Adepts in Self-Portraiture: Casanova, Stendhal, Tolstoy*. Translated by Eden and Cedar Paul, New York, 1928.

Index

INDEX

(Index by John Askling)